KU-206-073

STUDIES ON THE BOOK OF DEER

To Frances, Margaret and Isabel

Studies on the
Book of Deer

Katherine Forsyth

EDITOR

FOUR COURTS PRESS

Typeset in 10.5 pt on 12.5 pt Ehrhardt by
Carrigboy Typesetting Services for
FOUR COURTS PRESS LTD
7 Malpas Street, Dublin 8, Ireland
e-mail: info@fourcourtspress.ie
and in North America for
FOUR COURTS PRESS
c/o ISBS, 920 NE 58th Avenue, Suite 300, Portland, OR 97213.

© the various contributors and Four Courts Press 2008

A catalogue record for this title is available
from the British Library.

ISBN 978–1–85182–569–1

Printed in England
by MPG Books, Bodmin, Cornwall.

Contents

LIST OF ILLUSTRATIONS   vii

CONTRIBUTORS   xi

PREFACE AND ACKNOWLEDGMENTS   xiii

THE GOSPEL BOOK

1   The biblical text of the Book of Deer: evidence for the remains
of a division system from its manuscript ancestry   3
APPENDIX: A concordance of the display initials of the Book of
Deer with the Ammonian sections / Eusebian canons
Thomas O'Loughlin

2   Understanding the figurative style and decorative programme
of the Book of Deer   32
Isabel Henderson

3   The sick and the dying in the Book of Deer   67
APPENDIX: Four rites compared
Gilbert Márkus

4   The Book of Deer after *c.*1150   98
APPENDIX: Unpublished writings by Henry Bradshaw
concerning the Book of Deer
Patrick Zutshi

THE PROPERTY RECORDS

5   The property records: Diplomatic Edition including accents   119
Roibeard Ó Maolalaigh

6   The property records: text and translation   131
Katherine Forsyth, Dauvit Broun & Thomas Clancy

7   On the possible functions of the accents in the Gaelic Notes
in the Book of Deer   145
Roibeard Ó Maolalaigh
APPENDIX: Statistical analysis by *Heidi Ann Lazar-Meyn*

8   The Scotticisation of Gaelic: a reassessment of the language and
     orthography of the Gaelic Notes in the Book of Deer   179
     Roibeard Ó Maolalaigh

9   The toponymic landscape of the Gaelic Notes in the Book of Deer   275
     APPENDIX: Early forms of place-names discussed in the text
     Simon Taylor

10   The syntax of the place-names   309
     Richard Cox

11   The property records in the Book of Deer as a source for
     early Scottish society   313
     Dauvit Broun

                          DEER IN CONTEXT

12   Deer and the early church in North-Eastern Scotland   363
     Thomas Clancy

13   The stones of Deer   398
     Katherine Forsyth

14   The Cistercian abbey of Deer   439
     APPENDIX: Old Deer parish church
     Richard Fawcett

15   Deer and its abbots in the late Middle Ages   463
     Mark Dilworth

INDEX   475

Illustrations

PLATES

Reproduced by permission of the Syndics of Cambridge University Library.

1, 2   1st opening 1v, 2r
3   Property record 3r
4, 5   Property records 3v, 4r
6, 7   2nd opening 4v, 5r
8, 9   3rd opening 16v, 17r
10, 11   The Office for the Visitation of the Sick 28v, 29r
12, 13   4th opening 29v, 30r
14   Property record VII 40r
15, 16   5th opening 41v, 42r
17, 18   6th opening 84v, 85r
19, 20   7th opening 85v, 86r
21   Sample text and marginalia (detail) 54v
22   Sample text and marginalia (detail) 71v

FIGURES

2 *Understanding the figurative style and decorative programme of the Book of Deer* ISABEL HENDERSON

2.1   Crucifixion plaque. St John's, Rinnagan, near Athlone, Co. Westmeath. Courtesy of the National Museum of Ireland.   34
2.2   Crucifixion. Cambridge, St John's College, C.9 (59) (Southampton Psalter), fol. 38v. Courtesy of the Master and Fellows of St John's College, Cambridge.   35
2.3   Symbol of Matthew. Man. Paris, BN Latin 9389 (Echternach Gospels), fol.18v. Cliché Bibliothèque nationale de France, Paris   38
2.4   Portrait of Mark. Lichfield Cathedral Library (St Chad's Gospels at Lichfied), p.142. Courtesy of the Dean and Chapter of Lichfield Cathedral.   39
2.5   St Matthew initial, *Xpi autem* Dublin, Trinity College MS 56 (The Garland of Howth), fol. 1v. Courtesy of the Board of Trinity College Dublin.   43
2.6   The anointing of David by Samuel and David beheading Goliath. St Petersburg Public Library Cod Q.v.XIV.1, Paulinus of Nola, *Carmina*, fol.1r (flyleaf). Courtesy of St Petersburg Public Library.   47

2.7   Cross-slab fragment. Wester Denoon, Glamis, Angus, front.
       (Photo. © Tom and Sybil Gray Collection).   58
2.8   Cross-slab fragment. Wester Denoon, Glamis, Angus, back: body
       of a female figure. (Photo. © Tom and Sybil Gray Collection).   58
2.9   Cross-slab. Lethendy, Perthshire, back: angel, enthroned persons
       and David composing the Psalms. (Photo. © RCAHMS)   60
2.10 Cross-slab fragment. Dunkeld, Perthshire. 'The Apostles Stone'.
       Narrow face (right side): large scale nimbed figure with three
       smaller scale figures beneath. Broad face (back): The Apostles
       (Photo. © Tom and Sybil Gray Collection).   60

5   *The property records: Diplomatic Edition including accents*
     ROIBEARD Ó MAOLALAIGH

   5.1   The property records: key to numbering   118

9   *The toponymic landscape of the Gaelic Notes in the Book of Deer*
     SIMON TAYLOR

   9.1   The medieval parish of Deer and its contiguous parishes   276
   9.2   Land-holding within the medieval parish of Deer   287

12 *Deer and the early church in North-Eastern Scotland*
     THOMAS CLANCY

   12.1 Sites associated with Nechtán/Nathalan and Uineus/Finan   369
   12.2 Sites associated with Ethernan/Etharnon, Talorcan, Machar,
          Gartnait, and Uoloch   376
   12.3 Sites associated with Drostán and Fergus   380
   12.4 Sites associated with Gaelic influence: Mael Ruba, Mo-Ernóc,
          Mo Luag and Ternán   386

13 *The stones of Deer*
     KATHERINE FORSYTH

   13.1 OS 6" map, 1st Edition (1874) Aberdeenshire and Banffshire,
          Sheet XXI. Detail showing proposed enclosures, Old Deer.   401
   13.2 Cross-marked symbol stone, Deer Abbey (Stuart 1856, pl. 11)   403
   13.3 Early medieval carved stones from Buchan   404
   13.4 Symbol stones from Buchan: (a) Fetterangus (SC1081353),
          (b) Fyvie I (SC 1081334), (c) Fyvie II (SC 1081329), (d) Turriff
          (SC 1081271), (e) Tyrie (SC 1081266) (all Crown Copyright:
          RCAHMS) (drawings: John Borland)   408–409
   13.5 Cross-marked stone, Ellon (Crown Copyright: RCAHMS;
          SC 1090350; drawing: John Borland)   410

13.6 Relief-carved 'pillar', Fyvie III (Crown Copyright: RCAHMS; SC 1090346, John Borland)   415

13.7 Inscribed cross-slab fragment, Ravenscraig (Crown Copyright: RCAHMS; SC 1094917)   418

13.8 Inscribed cross-slab fragment, Ravenscraig (Crown Copyright: RCAHMS; SC 1092050, John Borland)   418

13.9 Detail of inscription, Ravenscraig fragment (from a rubbing by the author).   421

13.10 OS 6" map, 1st Edition (1874) Aberdeenshire and Banffshire, Sheet XIII. Detail showing possible watermill remains, South Skillymarno   427

14   *The Cistercian abbey of Deer*
RICHARD FAWCETT

14.1 A plan of the abbey in 1789 (N.L.S. Adv. MS 30.5.22 no. 7g, reproduced by permission of the Trustees of the National Library of Scotland)   443

14.2 A view of the abbey in 1927 before the demolition of the Ferguson Mausoleum (© Crown Copyright, reproduced by permission of Historic Scotland)   445

14.3 Excavations within the cloister in 1927 (© Crown Copyright, reproduced by permission of Historic Scotland)   445

14.4 The carved oak foliate cresting found in 1939 (© Crown Copyright, reproduced by permission of Historic Scotland)   447

14.5 The south claustral range in the course of cutting back ivy growth in 1927 (© Crown Copyright, reproduced by permission of Historic Scotland)   447

14.6 Plan of the abbey (© Crown Copyright, reproduced by permission of Historic Scotland)   448

14.7 A view southwards across the site of the church towards the cloister (© Crown Copyright, reproduced by permission of Historic Scotland)   449

14.8 Comparative plans of the Scottish Cistercian abbeys (Martin Wilson; © Crown Copyright, reproduced by permission of Historic Scotland)   451

14.9 A section of small-scale decorative arcading, possibly from some liturgical fixture (© Crown Copyright, reproduced by permission of Historic Scotland)   452

14.10 A view along the outer face of the south claustral range, compare with fig. 5 (© Crown Copyright, reproduced by permission of Historic Scotland)   455

14.11 The interior of the south claustral range (© Crown Copyright, reproduced by permission of Historic Scotland)   456

Contributors

DR DAUVIT BROUN Department of History, University of Glasgow

PROFESSOR THOMAS O. CLANCY Department of Celtic, University of Glasgow

DR RICHARD A.V. COX Sabhal Mòr Ostaig

PROFESSOR RICHARD FAWCETT Historic Scotland, Edinburgh and School of Art History, University of St Andrews

DR KATHERINE FORSYTH Department of Celtic, University of Glasgow

DR ISABEL HENDERSON Nigg, Easter Ross

GILBERT MÁRKUS Department of Celtic, University of Glasgow

PROFESSOR THOMAS O'LOUGHLIN Department of Theology and Religious Studies, University of Wales, Lampeter

PROFESSOR ROIBEARD Ó MAOLALAIGH Department of Celtic, University of Glasgow

DR SIMON TAYLOR Department of Celtic, University of Glasgow

DR PATRICK ZUTSHI Keeper of Manuscripts and University Archives, Cambridge University Library

DR MARK DILWORTH OSB† Formerly, abbot of St Benedict's Abbey, Fort Augustus

Preface and acknowledgments

This project has had a long gestation. In a sense, the seed was planted exactly twenty years ago in an undergraduate codicology class led by David Dumville in the manuscripts reading room of Cambridge University Library. My classmates and I had the privilege of encountering the Book of Deer first-hand and I, for one, was happy to concur with the scribe's judgement—expressed in the colophon which ends the manuscript—that this was indeed *lebrán co-llí*, 'a splendid little book'.

The calligraphic quality of the Book of Deer's illuminations engenders—to the modern eye—a certain quirkiness which some have found 'crude', but to me they lend an appealing touch of zanyness. While the Book of Kells may seem to be 'the work of angels', the Book of Deer is more obviously the work of human hands. Its humble scale renders its idiosyncracies and flaws the more obvious, but—to me at least—this makes it somehow easier to 'connect' with the Book of Deer and the people who created it. That sense of connection is all the greater for someone, like myself, who grew up in the North-East.

Having read Kenneth Jackson's (1972) and Kathleen Hughes's (1980) accounts of different aspects of the Book, I felt a mounting sense of frustration that their pronouncements appeared to have put an end to further discussion; notwithstanding critical reviews of Jackson 1972 by Greene (1973) and Black (1972). The Book of Deer was noticeable by its absence from works of both Scottish and Irish scholarship (see Black's comments (1986) on its omission from the *Catalogue of Irish Manuscripts in Cambridge Libraries*). I took heart, however, from Ronald Black's repost to de Brún and Herbert's assertion that the Gaelic *notitiae* had been dealt with exhaustively in print: 'while print may be exhausted, however, arguments are not' (1986, 120). I was further encouraged by the summary account of Isabel Henderson's lecture on the art of the Book to the 7th International Celtic Congress in Oxford (Henderson 1986): there was indeed a great deal more to be said about the Book of Deer.

A full decade passed before I was able to act on any of this. Early in 1996, as my PhD was coming to a close, I hatched a plan for a book of studies on diverse aspects of the Book of Deer and its context. This was, in part, a follow-up to the successful 'Pictfest' gathering of 1995 and the first to enlist were Pictfest veterans: Dauvit Broun, Thomas Clancy, Stephen Driscoll, Simon Taylor, and Alex Woolf. At this initial stage I also approached Gilbert Márkus, Roibeard Ó Maolalaigh, Tom O'Loughlin and two of my former undergraduate teachers, Isabel Henderson and David Dumville. From the outset the project was conceived of as a collaborative venture in which participants would discuss and comment on each others' work. To facilitate this I organised a little symposium at Forglen, Banffshire, in September 1997, attended by Broun, Clancy, Driscoll, Márkus, Taylor, Woolf and myself. Henderson was unable to attend but contributed a written text for discussion. Over the course of several days we discussed one another's pre-circulated papers, and explored the Buchan landscape of our texts, including visits to Deer and Aberdour.

We were not alone at this time in developing a greater interest in the Book of Deer. Our plan was already well advanced when we were approached by James Porter of the Elphinstone Insitute, University of Aberdeen, who was planning a 'study day' on the Book of Deer as part of an international conference he was organising: 'After Columba, after Calvin: Community and Identity in the Religious Traditions of North East Scotland', 5–7 September 1997 (the non-Book of Deer part of which was published as Porter 1999). We were able to align our dates and so ended our Forglen stay with a trip to Aberdeen where papers were given by Dumville, O'Loughlin, Márkus, Ó Maolalaigh, Taylor, Clancy, and Broun. Two papers, one on archaeology by Ian Fraser of the RCAHMS and one on art historical aspects of the Book of Deer by Jane Geddes, University of Aberdeen, were commissioned especially for the conference (the latter was subsequently published as Geddes 1998). On the day each paper was followed by a response, and I am most grateful to one of the respondents, Richard Cox, for consenting to publish his response as a short paper in this volume. David Dumville submitted a revised version of his conference paper for inclusion in this volume in May 2005. Only after the book had been typeset did I learn that he had, in fact, published the paper himself, just a few months previously, in November 2007. I regret that the paper is not being included here.

The Aberdeen conference was the academic response to a growing local interest in the Book of Deer, the catalyst for which was said to have been an event organised to mark the opening of the North Sea gas processing plant at St Fergus in 1982 in which the Total company featured the Book of Deer as a local link to the 'Dark Ages' to put beside an industrial venture set to take Buchan into the twenty-first century (Webster 1997). Heightened public awareness of the Book of Deer locally led to calls for its repatriation by the SNP and others, spurred on, no doubt, by the return to Scotland of the Stone of Destiny in November 1996. Indeed a Stone of Destiny-style theft of the Book of Deer on the eve of the 1997 devolution referendum was the central theme of a novel, as yet unpublished, by librarian James Christie. The threat of such an occurrence was taken sufficiently seriously for one of our contributors to be denied access to the manuscript at this time, apparently because he was suspected of being, as he put it, 'a palaeo-codico-ethno-terrorist'. Another contributor, whose Scottish accent had aroused suspicion, was eventually permitted to examine, but not touch, the manuscript and then only under the strict supervision of library staff.

Local interest in the Book was given a new focus in 1996/7 when 'The Book of Deer Project' was established by the Central Buchan Tourism Group, Maud, with the support of Aberdeenshire Council and of the local MP—SNP party leader and now First Minister—Alex Salmond. Graham Noble was appointed the Project's Development/Education officer and worked with Maureen Stephen of Aberdeenshire Council, Roy Chillingworth, and local volunteers, including enthusiasts George Smart, Sandy Ritchie, Bunty Penny and others to put the Book of Deer 'on the map'. Advice and assistance was provided by Donald Meek, Colm Ó Baoill and others at Aberdeen University. The Project's aim was to stimulate interest in the Book as a means of community regeneration and development. To this end, with the cooperation of the Library of Cambridge University, and generous sponsorship from BT Scotland, the Book of Deer Project funded the photographic digitization of the manuscript for SCRAN (www.scran.ac.uk), and created their own web-site, launched in November 1998 (www.bookofdeer.co.uk). Cambridge University Library followed with an on-line 'virtual' Book of Deer where the viewer can 'turn' the facing pages of the manuscript: http://www.lib.cam.ac.uk/ under 'Digital Library'.

While it was always clear that the Book of Deer's home would remain in Cambridge, a visitors' centre was created at Deer (in Aden Country Park, Mintlaw) to provide a physical focus for local interest. Opened in the summer of 2002 and manned by volunteer 'Friends of the Book of Deer project', it houses displays on the Book and related topics. The Friends have organised a series of seminars on topics related to the Book, and annual local pilgrimages since 2000. In the meantime academic interest in the Book continued to grow. Dr Dominic Marner's work on a catalogue of illuminated manuscripts in Cambridge University Library led to his paper on art historical aspects of the manuscript and its possible place of origin (Marner 2002) and an on-line translation of the Gaelic Notes, following Jackson 1972, appeared as part of University College, Cork's Corpus of Electronic Texts (CELT) project (http://www.ucc.ie/celt/).

All the while, the present book was slowly and intermittently taking shape. Three further contributors had kindly agreed to participate—Zutshi, Fawcett, and Dilworth—and the discovery of the Ravenscraig fragment prompted me to contribute a paper of my own. Pressures of work, however, and my changing family circumstances caused many delays and false alarms of completion. Almost a decade elapsed between the submission of the first paper and the arrival of the last. Some contributors have taken advantage of the delays to revise their papers, others have preferred to publish their original submissions. My first debt of gratitude is to all of them: for their forbearance—I'm sure many of you must have doubted this book would ever appear—and for their encouragement. I would particularly like to thank those who, at various stages, have taken the time to comment on one anothers' papers, including my own. The book has been enriched by this spirit of co-operation. I would also like to thank three people who did not, in the end, contribute written papers to this volume, but who have, nonetheless, contributed significantly to the arguments contained therein: Alex Woolf, Stephen Driscoll and Ian Shepherd. Though I retain full responsibility for errors of fact, and of editorial and scholarly judgement, as editor I offer particular thanks to Robby Ó Maolalaigh, Thomas Clancy, Simon Taylor and Dauvit Broun for saving me from the worst of my ignorance.

I am also most grateful to Graham Noble for his continued interest in the project and to him and to Andrew Kellock for help with digital images of the manuscript; to John Borland of the RCAHMS; to Ingrid Shearer for her clear design of the maps; and to Carol Smith and Stephen Driscoll for help in preparing digital versions of two papers. I am most grateful to the copyright holders of the various images reproduced here, in particular to the Syndics of Cambridge University Library for permission to reproduce plates 1–22. Also I thank the Abbot President of the English Benedictine Congregation for consenting to the posthumous publication of Dr Dilworth's paper.

I am greatly indebted to Martin Fanning and all at Four Courts Press: for taking on the project in the first place and for keeping faith in it despite the delays and what must have seemed like repeated cries of 'wolf!'

The book has received generous financial assistance from a number of bodies and it is my pleasure to acknowledge this and record my gratitude to: the Russell Trust, the Hunter Archaeological Trust, the Catherine Mackichan Trust, and the Ross Fund (Hunter Marshall bequest) of the University of Glasgow. I would like to register a particular debt to the Carnegie Trust for the Universities of Scotland which has enabled the colour reproduction of pages from the manuscript. All of these funders have been most under-standing of the long delay in bringing this project to completion.

A lot has happened in the decade since this book was begun. At the beginning I was circulating a black and white microfilm of the manuscript: today a high resolution colour digital image of every page is available with the click of a mouse via the Web. At the beginning, only two of the contributors, Broun and Clancy, were employed by the University of Glasgow, today that total has risen to six, including myself, of whom five are in the Department of Celtic. In the same time, five contributors have moved (back) to Scotland, including myself. When I began this project I was a single woman, now I am a married mother of three, and that, in essence, is why it has taken so long. My greatest debt is to Stephen Driscoll who has lived with this book as long as I have and without whose support and encouragement it would not have happened. I dedicate this book, with love, to our three daughters, a daily reminder of the future of Gaelic to one who has been so distractedly immersed in its past. Without them this book might have appeared in the twentieth century, but it would not have been the better for it.

REFERENCES

Black, Ronald (1973) Review of *The Gaelic Notes in the Book of Deer* by Kenneth Jackson, *Celtica* 10, 264–67.

—— (1986) Review of *Catalogue of Irish manuscripts in Cambridge Libraries* by Pádraig de Brún and Máire Herbert, *Cambridge Medieval Celtic Studies* 12, 120–2.

Dumville, David N. (2007) 'The palaeography of "The Book of Deer": the original manuscript and the liturgical addition', in *Celtic Essays, 2001–2007*, vol. 1, Aberdeen, 183–212.

Geddes, Jane (1998) 'The art of the Book of Deer', *Proc Soc Antiq Scot* 128, 537–49.

Henderson, Isabel (1986) 'The Book of Deer' (Abstract of a lecture), in *Proceedings of the Seventh International Congress of Celtic Studies*, (eds) D. Ellis Evans, J.G. Griffith, and E. M. Jope, Oxford, 278.

Greene, David (1972) Review of *The Gaelic Notes in the Book of Deer* by Kenneth Jackson, *Studia Hibernica* 12, 167–70.

Marner, Dominic (2002) 'The sword of the Spirit, the word of God and the Book of Deer', *Medieval Archaeology* 46, 1–28.

Porter, James (ed.), (1999) *After Columba, after Calvin: religious communities in North-East Scotland*, Aberdeen.

Webster, Jack (1997) 'Fully booked. The things that we hold dear', *Glasgow Herald,* 17 November 1997, 15.

THE GOSPEL BOOK

The biblical text of the Book of Deer (C.U.L. Ii.6.32): evidence for the remains of a division system from its manuscript ancestry

THOMAS O'LOUGHLIN

BIBLICAL TEXT

Bradshaw and Stuart

From the time that the Book of Deer[1] was first brought to scholarly notice in 1860 by Henry Bradshaw,[2] one topic that has proved to be of constant interest is the nature of its biblical text. Within a few years Westcott was referring to it as a witness to the Vulgate,[3] and one of the great strengths of Stuart's edition is that he collated Deer's text with other Insular gospel books and consistently noted where its text diverged from the Codex Amiatinus.[4] This collation, incidentally, must be seen as one of the glories of nineteenth-century scholarship in our area as he undertook it when the study of the textual history of the Vulgate was still in its infancy. Almost thirty years before Wordsworth and White published their edition of the Vulgate Gospels which established the so-called 'Irish family' of manuscripts (codices D, E, L, Q, R[5]), Stuart in selecting his comparisons picked both D (the Book of Armagh) and Q (the Book of Kells). His choice of the Codex Amiatinus as his basic comparison text was also particularly fortunate. The manuscript has a unique place in both Vulgate and Insular studies,[6] yet Stuart's choice was made eighteen years before F.J.A. Hort showed that this magnificent codex was an Anglo-Saxon manuscript, a product of Coelfrith's Jarrow.[7] Similarly, if less inspired, his choice of the Lindisfarne Gospels (BL Cotton Nero D. iv—codex Y in

1 Lapidge and Sharpe 1985, nn. 1032 and 1155.   2 Cf. Stuart 1869, clviii.   3 Cf. Stuart 1869, xxvii.   4 Stuart 1869, *passim*; and cf. xxxiv–xlv, and clviii.   5 Wordsworth and White 1898. The family D, E, L, Q, and R is first referred to on p. x; but in the light of the subsequent use of this as a touchstone of what is specifically 'Irish' and upon which some very elaborate edifices have been built, it is worth quoting the editors' more sober statement: *Ex una familia sunt D, E, L, Q, R, uel ex Hibernia, uel ex Gallia, uel etiam ex Brittania orta.* For a survey of the arguments since Wordsworth, cf. Loewe 1969 (note especially the schema on pp. 104–5 which presents the 'Irish Type' as an established 'fact' within the evolution of the text); for the most recent survey of the whole question, cf. Fischer 1985.   6 Cf. Fischer 1985, ch. 1; Bruce-Mitford 1967; and Nordhagen 1977. 7 He announced his identification of Amiatinus with the codex brought by Coelfrith on his final journey to Rome in a letter in *The Academy* n. 773 (26 Feb 1887), p. 148, col. 2. (cf. Bruce-Mitford 1967, 6).

Wordsworth and White)[8] was sound, for (as with the text witnessed in D and Q) this represents, if not an 'insular text' (I am wary of all such designations), then at least a text that was present in the Insular area. Hence Lindisfarne is a text against which a worthwhile comparison with any other Insular gospel book's text can be made. Likewise, his choice of the Book of Durrow (Dublin, TCD 57) was a good one as it compared Deer with another gospel book with connections with Iona.[9] Moreover, his decision to compare Deer's text with that of the Book of Dimma (Dublin, TCD 59), the Book of Mulling [Edition: 'Moling'] (Dublin, TCD 60), and Durham A. II. 17 was correct, as all four belong to the class of texts we now refer to as 'pocket gospel books.'[10]

Kathleen Hughes
This interest in the biblical text of the Book of Deer has continued. Kathleen Hughes, in an article published in 1980, described the biblical text thus:

> The text of Deer is Vulgate, but with quite a lot of Old Latin admixture. (Though it is a mixed version, it is not the same mixed version as Kells.) It has Irish-type idiosyncratic spelling and an extraordinarily large number of mistakes. Some of the mistakes, such as omitted passages, could easily be due to carelessness, but it seems to me that an expert latinist would not make senseless mistakes, and that an inexpert latinist would automatically construe as he wrote, so that some of the mistakes here could not be made by anyone with any understanding of the text. Let us take a page at random, fo 45v. John XI.13 reads 'And the pasc of the Jews was near', in the Vulgate *et prope erat pascha Iudaeorum*, but Deer (line 2) has *et properabat phasca Iudiorum*. The text goes on 'This temple was built in forty-six years, and you will raise it again in three days', in the Vulgate *Quadraginta et sex annis aedificatum est templum hoc, et tu tribus diebus excitabis illud*. In Deer this has become *Quadraginta et sex annis edificatum est hoc et tucribus diebus illut excitabis*. I think this sort of mistake, especially *tucribus* which is not a word at all, suggests someone whose understanding of Latin was very slight. Examples could be repeated at length.[11]

Her judgements about the text will have to be revised in the light of more recent work, and I think she was a little harsh in her judgement of the scribe's Latinity. There are, no matter how one cares to describe the relationship of Deer's text to the 'pure' Vulgate (on which I shall comment below), an awful number of errors in Deer, but the blunders may be due to extreme

---

8 1889, xiv.   9 Cf. Meehan 1996, 11–12.   10 Cf. McGurk 1956; and Hughes 1980, 22–37, where at the beginning of her article she lists the common elements of Deer and the 'pocket gospels.'   11 Hughes 1980, 25–6.

carelessness as much as they are a reflection on the scribe's knowledge of Latin. To take her final example again: the scribe had already, two lines earlier, written *et in tribus diebus* as the words of Christ, so *tucribus* is more likely to be a slovenly scribe who forgot to cross the 't' of *tu tribus* than the fool who imagined there was a word *tucribus*. Moreover, as is common in the period, while he practised word division, he was none too consistent, and especially when it came to words of only two or three letters such as *in*, *non*, *et*, *ex* and parts of the verb 'to be.' Whether replaced by abbreviations or not, he often let the next word follow these 'little words' without a space. Thus on this same page we have ₇*indieb*[*us*] and ₇*tucrib*[*us*].[12] Seen in this way, if he were not very sloppy, he was a complete fool rather than someone simply incompetent in Latin. Yet the consistency of the script, and mastery of a large range of abbreviations—which he used correctly—show him to be less than foolish. Hence I do not believe we can judge the quality of his Latin, but assert with confidence that he was careless, and never read back over what he had transcribed.[13]

Bonifatius Fischer

More recently, Deer was one of the one of the 471 gospel manuscripts from before AD 900 which were collated by Bonifatius Fischer in his *Die Lateinischen Evangelien bis zum 10. Jahrhundert*.[14] Deer, given the siglum 'Hc', was one of 22 Irish/Welsh/Scottish manuscripts (alongside 9 Northumbrian, 22 'other' English, and 26 Breton) whose variations he listed for four long excerpts in each of the four gospels.[15] Deer was considered in one of the excerpts from Matthew, one of the excerpts from Mark, in all four excerpts from John, but not in Luke since Deer stops as Luke 4:2 and his first excerpt is from Luke 6. The great value of the work is that it allows one to see, almost by glancing at the lists supporting each variant, just how distinctive (orthography apart) a particular manuscript is. When we look for Deer, we find that it is almost always there among the majority of witnesses to the Vulgate, and that blunders apart, it is not a significantly distinctive text. When it does stand out, it is often where a blunder, or possible blunder, has been considered more than a matter of orthography by Fischer. Thus at variant 41027v he notes that Deer has *cribus* instead of *tribus*, but since it is still cited as 41027v[16] we know

---

12 In Stuart's 1869 edition all omissions of space have been retained, and on this page of the MS (fol. 45v [Stuart 1869, 41]) we have for example: *nonmultis, intemplo,* ₇*oues,* ₇*columbas,* ₇*cum, defuniculis,* and *detemplo.* However, in support of Hughes' contention that he did not know Latin we could point to ₇*num mularios* [*et nummularios*] which occurs twice (in verse 14 and verse 15) with this spacing as if he read '*et num mularios.*'   13 We must also raise the question as to how much, if any, this codex was ever actually used in reading as there are no signs of a corrector at work pointing out dittography and the like.   14 Vetus Latina Institut 1988; 1989; 1990; and 1991.   15 Fischer explains his method (pp. 7*–11*) and gives his list of manuscripts (pp. 11*–48*) of each volume.   16 Within Fischer's

that Fischer did not consider it significant. Moreover, in the few cases when Deer does stand out, it is usually either alone (e.g. at John 3:8 it reads *non uos* for *non scis* [41166t]);[17] or with just one other manuscript (e.g. at John 3:8 it omits *sed* with a Spanish liturgical manuscript (Wo) [41165f]). But such agreements exhibit no consistency, and so we must view them as coincidences rather than as indicative of a distinctive text. And, in the less than handful of places where its variant has wider support, these are Irish manuscripts. The most interesting case I have noticed is at Jn 3:9 (41182h) where for *ei quomodo*, Deer has *ei et quomodo* along with MacRegol (Wordsworth's R; Fischer: Hr), the Stowe Missal (Ht), and BL Additional 40618 (Ha),[18] and this reading agrees with one manuscript of the Vetus Latina: Verona, Biblioteca Capitolare, VI.[19] However, when all such variants involving Deer are taken together they do not amount to a significant base upon which to venture any general solution to explain them. There is *some* interference from a Vetus Latina substrate, but no more than seems to affect the majority of the witnesses to some degree. Indeed, since there is such a lack of consistency when another manuscript, or manuscripts, agree with Deer against the majority, that we must be wary of 'family' groupings for such are functions of statistics, and here they are based on a tiny numerical base. It may be objected that this is only based on an analysis of 241 verses from the whole of the gospels,[20] and an analysis of the whole or of some other section might provide a significantly different picture. This is true, but it is also an unreasonable doubt—and humanly daunting when we look at the four large volumes of Fischer's work; suffice to say that this is a much larger sampling than Stuart's, or most collations which are intended to show family similarities, and that the *onus probandi* lies decisively with anyone who wishes to challenge Fischer.

BIBLICAL APPARATUS

The question
Concern about the biblical text to be found in early medieval manuscripts has been one of the abiding passions of the last couple of centuries and stems from the more general scholarly desire that we have accurate editions of the Scriptures. However, this emphasis on the text, while important for our understanding of the history of the Vulgate as a version, or of the Vulgate in these islands, has been carried out at the expense of exploring what an individual manuscript can tell us about how Scripture was understood at a

codes, this indicates that this reading is taken to be the Vulgate.   **17** Another example is 41183q: *haec ex fieri* for *haec fieri* at Jn 3:9.   **18** Cf. *CLA* 179.   **19** Cf. *CLA* 481.   **20** Deer is considered in Excerpt 1 of Mt (Mt 2:19—4:17 = 39 verses), Excerpt 1 of Mk (Mk 2:21—3:21 = 37 verses, and all four of Jn (2:18—3:31 = 39 verses; 7:28—8:16 = 47 verses;

particular place or time.[21] In other words, can the text of Deer tell us about how its scribe, or his monastery, understood the gospels? Iconography apart, evidence to answer such a question centres on finding out how the scribe's work reflects how they viewed the text in terms of understanding it as a piece, or pieces of narrative. And the evidence is found in the apparatus that is supplied with the text: this includes the apparatus that is supplied in addition to the text such as prologues,[22] onomastica,[23] and *argumenta*;[24] that apparatus supplied alongside the text such as Eusebian canons *qua tale*[25] (or other cross-references) and *capitula*-titles;[26] and that which is supplied within the text such as sectioning,[27] capitulation, devices for emphasis, or a search/reference system.[28] These questions—which are relatively new concerns in the history of exegesis—are similar to, but distinct from, those concerning what is becoming known in palaeography as the 'grammar of legibility.'[29] Where the grammar of legibility is concerned with how any piece of text or writing appears on the page, and how this appearance assists the reader to understand it in the sense of making it easier to read with assurance (its verbal meaning), these additions to a text as it appears on the page, enable its presumed intentional meaning to be understood, indeed they add to its meaning, and could be termed a 'grammar of intelligibility.'

The state of the question

Posing this question to the Book of Deer we note, first, that almost nothing has been written on this topic, and, second, that the text contains no obvious

12:17—13:6 = 44 verses; and 20:1—21:4 = 35 verses).   **21** A major exception to this is the study of iconography (e.g. the numerous studies of Kells), but this is carried out by those whose primary approach to this area is from the history of graphic images rather than the history of theology.   **22** E.g. cf. Wordsworth and White 1889, 11–14 and 15–16 (and on the latter cf. Livingston 1997, s.v. 'Monarchian Prologues, The').   **23** The first folio of Kells contains an excerpt from Jerome's *Liber interpretationis Hebraicorum nominum*.   **24** For an example, cf. Wordsworth and White 1889, 5.   **25** I wish to distinguish between the actual units into which the gospels can be broken down as either common to several of the gospels or proper to one of them, i.e. Ammonian Sections, and the system for cross-referencing and harmonising the gospels one to another which is carried out with the Eusebian canons. We can see this in the standard fraction that makes up a Eusebian canon in the margin of the text (e.g. 11/10 at Jn 1:24): the '11' points to a section in the text, what makes it a canon is the '10' which points to the list (*kanon*) / table which is to be consulted to see how this section stands in relation to pieces in the other gospels.   **26** We must distinguish between breaking the text into smaller units (*capitula*) and giving these units descriptive names which function as running headings, and which can be placed together at the front of the text as a summary.   **27** Primarily those which we call 'Ammonian Sections,' but also other sectioning such as those which derive from the identification of liturgical pericopes.   **28** It should be remembered that our division system into 'chapters' and 'verses' (although the numbering of verses is far more recent) which we now see as no more than a referencing system originated as one more system of *capitula* and represented a position on what is actually there in each division.   **29** For an introduction see the collection of essays edited by Maieru (1987), and especially the essay by Parkes (1987).

enhancements, in the usual forms that a grammar of intelligibility takes, apart from the display capitals (enlarged initials, sometimes with, and sometimes without, rubrication) found throughout the gospels.

The lack of apparatus was first commented upon by Westcott when he said that Deer was 'very carelessly written. [And contained] No Ammonian Sections or Capitula.'[30] Stuart took issue with this last comment thus:

> This last statement requires a very slight qualification, inasmuch as a solitary exception occurs in the first chapter of St John (p. 38), where by the letter u (v), there inserted, is to be understood that here commences the fifth Ammonian Section which belongs to the third canon of Eusebius, thus indicating that the substance occurs in the three Evangelists—St Matthew, St Luke, and St John.
>
> This is the only reference of the kind which occurs in the volume, and it would seem that the letter had been inserted or copied by the scribe without any comprehension of its original meaning. Its occurrence (which was first pointed out to me by Mr Bradshaw) is worthy of notice in judging of the source from which the Book of Deer may have been derived.[31]

I quote Stuart at length as my own work has done no more than bolster, and flesh out, his judgement.

The decorated initials as a grammar of intelligibility

This leaves us with the question of the display initials. While these occur throughout all four gospels, it is clear that they were inserted according to some kind of logic, for while on some pages there can be upwards of half-a-dozen (e.g. fol. 54r has six: *Dixit*; *Omne*; *Et*; *Hec*; *Murmurabant*; and *Respondit*), other have none (e.g. fol. 49r), while most have two (e.g. fol. 50v: *Dicit* and *Et*) to four (e.g. fol. 51r: *Respondit*; *Amen*; *Qui*; and *Amen*). (The average is three per page of gospel text.)[32] However, as we read through the text no all embracing solution recommends itself: often the initials come at a point when there are obvious shifts in the narrative (e.g. at Matthew 5:1 [*Uidens autem Ihesus*] and the beginning of the 'Sermon on the Mount'), on other occasions they highlight the words of Christ (such as the number of times *Amen* in the 'Amen, amen' logia are initialed), but often they occur in the middle of sentences (e.g. at John 1:19: *Et hoc est*) or where the scribe has punctuated in mid-sentence (e.g. John 5:28 reads: *nolite mirari hoc, quia uenit hora in qua omnes qui in monumentis sunt audient uocem eius*; but Deer breaks it thus: … *quia uenit hora. In qua omnes* …). So the question is this: can we find

---

30 Quoted in Stuart 1869, xxvii, n. 2.   31 Stuart 1869, xxvii, n. 2.   32 There are some 453 initials (Mt: 82; Mk: 63; Lk: 39; and Jn 269), while there are 155 pages of gospel text.

a logic underlying these initials, and one which we can test as to whether it was operative in some way in the mind of the author.[33]

Given, first, the presence of the single letter *u* which is found in the middle of a sentence—showing that the scribe had no notion of its meaning—thus: *... ex dõ nati sunt 'u' ⁊uerbum caro ...* (Jn 1:13–4); and, second, that in other Insular gospel books, such as the Book of Durrow, the decorated initials are linked to Ammonian Sections (this is clearly visible in that beside the decorated initial one can see the Eusebian Canon in the margin in red);[34] the obvious place to start an analysis of Deer is to compare it with Ammonian Sections/Eusebian Canons.[35]

The crude evidence is as follows: in the excerpt from Mt there are 82 display initials in all. Of these 47 (57%) are coincident with the beginnings of Sections. Viewed the other way round, in that excerpt there are 60 Sections, and Deer fails to identify 13 (21%) of them by not illuminating their first letter. In the excerpt from Mark there are 63 display initials in all. Of these 39 (63%) are coincident with the beginnings of Sections. Viewed the other way, in that excerpt there are 49 Sections and Deer fails to identify 10 (20%) of them by not illuminating their first letter. In the excerpt from Luke there are 39 display initials in all. Of these 14 (36%) are coincident with the beginnings of Sections. Viewed another way, in that excerpt there are 15 Sections and Deer fails to identify only one (7%) of them by not illuminating its first letter. Lastly, in Jn there are 269 display initials in all. Of these 147 (55%) are coincident with the beginnings of Sections. Viewed the other way, in John there are 232 Sections and Deer fails to identify 85 (37%) of them by not illuminating their first letter. This averages out as 247 of the overall total of 453 initials are coincident with Section beginnings (55%). While these account for 79% of the Sections in text which we have in Deer.[36] These figures taken alone are not very impressive, but when we look at how they relate to the actual text, and the cases where the initials do not coincide with Section beginnings, it becomes clear that the basic inspiration for the display initials came from a text where highlighting served to indicate the text as

33 We shall see the solution to these later in the paper. The solution to the first punctuation lies in the division of the text into Ammonian Sections: Jn 1:19, *Et hoc est* is the beginning of Section 9; the second case, in Jn 5:28, is one of those we shall refer to as 'bad breaks.' **34** See fol. 235v which is reproduced in Meehan 1996, 72. This page contains Jn 18:35—19:2 and has six illuminations, five of which correspond to the beginning of Ammonian Sections, and the canons are visible in the left margin; these are: *Respondit*—this corresponds to no section divide, but the reason for the illumination may be similar to that we will advance for such words being illuminated in Deer; *Dixit* (Jn 18:37) at Section 180; *Ego* (Jn 18:37) at Section 181; *Et dicit* (Jn 18:38) at Section 182; *Est* (Jn 18:39) at Section 183; *Clamauerunt* (Jn 18:40) at Section 184; and *Tunc* (Jn 19:1) at Section 185. **35** In the Book of Mulling the text is clearly divided into Ammonian Sections to fit it to the Canons in the margins, cf. Willis 1966, 90–2. **36** That is: the average miss rate is 21% (i.e. the simple average of 21% in Mt, 20% in Mk, 7% in Lk, and 37% in Jn. The remainder

divided by Ammonius and Eusebius. Here I shall confine my examination to Matthew and John, as these two gospels are sufficient to illustrate what is happening in Deer.[37]

The Gospel of Matthew   Leaving aside 1:1 which must be a Section beginning by the nature of the text, we find that the next three initials coincide with Section openings at 1:17, 1:18; and 1:19. Yet 1:17 does not constitute a new theme in the text, but the conclusion of the whole matthaean genealogy. Likewise, while 1:18 does mark an major shift in the narrative and so would be likely place for a division, the next verse (v. 19) does not, and can only be explained by it being a Section beginning. We see other such sequences where there are several initials all within narrative units of the text and where, unless one supposes the Sections, one could not see why particular letters (some beginning sentences when not all such beginnings are so marked; others which begin clauses within sentences, where sometimes the actual sentence beginning is not marked) are highlighted. The sequence of initials at 3:1, 3:3, 3:4, 3:7, 3:11, and 3:12 (he missed this last Section by a comma, see below) corresponding to Sections 7 to 12 is an example.

This leaves the question of the other initials. It is significant that most of the initials which do not match up with Section beginnings are found not haphazardly scattered—a few verses out each time—in those parts of the text where Sections are relatively common, but in clumps in parts of the text where Sections are widely separated. For example, after two Sections separated by only one verse near the beginning of our Chapter 2 (Section 5 at 2:5, and Section 6 at 2:7) there is no Section beginning in the 16 verses between 2:7 and 3:1. So here we find that Deer has inserted an initial at two natural breaks in the narrative at 2:9 (in the middle of one of our verses) and at 2:19. Something analogous happens with those Section beginnings which he misses. For example Section 12 begins at 3:12 with the words *cuius uentilabrum*. But Section 11 began at verse 11 with the words *Ego quidem uos baptizo*; so when the scribe found a new beginning just a little further on at *cuius uentilabrum* it seemed odd since the *comma* that relates to *Ego quidem* is *ipse uos baptizabit*. He missed the correct point by a single line in a text laid out *per cola et commata*, and opted for what seemed the obviously 'correct' phrase beside it; thus his action in illumination shows a curious consistency. He then missed Sections 13, 14, and 15 without inserting any emphasis of his own. However, he came back into harmony with the sections at Section 16 at the words: *et cum ieiunasset* (4:2) which only attracts attention if one has a text with sections; whereas the natural break at 4:1 (*Tunc Ihesus ductus est in*

(79%) equals the number of hits.   **37** The raw evidence which shows the same phenomena occur in Mk and Lk is available in the appendix.

desertum), which is also the beginning of Section 15, was ignored. In other places he followed the section divides, but then consistently extended what he took to be the pattern of this sectioning to parts of the gospel which do not figure in the divisions of Ammonius/Eusebius. For example, Deer recognises 5:1 as a significant point in the text (it corresponds to Section 24). It fails to note *et aperiens* in the middle of 5:2 as significant (i.e. Section 25) and high-lights the natural break at *Beati* (5:3), which is part of Section 25, instead. The next four highlights fall on the word *Beati* (at 5:4, 5:5, 5:6, and 5:7) and these correspond to the beginnings of Sections 26, 27, 28 and 29; but the scribe continues to emphasise this word in verses 8, 9, and 10 which is consistent, but where the word does not mark the beginning of a section. However, Deer and the Ammonian system come back into agreement on the last occurrence of *Beati* (v.11) which begins Section 30, and they remain in sequence for the next three sections. Clearly, what is happening is this: a scribe was following a manuscript where the first letter of each Section was highlighted. However, he failed to recognise these as such (perhaps the beginnings were marked by display initials, but someone forgot—as happened in the Book of Kells—to add the Eusebian Canons in the margin) as he did not understand their nature.[38]

The Ammonian Sections are not divisions of the text into units of sense, nor do they highlight words or events of significance, nor the words of Christ, nor any of the things we might think initially of emphasising, rather they are pieces, sometimes not more than half a sentence, from the individual gospels which can be identified in relation to the gospels as a quartet. That is some 'bits' are common to all four, some to just a combination of three of the four, some to just two, and some are unique to an individual gospel. So while our first thought, and our scribe's first thought, upon seeing markings within a text is that these are divisions relating to the narrative of the text, these Sections are nothing of the sort. Likewise, since the numeration of these sections as Eusebian Canons proceeds sequentially through the text, a first thought is that it is a referencing system to the subdivisions of the text; yet while they can function (almost as well as our chapters and verses) as a referencing system, they were intended solely as a key to the harmonisation of the divergent accounts which would show that they did not contradict, but complemented, one another. Our scribe assuming that they indicated places of note or episodes of text, followed them, but on occasion 'corrected' his text by adding them where he did not find them yet where he correctly observed a division in the text. In other places he added them to make the text 'consistent,' or having thus 'corrected' the text, he ignored some other

---

38 This inference is proven by its converse: if he did understand the nature of the Canons/Sections, he would have recognised the divisions in his exemplar.

emphases as redundant. On the hypothesis that he based his work on an exemplar with sections whose nature he did not recognise we can account for all the initials in Deer's text of Matthew.

The Gospel of John   What we have observed for Matthew holds equally true of John, and indeed is even more visible in that Jn has far few sections in common with the other gospels, than the synoptics have with one another. Thus there are some very large sections in Jn, simply because they are pointing out pieces of text which are proper to him alone.

The scribe's lack of understanding of what he was dealing with is illustrated in his treatment of our Chapter 1. Here Deer's first ten highlights correspond to the first eleven canons, the exception being at 1:14 when he failed to understand the meaning of the 'u' as being the number of a section. Deer falls out of sequence at 1:25 (*Neque*) when the next section is at 1:26 (*Respondit*) which are only a colon apart, and then it proceeds in and out of sequence to Section 24 (2:19). At that point Jn proceeds independently of the other evangelists and the next section does not begin until 3:23. The intervening 28 verses contain shifts in narrative (changes of location and the Nicodemus episode) and statements by Christ which deserved emphasis just as the copyist imagined other statements had been picked out. So into this vacuum of sections he supplied 10 points of emphasis of his own. When we examine these we see he makes them with approximately the same frequency as he found initials in the first two chapters, and they superficially resemble the sections. His first addition is at 2:22: *recordati*; already at an earlier *recordati* at 2:17 he found a section beginning (Section 22), so here he is following suit. His next emphasis is upon *erat autem* at 3:1 which is intelligible as the beginning of the Nicodemus story. He then highlighted accurately a sequence of oracular sayings by Christ: the *Amen, Amen* at 3:3 and 3:5; the comparison at 3:8; the *Amen, Amen* at 3:11; and the comparisons at 3:16 and 3:17. His next emphasis picks out the *Post haec* at 3:22 by which the evangelist moved the structure of his narrative forward.[39] He rejoins the Ammonian sections (Section 25) one verse further on at *Erat autem* (3:23). This process of intelligent 'correction' of what he did not understand can be seen throughout his gospel. Moreover, since so many of the sections in Jn begin with those characteristically Johannine expressions such as '*Amen, amen*'; '*Ego ...* '; '*Respondit ...* '; and '*Dixit ...* ', it is not surprising, having seen these words already receive emphasis, that he added emphasis whenever he met them beginning, or introducing, a dominical saying. Indeed, of the 122 initials in John which do not coincide with the beginnings of sections, no fewer than

39 The quality of his own work in picking out items for emphasis can be gauged by comparing it with the lay-out of the Jerusalem Bible, which of all the printings of the scriptures available today has probably the most elaborate division apparatus.

56 belong to just seven words: *Amen*, in the formula *Amen, amen*; *Dixit* (or *Dicit* or *Et ait*) *Ihesus*; *Ego*; and *Respondit*. In these cases the scribe is following what he believed was the rationale of the emphasis of his exemplar.

However, there are several places in John, a few in Mark, and one in Luke where we have emphasis added which cannot be explained by the above hypothesis. These are, in the jargon of proof-readers, bad breaks. I shall take two of those in Mark as illustrations of this phenomenon. Mark 2:4 reads in part: *et cum non possent offerre eum illi*, yet it is divided in Deer thus: *et cum non possent. Offerre eum illi* which destroys the meaning. Moreover there is no possibility that this was a simple slip: there is a full punctuation after *possent* (two points at middle height: · ·) and the rest of the line left blank[40] with *offerre* beginning a new line. The other example comes from Mark 5:31 which reads in part: … *uides turbam comprimentem te* … , but which is rendered thus: … *uides turbam. Conprimentem te* … with a full punctuation (· · ›) between *turbam* and *conprimentem*, and the second phrase is meaningless. Indeed, this last division reminds one of Kathleen Hughes' judgement of the scribe of Deer's Latinity; it is certainly the height of carelessness.

We can make sense of this seemingly erratic behaviour in this way. We are dealing with a tradition of copying where there was no understanding of the nature of Ammonian Sections / Eusebian Canons, and where the original exemplar had the beginning of each section indicated by an illuminated initial. Not recognising what these initials indicated, a careful scribe—who was attentive to the meaning of the text and sensitive to shifts in the narrative— assumed they indicated places of importance, or new departures in the text, and acted accordingly. This meant that he added extra points of emphasis, and, albeit far more rarely, dropped initials which upon his reckoning were not needed. Later, this scribe's work came into the hands of another copyist— most probably the actual scribe of Deer—who, though competent with a pen, was careless in the extreme. He either was like the scribe of his exemplar and did not understand Ammonian Sections / Eusebian Canons, or was simply too careless to bother about them. Thus he introduced several extra initials without a moment's thought (the 'bad breaks'), and indeed it is possible that his exemplar had other initials which he carelessly ignored, and this may explain the absence of some of the initials we know are missing (i.e. where there is section division that is not indicated by a display initial), for example, it is curious that the ' 'u' ' survives from the original exemplar-with-Canons at John 1:14, but the 'E' of *Et uerbum* is not emphasised, this could be an initial dropped by the actual scribe of Deer.[41]

40 What fills the remainder of this line is actually a run-on from the next line (i.e. the line which begins *Offerre*); this is a common Irish scribal technique known as *cenn fo eite* ('the head under the wing'). This practice is common in Deer, usually the *cenn fo eite* is indicated by two ʃ-shaped oblique dashes, but here (fol. 20r, line 12) by a little drawing of a wing.
41 Suggesting that there are *at least* two scribes after the exemplar does not contradict

IMPLICATIONS

This leaves us with a fascinating question about the community/communities where this tradition of copying took place: what level of theological sophistication existed in a place where someone could copy the gospels without any understanding, or even recognition, of Eusebian Canons?

The full significance of this question is probably not apparent. While today the Canons are still printed in all critical editions of the Latin, and in the standard critical edition of the Greek (Nestle-Aland), they are never actually used,[42] and a few articles and notices in books on editing apart,[43] most interest is focused, with a few notable exceptions,[44] on the Canons as an artistic phenomenon in the form of the arcaded tables with evangelist symbols that are found at the beginning of many gospel manuscripts. Yet, in the early Middle Ages a scholar who was not acquainted with them would be as poorly educated as a modern theology graduate who had never heard of the Synoptic Problem. Not only do we find the Canons in the front of gospel manuscripts, but we find explanations and guides to the use, for example in the Book of Armagh (fols 25v and 29r–32r), and short teaching works to introduce their use to students, that by Ailerán being not only simple but incredibly precise.[45]

So in what sort place could someone as immune to scholarly concerns as these scribes have been? This is all the more perplexing if, given the links between Deer and Iona, we assume that the book was produced in Deer. Other scholars in this volume, such as Thomas Clancy, have pointed to the differences between Deer and Iona, and if the book is a product of Deer, then its lack of sophistication in the canons is one more argument in favour of a separation between the two places. The least we can say is this: wherever it was produced, in Deer or elsewhere, that was a place that was not in close intellectual contact with Iona.[46] The fundamental problem that the Eusebian Canons addressed was the possibility that someone might seek to discredit the gospels due to 'apparent' discrepancies between them. Rebutting such objections, whether actually or rhetorically posed, became a theme in Latin

Occam's Razor for we must account for both careful sensitivity to the text's own structure (scribe 1) and for a thorough disregard to the meaning of the text (scribe 2). **42** Despite the plea for their utility in Oliver 1959; I was recently asked by a well-known New Testament scholar what 'those funny little numbers on the edge of the *new* Nestle-Aland' were? This scholar had never even noticed them in several decades of teaching the gospels in Greek! **43** For example, McArthur 1965; or Metzger 1981, 42–3. **44** For example, Willis 1966; and McGurk 1993; 1994, 13. **45** A proper study of the exegetical precision of Ailerán's *Canon euangeliorum* is needed, in the meanwhile cf. Howlett 1996, 11–20. **46** It might be argued that if we accept David Dumville's later dating of the book that this lessens the problem, however since this incompetence with the canons is not just unique to this scribe but belongs to his textual tradition—there is at least one scribe between a gospel text with canons and the scribe of the codex—the slightly later date does not affect my argument.

writing from Augustine onwards.[47] Yet few were as competent in these matters as Adomnán, and his *De locis sanctis* not only tackled some of the most notorious of these problems head-on,[48] but was valued for several centuries for this very reason.[49] Yet, we have not even a hint of this problem in the Book of Deer. So were these monasteries talking to one another, what were they reading in the place it was produced and/or used? If that place was Deer, could they have forgotten the work of an illustrious writer who was one of their own brethren?[50] I suspect this parting problem will be much harder to solve than the questions of the Book of Deer's biblical text or of its textual apparatus with which I set out.

APPENDIX

A concordance of the display initials of the Book of Deer with the Ammonian sections / Eusebian canons

Column **A** gives the location in the text of each gospel using the standard reference system of chapters and verses. All numeration follows the edition of Wordsworth and White (1898).

Column **B** indicates the initial in the Book of Deer which is emphasised at the point.

Column **C** indicates the opening of an Ammonian Section, and so the point at which a Eusebian Canon would be inserted.

Column **D** contains notes on particular points.

Blank Spaces in Column B indicate the beginning of an Ammonian Section that is not reflected in Deer; such spaces in Column C indicate an emphasis in Deer which does not correspond to the beginning of an Ammonian Section.

THE GOSPEL OF MATTHEW

A	B	C	D
1:1	L	1	
1:8	A		Emphasised in error in Stuart 1869
1:17	O	2	
1:17			Comment on end of Prologue

---

47 Cf. Penna 1955 (on the role of the Canons in this regard); and O'Loughlin 1993 (on how the theme developed). **48** Cf. O'Loughlin 1997. **49** I sketched this in O'Loughlin 1995; and see O'Loughlin 2000. **50** I say who *was* rather than who *had been* as the family of the monastery extended over time into the Communion of Saints.

THE GOSPEL OF MATTHEW *(contd)*

A	B	C	D
1:18			Comment on Gospel beginning[1]
1:18	C	3	
1:19	I	4	This initial is not in the margin.
1:20	E		
1:22	H		
1:24	E		
2:1	C		
2:3	A		
2:5	A	5	
2:7	T	6	
2:9	E		
2:19	D		
3:1	I	7	
3:3	H	8	
3:4	I	9	
3:7	U	10	
3:11	E	11	
3:11	I		
3:12		12	
3:13		13	
3:16		14	
4:1		15	
4:2	E	16	
4:4			Emphasised in error in Stuart 1869
4:10			Emphasised in error in Stuart 1869
4:11	T	17	Initial missed in Stuart 1869
4:12	E	18	
4:13	U	19	
4:17	E	20	
4:18	A		
4:19	E	21	
4:21	?	22	While the word *procedens* is not given an initial, it does follow a full punctuation.
4:23	E	23	Initial missed in Stuart 1869
5:1	U	24	
5:2		25	
5:3	B		
5:4	B	26	
5:5	B	27	
5:6	B	28	
5:7	B	29	

1 Comments at this point are found in the Lindisfarne Gospels (BL Cotton Nero D.iv (Wordsworth: Y) and BL Harley 1775 (Wordsworth: Z); cf. Wordsworth and White, 1889, 44.

THE GOSPEL OF MATTHEW *(contd)*

A	B	C	D
5:8	B		
5:9	B		
5:10	B		
5:11	B	30	
5:13	U	31	
5:14	U	32	
5:17	N	33	
5:18		34	
5:19		35	
5:20	D		
5:23	S		
5:25	E	36	
5:26	A		
5:27	A	37	
5:30	S		
5:31	D		
5:32	E		
5:33			Emphasised in error in Stuart 1869
5:34	E		
5:36	N		
5:38	A		
5:39		38	
5:41		39	
5:44	E	40	
5:46		41	
6:1		42	
6:2	C		
6:5	E		
6:5	A		
6:7		43	
6:8	N		
6:9	P		The *Pater noster*
6:14	S	44	
6:16	C	45	
6:16	A		
6:19	N		' ... *Nolite* ... ' This word does begin two Sections (at 7:1 and 7:6) and Deer has extended the practice to each occurrence.
6:20	T	46	
6:22		47	
6:23	S		
6:24	N	48	
6:25	I	49	
6:31	N		' ... *Nolite* ... '

THE GOSPEL OF MATTHEW *(contd)*

A	B	C	D
6:33	Q		
6:34	N		' ... *Nolite* ... '
7:1	N	50	' ... *Nolite* ... '
7:3		51	
7:6	N	52	' ... *Nolite* ... '
7:7	P	53	
7:8	E		
7:12	O	54	
7:13	I	55	
7:15	A	56	
7:15	O		
7:16	N	57	
7:17		58	
7:17	M		
7:21	N	59	
7:22	M	60	The end of the text in Deer corresponds to the end of this Section.

THE GOSPEL OF MARK

A	B	C	D
1:1	I	1	
1:2	E		
1:3	U	2	
1:4	F	3	
1:5	E		
1:6	E		
1:7		4	
1:9	E	5	
1:12	E	6	
1:13	E	7	
1:14		8	
1:14	P	9	
1:17	E	10	
1:19	E	11	
1:21	E	12	
1:22		23	
1:23	E	14	
1:25	E		
1:29	E	15	
1:32	U		

THE GOSPEL OF MARK *(contd)*

A	B	C	D
1:34	E	16	
1:35	E	17	
1:40	E	18	
1:45	A	19	
2:1	E	20	
2:4	O		bad break
2:7	Q		
2:8	Q		
2:10	U		
2:13	E	21	
2:15	E	22	
2:16	C		bad break
2:17	H	23	
2:21	A		
2:23	E	24	
2:27	E	25	
3:1	E		
3:5	C		
3:6	E	26	
3:7	E	27	Initial missed in Stuart 1869
3:10	M		
3:11	E	28	
3:13	E	29	
3:16	E	30	
3:20	E	31	
3:22		32	
3:23	E	33	
3:28	A	34	
3:31		35	
3:32	E		
3:34	E		
4:1		36	
4:3	E		
4:10	E		
4:11	I	37	
4:11	O		Bad break
4:13	O		Bad break
4:14		38	
4:20			Emphasised in error in Stuart 1869
4:21	E	39	
4:22		40	
4:24	E	41	
4:25		42	
4:26	E	43	

THE GOSPEL OF MARK *(contd)*

A	B	C	D
4:30	E	44	
4:33	E	45	
4:34	S	46	
4:35		47	
4:36	E		
4:38	E		
5:2	E		
5:7	E		
5:18	C	48	
5:21	E	49	
5:31	C		This is a bad break; and the text of Mk in Deer ends in a bad break.

THE GOSPEL OF LUKE

A	B	C	D
1:1	Q	1	
1:4			Emphasised in error in Stuart 1869
1:5	F		
1:19	E		
1:20	E		
1:25	Q		
1:34	D		
1:35		2	
1:36	E	3	
1:42	E		
1:46	M		*Magnificat* ...
1:56	M		
1:57	E		
1:68	B		*Benedictus* ...
1:80	P		
2:1	F		
2:4	A		
2:8	E		
2:9	E		
2:13	E		
2:15	E		
2:15	Q		
2:19	M		Initial missed in Stuart 1869
2:21	E		
2:25	E		

THE GOSPEL OF LUKE *(contd)*

A	B	C	D
2:29	N		*Nunc dimitt[is]* ... [2]
2:34	E		
2:40	P		
2:42	E		
2:47	S	4	
2:48	D	5	
3:1	A	6	
3:2	F		
3:3		7	
3:7	D	8	
3:10	E	9	
3:16	E	10	
3:17	C	11	
3:19	H	12	
3:21	E	13	
3:23	E	14	
4:1	H	15	The end of the text in Deer corresponds to the end of this Section.

THE GOSPEL OF JOHN

A	B	C	D
1:1	I	1	
1:6	F	2	
1:9	E	3	
1:11	I	4	
1:14	•	5	Section number in Deer's text
1:15	I	6	
1:16	E	7	
1:18	D	8	
1:19	E	9	
1:23	A	10	
1:24	E	11	
1:25	N		bad break
1:26		12	
1:28	H	13	
1:29	E		

2 The text reads *dimitte*; since these are the opening words—and so also the name—of one of the three most liturgically used gospel canticles (most probably in compline each night), this error seems to point to the scribe's carelessness; however, the same reading is found in codices D, L, Q, and R, among others (cf. Wordsworth and White, 1889, 319).

THE GOSPEL OF JOHN *(contd)*

A	B	C	D
1:30	H	14	
1:32		15	
1:35	A	16	
1:39	D		
1:41	I	17	
1:43	I	18	
1:48	R		
1:51	A		
2:1	E		
2:6	E		
2:12	P	19	
2:13	E	20	
2:14	E	21	
2:17	R	22	
2:18		23	
2:19	R	24	
2:22	R		
3:1	E		
3:3	A		
3:5	A		
3:8	S		
3:11	A		
3:13	E		
3:16	S		
3:17	N		
3:22	P		
3:23	E	25	
3:24	N	26	
3:25	F	27	
3:28		28	
3:29	Q	29	
3:35	P	30	
3:36		31	
4:3	R	32	
4:4		33	
4:6	I		
4:10	R		
4:13	R		
4:17	Q		bad break
4:25	C		
4:43	P	34	
4:44		35	
4:45	C	36	
4:46	E	37	

THE GOSPEL OF JOHN (*contd*)

A	B	C	D
4:53	C		
5:1	P	38	
5:5	E		
5:8	D		
5:11		39	
5:18	R		
5:19	A		
5:23	Q	40	This begins mid-sentence, so the emphasis must be due to the influence of the section (the word breaks the narrative in no way).
5:24	A	41	
5:25	A		
5:28	I		bad break
5:30	Q	42	See note at 5:23, same applies here.
5:31	S	43	
5:37	N	44	See note at 5:23, same applies here.
5:38		45	
5:43	E		
6:1	P	46	
6:3		47	
6:4	E	48	
6:5	C	49	
6:14		50	
6:15	F	51	
6:22	A	52	
6:23	A		
6:26	A		
6:29	R		
6:30		53	
6:31		54	
6:32	A		
6:35	D	55	
6:37	O		
6:37	E	56	
6:38		57	
6:39	H	58	
6:41	M	59	
6:43	R	60	
6:46		61	
6:47	A	62	
6:49	E	63	At 6:49 an error occurred in the numeration of Stuart 1869; until 6:71 its numeration is one behind.
6:49		64	

THE GOSPEL OF JOHN *(contd)*

A	B	C	D
6:51		65	
6:53	L	66	
6:54	A		
6:56	C	67	
6:57	Q	68	
6:58	S		
6:60	H		
6:63	S	69	
6:64		70	
6:64	U	71	See note at 5:23, same applies here.
6:65	S	72	
6:66		73	
6:69	R	74	
6:74	R	75	
7:1	P		
7:3	D		
7:6	D		
7:16	R		
7:19	E		
7:21	R		
7:23	S		
7:28	C	76	
7:30	Q	77	
7:31		78	
7:32	E	79	
7:33		80	
7:34		81	
7:34	H		
7:40	E	82	
7:41	Q	83	
7:43		84	
7:44	Q	85	
7:45		86	
7:51	N		
7:52	R		
8:1			Emphasised in error in Stuart 1869
8:3	A		
8:12	E		
8:13	D		
8:14	R		
8:19	R	87	
8:20	H	88	
8:21	D	89	
8:28	D		

THE GOSPEL OF JOHN *(contd)*

A	B	C	D
8:29			Emphasised in error in Stuart 1869
8:34	A		
8:36	S		
8:42	S		
8:51	S		
8:52	D		
8:57	D		
8:58	A		
9:1	E		
9:3	R		
9:4	U		
9:16	A		
9:17	E		
9:28	F		
9:38	C		
10:1	A		
10:3	H		
10:7	A		
10:11	E		
10:12	M		
10:15		90	
10:15		91	
10:16	E	92	
10:19	D		
10:22	F		
10:24			Emphasised in error in Stuart 1869
10:37	S		
10:39	Q	93	
10:41	E	94	
11:1	E		
11:9	R		
11:11			Emphasised in error in Stuart 1869
11:14	T		
11:17	U		
11:20	M		
11:21	D		
11:26	C		
11:29	E		
11:39	D		
11:49	C		
11:51			Emphasised in error in Stuart 1869
11:53	A	95	
11:55	P	95	
11:55		97	

THE GOSPEL OF JOHN *(contd)*

A	B	C	D
12:1			Emphasised in error in Stuart 1869
12:2	F	98	
12:7	D		
12:9		99	
12:12	I	100	
12:14	E	101	
12:16	H	102	
12:20	Q		
12:22	U		
12:23		103	
12:24	A	104	
12:25		105	
12:26		106	
12:27		107	
12:27	S	108	
12:30	R		
12:32	E		
12:35	D		
12:39		109	
12:41	H	110	
12:44	I	111	
12:46	E	112	
13:1	A		
13:2		113	
13:3		114	
13:4	S	115	
13:7	R		
13:8	R		
13:10			Emphasised in error in Stuart 1869
13:13		116	
13:14	S	117	
13:16	A	118	
13:18	N	119	
13:20	A	120	
13:21	C	121	
13:21	A		
13:22	A	122	
13:23		123	
13:26		124	
13:27	D	125	
13:31	C		
13:33	F		
13:36	D	126	
13:38	A		

THE GOSPEL OF JOHN *(contd)*

A	B	C	D
14:1	N	127	
14:6	E		
14:7	S		
14:9	D		
14:12	A		
14:13	E	128	
14:21	Q	129	
14:22	D	130	
14:24	E	131	
14:26	P	132	
14:29	E		
15:5	E		
15:7		133	
15:8	I	134	
15:13	M	135	
15:14		136	
15:16		137	
15:17	H	138	
15:20	M	139	
15:20	S	140	
15:21	S	141	
15:21		142	
15:22	S	143	
15:23		144	
15:24	S	145	
16:2		146	
16:5	H	147	
16:15	O	148	
16:15		149	
16:20	A		
16:23	A	150	
16:25	H	151	
16:31	R	152	
16:33	H	153	
17:3	H		
17:11	E		
17:12	E		
17:17	S		
17:19	E		
17:25	P	154	
17:25	E	155	See note at 5:23, same applies here.
18:1	H	156	
18:2	S	157	
18:3	I	158	
18:4	I	159	

THE GOSPEL OF JOHN *(contd)*

A	B	C	D
18:10	S	160	
18:11	C	161	Initial missed in Stuart 1869
18:12	C	162	
18:13	E	163	
18:15	S	164	
18:15		165	
18:16	P	166	
18:16		167	
18:17	D	168	
18:18	S	169	
18:20	R	170	
18:21		171	
18:22		172	
18:23		173	
18:24		174	
18:25		175	
18:28		176	
18:28		177	
18:29	E		
18:33		178	
18:34	E		
18:35		179	
18:36	R		
18:37		180	
18:37		181	
18:38		182	
18:39		183	
18:40		184	
19:1	T	185	
19:4	E	186	
19:5	E	187	
19:6		188	
19:6		189	
19:6		190	
19:7		191	
19:8		192	
19:10		193	
19:11	R		
19:15		194	
19:15	D	195	
19:16		196	
19:16		197	
19:17		198	
19:19		199	
19:20		200	

THE GOSPEL OF JOHN *(contd)*

A	B	C	D
19:20	E		
19:23		201	
19:25	S	201	
19:26	D		
19:28		203	
19:28	D		
19:30		204	
19:31		204	
19:35			
19:38		206	
19:39		207	
19:40		208	
20:1	U	209	
20:2		210	
20:3	E		
20:11	M	211	
20:13	D	212	
20:19	C	213	
20:20	G	214	
20:23	Q	215	
20:24	T	216	
20:26	P	217	
20:26	E		
20:28		218	
20:30	M		
20:31	H		
21:1	P	219	
21:2			Emphasised in error in Stuart 1869
21:7	D	220	
21:8	A		
21:9	U	221	
21:11	A	222	
21:12	D	223	
21:12	E	224	
21:13	E	225	
21:14	H	226	
21:15	D		
21:15		227	*Dicit* occurs twice in v. 15: once where emphasised, then at the section beginning.
21:16	D	228	
21:16		229	
21:17	D	230	
21:17	D	231	
21:18		232	
21:23	D		

ACKNOWLEDGMENTS

I wish to extend my thanks to the following who have assisted me in writing this paper: first and foremost, to Helen Davis (Boole Library, University College Cork); to my former colleagues Professor Martin McNamara (Milltown Institute, Dublin) and Alex Woolf (University of St Andrews); and to my friend Katherine Forsyth (University of Glasgow) who first interested me in the topic. The usual disclaimer applies.

REFERENCES

Bruce-Mitford, R.L.S. (1967) *The art of the Codex Amiatinus* (Jarrow Lecture 1967), Newcastle-upon-Tyne.

CLA = Lowe, E.A. (1934–1972) *Codices latini antiquiores: a palaeographical guide to Latin manuscripts prior to the ninth century*, 11 vols, Oxford.

Fischer, B. (1985) *Lateinische Bibelhandschriften im Frühen Mittelalter*, Freiburg.

Howlett, D. (1996) 'Seven studies in seventh-century texts', *Peritia* 10, 1–70.

Hughes, K. (1980) 'The Book of Deer (Cambridge University Library MS Ii.6.32)' in *Celtic Britain in the early Middle Ages*, ed. D.N. Dumville, Woodbridge, 22–37.

Lapidge, M., and R. Sharpe (1985) *A bibliography of Celtic-Latin literature*, Dublin.

Livingston, E.A. (ed.), (1997) *Oxford dictionary of the Christian church*, 3rd ed., Oxford (1st ed. 1957, ed. F.L. Cross, London).

Loewe, R. (1969) 'The medieval history of the Latin Vulgate', in *The Cambridge history of the Bible: the West from the Fathers to the Reformation*, vol. 2, ed. G.W.H. Lampe, Cambridge, 102–54.

Maieru, A. (ed.) (1987) *Grafia e interpunzione del Latino nel Medioevo*, Rome.

McArthur, H.K. (1965) 'The Eusebian sections and canons', *Catholic Biblical Quarterly* 27, 250–6.

McGurk, P. (1956) 'The Irish pocket gospel book', *Sacris Erudiri* 8, 249–70.

—— (1993) 'The disposition of numbers in latin Eusebian canon tables', in *Philologia Sacra: Biblische und patristische Studien für Hermann J. Frede und Walter Thiele zu ihrem siebzigsten Geburtstag*, 1 (*Altes und Neues Testament*), ed. R. Gryson, Freiburg, 243–58.

—— (1994) 'The oldest manuscripts of the Latin Bible,' in *The early medieval Bible: its production, decoration and use*, ed. R. Gameson, Cambridge, 1–23.

Meehan, B. (1996) *The Book of Durrow*, Dublin 1996.

Metzger, B.M. (1981) *Manuscripts of the Greek Bible: an introduction to palaeography*, Oxford.

Nordhagen, P.J. (1977) *The Codex Amiatinus and the Byzantine element in the Northumbrian Renaissance* (Jarrow Lecture 1997), Newcastle-upon-Tyne.

O'Loughlin, Thomas (1993) 'Julian of Toledo's *Antikeimenon* and the development of Latin exegesis', *Proceedings of the Irish Biblical Association* 16, 80–98.

—— (1995) 'Adomnán the Illustrious', *Innes Review* 46, 1–14.

—— (1997) '*Res, tempus, locus, persona*: Adomnán's exegetical method', *Innes Review*, 95–111.

—— (2000) 'The diffusion of Adomnán's *De Locis Sanctis* in the medieval period', *Ériu* 51, 93–106.

Oliver, H.H. (1959) 'The Epistle of Eusebius to Carpianus: textual tradition and translation', *Novum Testamentum* 3, 38–45.

Parkes, M.B. (1987) 'The contribution of Insular scribes of the seventh and eighth centuries to the "Grammar of Legibility"', *Grafia e Interpunzione del Latino nel Medioevo*, (ed.) A Maieru, Rome, 15–30.

Penna, A. (1955) 'Il "De consensu evangelistarum" ed i "Canoni Eusebiani"', *Biblica* 36, 1–19.

Stuart, J. (ed.), (1869) *The Book of Deer* (Spalding Club), Edinburgh 1869.

Vetus Latina Institut (1988) *Aus der Geschichte der Lateinischen Bibel*, vol. 13 *Varianten zu Mattheus*, Freiburg.

—— (1989) *Aus der Geschichte der Lateinischen Bibel*, vol. 15 *Varianten zu Markus*, Freiburg.

—— (1990) *Aus der Geschichte der Lateinischen Bibel*, vol. 17 *Varianten zu Lukas*, Freiburg.

—— (1991) *Aus der Geschichte der Lateinischen Bibel* vol. 18 *Varianten zu Johannes*, Freiburg.

Willis, G.G. (1966) 'Textual divisions in the Book of Mulling', *Journal of Theological Studies*, n. s., 17, 89–95.

Wordsworth, J., and H.J. White (1889) *Nouum Testamentum Domini Nostri Iesu Christi Latine secundum editionem Sancti Hieronymi*, part 1: the Gospels, Oxford.

Understanding the figurative style and decorative programme of the Book of Deer

ISABEL HENDERSON

For its small size the Book of Deer is a heavily illuminated manuscript. The programme consists of three cruciform pages, five gospel incipits with decorated initials, five full-page and one half-page figurative miniatures, and a variety of marginalia. The decoration, therefore, played an important part in the conception of the book.

Understanding exactly what that conception was is not straightforward. The size precludes its use as a display altar-book and its lack of prefatory apparatus shows that it had no scholarly function. It is still debatable whether it was ever intended to provide complete texts of all four Gospels. Is it as has been argued (Hughes 1980, 24–5) an unfinished gospel-book? The excerpts of the synoptic gospels end somewhat arbitrarily, but a scribe who knew the gospel texts well might easily run on a little past his intended excerpt. The Matthew excerpt ends at the climax of the Sermon on the Mount. The Mark chapters give a sample of Christ's healing ministry, stopping short of his miracle of raising the dead. The Luke chapters cover the annunciations to Zacharias and to Mary, Christ's baptism, and end with the beginning of the Temptation. To choose to give the full text of John is readily explained by the veneration of the Insular church, generally, for this Gospel (Brown 1969; Hughes 1980, 35; Werner 1997, 30–9).

On the basis of the shared style of the textual embellishments and the decoration the scribe was also the artist. The arrangement of the gatherings neatly accommodates the three excerpts and the complete Gospel together with their frontispieces. On the face of it what we have may well be what was intended; an abbreviated gospels enhanced by imagery and decoration suitable for personal devotion and informal pastoral use. The provision of illuminated frontispieces for gospel excerpts has a parallel in the ninth-century southern English gospel-book known as the Book of Cerne (Alexander 1978, no. 66).

The scribe was copying from a complete gospel-book which had some prefatory material for, as Stuart pointed out, a mark in John 1 referring to the third canon of the Eusebian canon tables has been copied, possibly by mistake (Stuart 1869, xxvii, n.2). Certainly there was no point in copying such marks, which have no purpose when three of the gospel texts are excerpts. On the other hand the retained reference, to section 5, naturally only occurs once in

32

the canon tables. In Canon III it is noted as a parallel to the Matthean and Lucan genealogies of Christ. The signalling of this passage in John, 1:14, '*et verbum caro factum est*' with its genealogical connotation could well be deliberate (for both genealogies are excerpted), or if inadvertent, be the result of familiarity, rather than ignorance.

If the scribe had a gospel-book with prefatory canon tables to hand then the likelihood must be that it was illuminated and that it, or similar books in his scriptorium, account for his evident familiarity with the basic conventions of Insular book illumination and text organisation. He knew that it was usual to have a decorative emphasis at the beginnings of the gospel texts that consisted of heavily decorated initial letters followed by graduated letter height which merged into the standard text height ('the diminuendo effect'); that the first page of the text could be framed, and that it was desirable for each gospel to have a decorative opening with a miniature on a verso facing decorated text on a recto. The Deer scribe's ruling for the text and frames is regular and the general impression of lay-out on the page and of the hand is disciplined.

The figure style of Deer belongs to a long tradition of frontally viewed stylized figures found in earlier Insular manuscripts such as the Book of Durrow and the Echternach and Lichfield Gospels, later *de luxe* books such as the Book of Kells and the St Gall Gospels and smaller books like the Book of Dimma and the Cadmug Gospels. In the tenth century it was used in Psalter illustration. This conventional frontal style was used, therefore, at the same time as the naturalistic, three-quarter view style, which for the Evangelists' portraits was derived from classical author portraits. This naturalistic style is the one used for the portraits in the Lindisfarne Gospels (Alexander 1978, no. 9). Artists could move from the stylized to the naturalistic style at will. It was an aspect of repertoire, the choice of representation being based on the function intended for the imagery or the taste of the patron. There is, of course, no question of an Evangelist portrait represented in terms of a classical author portrait being superior, more civilised, than one drawn in a hieratic geometric style, or any falling away from the naturalistic and humanistic to the merely decorative. Werckmeister in a well-known paper (1963) accounted for the nature of the Insular stylized figure style by proposing a direct derivation from the geometric shapes of metalwork. Such a style could not be termed degenerate for it never had any relationship to naturalistic Mediterranean art. Kitzinger, more positively, and with a wider application for Insular art generally, pointed out that, 'Christian imagery was not turned into ornament', rather 'it was invested with the same powers that spirals, knot-work, and zoomorphic interlace had possessed all along. It was integrated into the repertory of potent signs, to which it added a new force and a new quite specific content' (Kitzinger 1980, 160). A readily recognizable

2.1 Crucifixion plaque. St John's, Rinnagan, near Athlone, Co. Westmeath.
Courtesy of the National Museum of Ireland.

2.2 Crucifixion. Cambridge, St John's College, C.9 (59) (Southampton Psalter), fol. 38v. Courtesy of the Master and Fellows of St John's College, Cambridge.

example of the creation of what he calls 'the potent religious image' is the so-called Athlone crucifixion plaque (Youngs 1989, no. 133; fig. 2.1). Its forms lack naturalism, but Christ's weighty head and his breast-plate of spirals gives the image a unique force.

On the other hand Kathleen Hughes felt that the miniature of the crucifixion in the Southampton Psalter, drawn in this style, 'lacked emotional impact' (Hughes 1980, 35; fig. 2.2). This is an anachronistic expectation of any figurative representation in the manuscript art of this period. The Christ in the Southampton miniature is not the suffering Saviour or indeed Christ the King, nor is the miniature an illustration of the historical event. Instead, it focuses the mind of the viewer on the timeless fact of the crucifixion in a totally abstract way. The emotional impact has to come from within. If artistic forms in this style show an unrealistic tendency to interlace, as in the case of Christ's interlaced fingers blessing in the Last Judgement miniature of the St Gall Gospels (Alexander 1978, ill. 206) this is not evidence for an obsessive preoccupation with ornament, but, as Kitzinger suggests, an investiture of the act of blessing with the acknowledged potency of the knotted form. Similarly in the Southampton crucifixion the fact that Stephaton's pole with the sponge of vinegar pierces his own brow, is not due to a slack kind of whimsy but is a device which establishes a relationship between Stephaton and Christ in a strikingly succinct way.

Meyer Schapiro too, has criticized the separation of decoration and representations of people in Insular art, where a high artistic value is placed on its ornament while its figural art is judged to be clumsy and artless. Schapiro concludes that this dogmatic norm of naturalism is 'an obstacle to critical insight into the art as a whole' (1980b, 240). The figure style of Deer should be compared to the norm implicit in miniatures like the *Imago Hominis*, the symbol of Matthew, on folio 18v of the Echternach Gospels (fig. 2.3). When such a style is controlled and symmetrical the modern viewer can accept it as ornament, or even as symbolic, but when its execution is careless and misshapen, as it often is in the figurative art of Deer, then the viewer is disconcerted, for it is neither natural nor cunningly crafted. Even so, to look in Deer for rationally disposed anatomy or drapery is surely mistaken. The assessment of the art of Deer, and of much art of Irish origin, without acknowledging the existence of the values and aesthetic principles that lie behind the geometric figure style results in a simplistic, 'common-sense', ultimately patronising, analysis which is entirely irrelevant.[1]

---

1 Compare Hughes 1980, 27–8. 'If we look at a picture like the MacDurnan St Mark we can see something mid-way in the transformation of a realistic prototype to a figure composed of non-realistic ornament'. Dr Hughes seems to distinguish three figure styles, one naturalistic, a second stylized style made up of patterns ('superbly achieved' in the Lichfield Gospels) and thirdly an ornamental style which has lost its naturalism. For her

While the figure style is the most alienating aspect of the Book of Deer the expectations brought to the subject-matter of the miniatures ought also to be put into context. The 'building blocks' of the illumination of Insular gospel-books consist of a repertoire of decorated prefaces and canon tables, cruciform 'carpet' pages, portraits of the Evangelists and their symbols, and cruciform pages with the four Evangelists' symbols in the angles of the cross arms. The text has five decorated initial pages, four for the beginning of the Gospels and a second initial for Matthew 1:18. The decorative repertoire was a similarly restricted package of patterns; spiral, interlace, geometric, zoomorphic, anthropomorphic and foliate ornament. The palette too was based on a surprisingly uniform range of pigments (Fuchs and Oltrogge 1994, 149). However, all these standard elements were regularly subject to omission, addition and conflation in individual books. In particular, the figurative art of the gospel-books is not confined to author portraits of the Evangelists. Indeed even within the portrait pages additional attributes or figures can appear. By the time of the Book of Kells there was a range of other miniatures, and the decorated initials themselves could contain human figures.

Whereas in Kathleen Hughes' view the art of the Book of Deer demonstrated that its scriptorium had no 'well-established iconographical patterns' (Hughes 1980, 32), there is no evidence that there was ever a scriptorium in Ireland or Britain that was consistent in its iconography. Each book has iconographical and decorative individuality.

In the analysis that follows the illumination will be discussed as a sequence, for separating the figurative pages from the decorated initial pages obscures the artist's intentions.

THE FIRST OPENING: FOLIOS 1 VERSO–2 RECTO (PLATES 1 AND 2)

The first gathering may originally have been of four folios, with the second either missing or deliberately cut out. If the latter, then 1v and what became, as it is now, 2r, was planned to create a decorative opening for the first seventeen verses of Matthew, the prologue, which was contained in the first gathering. This has the additional benefit of allowing for the conventional

the Deer style belongs to the Lichfield tradition 'in a very degenerate form', but also to her third style where there is a move from 'reality' to an ornamental system. The possibility that the stylized style had a validity beyond the 'ornamental' is never addressed. For the figure style of the Lichfield Gospels see fig. 3.4. Webb 1983, remains, to my knowledge, the most perceptive account of the nature of the Southampton style and iconography, and related miniatures. Of recent writers on Deer, Alexander (1978, no 72) and Brown, M (1996) give the best, if brief, insights into the context of its art. See also the sensitive critique of Peter Meyer who, however, underplays the positive aspects of a style which he describes as 'the antipodes of all Hellenic illusionism' (Duft and Meyer 1954, 130, 134–6).

2.3 Symbol of Matthew. Man. Paris, BN Latin 9389 (Echternach Gospels), fol.18v. Cliché Bibliothèque nationale de France, Paris.

2.4 Portrait of Mark. Lichfield Cathedral Library (St Chad's Gospels at Lichfield), p. 142. Courtesy of the Dean and Chapter of Lichfield Cathedral.

second opening for Matthew at verse 18, with a figurative miniature at the beginning of the second gathering on 4v facing the genealogy of Christ with its standard Chi-Rho monogram for the genealogy of Christ on 5r. Julian Brown called this arrangement ingenious and Kathleen Hughes acknowledged that it suggested that the Deer scriptorium knew how to construct books (Brown, quoted in Hughes, 1980, 23, n.8). Because of this arrangement 1r and 4r are blank. The illumination of Deer throughout shows no pressing need for an economic use of parchment, such as is apparent in some other small format Irish gospel-books.

A noteworthy feature of the first opening is the regularity of the framing. The lay-out of the text and of the spaces to be decorated are carefully constructed. The pages are dry-point ruled on one side, with vertical margins to guide the framing. The writing space is 65mm x 105mm. The number of lines per page varies with the letter height chosen—eighteen lines for the first page of Matthew, thirteen for the spaciously laid out text for the beginning of Mark on 17r.

The interior of the frame on 1v is divided into four panels by a shafted cross. A circle at the crossing contains an encircled six-point 'marigold' cross, with the 'petals' meeting at a central ring. The points of the 'petals' are linked by curves. The 'marigold' cross is correctly constructed and the circles are concentric and regular.

The other decorative openings in the manuscript, where framed miniature faces framed text, have frames of approximately the same size. Only this first opening is significantly discrepant, with a difference of 12mm in the heights of the frames. The equivalent opening at the end of the manuscript, 85r and 86v, have frames that at 102mm are identical in height. The difference in size of the frames in the first opening would support the conjecture that there was a lost framed miniature on an original 2r. If there was such a miniature then we could speculate on what it contained; a four-symbols page or a crucifixion are possibilities.

Alternatively an original folio 2, ruled up when the first gathering was prepared, could have been cut out to create the existing openings and subsequently used for the singleton in the fourth gathering, folio 28. That folio's verso together with the blank 29r was used for part of the Office for the Visitation of the Sick—a useful adjunct to a portable gospel-book.

The four figures in the angles of the cross are differentiated in scale, the two larger flanking the shaft and the two smaller the top arm. In Insular book illumination a hierarchy of scale is regularly observed. The four figures have been interpreted variously as the four Evangelists, a duplication of Matthew with his man symbol, or as two of the Evangelists with two angel witnesses. In her review of how the Evangelists are depicted and identified in Insular manuscripts, Michelle Brown suggests that the four figures in Deer 1v, 85v and 86r is a variant of a four-symbols page with substitute human figures—Evangelist portraits as it were standing for their symbols.[2] Certainly the cross lay-out resembles four-symbols pages in other manuscripts, and the four-symbols page in the Book of Kells forms part of the frontispiece material for all four Gospels. In other words a repetition of the four symbols in this format would be much more likely than the repetition of the portraits. On the other hand Brown is conscious of the discrepant scales of the pairs of figures—present in all three miniatures—and of the further differentiation that only the larger figures hold books. She accepts the possibility that two Evangelists accompanied by angels is the intended iconography (Brown, M.P. 1996, 99). This seems the natural interpretation.

The lower figures are simple geometric constructions with recognizable affinity with the Echternach *Imago Hominis* prototype. The angels, being minor figures, are even more radically reduced.

All four figures are attached by strips to the inner frame. These strips, here and elsewhere in the manuscript, are not to be interpreted as misunderstood furniture (Hughes 1980, 28). To comply with the convention of avoiding imagery floating on blank parchment the image was either attached to its frame or intruded upon by cruciform shapes and the like (Henderson, G. 1987, ills. 108 & 109). The man symbol in the Book of Durrow does stand isolated within a framed space and it is not clear whether frame and figure are on the same plane, whereas the enthroned Matthew symbol in the Echternach Gospels is attached to the frame by panels emerging from it (fig. 2.3). This is the simplest form of the principle of false connections detailed by Meyer in his study of the St Gall miniatures (Duft and Meyer 1954, 129–30). The plane is often further defined by dotting. Simple lines of dots were often used for contouring decoration, or enhancing a surface, as on the cross on Deer IV, but it was also used for filling wider areas, as for example, the background of the letters '*Quoniam quidem*' on folio 139r of the Lindisfarne Gospels (Alexander 1978, ill. 33).

The lay-out of IV recalls, in particular, the prefatory four-symbols page on the corresponding folio of the Macdurnan Gospels, an Irish manuscript datable to the late ninth- or early tenth-century (Alexander 1978, ill. 325). Here the page is divided by a cross with barred terminals. It defines its shape with key-pattern. A circular panel at the crossing of the arms is filled with a cross of spirals. In the cruciform four-symbols page of the Trier Gospels, also on folio IV, the circular panel contains a bust of Christ holding a book, rather than the symbolic cross (Alexander 1978, ill. 114). For the Deer artist the cross of arcs would have been a reference to Christ. The repeated occurrence

2 The four-symbols page in the Trier Gospels (Alexander 1978, ill. 114) has human heads at each corner of the frame. These must represent the Evangelists. There is a precedent, therefore, for the conflation of symbols and Evangelists within a cruciform format.

of a cruciform page with the explicit or encoded reference to Christ within a circular panel at the crossing lends weight to Michelle Brown's observation that the Deer scribe's iconography for his IV shows knowledge of four-symbols pages. Nonetheless, for his own purposes, he chose to adapt the imagery. For his book the complexities of the Evangelists' symbols were not required. This is a matter of intelligent omission not ignorance.

Facing the cruciform page, on folio 2r, the Gospel of Matthew begins with an illuminated 'L' made up of two animals with strap-work bodies interwoven at the mid-points. This is a well-known type of decorated initial that appears in Insular manuscripts from the ninth to the eleventh century (Edwards, 1995). A third animal head is attached to the upper edge of the frame. The curl at the top of the left edge represents the end of its body. The animalising of frames with the heads and hindquarters widely separated is a common feature of Insular illumination, for example, in the Lindisfarne Gospels folio 139r and the Book of Kells, folio 285v (Alexander 1978, ills. 33 & 254). The simple pelta at the top of the letter is a faint echo of the spiral patterns invariably used to crown the display initials in the *de luxe* Gospel-books of the eighth and early ninth centuries. The bowl of the 'L' is formed from the attenuated body of one of the animals which terminates in a triangular shape, frilled at the base. 'Frilled triangles', often strung together, are the commonest form of text embellishment in Deer. It is a mannerism found in the earlier Gospel-books such as the Cambridge-London Gospels and the Durham Gospels. The extent to which it is used in Deer is, however, best paralleled in the eleventh-century Celtic Psalter (Finlayson 1962, xvii n.3).

The bowl of the 'L' is filled with an irregularly constructed grid with a circle and dot at three meeting points. This motif is used in the St Petersburg Bede, for example on folio 3v and 26v, but without the circle and dot feature. When drawing attention to this decorative device in the Bede manuscript Schapiro described it as irregular chaotic plaid, comprising a sophisticated confusion of intervals, background and colour (Schapiro 1980a, 206–12, figs. 1 & 4; Alexander 1978, ills. 83 & 84). It is unlikely that this eighth-century book from Bede's monastery at Jarrow/Wearmouth was even an indirect source for the Deer artist, but its occurrence in such a manuscript shows that the device, which pervades Deer, is an established one.[3]

---

3 The brilliant discussion of this motif by Schapiro (1980a, 206–12) has to be read in full. He traces its influence through a range of Insular books which includes the decoration of the Cambridge/London Gospels and the Book of Mulling. The exact placing within his analysis of the versions in the Book of Deer merits further study.

2.5 St Matthew initial, *Xpi autem* Dublin, Trinity College MS 56
(The Garland of Howth), fol. 1v. Courtesy of the Board of Trinity College Dublin.

THE SECOND OPENING: FOLIOS 4 VERSO–5 RECTO (PLATES 6 & 7)

The excerpt from Matthew occupies the second gathering, of twelve folios. Folio 4r was blank. Folio 4v is a full-page figurative miniature consisting of a seated figure with two small figures flanking his head. The frame has square panels with saltires at the corners. The same cruciform key-pattern fills the vertical edges of the frame. The left edge has eleven units of the design and the right eight units, so that the edges were evidently decorated free-hand. In spite of this irregularity each unit is accurately drawn. The key-pattern belongs to a group numbered 1002–1004 by Allen (Allen and Anderson 1903, 1, 358–9). One of these, no. 1003, fills the top right-hand corner of folio 172r of the Macdurnan Gospels. The patterns in the group, the related pattern no. 995, and the version used to fill circular panels, occur in Pictish, Irish, Northumbrian and Welsh sculpture.

The pattern within the upper horizontal edge is made of interlocking straight-line spirals. Its cruciform shape is articulated by black triangles, a feature of manuscript art, which is copied in relief Pictish sculpture. Six units are used. Here too the drawing is controlled but the free-hand technique has left a blank area to the right of the frame. In a small manuscript this kind of miscalculation leaps to the eye but in fact such mistakes occur in many of the most ambitious books. The bottom edge is filled with six units of a simpler but effective pattern made up of an equal-armed cross with a lozenge shape at the crossing and a superimposed saltire articulated by black squares at the corners and black expanded terminals for the equal-armed cross. This kind of cob-web pattern is very common in the interlinear decoration of the Book of Kells.

In the Macdurnan Gospels the portrait of Matthew is on folio 4v and the '*Christi autem*' initial on 5r (Alexander 1978, ills. 326 and 322). The natural interpretation of the Deer figure on 4v is that it too is a portrait of Matthew. Whereas he is shod in Macdurnan, in Deer his feet are bare, unlike all the other figures which have marks on the upper part of the foot, as if of sandal straps. The Deer figure has a moustache (difficult to see in reproduction because of a disfiguring stain) and a forked beard. Such facial hair is quite common in Insular Evangelist portraits for example, in the Matthew portrait in the St Gall fragment (Alexander 1978, ill. 281). However, the sword held in the figure's right hand between his knees is unusual and requires inter-pretation. In later art Matthew is evidently shown with a sword because of his traditional martyrdom by decollation but the attribute has no precedent in early medieval art. Hughes suggested that the sword was a misunderstood version of the Tau-shaped crozier held by Matthew in a panel on the north side of the Cross of the Scriptures at Clonmacnoise (Hughes 1980, 32). Doubt has now been cast on the identification of this figure as Matthew (Harbison 1992, 1, 53). Alexander and Hughes who were writing about Deer around the same time, compared the Deer sword-bearer with a similar figure in the eighth- to ninth-century Irish manuscript known as the 'Garland of Howth' (Alexander 1978, no 59; fig. 2.5). Here, within the first lines of the '*Christi autem* ...' text, a rectangular space is divided into four panels. Two frontal figures depicted in a linear style sit within the lower panels. Above, the smaller panels each contains a bust-length angel. The lay-out is therefore comparable to the cruciform page on folio 1v of Deer.

In the Howth miniature the figure to the left has a moustache and forked beard. He raises his right arm in a gesture of profession. He holds a book in his left hand. The figure in the right-hand panel holds a sheathed sword. His elbow is bent and the sword appears to lie across his shoulder. He holds a book on his lap. Alexander interpreted the figure on the left as Matthew with his symbol in the form of an angel above him but he could offer no explanation for the pair on the right (Alexander 1978, 80). Hughes thought this figure could be a second representation of Matthew, which therefore, she reluctantly conceded, would provide a parallel for the attribute of a sword for Matthew in Deer (Hughes 1980, 32). Against the duplication of Matthew imagery is the difference in appearance of the two figures, one bearded and the other clean-shaven. Nor indeed are Evangelists normally portrayed in amongst display lettering. On the other hand, the interspersing of figures in this position is commonplace in Kells. On precedent the Howth figure framed by '*Christi autem* ...' should represent some aspect of the text. In an unpublished lecture given in 1983 (Henderson, I. 1986; Meek, 1993) I proposed that the two figures could illustrate the beginning of Matthew, '*Liber generationis* ...', 'the Book of the generation of Jesus Christ, the son of David, the son of Abraham ...', and were representations of these two ancestors of Christ, the proclaiming figure to the left showing David as Prophet and Psalmist' and the adjacent figure Abraham, holding the sword with which he was willing to sacrifice his son in obedience to God's command. This right-hand figure also holds the Scriptures which record the ultimate fulfilment of God's promise to Abraham that he would be father of Israel.[4]

As mentioned earlier, the style of the figures in the 'Garland of Howth', the presence of angel witnesses, and the placing of the figures within separate compartments are comparable to Deer's miniature on 1v. The sword-bearing figure in 4v could reflect an iconographical tradition of representing precursors of Christ at this point in Matthew. The Howth artist put his David

---

4 The figure standing within the initial of the beginning of St Mark (Alexander 1978, ill. 275) is certainly to be identified as St Mark, for the decorative, but unambiguously leonine, animal above his head is his symbol. This, presumably is how Matthew would have appeared within the Liber initial for Matthew, now lost. An alternative interpretation of the proclaiming figure to the left is as Isaiah, whose prophecy' Ecce virgo ...' (Isaiah 7:14) is quoted in Matthew 1:23. His name, omitted in the Vulgate, is included in the text of Deer, fol.5v, with the spelling 'issias'.

and Abraham adjacent to the words telling of the birth of Christ. The Deer artist put Abraham on a miniature opposite the text.[5]

The small head in the angle of Chi in the '*Xpi*' lettering on folio 5r must represent Christ. In the Chi-Rho page in the Book of Kells (folio 34r) the head at this precise point and another, terminating Rho, are accepted as images of Christ (Meehan 1994, 50; Lewis 1980, 144). In the Macdurnan Gospels (folio 5) the Chi begins with a human head. The heads in these heavily illuminated books are given no special emphasis, indeed they are almost concealed from the viewer. The placing of the head in the angle of the Chi in the Book of Deer is evidence therefore for intimate knowledge and understanding of an iconographical convention present in *de luxe* books whether of the altar class or of the group produced in a smaller format for more informal use.

However one interprets the figure on folio 4v one cannot dismiss the presence of the sword as due to some sort of misunderstanding. A sword was intended and just because there is no certain parallel in the surviving books does not mean that the Deer artist did not know what he was doing. Stuart, following Westwood, drew attention to the unusual nature of the sword, with its hand guard turning down and a second guard curving up on either side of a sub-triangular, arch-shaped pommel (Stuart 1869, xix). Westwood compared it with Danish and Norwegian long swords engraved by Hewitt (1855, 33, pl.v).

In manuscript art of the period the closest analogy is the sword held by David in a drawing on a flysheet (folio 1) of a manuscript of the *Carmina* of Paulinus of Nola (Alexander 1978, ill. 179; fig. 2.6). The sword has the same arrangement of guards as the Deer sword except that the upper guard does not curl round at the tips. In Irish sculpture, where there are several representations of the Sacrifice of Isaac, Abraham's sword is long, quite different from the native short sword which seems to be represented in the 'Garland of Howth' (Hughes 1980, 32). Abraham wields a similarly long sword in the illustration of the Sacrifice in the Antwerp *Carmen Paschale* of Sedulius (Alexander 1978, ill. 286). The length of the sword is not in itself adequate evidence to confirm the identification of the figure on folio 4v of Deer as Abraham, but the representation of the double guarded hilt in Insular manuscript art allows for its design, as well as the depiction of Abraham as a

---

5 Another blade-bearing figure is the enigmatic and still unexplained miniature of what is known as the Tetramorph in the Trier Gospels (Alexander 1978, ill. 110). This unique, hybrid image certainly brings weaponry within the context of the iconography of the Evangelists. But the figure is so obscure that an association with Matthew cannot be argued. The equipment held by the figure may be liturgical in nature, a flabellum and a knife. The nature of the evidence for the use of a liturgical knife or other implement in the division of the host at this period is discussed by Wilson (1973, 1, 117–18).

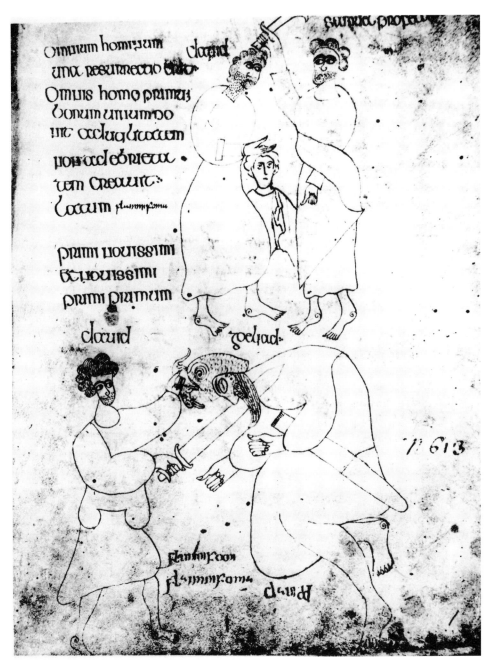

2.6 The anointing of David by Samuel and David beheading Goliath.
St Petersburg Public Library Cod Q.v.XIV.1, Paulinus of Nola, *Carmina*,
fol.1r (flyleaf). Courtesy of St Petersburg Public Library.

frontispiece in Matthew, to be ultimately derived from models. Similarly the long swords associated with Abraham and Peter in Irish sculpture are not native types but based on a model (Harbison 1992, 3, figs. 681 & 683b).[6]

The decoration of the frame for the text on folio 5r is consciously varied from that of the frame for the figure facing it on 4v. A loose broad-band interlace fills the horizontal edges. Both vertical frames are divided into two panels with the top left and bottom right panels filled with a simple version of the saltire pattern on the lower horizontal edge of the frame on folio 4r, and the top right and bottom left panels with the straight-line spiral ornament of its upper horizontal edge. Alternation of the location of the patterns is therefore observed within the frame on 5r and also vis à vis the frame on the facing folio. Such alternation is typical of Insular art. The margins of both the inner and outer frame are divided into short lengths by two parallel lines. This device is found in a number of books, for example in the portrait of Matthew in the Barberini Gospels (Alexander 1978, ill. 178). This is a minor decorative convention only likely to have been adopted by an artist thoroughly familiar with the Insular repertoire.

THE THIRD OPENING: FOLIOS 16 VERSO–17 RECTO (PLATES 8 & 9)

The frame for the figure on folio 16v, the frontispiece for the Mark excerpt, is more elaborate than those described so far. It has corner-pieces projecting from the frame, made out of extensions of the inner and outer margins which end in spirals. Such corner pieces are very common in Insular manuscripts from the earliest period.

The incorporation of small heads into frames has been mentioned above in connection with four-symbols pages. The bottom right-hand corner of the frame on folio 16v contains two small heads within the corner-pieces. Both are secured to the frame by bands. The incorporation of heads into frames is paralleled in this position, for example, in the Macregol Gospels opening page for St John (Alexander 1978, ill. 269).

6 For the identification of the sword in Deer with a Viking type, an example of which is found in north-east Scotland, see Geddes 1998, 545–7. Dr Lloyd Laing has been working for some time on the representations of swords on Pictish sculpture, a number of which he sees as Viking in nature. For example, on the basis of the sword types depicted in the battle-scene on the reverse of the Aberlemno Churchyard he would date that monument to the second half of the ninth century (Laing 2001). On the dating of the Abevlemno sword types to the eighth century see Graham-Campbell 2002, 37–8. On the general issue of seemingly native or other contemporary material culture being represented in manuscripts and sculpture see Carver 1986 and Henderson, I., 1998. Occasional substitution of contemporary objects for unfamiliar ones in imported models undoubtedly occurred.

The decorated initial '*In*' which introduces Mark is the most elegant in the book. The letters are made out of two strap animals, the smaller of which penetrates the slit body of the larger to form a woven knot. The space within the letter strokes is filled with two units of the plaid motif with encircled dots at the corners of the lower unit. The larger animal has a pricked ear, a slit for a jaw and a long lappet running forward from its brow. The '*In*' initial in Deer is markedly similar to the '*Ini*' initial of the Gospel fragment placed in the *cumdach* of the Book of Mulling (Alexander 1978, ill. 216), dated by Lowe to the eighth or ninth century (Lowe 1972, 11, no. 277). The animal's brow-lappet in Deer turns in towards the words '*Vox clamantis inde serto* [sic]'. The text is spaciously laid out and elegantly written. '*Vox*' is further emphasised by a marginal animal head. '*Fuit Johannis*' is given a line to itself. The decoration appears to be articulating the text. There is a possibility therefore that the figure opposite is intended to be John the Baptist, a figure frequently represented in early medieval art, and in Insular manuscript art in a lost miniature in the Royal Bible fragment (Alexander 1978, no. 32; Henderson, G. 1982, 26, ill. 6). The figure in 16v may have a halo—the only figure in the book to have this attribute. He holds a book perhaps illustrative of the opening of the text 'as it is written in the prophet Isaiah'. A more probable identification, therefore, is as Isaiah. The book has a carefully constructed saltire version of the key-pattern used to decorate the lower edge of the frame.

In spite of the gracious flow of the hand, the elegant initial and the ambitious frame there are clear signs on folio 16v of indifference to exact measurement and completion. Such imperfections abound in many *de luxe* manuscripts but the comparative simplicity of the decoration of Deer makes them disconcertingly obvious. What caused the artist to abandon the contouring of the interlace which fills the left-hand edge of the frame? Laziness, hurry, or some deeper sense of the part being adequate to express the whole?

The excerpt from Matthew ended with Christ's warning against false prophets and false healers. The Mark excerpt ends on folio 27v with his teaching that healing comes through faith. Folio 28, the singleton, is blank on the recto. The verso opens the portion of the office for the Visitation of the Sick, which ends on folio 29r. The congruence of these texts one to the other is evident.

THE FOURTH OPENING: FOLIOS 29 VERSO–30 RECTO
(PLATES 12 & 13)

The frames for both pages are simply decorated but maintain the principle of alternation, interlace for the vertical edges on 29v and the horizontal ones on 30r. Both have the 'leaf' motif at the corners, found, for example, in the more elaborate frame for the portrait of Mark in the Macdurnan Gospels (Alexander

1978, ill. 354). On 29v the vertical frames are penetrated under and over by the wrists and hands of a figure with outstretched arms. The importance of the gesture is heightened by a change of pattern within the frame above the arms, from interlace to cruciform key-pattern. The penetration of the frame is a sophisticated treatment of space, not an oddity. The hands are anatomically correct and the ball of the thumb is clearly defined. The Deer artist could draw naturalistic hands, and in one case, that of Abraham, naturalistic feet. The formula for sandaled feet is a calligraphic curve and a few vertical strokes.

A figure with arms outstretched would be a very unusual depiction of an Evangelist, but there are precedents for an outstretched right arm. In the Barberini Gospels it is Matthew whose silhouette is broken by his right arm reaching out to refresh his pen in the inkwell, but in Cerne this gesture is given to Luke. The brow lappet of the lowest of the three animals that make up the opening initial '*Q*' on the facing folio points to '*viderunt*'. This refers to the eye-witnesses who had written accounts of Christ's ministry and death, so the gesture of the left hand across to the text might indicate that St Luke too was going to set out his version of the events (Luke 1:3).

The gesture of spread arms, however, is an eloquent one. It inevitably recalls the crucified Christ, just as arms raised above the shoulders, in the traditional 'orans' attitude of prayer and blessing evoke the cross. It is above all the gesture of a celebrant priest. If the figure on 29v might on the principle of multivalence, also depict a priest, then the priest could be Zacharias. The opening chapter of Luke is devoted to Zacharias the priest, recounting the annunciation to him, as he was serving at the altar of incense, by the Angel of the Lord, of the birth of John the Baptist. The figure of St Luke, prefacing his Gospel in the Lichfield Gospels, holds a flowering plant which has been interpreted as referring to Aaron's Rod, and to the rituals of the Old Testament, over which Zacharias in his time presided.

The early chapters of Luke, as is well known, present the stories of the birth and ministry of John the Baptist and Christ, in parallel. The first chapter ends with the prophecy of Zacharias that God's covenant with Abraham is fulfilled by the birth of John the Baptist who prepares the way for the Lord, who will, through Christ, bring Salvation and the forgiveness of sins. Luke is the only gospel writer to record the Annunciation to Zacharias so the emphasis on his testimony, signalled by the initial, is appropriate. In Insular art the theme of the Annunciation of the birth of John the Baptist was illustrated in the Royal Bible, although the miniature is lost (Henderson, G. 1982, 26, ill. 7). It is also one of the scenes illustrated in St Augustine's Gospels, an Italian book brought to Canterbury at the time of the conversion (Henderson, G. 1982, 16, ill. 5). Two Carolingian books, the Harley Gospels and the fragment in BL Cotton (MS Claudius B V) place the scene within an initial at the beginning of Luke (Henderson, G. 1994, 260). There is precedent therefore for an allusion to the Annunciation to Zacharias forming a frontispiece for Luke.

The Luke excerpt ends at chapter 4, verse 1, the point immediately after the genealogy of Christ, when Christ, full of the Holy Spirit, departs into the wilderness to be tempted by the Devil. The genealogy takes up folio 39, recto and verso and eight lines of folio 40r. Its inclusion is further evidence of the scribe's interest, or perhaps the patron's interest, in the ancestry of Christ. The Lucan genealogy goes back to Adam, son of God, whereas the Matthean ancestry is concerned with Christ's connection with the royal line of David and Abraham. The Deer scribe miscopied the end of the Lucan genealogy. In the exemplar the last six names must have been written in two columns and unthinkingly, he read them down the way instead of across with the result that Maleel followed by Cainan, Enos, Seth, Adam and God became Maleel, Enos, Adam, Cainan, Seth and God. It would seem, therefore, that this unorthodox order, which has caused much scorn, is due to carelessness rather than ignorance.

Nonetheless the text on folio 30r is handsomely set out and the decoration of the initial 'Q' is ingeniously varied. It consists of two animals with strap-like bodies but not split along their length and with no central knot. The decoration filling the bowl of the Q is a conflation of the cruciform key-pattern and the plaid with encircled dot. The top of the letter has a shallow pelta. The animals share a body decorated with dots of blank parchment within the solid paint. The upper animal has a forward running lappet loosely knotted. The lappet of the lower animal penetrates a ring. A third animal head belongs to the upper edge of the frame. Its forward running lappet bends sharply to end in a curl.

THE FIFTH OPENING: FOLIOS 41 VERSO–42 RECTO
(PLATES 15 & 16)

The fifth gathering begins with folio 41. The recto was blank. The verso shows a figure framed in the usual way, and the framed initial for the beginning of the Gospel of St John is on folio 42r facing the figure.

The figure is enthroned, flanked by six small figures, three on either side, one below the other. Once again this would be very unusual iconography for an Evangelist. It is certainly not a composition that could arise from the misunderstanding of an Evangelist portrait. For a figure to be flanked by other personages is a sign of the importance of the central figure. The most straightforward interpretation is that the principal figure is that of St John, holding his authentic testimony of Christ's life and death, and the witnesses of the truth of his testimony (John 21:24) gathered around him to magnify his image. In the margin, under St John's feet, is the image of the Lamb of God, hailed by the Baptist in John 1:29. In the Book of Kells, however, the portrait of John has overtones of a portrait of Christ. Another possible interpretation of the Deer figure is that it is a portrait of Christ, such as occurs among the preliminary decorated pages for Matthew in the Book of Kells. There, on folio 32v, Christ is shown, his head flanked by peacocks, symbolic of immortality, and his body by four small-scale angels (Alexander 1978, ill. 243). The Kells Christ has no halo, but a cross is placed above his head, suspended as it were from the keystone of the arch, under which he sits. His feet touch two discs filled with cruciform key-pattern. Similarly, the Antwerp Sedulius shows Christ enthroned, holding a book, within an arch which is topped with a disc containing a Latin cross, with a tenon at the end of the shaft and circles within the angles of the arms (Alexander 1978, ill. 285). The figure on folio 41v of Deer has a linear Latin cross with expanded terminals between his feet. Outside the lower edge of the frame the lamb signals towards the cross and a flourish of six 'frilled triangles' ends in an animal head looking in the same direction. The case for this figure being a representation of Christ is comparatively strong. If this identification is acceptable, then the likelihood of the other three prefatory miniatures reach beyond conventional Evangelist portraits increases. The decoration of the '*In*' of '*In principio* …' which introduces John on folio 42 recto is virtually identical in construction to the '*In* …' of the Mark '*Initium* …' On folio 42r the brow-lappet of the lowest and largest creature points to the passage '*inipso vita est et vita erat lux hominum etlux intenebris lucet ettenebre eam nonconprehenderunt* [sic]'. The keyword is '*lux*'. John the Baptist was 'not the light but was to give testimony of the light,… and the word was made flesh'. On folio 292r of the Book of Kells, Christ, 'the incarnate Word' is depicted among the letters of '*In principio*'. He has a glory of flame round his head, to express visually, the identity of 'the light' and Christ, the Word made flesh (Alexander 1978, ill. 252).

A suggested iconographic programme for the four main figurative pages in Deer is therefore Christological, with Abraham, the ancestor of Christ (folio 4v), Isaiah the prophet of Christ (folio 16v), the Annunciation to Zacharias of the birth of the precursor (folio 29v), and Christ the Word made flesh (folio 41 recto). The climax of the programme prefaces, appropriately, the full text of the Gospel of St John with its prologue's emphasis on Jesus, as God on earth.[7]

---

7 Readers are referred to Geddes 1998, for another analysis of the Deer miniatures, one which is different from but more sympathetic to the views of Kathleen Hughes. See also Marmer 2002, who concludes that the makers of the Book of Deer were 'quite sophisticated in their approach to the relationship between text and image'. That there is room for many conjectures on the specific interpretation of the iconography goes without saying.

THE SIXTH OPENING: FOLIOS 84 VERSO–85 RECTO
(PLATES 17 & 18)

John ends on folio 84v, having taken up three gatherings. After the *explicit* which is written with flourishes and a bold, cross-like abbreviation for '*secundum*', a double frame contains a single figure in each compartment. The frame has leaf shapes at the corners, and on its vertical edges, two panels, separated by a small square panel at the level of the figures' arms. The colouring of the panels is alternated in the usual fashion. The dividing strut is more elaborately decorated with a variety of patterns. The second panel from the bottom may contain a representation of an object, just possibly an inkwell similar to the one used by John on folio 170v of the Macdurnan Gospels (Alexander 1978, ill. 328).

Both figures are drawn in formulaic style. At the conclusion of John, Christ reveals himself as risen and charges Peter, 'Feed my sheep'. If the tail-piece illustrates the text then the two figures could represent either Christ and Peter, or Peter and John 'which testifies of these things'. Hughes thought that they 'presumably represented Peter and John' thereby silently acknowledging that the artist had access to an illustrated New Testament (something of a rarity) or was capable of innovation (Hughes 1980, 29). Of the two, the figure at the viewer's right is given slightly more emphasis, for example his head is larger. His right hand is placed over his book, whereas the other figure holds his book in the conventional handless way, although his book is given a more eye-catching double frame. Since this artist, and all his fellow Insular book decorators, tends to relate his picture on the verso to what follows on the recto, it is reasonable to relate this pair of seated figures to the text of the Creed, and in particular to the lines on a level with their heads, *sedit addexteram dei patris* [*sic*], that is Christ, the Word, holding a symbol of himself, is literally seated at the right hand of God, the right hand itself being used as an attribute and identifying signal of the Father. If an iconographic argument is needed for the Pictish origin of the Book of Deer, it is the fact that the image of God the Father and God the Son seated side by side, precocious in this period, may be recognised in the cross-slabs at Lethendy (fig. 2.9), Aldbar and St Vigeans No. 11.[8]

The Apostles' Creed and the colophon fill folio 85r opposite. The Creed is introduced with a delicately drawn 'C' made out of a sharply bent strap animal. Two interlocked animal heads of the usual type float above the first line. The last words of the Creed are centred and the colophon, with a slightly enlarged initial, follows.

---

8 Henderson, G. and Henderson, I. 2004, 143–44, ills. 210, 193 and 209.

THE SEVENTH OPENING: FOLIO 85 VERSO–86 RECTO
(PLATES 19 & 20)

This final opening creates what in effect are decorative end-papers. They belong to the last gathering which has ten folios rather than the twelve of those preceding.

The miniature on folio 85v is divided into four panels by a shafted cross similar to the arrangement on folio 1r. Here, the cross has slightly expanded terminals. There are three concentric circles at the crossing of the arms—a simpler arrangement than the marigold cross in this position on the first miniature. Here, too, there are two larger, more elaborately drawn figures below the arms, on either side of the shaft, and two smaller figures above them. Hughes treats this miniature as yet another representation of the four Evangelists. None of the figures holds a book. The upper, minor, figures raise their arms in a gesture of prayer and acclaim. The lower figures have high head-dresses, or perhaps elaborate hairstyles recalling the portrait of Matthew in the St Gall Gospels, and of Mark in the Macdurnan Gospels (Alexander 1978, ills. 204 & 354). It is possible that the Deer head elaboration represents glories of light.

The figure at the bottom right extends his arms from the elbows and displays the palms of his hands. Insular depictions of Christ crucified include examples where the elbows are bent. It is a type with a long history. The lower arms of the Deer figure penetrate the shaft of the cross and the right-hand edge of the frame. This is a similar arrangement, a sophisticated one it should be stressed, to that of the figure with spread arms on folio 29v, but the bent elbow position is found on 85v only and is significant. This pose is certainly taken from crucifixion imagery but in the absence of any other positive indications of crucifixion, the position and the display of hands suggest that Christ Risen or Christ the Judge is intended. In the Judgement, 'every eye shall see him, and they also that pierced him'. The Crucifixion and Resurrection, the basis for the Christian hope of life after death, are conflated in the miniature in the Durham Gospels. Christ on the cross has his arms bent sharply at the elbow. There an inscription expounds the complex iconography (Henderson, G. 1987, 81–4, ill. 114). In Deer, the whole scene, dominated by the acclaiming or witnessing angels, moves the event beyond the passion to its eternal consequences.

In Deer, the figure at the lower left is markedly ungesturing in comparison with the other three figures, but nonetheless has head elaboration. He is presumably symbolic of the blessed, to whom the Risen Christ, as Judge, offers a place in Paradise. Christ touches the shoulder of his saintly companion, and with his other hand indicates the framed panel on the opposite recto, a segmented inhabited rectangle which could adequately stand for the diagrammatic description in Revelation 21 of the Heavenly Jerusalem, and the whole opening relates to the belief, stated in the Creed, in the Judgement, the resurrection of the dead, and the life everlasting.

This last miniature in the manuscript, on folio 86r, is the most elaborate of the three cruciform pages. It makes a fitting end to the book and dispels the sense of haste in some of the earlier illuminated pages. The frame is of virtually the same size and type as that on the verso opposite. The interior space is divided by a saltire cross. Its crossing point provides the centre point for three concentric circles of much larger diameter than those on folio 1v and 85v. The segments created within the innermost circle are filled with straight-line spirals, themselves creating a cruciform shape. The arms of an equal-armed cross project from the circular panel to meet the frame and further segment the page. Immediately above the cross-arms single units (one on either side) of cruciform key-pattern are tailored to conform to the curve of the circular panel. Immediately above these is a triangular space filled with plaid and carefully executed hatching of parallel curves. The upper arm and shaft of the cross are panelled but undecorated. The cross-arms are filled with interlace. Below the arms a sub-triangular space has plain panels, plaid and lattice hatching. Within the upper and lower spaces created by the saltire and equal-armed cross are four figures, the two lower holding books the two upper drawn without visible arms. All four are set on a background of plaid. The page forms a dense mat of varied decorative motifs within spaces created by the superimposed crosses. The four figures are set in a thicket of ornament—only their facial features differentiating them from the forms they, as it were, inhabit. The closest visual parallels for this page are to be found in the Book of Kells, and in the cruciform carpet page of the Turin Gospels fragment (Alexander 1978, ill. 278). The Turin manuscript also contains miniatures of the Ascension and Second Coming. In the Book of Kells, on folio 290v, the four-symbols page preceding the Gospel of St John is segmented by a saltire in the manner of the design of folio 86r in the Book of Deer (Alexander 1978, ill. 250). At the crossing there is a lozenge shape rather than a circle. This, and other lozenge-shapes in Insular art, have been convincingly shown to be symbolic of Christ, the second person of the Trinity, personifying the Word (Richardson 1996).

In the Macdurnan Gospels, the four-symbols page, on folio 1v has a circle at the crossing of an equal-armed cross (Alexander 1978, ill. 325). It encloses a cross of spirals which creates a lozenge-shape at the centre. In the Trier Gospels the prefatory four-symbols page displays a bust-length Christ within the circle at the centre of its cross (ibid. ill. 114). The triple concentric circles on the three full-page cruciform miniatures in Deer are likely to be symbolic of Christ, and possibly, of the three persons of the Trinity, in its most compelling scale, in the last miniature. Here, closing the whole book, we have the image of Christ, symbolically within the New Jerusalem, the Light of the men and angels who dwell therein.[9]

If as was hypothesised above, folio 1v did have a miniature facing it on an original 2r then the subject matter for it would most appropriately have been the Crucifixion, balancing the Risen Christ of the verso of the last opening.

MARGINALIA

In the discussion of the seven illuminated openings many of the analogies made have been with the Book of Kells. Another similarity, in kind if not in quantity, is the occurrence in Deer of 'floating' animal studies in the spaces outside the framed areas and on the text pages. Hughes described some of the marginalia as 'humble descendants of the Kells cocks and dogs'. She compared them also to isolated studies of animals in the margins of the much later Celtic Psalter (Hughes 1980, 27). Hughes associated such marginal animals with drollery in later medieval books. Recent scholarship makes such a view of the minor, interlinear or marginal decoration in the Book of Kells and other Insular manuscripts increasingly difficult to sustain (O'Reilly 1994: Meehan 1994). The likelihood is that such decoration, along with minor initials and colour coding represent a conscious articulation and enhancement of the meaning of texts. The possible significance of the creatures outside the frame on folio 41 verso has already been mentioned, and the two heads beneath the double-frame on folio 84 recto do not look like idle doodling. The alert bird with a leaf in its beak and the spirited quadruped on folio 54v (plate 21) may draw attention to the Eucharistic passage in John 6:56, written immediately above. Christ is the bread of life which nourishes creation just as he is the vine whose fruit symbolises his life-giving blood. The Deer creatures can be compared to the vine-scroll inhabited by birds and animals frequently depicted in Insular art. The figure of a man at the bottom of folio 71v (plate 22) draws the eye to another important passage, the account in John 14:16–26, of the gift of the Holy Spirit. The figure is drawn in the basic formulaic style, although the skirt of his robe is reduced to a unit of cruciform key-pattern. His arms are raised in the familiar gesture of prayer and praise.

Some of the incidental ornament consists of the usual scribal aids to guiding the reader. The detached head or pairs of heads placed crown to crown, and at the ends of flourishes of frilled triangles may all be susceptible to decoding. They are a distinctive aspect of the book which evokes an artist/scribe well in control of form and line.

9 For another interpretation of this miniature see Geddes 1998, 541. The increased size of the circle at the crossing at this point in the manuscript is certainly an indicator of specific iconography. See the important discussion of such medallions, which may have relevance for Deer, in Nees 1983.

THE ART OF THE BOOK OF DEER AND INSULAR
SCULPTURE IN SCOTLAND

In his introduction to his edition of the Book of Deer John Stuart discussed the question of the origin of the book. He was aware of its many similarities with surviving Irish gospel-books but there seemed to him nothing improbable in concluding that its known provenance in Deer was also its place or origin and that the scribe was a native of Alba (Stuart 1869, xxi–xxv).

Stuart was very familiar with the early medieval sculptured stones of Scotland and argued that the nature of the sculpture implied the existence of art in other media. In contrast Hughes felt that what she saw as the oddities in Deer made it 'alien in an Irish context' and that while the scribe knew about sculpture, he had no access to manuscripts other than a few hasty, misunderstood, sketches (Hughes 1980, 37). Quite rightly she drew attention to the iconography on the front of the symbol-bearing cross-slab now standing in the grounds of Elgin Cathedral. Following the drawing published by J. Romilly Allen she describes it in detail as

> showing four figures in the arms of a cross, and front-face, which is rather unusual on a Pictish monument. The bottom figure on the left has an angel beside him, that on the right has an eagle, so these are clearly the four evangelists, and suspended round their necks are Gospels on short straps, as in the Book of Deer. It is rather interesting that this unusual representation which antedates the manuscript is only some fifty or sixty miles from Deer (Hughes 1980, 28).

Evangelist iconography is rare on Insular sculpture, understandably, for it belongs with gospel-books. The Evangelist iconography on the Elgin cross-slab is certainly a strong argument for the existence of illuminated gospels in Pictland. The Elgin slab is made of very rough gneiss and is worn. That Allen was able to draw out the designs on the slab at all is remarkable. His verbal description is less confident than his drawing and no mention is made there of book satchels.[10] The iconography of the Elgin cross-slab cannot be discussed in terms of Allen's drawing.[11]

---

10 A number of Pictish monuments show clerics wearing book satchels suspended from their shoulders. Interestingly the bearer of the book is always at the rear of a procession. The case for the depiction of figures wearing suspended satchels being represented in Deer depends on how one interprets the formulae for drapery. The suggestion that the figures hold reliquaries can be set aside (Jackson 1972, 10–11). On balance, the books would seem to function as an attributive label for the scriptures generally or for Gospel-books specifically. The placing of the book horizontally is an aspect of Deer figurative iconography that might be profitably explored.   11 Dr Geddes has also been misled by Allen's drawing. See Geddes 1998, 538.

2.7 Cross-slab fragment. Wester Denoon, Glamis, Angus, front. Photo: © Tom and Sybil Gray Collection.

2.8 Cross-slab fragment. Wester Denoon, Glamis, Angus, back: body of a female figure. Photo: © Tom and Sybil Gray Collection.

I have written elsewhere about the damaged top of the Elgin cross-slab. Stylistically and iconographically the figures in the angles of the cross-arms are very different from those in the Book of Deer. They are bust-length, carved, not front-face but in three-quarter view in the manner of the David and other figures on the St Andrews Sarcophagus and the hermit saints on the Nigg cross-slab. The Elgin evangelists are remarkable pieces of naturalistic, plastic, sculpture, virtually three-dimensional. The two remaining complete images show the Evangelist with his symbol adjacent. The upper figures are not winged, as Allen drew them, the wings are the remains of the winged symbols of the calf and the lion (Henderson, I. 1994, 82; 1999a, 11–15 and ill). In his description Allen thought the figures held books. The Elgin cross-slab iconography has no direct bearing on the art of the Book of Deer. The book-holding symbols on the Brechin slab show that other types of Evangelist symbol iconography were also available to artists (Okasha 1985, 49–51, ill. 1). In other words, on the evidence of the sculpture and of the scripts displayed in inscriptions on sculpture (ibid.), there was access to a range of illuminated gospel texts in eastern Scotland in the early medieval period, some of which could be reflected in the art of the Book of Deer.

More directly relevant to the Book of Deer are the frontal-facing, often paired, ecclesiastical figures carved on cross-slabs in Angus and Perthshire. These figures represent a change in emphasis for Pictish sculpture both in subject matter and style. The predominantly profile art, so often representing riders in motion, gives way to pairs of static ecclesiastical figures standing, or enthroned side by side. They carry books, croziers or other less readily identifiable objects. Hughes rightly cited the enthroned pair at the top of the reverse of the Aldbar cross-slab as particularly similar to the pair of figures in the miniature in Deer at the end of John (Hughes 1980, 31, fig. 3)[12] although she failed to recognise the iconographic significance of this comparison.

There is no doubt that a sculptural artistic context for the art of the Book of Deer can be found in these slabs and the more elaborate iconography of the Brechin cross-slab and the Dunkeld 'Apostles' stone (RCAHMS 1994, 89, ill. B; fig. 2.10)—both fragments of cross-slabs. It is an interesting fact, and one relevant to the extended iconography of Deer, that this later phase of early medieval sculpture has a new range of imagery. A recently discovered northern example is the slab fragment found in the crypt of the twelfth-century church at Portmahomack, Tarbat. It shows a row of figures, one holding a book, wearing classical dress on its reverse, probably another representation of the Apostles, and above them an enigmatic scene involving the butchering of an animal which may represent a reference to an animal rite connected with the ratification of God's covenant with Abraham in *Genesis* 15—an episode illustrated in Aelfric's Hexateuch, a heavily illustrated English manuscript of the eleventh century (Henderson, G. and Henderson, I. 2004, 142, ill. 206). This expansion of iconography undoubtedly owed much to the intensification of contacts with Iona in the ninth century but there is no question of a cultural take-over (Henderson, I. 1978; 1999b). This later sculpture retains many distinctive features but the essentially synthetic nature of the art through-out the period, the seventh to the tenth century, remains. The seemingly innovative nature of the iconography of the Book of Deer fits well into this phase in sculpture.

Stylistically, comparison between sculpture and the art of Deer is not very fruitful for the essence of the Deer style is its calligraphic quality. The figures in Deer and on the slabs with ecclesiastics are depicted in geometric style, but that is the extent of the similarity. The figures on Aldbar are rounded and plastic. The enthroned figures on a cross-slab from Lethendy, Perthshire (fig. 2.9) have the Deer head proportion and Abraham's feet but the tubular drapery belongs to a chiselled sculptural style used, for example, for the neat

---

12 Again Dr Hughes was content to rely on Allen's drawing.

2.9 Cross-slab. Lethendy, Perthshire, back: angel, enthroned persons and David composing the Psalms. Photo: © RCAHMS.

2.10 Cross-slab fragment. Dunkeld, Perthshire. 'The Apostles Stone'. Narrow face (right side): large scale nimbed figure with three smaller scale figures beneath. Broad face (back): The Apostles. Photo: © Tom and Sybil Gray Collection.

row of clerics on a slab from Invergowrie, Angus (Allen and Anderson 1903, fig. 277B). The Deer figures have the fluency of a pen and the quite specific formula for their robes connects its style with the surviving Irish manuscripts rather than early medieval Scottish sculpture. The growing predominance of the frontal viewpoint is a significant development in Pictish sculpture but it is equally a development in Irish book illumination. In this respect Pictish sculpture maintains its responsiveness to and participation in the Insular art style.[13]

The ornament in Deer can be paralleled in sculpture. For example, the inner circle at the crossing of the saltire on folio 86r is a version of straight-line spiral motifs, described by Allen as nos. 1014 and 1015, which appear in square panels as nos 995, 1002 and 1004. Allen's examples are taken from a wide range of Insular art but it is not comprehensive for there is always a creative element in decoration which modifies basic types making it difficult to systematise. For what it is worth, Allen's Pictish examples come from what is conventionally considered to be later sculpture, the Dupplin Cross and slabs at St Andrews, Invergowrie 1 and Monifieth 1.[14] The clear motivation behind the choice of ornament by the Deer artist is a desire to employ motifs with cruciform frameworks whether in a saltire or Greek type. The appreciation of the cruciform nature of much Insular ornament in all media was noted by Allen and developed by Robert Stevenson (1982).

13 A comparatively recent find demonstrates the extent to which we are at the mercy of surviving material. In 1994, Norman Atkinson identified a Pictish cross-slab at Wester Denoon, Glamis, Angus (figs 2.7 & 2.8). On the front is a cross covered with median-incised interlace of a character and weight similar to the interlace of Deer. To the right and left of the shaft are raised panels decorated with units of a geometric motif consisting of a cross with horizontally laid square brackets on the top and bottom of the shaft. This seems to me a skeleton form of the geometric patterns in Deer. The arrangement on the raised panels also recalls the Deer frames. That the figure on the reverse is in an extreme version of the formulaic geometric style would seem to clinch the connection showing that this style, without, of course, the calligraphic fluency, was part of sculptural repertoires. Of particular interest is the use of a pennanular brooch centrally placed within the sub-rectangular garment. This location is strongly indicative that a woman is intended (Ó Floinn 1989, 89) and to complete the picture the Pictish mirror and comb symbolic pair is placed to the figure's right, and what may be serpentine interlace to the left. Regrettably, I have not yet seen this slab and I am most grateful to Norman Atkinson for an account of his identification and to Tom E. Gray for permission to reproduce his excellent photographs.　　**14** I have been unable to see the apparently unpublished fragments of key-pattern paralleling those in Deer, from Aberdeenshire referred to in Geddes 1998, 541–43. The Lindisfarne analogy cited in that paper from Allen's listing, is from the incomplete cross-shaft, Lindisfarne 6, see Cramp 1984 (vol. 1, part 2, ill. 1073). Professor Cramp dates Lindisfarne 6 to the last quarter of the ninth to the first half of the tenth, a date which, as it happens, accommodates the production of the Book of Deer. On the difficulties of classifying key-patterns and the range of designs see Lionard 1961, Crawford 1980 and Edwards 1987 (114–15).

CONCLUSIONS

A close examination of the art of the Book of Deer reveals that it is the production of an artist familiar with many of the conventions of Insular book art. This being so, the proposition that the distinctiveness of the figurative art was the result of ignorance cannot be sustained. A figure holding a book is, after all, not an arcane image. The figurative art of the frontispieces can be understood as a coherent Christological programme. The alternative, that there are three representations of the four Evangelists (1v, 85v and 86r), and 4 representations of individual Evangelists (4v, 16v, 29v and 41v) seems highly unlikely in a book of this scale, and given the unusual nature of three of the frontispieces (4v, 29v and 41v) require unacceptably procrustean arguments to support the identifications.

To assess the Book of Deer properly weight has to be given to its function, a subject discussed elsewhere in this book. On the grounds of its size it is probable that Deer was written and decorated for private and intimate pastoral use. The imagery provides, as it were, resting places for reflection and consolation, the text an *aide-mémoire*. The miniatures are concerned with central themes of scriptural testimony; the ancestry of Christ, the role of the prophets and patriarchs, the assurance of the Resurrection. The Apostles' Creed and the abbreviated Eucharist complete the manual. This imagery may have been available in a single model or models but in Insular art, almost from the beginning, specific iconography could be created afresh or constructed in different ways to serve different purposes. The spacious lay-out of the text sets Deer apart from some of the very compressed, small Gospel-books.[15] The excerpts, together with the full text of John, appear to have had their own significance (Hughes 1980, 36, with reference to Brown, T.J. 1969, 36, n.1). If Deer had the amuletic function claimed for the beginnings of the Gospel texts this does not necessarily tell us about its artistic models, or of the resources of the scriptorium in which it was produced.

Some of the art of Deer may seem flagrantly careless and excessively formulaic but this is to some degree evidence for the minimalist requirements of the artist and his patron, not an indicator of cultural impoverishment

---

15 I have deliberately refrained from stressing the connections between the Book of Deer and the category of manuscripts termed by McGurk the Irish pocket gospel-book (1956). The category, while undoubtedly useful in broad terms, does not provide a norm against which Deer must be evaluated. See the reservations of Françoise Henry on the usefulness of the term and the need to examine 'these humbler volumes anew' (Henry 1965, 199–202). There are after all no surviving Irish Gospel-books of the tenth century with which to compare the Book of Deer (Henry 1967, 105). On the other hand, if left out of discussions of these small format Irish manuscripts the book can be neglected. See, for example, the position described by Black, 1986.

either of the place of origin or of the entirety of the society of which that place was a part (Sims–Williams 1985).

From the art-historical point of view the context of the Book of Deer is most readily detectable in the nature of its decorated initials (Alexander 1978, 87). The type had a long history, from the ninth to the eleventh century. The Deer version is entirely competent with no hint of undue dependency or degeneration. Because of the many small details that link the book with the Book of Kells and the Macdurnan Gospels a date towards the middle of this period, that is the late ninth to early tenth century, seems most probable. As is notorious, the productions of Insular art do not readily proclaim their date and place of origin, and from the point of view of art, the Book of Deer is no more likely to reveal certainty as to its origin.

The way forward towards a full understanding of the Book of Deer is to concentrate on the evidence which its confident and often innovative art provides. To explain it away, in terms of comparison with other art, whether to its credit or discredit, obscures what it has to tell us about the principles that were devised in Insular art from the beginning, for making connections between text and image in an abbreviated non-classical style. A study of these principles is overdue. When it is made we can be confident that the artist/scribe of 'this splendid little book' will be revealed as an intelligent exponent of this austere, cerebral style where the standard of nature is irrelevant, and the participation of an informed viewer expected.

MANUSCRIPTS CITED

Antwerp
Museum Plantin-Moretus
MS M.17.4 (Sedulius, *Carmen Paschale*)

Cambridge
Corpus Christi College
MS 197B+ London, BL, Cotton Otho C.V
(Cambridge/London Gospels)
MS 286 (St Augustine's Gospels)

St John's College
C.9 (59) (Southampton Psalter)

University Library
MS Ii. 6. 32 (Book of Deer)
MS Ll.1.10 (Book of Cerne)

Dublin
Trinity College
MS 56 (Garland of Howth)

MS 57 (Book of Durrow)
MS 58 (Book of Kells)
MS 59 (Book of Dimma)
MS 60 (Book of Mulling)

Durham
Cathedral Library
MS A. II. 17 (Durham Gospels)

Edinburgh
University Library
MS 56 (Celtic Psalter)

Fulda
Landesbibliothek
Cod Bonifatianus 3 (Cadmug Gospels)

Lichfield
Cathedral Library
s.n. (Lichfield Gospels)

London
British Library
Cotton MS Nero D. IV (Lindisfarne Gospels)
Cotton MS Claudius B. IV (Aelfric's
    Hexateuch)
Cotton MS Claudius B.V
Harley 2788 (Harley Gospels)
Royal MS I. E. VI (Gospel-book, fragment
    of a Bible)

Lambeth Palace
MS 1370 (Macdurnan Gospels)

Oxford
Bodleian Library
Auct. D.2.19 (MacRegol Gospels)

Paris
Bibliothèque Nationale de France
Latin 9389 (Echternach Gospels)

Rome, Vatican
Biblioteca Apostolica

MS Barberini Lat. 570 (Barberini or Rome
    Gospels)

St Gall
Stiftsbibliothek
Cod 51 (St Gall Gospels)
Cod 60 (Gospel of St John)
Cod 1395 (Gospel-book fragment)
    pp 418–19.

St Petersburg
Public Library
Cod Q.v.I.18 (St Petersburg, formerly,
    Leningrad, Bede)
Cod Q.v.XIV.1 (Paulinus of Nola, *Carmina*)

Trier
Domschatz
Cod. 61 (The Trier Gospels)

Turin
Biblioteca Nazionale
Cod. O.IV.20 (Turin Gospels)

REFERENCES

Alexander, J.J.G. (1978) *Insular manuscripts: 6th to the 9th century* (A Survey of Manuscripts Illuminated in the British Isles, I), London.

Allen, J.R., and J. Anderson (1903) *The early Christian monuments of Scotland*, 3 parts, Edinburgh (repr. Balgavies, 1993, 2 vols).

Black, R. (1986) Review of P. De Brun and M. Herbert, *Catalogue of Irish manuscripts in Cambridge libraries*, Cambridge 1986, *Cambridge Medieval Celtic Studies*, 12 (1986) 120–1.

Brown, M.P. (1996) *The Book of Cerne: prayer, patronage and power in ninth-century England*, London and Toronto.

Brown, T.J. (1969) *The Stonyhurst Gospel of St John*, Oxford. [facsimile ed.]

Carver, M.O.H. (1986) 'Contemporary artefacts illustrated in Late Saxon manuscripts', *Archaeologia* 108 (1986), 117–45.

Cramp, R. (1984) *Corpus of Anglo-Saxon stone sculpture. Volume 1, County Durham and Northumberland*, 2 parts, Oxford.

Crawford, H.S. (1980) *Handbook of carved ornament from the Irish monuments of the Christian period*. Dublin 1926. (Repr. 1980 with the title *Carved ornament*.)

Duft, J., and P. Meyer (1954) *The Irish miniatures in the Abbey Library of St. Gall*, Berne, Olten and Lausanne.

Edwards, N. (1987) 'Abstract ornament on early medieval Irish crosses: a preliminary catalogue', in *Ireland and Insular art AD 500–1200*, ed. M. Ryan, Dublin, 111–17.

——, (1995) '11th-century Welsh illuminated manuscripts: the nature of the Irish connection', in *From the Isles of the North: early medieval art in Ireland and Britain*, ed. C. Bourke, Belfast, 147–55.

Finlayson, C.P. (1962) *Celtic Psalter: Edinburgh University Library MS 56*, Amsterdam. [facsimile ed.]

Fuchs, R., and D. Oltrogge (1994) 'Colour material and painting technique in the Book of Kells', in *The Book of Kells: Proceedings of a conference at Trinity College Dublin 6–9 September 1992*, ed. F. O'Mahony, Dublin, 133–71.

Geddes, J. (1998) 'The art of the Book of Deer', *Proc. Soc. Antiq. Scot.* 128, 537–49.

Graham-Campbell, J. (2003) *Pictish silver: status and symbol* (H.M. Chadwick Memorial Lectures, 13), Cambridge.

Harbison, P. (1992) *The high crosses of Ireland: an iconographical and photographic survey*, 3 vols (Römisch-Germanisches Zentralmuseum Forschungsinstitut für Vor-und-Frühgeschichte, Monagraphien, 17), Bonn.

Henderson, G. (1982) *Losses and lacunae in early Insular art* (University of York Monograph Series, 3), York.

—— (1987) *From Durrow to Kells*, London.

—— (1994) 'Emulation and invention in Carolingian art', in *Carolingian Culture: emulation and innovation*, ed. R. McKitterick, Cambridge, 248–73.

Henderson, G., and I. Henderson (2004) *The art of the Picts: sculpture and metalwork in early medieval Scotland*, London.

Henderson, I. (1978) 'Sculpture north of the Forth after the take-over by the Scots', in *Anglo-Saxon and Viking Age sculpture and its context*, ed. J. Lang (BAR British Series 49), Oxford, 47–74.

—— (1986) 'The Book of Deer' [Abstract of a lecture], in *Proceedings of the Seventh International Congress of Celtic Studies*, ed. D. Ellis Evans, J.G. Griffith, and E.M. Jope, Oxford, 278.

—— (1994) 'The Insular and Continental context of the St Andrews sarcophagus', in *Scotland in Dark Age Europe*, ed. B.E. Crawford, St Andrews, 71–102.

—— (1998) 'A note on the artefacts depicted on the surviving side panel', in *The St Andrews Sarcophagus: a Pictish masterpiece and its international connections*, ed. S.M. Foster, Dublin, 156–65.

—— (1999a) 'The social function of Pictish sculpture at Elgin and Kinneddar, Moray, and Portmahomack, Tarbat, Easter Ross', in *Pictish art*, ed. S. Bennett (The Moray Society), Elgin, 11–15.

—— (1999b) 'The Dupplin Cross: a preliminary consideration of its art-historical context', in *Northumbria's Golden Age*, ed. J. Hawkes and S. Mills, Stroud, 161–77.

Henry, F. (1965) *Irish art in the early Christian period (to 800 AD)*, London.

—— (1967) *Irish art during the Viking invasions (800–1020 AD)*, London.

Hewitt, J. (1855) *Ancient armour and weapons in Europe*, Oxford and London.

Hughes, K. (1980) 'The Book of Deer (Cambridge University Library MS Ii. 6. 32)', in *Celtic Britain in the early Middle Ages: studies in Scottish and Welsh sources by the late Kathleen Hughes* (Studies in Celtic History II), ed. D.N. Dumville, Woodbridge and Totowa, NJ, 22–37.

Jackson, K. (1972) *The Gaelic Notes in the Book of Deer*, Cambridge.

Kitzinger, E. (1980) 'Christian imagery: growth and impact', in *Age of spirituality: a symposium*, ed. K. Weitzmann, New York, 141–63.

Laing, L. (2001) 'The date of the Aberlemno churchyard stone', in *Pattern and purpose in Insular art: Proceedings of the Fourth International Conference on Insular Art … Cardiff …1998*, ed. M. Redknap et al., Oxford, 241–51.

Lewis, S. (1980) 'Sacred calligraphy: the Chi Rho page in the Book of Kells', *Traditio* 36, 139–59.

Lionard, P. (1961) 'Early Irish grave-slabs', *Proc. RIA* 61C (1960–1), 95–169, (ed. F. Henry).

Lowe, E.A. (1972), (ed.) *Codices Latini Antiquiores: a palaeographical guide to Latin manuscripts prior to the ninth century. Vol II, Great Britain and Ireland* (2nd ed.), Oxford.

Marner, D. (2002) 'The sword of the Spirit, the word of God and the book of Deer', *Medieval Archaeology* 46, 1–28.

McGurk, P. (1956) 'The Irish pocket gospel book', *Sacris Erudiri* 8, 249–70.

Meehan, B. (1994) *The Book of Kells*, London.

Meek, D.E. (1993) 'The Book of Deer', in *The dictionary of Scottish church history and theology*, ed. N. Cameron et al., Edinburgh.

Nees, L. (1983) 'The colophon drawing in the Book of Mulling: a supposed Irish monastery plan and the tradition of terminal illustration in early Medieval manuscripts', *Cambridge Medieval Celtic Studies* 5, 67–91.

Ó Floinn, R. (1989) 'Secular metalwork in the eighth and ninth centuries', in *'The work of angels': masterpieces of Celtic metalwork, 6th–9th centuries AD*, ed. S. Youngs, London, 72–91.

O'Mahony, F. (1994), (ed.) *The Book of Kells: Proceedings of a conference at Trinity College Dublin, 6–9 September 1992*, Dublin.

O'Reilly, J. (1994) 'Exegesis and the Book of Kells: the Lucan genealogy', in *The Book of Kells: Proceedings of a conference at Trinity College Dublin, 6–9 September 1992*, ed. F. O'Mahony, Dublin, 344–97.

Okasha, E. (1985) 'The non-ogam inscriptions of Pictland', *Cambridge Medieval Celtic Studies* 9, 44–69.

RCAHMS (1994) *South-East Perth: an archaeological landscape*, Edinburgh.

Richardson, H. (1996) 'Lozenge and logos', *Archaeology Ireland* 10, 24–5.

Schapiro, M. (1980a) 'The decoration of the Leningrad manuscript of Bede', in *Late Antique, early Christian and medieval art: selected papers*, London, 199–224.

—— (1980b) 'The place of Ireland in Hiberno-Saxon art', in *Late Antique, early Christian and medieval art: selected papers*, London, 225–41.

Sims-Williams, P. (1985) [Review of K. Hughes 1980], in *Journal of Ecclesiastical History* 36, 306–8.

Stevenson, R.B.K. (1982) 'Aspects of ambiguity on crosses and interlace,' *Ulster Journal of Archaeology* 44–5 (1981–2), 1–27.

Stuart, J. (1869), (ed.) *The Book of Deer* (Spalding Club), Aberdeen and Edinburgh.

Webb, N. (1983) 'Finding a context for the Southampton Psalter', unpublished undergraduate dissertation, History of Art Department, University of Cambridge.

Werckmeister, O.-K. (1963) 'Three problems of tradition in pre-Carolingian figure-style: from Visigothic to Insular illumination', *Proc. RIA* 63C (1962–64), 167–89.

Werner, M. (1997) 'The Book of Durrow and the question of programme', *Anglo-Saxon England* 26, 23–39.

Wilson, D. (1973) 'The treasure', in *St Ninian's Isle and its treasure*, 2 vols, ed. A. Small, C. Thomas, and D. Wilson, Oxford, vol. 1, 45–148.

Youngs, S. (1989), (ed.) *'The work of angels'. masterpieces of Celtic metalwork, 6th–9th centuries AD*, London.

The sick and the dying in the Book of Deer

GILBERT MÁRKUS

An extra folio has been inserted into the original Book of Deer, the present folio 28. It is bound following the partial text of Mark's Gospel (which comes to an abrupt halt at 5:35, half way through the verse, on folio 27v) and before the beginning of Luke. On the *verso* of this inserted folio, and on the *recto* of folio 29—which was originally the blank *recto* side of the first folio of the gathering containing Luke's Gospel—there is the text of a ritual for the giving of communion. The ritual section has often been said to have been inserted some centuries later than the original manuscript. Lapidge and Sharpe, for example, date it to the early twelfth century,[1] as does David Howlett in his essay on this ritual text, where he states that 'the prayer may have been composed as early as the seventh century, though the copy in this manuscript was written early in the twelfth century.'[2] David Dumville has cast doubt on this conventional dating on palaeographic grounds, however: the script is 'Late Celtic miniscule', and should accordingly be dated to *c*.850 x 1000,[3] that is more or less contemporary with the script and illumination of the original Gospel text of the manuscript. I wholly accept Professor Dumville's view. Why some scholars have dated it to the twelfth century is not clear, but it may be simply that some additions to the Book of Deer are clearly dateable, namely the property records, and that as those additions are dateable to the twelfth century people have supposed that the ritual addition was also made at about the same period. The palaeographic evidence that the ritual was inserted in the ninth or tenth century is supported by the single line of Gaelic in the text, the instruction *hisund dub[eir] sacorfaicc dau*, 'here he gives him the sacrifice', which is straightforward Old Gaelic.[4]

Kathleen Hughes refers to this ritual as a 'mass for the sick',[5] though strictly speaking it is not a mass at all in the usual sense of the word, which generally refers to the full eucharistic liturgy of the church, but is rather a truncated rite of communion outside mass. Furthermore, there is little clear internal evidence in the text that the sick are envisaged as the recipients of communion, though it is perfectly clear from a comparison with other manuscripts that this was indeed a rite for the sick, indeed for the dying, as we

---

1 Lapidge and Sharpe 1985, no. 1032. 2 Howlett 2000, 1. 3 Personal communication; also see Dumville 2001, 455. 4 Of course, it is possible that the Old Gaelic rubric was copied in the twelfth century from an earlier manuscript, but given the palaeographic evidence, this linguistic evidence is at least suggestive. 5 Hughes 1980, 35.

shall see. The Book of Deer was clearly not originally intended as a missal or ritual book, but as a gospel book. Nor was it intended for ordinary liturgical use in a church. It is a tiny volume, one of those books referred to as 'pocket gospels' because of their size, and which Patrick McGurk has identified as a group which is 'so obviously eccentric and Irish in its connection as to make certain that Ireland was the home of this particular tradition of book making.'[6] For Ireland, here, read the Gaelic-speaking world. Nobody would be likely to produce such books, with their tiny and cramped script, unless portability was a prime consideration. These books were made for walking.[7] In this article I propose to examine the ritual text itself, to compare it with three similar texts from the Gaelic-speaking world, and to place it within the context of the development of Christian rites for the sick and the dying. The ritual text is as follows:[8]

[f. 28v]
Item oratio an[te] dominicam orationem
Cre[a]tor naturarum omnium d[eu]s
$_7$ parens uniu[er]sarum in c[e]lo $_7$ in t[er]ra
originum hás trementis p[opu]li tui
relegiosas p[re]ces ex illo inaccessibileis
lucis trono tuo suscipe $_7$ int[er] hiruphín
et zaraphin indefessas circum
stantium laudes exaudi spei n[on] am
bigue precationes. P[ate]r n[oste]r q[ui] es . us[que] i[n] fin[em]

Lib[er]a nós D[omi]ne a malo D[omi]ne Xr[ist]e Ih[es]u
custodi nos semp[er] in omni op[er]e bona
fons et auctor omnium bonorum
d[eu]s euacua nos uitiis . et reple nos
uirtutibus bonis . p[er] te Xr[ist]e Ih[e]s[u]

hisund dub[eir][9] sacorfaicc dau . $_7$

6 Cited in Hughes 1980, 22. McGurk excluded Deer from his list, perhaps because he thought it was Scottish rather than Irish. 7 Stuart noted of the illuminations that 'the worn and stained condition of some of them would suggest that the volume had at times been carried about by those who used it' (1869, clix). 8 The text is taken from a photograph of the original manuscript, with enlarged initials and original line arrangement retained. Expanded contractions are placed in square brackets. Spelling irregularities have been retained: *inaccessibileis* for *inaccessibilis*; *opere bona* for *opere bono*. 9 I expand this to *dubeir* 'he gives', but the scribe may have intended *dubir* 'you give'. Note that the parallel instruction in the rite of Dimma, in the appendix below, has *das ei eucharistiam* 'you give'.

Corpus cum sanguine d[omi]ni n[ost]ri Ih[es]u
X[rist]i sanitas sit tibi i[n] uitam p[er]petua[m]
        et salutem
Reffecti X[rist]i corpore et sanguine
t[ib]i semper dicamus d[omin]e al[leluia] al[leluia]
Q[ui] satiauit animam inanem et anima[m]
essurientem satiauit bonis al[leluia] al[leluia]
Et sacrificent sacrificium laudis ⁊
usque exultatione . al[leluia] al[leluia]

[f. 29r]
Calicem salutaris accipiam et nomen
d[omi]ni inuocabo . al[leluia] al[leluia]
Reffecti Xr[ist]i corpore . al[leluia] al[leluia] ..
Laudate d[omi]n[u]m omnes gentes al[leluia] al[leluia]
Gloria .. reffecti Xr[ist]i . al[leluia] al[leluia]
et nunc . Et semper. Reffecti
Sacrificate sacrificium iustitiæ

      ⁊ sperate in d[omi]no

d[eu]s t[ib]i gratias agimus p[er] quem mist[er]ia
s[an]c[t]a celebrauimus et a te s[an]c[t]itatis
dona deposcimus miserere nob[is]
d[omi]ne saluator mundi . qui regnas
in secula seculorum amen . Finit

Note that the whole of this communion ritual appears across two facing pages at a single opening of the book. No turning of pages would be required from the beginning to the end of the rite, leaving the minister's hands free—to handle the host, for example.

It is also instantly recognisable that the structure of the rite broadly follows that of the communion rite in the Mass, beginning with the introduction to the Lord's prayer, then the *Pater Noster* itself, followed by the embolism or prayer *Libera nos*, as in many missals, and then the giving of communion. The following antiphons and responsory reflect the common practice during Mass of singing during and after the reception of communion, and the concluding prayer is just as one would expect at the end of a Mass. So much for the overall structure of the Deer ritual. The content has been closely studied by F.E. Warren, who pointed to many of the sources used in this rite, and compared it to other rituals, both Insular and Continental.[10]

10 Warren 1881, 163–6.

The communion antiphons in Deer are generally taken from the Psalms, although the first one, *Reffecti Christi corpore et sanguine*, is not, but first appears as a communion antiphon in the Mozarabic rite of the Mass.[11] The next two antiphons in Deer, *Qui satiavit* and *Et sacrificent sacrificium*, are from Vulgate Psalm 106, verses 9 and 22 respectively. Psalm 106 praises the God who delivers his people from danger and distress, forgiving their sins, raising them from sickness and closeness to death. The eighteenth verse, *usque ad portas mortis*, is particularly appropriate given the circumstances in which this ritual was performed. Its final request is that God should raise the needy out of affliction, giving them families like flocks of sheep.

The antiphon *Calicem salutaris accipiam* is from Psalm 115:13, another psalm of deliverance in time of distress, and particularly useful for someone sick unto death who is now receiving communion. The fifteenth verse of this psalm does not suggest that there was necessarily any great confidence that God would save the person from dying, but rather that God would save them from judgement when they died: 'precious in the sight of the Lord is the death of his holy ones.' The psalm makes the promise: 'I will pay my vows unto the Lord, before all his people, in the courts of the house of the Lord.'

The next communion prayer in Deer is a responsory, a song in which one line is recited, usually by cantor or minister, and that line repeated as a response by the choir or congregation. The response here seems to be the whole antiphon given earlier, *Reffecti Christi corpore et sanguine, tibi semper dicamus, Domine, alleluia, alleluiai*. The cantor then sings the verse *Laudate Dominum omnes gentes*, the first verse of Psalm 116, and the response is sung again by the choir or congregation; then *Gloria Patri et Filio et Spiritui Sancto*, followed by the response, then *sicut erat in principio et nunc et semper et in saecula saeculorum, Amen*, again followed by the choral response.[12]

The final antiphon, *Sacrificate sacrificium iustitiae* is Psalm 4:6, a psalm which rejoices that 'the Lord hears me when I call him,' and invites believers to trust in God as they lie on their beds, and assures them that when they fall asleep, when they rest, God alone will give them hope. Again the psalm is particularly fitting for those close to the long sleep of death.

Communion antiphons such as those in Deer are typical of communion rites for both *viaticum* and the celebration of the mass as found in early Irish sources.[13] The actual verses chosen for the prayers differ greatly among the various texts, but the style is fairly consistent. They represent a continuation of the practice in the ancient liturgies of singing a psalm during communion. By the tenth century the practice had ceased, or rather the singing of the

11 Hammond 1878, 357.   12 It may be unusual to have the *Gloria Patri* separated from the *Sicut erat* sections by a response.   13 For the other rituals for the sick, see the comparative table of rituals below. For the use of antiphons during Mass, see the *Stowe Missal* (Warner 1915, 17–18) and *The Antiphonary of Bangor* (Warren 1895, 30–1).

whole psalm had been replaced in most places by the singing of a short antiphon from the psalm. It is not clear whether the Deer ritual envisages the singing of all the antiphons, or just a selection.[14]

The concluding prayer of the Deer ritual, *Deus tibi gratias agimus*, is found in the mass of the Gallican Sacramentary, *c.*AD700, as well as in several Irish sources—the rites of *viaticum* in Dimma, Stowe and Mulling, as we shall see below, and in the closing prayers of Stowe's baptismal ritual.[15] Its *incipit* corresponds to that of a concluding prayer in the rite of the Mass in the Stowe Missal, but the Stowe prayer is longer and more elaborate.[16] I would suggest that the few words towards the end of Deer's concluding prayer, *Miserere nobis domine, salvator mundi*, are not part of the original prayer. They look like additional material which has been inserted, perhaps erroneously, at this point, separating the body of the prayer from its concluding formula, *qui regnas*. This is confirmed by the three Irish texts which we shall examine shortly, all of which lack the *miserere nobis* element at this point, as does the *Missale Gothicum* version of the same prayer.[17]

DEER AND ITS COGNATES

The ritual section in the Book of Deer bears a close resemblance to ritual texts in three other manuscripts, all of Irish origin: the Book of Dimma, the Book of Mulling, and the Stowe Missal.[18] Warren listed a fifth rather different text in a manuscript at St Gall as another example of an eighth- or ninth-century Irish rite *De Visitatione Infirmorum*,[19] but the prayer he cites appears to be rather a rite for someone who has just died, the commendation of a soul now returning to God (*animam servi tui ... revertentem ad te*), and the same prayer appears in the Gelasian Sacramentary in a section headed *Orationes post obitum hominis*.[20] Leaving the St Gall prayer aside, these four manuscripts, all of Irish or Scottish origin, form a closely related family of similar rites, as set out in the appendix below. They have no such close approximations to rites in any continental manuscripts.[21]

---

14 Eisenhofer and Lechner 1961, 328–9. The communion rite in the *Stowe Missal* has 24 antiphons after communion at Mass. Perhaps a suitable selection was made on different occasions (Warner 1915, 18). 15 Warner 1915, 33. 16 Warner 1915, 19. 17 Warren 1895, 165. 18 Respectively TCD 59 (A.4.23), probably made in the late eighth or early ninth century (Kenney 1929, 703–4); RIA Stowe D.II.3, dated around AD 800 (Warner 1915, xxxiv); TCD 60, possibly to be dated to the seventh or eighth century, but its liturgical sections were written by a later hand in the eighth or ninth century (Kenney 1929, 632, 703). 19 St Gall, Stiftsbibliothek, Cod. 1395 (Warren 1881, 182–3). 20 Wilson 1894, 296. See also Mohlberg 1968, 236–7. 21 For Dimma and Mulling I have used here the texts of the rites found in Warren (1881, 167–71 and 171–3 respectively), and for Stowe the text given by Warner (1915, 33–6). I have left these texts as their editors published them, apart from italicising the rubrics and substituting references for the

There is much that could be said of all of these rituals, in terms of the origin of their materials, their scribal errors and even their theological peculiarities,[22] but here we will focus on those things which illumine our reading of the Deer text. The similarity of the four rites becomes immediately apparent when they are placed side by side (see Appendix), both in their structure and their content. But there are also significant differences at several points. Deer and Mulling in the two left hand columns form a more closely similar pair, as do Stowe and Dimma on the right. At one point, however, Stowe is closer to Deer, at the antiphon *Quia satiavit animam inanem*. The biggest single difference, of course, is that Deer has no anointing ritual at all. It has not been lost from the manuscript, as its arrangement on the two folios makes it clear that this is the whole rite as it was written down.[23] The Deer scribe (or perhaps the scribe of his exemplar) has simply decided to omit the rite of anointing, as if the *viaticum* itself was quite sufficient for his needs.

The question of the relationship between anointing and *viaticum* leads us to look at an even wider circle of rituals. Where did these liturgies come from? What kind of changes in the Church's ministry to the sick took place in the centuries up to this point, and what needs were these rites shaped to answer? If we look at the development of the Church's rituals surrounding the sick and the dying, and at some of the forces which shaped that process, we can see every liturgy as the result of a negotiation between different needs, changing perceptions and expectations. Our family of four rituals reflects the state of the rites at one moment in a long history of development.

WHO ANOINTS?

In the early church, anointing the sick with oil was seen as a way of making them better, or asking God to do so. When Jesus sent out the twelve disciples, Mark says that 'they cast out many demons, and they anointed with oil many that were sick and healed them.'[24] Perhaps more commonly cited is the Epistle of James: 'Is anyone sick among you? Let him call for the elders of the church, and let them pray over him, anointing him with oil in the name of the Lord; and the prayer of faith will save the sick man, and the Lord will raise him up; and if he has committed sins, he will be forgiven.'[25] The early church's concern here, as manifested by these texts, is the power to heal. Anointing and

scriptural texts themselves. **22** Dimma's blessing seems to require some kind of facial acrobatics (reading *ulutum tuum* for *ultum suum*); Mulling's third prayer, *Pater omnipotens*, suggests that the sick person has been sanctified and redeemed by the blood of the Father, rather than that of the Son—an error avoided by the parallel prayer in Stowe, *Domine sancte pater*. **23** Folio 28r, immediately before the *Creator naturarum*, is blank. The rite ends on 29r with *finit*, followed by half a page of empty space. **24** Mk 6:13. **25** Jas 5:14–15.

prayer over sick people can make them better. But there are already hints of another dimension to the ritual. In Mark the twelve are also casting out demons, concerned not only with physical sickness, but also with spiritual affliction. In James, the ritual of anointing the sick shows a concern also for moral and spiritual sickness and its healing: 'if he has committed sins, he will be forgiven.' So when we are told that the prayer of faith 'will save the sick man' we might be left wondering whether this salvation is physical or spiritual. Greek *sozo* and Latin *salvo* are both usefully ambiguous, capable of referring to restored physical health or eternal destiny. Likewise, when we are told that 'the Lord will raise him up', it is not clear whether the Lord will raise him from his sick-bed to health, or from death to eternal life.

In fact, most of the early rites for blessing the oil used for anointing the sick lay a fairly heavy stress on physical healing. That seems to be what is being asked for in the liturgy of Hippolytus' *Apostolic Tradition* in the third century, for example: 'O God, who sanctifiest this oil, ... grant that it may give strength to all that taste it and health to all that use it.'[26]

We have no rituals from this early period for the actual anointing of the sick, but rather rituals for the blessing of the oils—oil which would subsequently be used in apparently unstructured ways, and used for healing not just when administered by clergy, but by all Christians, clergy and laity alike. Thus Pope Innocent I wrote in the early fifth century to interpret the letter of James: 'they can be anointed with the holy oil of anointing, which has been prepared by the bishop to be used for anointing, not only by priests but by all Christians for their own need or that of their dear ones.'[27] It is well known that oil was used throughout the Mediterranean world as part of ordinary medical techniques—both by anointing and by swallowing it—so that what the church was doing was not creating a new ritual practice *ex nihilo*, but rather adding a ritual depth of prayer to an existing medical practice.

We can see the rather loosely organised practice of anointing in fourth and fifth century Gaul, and the freedom with which the holy oils were treated by clergy and laity. A woman sends a flask of oil to Martin of Tours 'so that he might bless it, as is the custom, which is necessary for various causes of illness.'[28] The biographer of St Genovefa (423–502), writing about 520, shows her restoring the health of the sick by anointing them with the holy oil which she carried around with her,[29] while Monegund seems to have taken onto herself the normally episcopal prerogative of blessing the oil, as people ask her to 'bless the oil and the salt with which we may minister your blessings to

---

26 Apostolic Tradition, I, vii. VIII, 29 (Dix 1992, 10). 27 ... *qui sancti oleo chrismatis perungi possunt, quod ab episcopo confectum, non solum sacerdotibus sed et omnibus christianis licet in sua aut in suorum necessitate unguendum.* From the letter to Decentius, cited in Poschmann (1964, 240). 28 Sulpicius Severus, *Dialogi* III, iii: *Auitiani comitis uxorem misisse Martino oleum, quod ad diversas morborum causas necessarium, sicut est consuetudo, benediceret* (Halm 1866, 200). 29 McNamara et al. 1992, 35.

supplicating invalids.' She blessed the oil and gave it to them, and they took it and saved it most carefully.[30] Even as late as the eighth century, religious women were being portrayed as doing the anointing themselves. The *Life of Austroberta* shows her anointing one of her nuns who has been crushed by a falling wall, and restoring her to health.[31]

Clearly the administration of the holy oils to the sick had not yet become an exclusively clerical prerogative. But in the early ninth century, three French church councils commanded the clergy to keep the oils locked up, to give them to no one else to administer but to reserve the office of anointing the sick to themselves. The councils sometimes state their anxiety in terms of preventing abuses. They are concerned, for example, that people are taking the oils to rub on criminals and evil-doers in the belief that those who are so anointed will escape discovery and punishment.[32] The *Statuta Bonifatii*, documents of a Burgundian synod between 800 and 840, forbid clergy, on pain of deposition, to give the holy oils to lay-folk for use as a remedy, but now on the grounds that it is a sacrament, and so should be administered only by clergy.[33]

The concern of the clergy about superstition impacted on the rite of anointing in other ways, too. Caesarius of Arles, bishop from 502 till his death in 542, stresses the rite of anointing as involving both physical and spiritual healing, but he does so in a context which suggests that part of his aim is to woo people away from various kinds of divination and pagan healing practices, to get them back into church and away from unchristian places. Such an agenda might well lend itself to establishing clerical control.

> Whenever some infirmity comes on someone, let him have recourse to the church and receive the body and blood of Christ, and let him be anointed by the priests with blessed oil, and let them ask the priests and deacons to pray over them in the name of Christ, because if they do they will receive not only bodily health, but also forgiveness of sins … Why therefore should someone kill his own soul with magicians and diviners, with chanters and diabolical phylacteries, when he could heal his soul and his body by the prayer of the priest and the holy oil?[34]

30 Monegund's story appears in Gregory of Tours' *De Vita Patrum*, cap. 19, written around AD 570 (see McNamara et al. 1992, 58). The *Lives* of these Frankish women saints also show their association with healing oil in a less deliberate sense: after their deaths, the oil from the lamps at their altars is shown to have healing properties (see McNamara et al. 1992, 110–11; 232). **31** McNamara et al. 1992, 316. Austreberta died in AD 703 and her Life was written shortly thereafter. **32** The three councils are those of Mainz, Arles and Tours, all held in AD 813. Tours directed: *Item presbyteris iniungendum est, ne sacrum chrisma foras conclavi dimittant, ubi a quolibet attingi possit. Nam criminosos eodem chrismate unctos aut potatos nequeqam ullo examine deprehendi posse a multis putatur.* MGH, *Concilia* II, 289. **33** PL 89:821, *genus enim sacramenti est; non ab aliis nisi a sacerdotibus contingi debet.* Others forbid sending the oils to laymen: Hincmar, PL 125.779; Rather of Verona, PL 80.443. **34** Sermon xix, 5: *Praeterea,*

What we see is a practice of anointing, whose clerical element was originally confined to the episcopal rite of blessing the oil during mass while the actual anointing was often done by lay people, being drawn into the sphere of clerical control. Perhaps the early lay administration of the sacrament partly explains the scarcity of ritual texts in the western church before the ninth century, even though the practice of anointing was well established for centuries before that.[35] Rituals performed by lay people in a domestic context would be less likely to have fixed written forms than those performed solely by clergy.

The move towards exclusively clerical administration of anointing may have led to far more elaborate and complex rites.[36] From the ninth century onwards this elaboration meant that there might be several clergy involved, who would arrive and sprinkle the sick person with water. The patient might be anointed every day for a week. There might be a small choir to sing the necessary psalms and antiphons. All the clergy would lay their hands on the sick person, who would then be anointed several times—the rituals recommend anything from three to twenty anointings of various body-parts, and some suggest that you should also anoint the part where the pain is greatest,[37] or even, according to Raymond Lull (d. 1315), 'the parts with which the sick person has sinned.'[38]

These elaborate rituals share the same basic structure as our Irish family of rituals: prayers, antiphons, anointing, more prayers, communion and concluding prayers or antiphons. But in their complexity, verbosity and elaboration, and in the teams of ministers envisaged as conducting them, whether in church buildings or in the homes of the sick, they are a long way from the stark simplicity of Stowe, Dimma and Mulling.

'SALUS': FROM HEALTH TO SALVATION

Another shift in the practice of anointing took place in the centuries before Deer was produced. We saw that in the beginning the ritual focussed more or less on the healing of the sick, praying that they should recover their health.

quotiens aliqua infirmitas cuicumque supervenit, ad ecclesiam recurrat, et corpus et sanguinem Christi accipiat, et oleo benedicto a presbyteris inunguatur, eosque presbyteros et diaconos petant ut in Christi nomine orent super eos: quod si fecerint, non solum sanitatem corporis sed etiam indulgentiam accipient peccatorum ... Quare ergo per caraios et divinos, praecantatores et filacteria diabolica occidat animam suam, qui per orationem presbyteri et oleum benedictum potest sanare animam suam et carnem suam? (Morin 1953, vol. 1, 90). See also Sermon clxxiv, 4–5 (Morin 1953, vol. 2, 751), which makes exactly the same point. **35** The earliest rituals for anointing are found in the Spanish *Libri Ordinum* whose manuscripts of the tenth century and the eleventh contain material from between AD 550 and 750 (Paxton 1990, 69–73). The anointing rite is said by most scholars to date from the eighth century (Ziegler 1987, 56). But outside Spain we have no texts for a rite of anointing from before the ninth century (Porter 1956). **36** Paxton 1990, 151ff. **37** The Carolingian ritual (Paxton 1990, 151). **38** Raymund Lull, *Liber de septem*

This expectation is also clearly implicit in some later Gaulish rites, as it was also in Spain.[39] So also Caesarius says that the priest's prayer and the anointing with oil will heal both body and soul.[40] But already he is beginning to lay the stress on the soul, and he even tells his congregation that physical illness can be a sign of holiness: 'sickness of the body leads to health of the heart, for the Lord scourges those whom he loves.'[41] It almost discourages the quest for physical healing as the stress shifts towards the spiritual. This soul-wards drift is apparent in most of the continental rites, though the Roman ritual did continue more than others to stress the hope for physical healing. On Maundy Thursday, when the oils which would be used to anoint the sick for the rest of the year were blessed, the rites asked for healing both of mind and body,[42] but the liturgy of the Bobbio missal for the exorcism and blessing of oil originally made no mention at all of physical healing, but focussed on grace and the forgiveness of sins.[43]

Of course, if the quest for healing of the body was giving way to the quest for salvation of the soul, one might expect that the rite of anointing would be drawn into the rites for the dying, whose concern for bodily health is being overshadowed by the desire for eternal salvation. This is exactly what happened, in fact, as the anointing of the sick gradually became 'extreme unction', and the pouring of oil became part of the complex of rites of Christian death. By the eighth century the *Penitential* of Egbert (d. 767) stated: 'anyone who avails himself of this custom (anointing), his soul shall be as pure after death as that of a child who dies immediately after baptism.'[44] That is not to say that the older expectation of healing had disappeared, but anointing was certainly entering into the rituals for the dying, especially in the

sacramentis sanctae ecclesiae, Sermo 7, linea 15. CETEDOC.   **39** Paxton 1990, 70.   **40** *Quod si fecerint, non solum sanitatem corporis sed etiam indulgentiam accipient peccatorum*, Sermon xix, 5 (Morin 1953, vol. 1, 90); *non solum sanitatem corporum, sed etiam remissionem acciperent peccatorum*, Sermon clxxxiv, 5 (Morin 1953, vol. 2, 751).   **41** *Quia infirmitas corporis ad sanitatem pertinet cordis: quia deus quos amat in hoc mundo flagellat*, Sermon xix, 5 (Morin 1953, vol. 1, p. 90).   **42** The blessing of the oils in the tenth century Egbert Pontifical (Banting 1989, 128) suggests physical and spiritual healing (*tutamen tum mentis et corporis*), though the physical is still more explicit here than it will be later: *ad evacuandos omnes dolores omnesque infirmitates, omnem egritudinem corporis*. This rite is said to reflect seventh century Roman usage (Banting 1989, xxvi). The same sense is found in the Gelasian, where prayer is made over oil for *refectionem mentis et corporis*, where every anointing, tasting and touching with the oil leads to protection of body, soul and spirit— *tutamentum corporis, animae et spiritus* (Wilson 1894, 70; Mohlberg 1968, 61); note there is still a strong sense of the physical here: *ad evacuandos omnes dolores, omnem infirmitatem, omnem aegritudinem mentis et corporis*. The phrase is also found in the tenth century Romano-Germanic Pontifical (Vogel and Elze 1963, 70).   **43** Actually, a later (eighth century) hand has added a *benedictio olei* which prays that all who are anointed with it or ingest it may have health of body and protection of soul (Lowe 1991, 173).   **44** *Quoniam scriptum est quod quicumque hanc disciplinam habuerit, anima ejus aeque pura sit post obitum ac infantis qui statim post baptisma moritur*, Egbert, *Poenitentiale*, lib.1, pars altera, cap 15 (PL

Gallican books. By the mid-eighth century the Gelasian sacramentary, probably compiled at Chelles, was placing the rites of care of the sick in the same continuous sequence as the rites for the dying (*viaticum*) and the dead, fully in accord with the Gallican tendency to see sickness as a preparation for death, and so also seeing the sacrament of the sick as part of the preparation for death, geared to spiritual rather than physical healing.[45]

There was an attempt in the early ninth century, as part of the Carolingian liturgical reforms, to re-establish anointing as a sacrament for the healing of the sick, in which the prayers focus on the restoration of health. We see the attempt in the Canons of Chalons and Tours in 813, for example, where anointing the sick is commended as an alternative to pagan magical cures, suggesting that curative rites are beginning to make a come-back, 'as an aid to recovery rather than transition to the other world.'[46] But even the Carolingian reform ritual—possibly the work of Benedict of Aniane—continued to run together anointing and communion in a seamless rite, which would of course have continued to lend itself to seeing anointing as part of the last rites. Indeed the structure of the reform ritual, dated to the years 815–45, is pretty much the same as that of Stowe, Dimma and Mulling. And in spite of the energy with which secular rulers promoted liturgical reform, the old Gallican ideas, the spiritualised conception of the rite, continued. Throughout the ninth century, synods and bishops began increasingly to urge anointing as a rite for the dying, and by 858 a bishop such as Herard of Tours could write:

> Those who become ill are to be reconciled without delay; they should receive *viaticum* while still alive and they should not lack the benediction of sanctified oil.[47]

A similar thrust can be seen in the documents of the Synod of Mainz in 847, that those who are sick and in danger of death should be offered 'the prayers and consolations of the Church, with the holy anointing of oil, while they are still alive, and with the communion of *viaticum* according to the statutes of

---

89:416). **45** Paxton 1990, 155. The continuous sequence is as follows: Prayer over the sick person at home; Prayers at a mass for the sick; Prayer for the return of health; Prayer after a person's death and the commendation of the soul; Mass for a dead priest, and then several other masses for the dead of various classes. **46** These reforms are beginning to draw anointing back into the realm of physical healing rather than preparation for death. Canon 42 of the Council of Tours says: 'Let the priests admonish the faithful people, that they may know that magic arts and incantations cannot confer healing on any of the diseases of men ... nor ligatures of bones or herbs, but that these are snares and traps of the ancient enemy' (cited in Paxton 1990, 130, n. 7). Aix-la-Chapelle in 836 taught that if someone fell ill they should confess their sins and receive anointing, and if the illness looked fatal the priest should make over the sick person a *commendatio animae* and give the Eucharist as *viaticum*. But the clear implication from the outset is that anointing *would* be done when the person was not in danger of death. **47** PL 121:765–6.

the holy fathers.'[48] The rite of anointing was becoming so firmly drawn into the rites of death, that by the time of Raymond Lull it had been detached from any sense of healing. Indeed, he thought that whoever underwent anointing whilst still hoping to live was actually deforming the character of the sacrament.[49]

In this context, there is nothing strange in the appearance of anointing and *viaticum* as a single, almost seamless rite in Dimma, Stowe and Mulling. Other Irish sources suggest much the same trend away from healing and towards salvation. The Irish text known as the *Tractatus Hilarii in Septem Epistolas Canonicas*, probably written around AD700, can be seen pushing strongly towards a spiritual account of anointing. Commenting on James 5:14, Pseudo-Hilary by-passes the physical reality of sickness, and heads straight for its moral and spiritual meaning: 'Is anyone sick among you? This sickness is the sickness of sin.' And the cure is equally regarded as a spiritual one: 'And God will relieve him—that is, from the ruin of sin.'[50]

In our Irish rites of anointing the prayers also fit into this pattern of the drift to the spiritual. Deer must of course be excluded, as it has no rite of anointing. Its only rite, *viaticum*, is a rite for the dying. Most of the prayers of anointing in the other three are usefully ambiguous, using words like *salus, corroborare, curare, conservare, caelestis gratiae medicamentum, det tibi pacem et sanitatem*, and so on, which are capable of being understood either physically or spiritually. But there are some relics of the older concern for physical healing. Mulling prays *ut dominus ei reuelationem* (for *releuationem*) *dolorum presentet*, for example, while Stowe and Dimma recognise that prayer might be answered by the hand of God *aut in reparando aut in recipiendo*, and they also ask of God *ut corporis huius infirmitatem sanet*.

The bible readings selected for the Irish rites (Stowe and Dimma) also suggest spiritual rather than medical concerns. Stowe's readings are concerned respectively with the life of the body in the resurrection (Matthew 22) and the coming of the Son of Man in judgement (Matthew 24). Dimma shares Matthew 22 with Stowe, but has a reading from 1 Corinthians 15, about how those who have fallen asleep in Christ have not perished. In other words the readings place the entire stress on death, resurrection and judgement—to inspire fear, repentance and hope—and offer no reflection on physical healing at all. Generally speaking, then, the Irish anointing rituals seem to be behaving much as the continental ones did (apart from those of the Carolingian reform), concerning themselves with spiritual matters rather than medicinal ones.

Other sources suggest strongly that anointing in Ireland had become part of the rite for the dying rather than for the sick by the time when Stowe,

48 MGH, *Concilia* 3, 173–4, c.26.   49 Dominguez and Soria 1987, 49–50, *De Septem Sacramentis*.   50 *Tractatus in Epistola Jacobi* 5.14: Infirmatur quis in uobis? Infirmatio ista peccati infirmitas est … Et alleuiabit eum Dominus, id est de ruina de peccati (McNally

Dimma and Mulling were written. Versions of the *Cáin Domnaig*, the Law of Sunday, list exceptions to the prohibition on travelling on the day of rest. In one version of the text people are allowed to make a journey for the sake of 'ministering to a sick person in the pangs of death',[51] while another version of the *Cáin* describes this, it seems, as the 'anointing of death'.[52] As elsewhere in Europe, anointing has been absorbed into the rites of death, and attached to the rite of *viaticum* for the salvation of the soul.

COMMUNION AS 'VIATICUM'

The one thing that all four of these Irish-Scottish rites have in common, of course, is the rite of communion. From the very earliest centuries communion was given to the sick when on the point of death.[53] This was never something which was seen as primarily for the sick *as sick*, but rather for the sick as people in danger of death. It is *viaticum*, food for the journey into the next world. It is a protection from judgement, because as the Roman *ordo defunctorum* says, 'the communion will be his defender and advocate at the resurrection of the just. It will resuscitate him.' After the reception of communion, the Gospel accounts of the passion and death of the Lord are to be read to the sick person by priests or deacons, until his soul departs from his body.[54]

The reception of communion remains one of the most stable elements in the rites surrounding the care of the sick. It is perhaps one of the things that turns anointing of the sick into a spiritual rather than a physical matter. In order to receive communion you had to be baptised, so death-bed *viaticum* must be preceded by baptism if the person was not already baptised—and people had commonly delayed baptism in earlier centuries. If the sick person was already a baptised Christian and was noticeably sinful, they could not receive communion without being reconciled and receiving a penance. And

1973, vol. 1, 75). **51** O'Keeffe 1905, 210. This exception also appears in *The Monastery of Tallaght*, §71, where one may travel on Sunday 'for watching a sick man and bringing communion to him' (Gwynn and Purton 1911, 156). **52** *imgnu báis* (Hull 1966, 161). Hull translates *imgnu* as agony, but I do not know why. DIL suggests 'anointing' as more likely, though *ongad* (< *ungere*) seems to be the more usual word for this (DIL s.v.). See also *Ríagal Pátraic*, §12, where a priest is permitted to abandon his normal duties for the sake of (presumably urgent) anointing and baptism, *ongad 7 baithis* (O'Keeffe 1904, 216–24). **53** In Ireland it is required by the sixth century *Penitential of Finnian*, where *viaticum* was given on the death-bed to sinners who repented and who would be given a penance at the time. If they recovered they were expected to perform the penance (Bieler 1975, 86). **54** Paxton 1990, 38–9. The *Ordo defunctorum* has its roots in Roman practices of the fourth and fifth centuries, In some strange cases communion was even put into the mouths of the dead, as we know from the fact that Councils tried to stop people doing it. See, for example, *Sinodus Autisioderensis* (Auxerre), 561 x 605: *Non licet mortuis nec eucharistia nec usculum tradi, nec de vela vel pallas corpora eorum involui* (De Clercq 1963, ii, 267).

anointing, like any other sacrament, can only be received by baptised Christians who are in good standing with the church. It was therefore natural that the anointing of the sick came to be connected with these rites of incorporation (baptism) and re-incorporation (penance). Besides this, if you are inclined to think of it as a sign of spiritual rather than physical healing, anointing will naturally gravitate to the death-bed scene as well, and become incorporated into the rite of reconciliation. The *viaticum* seems to have such a gravity that it pulls other rites into its orbit—rites that were not originally designed for the dying. We have seen how this happened in the Frankish Gelasian rites, and how it continued into the ninth century and beyond, in spite of attempts at reform. That the same process appears to have taken place in Ireland need be no surprise, of course. It is evidence of a long-lasting and fairly close connection between the Gallican and Irish churches in terms of ritual, much as Jane Stevenson has shown that, in terms of hymnody, 'the monasteries of Aquitaine were crucial to the formative centuries of Irish Christianity.'[55]

All our Irish-Scottish rites involve the administration of *viaticum*, and all of them apart from Deer have been joined with the rite of anointing in a way which suggests that this anointing of the sick envisages eternal salvation rather than medical healing. If anything, the Gaelic rites would have represented in the late eighth century, or the early ninth, a conservative manifestation of this kind of pastoral care. They continue that spiritualised version of the rites which in Europe the Carolingian reforms were seeking to counteract.[56]

These small books, with their gospels and ritual contents, are for a mobile clergy ministering to a widely scattered non-urban flock. The priests are not able to go in crowds to the bedsides of the sick and the dying, as some continental sacramentaries envisage, nor are they inclined to drag them off to the church. Where people are dying, the clergy see it as their prime duty to snatch them from the jaws of hell with anointing and the *viaticum*, the rite of participation in the body and blood of Christ. 'Whoever eats my body and drinks my blood has eternal life, and I will raise him up at the last day.'[57]

POLLUTION AND IRISH PECULIARITY

Paxton has noted this tendency in the Irish sources toward a more spiritual meaning for anointing around 800, and its use as part of a rite for the dying rather than for the merely sick. Although we saw that this kind of drift had taken place in Gallican rituals too, up to the reforms of the early ninth century, Paxton has suggested that the Irish-Scottish liturgies may have

---

55 Stevenson 1995, 109.   **56** Paxton 1990, 139–40.   **57** Jn 6:54. The *Hibernensis* (CCH, xlvii, especially chapters 9–16) make it clear that the Irish church was connecting *viaticum* with repentance and reconciliation (Wasserschleben 1885, 199–201).

reached their present form because of a peculiarly Gaelic need to maintain ritual purity in the face of the threat of pollution.[58] He has noted that in Irish and Scottish sources from the seventh century to the ninth, there are references to clergy avoiding contact with the dead, because of the danger of ritual impurity which such contact imparted, and suggests that this pollution anxiety affected the rituals of anointing and *viaticum*:

> Since priests had to shun the dead in order to avoid ritual pollution, they were led to give special attention to the sick and the dying. This practice resulted in the rewriting of an old ritual for the visitation of the sick to make it appropriate as a preparation for death—the last time a dying individual would be attended by a priest.[59]

This interesting observation deserves further discussion, as it may shed light on the absence of anointing in the Deer ritual. I hope therefore that the reader will forgive a substantial digression into the strange world of ritual purity. The earliest surviving reference to the Irish fear of pollution by a corpse seems to be in the late seventh century, in Adomnán's *Vita Columbae*, where the saint departs from the death bed of a monk to avoid being there when he died:

> At another time, when the holy man was living on the island of Iona, one of his monks, a Briton much given to good works, was seized by a bodily affliction and brought to the point of death. When the venerable man visited him in the hour of his death, after standing for a little while beside his couch, and blessing him, he quickly went out of the house, being unwilling to see him die. And immediately after the holy man had gone away from the house, he (the monk) ended the present life.'[60]

Two later texts from the early ninth century also reflect this pollution fear, and both are associated with the monasteries of the *Céli Dé* reform movement, as was Columba's Iona of course. The document known as *The Monastery of Tallaght* offers a full explanation for what might seem strange behaviour on Columba's part in the passage just quoted:

> Now to eat a meal with a dead man (though saintly) in the house is forbidden; but instead there are to be prayers and psalm-singing on such occasions. Even one in orders who brings the sacrament to a sick man is

---

58 Paxton 1990, 78–88.   **59** Paxton 1990, 86.   **60** *Vita Columbae* iii, 6: *Alio in tempore, cum vir sanctus in Ioua commoraretur insula, quidam de suis, monacus Brito bonis actibus intentus, molestia correptus corporis ad extrema perductus est. Quem cum vir venerandus in hora sui visitaret exitus, paulisper ad lectulum eius adsistens et ei benedicens ocius domum egreditur, nolens videre morientem; qui eodem momento post sancti de domu secessum viri praesentem finit vitam* (trans. Anderson and Anderson 1981, 191).

obliged to go out of the house at once thereafter, that the sick man die not in his presence; for if he be present in the house at the death, it would not be allowable for him to perform the sacrifice until a bishop should reconsecrate him. It happened once upon a time to Diarmait and to Blathmac mac Flaind that it was in their hands that Curui expired. When he died, they were about to perform the sacrifice thereafter, without being reconsecrated, till Colchu hindered them from doing so. The authority is Leviticus; and Diarmait also, the abbot of Iona, was with him on that occasion.[61]

Note again the *Céli Dé* connection with Iona. A similar pollution anxiety appears in the *Prose Rule of the Céli Dé*, though this time it is not concerned with the pollution of the clergy by a corpse, but with pollution of food.

The food which is in the house, when anyone dies in it, should be divided and distributed to the poor, because food ought not to be kept and eaten in the same house with a sick person or a corpse.[62]

The biblical reference in the Curui story is of course to Leviticus 21:1–11, in which we read:

The Lord also said to Moses, 'Speak to the priests, the sons of Aaron, and say to them: Let not a priest be defiled by the dead of his people, except for the nearest of his kin, that is his father and mother, his son and his daughter, and his brother or his virgin sister who is not married to a man. But he shall not be contaminated by a ruler of his people. ... A pontifex, that is a high priest among his brethren, on whose head the oil of anointing has been poured, and whose hands are consecrated to the priesthood, and who is clothed in holy garments—he shall not uncover the hair of his head, nor tear his garments; and let him not go in to any dead person at all; let him not be defiled by his father or his mother.'[63]

Paxton suggests that because the priest was forbidden to be in contact with the dead, for fear of Levitical pollution, the ritual focus was brought forward

---

61 Gwynn and Purton 1911, 153. 62 Reeves 1994, 91. 63 This translation is from the Vulgate. The former of these injunctions is the one which would have applied to priests in the early Irish church—that relating to the ordinary priestly 'sons of Aaron', rather than the high priestly *pontifex*, which title was applied to bishops in the early medieval church. The prefiguring of ordinary priests by the Sons of Aaron in the Old Law, and of bishops by Aaron himself, is stated explicitly in the *Hibernensis*, for example (CCH I, 3 and II, 2). If the Levitical code was strictly applied to the Irish clergy, it would suggest that priests may attend to the dead members of their immediate family, but not to others, while the bishop (the *summus sacerdos* of CCH I, 3) could not make contact with any dead person, not even

to the period of the patient's illness, prior to his actual death, and that this shaped the Irish rites of anointing and *viaticum*. However, I find this less than convincing for a number of reasons. First the use of anointing and *viaticum* together as a rite for the terminally ill, as the Irish sources suggest, would hardly reduce the risk to a priest of being in a house when someone actually died. Neither anointing nor *viaticum* were rites for the dead, so there is no reason to think that there is anything peculiar about their application to the dying in Ireland which might be intended to protect the clergy from pollution. Furthermore, Irish rites which do have anointing and *viaticum* together have the same kind of structure as the continental ones. Even the Carolingian reform ritual, more or less contemporary with our Irish sources, has the same structure, broadly speaking: prayers and antiphons, followed by anointings, more prayer and communion.[64] It makes little sense to explain this structure in Ireland as necessitated by pollution anxiety, while no such explanation is sought for the very similar Frankish structure. If there is a difference between Irish and Carolingian rites, it lies in the Irish emphasis on salvation in comparison to the Carolingian quest for healing. But even this, as we saw above, is not a clear-cut opposition between Irish and other rites, as the reform of Benedict of Aniane did not displace the older spiritualising rites, and these seem to have gained new influence on the continent in the mid-ninth century, while in Ireland it is not true that the rites have entirely abandoned the quest for physical healing. Generally, the differences between the Irish and continental rites, in structure or in content, are not so great as to require explanation by such a radically new principal as that of ritual purity and fear of pollution. The Irish texts seem rather to represent one part of a spectrum of rituals of greater or lesser complexity, of more or less concern with physical healing, but still with much the same kind of activity taking place around the beds of the seriously ill.

Secondly, the fear of corpse-pollution does not seem to be a widespread or long-lasting phenomenon even in the Irish church. It is mentioned in only three texts, to the best of my knowledge, and all of these texts are connected to monasteries where some degree of *Céli Dé* practice was observed. We can not assume that these three texts represent a general and persistent point of view in Ireland. Pollution by dead bodies is not mentioned at all in any of the surviving Irish penitentials, although they do show concern with several other forms of pollution, sexual and dietary, which might occur. There is a general concern with pollution among Irish writers, and it does seem that the Irish church took the Levitical laws more seriously, or at least more literally, than continental churches did.[65] There are additional Irish purity rules (strange to modern ears) where Leviticus saw no need for them:

his own father and mother. **64** Paxton 1990, 151. **65** Eating scabs from your own body, drinking blood or urine, eating what is tainted by a cat, or by a pregnant woman, and much

A basin or cauldron which is used for washing, or in which a bath is prepared, in such cauldron it was not their custom to brew liquor or boil flesh-meat or to make porridge (a rule which no one now observes) until it has been sent to the smith and until it has been tapped all round three times with the craftsman's hammer.[66]

To bathe in *imsitim* (semen? urine?) is prohibited, and it is pollution to everyone who puts this liquid upon his head. It is defilement to those in orders on whose head it is put; they are to be anointed and consecrated after it.[67]

It is not the practice of the *Céli Dé* for one to drink anything after making water.[68]

Now if spittle falls on a man's hand at meals, their use is to pour water thereupon, after the spittle touches the hand.[69]

We should bear in mind, however, that all four of these examples of pollution fear come from a *Céli Dé* environment, and we can not assume that they were a general concern in the wider Irish church. On the contrary, in respect of fears of pollution by a corpse, early medieval stories about Irish saints include several incidents in which a person dies in the presence of a cleric, and there is no hint of a pollution anxiety in any of them apart from the one we have seen in the *Vita Columbae*. Tírechán, for example, has Patrick's charioteer die, apparently in the presence of the saint, and no anxiety about pollution is mentioned.[70] He tells the story of two king's daughters who meet Patrick at a well. Given communion by the saint, they immediately 'fell asleep in death'.[71] Muirchú describes the baptism of Monesan by Patrick, followed by her immediate death, apparently in Patrick's presence,[72] and the death of Patrick himself, having received *viaticum* from the hands of bishop Tassach.[73] These texts, written perhaps only twenty or thirty years before the *Vita Columbae*, have no sense of pollution anxiety. The eighth-century *Navigatio Brandani* describes the death of its subject 'strengthened by the divine sacraments and in the hands of his disciples',[74] and it is very often the case that in a saint's *Life*, his or her death takes place, often after receiving communion, in the presence of disciples.[75] The tale *Buile Shuibhne*, although a good deal later in

more, as well as the Levitical rules on carrion—attributed, interestingly, to Adomnán, abbot of Iona (Bieler 1975). **66** Gwynn 1927, 104. **67** Reeves 1864, 92. **68** Gwynn and Purton 1911, 142. **69** Gwynn and Purton 1911, 142. **70** Bieler 1979, 152. **71** Bieler 1979, 144. **72** Bieler 1979, 98–100. **73** Bieler 1979, 119. **74** Selmer 1959, 81–2. **75** It is not usually explicitly stated that these disciples include clergy, but neither are they excluded, and the typical picture seems to be that the whole monastery is gathered around the dying saint. It would be strange were ordained monks to be excluded from such an important scene in the monastery's life. For other examples of saints receiving communion at their death, without pollution being a problem, see Heist 1965, 144 (§68); 152–3 (§§22–3); 170–1 (§11), 180 (§48),

its present form, has its roots in the ninth or tenth century, and here at the door of the church, having confessed, received communion and been anointed by Moling's clerics, Suibhne dies holding the hand of the cleric Moling.[76] Later texts make a similar point: at the death of Áed Alláin, it is reported that he died in the presence of a cleric: 'Then the king was anointed, and he received the Body of the Lord, and he died at once and went to heaven.'[77] Mael Sechnaill, another king whose death involved the presence of clergy who seem to have been unafraid of pollution, died in 1022, and according to the Annals of the Four Masters he received the Body and Blood of Christ, and was anointed by Amalgaid the *comarbh* of Patrick (died AU 1049) in the presence of the heirs of Columcille and Ciarán.[78] It does not matter whether these stories are historically 'true' or not; the important thing is that they represent a pattern of expectation at the times of their composition, and a lack of interest in ritual purity, a lack of fear of pollution by corpses.

Even in texts from the Columban *familia* there are tales which show an absence of pollution threat. In the tenth century *Betha Adomnáin*, probably written in Kells, Adomnán himself is in contact with a corpse in a house:

> One time the body of Bruide mac Bile, king of the Picts, was brought to Iona. And Adomnán was distressed and grieved at the death. And he said to bring the body of Bruide to him in the house that night. Adomnán watched over the body till morning in that house. On the morrow's morning the body began to move and to open its eyes, and it is then came another unsympathetic pious one to the door of the house and said, 'If, as seems likely, the dead are being raised by Adomnán, I declare that no cleric will be appointed abbot to succeed him unless he too raises the dead.'

Adomnán thought again after this remark, and uttered a blessing over the body and for the soul of Bruide, who then lay down again like a respectable corpse.[79] Another text adds weight to the argument, this time one from twelfth century Derry, and so also from the hand of a Columban monk. The *Betha Choluim Cille* claims that Buite was in the company of his community (*a muintir*) when he died. Were the priests excluded? There is no suggestion that this was envisaged.[80]

198 (§ 60), 204 (§23), 208 (§35), 217 (§23), 230f (§§22, 26). Several of these accounts appear in *Vitae* which Sharpe dates to 'before or around 800' (Sharpe 1991, 338). **76** O'Keeffe 1913, 147, 158. **77** *Fragmentary Annals of Ireland s.a.* 605 (Radnor 1975, 8). **78** I am grateful to Dr Martin Holland for this reference, and for several other helpful comments he has made on an earlier draft of this chapter. **79** Herbert and Ó Riain 1988, 59. **80** Herbert 1988, 252. Of course, by the time *Betha Choluim Cille* was written the Irish church was undergoing a process of reform in which men like Gille of Limerick were insisting both on the potential of physical healing in anointing with oil, and apparently on

Even within the *Vita Columbae*, which first suggests the presence of such a
pollution fear, the saint goes alone into a building where a newly dead boy is
lying, prays for him and raises him from death.[81] Again, there is no sense of
pollution anxiety.

Furthermore, even from monasteries connected with the purity-minded
Céli Dé reform, we have signs that another view of the dead and dying was
held. Admittedly, there was a strong concern generally with visiting the sick
and caring for them, but this concern did not cease when death approached.
The *Teaching of Mael Ruain* states that when a monk was at the point of
death, and immediately after his soul departed, the *Canticum Salomonis* was
sung, and there is no suggestion that clergy were excluded from this important
community ritual.[82] The same text observes that the sacrament was given to
people *in articulo mortis*. The only question about the propriety of such a
thing was whether or not they had properly repented of their sins.[83] Again,
'This is what Colchu approves: to give the sacrament to those that are lying sick
at the hour of death, provided that they have made a renunciation of every
vanity.'[84] Such pastoral concern for the dying seems to outweigh any anxiety
about pollution. Indeed it was seen as so important that it outweighed the
Sunday obligations. The same concern is found in the Penitential of Finnian:

> If any man or woman is at their last breath, even if she or he is a sinner,
> and requests the communion of Christ, we say that it is not to be denied
> to them if they should make a vow to God, and do well and be received
> by him ... We must not cease to seize the prey from the mouth of the
> lion or the dragon, that is from the devil's mouth, who never ceases to
> snatch at the prey of our souls, even if we have to pursue him and strive
> for him at the last moment of a man's life.[85]

The *Hibernensis* also insists that 'communion is not to be denied, even to
penitents at the last breath of their life,'[86] and that 'if [the sick person] is
thought to be about to die, let him be reconciled by the laying on of hands,
and let the Eucharist be poured into his mouth.'[87] Others stress the possibility
of communion or anointing right up to the last moment: 'If you go to give

the necessity of the priest being present at the death of the faithful: 'He can anoint any
member of the faithful once in any grave danger, since the holy anointing gives healing not
only of the soul but also often of the body (*non solum animae sed et corporis saepe*) ...
Praying, he ought to commend the souls of the faithful as they leave their bodies and
celebrate their memory at Mass and in prayer' (Fleming 2001, 157). **81** Vita Columbae,
II, 32 (Anderson and Anderson 1991, 138–40). **82** Gwynn 1927, 18. Paxton (1990) 90
compares this to the Roman practice in the *Ordo Defunctorum* in which after death a series
of psalms were sung. The death ritual in the Spanish *Libri ordinum* prescribes a sequence of
thirty-six psalms to be sung during the agony. **83** Gwynn 1927, 10. **84** Gwynn and
Purton 1911, 148. **85** Bieler 1979, 86. **86** CCH xlvii, 12, c. (Wasserschleben 1996, 200).
87 CCH xlvii, 16 (Wasserschleben 1996, 201).

Holy Communion at the very moment of death, you shall accept their confession without shame and without reserve.'[88] 'He makes much of going the thousand paces or more ... for watching a sick man and for administering the communion to him.'[89] Another text refers to the exception to the Law of Sunday as 'tending a sick person in the pangs of death.'[90] Admittedly, some of these texts concern the dying rather than the dead, but ministering to folk at their last gasp is hardly a reliable way of avoiding contact with the newly dead corpses of one's flock. And many of the texts cited make it quite clear that the clergy *are* staying with the dying person until after his death.

In short, the fear of pollution by the dead is one which appears in only three sources, restricted geographically to Iona, Tallaght and possibly Clonmacnoise. Even within the Iona *familia*, even within the *Vita Columbae*, the pollution taboo is not observed consistently. The pollution anxiety is not widespread, nor long-lasting, and is far less important than the need to care for the sick and the dying. Columba's hasty retreat was an anomaly. It is hard, therefore, to accept Paxton's suggestion that all the Irish rites of anointing and communion for the sick were formed by such a temporary and local fear, especially when, as we have seen, the Irish rites do not differ in any radical way in content or structure from some of the continental ones.

CONCLUSION

The rites from Ireland and Scotland are simpler, smaller-scale, more domestic-looking than some of their continental contemporaries, but in their basic liturgical approach to death they differ neither in the tone of their prayers of anointing and *viaticum*, nor in their structure.[91] The differences in scale may have more to do with social geography, and with the pattern of church organisation in Ireland and Scotland.[92] But even on the Continent there must have been rites practised on a smaller scale, with or without books like ours, in rural areas, by single clergy in emergencies, improvised as necessary. The *Statuta Bonifatii*, from a Burgundian synod in the early ninth

88 From the 'Rule of Carthage' (Ó Maidín 1996, 65). 89 Gwynn and Purton 1911, 158. As this is an exception to not walking distances on a Sunday, we can assume that it represents an urgent need to visit someone, and therefore a visit to someone who is dying, someone who needs *viaticum*. 90 O'Keeffe (1905) 211. 91 The reduction in the scale of the rite corresponds, perhaps, to the scaling down of the book itself, and to the 'drastic reduction of forms' noted by Isabel Henderson in the illuminations of Deer (Henderson 1986, 278; and in this volume). 92 For recent studies of widespread provision of pastoral care on a very local basis in Irish and Scottish churches, see Charles-Edwards (1992) and Sharpe (1992). I am also grateful to Rachel Butter for her observations about the very local level of pastoral provision suggested by the high density of *cill*-names in, for example, Mid-Argyll, Kintyre and Knapdale, and the implications of this for our understanding of the level of pastoral provision in the early medieval period.

century, require priests to carry both Eucharist and oil on their journeys, presumably in case they need to take care of a dying person. We might imagine that when their ministrations were carried out *en route* the ritual would have been scaled down from those recorded in the sacramentaries, and would perhaps have been closer in scale and simplicity to the Irish rites.[93] In 852, Hincmar required every priest to learn by heart the rites of reconciliation and the anointing of the sick,[94] perhaps envisaging a more mobile pattern of pastoral visitation in which books would not always be available to the clergy. Again, in such circumstances we might imagine that the rites that were learned by heart were simpler than those in the sacramentaries, perhaps similar to those in the Irish and Gaelic manuscripts.

Finally, it might be worth asking why Deer, alone of these four rites, has no rite of anointing. Warren called the rite in Deer a 'fragment', implying that it was partially copied from another, more complete, rite. This is possible. Or he may have meant that it was fully copied, but that part of it was subsequently lost. This latter explanation seems to me impossible, as I have said, given the blank folio 28r which precedes it and the way it finishes half way down folio 29r with the word *finit*. But there are various other possible explanations, all of them fairly speculative.

It may be that the scribe or the intended user of the Deer ritual did not think the rite of anointing was required. Indeed, throughout the Middle Ages it seems that anointing was neglected for a number of reasons. Jonas of Orleans (d. 843/4) wrote that, 'This anointing with oil has declined in use among many out of ignorance, and many others out of negligence.'[95] Irish and Scottish clergy, aware of pastoral practice in continental churches, may simply have been sharing in that 'negligence'.

It may also be that it was difficult for bishops in the north of Scotland to procure the necessary oil, and whatever they could obtain was therefore not used for the 'unnecessary' anointing of the sick, but kept for the more 'important' anointings of baptism and ordination—rites in which oil might also have been used in smaller quantities. An explanation based on the scarcity of oil is supported by a letter written by Alcuin of York to his spiritual father and teacher, Colcu of Clonmacnoise: 'I have sent you, my friend, some oil, which is hardly obtainable in Britain, for you to share out wherever the bishops need it, to use in God's worship.'[96]

93 There is, however, no mention of the need to carry a book: *Ut presbyteri sine sacro chrismate, et oleo benedicto, et salubri eucharistia, alicubi non proficiscantur. Sed ubicunque vel fortuitu requisiti fuerint, ad officium suum statim inveniantur parati in reddendo debito* (PL 89.821). **94** *Capitula Synodica*, cap. IV: *Ordinem reconciliandi ... atque ungendi infirmos ... memoriter discat* (PL 125:773–4). **95** *De Institutione laicale*, III, xiv (PL 106.261). **96** *Misi caritati tue aliquid de oleo, quod uix modo in Britannia inuenitur, ut dispensares per loca necessaria episcoporum ad utilitatem honoris Dei* (Chase 1975, 26). I am grateful to Dr Jane Stevenson for pointing out this passage, and for other guidance. A story in the *Vita S.*

Another possibility, just as speculative, is that clerical abuses were taking place in which the laity were charged for the anointing, as happened elsewhere. This would have reduced its appeal, discouraging people from seeking the sacrament.[97] Others may have failed to use it because anointing was seen in many contexts as entailing a certain penitential commitment, and if the anointing 'worked' and the patient recovered, he or she would have to live a life of vowed penance, a quasi-monastic existence whose rigours might have persuaded the lay faithful to defer sacramental reconciliation until the last possible moment, making anointing less important than *viaticum*. This also touches on the question we addressed earlier, concerning the relationship of anointing, penance and Eucharist. It does seem that, at least in the late eleventh century, the Scottish church was regarded by its English neighbours as having a deficient sacramental practice. Turgot, in his *Life of Margaret*, states that the saintly queen confronted Scottish churchmen in a dispute about, among other things, their irregular use of the Eucharist. They refused to receive communion even at Easter, on the grounds of their unworthiness: 'We fear to approach that mystery, lest we should eat and drink judgement on ourselves.'[98] The way to avoid unworthy eating and drinking would have been to confess and do penance, preparing for the Easter communion during Lent. But if people were refusing to do penance until they lay on their death-beds, because of the quasi-monastic ascetic rigour we discussed above, then they would not be able to communicate at Easter. If communion was being neglected until the moment of death because of such a reluctance to undergo penance, perhaps anointing was being neglected too, for the same reason: that being anointed might commit you to years of ascetic penitential observance.[99]

Other explanations for the absence of an anointing rite might include the possibility that the scribe of Deer was working from the assumption that anointing was indeed necessary but that it was not thought necessary to give a written formula. As we have seen, up to the eighth century there were no

Colmani de Land Elo, § 13, may also illustrate a concern with the difficulty of procuring the holy oils (Heist 1965, 214), though here the story suggests that it is more available in Scotland than in Ireland. **97** Poschmann 1964, 244ff. **98** Life of Margaret, § 19 (Hodgson Hynde 1868). **99** It is worth considering in this context a passage in the *Hibernensis* (CCH II, 16) which suggests that there was an Irish school of thought, as early as the early eighth century, in which communion had been more or less completely assimilated to *viaticum*, the rite for the dying: *Communionis nomen hoc est, viaticum, id est viae custodiam*, 'This is the name of communion: viaticum, that is guardian on the way' (Wasserschleben 1885, 17). Another version is cited in a footnote: *Communio dicitur, quia omnium fidelium in exitu vitae communis est victus*, 'It is called communion because it is the common food of all the faithful in their departure from life.' Might this relate to the same sense that an ordinary Christian is unworthy to receive the sacrament *in medio vitae*, and that its reception should be deferred until death-bed penance is accepted? It is certainly saying more than that communion is a *viaticum* in the more general sense of the word, as is sometimes found in the medieval church when speaking of baptism, vows, good works and

written formulae anywhere outside Spain for the administration of unction, and it seems to have been left to the minister (clerical or lay) to apply the oil with whatever prayers he knew, without any book-ritual. It is possible that, even if the scribe of Deer had known of formal prayers for the rite of anointing, they were excluded because it was *still* acceptable in the ninth century for a priest to perform the rites from memory. Hincmar, as we have seen, required every priest to learn by heart the rite of reconciliation and anointing of the sick.[100] It may therefore be significant that there is a text of the Creed on the last written folio (85r) of the Book of Deer, since both Mulling and Dimma use a version of the Creed in their anointing ritual, while none of the four rites uses any form of the Creed in the *viaticum* ritual. If the cleric using Deer was indeed meant to anoint the sick person, the text of the Creed might have been a useful element.

There may have been other reasons for not including anointing in the Deer rite. Does the fact that the saints are almost never shown being anointed,[101] though they very often receive *viaticum* in the last chapters of their *Vitae*, suggest that anointing was not seen as terribly important at a person's death, and as Deer was a ritual for the dying then anointing would not be required? In that case it would seem that the Deer scribe had in a sense come fairly close to the thinking of the Carolingian reformers, driving a wedge between the sacrament of the sick and the sacrament of the dying.

Another possibility hinges on the stress laid on the healing power of saints in medieval *vitae*. If the community which used the Book of Deer had a reason for *not* anointing the sick, because they would rather people sought healing through the intercession of their patron saint or saints, perhaps saints whose relics they might possess, this might help to explain the lack of a rite of anointing. There may have been a relic associated with Deer whose healing *virtus* was preferred to the effects of the sacrament, and here either Columba or Drostan would be ideal candidates. After all, it was their prayers that had saved the life of the son of the mormaer Bede.[102]

Leaving aside the issue of anointing, the rite in the Book of Deer, like the other Gaelic rites, was a ritual of communion for the sick who were dying attended by a priest. Whether or not the priest remained present till the

so on, of being a general help in the journey of life.   **100** See note 94 above. We tend to underestimate the capacity for memorisation of large amounts of material in the Middle Ages. It was common for monks and clergy to be able to recite the entire Psalter from memory.   **101** See Paxton 1990, 50, for four interesting exceptions: saints of the fifth and sixth centuries who were anointed before their deaths. Note, however, that these Lives were written in the ninth century, when anointing was becoming associated with the dying. **102** Stuart 1869, 91–2. I am assuming here that the Book of Deer was actually made at Deer, and was used there at the time when the ritual for the sick was in use. This is not by any means proven, but an eastern Scottish origin is thought, for art-historical reasons, to be most likely. See Geddes 1998; Marner 2002.

moment of death would make no difference to the rite as we have it at the moment. Its present character is consistent with the kinds of development we find in continental sources, a drift towards the spiritual, a drawing together of the rites of the sick and the rites of the dying. If it differs from some of them in scale and complexity, this may have much more to do with the sociology of the church, its demography and the distribution of its clergy than with the pollution fears that we find in a very narrow stratum of sources.

APPENDIX

Four Rites Compared

Deer	Mulling	Stowe	Dimma
	Oratio communis pro infirmo incipt: Oremus, fratres carissimi, pro spiritu cari nostri .N. qui secundum carnem egritudinem patitur, ut dominus ei reuelationem dolorum presentet, uitam concedet, tutellam salutis remunerationem bonorum operum impertiat, per dominum]		
	Prefatio communis incipt: Oremus fratres carissimi pro fratre nostro .N. qui incommodo carnis et egritudine uexatur, ut domini pietas per angelum medicinae celestis uisitare et corroborare dignetur, per dominum.		
		Oremus fratres dominum deum nostrum pro fratrae nostro [.n. quem duri] ad pressens malum langoris adulcerat ut eum domini pietas caelestibus dignetur curare medicinis; qui dedit animam det et salutem: - per	Oremus, fratres, dominum Deum nostrum pro fratre nostro .n. quem duri adpresens malum langoris adulcerat, ut eum domini pietas caelestibus dignetur curare medicinis; qui dedit animam det et salutem, per dominum nostrum.
		Deum uiuum omnipotentem cuo omnia opera restaurare [et] confirmare facillimum est fratres carissimi pro fratre nostro infirmo .N. supliciter oremus quo cr[e]atura manum sentiat creatoris ut aut in reparando aut in recipiendo in nomine suo pius pater opus suum recreare dignetur:- per dominum nostrum Iesum Christum.	Deum uiuum omnipotentem, cui omnia opera restaurare [et] confirmare facillimum est, fratres carissimi, pro fratre nostro infirmo supliciter oremus, quo creatura manum sentiat creatoris aut in reparando aut in recipiendo; in nomine suo pius pater opus suum recreare dignetur, per dominum nostrum.
		Domine sancte pater uniuersitatis auctor omnipotens aeternae deus cui cuncta uiuunt qui uiuificas mortuos et uocas ea quae non sunt tamquam ea quae sunt tuum solitum opus qui es magnus artifex pie exercere in hoc tuo plasmate :- per christum:-	Domine sancte pater, uniuersitatis auctor, omnipotens aeternae deus, cui cuncta uiuunt, qui uiuificas mortuos et uocas ea quae non sunt, tanquam ea quae sunt, tuum solitum opus, qui es artifex, pie exerce in hoc plasmate tuo, per dominum.

Deer	Mulling	Stowe	Dimma
		Deum in cuius manu tam alitus uiuentes quam uita morientis fratres dilectissimi diprecemur ut corporis huius infirmitatem sanet et animae salutem prestet ut quod per meritum non meretur misseriecordiae gratiae consequatur orantibus nobis prestet per dominum nostrum Iesum Christum.	Deum, in cuius manu tam alitus uiuentis quam uita morientis, fratres dilectissimi, deprecamur ut corporis huius infirmitatem sanet et animae salutem prestet; ut quod per meritum non meretur, misericordiae gratia consequatur, orantibus nobis, per dominum.
	… [Pate]r omnipotens, et conserua famulum tuum hunc .n. quem [sancti]ficasti et redemisti pre[tio] magno sancto sanguinis tui, in secula seculorum.	Domine sancte pater omnipotens aeternae deus qui es uia et ueritas et uita exaudi et conserua famulum tuum hunc .N. quem uiuificasti et redimisti pretio magno sancti sanguinis filii tui qui regnas etc:-	
	Benedictio super aquam: Oremus et postulemus de domini misericordia ut celesti spiritu hunc fontem benedicere et sanctificare dignetur, per dominum.]		
	Benedictio Hominis: Benedicat tibi Dominus et custodiat te; illuminet dominus faciem suam super te, et misseriatur tui, conuertatque dominus uultum suum ad te, et det tibi pacem et sanitatem. Misserere n.d.a.		
		Deus qui non uis mortem peccators sed ut conuertatur et uiuat huic ad te ex corde conuerso peccata dimite et perennis uitae tribue gratiam per dominum.	Deus qui non uis mortem peccatoris, sed ut conuertatur et uiuat, huic ad te ex corde conuerso peccata dimite, et perennis uitae tribue gratiam, per dominum.
		Deus qui facturam tuam pio semper donaris affectu inclina aurem tuam supplicantibus nobis tibi ad famamulum tuum. N. aduersitate uelitudinem corporis laborentem placidus respice uissita eum in salutari tuo et caelestis gratiae concede medicamentum: per:-	Deus, qui facturam tuam pio semper do[mi]naris afectu, inclina aurem tuam suplicantibus nobis tibi; ad famulu tuum .N. aduersitate ualitudinis corporis laborantem placitus respice; uisita eum in salutare tuo, et caelestis gratiae ad medicamentum, per dominum.
		Lect: Matt 22:23, 29–33	*Lect: 1 Cor. 15:19–22*
		Lect: Matt 24:29–31	*Lect. Matt 22: 23–33*
			Diuino magisterio edocti, et diuina institutione formati, audemus dicere.
			Credo in deum patrem omnipotentem; credo et in Ihesum christum filium eius; Credo et in spiritum sanctum; Credo uitam post mortem; Credo me resurgere.
	Tunc unges cum oleo Unguo te de oleo sanctificationis in nomine dei patris, et filii, et spiritus sancti, ut saluus eris in noimine sanctae trinitatis.	Ungo te de oleo sanctificato ut salueris in nonomine patris et filii et spiritu[s] sancti in saecula:	Ungo te de oleo sanctificato in nomine trinitatis, ut salueris in saecula saeculorum.

Deer	Mulling	Stowe	Dimma
	Simul canit: Credo in Deum Patrem. *Tunc dicitur ei ut dimittat omnia.*		
[f.28*v*] *Item oratio ante dominicam orationem.* Creator naturarum omnium deus et parens uniuersarum in celo et in terra originum hás trementis populi tui religiosas preces ex illo inaccessíbileis lucis trono tuo suscipe et inter hiruphín et zaraphin indefessas circumstantiam laudes exaudi spei nonambigue precationes.	*Collectio orationis dominicae*: Creator naturarum omnium, deus et pariens uniuersarum in celo et in terra originum has trinitatis populi tui religiosas preces ex illo inaccessae lucis throno tuo suscipe, et inter hiruphin et saraph[in i]n-defessas circu[m]st[an]tium laudes exaudi spei non ambi[gue] precationes.		
		Concede domine nobis famulis tuis ut orantibus cum fiducia dicere meriamur:	Concede nobis famulis tuis ut orantes cum fiducia dicire mereamur:
Pater noster qui es. *usque in finem*	P[ater] noster.	Pater Noster.	Pater Noster.
			Infirmus canit si potest; si non, persona eius canit sacerdos.
			Agnosce, Domine, uerba quae precipisti; ignosce presumpsioni quam imperasti; ignorantia est nobis, non agnoscere meritum; contumacie non seruare preceptum, quo iubemur dicere: Pater Noster.
Libera nós Domine a malo, Domine Xriste ihesu, custodi nos semper in omni opere bona; fons et auctor omnium bonorum deus, euacua nos uitiis et reple nos uirtutibus bonis per te Xriste ihesu:.-	*Collectio nunc sequitur* Libera nos a malo, domine christe Ihesu, et custodies nos in omni opere bono, auctor omnium bonorum, manens et regnans in saecula saeculorum. Amen	Libera nos domine ab omni malo et custodi nos in omni bo[no] Iesu Christe aucto[r] omnium bonorum qui regnas in saecula saeculorum: -	Libera nos Domine, ab omni malo, et custodia nos semper in omni bono, Christe Ihesu, auctor omnium bonorum, qui regnas in saecula.
		Oramus te domine pro fratre nostro .N. cui infirmitate sua officium commonionis ut si qua eum saecularis macula inuassit aut uitium mondialem ficit dono tuae pietatis indulgeas et extergas :- per etc.	
		Domine sancte pater te fideliter deprecemur ut accipiendi fratri nostro sacrosanctam hanc aeucharistiam corporis et sanginis domini nostri iesu Christi tam carnis quam animae sit salus: per dominum: -	
		Exaudi nos domine iesu christe deus noster pro fratre nostro infirmo te rogantes ut tua sancta euchoristia sit ei tutella: per dominum: -	
		Pax et caritas domini nostri iesu christi et commonicatio sanctorum turorum sit semper nobiscum . *respondeat*: Amen.	Pax et caritas Domini Nostri Ihesu Christi sit semper nobiscum. *Hic pax datur ei, et dicis.* Pax et commonicatio sanctorum tuorum, Christe Ihesu, sit semper nobiscum. *Respondit*: Amen.

Deer	Mulling	Stowe	Dimma
hisund dub sacorfaicc dau. Corpus cum sanguine domini nostri ihesu Xristi sanitas sit tibi in uitam perpetua[m] et salutem	*Tunc reficitur corpore et sanguine* Corpus cum sanguine domini nostri Ihesu Christi sanitas sit tibi in uitam aeternam.	Corpus et sanguis domini nostri iesu christi filii dei uiui altisimi. *reliqua*	*Dás ei euchari[s]tiam dicens:* Corpus et sanguis domini nostri Ihesu Christi filii dei uiui conseruat animam tuam in uitam perpetuam.
		Accepto salutari diuini corporis cibo nostro iesu christo gratias agimus quod sui corporis et sanguinis sacramento nos a morte liberauit et tam corporis quam animae homano generi remedium donare dignatus est qui regnat.	
	Oratio post sumptum eucharistiam Custodi intra nos, domine, gloriae tuae munus, ut aduersus omnia presentis saeculi mala euchari[s]tiae quam percipimus uiribus muniamur, per dominum.		
		Agimus deo patri omnipotenti gratias quod terrenae nos originis atque naturae sacramenti sui dono in caelestem uiuificauerit demotationem : per dominum :-	*Post adsumptum ait:* Agimus deo patri omnipotenti gratias quod terrenae nos originis atque naturae, sacramentae sui dono in celestem uiuificauerit demotationem.
Reffecti Xristi corpore et sanguine, tibi semper dicamus domine alleluia alleluia.			
			Item oratio Ostende nobis, domine, misericordiam.
		Conuerte nos deus salutum nostrarum et inrmirmorum presta salutem nostrorum.	Conuerte nos deus salutum nostrarum, et firmare presta salutem nostrorum; qui regnas in saecula saeculorum.
Qui satiauit animam inanem et animam essurientem satiauit bonis, alleluia alleluia.		Quia satiauit animam inamem et animam essurientem satiauit bis alleluia alleluia.	
Et sacrificent sacrificium laudis *usque* exultation. alleluia alleluia.	Allelia Et sacrificent sacrificium laudis *usque* annuntiant opera eius in exultatione allleluia.		
		Uissita nos deus in salutari tuo: Alleluia	
		Fortitudo mea *usque* salutem: Alleluia	
[f.29r] Calicem salutaris accipiam et nomen domini inuocabo. alleluia alleluia.	Calicem salutaris accipiam, et nomen domini inuocabo.	Calicem salutaris accipiam usque inuocabo: Alleluia	Alleluia. Calicem salutaris *usque* inuocabo. Alleluia. Fortitudo mea *usque* salutem.
Reffecti Xristi corpore. alleluia alleluia ..	Reffecti Christi corpore et sanguine, tibi semper, domine, dicamus, alleluia.	Refecti christi corpore et sanguine, tibi semper domine dicamus. Alleluia	Alleluia. Refecti Christi corpore et sanguine, tibi semper dicamus.
Laudate dominum omnes gentes, alleluia alleluia. Gloria .. reffecti Xristi. alleluia alleluia. et nunc. Et semper. Reffecti	Laudate dominum omnes. Glo[ria patri].	Laudate dominum omnes gentes *usque in finem.*	Alleluia. Laudate dominum omnes gentes, *usque in finem.*
Sacrificate sacrificium iustitiae et sperate in domino	Sacrificate sacrificium iustitiae, et sperate in domino.	Sacrificate sacrificium iustitiae et sperate in domino.	Alleluia. Sacrificate sacrificium iustitiae *usque* in domino.

Deer	Mulling	Stowe	Dimma
			Tunc signas et dicis: Pax tecum. Benedicat tibi dominus, et custodiat te, conseruat uultum tuum ad te, ut det tibi pacem.
			Respondit
Deus tibi gratias agimus per quem misteria sancta celebrauimus et a te sanctitatis dona deposcimus miserere nobis domine saluator mundi. Qui regnas in secula seculorum amen. *Finit*	Deus, tibi gratias agimus, per quem misteria sancta celebrauimus, et a te sanctitatis dona deposcimus, per dominum nostrum Ihesum Christum filiium tuum, cui gloria in saecula saeculorum.	Deus tibi gratias agimus per quem misteria sancta celebrauimus et ad te sanctitatis dona deposcimus qui regnas in saecula saeculorum: -	Deus, tibi gratias agimus per quem ministeria sancta celebramus, et a te dona sanctitatis desposcimus, qui regnas in saecula:
		Benedicat tibi dominus et custodiat te ostendatque dominus faciam suam tibi et misseriatur tui conuertat dominus uultum suum ad te et det tibi pacem: *et respondit*: Amen.	
		Tunc signans eum dicito: Signaculo crucis christi signaris.	
		Pax tecum in uitam aeternam. *Et respondit*: Amen. *Finit ordo commonis*.	

ABBREVIATIONS

CCH   *Collectio Canonum Hibernensis* (see Wasserschleben, 1885).

CETEDOC   CETEDOC *Library of Christian Latin Texts*, Louvain 1991, on CD-ROM.

DIL   *Dictionary of the Irish Language based mainly on Old and Middle Irish Materials*, ed. E.J. Quin et al., Dublin 1973-76, Compact edition, Dublin, 1983 (reprinted 1990).

MGH   *Monumenta Germaniae Historica*

PL   *Patrologia Latin* (ed. J.-P. Migne, Paris, 1841-64).

REFERENCES

Anderson, A.O., & M.O. Anderson (eds), (1991), *Adomnán's Life of Columba*, Oxford.

Banting, H.M.J. (1989), *Two Anglo-Saxon pontificals (the Egbert and Sidney Sussex Pontificals)*, (Henry Bradshaw Society, 104), Woodbridge.

Bieler, L. (1963), *The Irish Pentitentials* (Scriptores Latini Hiberniae 5), Dublin (reprinted 1975).

—— (1979), *The Patrician texts in the Book of Armagh* (Scriptores Latini Hiberniae 10), Dublin.

Blair, J., and R. Sharpe (eds) (1992), *Pastoral care before the parish*, Leicester.

Breen, A. (1984), 'Some seventh-century Hiberno-Latin texts and their relationships', *Peritia* 3, 204–14.

Charles-Edwards, T. (1992), 'The pastoral role of the church in early Irish laws', in Blair and Sharpe (1992), 63–80.

Chase, Colin (ed.), (1975), *Two Alcuin letter-books*, Toronto.

De Clercq, C. (ed.), (1963), *Concilia Galliae* (Corpus Christianorum, Series Latina, 148 and 148a), Turnhout.

Dix, G. (1937), *The Treatise on the Apostolic Tradition of St Hippolytus of Rome, bishop and martyr*, edited by G. Dix and reissued with corrections, preface and bibliography by Henry Chadwick, London (1992).

Dominguez Reboiras, F,. and A. Soria Flores (eds), (1987), *Raimondus Lullus: opera latina sive in languam Latinam translata*, Turnhout.

Dumas, A. (1981), *Libert Sacramentorum Gellonensis* (Corpus Christianorum, Series Latina 159), Turnhout.

Dumville, D. (ed.), (1980), *Celtic Britain in the early middle ages*, Woodbridge.

—— (2001), review of David Howlett, *Caledonian craftsmanship: the Scottish Latin tradition, English Historical Review* 116, 455–6.

Eisenhofer, L., and J. Lechner (1961), *The liturgy of the Roman rite*, Edinburgh and London.

Geddes, J. (1998), 'The art of the Book of Deer', *Proc. Soc. Antiq. Scot.* 128, 537–49.

Gwynn, E. (1927), 'The Rule of Tallaght', *Hermathena* 44, second supplementary volume, 1–63.

—— and W.J. Purton (1927), (eds) (1911), 'The Monastery of Tallaght', *Proc. RIA*, 49C, 115–79, Dublin.

Halm, C. (ed.), (1866), *Sulpicii Severi Libri Opera*, Vienna.

Hammond, C.E. (1878), *Liturgies Eastern and Western*, Oxford.

Heist, W.W. (1965), *Vitae Sanctorum Hiberniae ex codice olim Salamanticensi nunc Bruxellensi*, Brussels.

Henderson, I. (1986), 'The Book of Deer (Cambridge University Library MS Ii.6.32)', in D.E. Evans et al. (eds), *The Proceedings of the Seventh International Congress of Celtic Studies*, Oxford, 186.

Herbert, M. (1988), *Iona, Kells and Derry: the history and hagiography of the monastic Familia of Columba*, Oxford.

—— and Ó P. Riain (1988), *Betha Adomnáin*, Dublin.

Hodgson Hynde, J. (ed.), (1868) *Vita Margaretae Reginae* in *Symeonis Dunelmensis Opera et Collectanea* (Surtees Society), London.

Howlett, D. (2000) *Caledonian craftsmanship: the Scottish Latin tradition*, Dublin.

Hughes, K. (1980), 'The Book of Deer (Cambridge University Library MS Ii.6.32)', in Dumville (1980), 22–37.

Hull, V. (1966), 'Cáin Domnaig', *Ériu* 20, 151–77.

Kenney, J.F. (1929), *The sources for the early history of Ireland: ecclesiastical: an introduction and guide*, Dublin (reprinted 1966 with Addenda and Corrigenda by Ludwig Bieler).

Lawrie, A.C. (1905) *Early Scottish charters prior to AD 1153*, Glasgow.

Lapidge, M., and R. Sharpe, (1985), *A bibliography of Celtic-Latin literature, 400–1200*, Dublin.

Lowe, E.A. (1917–24), *The Bobbio Missal: a Gallican mass book (MS Paris, Lat. 13246)* (Henry Bradshaw Society 53, 58, 61), London, reprinted 1991, Woodbridge.

McGurk, P. (1956), 'The Irish pocket gospel book', *Sacris Erudiri* 8, 249–70.

McNally, R.E. (ed.), *Sriptores Hiberniae Minores*, 2 vols, (Corpus Christianorum, Series Latina 108), Turnhout.

McNamara, J.A., J. Halborg and G. Whatley (1992), *Sainted women of the Dark Ages*, Durham NC.

Marner, D. (2002), 'The sword of the spirit, the word of God and the Book of Deer', *Medieval Archaeoogy* 46, 1–28.

Mohlberg, L.C. (1968), *Liber Sacramentorum Romanae Aeclesiae ordinis anni circuli (Cod. Vat. Reg. lat. 316/Paris Bibl. Nat. 7193, 41/56) Sacramentarium Gelasianum*, Rome.

Morin, G. (1953), *Caesarii Arelatensis Opera* (Corpus Christianorum, Series Latina, 103 and 104), Turnhout.

O'Keeffe, J.G. (1904), 'The Rule of Patrick', *Ériu* 1, 216–24.

—— (1905), 'Cáin Domnaig: the Epistle concerning Sunday', *Ériu* 2, 189–213

—— (1913), *Buile Suibhne, The Adventures of Suibhne Geilt*, London.

Ó Maidín, U. (1996), *The Celtic monk: rules and writings of early Irish monks*, Kalamazoo, MI.

Paxton, F. (1990), *Christianizing death: the creation of a ritual process in early medieval Europe*, Ithaca/London.

Porter, H.B. (1956), 'The origin of the medieval rite for anointing the sick or dying', *Journal of Theological Studies*, n.s. 7, 211–25.

Poschmann, B. (1964), *Penance and the anointing of the sick*, London.

Radnor, J.N. (1978), *Fragmentary Annals of Ireland*, Dublin.

Reeves, W. (1864), *The Culdees of the British Islands as they appear in history, with an appendix of evidences*, Dublin (reprinted 1994, Llanerch).

Selmer, C. (ed.), (1959), *Navigatio Sancti Brendani Abbatis from early Latin manuscripts*, Notre Dame, IN.

Sharpe, R. (1991), *Medieval Irish Saints' Lives: an introduction to Vitae Sanctorum Hiberniae*, Oxford.

Stevenson, J. (1995): see Warren, F.E. (1881).

Stuart, J. (1869), *The Book of Deer*, edited for the Spalding Club, Edinburgh.

Warner, G.F. (1915), *The Stowe Missal, MS D. II. 3 in the Library of the Royal Irish Academy, Dublin*, vol. II , Dublin (reprinted with vol. I for Henry Bradshaw Society, 1989, Woodbridge).

Warren, F.E. (1881), *The liturgy and ritual of the Celtic church*, London (2nd edition with a new introduction and bibliography by Jane Stevenson, 1987, Studies in Celtic History, Woodbridge.)

—— (ed.) (1895), *The Antiphonary of Bangor: an early Irish manuscript in the Ambrosian Library at Milan*, part II, London.

—— (1906, 1915), *The Stowe Missal: Ms DII.3 in the Library of the Royal Irish Academy, Dublin*, London (reprinted 1989, Henry Bradshaw Society, 31, 32, Woodbridge).

Wasserschleben, H. (1885), *Die Irische Kanonensammlung*, Leipzig (reprinted 1996, Leipzig).

Wilson, H.A. (1894), *The Gelasian Sacramentary: Liber sacramentorum Romanae Ecclesiae*, Oxford.

Ziegler, J. (1987), *Let them anoint the sick*, Collegeville, MN.

The Book of Deer after *c*.1150

PATRICK ZUTSHI

The purpose of the present essay is to trace the wanderings of the Book of Deer (Cambridge University Library, MS Ii.6.32) from its first documented appearance at Deer in Aberdeenshire in the twelfth century until its arrival in Cambridge University Library in 1715 and to sketch its subsequent history in the Library.[1] Unfortunately the sources concerning the fate of the manuscript prior to its arrival in Cambridge are sparse, and the story contains long gaps, as well as a certain amount of speculation.

The Book of Deer, now generally dated to the tenth century,[2] is a Gospel book known chiefly for a series of entries in Gaelic added at different times to the manuscript.[3] One of these, Text III, bears the date 8 David I (1131–32), and the most recent editor of another addition, Text VII, a Latin brieve of King David I, has dated it '1139 x 1153, perhaps 1145 x 1153'.[4] It is likely that some of the texts were entered in the Book of Deer not long after the transactions to which they refer. The additional material includes an account of the foundation of a monastery by St Columba and St Drostan, land grants to the monastery, and the brieve of King David I in favour of the 'clerici de Der', which grants them immunity from lay control and unjust exactions, 'sicut in libro eorum scribtum est'—evidently a reference to the Book of Deer itself. Quite apart from the explicit reference to Deer in the brieve of King David, there is a play on words alluding to Deer in the foundation account, and some of the lands mentioned in the grants later belonged to the Cistercian abbey of Deer.[5] It is reasonable, therefore, to conclude that the manuscript was at Deer by the time that the additions were made to it, that is, by the first half of the twelfth century; and it is carrying scepticism too far to suggest that these entries are insufficient to associate the manuscript with a foundation at Deer.[6] Nonetheless, the nature of the institution which existed

---

1 I am grateful to Dr Katherine Forsyth, Professor Geoffrey Barrow, Dr Martin Brett and Dr Nigel Ramsay, and to my colleagues Miss Jayne Ringrose, Mr Alan Farrant amd Mr Arthur Owen for their valuable assistance in preparing this article. I am indebted to the Syndics of Cambridge University Library for permission to print extracts from manuscripts in their custody.   2 E.g., Hughes 1980, 25; Dumville 2007, 183–212. Henry Bradshaw, who was the first to realise the significance of the Book of Deer, suggested a date of late ninth to early tenth century: see his description in Bond and Thompson 1883 (facing pl. 210); and see the Appendix below, nos. 5–16.   3 For what follows see especially Stuart 1869; Jackson 1972; Broun 1995.   4 Barrow 1999, 119 no. 136. See also Jackson 1972, 89; Lawrie 1905, 180–1, no. 223.   5 See Jackson 1972, especially p. 3 and n. 1. 6 See Jackson 1972, 97–102.

there in the twelfth century is unclear. The term 'clerici de Der' in King David's charter, which is the only one of the additions which refers explicitly to Deer, suggests not so much a monastery as a community of secular clergy.[7] Such communities, with pastoral responsibilities for a wide area, were a feature of the pre-parochial organization of the church in Scotland.[8]

The subsequent history of this community at Deer is completely obscure. In 1219 William, earl of Buchan, established a Cistercian monastery at Deer. It has generally been assumed that the Book of Deer was in the possession of this Cistercian house,[9] although both Henry Bradshaw and M.R. James expressed themselves cautiously on this point.[10] The deed by which the abbey of Deer was in effect dissolved states that 'the monastical superstitioun for the quhilk the said Abbay of Dier was of auld erectit and foundit is now be the lawis of this realme alluterlie abolischeit sua that na memorie thairof sall be heirafter'.[11] In the case of Deer, the eradication of 'monastic superstition' was remarkably successful, for the monastery is poorly documented, and such sources as exist are almost exclusively concerned with the monastery's landed possessions.[12] Although it did not occupy the same site as the earlier establishment, it took over some of the latter's lands.[13] It is quite possible that it also took over moveable property, including books. There is, in fact, one specific piece of evidence which may associate the Book of Deer with the Cistercian abbey. A small register of the house, dating from the sixteenth century, survives at Trinity College, Cambridge.[14] This forms part of the library which Thomas Gale assembled and which his son Roger, himself a notable collector of books, presented to the College.[15] The Book of Deer itself was in the possession of Thomas Gale in 1695.[16] Although it is possible that Gale acquired the two volumes from different sources, it is at least as likely that they had remained together since the dissolution of the Cistercian abbey of Deer. If this is so, the Book of Deer not only belonged to the abbey, but also remained there until the dissolution, for the register dates from the last phase of the abbey's history. I should, however, stress that there is no still no direct evidence that the manuscript was ever the property of the Cistercian abbey.

It may be worth asking whether other books from the abbey throw any light on the question. A fifteenth-century manuscript of Aristotle's *Politics* in William of Moerbeke's translation in St Andrews University Library bears

---

7 Cowan and Easson 1976, 47.   8 Cowan 1961, 43–55, especially p. 46. Cf. Jackson 1972, 7. See also Morgan 1947, 135–49.   9 See especially Ker 1964, 57.   10 For Bradshaw see the Appendix below, no. 7. In his unpublished description of MS Ii.6.32 kept in the manuscripts department at Cambridge University Library, James stated: 'This book may have passed to the later foundation, the Cistercian abbey of Deer ... but there is no evidence of this.'   11 *A. B. Ill.*, ii, 437.   12 The most detailed account of the abbey remains the one in *A. B. Ill.*, ii, 409–42. See also *A. B. Coll.*, 185–92. Mitchell (n.d.) is of relatively little value.   13 Jackson 1972, 2; Cowan and Easson 1976, 47.   14 MS O.7.42. See below at n. 22.   15 See McKitterick 1995, 61–4.   16 See below at n. 38.

the signature 'Rꙍertus Steφanus Deirensis cenobii'.[17] This man was subprior
of Deer in 1537 and prior in 1566.[18] The only other manuscript known to
come from Deer is a Cistercian Ordinal of the fifteenth century now in the
National Library of Scotland.[19] In addition, four printed books have associations with the abbey.[20] The Ordinal now in the National Library of
Scotland comes from the muniments of the Keith-Murray family of Ochtertyre.
From the same source, and also in the National Library of Scotland, is a small
register with entries dating from the years 1542–9 and later.[21] Of greater
interest from our point of view is the other register, at Trinity College,
Cambridge, already mentioned.[22] This likewise contains mainly documents
from the last phase of the abbey's existence, visitation records and directions
concerning regular observance of 1531 and 1535 (fos. 1–22v) and later
financial accounts (fos. 25v–30v). There is also a charter of William Lindsay
making a gift to the abbey for the anniversaries of his two wives, Alice and
Margaret, countess of Buchan. It is undated, but a charter immediately
following it is dated St Lambert's day (17 September), 1246 (fos. 24v–25).
The book bears the ownership inscription 'Robertus Stephanussonus' (fo.
30v), the same prior of Deer who owned the manuscript of Aristotle's *Politics*
in St Andrews University Library.[23] Another, later ownership inscription
appears at the foot of folio 1: 'Sum Johannis Aubrii Wiltoniensis'.[24] We shall
consider the significance of John Aubrey's ownership of this manuscript later.
In addition to the two cartularies, there is a small collection of charters,
likewise among the muniments of the Keith-Murray family and dating from
the final period of the abbey's existence.[25] Other charters were thought to
have been destroyed in the eighteenth century.[26]

    Although the cartularies and charters throw no light on the Book of Deer,
they do at least mean that the period of the abbey's dissolution is better
documented than any other period in its history.[27] The abbey's fate became

17 St Andrews University Library, MS PA.3895.P6, fo. 74v. His use here of Greek letters
for 'o' and 'ph' is no doubt an affectation.   **18** Ker and Piper 1992, 250; Dilworth 1997,
155.   **19** Ker 1964, 57; Watson 1987, 15. See also McRoberts 1953, 8, no. 42.   **20** Durkan
and Ross 1961, 82, 101, 120, 165.   **21** National Library of Scotland, MS 21183. See
Cunningham 1997, 3.   **22** MS O.7.42. It is described in James, 1902, 382. Robertson (*A. B.
Ill.*, ii) and Lawson (1896) made use of the manuscript. It does not appear in Davis 1958, or
in Cunningham 1997.   **23** See above at n. 17.   **24** There is no parallel to this inscription
in the numerous examples of Aubrey's ownership inscriptions given in Powell (1963, 295–
309). However, a frequently occurring form of his inscription was (with varying spellings)
'Jo. Aubrey de Easton Piers', described (Powell 1963, 307) as 'in agro Wiltoniensi'. Easton
Piers, Wiltshire, was Aubrey's birthplace.   **25** National Library of Scotland, Charters
17125, 17126, 17135, 17141, 17142, 17144, 17167–9, 17171, 17172.   **26** Letter of 28
December 1860 from John Stuart to Henry Bradshaw (CUL, Add. MS 2591/69): 'The
Deer property came by many intermediate sales and descents into the hands of Mr
Ferguson of Pitfour—and the old Deeds were said to have been destroyed by someone in
the end of the last century.'

closely interlinked with the Keith family, Earls Marischal, whose presence in
the parish of Deer dates back to at least 1324.[28] The Queen Dowager Mary in
1543 recommended Robert Keith, brother of William, fourth Earl Marischal,
to the pope for appointment to the abbey,[29] and two years later she requested
that the abbey be conferred on him *in commendam*.[30] This letter refers to him,
in a restrained tone, as 'modesto, & non illiterato adolescenti'. The pope provided Robert Keith to the abbey in 1546.[31] Robert only survived until 1552, in
which year he died at Paris.[32] He was succeeded by the Earl Marischal's son,
also called Robert and still a youth.[33] He is generally styled commendator of
Deer.[34] In 1587 he arranged for the resignation of the lands, tithes and other
property of the abbey into the king's hands; they were to be erected into a
temporal lordship (the lordship of Altrie). He was to hold the lordship for his
lifetime and it was then to pass to George, Earl Marischal, and his heirs.[35] The
deed of resignation makes no explicit mention of the moveable property of the
abbey,[36] nor, as far as I am aware, does any other source; and we know nothing of
the fate of the library at the time of the dissolution. It is worth mentioning that
three monks of Deer became ministers in the Reformed Church of Scotland.
They included Gilbert Chisholm, mentioned as a monk of Deer in 1536 and
as prior in 1554–60. He was minister at various times of several parishes,
among them Deer itself. He held the latter until his death in 1585.[37]

It is not until over a century after these events, in 1695, that the Book of
Deer re-surfaces. An entry in John Evelyn's *Diary* for 10 March of that year
records that 'Dr. Gale shewed me a MS of some parts of the New Test. in
vulg: Lect: that had belonged to a Monastery in the north of Scotland, which
he esteemed to be above 800 years old: some considerable various readings
observable as in i. John: & Genealogies of St Luke, left out &c: ...'[38] This is
almost certainly the Book of Deer.[39] The question naturally arises of how
Thomas Gale, who at the time was High Master of St Paul's School, may
have acquired this manuscript. Gale was a scholar of wide interests and
learning, whose contributions to the study of Anglo-Saxon history were
especially noteworthy.[40] Little is known about how he obtained his manuscripts,[41] and there is no evidence in the case of the Book of Deer. However,
the other manuscript from Deer which Gale owned, the register of the abbey,
may provide a clue. The register bears the ownership inscription of John

27 See Dilworth 1997, 155–6. See also Dilworth 1994, 218–20. 28 Lawson 1896, 80.
29 *ERS*, ii, 156, where the letter is undated. For the date (3 May 1543) see Warner and
Gilson 1921, ii. 286, no. 317. See also Lawson 1896, 45; *A. B. Coll.*, 187 n. 30 *ERS*, ii,
235–6 (dated 12 February 1545). 31 Royal Commission on Historical Manuscripts (1872),
Appendix, 412. 32 Pollen 1901, 415. 33 Stuart 1869, xii. 34 E.g., *A. B. Ill.*, ii , 437.
For the income of the abbey at around this time, *c.*£2400 *per annum*, see Kirk 1995, lvi,
457–9. 35 Stuart 1869, xiii. 36 It is printed in *A. B. Ill.*, ii , 437–9. 37 Dilworth 2003.
38 de Beer 1955, 206. 39 Mackay 1942, 50. 40 Douglas 1951, 59–61, 170–4.
41 McKitterick 1995, 63.

Aubrey.[42] Might Gale have acquired the Book of Deer in the same way that he acquired the register, that is, from Aubrey?[43]

The suggestion that Aubrey may be one of the missing links in the peregrinations of the Book of Deer has something to recommend it. Aubrey enjoyed close and cordial relations with Gale and respected him. He apparently wrote a life of him, and in a letter written when he thought that he was dying Aubrey referred to Gale as 'my faithful friend'.[44] Gale was one of the friends to whom Aubrey showed the *Monumenta Britannica*, and Gale added some notes to it.[45] He also provided notes for Aubrey's *Naturall Historie of Wiltshire*.[46] The ownership of the Book of Deer would accord reasonably well with Aubrey's known preoccupations. He was sufficiently interested in palaeography to include a section entitled 'Chronologia graphica' in his *Monumenta Britannica*.[47] However, the 'Chronologia graphica shows no trace of the use of the Book of Deer. The study of Scottish antiquities was not one of Aubrey's main interests, but from 1692 to 1695 he corresponded with James Garden, Professor of Divinity at King's College, Aberdeen, on this subject. Garden's letters to Aubrey have been published, and they discuss highland customs, stone circles, second sight and other topics.[48]

John Aubrey's library did not remain intact. He was obliged in 1677 for financial reasons to sell many books, and this was not the only sale.[49] There were also donations and bequests of books. The largest of these was to the Ashmolean Museum, Oxford.[50] If Aubrey ever owned the Book of Deer, it is likely that it passed from him to Thomas Gale by gift.

Gale did not retain the manuscript for long after John Evelyn saw it in his possession. It does not appear in the catalogue of his library published in Edward Bernard's *Catalogi*.[51] But in the same work we find it in the library of John Moore, bishop of Ely, one of the greatest collectors of manuscripts and printed books of his day.[52] Moore's books are described in four places in volume ii, part 1 of the *Catalogi*: (1) the main catalogue (pp 361–84, of which pp 379–84 concern printed books); (2) a section of the 'Appendix Librorum quorundam omissorum in Tomo 2do.' headed 'Libri MSS. & rariores impressi penes R.P. Joannem Morum Ep. Norvicensem' (pp 390–1); (3) the 'Modicum Catalogi Manuscriptorum, penes Reverendum admodum in Christo Patrem D.D. Joannem More Ep. Norwicensem, Auctarium' (pp 393–99); and (4)

---

42 See above at n. 24.   43 Lawson (1896, 31) hinted at this.   44 Powell 1963, 225; 233–4. 45 Britton 1845, 90; Hunter 1975, 206.   46 Powell 1963, 272.   47 Oxford, Bodleian Library, MS Top.gen.c.25 (S.C. 28427), fos. 185–196. This section of the *Monumenta Britannica* does not appear in the facsimile edited by Legg et al. (1980, 1982).   48 Gordon 1960. See also Britton 1845, 63–4.   49 Britton 1845, 53–4; Hunter 1975, 245.   50 Hunter 1975, 243–6.   51 Bernard 1697, ii, part 1, 185–95. Despite the date on the title-page, the final sheets of the *Catalogi* were not printed until summer 1698: McKitterick 1986, ii, 102. 52 On Moore as a collector see McKitterick 1986, chapters 3 and 4; Ringrose 1998.

'Addenda & Emendanda in priore Catalogo Codicum MSS.' (pp 399–403). The Book of Deer appears towards the end of the main catalogue, as no. 663.[53] Its position there, immediately before a group of manuscripts that Moore purchased on 22 May 1697, suggests that Moore acquired it, presumably from Gale, in the spring of 1697. There is a fuller description of the manuscript among the 'Addenda & Emendanda': 'Codex hic vetustissimo Hibernorum Charactere exaratus, continet tantum principia Evangeliorum secundum Mathaeum, Marcum, & Lucam, integrum vero Evang. Johannis. Habentur in margine quaedam Geneologiae Hibernicae'.[54] With the references to the Irish script and 'genealogies', this comes closer than any previous description to pointing out the nature and interest of the manuscript.

Henry Bradshaw stated that the manuscript showed 'marks of Bentley's use of it for textual purposes'.[55] It is quite possible that Bentley had access to the manuscript and that this occurred when it was still in the possession of Bishop Moore, for his use of Moore's library is well documented.[56] However, what these marks are I do not know.

Moore died in 1714. The following year King George I bought his library for £6,450, and presented it to the University of Cambridge.[57] It has been know since then as the Royal Library, a description which preserves the memory of a king's generous benefaction but disguises the nature of the library as one assembled by a private collector. Given the sheer scale of John Moore's library, it is perhaps not surprising that there should have been a delay before the books were arranged and catalogued. In 1752 they were placed in the Library's Dome Room, integrated with the Library's other holdings and assigned new class-marks.[58] Most of Moore's manuscripts are in the two-letter classes Dd to Mm. The following year, Thomas Goodall compiled a concordance between the old numbers (which derive from Bernard's *Catalogi*) and the new classmarks. In 1754–6 he prepared a new, very summary catalogue of the manuscripts.[59] Towards the end of the century, the Library commissioned James Nasmith to prepare a catalogue of its manuscripts, which he completed in 1798.[60] Nasmith's description of the Book of Deer is fuller than Goodall's, but it is hardly an advance on the account in the 'Addenda and Emendanda' to Bernard,[61] and Nasmith describes the script less satisfactorily. His entry reads:

---

53 McKitterick 1986, 129; Ringrose 1998, 82.   **54** Bernard 1697, ii, part 1, 403, no. dclxiv. **55** See the description of the manuscript in Bond and Thompson 1883 (facing pl. 210). **56** See McKitterick 1986, 71–3.   **57** McKitterick 1986, 148–52.   **58** Cambridge University Library (henceforth CUL), MS Oo.7.56 contains two copies of the concordance. The Book of Deer appears on fos. 7 and 21. See McKitterick 1986, 217 n. 170.   **59** CUL, MS Oo.7.53–5. The Book of Deer appears in MS Oo.7.55, fo. 31. See McKitterick 1986, 215–7.   **60** McKitterick 1986, 344.   **61** See above at n. 54.

Codex membranaceus forma minori, venerandae antiquitatis priscis
literis saxonicis scriptus, sed quod dolendum inutilus [*sic*], in quo
habentur,

1. Capita priora Evangeliorum Matth. Marc. et Luc. cum notis Hybernicis
2. Evangelium Johannis
3. Cartae quaedam Davidis regis Scottorum
4. Symbolum apostolorum etc.[62]

A major turning point in the study of the Book of Deer came in 1857 when
Henry Bradshaw, to use his own term, 'discovered' it.[63] He observed how his
possession of 'the most considerable private library' of Irish books 'led Mr
Hardwick (the Editor of the new printed Catalogue of Cambridge MSS.) to
draw my attention to the volume as containing the Gospels in "handwriting
Anglo-Saxon not later than the 10th. Century" with some notes apparently in
the Old Irish language. This was last autumn, and I at once set to work, & was
happy enough from these "notes" to discover the true nature of the book'.[64]
Bradshaw wished to edit the Book of Deer himself; but in his personality
'astonishing powers of industry went hand in hand with a monumental
capacity for procrastination',[65] and he could never bring himself to complete
his work on the volume. His biographer ascribes this to 'his reluctance to
publish anything so long as any point, however minute, remained to be
explained, and to the difficulty which he always laboured under of con-
centrating himself on one subject for any length of time'.[66] Bradshaw left it to
John Stuart to publish an edition of the manuscript in 1869, by which time
Bradshaw had been elected University Librarian.[67]

As we have seen, Bradshaw's initial work on the Book of Deer coincided
with the preparation of a new catalogue of the University Library's western
manuscripts, which had begun in 1850–1. A team under the general direction
of Charles Hardwick, and from 1866 of H.R. Luard, undertook the work.
The catalogue appeared with remarkable speed between 1856 and 1867 in six
volumes.[68] Bradshaw was far from being satisfied with the standard of the
catalogue. In a memorandum for the Library Syndicate, he made some severe,
although courteous, criticisms of it. Among the manuscripts that he chose to
illustrate his observations was the Book of Deer:

Ii.6.32 is a very early unfinished copy of the Latin Gospels written in
Aberdeenshire, and containing many entries in Gaelic of deeds of gift

62 CUL, MS Nn.6.42–4 (bound in one volume), no. 1896. 63 For a fuller discusion of
Bradshaw's interaction with the manuscript, see Zutshi 2004. 64 Draft of a letter of 15
May 1858 to John Stuart: CUL, Add. MS 2591/31. 65 Oates 1970, 279. 66 Prothero
1888, 71. 67 Stuart 1869. 68 *A catalogue of the manuscripts preserved in the Library of the
University of Cambridge* (Cambridge, 1856–67). See McKitterick 1986, 543–51.

etc. to the religious house in which it was preserved, and the volume is remarkable as containing the only contemporary records now remaining of those houses which existed before the introduction of Italian monachism in the 12th. century. The description first printed (afterwards cancelled and re-written) called it a *mutilated* copy of the Gospels in the *Anglo-Saxon* character, with some notes at the beginning in the Old Irish language![69]

It is clear from this passage that Bradshaw was consulted about the description of the manuscript in the printed catalogue.[70] The entry as published, for instance, the dating of the different sections of the manuscript and the description of the hand as Irish, reflects his study of the Book of Deer.[71] The survival of the full text of the entry among Bradshaw's papers and in his handwriting shows that he was indeed its author, although his authorship is nowhere noted in the *Catalogue*.[72]

Bradshaw's interest in the manuscript seems to have revived in 1879, at the prompting of Edward Maunde Thompson,[73] who requested an account of it for the Palaeographical Society. Bradshaw completed this in 1882. It was thus not until twenty-five years after his 'discovery' of the Book of Deer, and twenty-four years after the publication of the unattributed catalogue entry, that Bradshaw published a brief account of the manuscript.[74]

This is not the place to discuss scholarship concerning the Book of Deer since the time of Bradshaw. However, it may be worth drawing attention to a few aspects of its physical custody and preservation in the last century and a half. In Bradshaw's day, it was common practice for many libraries to lend even their most precious manuscripts to scholars who wished to study them. Thus, as Librarian of the University of Cambridge, Bradshaw arranged for Joseph Robertson, who had undertaken to edit the Book of Deer for the Spalding Club, to borrow the manuscript.[75] A more unexpected outing for the manuscript was its production in the Mar peerage case in 1870.[76] More recently, the University Library lent the Book of Deer to Glasgow City Council's Museums and Art Galleries for the exhibition 'Scotland creates' which took place in the McLellan Galleries from 17 November 1990 to 1 April 1991.[77] The entire manuscript has been photographed digitally and may be viewed on the website of Cambridge University Library (http://www.lib.cam.ac.uk/under 'Digital Library').

69 CUL, Add. MS 6419, fo. 260.   **70** See also the Appendix below, no. 1.   **71** *Catalogue of the manuscripts preserved in the Library of the University of Cambridge*, iii. 530–2.   **72** See the Appendix below, no. 21.   **73** See Bradshaw's letter to Thompson of 31 December 1879: CUL, Add. MS 2592/578.   **74** See the Appendix below.   **75** CUL, Add. MS 8916/A64/62, A65/47, 76, 77. Robertson died in 1866, and John Stuart took over the editorship.   **76** Prothero 1888, 72. On the Mar peerage case, see Cokayne 1932, Appendix G.   **77** See Kaplan 1990.

The present binding of the Book of Deer dates from 1963, when Douglas Cockerell & Son, then of Letchworth, Hertfordshire, repaired and rebound the volume. Evidently the spine folds were seriously damaged, and they were repaired with vellum. Loose guards, in the form of narrow strips of folded hand-made paper, were placed around each gathering. This was a technique which Sidney Cockerell developed to prevent the adhesive used in the rebinding process coming into direct contact with the manuscript. New vellum end-leaves and doublures were added. The sewing uses unbleached linen thread on four double raised cords, laced into boards of sawn English oak. The ends were sewn with unbleached linen thread at the head and tail. The binding is in full dyed Niger (goatskin). The manuscript's custom-made box contains the previous binding, of full brown calf, as well as fly-leaves and pastedowns. This binding may derive from the major exercise of repair and rebinding which the University Library's books underwent in the late eighteenth century,[78] or it may be a little later in date. No trace of any earlier binding, or of any medieval pastedowns or fly-leaves, survives.

APPENDIX

Unpublished writings by Henry Bradshaw concerning the Book of Deer

The main purpose of this appendix is to describe some of the manuscript papers of Henry Bradshaw in Cambridge University Library which concern the Book of Deer. The papers fall into two distinct groups. Items 1–4 and 17–21 represent Bradshaw's early work on the manuscript, dating from the years 1857– c.1861. The University Library holds a good deal of Bradshaw's correspondence with John Stuart and others concerning publication plans for the Book of Deer, and I have printed extracts from two letters from the correspondence (nos. 1–2).[79] The second group of papers almost all concern the description of the manuscript which Bradshaw prepared at the request of Edward Maunde Thompson of the British Museum for publication by the Palaeographical Society. Among the papers is a copy of Bradshaw's letter of 10 March 1882 addressed to Thompson, which accompanied the description. I print the letter (no. 5), together with some extracts from the other papers insofar as they supplement the published description.

The entries in the Appendix are in the order of Cambridge University Library's Additional Manuscript numbers.

78 See McKitterick 1986, 309–14.   79 See also Zutshi 2004.

1. CUL, Add. MS 2591/25. Draft of a letter of 21 April 1858 from Henry Bradshaw to John Stuart:

> The enclosed papers will go some way towards answering the two queries in your letter of the 15th. to Mr. Gordon, and but for illness the greater part of these last few months, and the pressure of work in consequence, you should have had your curiosity satisfied before this.
>
> My own extreme interest in finding any remains of the old Irish language, as well as tracing new facts in the history (however legendary) of the Irish Apostles of Scotland, has led me to go as thoroughly into the matter as lies in my power. It requires time, but I find that, by patiently working right through the chartularies published by the Spalding, Bannatyne and Maitland Clubs, I have been able to verify names, & a few places, so as to exceed my utmost expectations. I wish very much Mr. Robertson could have had the benefit of the knowledge for his 'Collections'.
>
> I enclose a transcript of the description of the volume, as it stands in the printed catalogue of the MSS. in the Public Library here, but as this is so extremely meagre (owing to the sheet having been printed off, before the writer became aware of what the MS contained) I may say briefly thus:–[80]
>
> P.S. I must trust to your patience to make some thing out of the papers I enclose which with the book ought to give you a fair notion of the MS. I will gladly answer any queries. I have worked so much at the Gaelic grants & lists, that I know them all by heart, and have made out almost all the words, which considering that no dictionary contains half of them, I look upon as successful. My materials have been O'Donovan's invaluable Irish Grammar, & the publns of the Irish Archaeological Society, which both contain words & translations to be found in no other printed works.
>
> I am anxious to make out a satisfactory account of what the MS. contains, & this is the real reason that I have been so long about it, having only intervals of time to work in, & feeling so strongly that half information on such matters is little better than none.
>
> You will be able to make out what I have written in pencil at the beginning and end of the book. My friend to whom I sent it rubbed out some of the pencil writing in order to send it open through the post.[81]
>
> Two things which I want very much are (1) a map to enable me to verify townlands in the way that the Ordnance Survey of Ireland does, and (2) a reference to any work where I can find information on the

---

80 The draft does not include Bradshaw's description.   81 See no. 4 below.

jurisdiction of the 'Mormar' of the district, and the 'Tosec' or Chieftan of the Clan, over the same ground, as I find in several instances these two uniting (in the same charter) to grant immunities to the convent ...'

At the end of the letter is a page of notes:

This is the evident chronological order of the handwritings used:
1. Gospels, Creed & Subscription.
2. Visitation Office.
3. Legend and list of grants.
4. Two charters of Gartnat son of Cannec and Ete daughter of Gillemichel, his wife.
5. Grant of Doncad son of McBead.
6. With supplement to no. 5, list of Grants further.
7. Latin Charter of King David in favour of the Clerics of Deer.
8. Grant of Colban, Mormar of Buchan & Eva d. of Gartnat his wife, and Clan Magan, together with supplements to nos. 3 and 6.'

This is followed by a more detailed description of the contents of these eight sections.[82]

2. CUL, Add. MS 2591/28. A letter of 10 May 1858 from Henry Bradshaw to John Stuart. It contains the following paragraph:

Of the precise nature of the MS there is no doubt. It is an unfinished MS of the Vulgate version of the four Gospels, with the Apostles' Creed, written by a scribe who[se] vernacular language was Gaelic, in which the subscription at the close is written. The first three Gospels are unfinished (not mutilated); St. John is complete. The cursive character, the size of the volume, & the position of the visitation office (in a slightly later hand) corresponding almost verbatim with that in the Book of Dimma, lead one to believe that its original use was to be carried about the person, not used in the choir, while the transcripts of documents, & lists of possessions inserted in the blank spaces at the beginning &c. as in the Book of Kells, show that it was venerated as a relic & so used, as a depository for these documents; and as the book, apparently, on which they swore in claiming their lands, while finally from the known history of the Culdees, and the fact that *at Deer* the only known religious house was a Cistercian convent founded in 1219 or thereabouts, it is natural to believe that these insertions in the volume which refer to David's reign were written in, some time between that

82 Stuart's reply is CUL, Add. MS 2592/27.

and the year 1219, that is at some time when they were likely to be of some service.

3. CUL, Add. MS 2591/81. A brief description of the Book of Deer, left incomplete apparently and intended to be the first part of a projected series of Cambridge Literary Remains. The title reads *A single specimen of the Scottish Communion Service as used by the Clerics of Deer in Aberdeenshire. From the Book of Deer, now MS Ii.6.32 in the Public Library of the University of Cambridge.* The design for the title page (CUL, Add. MS 2591/80, 82) bears the dates 1858 and 1861.

4. CUL, Add. MS 4594. A small notebook of 86 numbered pages containing tracings and transcripts from the Book of Deer. At the beginning is a letter from Bradshaw lending this notebook to a friend. The letter is written in pencil, and parts of it, notably the name of the addressee, have been rubbed out and are too faint to be read:

> I have but just returned & found your letter. 5th. century is absurd of course, but I don't think it can be later than the 8th. century taking all things into consideration. You must take this until I can send you a collation, as a mere specimen of handwriting & illumination.
>
> It was the sacred book upon which the Culdees of Old Deer in Aberdeenshire swore upon [*sic*], in pleading for their right to lands in the beginning of the 12th century, and is of very special interest as containing the only extant account of this house, & it is invaluable for the early Gaelic which it contains.
>
> I want to find what MSS. have the *Genealogy* followed by 'Finit Prologus. Item incipit nunc Evangelium secundum Matheum'. For one the Lambeth Book of McDurnan has—you know may I dare say. By its containing part of the Off. for Visitn. of the Sick, it must have been apparently for carrying about, & the size of [*recte* and] cursive character agree with this. The number and arrangement of the leaves are accurately represented in this volume, & you will see that one signature in St John is disarranged.
>
> I write this in the railway carriage, & wd bring it on to you, but that as Junior Dean I am compelled to be in College …

A list of tracings at the end of the notebook bears the date 23 December 1857.

5. CUL, Add. MS 4602, fos. 16–18. A copy of a letter of 10 March 1882 to Edward Maunde Thompson of the British Museum concerning the description of and illustrations from the Book of Deer, which were to appear in the

second volume of the Palaeographical Society's series of *Facsimiles of Manuscripts and Inscriptions*, to which is appended a description of the manuscript. The letter reads as follows:

> I have not been able to give any mind to the Book of Deer until the last three days, and it has taken me even with your kind help much more time than I counted upon, but I could not do the thing in a slovenly way. I know my notes are much too long for your purpose, but it has been of really great service to me to work them out & put them into shape.
>
> The little 'Communion of the sick' is I think important for the consideration of date. These things become treasures from perhaps being associated with some dead member of the fraternity, & eventually they come to be placed in silver or jewelled cases, & used as receptacles for deeds of importance. My point is (which of course I have not argued out in my notes) that an xith cent. entry of a service for practical use would not be entered in a book which had already become a sacred relic. This falls in so well with your views about the a and q, that I am more than ever satisfied to place the book as "late 9th or early 10th century".[83]
>
> I should like to see a proof of whatever you print, especially of the transcript of text. You know I shall not be hurt even if you do not use my notes at all. So do as you like in that. I hope you will not put I.i.b. 32 on the Plate as the name of the MS. Our books are all marked with double *letters* & shelf & volume *numbers*, this being Ii.6.32. Stuart's work though good in some points is most objectionable in others. He never could bear the notion of an Englishman interesting himself in these things. Write a line when you have time, and tell me what you do.

There follows a description of the manuscript which does not differ significantly from the one published in *Facsimiles of Manuscripts and Inscriptions* (Bond and Thompson 1873–83, facing plate 210).

6. CUL, Add. MS 6420, fo. 40. Notes on the Book of Deer under the headings 'Gatherings', 'Ruling', 'Writing', 'Spelling' and 'Contractions'. A list of headings at the top of the sheet shows that Bradshaw intended to cover twelve headings, but he seems to have broken off after the first five. Under 'Writing' Bradshaw expresses himself more fully than in *Facsimiles of Manuscripts and Inscriptions*: 'Hiberno-Saxon minuscule of the ix–xth century, not so free as the early ixth century Book of Armagh, yet showing no traces of the angular, or purely Irish, character noticeable in the x–xith century. The uppermost portion of letters rests on the line, the rest depending from it. Words are separated, but conjunctions and prepositions are generally joined

83 I have not been able to locate any letter from Thompson to Bradshaw about the 'a' and 'q'.

to the succeeding word. The vacant space at the end of a paragraph is frequently (not uniformly) filled up by continuing on it the first line of the succeeding paragraph, this continuation being marked off from the end of the preceding by SS, sometimes a hand.' The heading 'Spelling' has no parallel in the published description. Here Bradshaw lists the most frequent peculiarities of spelling. The other sections do not differ significantly from the equivalent passages in the description prepared for the Palaeographical Society.

7. CUL, Add. MS 6240, fo. 41. Further notes, beginning with 'Gatherings' and 'Rulings' (as on fo. 40). They are followed by a paragraph that has been crossed through: 'One 2-sheet quire of prologue, that is, the Genealogy of Christ treated as such (Matth. 1,1–1,17), ending on leaf 3a, the rest of lf 3 left blank originally, and leaf 4 also, which last had disappeared before entries made early in the twelfth century. One 6-sheet quire of St Matthew (1,18–7,23).' Bradshaw provides a brief account of the contents and provenance of the manuscript. The final sentence breaks off incomplete: 'It bears no trace of its possession by the Cistercian monastery of Deer founded in 1219; but it ...' At the foot of the page Bradshaw has attempted to copy and describe some of the letter-forms.

8. CUL, Add. MS 6420, fo. 64. A six-line description of the manuscript prepared for an exhibition.

9. CUL, Add. MS 6425, fo. 73. A draft of the beginning of Bradshaw's description of the manuscript prepared for Thompson, the final paragraph crossed out.

10. CUL, Add. MS 6425, fo. 74. A draft of the beginning of Bradshaw's description of the manuscript, earlier than no. 9 above.

11. CUL, Add. MS 6425, fos. 75–80. A draft, later than nos. 9 and 10 above, of Bradshaw's letter of 10 March 1882 to Thompson together with the description of the manuscript that Bradshaw prepared for publication.

12. CUL, Add. MS 6425, fo. 80a. A draft of the beginning of Bradshaw's description of the manuscript, apparently earlier than nos. 9 and 10 above.

13. CUL, Add. MS 6425, fo. 80b. A draft of the section on 'Ornamentation' in Bradshaw's description of the manuscript.

14. CUL, Add. MS 6425, fo. 81. A draft description of the manuscript with the headings 'Gatherings', 'Ruling' and 'Writing'. Under the first heading, Bradshaw expresses himself more fully than in his published description:

6-sheet quires; no trace of signatures. Each Gospel commences (as is commonly the case in MSS. of this school) on a fresh quire, the text beginning with an illuminated initial and border on leaf 2a, with a representation of the Evangelist facing it on leaf 1b, the first page of each quire being left blank. A further characteristic of this school is seen in this MS The text facing the picture of St Matthew begins with Matth.i.18, and the Genealogy (Matth.i.1–17) is treated as a prologue to the whole book, is written on a separate preliminary quire, with a frontispiece representing all the four evangelists facing the commencement, and the close of the genealogy (Matth.i.17) is followed by the rubric: 'Finit prologus. Item incipit nunc evangelium secundum matheum'.

15. CUL, Add. MS 6425, ff. 82–85. Draft of the entire description of the Book of Deer prepared for publication by the Palaeographical Society.

16. CUL, Add. MS 6425, ff. 86–88. Draft of part of the published description of the Book of Deer.

17. CUL, Add. MS 8916/K (39 ff.). Transcript by Bradshaw of the entire register of the abbey of Deer at Trinity College, Cambridge (MS o.7.42).

18. CUL, Add. MS 8916/L. Miscellaneous notes in Bradshaw's hand: /1, genealogy of the Earls of Buchan; /2, ten-line description of the Book of Deer; /3, notes on Trinity College MS o.7.42; /4–29, transcripts of the additions to the Book of Deer with notes on the individuals named in them; /30, eight-line description of the manuscript; /31, genealogy of the Earls of Buchan; /32, transcript of office for visitation of the sick; /33, translation of Gaelic Notes.

19. CUL, Add. MS 8916/M. Miscellaneous notes on the Book of Deer in Bradshaw's hand: /1–9, transcripts of Gaelic Notes and visitation office; /11, 'Documents relating to the monastery of Deer, ... I. Legend of the origin of the house, together with a list of the benefactors and their gifts (about AD 1125?)', with six lines of transcript; /12, further transcripts of Gaelic passages; /13, brief description of the manuscript; /13, comparison of passages in the Books of Deer, Dimma and Mulling.

20. CUL, Add. MS 8916/N. Miscellaneous notes, mainly on the Book of Deer, in Bradshaw's hand, including: /1, transcript with partial translation of Gaelic passage; /2, end of a description of the manuscript (five lines); /3, description of the manuscript; /4–15, transcript and translation of Gaelic entries and transcript of visitation office; /15, 17, brief descriptions of the manuscript; /23, partial transcript of foundation account; /39–42, tracings;

/43, transcript of visitation office; /44–5, partial transcript of foundation account and lists of Gaelic words and names; /46, transcript of opening of Gospel text; /47–51, notes on the Earls of Buchan and Angus; /52–4, collations; /55, list of kings of Scots; /56, list of Earls of Fife; /57–60, transcripts of Gaelic passages; /61, brief collation; /65, notes headed 'A small cartulary of the Clerics of Deer in Aberdeenshire, written by more than one scribe, most probably in various parts of the XIIth. Century'; /66, copy for the press dated 5 April 1861 and headed 'A single specimen of the Scottish Communion Service as used by the Clerics of Deer in Aberdeenshire ...', with introductory remarks, 'The "Book of Deer" is a copy of the Latin Gospels, written possibly in the eighth century. What is here given is found on two pages (ff. 28b, 29a) immediately preceding the Gospel of St Luke. From the fact that f. 28 is an inserted leaf, the *recto* of which is blank, it is clear that there is no defect arising from any mutilation of the volume. The handwriting may be assigned to the eleventh century ...'

21. CUL, Add. MS 8916/O. Descriptions of the manuscript in Bradshaw's hand prepared for volume three of the *Catalogue of manuscripts preserved in the Library of the University of Cambridge,* which was published by Cambridge University Press in 1858: /1, draft description which breaks off at line 10; /2, description as published in the *Catalogue,* iii. 530–2, marked 'Proof to Mr Bradshaw'; /3, draft of the previous.

REFERENCES

A. B. Coll.   Robertson, J. (1843) *Collections for a history of the shires of Aberdeen and Banff* (Spalding Club), Aberdeen.

A. B. Ill.   Robertson, J. (1847) *Illustrations of the topography and antiquities of the shires of Aberdeen and Banff,* ii (Spalding Club), Aberdeen.

Barrow, G.W.S. (ed.), (1999) *The charters of King David I,* Woodbridge.

Bernard, E. (1697) *Catalogi librorum manuscriptorum Angliae et Hiberniae,* Oxford.

Bond, E.A., and E.M. Thompson (eds), (1873–83) *Facsimiles of manuscripts and inscriptions,* ii (Palaeographical Society), London.

Britton, J. (1845) *Memoir of John Aubrey, F.R.S.,* London.

Broun, D.E. (1995) *The charters of Gaelic Scotland and Ireland in the early and central Middle Ages* (Quiggin Pamphlets on the Sources of Mediaeval Gaelic History, 2), Cambridge.

Catalogue of the manuscripts preserved in the Library of the University of Cambridge (Cambridge, 1856–67).

Cokayne, G. (1932) *The complete peerage,* viii, London.

Cowan, I. B. (1961) 'The development of the parochial system in medieval Scotland', *Scottish Historical Review* 40, 43–55.

Cowan, I.B., and D.E. Easson (1976) *Medieval religious houses: Scotland* (2nd ed.), London.

Cunningham, I.C. (1997) 'Medieval cartularies of Great Britain: Amendments and additions to the Scottish section of Davis', *Monastic Research Bulletin* 3, 1–7.

Davis, G.R.C. (1958) *Medieval cartularies of Great Britain*, London.

de Beer, E.S. (ed.), (1955) *The diary of John Evelyn*, v: *Kalendarium, 1690–1706*, Oxford.

Dilworth, M. (1994) 'Franco-Scottish efforts at monastic reform 1500–1560', *Recs Scottish Church History Soc.* 25, pt 2 (1994), 215–20.

—— (1997) 'Scottish Cistercian monasteries and the Reformation' *Innes Review*, 48, 144–64.

—— (2003) 'Deer abbey's contribution to the Reformed Church', *Innes Review* 54, 216–25.

Douglas, D. (1951) *English scholars, 1660–1730* (2nd edn), London.

Dumville, D.N. (2007) *Celtic essays, 2001–2007*, 2 vols, Aberdeen.

Durkan, J., and A. Ross (1961) *Early Scottish libraries*, Glasgow.

ERS   Epistolae ... Regum Scotorum, ed. T. Ruddiman (1722–4), 2 vols, Edinburgh.

Gordon, C. (1960) 'Professor James Garden's letters to John Aubrey, 1692–1695', in *The Miscellany of the Third Spalding Club*, iii, 1–56.

Hughes, K. (1980), 'The Book of Deer (Cambridge University Library MS Ii.6.32)', in K. Hughes, *Celtic Britain in the early Middle Ages*, ed. D. Dumville, Woodbridge, 22–37.

Hunter, M. (1975) *John Aubrey and the realm of learning*, London.

Jackson, K.H. (1972) *The Gaelic Notes in the Book of Deer*, Cambridge.

James, M. R. (1902) *The Western manuscripts in the library of Trinity College, Cambridge: a descriptive catalogue*, iii, Cambridge.

Kaplan, W. (ed.) (1990) *Scotland creates: 5000 years of art and design*, London.

Ker, N. R. (1964) *Medieval libraries of Great Britain: a list of surviving books* (2nd ed.), (Royal Historical Society), London.

Ker, N.R., and A.J. Piper (1992), *Medieval manuscripts in British libraries*, iv Oxford.

Kirk, J. (ed.), (1995) *The Books of Assumption of the Thirds of Benefices*, Oxford.

Lawrie, A. C. (1905) *Early Scottish charters prior to AD 1153*, Glasgow.

Lawson, A. (1896) *A book of the parish of Deir*, Aberdeen.

Legg, R., W. Hoade, R. Briggs, and J. Fowles (eds), (1980, 1982) *Monumenta Britannica, or, A miscellany of British antiquities* by John Aubrey (facsimile), 2 vols, Sherborne.

Mackay, D. (1942) 'New light on the Book of Deer', *Scottish Gaelic Studies* 5, 50.

McKitterick, D. (1986) *Cambridge University Library: a history*, ii: *The eighteenth and nineteenth centuries*, Cambridge.

—— (ed.), (1995) *The making of the Wren Library, Trinity College, Cambridge*, Cambridge.

McRoberts, D. (1953) *Catalogue of Scottish medieval liturgical books and fragments* Glasgow.

Mitchell, J. (n.d.) 'A history of the Abbey of Deer' (Edinburgh, National Library of Scotland, MS 2098).

Morgan, M. (1947) 'The organisation of the Scottish church in the twelfth century', *Transactions of the Royal Historical Society*, 4th series 29 , 135–49.

Oates, J.C.T. (1970) 'Young Mr. Bradshaw', in *Essays in honour of Victor Scholderer*, ed. D.E. Rhodes, Mainz, 276–83.

Pollen, J. H. (1901) *Papal negotiations with Mary Queen of Scots*, ed. J.H. Pollen (Scot. Hist. Soc. 37), Edinburgh

Powell, A. (1963) *John Aubrey and his friends*, London, 2nd edn.

Prothero, G. W. (1888) *A memoir of Henry Bradshaw*, London.

Ringrose, J. (1998) 'The Royal Library: John Moore and his books', in *Cambridge University Library: the great collections*, ed. P. Fox, Cambridge.

Royal Commission on Historical Manuscripts (1872) *The Third Report*, London.

Stuart, J. (ed.), (1869) *The Book of Deer* (Spalding Club), Aberdeen.

Warner, G.F., and J.P. Gilson (1921), *Catalogue of western manuscripts in the Old Royal and King's collections in the British Museum*, London.

Watson, A.G. (1987) *Medieval libraries of Great Britain: supplement to the second edition* (Royal Historical Society), London.

Zutshi, P. (2004) 'Henry Bradshaw and the Book of Deer', in *The medieval book and a modern collector: essays in honour of Toshiyuki Takamiya*, ed. T. Matsuda, R.A. Linenthal and J. Scahill, Woodbridge and Tokyo.

THE PROPERTY RECORDS

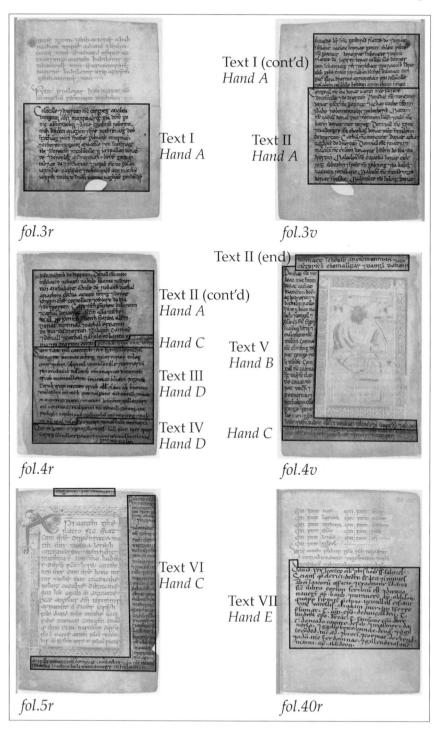

Text I (cont'd)
Hand A

Text I
Hand A

Text II
Hand A

fol.3r

fol.3v

Text II (end)

Text II (cont'd)
Hand A

Hand C

Text V
Hand B

Text III
Hand D

Text IV
Hand D

Hand C

fol.4r

fol.4v

Text VI
Hand C

Text VII
Hand E

fol.5r

fol.40r

5.1 The property records: key to numbering.

The property records: Diplomatic Edition including accents

ROIBEARD Ó MAOLALAIGH

EDITORIAL POLICY

Except in one important respect, this edition does not differ from that of Jackson (1972), other than to correct a single transcriptional / typographical error (*cilli* for Jackson's *cille* (AVII5; Jackson 1972, 22, but cf. p. 32)). The identification of individual scribes (A–E) follows that of Jackson (1972). The lineation follows that of the MS (and Jackson, 1972), except lines II.28–29 where we deviate slightly in order to group the writing of individual hands as closely as possible together. The only significant departure from Jackson, and the main purpose in presenting a new edition here, is the inclusion of the many suprasegmental diagonal strokes ('accents') which pepper the text. The characteristics and possible functions of these accents, and the reasons for reproducing them here, are discussed in detail in Ó Maolalaigh, 'On the possible functions of the accents', this volume.

Underlining has been used to indicate the expansion of manuscript contractions. Capitalization and punctuation follows that of the manuscript. The method devised for representing manuscript accents is as follows: An accent may cover either one, two, or three letters. Bold characters are used to represent the 'coverage' of individual acute accents, e.g. **drostán** (AII, with accent over -*an*), **adál**ta (AII, with accent over *dal* centred over *a*). Since it is not always clear whether or not the accents have significance as individual letter markers or as syllabic markers, the use of bold in addition to the acute accent has the advantage of illustrating both letter and syllabic 'coverage'. There is a small number of instances where two successive accents cover adjacent series of letters; in cases where ambiguity might arise the bold characters have been italicised in order to illustrate the coverage of the second accent. For instance, as**á***ath*le (AI6) illustrates that the first accent covers the *a* beneath it, and the second accent covers the sequence *ath*, centred above the *t*. In our edition, the acute accent has usually been placed over the letter which receives maximum coverage, i.e. over the letter which occurs immediately under the centre of the accent. In cases where the accent appears to cover two letters, one of which is a vowel, the accent has usually been placed over the vowel in such sequences (e.g. **drostán** (AII), **essé** (AI4));[1] in cases where the

[1] This includes cases of uncertainty where it is difficult to decide whether the accent

accent covers a sequence of two vowels, the accent has generally been placed over the first vowel (e.g. **ómormáer** (AI5)), although precedence is given to the principle of 'maximum coverage' where this can be applied, hence **dochuíd** (AI11) rather than **dochúid**.

In a number of instances—usually involving a sequence of a vowel and a consonant—the manuscript accent appears to occur above the consonant segment rather than the preceding vowel as might be expected. The rightward placement of accents in this manner is common in Gaelic manuscripts from all periods, and in some cases such accents may be due to the scribe avoiding a descending character from the previous line, e.g. **araginn** (AI4), **incathŕaig** (AI6), **bidbiń** (AIII0).[2] In cases where it seems reasonable to do so, our interpretation and practice in the diplomatic edition of the text has been to place the accent over the vowel rather than the consonant, although in such cases the actual manuscript form is given in the right-hand margin between brackets, e.g. **aragínn** {**araginn**} (AI4). There are approximately 27 instances of this (most examples occurring in Texts AI and AII) as follows:

Table 5.1: Rightward placement of accents. Distribution by scribe and text[3]

HAND	A	B	C	D	E
Per text	I 7	V 1	II 1	III 3	VII 2
	II 13		V 0	IV 0	
			VI 0		
Total	20	1	1	3	2

Notwithstanding the fact that we have more text from Hand A than any other hand, it is nevertheless noteworthy that Hand A seems to have a predilection for the rightward placing of suprasegmental accents. The editorial measures adopted by Best and Bergin (1929, xli) who 'put the accent over the vowel to which it belongs' have not been adopted in our diplomatic edition except in the case of rightwardly placed accents on contiguous segments.

At first sight the Gaelic Notes furnish 37 (14%) apparent instances of accents occurring centred above consonants. However, the restoration of rightwardly placed accents enables us to discard 27 of these, leaving us with a much smaller number of 10 (3.76%)—some of which may also be explained

covers more of the first or the second letter (e.g. the second accent in **ímácć** (AII9). 2 For other instances, see notes below. 3 The calculations of percentages based on the number of syllables with accents provides only a rough indication of accent usage by individual hands: note that Hand A on four occasions uses two accents over one syllable (**aǹím óhúnń ímácć** AII9, **catháĺ** AIII7).

The property records: Diplomatic Edition including accents   121

as misplacements. In other words, more than 96% (256/266) of all accents appear to cover vowels rather than consonants.

Table 5.2: Accents above consonants (Ć)

T	Ć	Ć removed	Remaining Ć	Total no. of accents
	13	7	6	85
	14	13	1	94
	27 (15%)	20	7	179 (100%)
	2	1	1	25
	2 (8%)	1	1	25 (100%)
	1	1	0	3
	0	0	0	3
	0	0	0	9
	1 (6%)	1	0	15 (100%)
DIII	4	3	1	32
DIV	0	0	0	6
Total D	4 (11%)	3	1	38 (100%)
E	3	2	1	9
Total E	3 (33%)	2	1	9 (100%)
Overall totals	37 (14%)	27	10	266 (100%)
%	14	10	3.76	

DIPLOMATIC EDITION INCLUDING ACCENTS

Text I   [Hand A, fo. 3r]

1 Columcille ⁊ drostán mac cósgreg adálta
2 tangator áhí marroalseg día doíb go
3 níc abbordoboír ⁊bedé cruthnec robomor
4 mǽr búchan aragínn ⁊ essé rothidńaíg doíb   {aragińn}
5 ingathraíg saín insaere gobraíth ómormáer   {gobraíth}
6 ⁊óthóséc• tangator asáaíhle sen incathŕaig   {óthóseć}
7 ele ⁊doráten ricolumcille sí iarfallán dóráth   {doráten}

8 dé ₇dorodloeg ari<u>n</u>mormáer •i• bédé gondas
9 tabrád dó ₇níthárat ₇rogáb m<u>a</u>c dó galár
10 iarn*éré* na gleréc ₇robomar*é*b act mádbec
11 iarsén dochuíd i<u>n</u>mor<u>m</u>aer dattác naglerec g*ón*d*é*nd<u>a</u>es
                    [Hand A, fo. 3v]
12 ernacde les i<u>n</u>m<u>a</u>c gondisád slán*té* dó ₇dórat
13 i<u>n</u>edbaírt doíb úaćloic i<u>n</u>tiprat goníce chloíc pette
14 m<u>e</u>c garnaít doronsat i<u>n</u>nernacde ₇ taníc
15 slante dó; iarsén dorat collu<u>m</u>cille dódros   {iarseń}
16 tán i<u>n</u>chadraíg sén ₇rosbenact ₇foracaib i<u>m</u>bre   {tań}
17 ther gebe tisad ris nabad blienec buadacc tan
18 gat<u>or</u> deara drostán arscarthaín fri collu<u>m</u>cille
19 rolaboir colu<u>m</u>cille bedeár á*ń*ím óhúnń ímácé ;

Text II   [Hand A, fo. 3v]

1 Cómgeall m<u>a</u>c éda dórat úaorti níce fúrené
2 docolu<u>m</u>cille ₇do drostán• Moridac m<u>a</u>c morcúnn   {drostań} {morcunń}
3 dorat pett m<u>e</u>c garnaít ₇áchád toche temní
4 ₇bahé robomormaír₇robothoséc• Mataín
5 m<u>a</u>c caerill dorat cuit mormoir i<u>n</u>ált<u>er</u>i ₇culí: m<u>a</u>c
6 batín dorat cuít toíség• Domnall m<u>a</u>c gíric
7 ₇malbrigte m<u>a</u>c chathail dorat pett i<u>n</u>mulenn•
8 dodrostán• Cathal m<u>a</u>cmorcunt dorat áchád   {dodrostań}
9 naglerec do drostán• Domnall m<u>a</u>c rúadri ₇   {drostań}
10 malcolu<u>m</u> m<u>a</u>c culeón doratsat bidbín dó dia ₇dó   {bidbiń}
11 drostán• Malcolou<u>m</u> m<u>a</u>c cinathá dorat cúit   {drostań}
12 rííg íbbidbín ₇i<u>n</u>pett m<u>e</u>c gobróig ₇dá dabég
13 uactaír rósábard• Malcolu<u>m</u> m<u>a</u>c moilbrigte
14 dorat i<u>n</u>delerc• Málsnecte m<u>a</u>c luloíg dorat
                    [Hand A, fol. 4r]
15 pett malduíb dó drostán; Domnall m<u>a</u>c meíc   {drostań}
16 dubbacín robaíth nahúle edbarta rodros
17 tán arthabárt áhule dó• robaíth cathá́l   {tań}
18 árachoír c<u>h</u>etna acuitíd t<u>h</u>óisíg ₇dorat   {acuitíd}
19 proínń chét cecnolloce₇ceccasc dó diá
20 ₇dó drostán• Cainnéch m<u>a</u>c meic dobarcon
21 ₇cathál doratsat<u>or</u> alt<u>er</u>ín alla uéthé   {alteriń}
22 na ca<u>m</u>me[?] gonice in• bé*íí*h edarda ált<u>er</u>in   {béí́h}
23 dorat domnall ₇cathál étdanin
24 dó dia ₇dó drostán• Robaíth cainnéc   {Robaíth}
25 ₇do<u>m</u>nall ₇cathál nahúle edbarta ri

26 dia ₇rí drostan óthós[Hand C]ach goderad issaére omór[maer] ₇othesech
culaithi brátha

{issaére}

[Hand A, fo. 4v]

27 ₇bennact inchomded ar cecmormar ₇ar
28 cectosech chomallfas ₇dansíl daneis

Text III   [Hand D, fo. 4r]

1 Gartnait mac cannech ₇éte ingengillemíchel
2 dóratsat petmec cóbrig ricosecrad eclasi
3 críst ₇petir abstoil ₇docolumcille ₇dodrostan
4 sér ónáhulib dolodib cónánascad dócórmac
5 éscob dunicallenn• innócmad blíádin• rígi•dan   {eścob}
6 testib[us] istis• néctan• escob abberdeon•₇léot áb bŕecini
7 ₇máledomni mac mecbead•₇álgune mac árcill•ŕúad   {aŕcill}
8 ri mórmar márr ₇matadin bríthem•₇gillecríst
9 mac córmaic•₇malpetir mac domnaill•₇domongart
10 ferleginn turbruad•₇gillecolaim mac muredig•₇dub
11 ni mac málcolaim %

Text IV   [Hand D, fo. 4r]

1 Dorat gartnait₇ingengillemicael báll dómin ipet ipúir {docrist ₇docolimcilli
₇dodrostan}
2 testi•gillecallinesacart•₇feradac mac málbrícin•₇mál girc mac tralin

Text V   [Hand B, fo. 4v]

1 Donchad mac mec
2 bead mec hídid
3 dorat acchad
4 madchór docrist
5 acus dodrostan ₇
6 docholuim cille
7 insóre gobrád ma
8 lechí ₇cómgell ₇
9 gille crist mac finguní   {finguńi}
10 innaíenasi intestus•₇
11 malcoluim mac
12 molíní• Cormac
13 mac cennedig do

14 rat goníge séa
15 li merlec• Com
16 gell mac cáenna
17 ig táesec clan
18 de canan dó
19 rat do crist ₇
20 dodrostán ₇
21 dócholuim cille
22 gonige ingort
23 he mór igginn
24 infrís isnesu daldín alenn ódubucí gólurchárí etarsliab ₇achad •
                              [Hand C, fol. 4v]
25 issaeri othesseach cubráth₇abennacht arcachhén chomallfas
26 araes cubrath₇amallact arcachén ticfa ris;

Text VI   [Hand C, fo. 5r]

1 Robaid colba
2 in mormér
3 búchan ₇e
4 ua ingen gar
5 nait a ben
6 phústa
7 ₇donnachac
8 mac sithig tœ
9 sech clenni
10 morgainn
11 nahuli edba
12 rta rí diá₇
13 ridrostan
14 ₇ ria colum
15 cilli ₇rípe
16 tar apstal
17 onahulib
18 dolaidib ar
19 chuit cetri
20 dabach do
21 nithíssad
22 arardmand
23 aidib alban
24 cucotchenn
25 ₇arhardchel

26 laib • tes[tibus] his
27 broccin ₇cor
28 m̱ac abb tur
29 bruaid ₇
30 morgunn
31 m̱ac donnch
32 id ₇ gilli petair m̱ac donncẖaid ₇ malæch́in ₇ da m̱ac matni•
33 ₇mathe buchan huli naiaidnaisse in helaín;

Text VII   [Hand E, fo. 40r]

1 Dauid • rex scotṯo̱ṟu̱m o̱mnuḇu̱s̱ p̱ṟo̱bis ho̱m̱i̱ṉibus su̱i̱s•salutes•
2 Sciatis q̱uo̱d clerici • dedér• sint q̱uieti ₇ i̱mmunes   {deder̀}
3 ab o̱m̱ni laaico̱ṟu̱m officio •₇ exactione i̱ndebita
4 sicu̱t i̱nlibro eorum scriptu̱m est•₇diratio
5 naueru̱nt apu̱d • bánb •₇ iaraueru̱nt apu̱d abḇe̱rdéon•   {bańb}
6 quap̱ro̱pter firmiṯer p̱ṟe̱cipio • utnullus eis• aut
7 eo̱ṟu̱m catellis• aliquam i̱niuriam i̱nferre
8 p̱ṟe̱sumat• T[este] Greg̱o̱ṟio • episc̱o̱po • deduncallden • T[este]
9 andrea epi̱sc̱o̱po decaṯe̱nes • T[este] samsone epi̱sc̱o̱po deḇṟe̱chin•
10 T[este] doncado comite• defíb •₇ malmori•dat
11 hótla• ₇ ggillebrite•comite•déngus• ₇ ggil
12 lecóm̱ded • m̱ac ǽd • ₇brocin•₇cormac • detu̱ṟbrud•
13 ₇adam• m̱ac ferdomnac• ₇gillendrias •m̱ac •
14 mátni• apu̱d • abḇe̱rdeon•

Hand C (collected)

Text II
26 [...] acẖ goderad issa̱ére omór[maer] ₇otẖesecẖ culaitẖi brátha   {issa̱ére}

Text V
25 issaeri othesseach cubráth₇abennacẖt arcacẖhén chomallfas
26 araes cubrath₇amallact arcacẖén ticfa ris;

Text VI
1 Robaid colba
2 in mormér
3 búchan ₇e
4 ua i̱ngen gar
5 nait a ben
6 phústa

7 ₇donnac<u>h</u>ac
8 m<u>a</u>c sithig tœ
9 sech clenni
10 morgainn
11 nahuli edba
12 rta rí diá₇
13 ridrostan
14 ₇ ria colum
15 cilli ₇rípe
16 tar apstal
17 onahulib
18 dolaidib ar
19 chuit cetri
20 dabach do
21 nithíssad
22 <u>ar</u>ardmand
23 aidib alban
24 cucotc<u>h</u>enn
25 ₇ar<u>h</u>ardc<u>h</u>el
26 laib • tes[tibus] hi
27 broccin ₇cor
28 m<u>a</u>c abb tur
29 bruaid ₇
30 morgunn
31 m<u>a</u>c donnch
32 id ₇ gilli petair m   ₇ malæchín ₇ da m<u>a</u>c matni•
33 ₇mathe buchan   sse in helaín;

NOTES

Text I
3 abbordob**o͘ír**: The i is written subscript.
4 m**æ**r: The æ ligature occurs with the stroke covering both symbols in the MS.
4 b**ú**c<u>h</u>an: Perhaps b**ú**c<u>h</u>can is intended?
4 rothid**ń**a**í**g: The stroke is clearly over the n. Although since the tail of the initial of robomor (A13) comes down near the top of d, it is possible that the stroke was intended to cover the preceding d (or possibly the i) rather than the n.
6 **óthóse**ć: The stroke is more over the final c than the preceding e, but this may be due to the fact that the final g of ga<u>th</u>ra**í**g (A15) from the previous line descends to the e of th**óse**ć; similarly, the first stroke, although it occurs above the o of the preposition, covers more of the following t; this may be due to the fact that the initial g of ga<u>th</u>ra**í**g (A15) descends to the o of the preposition.
6 <u>in</u>cath**ŕ**aig: The faint stroke occurs above the r, and not the following vowel sequence ai. Although there is sufficient space for a stroke above the i, this is not the case with a, since

the tail of the final r of **ómormáer** (A15) descends right down to the top of a. It is possible therefore that that the stroke was intended to cover the ai sequence but that the descending r prevented the scribe from doing so to avoid a clash.

7 **sí**: The i is written subscript.

9 **galár**: The stroke appears more over the r than the a, perhaps because the tail of the final s of gondas descends to the second a of **galár**.

10 **iarnéré**: The first stroke occurs slightly to the left and so covering the n, perhaps to accommodate the tall e.

10 **robomaréb**: The e has a point inserted both above and below it. Jackson (1972, 24) refers to these points as 'cancellation-points', and later as 'punctum delens both above and below the *e*, as if the scribe wrote by ear and then realised this was "incorrect" spelling' (1972, 135). However, the use of points above and below certain characters is used elsewhere by Hand A to signify insertion rather than cancellation, although in all instances the inserted letter occurs written superscript. Examples are dorodloeg (A18), deara (A118), edbarta (A1116), **proínn** (A1119). In the light of this evidence, it is possible (despite the fact that the e is not written superscript) that the e was understood as an insertion, the scribe recognising that the e would not 'normally' be written; cf. the use of upper and lower points separated by a diagonal line to indicate the insertion of **doíb** (A113).

11 **iarsén**: That the stroke covers the s to the left may perhaps be due to the fact that the tail of the second r in iarnéré of the preceding line descends to touch the e.

13 inedbaírt: The i in the final syllable is written superscript.

13 **doíb**: This is written in the left margin, signalled in the text by an insertion mark.

13 **úaćloic**: The stroke over the u may have been prevented from extending to the following a since the tail of les in the preceding line descends to approach the a.

13 **chloíc**: The scribe may have been forced to begin the stroke more to the left and so to cover the o because of the descending tail of the et compendium of the preceding line, which descends to the left hand side of the final c.

14 **taníc**: The stroke is slightly thicker than usual.

15 The semicolon which occurs following **dó** could be a colon which clashes with a possible stroke above dr of chadraíg in the following line.

18 deara: The e is written superscript and insertion points are used.

18 drostán: Note that the tail of s in ris descends to the final n of drostán.

19 **bedeár**: Note that the tails of both the s and r of scarthaín descend to the e and r of deár, perhaps restricting the scribe when applying the stroke.

19 **ímáċċ**: The second stroke appears to begin over the last minim of the m, perhaps indicating that a later hand added this taking it to be an i rather than the final minim of an m.

19 The use of the semicolon at the end of this line might suggest that the scribe intended to continue, thus adding weight to the suggestion that text I and II were written by the same hand.

Text II

1 **Cómgeall**: The stroke covers the m more than the preceding o, perhaps due to the fact that the tail of initial r in rolaboir of the preceding line descends over the left hand side of the o.

4 robothoséc: The stroke is very faint in the MS.

5 culí: : Jackson transcribes as culii but the MS clearly has culi: with a colon.

10 bidbiń: The stroke was possibly intended to cover the i but the scribe was restricted here since the tail of initial the r in rúadri in the previous line descends over the sequence in.

10 dia: There may be a very faint stroke above dia in the MS, but it is in a considerably higher position than other strokes in the MS, and as such has been ignored here.

11 cúit: The stroke was possibly intended to cover the i rather than the u but the scribe was restricted since the et compendium descends to touch the i of cuit.

16 edbarta: The d is inserted.

18 thóisíg: There appears to be a stroke above the o which clashes with the spiritus asper lenition sign above the t. At first sight the stroke has the appearance of being a left projection of the lenition sign but since this occurs nowhere else in the MS I have taken it to be a stroke. It is possible that the stroke was intended to cover the i but this may have been prevented by the descending tail of r in the preceding line which touches the i.

19 proínń: The i is written subscript.

21 alteriń: The stroke was perhaps intended for the i rather than the n, but was moved slightly to the right because of the MS contraction which appears over the t and which extends to the i.

22 camme [?]: There is a hole in the MS between cam and m[?]e. Jackson read *camse* and took this to be a possible genitive singular of *camus* (1972, 56–57), otherwise unattested, which he claims cannot 'be ruled out of court altogether […] considering the fact that we are dealing with such a remote part of Gaeldom, and that the Middle Irish period is notoriously one when a good many nouns changed their declensions'. Jackson has a full discussion (1972, 24–26) of this difficult reading which he acknowledges as being far from certain (26). There are two difficulties with Jackson's suggestion that the two 'tails' which appear under the hole in the MS after cam represent the tails of two s letters: firstly, the first one is quite thin and seems to come vertically downwards rather than slanting slightly to the left as the tails of r and s tend to in Hand A; secondly, if the scribe erased what he had previously written (apparently creating a hole in the MS as Jackson suggests), it is not clear why he failed to erase the parts now under the hole—unless of course it is argued that he did not wish to destroy any more of the MS by further erasing. There appears to be a stroke above and to the right of the m contraction over the a, which might suggest that the first 'tail' appearing under the hole is an i (in the light of our later discussion). The horizontal line through the top of the i might be taken as a MS contraction for n or, alternatively, the whole may itself be taken to be an n, connecting up with the other tail occurring below the hole. The following larger letters might be taken to represent ns or just m (with a small portion of the top left hand stroke of the m missing). Indeed, it could be argued that the MS contraction for m was added after an m was incorrectly written, the scribe trying to reinforce the m in two ways—by the use of a MS contraction and by trying to squeeze an m in before the e. The reason why an m would reach down further than expected might be due to the scribe trying to make it appear level with the suggested i appearing below the hole. This gives the further possible readings of caminse, camime, camme.

24 drostán: Note that the et compendium descends to touch the final n of drostán, perhaps preventing the stroke from covering the final n also.

24 Robaith: There may be a stroke above the o in robaith but this is more likely to be the curved descending tail of the h of cathál in the preceding line.

24 cainnéc: It could be argued that the stroke over the e of cainnec represents an exaggerated flourish of the semicolon at the end of the previous line, though I deem it unlikely.

25 nahúle: It might be argued that the stroke above the u here represents an upward rising flourish of the capital r in robaith in the previous line, though I deem this unlikely since all such flourishes in Hand A appear in a downward direction.

25 A stroke appears to the right of ri at the same level as the letters, *not* above them, and has therefore been discounted here. It is quite likely that it was intended as a sign to the reader to

proceed to the next line and to skip over the encircled addition in the right margin by Hand C. Indeed, this would seem to be supported by the fact that this stroke seems to be written in a different shade of ink, similar to that used by Hand C. (cf. note 7 to Text III below.)

26 omór[maer]: MS omór•

26 othesech: I have taken the stroke which appears over the e to be part of the lenition sign occurring over the preceding t; it is very similar to that occurring over the t in culaithi.

26 culaithi brátha: These two words are written at the end of line 44 in the MS and are partially encircled to show that they belong to the end of line 45.

27–28: At this point our lineation differs from that of Jackson, where his lineation follows exactly that of the MS. Our lineation refers to our diplomatic edition which seeks to group writing of individual hands as closely as possible together.

Text III

5 escob: It might be argued that the stroke was positioned to the right above the s rather than the e to accommodate the descending s of sér in the preceding line. However, against this the stroke comes quite close to the descending r of sér.

5 blíádin: The thick stroke above the final i, although it has a similar angle of ascent to the 'normal' strokes, is clearly a MS contraction for n. blíádin might also be transcribed as blíadin.

6 testib[us]: MS has testib;.

7 mecbead: There is a small hole in the MS between mecb and ead.

7 rúad: There appears to be a stroke (at the same level) following the final d of rúad. This may be an indication to the reader to read on to the next line (cf. note 26 to Text II above)

9 domongart: Jackson in his diplomatic edition transcribes this word as if there were a space between dom and ongart. This space is quite small and similar to that between the g and a in the same word; it is ignored here.

11 %: The insertion symbol (similar to '%') written by Hand D indicates that the following text {docrist ₇docolimcilli ₇dodrostan} is intended to follow at the end of the first line of Text IV.

Text IV

1 gillemicael: The lower a attached to the e in the final syllable is not at all clear; it may be a stain or some dirt. This would give the reading gillemicel, similar to that in Text III, line 1.

1 dómin: The stroke appears higher than the MS contraction for m.

1 ipúir: Perhaps ipáir is intended.

1 docrist ₇docolimcilli ₇dodrostan: This text is added with the insertion sign (similar to %) at the end of Text III.

2 feradac: There appears to be a point above the first a in this word.

2 feradac mac málbrícin: There appears to be a point above the b. Could this be a lenition marker?

2 tralin: There appears to be a faint stroke over the final n here. It is more horizontal than the 'normal' strokes. Could it be a MS contraction for n, thus altering the reading to tralinn?

2 girc mac tralin: These words are written below the second line of Text IV in the MS (i.e. below feradac [...]).

Text V

7–8 malechí: The stroke is clearly not a MS contraction for n.

9 gille: There appears to be a point above the g in the MS.

9 fin<u>gu</u>ńi: The stroke is written above the n, and the i is written subscript. The stroke may have been intended for the i.

14–15 sćali: The stroke appears over the c rather than the a perhaps because the a is written right up against the border of the picture drawn in the middle and right hand side of the page.

25 The final s no longer visible at the right margin.

26 arca<u>ch</u>én: The stroke above the e is very faint indeed.

Text VI

2 mormér: The stroke is very faint indeed.

3 búchan: The stroke over the u is more horizontal than other strokes.

6 phústa: The stroke is faint.

12 diá: The stroke is quite faint.

15 cilli: Jackson reads *cille* in his diplomatic edition (1972, 22) but had the correct form *cilli* in his edition (1972, 32).

26 tes[tibus]: MS has tes•.

27 cor: There may be a faint stroke following the r here, perhaps to indicate that the rest of the word follows on the next line.

33 There seems to be a rising stroke at the end of the line following the semicolon. Its significance is not clear; it may be merely decorative.

Text VII

5 ab<u>berd</u>éon: The e of the final syllable is written superscript with what appears to be a long thin stroke coming from it, though it is possible that it is merely part of an elaborate superscript e.

8 T[este]: The   oth occurrences).

9 T[este]: The

10 T[este]: Th

11 ggil: The fir   o have a point above it.

12 lećomded: vers the preceding e slightly.

12 de<u>tur</u>brud: s to be a long stroke in the right margin following the final d, perhaps intende   final syllable.

The property records: text and translation

KATHERINE FORSYTH, DAUVIT BROUN & THOMAS CLANCY

Jackson provided text and translation of the Deer property records with the needs of students in mind and with linguistic interests primarily to the fore (1972, viii). Both text and translation retain their original value, of course, but to complement them and to highlight other, perhaps more historical issues we provide here an edited text and facing translation arranged by grant. The edited text follows that of Ó Maolalaigh's diplomatic edition but with the omission of the problematic accents discussed in Ó Maolalaigh's article. While the numbering of the lines in the diplomatic edition follows the texts and lineation of the MS, the numbering system employed here is designed to highlight the different grants. Therefore Texts II and V are subdivided by act of granting. Sans serif type is used in Texts II and IV to indicate later additions by Scribe C. Latin is translated in small capitals.

Punctuation and vowel length marks have been added. There is a degree of ambiguity concerning the diphthongs in words such as *tosec/taesec* and *sore/saere* and whether, by this date, they were in fact still diphthongs. Following Jackson these have been left unmarked. Omitted letters are supplied selectively to clarify the underlying form, e.g. *ro-[f]alseg* and *na [f]iaidnaisse*, where the (silent) lenited *f* was omitted in the manuscript. In the Latin text all abbreviations have been silently expanded. In the Gaelic texts, suspensions of **n**, **m** and **h** have been silently expanded, as has the contraction *m̄c̄* where it is unambiguously *mac*. All other expansions are underlined.

There are three instances where *m̄c̄* is potentially ambiguous and these have been indicated with an underscore: *pett(e) m̲a̲c̲ Garnait* (IA14 and IIA3) and *pett m̲a̲c̲ Gobroig* (IIA12). There are linguistic and onomastic implications of the alternative expansions of this abbreviation so it is worth exploring the issue in detail. Leaving these three examples to one side for the moment, the various scribes of the property records use the abbreviation *m̄c̄* 39 times. In every case but one, this is unambiguously for *mac*. The sole exception is (*Male-Domni[g]*) *m̄c̄ m̄c̄ Bead* (IIID7) for *m̲a̲c̲ M̲e̲c̲Bead* 'son of Mac-Bethad' (the slip of *m̄c̄* for *m̲e̲c̲*—if slip it is—may have arisen from its following on directly after the abbreviated *m̲a̲c̲*; note also that there are spacing constraints in this line caused by the need to avoid a small tear in the vellum between *b* and *ead*). Conversely, the three certain examples of *mec* are written out in full: *pet Mec-Cobrig* (IIID2) and *Donchad m̄c̄ Mec|bead mec hIdid* (VB1–2). On the evidence of palaeography, *mac* is always (with that single exception) abbreviated

$\bar{m}\bar{c}$, and *mec* is always written out in full. On this basis we should read *pett(e) mac Garnait*, 'the holding of the sons of Gar(t)nait'. There remains, however, one difficulty: how to reconcile the contradictory forms *pett $\overline{mc}$ Gobroig* (IIID2) and *pet Mec-Cobrig* (IIID2), assuming these to be references to the same place. Jackson argued on phonological grounds that *mec Cobrig* was a corruption of *mec Gobroig* (1972, 51), and that both forms referred to the holding of a person called 'Mac-Gobraig'. Ó Maolalaigh (this volume) suggests the alternative reading *mac Gobroig* (III), 'of the sons of Cobrach', with genitive plural *mac* causing eclipsis of the following *c-*. This is consistent with the palaeographical argument just outlined. We are then, however, obliged to take the *mec* at IIID2—which is written out in full—as a later reinterpretation of the name: 'holding of the son of Cobrach' or 'holding of Mac-Cobraig'. This latter form occurs with reference to a grant which took place in the eighth year of the reign of David I, i.e. 1131/2, whereas the other, although written in the Book perhaps only a decade earlier, occurs with reference to a grant which took place over a century before (the donor Mael-Coluim mac Cinaeda died in 1034).

The translation is a collective effort. It is based on new translations by Clancy (Text I) and Broun (Texts II–VI)—both of which draw on Jackson's 1972 translation and linguistic notes—and is indebted to the specialist discussion in the contributions to this volume of Broun, Clancy, Cox, Ó Maolalaigh, and Taylor. It was thought desirable to provide a translation which sticks closely to the literal meaning of the text. Straightaway, however, we are confronted with the question: are the labels given to places in the property records actually place-names or are they descriptive phrases? There is no easy solution to this conundrum, which is discussed by Taylor, this volume. Jackson usually rendered them as place-names, others have gone to the opposite extreme and treated any name (if practicable) as if it were a simple description (see, for instance, Anderson 1922 ii, 175–6). The real situation will have lain at some indiscernible, and probably unfixed, point in-between. The policy here has been to provide the modern forms of all identified places and to take unidentified places on a case-by-case basis, prefixing the form with an asterisk and, where possible, providing a translation in square brackets. The reader is referred to Taylor, this volume, for detailed discussion of individual place-names. An attempt has been made to provide standardized forms of the personal names in the translation but this is not always straightforward and the reader is directed to Ó Maolalaigh's article 'Scotticisation of Gaelic' (this volume), and of course, Jackson's notes (1972, 37–84), for discussion of individual forms.

Another difficulty arises from the fact that the property records in the Book of Deer employ several Gaelic technical legal terms. The extent to which this technical force is lost by translating them is a moot point. Two terms refer to the act of granting: *edbart* and *báidid*. *Edbart* is the thing granted, as in *do-rat in edbairt* 'he gave as a bequest' and appears four times—dat. sg. *i-n-edbaírt* (I); acc. pl. *na h-ule edbarta* (II.10, 14), *na h-uli edbarta* (VI). The word is the verbal noun of *ad-opair*, 'offers, grants, bequeaths' and means, in a general sense, 'offering, sacrifice', and more specifically 'offering or presentation for religious purposes', 'alms, offerings to the poor' (DIL under *idbart*, MI *edbart*). As Jackson points out (1972, 40), the same verb— *ro edpair, ro edpratar* 'he, they granted'—is used in the property records in the Book of Kells (Herbert 1994). The use of the term *báidid*—literally 'submerges, drowns, quenches, destroys' (*DIL báidid*)—in connection with property alienation is unique to the Deer property records (*ro báid* I, VI; *ro báith* II.10, II.11, II.14): see Jackson 1972, 120–3; and Broun, this volume, who translates it 'extinguished'. It is possible there may be a further legal term contained within the grant of *achad toche temni* (II.2). Jackson suggested that *temni* might be connected to the Middle Gaelic word *timna* 'bequest', 'will, testament' (*DIL timn(a)e*); however, Taylor, this volume, would prefer to see it as the personal name *Temne* or *Teimen*. If the word *toche* is related to *toich*, 'inheritance', 'property' (as in the phrase: *is toich do* N, 'it is N's natural, hereditary right', *DIL*), the grant might be 'the field of Teimen's inheritance'. Alternatively, it might relate to *toichid* (*DIL* s.v., *toiched, toiche, toich*), verbal noun of *do-saig* 'act of seeking', 'act of suing', with the grant being, therefore, 'the field of Teimen's law-suit'. In either case it could hint at a dispute over ownership of the land in question.

Further Gaelic technical terms refer to that which was granted. The term *cathair* has a range of related meanings, including 'fortress, city, monastery, enclosure, major church' (*DIL*), it may also refer to a small unit of secular lordship (Barrow 2003, 54). Because of this ambiguity it is left untranslated here. The Deer property records refer to two units of land-holding, *pett* and *achad*. The meaning of these terms is discussed by Taylor, this volume. The former, which is borrowed from Pictish, refers to a unit of landholding roughly equivalent to a modern farm and is here translated neutrally as 'holding'. The latter appears to distinguish *enclosed* land and is perhaps best translated 'field'. The records also employ two units of assessment. Gaelic *dabach* (pl. *dabaig*) 'davoch', means, literally, a '(large) vat' and appears to have been used in Scotland as a unit of assessment for general dues and services: see Broun, this volume; Jackson 1972, 116–17; Ross 2006. Gaelic *cuit* means literally 'a share, a part, a portion' (*DIL*) but is being used here in some technical sense, as yet unclear (II.3a, 3b, 7, VI; *cuitid* II.11): see Jackson (1972, 119), Broun, this volume.

The Deer property records refer to a number of social roles, some of which are well established in the wider Gaelic world, while others—notably the *mormaer*—are restricted to Scotland. Record III is particularly rich in identifying these. The ecclesiastical offices are straightforward: *sacart* 'priest', *ab* 'abbot', *e(p)scob* 'bishop' and *fer léginn* (all in III), this last being one of the six officers of a monastery, namely the head of a *scriptorium*, usually translated by Latin *lector* (*DIL fer léiginn*). In the Deer foundation legend (I) Drostán is referred to as the *dalta* of Colum Cille. This is the legal term for a 'fosterling' or 'ward', someone under the care of a foster-parent. Since *de facto* it would often mean also 'pupil', 'apprentice', in the ecclesiastical realm it comes to mean 'disciple', but the connotation is of a close familial bond. It is translated by Latin *alumnus* (*DIL daltae*). One of the witnesses to III is identified as a *brithem* ('brehon'), a legal professional, literally a 'maker of judgements', 'judge', 'jurist', Latin *iudex* (*DIL breithem*). The Deer records have been regarded as crucial evidence for understanding *mormaer* and *toísech* (see Broun, this volume; Jackson 1972, 102–14). The term *mormaer* (pl. *mormaír*), which means literally 'sea steward' (although Jackson preferred to see it as *mór maer*, 'great steward'), is often translated 'earl'. The *toísech* (pl. *toísig*), 'leader, chief', has, in the past, been identified as an official in charge of a small unit of secular lordship. Broun, however, argues that this view is not supported by the evidence of the Deer records where, instead, the *toísech* appears as head of a kin-group. Both terms are left untranslated here.

We offer a few minor corrections to Jackson's text and translation but only two divergences of any substance. The first concerns a problematic area where the manuscript is damaged (fol.4r lines 7–8; II.12). Jackson read *Alterin Alla Ueth | na Camss[?]e....*, which he translated: 'Altrie of the cliff of the birch-tree of the river-bend'. (1972: 20, 24–6, 34, 56–7). Ó Maolalaigh ('Diplomatic edition', this volume, AII.21–22) suggests an alternative reading: *camme[?]*, while Cox, this volume, proposes a textual emendation: *Alterin alla uéthé[prat] | na [?]*, which he would translate: 'Altrie on this side [i.e.] from the well of the bend'. An alternative translation of a problematic passage in VI (*ó na h-ulib dolaidib ar chuit cetri dabach don-í thíssad ar ...*) is discussed by Broun, this volume. Note also in Text I *in cathraig ele* is read here as 'another *cathair*' against Jackson's 'the other'. Apart from that, any divergences from Jackson's translations are merely different interpretations which should be read alongside his in order to gain a fuller sense of the text's possible meaning. Note that Jackson omitted the following phrases from his translation of V.3: 'and to Colum Cille' and 'his blessing on everyone who shall maintain this thereafter till Judgement, and' (Davies 1982, 264 n.26).

We include the Latin invocation at the upper margin of folio 5r. This was noted by Stuart (1869, lvi) and reproduced in his Plate VII in a form identical to that which survives today, showing that the loss is not recent. Jackson considered it a 'scribal note' pre-dating the work of scribe C (1972, 13 n.2). With only the lower portion of each letter surviving it is difficult to assign this short section to one scribe or another, but it is written in brown ink, like the marginal note and unlike the black ink of the main text. Given the scribe's use of Latin *testibus* a few lines below, it is possible that *in nomine Sancte Trinitatis*, an attested charter invocation of the period, albeit rare (Flanagan 2005, 66–7), should be taken as the opening part of Text VI. The date and status of other additions in the upper margins are unclear: *xp* on folios 2v and 6or are the Greek letters chi rho, for 'Christ', but the *xb[-]* in the top left corner of folio 4r and at the top of folio 55r is puzzling (Dumville suggests *Christe, benedic*, 2007, 202), as is what appears to be Latin *quae* or *quia* at the top of folio 50r. The latter is uncertain, however, as only the lower portion of the letters have survived the binder (Dumville suggests *Macc* (??), 2007, 202).

TEXT AND TRANSLATION

TEXT

Text I   Scribe A   (Fol. 3r–v)

Colum Cille 7 Drostán mac Cosgreg a dalta tángator a hÍ mar ro-[f]alseg Dia
doib gonic' Abbordoboir, 7 Bede Cruthnec robo mormær Buchan ar a ginn 7
ess é ro thidnaig doib in gathraig-sain in saere go bráith ó mormaer 7 ó thosec.
Tángator as a athle-sen in cathraig ele, 7 do-raten ri Colum Cille sí, iar fa llán
do rath Dé. 7 do-rodloeg ar in mormær .i. Bede go-n-das tabrad dó, 7 ní
tharat. 7 ro-gab mac dó galar, iar n-ére na glérec 7 robo marẹb act mad bec. Iar
sen do-chuid in mormaer d'attac na glérec go ndéndaes ernacde lesin mac go
ndísad slánte dó; 7 do-rat i n-edbairt doib ua cloic in tiprat gonice chloic pette
mac–Gar[t]nait. Do-rónsat in n-ernacde, 7 tánic slánte dó. Iar sen do-rat
Collum Cille do Drostán in chadraig-sen 7 ros-benact 7 fo-rácaib i[n]
mbréther, ge bé tísad ris, ná bad blie[d]nec buadacc. Tángator déara Drostán
ar scarthain fri Collum Cille. Ro-laboir Colum Cille, 'Be[d] Déar [a] a[i]nim ó
[s]hun imacc.'

Text II   Scribe A   (Fol. 3v–4r)

1   Comgeall mac Éda do-rat ua Orti 'nice Fúréne do Colum Cille 7 do
      Drostán
2   Moridac mac Morcunn do-rat pett mac Gar[t]nait 7 achad toche
      Temni 7 ba h-é robo mormaír 7 robo thosec.
3a   Matain mac Caerill do-rat cuit mormoír i n-Alteri
3b   7 Cu-Lí: mac Batín do-rat cuit toíseg.
4   Domnall mac Giric 7 Mal-Brigte mac Chathail do-rat pett in mulenn
      do Drostán.
5   Cathal mac Morcunt do-rat achad na glérec do Drostán.
6   Domnall mac Ruadrí 7 Mal-Colum mac Culeón do-ratsat Bidbin do
      Dia 7 do Drostán.

TRANSLATION

Text I

Colum Cille and Drostán son of Coscrach, his *dalta* ['fosterson/pupil'], came from Iona as God revealed to them, as far as Aberdour; and Bede the Pict was mormaer of Buchan on their arrival; and it is he who granted that *cathair* ['church settlement'] to them in freedom from mormaer and toísech until Judgement. They came after that to another *cathair*, and it was pleasing to Colum Cille, for it was full of the grace of God. And he asked the mormaer, i.e., Bede, that he should give it to him, and he did not give [it]. And a son of his took sick, after the refusal of the clerics, and was all but dead. Then the mormaer went to beg the clerics to make a prayer for the boy, that health might come to him; and he gave as an *edbart* ['offering'] to them from *cloch in tiprat* ['the stone of the well'] as far as *cloch pette mac Gartnait* ['the stone of the holding of the sons of Gartnait'].[1] They made the prayer, and health came to him. Then Colum Cille gave that *cathair* to Drostán, and blessed it, and left the saying, that whoever might come against it should not be long-lived or successful. Drostán's tears [*déara*] came on account of parting from Colum Cille. Colum Cille said, 'Let *Déar* be its name from now onwards.'

Text II

1   Comgell son of Aed gave from *Orti* as far as *Púréne* to Colum Cille and Drostán.

2   Muiredach son of Morgann gave *pett mac Garnait* ['the holding of Gartnait's sons'][2] and *achad toche Temne* [?'the field of Teimen's inheritance/law-suit']; and he was mormaer and he was toísech.

3a   Matain son of Cairell gave a mormaer's 'portion' [*cuit*] in Altrie,

3b   and Culi[3] son of Batín gave a toísech's 'portion'.

4   Domnall son of Giric and Mael-Brigte son of Cathal gave *pett in Mulinn* ['the holding of the mill'] to Drostán.

5   Cathal son of Morgann gave *achad na clérech* ['the field of the clerics'] to Drostán.

6   Domnall son of Ruaidrí and Mael-Coluim son of Cuilén gave Biffie to God and to Drostán.

1 Alternatively, if the reading is *mec* for *meic*, 'the holding of Mac-Gartnait', or 'the holding of the son of Gartnait', see Taylor, this volume for discussion.   2 As above.
3 Jackson read *culíi* which he interpreted as *Cú Líi* an unattested variant of the familiar

7a   Mal-Coloum mac Cinatha do-rat cuit ríig i bBidbin
7b   7 in pett mec Gobroig
7c   7 dá dabeg uactair Ros a[n] Bard.
8   Mal-Colum mac Moíl-Brigte do-rat ind elerc.
9   Mal-Snecte mac Luloig do-rat pett Mal-Duib do Drostán
10   Domnall mac Meic-Dubbacín ro-báith na h-ule edbarta ro Drostán ar
        thabart a [t]hule dó.
11a   Ro-báith Cathal ar a[n] choir chétna a cuitid thoísig
11b   7 do-rat proinn chét cec Nolloce 7 cec Cásc do Dia 7 do Drostán.
12   Cainnech mac Meic-Dobarcon 7 Cathal do-ratsator Alterin alla uethe
        na camme[?] gonice in beith edar dá Alterin.
13   Do-rat Domnall 7 Cathal Etdanin do Dia 7 do Drostán.
14   Ro-báith Cainnec 7 Domnall 7 Cathal na h-ule edbarta ri Dia 7 ri
        Drostán ó thosach go derad i ssaere ó mormaer 7 ó thésech cu laithi
        brátha

Remaining half-page in rasura: *Apparently Text II originally filled all of fol.4r,
but the final portion has been erased and written over by Scribe D.*

Text III   Scribe D   (Fol. 4r)

Gartnait mac Cannech 7 Éte ingen Gille-Míchél do-ratsat pet Mec-Cobrig ri
cosecrad eclasi Críst 7 Petir abstoil, 7 do Colum Cille 7 do Drostán, sér ó na h-
ulib dolodib, co n-a nascad do Cormac escob Dúni Callenn, in n-oc[t]mad
bliadin rígi Dauíd.

Testibus istis: Nectan escob Abberdeon 7 Leót ab Brecini 7 Male-Domni[g]
mac Mec-Be[th]ad 7 Algune mac Arcill 7 Ruadrí mormar Marr 7 Matadín
brithem 7 Gille-Críst mac Cormaic 7 Mal-Petir mac Domnaill 7 Domongart
fer léginn Turbruad 7 Gille-Colaim mac Muredig 7 Dubni mac Mal-Colaim.

7   Mael-Coluim son of Cinaed[4] gave a king's 'portion' in Biffie and in *pett mac Gobraig* ['the holding of Cobrach's sons']5 and two davochs of *uachtar Ros an Baird* ['the upland of *Ros abard* ('the promontory of the poet')'].

8   Mael-Coluim son of Mael-Brigte[6] gave Elrick ['the deer-trap'].

9   Mael-Snechta son of Lulach[7] gave *pett Mael-Dub* ['the holding of Mael-Duib'] to Drostán.

10   Domnall son of the son of Dubaicín[8] 'extinguished' all *edbarta* ['offerings'] in favour of Drostán in return for giving him [Domnall] his [Drostán's] goodwill.

11   Cathal 'extinguished' his toísech's 'portion' on the same terms, and gave a feast for a hundred every Christmas and Easter to God and to Drostán.

12   Cainnech son of the son of Dobarchú[9] and Cathal gave the Altrie of the other birch tree of *camme* [?, 'the bend'] as far as the birch tree between the two Altries.

13   Domnall and Cathal gave *Etdane* to God and to Drostán.

14   Cainnech and Domnall and Cathal 'extinguished' all *edbarta* ['offerings'] in favour of God and of Drostán from beginning to end, free from mormaer and toísech until Judgement.

Text III

Gartnait son of Cainnech and Éte daughter of Gille-Mícheil gave *pett meic-Cobraig* ['the holding of Mac-Cobraig (or 'of Cobrach's sons')'], free of all burdens, to Colum Cille and Drostán for the consecration of a church to Christ and to Peter the apostle, with a pledge of this to Cormac, bishop of Dunkeld; in the eighth year of the reign of King David.[10]

WITH THESE WITNESSES: Nechtan bishop of Aberdeen,[11] and Léot abbot of Brechin, and Mael-Domnaig son of MacBethad, and Alguine son of Airchill, and Ruaidrí mormaer of Mar, and Mataidín the judge [*brithem*], and Gille-Críst son of Cormac, and Mael-Petair son of Domnall, and Domangart *fer léginn* of Turriff, and Gille-Coluim son of Muiredach, and Duibne son of Mael-Coluim.

---

name-form in *Cú* plus qualifying genitive. Alternatively, he suggested the reading *Culíin* which is a known name (1972, 47). There is, however, no trace of a horizontal suspension mark and instead the reading appears to be *culí:* (Ó Maolalaigh, Diplomatic Edition). While the medial point is used frequently to punctuate the text of the property records this is the only instance of ':'. The abbreviation *i:* for *ius* (Dumville 2004, 16) is unlikely to be relevant here and the significance of the double point remains unclear. **4** King of Alba, 1005–34. **5** Alternatively, if the reading is *mec* for *meic*, 'the holding of Mac-Cobraig', or 'the holding of the son of Cobrach'. Note DIII2 *petmeccobrig*. See Taylor and Ó Maolalaigh, this volume for discussion. **6** Ruler of Moray (and king of Alba in opposition to Máel Coluim mac Cinaeda, donor in II.7), d. 1029 **7** King of Moray, d. 1085. **8** Or, possibly, 'Domnall son of Mac-Dubaicín'. **9** Or, possibly, 'Cainnech son of Mac-Dobarchon'. **10** 24 April 1131 × 23 April 1132. **11** 1125–<1150.

Text IV   Scribe D   (Fol. 4r)

Do-rat Gartnait ꝛ ingen Gille-Mícael ball domin i Pet i[n] Púir do Críst ꝛ do Colim Cilli ꝛ do Drostán.
Teste: Gille-Callíne sacart ꝛ Feradac mac Mal-Bricín ꝛ Mal-Girc mac Trálín

---

end Text II ? Scribe A   (Fol. 4v)

ꝛ bennact in Chomded ar cec mormar ꝛ ar cec tosech chomallfas ꝛ da'n síl dan-éis.

Text V   Scribe B   (Fol. 4v)

1   Donchad mac Mec-Be[th]ad mec hIdid do-rat Acchad Madchor do Críst acus do Drostán ꝛ do Choluim Cille in sore go brád. Mal-[F]echí[n] ꝛ Comgell ꝛ Gille-Críst mac Finguni i nn-a [f]ie[d]nasi in test*us*, ꝛ Mal-Coluim mac Molíni.
2   Cormac mac Cennédig do-rat gonige Scáli Merlec.
3   Comgell mac Caennaig, taesec Clande Canan, do-rat do Críst ꝛ do Drostán ꝛ do Choluim Cille gonige in gorthe mór i gginn in fris is nesu d'Aldín Alenn ó Dubuci go Lurchari, etar sliab ꝛ achad, i ssaeri ó thésseach cu bráth; ꝛ a bennacht ar cach hén chomallfas ar a és cu bráth, ꝛ a mallact ar cach én ticfa ris.

Text VI   ?Scribe C   (Fol. 5r – top margin)

In nomine S[an]c[t]e Trinitatis

        Scribe C   (Fol. 5r – side margin)

Ro-báid Colbain mormér Buchan ꝛ Eua ingen Gar[t]nait a ben phústa ꝛ Donnachac mac Síthig tœsech Clenni Morgainn na h-uli edbarta ri Dia ꝛ ri Drostán ꝛ ria Colum Cilli ꝛ ri Petar apstal, ó na h-ulib dolaidib ar chuit cetri dabach don-í thíssad *ar* ard-mandaidib Alban cu cotchenn ꝛ ar [a] h-ard chellaib.

Text IV
Gartnait and the daughter of Gille-Míchéil gave *ball domain* ['the deep spot']
in Pitfour to Christ and to Colum Cille and to Drostán.

WITNESS: Gille-Caillíne the priest, Feradach son of Mael-Bricín, and Mael-
Giric son of Tráillín.

And the blessing of the Lord on every mormaer and on every toísech who
shall comply with it, and to their descendants after them.

Text V

1   Donnchad son of MacBethad son of Ided[12] gave Auchmachar to
Christ and to Drostán and to Colum Cille, in freedom till Judgement.
In witness of it, Mael-Feichín and Comgell and Gille-Críst son of
Finguine, as testimony, and Mael-Coluim son of Moílíne.

2   Cormac son of Cennéitech gave as far as Skillymarno.

3   Comgell son of Cainnech, toísech of Clann Chanann, gave to Christ
and to Drostán and to Colum Cille as far as the large standing stone at
the end of the thicket nearest *Ailldín Ailenn*, from the Black [i.e.
South] Ugie to *Lurchaire*, both enclosed and unenclosed land, free
from toísech till Judgement; and his blessing on everyone who shall
comply [with this] thereafter till Judgement, and his curse on everyone
who shall come against it.

Text VI

IN THE NAME OF THE HOLY TRINITY

Colbain mormaer of Buchan and Eva, daughter of Gartnait, his wedded wife,
and Donnchad son of Síthech, toísech of Clann Morgainn, 'extinguished' all
the offerings, in favour of God and of Drostán and of Colum Cille and of
Peter the apostle, from all burdens of that which would apply to the chief
districts of Alba in general and on its chief churches so far as concerns four
davochs.

12 or 'Idad'.

Testibus his: Bróccín ⁊ Cormac abb Turbruaid ⁊ Morgunn mac Donnchid ⁊ Gilli-Petair mac Donnchaid ⁊ Mal-[F]æchín ⁊ dá mac Matni, ⁊ mathe Buchan huli 'na [f]iaidnaisse i nHelain

Text VII   Scribe E   (Fol. 40r)

Dauíd   rum omnibus probis hominibus suis salutes. Sciatis quod
clerici   t quieti ⁊ immunes ab omni laicorum officio ⁊ exactione
indeb   libro eorum scribtum est, ⁊ dirationauerunt apud Banb ⁊
iurau   Abberdeon. Quapropter firmiter precipio ut nullus eis aut
eorun   uam iniuriam inferre presumat.
T[est   episcopo de Dúncallden
T[est   iscopo de Catenes
T[est   episcopo de Brechin
T[est   comite de Fíb ⁊ Mal-Mori d'Ath[f]ótla ⁊ gGille-Brí[g]te
comit   gGille-Comded mac Æd ⁊ Brócín ⁊ Cormac de Turbrud ⁊
Ádan   mnac ⁊ Gille-[A]ndrias mac Matni apud Abberdeon.

THESE BEING THE WITNESSES: Bróiccín, and Cormac abbot of Turriff, and Morgann son of Donnchad, and Gille-Petair son of Donnchad, and Mael-Feichín, and the two sons of Matain,[13] and all the 'good men' of Buchan in witness of it. At Ellon.

Text VII

DAVID KING OF SCOTS, TO ALL HIS 'GOOD MEN', GREETINGS. YOU ARE TO KNOW THAT THE CLERGY OF Deer ARE TO BE QUIT AND IMMUNE FROM ALL LAY SERVICE AND IMPROPER EXACTION, AS IS WRITTEN IN THEIR BOOK, AS THEY PROVED BY ARGUMENT AT Banff AND SWORE AT Aberdeen. WHEREFORE I STRICTLY ENJOIN THAT NO-ONE SHALL DARE TO DO ANY HARM TO THEM OR TO THEIR GOODS.

WITNESS: GREGORY BISHOP OF Dunkeld.
WITNESS ANDREW BISHOP OF Caithness.
WITNESS, SAMSON BISHOP OF Brechin.
WITNESS: DONNCHAD EARL OF Fife and Mael-Moire OF Atholl and Gille-Brigte EARL OF Angus, and Gille-Coimded son of Aed, and Bróiccín, and Cormac OF Turriff, and Adam son of Ferdomnach, and Gille-Aindrias son of Matain.[14] AT Aberdeen.

13 or 'Maitne'.   14 or 'Maitne'.

REFERENCES

Anderson, A.O. (ed.), (1922), *Early sources of Scottish history 500 to 1286*, 2 vols, Edinburgh (reprinted with preface, bibliographical supplement and corrections by M.O. Anderson, Stamford, 1990).

Barrow, G.W.S. (2003) *The kingdom of the Scots*, 2nd ed., Edinburgh.

Davies, W. (1982) 'The Latin charter-tradition in western Britain, Brittany and Ireland in the early mediaeval period', in *Ireland in early medieval Europe: studies in memory of Kathleen Hughes*, ed. D. Whitelock et al., Cambridge, 258–80.

DIL Dictionary of the Irish Language (compact edition), ed. E.G. Quin (Dublin, 1983). Repr. 1990.

Dumville, D. N. (2004) *Abbreviations used in Insular Script before AD 850: tabulation based on the work of W. M. Lindsay* (Anglo-Saxon, Norse and Celtic Manuscript-studies 2), Cambridge.

—— (2007) 'The palaeography of "The Book of Deer": the original manuscript and the liturgical addition", in *Celtic essays, 2001–2007*, vol. I, The Centre for Celtic Studies, University of Aberdeen, 182–212.

Flanagan, M.-T. (2005) *Irish royal charters: texts and contexts*, Oxford.

Herbert, M. (1994) 'Charter material from Kells', in *The Book of Kells: Proceedings of a conference at Trinity College, Dublin, 6–9 September 1992*, ed. Felicity O'Mahony, Aldershot, 60–77.

Jackson, K. H. (1972), *The Gaelic Notes in the Book of Deer*, Cambridge.

Ross, A. (2006) 'The dabhach in Moray: a new look at an old tub', in *Landscape and environment in Dark Age Scotland*, ed. Alex Woolf, St Andrews, 57–74.

Stuart, J. (ed.) (1869) *The Book of Deer* (Spalding Club), Edinburgh.

On the possible functions of the accents in the Gaelic Notes in the Book of Deer

ROIBEARD Ó MAOLALAIGH

One of the most salient characteristics of the Gaelic Notes is the use of suprasegmental strokes or accents throughout, although, as we shall see, these occur with different frequencies in each of the seven texts.[1] The significance of these accents has proved controversial in previous discussions and editions. On the one hand, there have been those who were careful to reproduce the accents as accurately as possible, e.g. Stokes (1872 [1866]), Stuart (1869, 91–5), MacBain (1885),[2] W.J. Watson (1929 [1915], 184–92), J. Cameron (1937, 205–11). On the other hand, there have been those who dismissed or ignored the accents, e.g. Strachan (1895), whose transcriptions show no traces of the accents. Although Diack reproduced them he claimed that their use was 'capricious'. He referred to them as 'length marks' which 'are distributed capriciously, partly it would appear from ornamental ideas' (Diack 1920–1, 128, 130). Fraser (1942, 59) notes that 'there can be little doubt that they [i.e. the accents] were written in by some one who was not acquainted with the language of the *notitiae*. They have not been reproduced'. Jackson, following Fraser (1942), chose not to include the accents in his edition of the Gaelic Notes:

> It should be mentioned that all texts except the Latin of no. vii are liberally sprinkled with what appear to be *acute accents*, such as *are normally used to indicate long vowels or diphthongs* in Irish and Scottish Gaelic MSS. *This cannot be their purpose here*, however, since many of them are written over short vowels, and others even over consonants. Actually, *their function is evidently to indicate that the language is vernacular, not Latin—that is to say, they are used very much as we use italics*. The same is true of the Irish words in Latin contexts in the notulae in the Book of Armagh; and the Andersons point out that short, roughly horizontal, over-dashes are used in the same way in the Schaffhausen manuscript of Adamnán's Life of St Columba. The late eighth-century fragments of Muirchú's Life of St Patrick also mark Irish names in the Latin with rows of accents; and the Old Welsh words in some Latin MSS glossed in Old Welsh are similarly distinguished, as

1 My sincere gratitude is due to Dr Heidi Ann Lazar-Meyn for performing the statistical analysis on the accent data and for kindly agreeing to write the Appendix to this article.
2 'In regard to the accents, the MS is scrupulously followed in every peculiarity' (MacBain

well as the Old Welsh names in Asser's Life of King Alfred. Since *the position of the accents in Deer is wholly meaningless*, I have followed the example of some editors in omitting them altogether (in the 'edited' texts I have, however, marked long vowels with the acute accent in accordance with the usual editorial practice). (Jackson 1972, 17–18) [italics mine]

One can certainly sympathise with Jackson's decision to ignore the accents as it is difficult to put forward convincing explanations of their placement in a number of cases. A number of reviewers of Jackson (1972) refer explicitly to Jackson's decision to jettison the accents. Ó Cuív (1972, 345–6) suggests that Jackson's interpretation is 'open to doubt' and adds that 'it is hard to see what advantage is gained by the omission of the "accents" when such great care has been taken to devise typographical means to represent other scribal marks, including abbreviations'. It is worth noting in this context that Ó Cuív (1994, 19–23), in his recent edition of *Aibidil Gaoidheilge & Caiticiosma*, chose to reproduce the length marks of the original source although they are not always placed over historically long vowels, and also that he could explain some, though not all, of these on orthographic and phonological grounds. R. Black (1973, 266) and MacAulay (1975, 84–5) criticise Jackson's omission of the accents, and both make comments relating to the accuracy of the placement of accents over historically long vowels.[3] R. Black's (1973, 266) discussion dwells on the function of the accents as vocalic length markers,[4] although he refers importantly to Greene's (1954) observation of the marking with accents of pretonic vowels in Irish medieval manuscripts, which is discussed further below.

The purpose of this essay is to explore what the possible orthographic and linguistic functions of the accents may have been. We shall see that Jackson may have been somewhat rash in dismissing the orthographic (and possibly linguistic) significance of a number of these accents. Previous commentators, with the exception of R. Black (1973, 266), have assumed that these accents were categorically used to indicate vocalic length. In what follows, we shall suggest a number of other possible explanations, arguing that the accents may have had a number of disparate functions. Although the numbers involved are too small in certain cases to enable us to draw firm conclusions about all of the proposed functions, we shall see that some, but not all, of the findings discussed below can be seen to be statistically significant.

1885, 143).   3 MacAulay notes that 'Hand C, keeps putting them [i.e. accents] appropriately on long vocalic segments' (1975, 85). MacAulay's statement is slightly misleading as we shall see; although 66% of his overall accents occur over historically long vowels, of all historically long vowels occurring in Text Cvi only 33% of these are marked with an accent.   4 My analysis below differs somewhat from R. Black's. Cf. also MacBain's comment that 'The spelling is wonderfully consistent throughout, but the accent marks,

We may begin by questioning Jackson's claim that the accents are intended to indicate that the language 'is vernacular, not Latin'. Supporting his argument, Jackson refers to a number of Latin manuscripts where either Old Irish or Old Welsh words in Latin contexts are marked with suprasegmental strokes or accents.[5] However, the Gaelic Notes (with the exception of Text VII) are quite unlike the examples he cites, since the majority of the Gaelic Notes can hardly be said to be in a Latin context,[6] unless one argues that they occur in a manuscript containing Latin texts. The Gaelic Notes are different from the examples to which Jackson refers, in that they form continuous independent texts in their own right, and it is not at all clear why such free-standing texts would require to be marked as 'vernacular'; a similar point is made by R. Black (1973, 266). In fact, Text VII is the only text which approximates to the examples cited by Jackson, where the relatively small number of Gaelic words occur in a Latin context. Moreover, it is important to note that some of the earlier Latin texts contained in the Book of Deer also contain similar strokes or accents, in most cases more faint than the main text.[7]

High levels of consistency in the use of accents in particular words, particularly in Texts AI and AII, would seem to suggest that the accents were not randomly placed in some instances, and furthermore, suggest that accents may have served several different functions (cf. R. Black 1973, 266 and MacAulay 1975, 85), e.g. an accent is placed: over the final vowel of *Drostán* in 11 instances out of 12 (i.e. 92%); over the unstressed vowel(s) of *mormáer / mormaír* 4 times out of 6 (i.e. 67%),[8] and of *Cathál* 4 times out of 6 (i.e. 67%); over *i* in *robaíth* 3 times out of 3, and *doíb* 3 times out of 3; over both *as* in *áchádh* 2 times out of 2; over *u* in *nahúle* 2 times out of 2. This consistency is reflected in some orthographic features also. Hand A consistently uses *o(i)* (with and without accents, 6 times out of 6) in the first syllable to spell Old Gaelic *toísech*; compare Hand C who uses *e* in the first syllable (2 times out of 2) in this word: t̲h̲e̲s̲e̲c̲h̲ (CII26), thesseach (CV25).

which do not mean accent at all, but only quantity, are irregular.' (1885, 143) **5** On the use of 'apices' to mark vernacular words in Latin texts, see Ó Néill (1993, 99 and n. 3 for further references). **6** Latin text (quite separate from, and not integrated with) the Gaelic text appears on the same folios in two instances (Text I, fol. 3r, Text VI, fol. 5r). **7** In many, though not all, instances these occur with proper names. The marking of proper names in the Notes does not appear to be significant except possibly in the case of Hand A: see further below. Latin examples include: fol. 2r: issác (ll. 3, 4), dethamár (l. 7), aminadáb (l. 9), nadáb (l. 10), solmón (l. 16), abiúd (l. 17); fol. 2v: mannassén (l. 5), babél (l. 12), mathán (l. 17); fol. 5r: insomnís (l. 12); fol. 5v: emanuél (l. 6), réx (l. 16); fol. 6r: israhél (l. 9), magís (l. 10), abéis (l. 11), éis (l. 12); fol. 7r: chíel (l. 2), illúc (l. 12), nazaréth (l. 15), uóx (l. 20), etc. Cf. Ó Cuív (1972: 346). The investigation of the use of accents in the Latin entries may shed some light on the use of the accents in the Gaelic Notes. However, such an investigation is outwith the scope of the present essay. I am grateful to Gilbert Márkus for discussing the Latin accents with me and for pointing out that many of these accents are not obviously markers of length. **8** Excluding mor̲m̲aer (AII1), where -*maer* is

Jackson (1972, 17) notes the occurrence of accents above historically short vowels and consonants, but does not propose any orthographic or linguistic explanations in such cases.[9] Jackson did not note that similar practices are evident in certain Irish manuscripts, including the near-contemporary *Lebor na hUidre*, the editors of which note:

> Besides the well marked accents, as clear as the rest of the text, there are many faint thin lines, often hard to distinguish from scratches on the vellum. In dealing with these we have been guided by probability. In the MS the accent is often written apart from the vowel to which it belongs, generally over the following letter. When the latter is a vowel some editors print e.g. *cián*, but this cannot be done when the accent is over a consonant, as in *tír* [*tiŕ*], with accent over the *r*. Frequently the accent is quite out of place, as if inserted carelessly after the line had been completed. For example, *do dénam* 443, *dódenam* MS; *hi rét* 461, *híret* MS. In line 134, here printed *Sléib Sína ‚ is e ro scríb cona láim fein*, the scribe has put the first accent over the *s* and the second over the *b* of *sleib*, the third over the *sc* of *scrib*, and the fourth over the *a* of *cona*. The principle we have adopted is to put the accent over the vowel to which it belongs. (Best and Bergin 1929, xli)[10]

The study of accent placement and function in Gaelic manuscripts has, understandably perhaps, not figured high on the agenda of Gaelic scholarship, such questions being seen mostly as representing what Thurneysen referred to in a different context as 'orthographical trifles' (1951, v). However, given the unique and central importance of the Gaelic Notes for the early history of Gaelic in Scotland, the accents which occur there deserve more attention than they have received hitherto for the light which they could potentially cast on medieval Gaelic scribal practices—especially in the light of Best's and Bergin's comments above, which suggest that the use of accents in medieval manuscripts is less straightforward than scholarly editions of such manuscripts might lead us to believe. The detailed study of accent placement in Gaelic medieval manuscripts, as well as providing a valuable contribution to palaeographic studies—with concomitant implications for modern editorial scholarship—could in addition offer new insights into earlier forms of the

represented in the MS by a contraction.   **9** MacBain implied that the placement of accents above consonants may have been intended in some cases, particularly in the marking of double consonants: 'What may be design appears in the accentuation mark placed over some double consonants, notably *nn* [but also] *cc*' (MacBain 1885, 143).   **10** Cf. the editors' comments on the edition of *Tochmarc Étaíne*: 'Marks of length, which throughout the Yellow Book, are often otiose or misplaced, e.g. over *dó*, *mó* 'to, thy, my', &c., are, notwithstanding, retained' (Bergin and Best 1938, 141). McCone (1996, 28) refers to the use of accents by the prima manus of the Würzburg Glosses as 'an experimental device

language. See especially the speculative comments below on the marking of final syllables in forms such as *tóséc*, *galár* and *Cathál*.

In what follows I put forward a number of very tentative suggestions with regard to the possible functions of the Deer accents, while recognising that Jackson's explanation of the accents may ultimately be correct. We begin with the hypothesis that the accents were not necessarily randomly placed in the majority of instances. Ideally, the interpretations offered below should be checked by means of a comparative statistical analysis of comparable contemporary texts. However, for various reasons, including time and space, this will not be attempted here. Best's and Bergin's (1929, xli) comments referred to earlier will suffice here to illustrate that there is similar material worthy of study on the Irish side.

DESCRIPTION

Before we proceed it will be necessary to describe briefly these suprasegmental accents. The first impression of most of the accents is that they are thinner and lighter in character and hue than the characters of the main text (including contractions),[11] which tend to be thicker and darker in substance. Compare, for instance, the three accents occurring in the first line of Text AI (**drostán** m**a**c c**ó**sgreg ad**á**lta AI1) with the contraction which occurs in mc̄ (AI1); cf. also the accent and the contraction in alter**í**n (AII21). Not all texts exhibit a difference in colour or shade between accents and text; they appear to be the same, for instance, in text DIII. Some accents appear lighter than others; compare, for instance, the relatively light accent occurring in **doíb** (AI4) with the darker accents in **essé** (AI4), **sí** (AI7), **iarnéré** (AI10). A further distinction between our accents and contractions can be seen in the different angles at which each are drawn. Contractions tend on the whole to be horizontal in the main (with slight raising from the horizontal line towards the end in some cases), e.g. **inmormaer** (AI11). Accents on the other hand tend to be raised 45 degrees from the horizontal. Such apparent contrasts in colour and character raise important questions with regard to the date and provenance of the accents. Can we be certain that all accents are to be ascribed to each of the individual scribes? Can we even be sure that the accents are contemporaneous with the texts themselves? Could it be that the accents, or at least some of them, were added later either by the same hand or conceivably by a number of different hands on one or more occasions? One could certainly

[...] where length was clearly not the criterion'.   11 Cf. Best and Bergin (1929, xli) who note in the case of *Lebor na hUidre*: 'But besides the well marked accents, as clear as the rest of the text, there are many faint lines, often hard to distinguish from scratches on the vellum.' The Deer accents discussed here are more substantial than mere scratches on the

imagine a later reader or readers reading over and marking, correcting or ticking what he or they had read, almost in the same way as a student might underline or tick certain parts of a printed text nowadays.[12] We may recall Fraser's (1942, 59) opinion that most if not all of the accents were due to the same hand and, furthermore, that they were 'written in by someone who was not acquainted with the language of the *notitiae*.' His opinion seems to be based, partly at least, on his interpretation of the accents as 'marks of length' and their occurrence over historically short vowels. It could be argued that the placing of the accent above the upper punctum delens of 'incorrect' *e* in marẹb (AII0) suggests that the punctum delens may already have been in place when the accent was added. It is difficult perhaps to see why Hand A would place an accent above a letter he had previously 'deleted'. Of course, it is difficult to know for certain which was written first, the accent or the punctum delens; we may note that there is ample space for the placement of a punctum delens beneath many of the accents.

In some cases the avoidance of descending characters from the immediately preceding line can account for the placement of accents to the left and right of target vowels.[13] This could suggest the accents may have been added after the texts (if not complete words or lines) had been written. This in itself does not, of course, rule out the possibility that the individual hands were responsible for the addition of the accents.

The lighter or thinner nature of many of the accents need not necessarily be ascribed to a 'later' thinner pen. It is possible that the accents were applied using the edge of a pen, perhaps even with a lighter touch—and being lighter they may have faded more with the passage of time as a result. In support of this suggestion note the lighter upward tail of the contraction for *m* in Colum (DIII3), which resembles in many ways the nature of the manuscript accents. In support of the accents being contemporary with the texts in which they appear, we may note that the colour of the ink of some accents resembles very closely that of the text underneath, e.g. bidbín (AIII2), dó (BVI8), ó (BV24). It is worth noting perhaps that Jackson, though he chose to ignore the accents in his edition, nowhere suggests that the accents were attributable to later scribes. There is further evidence to suggest that the accents may be attributed to the individual hands in some cases; the number of accents per syllable in texts attributable to these hands has been shown by Lazar-Mein in the Appendix below to be highly statistically significant. Similarly, the high

vellum. 12 Ní Dhonnchadha (1982, 179) notes that the length marks in the guarantor list of *Cáin Adomnáin* 'appear to have been added in a secondary hand and in a very light ink, now almost completely faded'. 13 See the notes on individual forms in the Diplomatic Edition, 119–130, e.g. Text I: 4 (rothidńaíg), 6 (óthóseć, incathŕaig), 9 (galár), 11 (iarsén), 13 (úaćloic, chloíc), 19 (bedeár); Text II: 1 (Cómgeall), 10 (bidbiń), 11 (cúit), 18 (thóisíg), 24 (drostán); Text III: 5 (eścob); cf. Text V: 14–15 (sćali).

levels of consistency in the use of accents with certain words by individual 'hands', already alluded to, also provides some admittedly weak support for the claim that the accents are attributable to the individual hands. Jackson noted palaeographic similarities between Hands A and B in contrast with Hand C. This is supported, as we shall see, by the patterns exhibited in the use of accents in texts attributable to these hands.

DISCUSSION OF STATISTICS

I calculate that there are 266 accents in total, the distribution of which is summarised in **Table 7.1** according to text and 'hand'.[14]

Table 7.1: Distribution of total accents by scribe and text

	HAND A		HAND B	HAND C			HAND D		HAND E	TOTALS
	I	II	V	II	V	VI	III	IV	VII	
	85	94	25	3	3	9	32	6	9	266
Total	179		25	15			38		9	266
%	67		9	6			14		3	100%

However, approximately 52% of the Gaelic Notes were written by Hand A. If we count the written syllables of the Gaelic Notes and compare this with the number of accents for each 'hand', we get a clearer picture of the rate of accent-use by individual 'hands':[15]

Table 7.2: Proportion of syllables with accents per scribe

	HAND A	HAND B	HAND C	HAND D	HAND E	TOTALS
Syllables	575	126	171	188	51	1111
Accents	179	25	15	38	9	266
% syllables with accents[16]	31	20	9	20	18	24

14 Cf. R. Black's calculation of 252 (1973, 266).   15 In counting syllables I have not included MS contractions. In Text VII, I have only counted the syllables of Gaelic words, not Latin; I take *de* in this text to be Latin rather than Gaelic. Given that the domain of accents is syllabic nuclei or syllables, it is preferable to count syllables rather than words. 16 The calculations of percentages based on the number of syllables with accents provides only a rough indication of accent usage by individual hands; note that Hand A on four occasions uses two accents over one syllable (**án̠ím óhúnn̠ ímácc** AI19, **catháí** AIII7).

The number of accents per syllable by individual 'hands' is highly statistically significant: see Lazar-Meyn, Appendix. We observe that Hand A uses accents far more frequently than the other hands, and that Hands B, D and E use accents roughly to the same extent. Hand C is distinctively different to all other hands, being the one least likely to utilise accents. A word of caution should be signalled from the outset: the relatively low number of accents, which Hands B, C, D and E provide, makes it dangerous to draw concrete significant inferences with regard to their usage.

FUNCTION OF ACCENTS: POSSIBILITIES

Five main environments may be discerned in which accents are found, and thus five functions may be tentatively suggested for the Deer accents. Accents are found with: (1) historically long vowels; (2) the grapheme *i*; (3) pretonic vowels / syllables; (4) stressed vowels / syllables preceded by pretonic vowels / syllables or genitive modifiers preceded by head nouns; (5) unstressed (post-tonic) vowels / syllables.

1 The marking of long vowels[17]
In the following analysis I have followed Jackson's edition in the identification of long vowels, although a small number of these are uncertain.[18] For a discussion of other possible long vowels, not interpreted as such for the present analysis, see the discussion of the preposition *dó* and the place-name *Buchan* below. The statistics for the marking and non-marking of inherently long historical vowels are presented in **Table 7.2** Stressed and unstressed (both pretonic and post-tonic) vowels have been distinguished.

The marking of historically long vowels accounts for 35% (92/266) of all MS accents. Our analysis shows that overall 48% of long vowels are marked with an accent, and that 52% are not marked at all.[19] The overall marking of long vowels in the Deer Notes reflects roughly the practice of Hands A and D although E comes close to this overall average. Hand C, however, is the least discerning of all in the marking of long vowels; he marks only 33% of all long vowels, although it should be added that the marking of long vowels represents 66% (10/15) of the total number of accents in texts attributable to

---

17 Taken to include diphthongs here.   **18** The three instances of *doíb* occurring in A1 could contain hiatus (i.e. *doïb*) rather than the long vowel *ó*, and are thus ignored for present purposes; see Jackson (1972, 147). For comments on the names *Éua* and *Féchín*, see Greene's discussion (1972, 170); cf. also R. Black (1973, 266–7; 2000a, 45–8).   **19** A random selection taken from the text 'De Liberatione Scandlani' from the late eleventh-century version of the Liber Hymnorum (if Bernard's and Atkinson's (1898, 187–8) edition is to be trusted) shows that long vowels are marked by accents in approximately 42% of all cases.

Table 7.3: The marking of long vowels

HAND/ TEXT	Long vowels marked		Long vowels not marked		Total no. of long vowels
	Stressed	Unstressed	Stressed	Unstressed	
AI	15	10	20	5	50
AII	13	15	14	11	53
Totals	28	25	34	16	
Totals A	53 (51%)		50 (49%)		103 (100%)
B	5	5	2[20]	4	
Totals B	10 (63%)		6 (38%)		16 (100%)
CII	2	0	1	2	5
CV	3	0	4	1	8
CVI	3	2	7	5	17
Totals	8	2	12	8	
Totals C	10 (33%)		20 (67%)		30 (100%)
DIII	8	3	2	6	19
DIV	1	2	3[21]	3	9
Totals	9	5	5	9	
Totals D	14 (50%)		14 (50%)		28 (100%)
E	4	1	3	5[22]	13
Totals E	5 (38%)		8 (62%)		13 (100%)
Overall totals	54	38	56	42	190
	92 (48%)		98 (52%)		190 (100%)

Hand C.[23] Hand B, on the other hand, who marks 63% of all long vowels, is the most likely to mark long vowels. The following ordering emerges with regard to the marking of long vowels, beginning with the hand with the highest proportion of marked long vowels:

B >> A >> D >> E >> C

21 If scáli (BV14) were interpreted as **scáli**, then the number of marked long vowels would be increased by one for Hand B.   **21** Following Jackson's reading *Trálín* of MS tralin (DIV2) without accents.   **22** Taking *Dún* of duncallden (EVII8) to be 'unstressed'.   **23** Our

There appears to be a slight differentiation in the marking of long stressed and unstressed syllables in some cases. Hand A is more likely to mark long vowels when they are unstressed than stressed. Stressed long vowels are marked by Hand A in 45% of cases (28/62) but unstressed vowels are marked in 61% of cases (25/41). However, this difference may be due to the high number of instances of the name *Drostán*, which Hand A marks with an accent 11 out of 12 times. This contrasts with Hands B and D who are more likely to mark long vowels when they are stressed. See **Table 7.3**.

Lazar-Meyn (see below) concludes, however, that these patterns have no statistical significance:

> There is no statistical significance to the marking of vowels by length for any one of the five hands. Further, there is no statistical significance to the marking of long vowels based on stress, either in the texts as a whole or by any one of the five hands.

2(i) The marking of the grapheme *i*
Although not mentioned by Denholm-Young (1954), accents or hair-strokes may be used in medieval manuscripts to mark the grapheme *i*, with the apparent original purpose of distinguishing it from other minims.[24] The marking of the grapheme *i*, though not consistent in the Gaelic Notes, occurs frequently. In 36% (83/233) of all instances the *i* grapheme is marked with an accent. The statistics for the marking of the grapheme *i* are presented in **Tables 8.4** and **8.5**, where historically short and long vocalic *i* are differentiated for the purpose of analysis.

There appears to be wide variation amongst the various hands in the marking of *i*. Hand A has by far the highest proportion of marked to unmarked instances of *i* as he marks *i* 54% (58/106) of the time. All other hands have much smaller instances of marked *i*, although Hand B (with a percentage of 42% (11/26)) is the nearest in practice to Hand A. Hands C, D and E exhibit similar rates of marked *i*, namely 13% (6/48), 16% (7/45) and 13% (1/7) respectively. The following ordering emerges, beginning with the most likely to mark the grapheme *i*:

A >> B >> D >> C = E

---

analysis here differs from that of R. Black (1973, 266), who claims that Hand A is 'the least discriminating' with regard to accuracy in the marking of long vowels. **24** 'The acute accent over *i*, which most often serves the purpose of a dot, has only been retained when the vowel is naturally long' (Bergin and Best 1938, 141); cf. Ó Concheanainn (1980, 56) and Ó Cuív (1994, 19). The 'Gaelic' scribe of the royal genealogy contained in an early thirteenth-

Table 7.4: The marking of *i* (marked/unmarked)

Hand/text	*i* marked		*i* not marked		Totals
	Short *i*	Long *i*	Short *i*	Long *i*	
AI	21	4	17[25]	2	44
AII	25	8	23[26]	7	62
Totals	46	12	40	9	
Total A	58 (54%)		49 (46%)		107 (100%)
B	7	4	14[27]	1	26
Total B	11 (42%)		15 (58%)		26 (100%)
CII	0	0	3	0	3
CV	0	0	4	0	4
CVI	3	3	31[28]	4	41
Totals	3	3	38	4	
Total C	6 (13%)		42 (88%)		48 (100%)
DIII	1	5	24[29]	1[30]	31
DIV	1	0	9[31]	4[32]	14
Totals	2	5	33	5	
Total D	7 (16%)		38 (84%)		45 (100%)
E	0	1	6	1[33]	8
Total E	1 (13%)		7 (88%)		8 (100%)
Overall totals	58	25	131	20	234
	83 (35%)		151 (65%)		234 (100%)

century Latin charter uses an accent above every minim which he intended as an *i*; see Broun (1998, 200 n. 44). **25** Twelve instances where a MS contraction appears above the *i* (i.e. in and im) have not been counted. **26** Six instances where a MS contraction appears above the *i* (i.e. in) have not been counted. **27** Seven instances where a MS contraction appears above the *i* (i.e. in) have not been counted. **28** One instance where a MS contraction appears above the *i* (i.e. in) has not been counted. **29** Six instances where a MS contraction appears above the *i* (i.e. in and im) have not been counted. **30** One instance where a MS contraction appears above the *i* (i.e. in) has not been counted. **31** One instance where a MS contraction appears above the *i* (i.e. in) has not been counted. **32** Two instances where a MS contraction appears above the *i* (i.e. in and im) have not been counted. **33** One instance where a MS contraction appears above the *i* (i.e. in) has not been counted.

Table 7.5: The marking of *i* (long/short)

HAND/ TEXT	Short *i* marked	Short *i* not marked	Total short *i*	Long *i* marked	Long *i* not marked	Total long *i*
A	46 (53%)	40 (47%)	86 (100%)	12 (57%)	9 (43%)	21 (100%)
B	7 (33%)	14 (67%)	21 (100%)	4 (80%)	1 (20%)	5 (100%)
C	3 (7%)	38 (93%)	41 (100%)	3 (43%)	4 (57%)	7 (100%)
D	2 (6%)	33 (94%)	35 (100%)	5 (50%)	5 (50%)	10 (100%)
E	0 (0%)	6 (100%)	6 (100%)	1 (50%)	1 (50%)	2 (100%)
Totals	58 (31%)	131 (69%)	189 (100%)	25 (56%)	20 (44%)	45 (100%)

Some interesting distinctions arise with regard to the marking of short and long *i* in some cases. All hands without exception are more likely to mark long *i* than short *i*—thus perhaps strengthening the case for some accents being used as indicators of length. The marking of short *i* is a priority only for Hand A (followed closely by Hand B). The marking of *i* accounts for 31% (83/266) of all MS accents.

Lazar-Mein (see below) concludes that, for the Notes as a whole, the marking of *i* for length is statistically significant, as it is in the case of Hands C and D (highly significant in the case of the latter); marking of *i* for length is not statistically significant in the case of Hands A, B and E.

2(ii) The marking of *i* next to *n* and *m* (i.e. in *ni*, *mi*, *in*, *im* sequences)[34]
Given the probable original function of the marking of *i* to differentiate it from other minims, it is worth considering the distribution of marked and unmarked *i* in the immediate vicinity of the graphemes *n* and *m*, even though *i* is usually clearly distinguished from a neighbouring *n* or *m* in the Notes. This is presented in **Table 7.6**. Although the Gaelic Notes considered as a whole provide an almost 1:1 ratio between marked and unmarked *i* in this environment, the situation is in fact quite different in the case of the individual hands. Hand A appears to be substantially different in this respect, as he marks 78% of all instance of *i* in the vicinity of *n* or *m*; and in Text I, he marks all such instances. Hand B is the closest, who marks 44% instances, whereas the remaining hands mark only a small percentage: C (22%), D (18%), E (0%).

Lazar-Mein (see below) concludes that the marking of *i* next to *n* and *m* is statistically significant by hand.

---

34 I make no distinction here between long and short *i*.

Table 7.6: The marking of *i* next to *n* / *m*

HAND/TEXT	*i* marked next to *n* / *m*	*i* not marked next to *n* / *m*	TOTALS
AI	9	0	9
AII	9	5	14
Total A	18 (78%)	5 (22%)	23 (100%)
B	4	5	9
Total B	4 (44%)	5 (56%)	9 (100%)
CII	0	0	0
CV	0	0	0
CVI	2	7	9
Total C	2 (22%)	7 (78%)	9 (100%)
DIII	1	5	6
DIV	1	4	5
Total D	2 (18%)	9 (82%)	11 (100%)
E	0	1	1
Total E	0 (0%)	1 (100%)	1 (100%)
Overall totals	26 (49%)	27 (51%)	53

3(i) The marking of pretonic syllables / vowels

Thurneysen notes the marking with accents of pretonic vowels in Old Irish (*GOI* 33–34) and the subject is further discussed by Greene (1954); cf. also Lindeman (1988, 108). There are similar examples to be found in the Notes as pointed out by R. Black (1973, 266), e.g. **áhí** (AI2), **ómormáer** (AI5), **óthóséc** (AI6), **ááthle** (AI6), **dóráth** (AI7), **níthárat** (AI9), **góndéndaes** (AII11), **dórat** (AII2), etc.

For the purposes of the present analysis the following categories have been recognised: prepositions, preverbal particles, possessive pronouns, definite article, copula. In addition, relatively unstressed *Ma(e)l*, *Moil* and *Cú* (in **culí:** AII5) have also been included. *Mac* and *meic* have not been included as *mac* always appears as **mac** in the MS; *mec* usually appears as **mec** (although three instances of **mec** occur DIII2, BVI, BV2), and are never written with an accent. **meic** occurs twice, once without an accent (AII20) and once with an accent (AIII5) although the latter instance is perhaps most likely to represent the marking of *i*.

The statistics for the marking of pretonic vowels / syllables are presented in **Table 7.7**.

Table 7.7: The marking of pretonic syllables / vowels, including genitive modifiers preceded by head nouns

Hand / Text	Pretonic syllables / vowels marked	Pretonic syllables / vowels not marked	Totals
AI	13	39	52
AII	16	47	63
Total A	29 (25%)	86 (75%)	115 (100%)
B	4	17	
Total B	4 (19%)	17 (81%)	21 (100%)
CII	0	5	5
CV	0	10	10
CVI	2	14	16
Total C	2 (6%)	29 (94%)	31 (100%)
DIII	6	3	9
DIV	2	6	8
Total D	8 (47%)	9 (53%)	17 (100%)
E	0	1	1
Total E	0 (0%)	1 (100%)	1 (100%)
Overall totals	43 (23%)	142 (77%)	185 (100%)

The marking of pretonic syllables accounts for 16% (43/266) of all accents. We note that overall 23% (43/185) of all instances of pretonic vowels are marked by accents. Once again the picture is quite different when we consider the individual hands. Hand D marks 47% of all instances of pretonic syllables in his texts—although this high figure may be misleading given that Hand D provides a relatively small amount of instances of pretonic syllables—only 9% (17/185) of the total number of pretonic syllables in the Notes. On the other hand, Hands A and B are quite close, which mark 25% and 19% respectively. It is worth noting that Hands A and B provide 74% (115+21/185) of all instances of pretonic vowels. Hand C marks only 2 (6.4%) of a total of 31 pretonic syllables. Little can be said of Hand E since he provides only one instance of a pretonic vowel, and it is not marked. The following hierarchical ordering for the marking of pretonic syllables / vowels emerges:

D[?] >> A >> B >> C

Lazar-Mein (see below) concludes that the marking of pretonic syllables and vowels by individual hand is weakly statistically significant, and that Hands A and B effectively mark at random.

3(ii) The marking of preverbal *do* (e.g. *dorat*) and prepositional *do* (e.g. *dodrostan*)

A total of 27% (50/185) of all instances of pretonic vowels involve prepositional or preverbal *do*. The statistics for the marking of both types of *do* are presented in **Table 7.8**. While only 30% (15/50) of all instances of *do* are marked (comparable to the overall marking of long vowels, the grapheme *i* and pretonic syllables), 73% (11/15) of these (which corresponds to 22% (11/50) of the total number of instances of *do* which occur in the Notes) represent the preposition *do*. We note also that the preposition *do* is more likely to be marked than the preverb *do*: 42% (11/26) of all instances of the preposition *do* are marked, whereas only 17% (4/24) of all instances of the preverb *do* are marked. This reflects the patterning of Hand A, which skews the statistics to a great degree since Hand A provides 64% (32/50) of the total number of instances of *do* in the Gaelic Notes, accounting for 73% (11/15) of all marked instances of *do*. The numbers are too small to draw inferences for the other hands; note, for instance, that Hand B marks the preverb *do* (33% = 1/3) more frequently than the preposition *do* (17% = 1/6).

Lazar-Mein (see below) concludes that the marking of *do* by category is barely statistically significant for the Notes as a whole, and highly statistically significant for Hand A.

Given that Hand A marks the preposition *do* to a high degree (i.e. 69% = 9/13 of the time), the question arises whether or not the marking of *do* may have another significance other than being a pretonic word. In particular, the question arises if in fact we should read *dó* with a long *ó*, thus suggesting the possibility that the simple preposition may have been replaced by the third person singular masculine form, as may have occurred in some Scottish Gaelic dialects with this very preposition.[35] Based on present knowledge, it would appear that the distribution of *d(h)a* forms, possibly deriving from an original *dó* form, suggests that they may have been a mainland feature of the north and east—although we must await the publication of the remaining morphological

---

35 Borgstrøm (1941, 116) notes the simple prepositional form *dha* /ɣa/ (which does not lenite a following noun) for certain western Ross-shire dialects. Ó Murchú (1989a, 328 s.v. *do*) also notes the simple prepositional form *da* /da/ (and *dha* /ɣa/) for East Perthshire dialects. MacBain (1894, 93) noted that 'do is always da' in Badenoch, south-east Inverness-shire. In addition to this we may note that the compositional form of this preposition with forms of the article is frequently *d(h)a* /da/, /ɣa/ in Scottish Gaelic dialects. Derivation from the original third person singular masculine form *dó* (generally *dha* /ɣa/ in Scottish Gaelic) is not the only possibility; it is possible that the original vowel of the simple preposition *d(h)o* was lowered to /a/, or that /a/ derives from the

volumes of the Linguistic Survey before this impression can be validated.[36] If correct, this interpretation would provide another possible dialectal feature. It is possible that the marking of the preposition *do / dó* may have influenced the marking of the preverb *do*.

Table 7.8: The marking of *do*

Hand / Text	*do* marked		*do* not marked		Totals
	Preposition	Preverb	Preposition	Preverb	
AI	2	I	0	5	8
AII	7	I	4	12	24
Totals	9	2	4	17	
Total A	11 (34%)		21 (66%)		32 (100%)
B	I	I	5	2	
Total B	2 (22%)		7 (78%)		9 (100%)
CII	0	0	0	0	0
CV	0	0	0	0	0
CVI	0	0	I	0	I
Totals	0	0	I	0	
Total C	0		1 (100%)		1 (100%)
DIII	I	I	2	0	4
DIV	0	0	3	I	4
Totals	I	I	5	I	8
Total D	2 (25%)		6 (75%)		8 (100%)
E	0	0	0	0	0
Total E	0		0		0
Overall totals	11	4	15	20	
	15 (30%)		35 (70%)		50 (100%)

compositional forms involving possessive pronouns (*dá(-)*). However, there is other supporting evidence for the replacement of simple prepositions by their third person singular masculine counterparts, e.g. *ar* ('on')→ *air* (< *aire*), *ag* ('at') → *aig* (< *aige*), in both Irish, Scottish Gaelic and Manx; see O'Rahilly (1932, 226), O'Brien (1956, 175) and Murphy (1944, 148, n. 14c); I am grateful to Liam Breatnach for the latter reference. **36** My own impression of Modern Scottish Gaelic is that the change *do* → *dha* as simple preposition is on the increase amongst younger speakers generally.

4(i) The marking of stressed syllables preceded by pretonic vowels or head nouns

Thurneysen refers to instances from Old Irish where accents are used in stressed syllables to mark 'any vowel in syllabic auslaut which is followed by a lenited consonant' (*GOI* 33). He cites four examples: *as-rúbart, dlíged, ro-chlúinetar, níme*. The occurrence of lenited consonants in these examples may, however, be irrelevant. It is possible that the accent was used in *dlíged* and *níme* in order to mark the grapheme *i*, and in the case of *as-rúbart* and *ro-chlúinetar* to mark the stressed syllable; with the latter we may compare rogáb (AI9), etc. Analysis of the Notes is here restricted to tonic syllables immediately preceded by pretonic syllables, where there is a close syntactic relation between these syllables; genitive modifiers preceded by head nouns are also included. In other words the following types are included: prepositional phrases (e.g. dóráth AI7),[37] noun phrases (e.g. adálta AII),[38] verb phrases (e.g. rogáb AI9, níthárat AI9), copula phrases (e.g. bedéar AII9), adverbs (e.g. ímácċ AII9).

The statistics for the marking of stressed syllables in the environments just defined are presented in **Table 7.9**.

Table 7.9: The marking of stressed syllables preceded by
pretonic vowels or head nouns

Hand / Text	Marked	{Containing long vowel or *i*}	Not marked	Totals
AI	24	{10}	36	60
AII	15	{9}	63	78
Total A	39 (28%)	{19}	99 (72%)	138 (100%)
B	8	{7}	18	26
Total B	8 (31%)	{7}	18 (69%)	26 (100%)
CII	3	{2}	3	6
CV	1	{1}	6	7
CVI	4	{3}	19	23
Total C	8 (22%)	{5}	28 (80%)	36 (100%)
DIII	8	{1}	11	19
DIV	2	{2}	8	10
Total D	10 (34%)	{3}	19 (66%)	29 (100%)
E	6	{4}	6	12
Total E	6 (50%)	{4}	6 (50%)	12 (100%)
Overall totals	71 (30%)	{39}	170 (71%)	240

37 Including phrases involving (*go*)*nice*; also úaċloic (AII3) where the accent occurs above a consonant.   38 Including noun phrases involving head nouns followed by genitival

We note that 30% (71/240) of all instances of such stressed vowels are
marked. The marking of the stressed syllables discussed here accounts for
27% of the total number of accents, or 12% if we discount all instances of
marked long vowels and marked *i*. Little weight should be given to Hand E
because of the relatively low numbers involved. The hierarchical ordering
which emerges is as follows:

$$B = D >> A >> C$$

The closeness of Hands A, B and C is noteworthy, although relatively low
numbers for Hands B and C warn us against making any concrete inferences.
Lazar-Mein (see below) concludes that there is no statistical difference
between the hands.

4(ii) The case of *Buchan*

The place-name Buchan occurs three times in the Gaelic Notes as follows:
mormǽr búchan (A13–4), mormér búchan (CvI2–3), mathe buchan
(CvI33) and has been assigned to the category discussed in the immediately
preceding section. The occurrence twice of *Búchan*, with an accent over the *u*,
raises the question of whether in fact the accents in these instances should be
regarded as indicating a long vowel *ú*. However, the statistical analysis of the
marking of long vowels demonstrates that no weight can be placed on this
evidence. Alexander (1952, 26–27) notes that in Braemar Gaelic the name was
pronounced with long *ú*; indeed, he transcribes the Gaelic pronunciation as
['bu.hən].[39] W.J. Watson (1926, 119) notes the Old Norse form *Búkan-siða*
('Buchan-side') where 'the *u* appears to be long', and also refers to the accent
in the Gaelic Notes. W.J. Watson further suggests a possible connection with
Welsh *buwch* ('a cow'), which, if correct, we might expect to yield a long *ú* in
Gaelic.[40] Jackson (1972, 39) casts doubt on the evidence cited by both W.J.
Watson and Alexander.

5 The marking of unstressed (post-tonic) vowels / syllables

Thurneysen referred to the marking with accents in Old Gaelic of unstressed
syllables containing unlenited *m*, *n*, *l*, *r* (*GOI* 32), although many of his

modifiers (e.g. culaithi brátha (CII26), mac cóscreg (AII), mormǽr búchan (A13–4),
mormér búchan (CvI2–3), áb bŕecini (DIII6), mórmar márr (DIII8), alla uéthé
(AII21)); also including nahúle (AII25), and ggillećomded (EvIII1–12), where the accent
occurs above a consonant.   39 In support of the long vowel Alexander notes the derivation
bó-cháin ('cow tribute'), ultimately traceable to Hector Boece's early sixteenth-century
derivation (1952, 26–27). Jackson (1972, 39) dismisses this derivation as 'fanciful'.
40 Jackson (1972, 39) agrees that this derivation 'might be correct' and adds 'in which case
it would be Pictish'. Cf. Thomas Owen Clancy's suggestion of a connection with Brythonic
bychan, which would argue for a short vowel.

examples may represent the marking of the grapheme *i*. The marking of unstressed syllables in the Notes differs from Thurneysen's Old Gaelic examples in that unstressed syllables containing unlenited sonorants are not usually marked with accents, the only example being morcúnn (AII2); contrast: Cómgeall (AIII), caerill (AII5), Domnall (AII6, 9, 15, 23, 25), mulenn (AII7), chomallfas (AII28), callenn (DIII5), docholuim (Bv6), malcoluim (Bv11).

The marking of post-tonic vowels / syllables in the Notes may be classified into two groups: (A) open syllables and (B) closed syllables, the evidence for which is presented in **Tables 7.10** and **7.11**. It is interesting to speculate whether or not the system used in the Notes represents a development of the system described by Thurneysen for Old Gaelic. It may be significant that practically all examples come from Hand A (with only two examples from Hand B), and as such that we are dealing primarily with a characteristic of Hand A.[41]

Table 7.10: The marking of post-tonic vowels / syllables. Group (A): Final unstressed open syllables

	-é	-á
	bedé AI3	cinathá AIII1
	bédé AI8	
	iarnéré AI10	
	slánté AII2	
	fúrené AIII	
	uéthé AII21	
Total	6/15 (40%)	1/23 (4%)
	7/45 (16%)	

41 Statistics are as follows: 27/29 (i.e. 93%) of such instances are attributable to Hand A.I have not included taníc (AI14), temní (AII3) as the accents in these cases are likely to mark the *i* grapheme.

Table 7.11: The marking of post-tonic vowels / syllables. Group (B): Final
unstressed closed syllables (Hand A)[42]

	-ád	-éc(h), -ác, -ég	-éb	-ár, -ál, -árt[43]
	tabrád Aı9	thóséc Aı6	maréb Aııo	galár Aı9
	disád Aıı2	gleréc Aı 10		cathál Aıı 17
	áchád Aıı3	dattác Aı 11		cathál Aıı 21
	achád Aıı8	thoséc Aıı4		cathál Aıı 23
		toíség Aıı 6		cathál Aıı 25
		dabég Aıı 12		thabárt Aıı 17
		Cainnéch Aıı 20		
		cainnéc Aıı 24		
Total	4/5 (80%)	8/20 (40%)	1	6/9 (67%)

It would be unwise to attach any significance to the seven examples in group
(A) as there are 38 instances by Hand A (15 in text Aı and 23 in text Aıı),
where no accent appears on the final unstressed vowel. Such accents may have
been intended to mark word boundaries—in this case the ends of words.[44]

Instances gathered under Group (B) may be purely orthographic and may
also serve to mark the end of a word boundary. Given the small number of
examples involved it would be rash to attach too much importance to the
fairly consistent marking of final syllables in *-ad*, *-ar*, *-al* by Hand A.
Nevertheless the clear patterns exhibited are suggestive of a linguistic
explanation as we shall tentatively suggest below. Hand A is not consistent
with regard to the marking of unstressed syllables in *-eg*, *-ec(h)*, *-ac(c)*, or
-al(l). In the following examples no accent appears: **cósgreg** (Aıı), roalseg
(Aı2), cruthnec (Aı3), glerec (Aıı 1, Aı9), dorodloeg (Aı8), benact (Aıı6),
bennact (Aıı27), blienec (Aıı7), buadacc (Aıı7), Moridac (Aıı2), tosech

---

42 Cf. gobróig (Aıı 12), madchór (Bv4).   43 Cf. lurchárí (Bv24).   44 We might compare
the marking with an accent of final consonants in the following cases: **óhúnń** (Aıı9, third
accent), **ímácć** (Aıı9, third accent), *l* in cathál (Aıı17, second accent), proínń (Aıı9, last
accent). Cf. words whose consonantal onsets are marked with an accent—perhaps as an
initial word-boundary marker, e.g. **úaćloic** (Aıı3, second accent); cf. scáli (Bv14–15); cf.
also sleib referred to above from *Lebor na hUidre*, the accents of which may have served to
indicate word boundaries (Best and Bergin 1929, xli). Indeed, this may account for the
accents considered above under the category of stressed vowel preceded by pretonic vowel,
and also in the following cases (where no pretonic syllable precedes): **Cómgeall** (Aıı1),
Rósábard (Aıı13), **Cómgell** (Bv8), **Dómin** (Dıvı), bédé (Aı8), **sén** (Aıı6), étdanin
(Aıı23), éte (Dıııı), éclasi (Dııı2), éscob (Dııı5), néctan (Dııı6), áním (Aıı9), áchád
(Aıı3), **áchád** (Aıı8), álterin (Aıı22), áb (Dııı6), álgune (Dııı7), báll (Dıvı), bánb
(Evıı5).

(AII28), chathail (AII7), Cathal (AII8), Domnall (AII9, 15, 23, 25). In the case of unstressed syllables containing the velar fricative, this means that Hand A marks these 8 (40%) times out of a total of 20, which suggests that the marking of such syllables with accents is not statistically significant.

We have suggested that clear unstressed vowels may have been a characteristic feature of earlier forms of Scottish Gaelic, and indeed that this feature may account, partially at least, for the reduction of long unstressed vowels (Ó Maolalaigh, *infra* 220). Given the possible existence of an elaborate short vowel system in unstressed syllables in earlier forms of Scottish Gaelic, it is tempting to suggest a linguistic explanation for the marking with accents of syllables containing unstressed *-ach*, *-ad*, *-ar*, *-al*. Could accents in such cases have marked the clear quality of these unstressed vowels? There is both diachronic and synchronic evidence to suggest that syllables containing non-oblique *-ach*, *-ech* contained clear vowels. Although oblique forms do not contain clear vowels in modern dialects, it is possible that such forms did exist in older forms of the language.[45] Indeed, the spellings *-ég* / *-eg* in oblique forms may even support this as argued above, e.g. toíség (AII6), dabég (AIII2), cósreg (AII1), cannech (DIIII, genitive). Compare also our earlier discussion of the forms thesseach (CV25), cáennaig (BVI6–17). This interpretation would suggest that *achad* with -ád (both instances by Hand A) may have contained unstressed clear *a*, i.e. [að] (possibly [aɣ]). However, I have no corroborative evidence for such a pronunciation in the case of *achadh* in the modern dialects.[46]

The evidence of modern Scottish Gaelic phonology suggests a phonological explanation for the accents above unstressed vowels which precede one of the sonorants *l* or *r*. In Scottish Gaelic clear unstressed vowels can occur for expected schwa in some words in the vicinity of the sonorants *l* and *r*, for instance, in words such as *coinneal, iodhal, iomcha(i)r*, and also, significantly, in the word *galar* itself; see Ó Maolalaigh (2006, 242).[47] The final syllable of the word *galar* ('disease') is realised with a clear [a] in practically all Scottish

45 I hope to argue elsewhere that the existence of clear vowels in oblique forms of *-ach* / *-ech* syllables may provide one explanation for the voiceless nature of the fricative in Scottish Gaelic: compare Irish *-igh* with Scottish Gaelic *-ich*. 46 It is perhaps possible that the preceding *ch* had the effect of lowering the following vowel, or that vowel harmony once operated across *ch* in the word *achad*[*h*], producing forms like [axað] (or possibly [axaɣ]. 47 For the geographical distribution of clear vowels in these words in Scottish Gaelic (which usually correspond to /ə/ in Irish dialects), see *aingeal* (*SGDS* 15), *coinneal* (*SGDS* 229, 230), *iodhal* (*SGDS* 523), *iomcha(i)r* (*SGDS* 524), *galar* (*SGDS* 454); cf. *àraid, atharrais* (Oftedal 1956, 335), etc. It seems reasonable to suggest that, in some dialects at least, a clear vowel may have occurred in unstressed syllables containing the sonorants *ll, nn, m* in an earlier stage of Irish. Indeed, this may be suggested by the existence of forward stress in such syllables in certain north-east Connacht dialects (Ó Sé 1989, 155–8). On the occurrence of clear vowels in some Donegal dialects in the likes of *galar* and *Cathal*, see further below.

Gaelic dialects outside the dialects of Lewis, Sutherland and most of Ross-shire.[48] Clear unstressed [a] notably occurs in the word *galar* in eastern Scottish Gaelic.[49] I have no evidence from the modern period which would suggest that *Cathal* is or ever was pronounced with a clear vowel in any variety of Scottish Gaelic. However, Professor Dónall Ó Baoill informs me that low clear vowels are attested in certain dialects of north-west Donegal in the name *Cathal* [kahal] and also, as it happens, in *galar* ([galɑr] ~ [galər]); cf. also *tuathal* [tuəh-əl] ~ [tuə-hal].[50] It seems plausible on the basis of Scottish Gaelic *coinneal, iodhal, iomcha(i)r, galar,* and on the basis of Donegal forms of the name *Cathal,* that *Cathal* may also have been realised in varieties of Scottish Gaelic with an unstressed clear vowel. The sonorant environment of unstressed *a* in *Cathal* may have led to this development, although vowel harmony may also be invoked as a contributory factor. It is tempting to speculate, based on this evidence, that accents in the unstressed syllables of *Cathál* (written 4 times out of 6 by Hand A with an accent over the final *a*) and *galár* may be indicative of unstressed clear vowels.[51] This interpretation, if correct, would suggest that historically long unstressed vowels and certain short unstressed vowels synchronically belonged to the same class, i.e. the class of short clear unstressed vowels. In other words, the function of the accent in *Drostán* (AII; AII8, 15, 20, 24, with historical long -*á*) and that in *galár* (AI9), *Cathál* (AII17, 21, 23, 25), etc. (with historically short *a*) may have been identical; both may have marked synchronically short clear unstressed vowels. If correct, it would follow that historically long unstressed vowels had

---

48 The phonological development in the case of *galar* may have been influenced by morphological factors. In particular, the agentive suffix -*a(i)r* may have influenced the pronunciation. This latter suggestion seems to be supported by the numerous attestations of *galar* with final palatalised *r*; see *galar* (*SGDS* 454).   **49** In the context of unstressed syllables containing sonorants marked with accents, mention should also be made of **Cómgeall** (AIII), where -*ea*- may be indicative of a clear vowel. Similarly, mention should also be made of **morcúnn** (AII2, MS **morcunń**), which may indicate a clear vowel—in this case perhaps [u].   **50** Also recorded by Professor Malachy McKenna from Rann na Feirste as [galɑr]. The occurrence of clear unstressed *a* in the name *Cathal* (possibly also in *tuathal*) may be due to vowel harmony across the segment /h/, in which case it may post-date the development *th* > *h*. Professor Ó Baoill also provides the following examples: *áthas* [a·h-əs] ~ [a·-has]; *snáthad* [sNa·h-əd] ~ [sNa·-had], where '-' indicates a syllable boundary; Professor Malachy McKenna has also recorded the following example from Rann na Feirste: *snáthad* [sNɛhɛḑ] (personal communication). For vowel harmony in the environment of *h* in Scottish Gaelic, see *athair* (*SGDS* 63, 64), *màthair* (*SGDS* 606), *beatha* (*SGDS* 92, 93), *saothair* (SGDS 740), etc.; however, the final syllable of *athair* and *màthair* may have been affected by agentive -*air*. One wonders if the general loss of intervocalic *h* (< *th*) in the majority of Scottish Gaelic dialects (i.e. southern and eastern dialects) surveyed in *SGDS* may have developed as a consequence of the existence in an earlier stage of ScG of vowel harmony across syllables of the structure V_xhV_x.   **51** If **deár** (AII9) represents a hiatus word, as we have tentatively suggested (Ó Maolalaigh, infra 210–1), it might be argued that the accent over the *a* may have marked a clear unstressed vowel -[ar].

been reduced in certain eastern Scottish Gaelic dialects by the twelfth century, thus providing possible corroborative evidence for our interpretation of mormar (AII27), mórmar (DIII8), cinathá (first *a*; AIII1) and helaín (CVI33), discussed in Ó Maolalaigh 'The Scotticisation of Gaelic', *infra* 220–5). It should be stressed that this interpretation is highly tentative and speculative, and rests on the assumption that accents could be used to mark historically long unstressed vowels, the marking of which, as we have seen, is statistically insignificant.

A further aspect of unstressed vowels in the Notes is that round vowels are used frequently in unstressed syllables where these would not be expected. It may be significant that in the vast majority of these the preceding stressed syllable contained a round vowel. One possible explanation of such forms may be a form of vowel harmony, perhaps indicating further the existence of clear short non-schwa-like vowels in the unstressed position in twelfth-century eastern Scottish Gaelic. Examples include:[52]

> tangator (AI2, 6), abbordoboír (AI3), dorodloeg (AI8) (which Jackson (1972, 132) refers to as 'unique'), rolaboir (AII9), morcúnn (AII2), mormoir (AII5), morcunt (AII8), gobróig (AIII2), luloíg (AIII4), nolloce (AIII9), abstoil (DIII3), dolodib (DIII4), domongart (DIII9), madchór (BV4), morgunn (CVI30).

Jackson (1972, 130, 132) lists some of these and notes the occurrence of a preceding labial consonant as 'significant' in four of these (domongart, abbordoboír, rolaboir, gobróig).[53] However, it may be more significant that in 11 of these 16 (69%) examples the preceding stressed syllable contains a round vowel.[54] Seven of these round vowels are flanked by *r* (usually in final position), five of which are marked by an accent although three of these contain the grapheme *i*. (The Poppleton Manuscript also has unstressed *o* in similar environments, e.g. *Domongrat, Conore, Labchore* (Broun 1999, 176, 177, 179).)

---

[52] Leaving aside historical spellings such as *Colum* (AII, 19, etc.), *e[p]scob* (DIII5, 6); the second *o* in the form Malcoloum (AIII1), if it is not an error, may have been written to reinforce the round nature of the stressed vowel and may be indicative of vowel harmony. Jackson (1972, 132) refers to the latter 'peculiar' form as 'a slip'; forms without unstressed round vowels also occur in the Notes, e.g. colaim (Diii10, 11), colim (DIvi). [53] mormoir (AII5) could possibly be added though *oi* could represent a variant spelling of the original *aí* diphthong. Cf. *cethror* and *uabor* (Ó Cuív 1990, 58).   [54] Counter examples exist in the Notes where such rounding is not indicated (e.g. dobar (AII20), domnall (AII23), chomallfas (AII28), cóbrig (DIII2), córmaic (DIII9), Cormac (BV12), dómin (DIvi), lurchárí (BV24), morgainn (CVI10), dolaidib (CVI18)), which suggests that the occurrence of round vowels in unstressed syllables may be purely orthographic and have no phonetic significance.

SUMMARY SO FAR

Table 7.12 provides summary statistics for each of the five categories discussed above, which may be summarised as follows. They each account for the following percentage of accents: (1) long vowels (35%), (2) the grapheme *i* (31%), (3) stressed syllables preceded by pretonic vowels or head nouns (16%), (4) stressed vowels / syllables preceded by syntactically related pretonic vowels /syllables, including genitive modifers preceded by head nouns (27% [or 12%]), (5) unstressed post-tonic vowels (11%). Since there is a certain amount of overlap between categories, the resultant percentages may not be simply added to give us a total of 'explicable' accents. However, a cursory glance at **Table 7.12** illustrates that the majority of accents fall within these categories.

Table 7.12: Summary statistics for categories discussed above

HAND / TEXT	Long vowels marked	Grapheme *i* marked	Pretonic vowels marked	Stressed vowels marked preceded by 'pretonic' element	Unstressed (post-tonic) vowels[55]	Total no. of accents
AI	25 (29%)	25 (29%)	13 (15%)	24 (28%)	11 (13%)	85 (100%)
AII	28 (30%)	33 (35%)	16 (17%)	15 (16%)	16 (17%)	94 (100%)
Total A	53 (30%)	58 (32%)	29 (16%)	39 (28%)	27 (15%)	179 (100%)
B	10 (40%)	11 (44%)	4 (16%)	8 (32%)	2 (8%)	25 (100%)
Total B	10 (40%)	11 (44%)	4 (16%)	8 (32%)	2 (8%)	25 (100%)
CII	2 (67%)	0	0	3 (100%)	0	3 (100%)
CV	3 (100%)	0	0	1 (33%)	0	3 (100%)
CVI	5 (56%)	6 (67%)	2 (22%)	4 (44%)	0	9 (100%)
Total C	10 (67%)	6 (40%)	2 (13%)	8 (53%)	0	15 (100%)
DIII	11 (34%)	6 (19%)	6 (19%)	8 (25%)	0	32 (100%)
DIV	3 (50%)	1 (17%)	2 (33%)	2 (33%)	0	6 (100%)
Total D	14 (37%)	7 (18%)	8 (21%)	10 (26%)	0	38 (100%)
E	5 (56%)	1 (11%)	0	6 (67%)	0	9 (100%)
Total E	5 (56%)	1 (11%)	0	6 (67%)	0	9 (100%)
Overall totals	92 (35%)	83 (31%)	43 (16%)	71 (27%) [32 (12%)][56]	29 (11%)	266 (100%)

55 Counting only final open syllables, and instances of *-ád*, *éc(h)*, *ác*, *ég*, *éb* and *galár*, *Cathál*. **56** The figures in square brackets represent the totals once all instances of marked long vowels and marked *i* have been discounted.

The following hierarchical orderings have emerged from the above study (occurring in decreasing order):

Accents per syllable:
   A (31%) >> B = D (20%) ≈ E (18%) >> C (9%)

Accents (unedited) above consonants:
   [E (33%) >>] A (15%) ≈ D (11%) ≈ B (8%) ≈ C (6%)

Long vowels:
   B (63%) >> A (51%) ≈ D (50%) >> E (38%) ≈ C (33%)

Grapheme *i*:
   A (54%) >> B (42%) >> D (16%) ≈ C = E (13%)

Grapheme *i* next to *n, m*
   A (78%) >> B (44%) >> C (22%) ≈ D (18%) [>> E (0%)]

Pretonic syllables:
   D (47%) >> A (25%) ≈ B (19%) >> C (6%) [>> E (0%)]

Pretonic *do*:
   A (34%) >> D (25%) ≈ B (22%) [>> C = E (0%)]

Stressed syllables preceded by pretonics, including genitive modifiers preceded by head nouns:
   E (50%) >> D (34%) ≈ B (31%) ≈ A (28%) >> C (22%)

Overall Hand C seems to be the least compliant with these categories with consistently low values except in the marking of long vowels. Otherwise Hands A, B and D seem the closest in overall practices, with Hands A and B being the closest of all. However, orthographically speaking Hands A and B seem to differ in their representation of final unstressed vowels following palatal consonants: Hand A uses -*e* far more frequently than -*i*, whereas Hand B tends to use both equally. The statistics for each hand are as follows:

Table 7.13: The use of final unstressed -*e* and -*i*

Hand / Text	-e#	-i#	Totals
Aɪ	16	0	16
Aɪɪ	13	3	16
Total A	29 (91%)	3 (9%)	32 (100%)
Bᴠ	8	7	15
Total B	8 (53%)	7 (47%)	15 (100%)
Cɪɪ	1	1	2
Cᴠ	0	1	1
Cᴠɪ	2	7	9
Total C	3 (25%)	9 (75%)	12 (100%)
Dɪɪɪ	6	6	12
Dɪᴠ	3	1	4
Total D	9 (56%)	7 (44%)	16 (100%)
E	3	2	5
Total E	3 (60%)	2 (40%)	5 (100%)
Overall Totals	52 (65%)	28 (35%)	80 (100%)

There is an overall preference for the use of final -*e* rather than final -*i*. For Hands B, D and E both *e* and *i* are used to similar degrees but Hands A and C, as well as being distinctly different in their practices from one another, are distinct from all other hands. Hand A uses *e* almost always whereas Hand C tends to use *i*. The percentage usages of *e* and *i* may be represented in a hierarchical ordering as follows:

e: A (91%) >> E (60%) ≈ D (56%) ≈ B (53%) >> C (25%)
i: C (75%) >> B (47%) ≈ D (44%) ≈ E (40%) >> A (9%)

Lazar-Mein (see below) concludes that the choice of final *e* or *i* is highly statistically significant for Hands A and C .

These general observations concur on the whole with Jackson's conclusions based on palaeographic grounds. He noted that Hand B was 'quite similar to A' (1972, 13), and that 'A and B are obviously contemporaries' (1972, 16). Jackson also notes how different Hand C is to Hands A and B, being 'comparatively rather spidery' (13). Jackson's conclusion that Hand D 'is of a somewhat different type from the others' (14) (i.e. Hands A, B and C) would appear to be at variance with the conclusions reached here, based on accent usage. The broad agreement in our conclusions based on accent usage and Jackson's conclusions based on other palaeographical considerations would seem to offer some support for (i) the accents being ascribed to the scribes themselves rather than a later scribe or scribes; and (ii) that the accents have palaeographical significance.

ACCENTS UNACCOUNTED FOR

Our discussion so far has suggested five possible functions for the accents, of varying statistical significance, which accounts in one way or another for approximately 239 of the accents (i.e. *c*.90% of all accents). This leaves approximately 27 accents to be accounted for (i.e. *c*.10% of the total). Unexplained accents are listed below in **Table 7.14** according to Hand/Text:

Table 7.14 Unexplained accents

Hand / Text	Unexplained accents
AI	rothidńaíg (4, first accent), i<u>n</u>cathŕaig (6), bédé (8, first accent), úaçloic (13, second accent), sén (16), áṇím (19, second accent), óhúnń (19, third accent), *ímá*ćć (19, third accent).
AII	Cómgeall (1), áchád (3), áchád (8, first accent), cúit (11), rósábard (13, first accent), catháí (17, second accent), proínń (19, last accent), étdanin (23).
BV	Cómgell (8), sćali (14–15).
DIII	Éte (1), éscob (5), blí*ád*i<u>n</u> (5, second accent), néctan (6), álgune (7).
DIV	báll (1), dó<u>m</u>in (1)
EVII	(ap<u>ud</u>) bánb (5, MS bańb)

The number of unaccounted for accents according to hand is presented in **Table 7.15**.

Table 7.15: Unexplained accents by scribe

Hand / Text	Unexplained accents	Total no. of accents
AI	8 (9%)	85
AII	8 (9%)	94
Total A	16 (9%)	179
B	2 (8%)	25
Total B	2 (8%)	25
CII	0	3
CV	0	3
CVI	0	9
Total C	0	15
DIII	6 (22%)	32
DIV	2 (33%)	6
Total D	8 (24%)	38
E	1 (11%)	9
Total E	1 (11%)	9
Overall totals	27 (10%)	266

We note that all accents from Hand C may be accounted for—in theory at least. The relatively high proportion of unexplained accents from Hand D is noticeable.

A variety of possible functions suggest themselves as explanations for the remaining accents (and others discussed above) although such functions are of course impossible to prove. The most obvious of these are listed here: (1) the leftward placement of accents might explain three of these, namely, incathŕaig (for *in cathraíg*), cúit (for *cuít*) sćali (for *scáli*)—in which case these examples could be assigned to one of the five categories discussed above; (2) the marking of word boundaries might explain a large number of these examples,[57] e.g. úaćloic (second accent); áchád, áchád, rósábard (first accent); étdanin, Éte, éclasi, éscob (allowing for slight rightward placement of accent in latter two examples), álgune; óhúnń, ímácć, proínń, catháí

---

[57] This type of marking (including the marking of stressed syllables preceded by pretonic vowels) may represent a development and extension of the marking of monosyllables which is attested in medieval Latin manuscripts (Denholm-Young 1954, 19).

Table 7.15: Proper names marked with accent

Hand / Text	With accent	Without accent	Totals
AI	11 (73%)	4 (27%)	15
AII	36 (67%)	18 (33%)	54
Total A	47 (68%)	22 (32%)	69
BV	11	10	21
Total B	11 (52%)	10 (48%)	21
CII	0	0	0
CV	0	0	0
CVI	3	18	21
Total C	3 (14%)	18 (86%)	21
DIII	14 (47%)	16 (53%)	30
DIV	2 (22%)	7 (78%)	9
Total D	16 (41%)	23 (59%)	39
E	9	18	27
Total E	9 (33%)	18 (67%)	27
Overall Totals	86 (49%)	91 (51%)	177

(last accent); (3) post-tonic marker or monosyllabic marker, e.g. **sén**; (4) high tense mid-vowels, e.g. **Cóm**geall, **Cóm**gell; cf. **dóm**in (DIVI), which has, however, been included under category 4 above; **éc**lasi, **ét**danin, **ésc**ob;[58] (5) the marking of syllables of middle length quantity (*síneadh meadhónach*; see Greene 1952), e.g. **márr** (DIII8), **báll** (DIVI), **bánb** (EVII5); possibly also the svarabhakti examples of **áńím** (AI19) and **maréb** (AI10); cf. **Cóm**geall, **Cóm**gell; (6) the marking of proper names.

The statistics for the marking with an accent of proper names is given in **Table 7.15**, which includes personal names and place-names but does not include common nouns used as place-name elements since the status of such names in some cases is unclear (see Taylor, this volume), e.g. **ć**loic i̱ntiprat (AI13), **chlóíc** pette m̱e̱c garna**ít** (AI13–14), etc. However, proper names in such place-names have been included, e.g. **garnaít**.

---

58 Note that high mid (tense) /e/ occurs before /g d s/ in many modern Scottish Gaelic dialects (cf. the retention of original //e// in these environments in certain Ulster dialects: Ó Maolalaigh 1997, 244–6, 283–9, 314–15).

There is no overall tendency to mark proper names with accents in the Notes. However, Hand A stands apart from each other hands in marking 68% of all proper names.

CONCLUSIONS ON ACCENTS

Our discussion of the neglected accents in the Gaelic Notes illustrates that it is difficult to provide convincing explanations for many of the accents. Nevertheless, we have established a number of facts regarding their placement. Importantly, their function was not to mark long vowels (cf. Jackson 1972, 17), the marking of which has been shown not to be statistically significant. Similarly, the marking of pretonic syllables cannot be claimed as a significant function in the Notes. On the other hand, the numbers involved in some cases are so small that it is impossible to make valuable or meaningful judgements. Nevertheless, we have seen that some aspects of accent usage can be shown to be statistically significant, e.g. the number of accents per syllable by individual 'hands', the marking of *i* for length, and the marking of *i* next to *n* and *m*. This would suggest that the placement of accents is not 'wholly meaningless' as Jackson (1972, 18) claimed.

Some of the accent usage discussed is attested in contemporary medieval Irish manuscripts but a full comparison with such sources will not be possible until this aspect of medieval palaeography has been more widely studied. The placement of the accents in the Notes may represent an adaptation and development of that which we find in contemporary sources in Ireland. This process of adaptation is paralleled in other aspects of the orthography and language of the Notes, as has been argued in 'The Scotticisation of Gaelic'. However, the variation in accent usage witnessed in the Notes suggests strongly that in most cases the accents were not placed according to fixed principles. Accordingly, it is difficult to see how these accents could have served to elucidate the texts in which they appear.[59] Nevertheless, despite this conclusion, the accents have been reproduced in the Diplomatic Edition (this volume) to enable future researchers to compare accent usage in the Notes with other texts, and also with the possibility in mind that different patterns in the distribution of the accents may yet be discovered in the future.[60]

---

[59] Cf. Denholm-Young's comments on the placing of stress accents only on syllables 'that might be misread by a not too learned monk' (1954, 20).   [60] Denholm-Young (1954, 19) comments that 'all medieval reading was, as is well known, reading aloud, and that a […] system of rhythmical accents was in use at least as late as the twelfth century in Latin manuscripts'. Cf. Keller's observations on the Caedmon manuscript (in Denholm-Young 1954, 19) quoted above. I see no rhythmical basis for the placement of the accents in the Notes.

SYMBOLS

>>   occurs more commonly than

ABBREVIATIONS

GOI   *A Grammar of Old Irish*, by R. Thurneysen (Dublin, 1946). Repr. 1993.
SGDS   *Survey of the Gaelic Dialects of Scotland*, 5 vols, ed. by C. Ó Dochartaigh (Dublin, 1994–97).

REFERENCES

Alexander, W.M. (1952) *The place-names of Aberdeenshire* (Third Spalding Club), Aberdeen.

Bergin, O., and R.I. Best (1938) 'Tochmarc Étaíne', *Ériu* 12, 137–96. Also publ. sep. as Bergin, O. and R.I. Best (1938) *Tochmarc Étaíne*, Dublin.

Bernard, J.H. and R. Atkinson (1898) *The Irish Liber Hymnorum: edited from the MSS with translations notes and glossary* (Henry Bradshaw Society), London.

Best, R.I. and O. Bergin (1929) *Lebor na hUidre: Book of the Dun Cow* (RIA), Dublin.

Black, R. (1973) Review of Jackson (1972), *Celtica* 10, 264–7.

Borgstrøm, C. Hj. (1941) *The dialects of Skye and Ross-shire*, Oslo.

Broun, D. (1998) 'Gaelic literacy in Eastern Scotland between 1124 and 1249', in *Literacy in medieval Celtic societies*, ed. Huw Price, Cambridge, 183–201.

—— (1999) *The Irish identity of the kingdom of the Scots in the twelfth and thirteenth centuries*, Woodbridge.

Cameron, J. (1937) *Celtic law: The "Senchus Mór" and "The Book of Aicill," and the traces of an early Gaelic system of law in Scotland*, London and Glasgow.

Denholm-Young, N. (1954) *Handwriting in England and Wales*, Cardiff.

Diack, F.C. (1920–1) 'Place-names of Pictland [I]', *Revue celtique* 38, 109–32.

Fraser, J. (1942) 'The Gaelic *Notitiae* in the Book of Deer', *Scottish Gaelic Studies* 5, 51–66.

Greene, D. (1954) 'Miscellanea: the mark of length on pretonic vowels', *Celtica* 2, 334–40 (339–40).

—— (1972) Review of Jackson (1972), *Studia Hibernica* 12, 167–70.

Jackson, K.H. (1972) *The Gaelic Notes in the Book of Deer*, Cambridge.

Lindeman, F.O. (1988) 'Notes on two biblical glosses', *Celtica* 20, 108–9.

MacAulay, D. (1975) Review of Jackson (1972) *Scottish Historical Review* 54, 84–7.

MacBain, A. (1885) 'The Book of Deer', *Transactions of the Gaelic Society of Inverness* 11 (1884–5), 137–66.

—— (1894) 'The Gaelic dialect of Badenoch', *Transactions of the Gaelic Society of Inverness* 18 (1891–2), 79–96.

McCone, K. (1996a) *Towards a relative chronology of ancient and medieval Celtic sound change*, Maynooth.

—— (1996b) 'Prehistoric, Old and Middle Irish', *Progress in Medieval Irish Studies*, ed. Kim McCone and Katharine Simms, Maynooth, 7–53.

Murphy, G. (1944) 'A poem in praise of Aodh Úa Foirréidh, bishop of Armagh (1032–1056)', in *Measgra i gCuimhne Mhichíl Uí Chléirigh* […], ed. S. O.Brien, Dublin, 140–64.

Ní Dhonnchadha, M. (1982) 'The guarantor list of *Cáin Adomnáin*', *Peritia* 1, 178–215.

O'Brien, M.A. (1956) 'Etymologies and notes: 12. *oc* in Mod.Ir', *Celtica* 3, 175–7.

O Concheanainn, Tomás (1980) 'The YBL Fragment of *Táin Bó Flidais*', *Celtica* 13, 56–7.

Ó Cuív, B. (1972) Review of Jackson (1972), *Éigse* 14.4, 341–6.

—— (1990) 'The Irish marginalia in Codex Palatino-Vaticanus No. 830', *Éigse* 24, 45–67.

—— (1994) *Aibidil Gaoidheilge & Caiticiosma: Seaán Ó Cearnaigh's Irish Primer of Religion published in 1571*, Dublin.

Oftedal, M. (1956) *The Gaelic of Leurbost Isle of Lewis*, Oslo.

Ó Maolalaigh, R. (2006) 'On the possible origins of Scottish Gaelic iorram "rowing song"', in *Litreachas & Eachdraidh : Rannsachadh na Gàidhlig 2, Glaschu 2 / Literature & History: Papers from the Second Conference of Scottish Gaelic Studies, Glasgow 2002*, ed. Michel Byrne, Thomas Owen Clancy and Sheila Kidd, Glaschu, 232–88.

Ó Murchú, M. (1989a) *East Perthshire Gaelic: social history, phonology, texts, and lexicon*, Dublin.

Ó Néill, P.P. (1993) 'Some remarks on the edition of the Southampton Psalter Irish glosses in *Thesaurus Palaeohibernicus*, with further addenda and corrigenda', *Ériu* 44, 99–103.

O'Rahilly, T.F. (1932) *Irish dialects past and present*, Dublin.

Ó Sé, D. (1989) 'Contributions to the study of word stress in Irish', *Ériu* 40, 147–78.

Strachan, J. (1895) 'The importance of Irish for the study of Scottish Gaelic', *Transactions of the Gaelic Society of Inverness* 19 (1893–94), 13–25.

Stokes, W. (1872 [1866]) *Goidelica: Old and Early-Middle-Irish glosses, prose and verse*, 2nd ed., London.

Stuart, J. (1869) *The Book of Deer*, edited for the Spalding Club, Edinburgh.

Thurneysen, R. (1951 [1935]) *Scéla Mucce Meic Dathó*, Dublin.

Watson, W.J. (1926) *The history of the Celtic place-names of Scotland*, Edinburgh.

Watson, W.J. (1929 [1915]) *Rosg Gàidhlig: specimens of Gaelic prose*, Glasgow.

APPENDIX

STATISTICAL ANALYSIS OF TABLES 7.2–7.9 AND 7.13

HEIDI ANN LAZAR-MEYN

At Dr Ó Maolalaigh's request, statistical analysis has been performed on the accent data in those tables (7.2–7.9 and 7.13) for which such analysis is meaningful. Caution must be used in interpreting the results because of the limited amount of data available in some categories, and the lack of suitable texts for comparison. Keeping this in mind, it is nonetheless worthwhile to examine the data that do exist objectively as well as subjectively.

For each of the abovementioned tables, the chi-square (X^2) test was used to determine the probability (P) that the distribution of accents in the linguistic environment in question, either within the document as a whole or by a given hand, happened by chance. A P value of $\leq$ .05 ordinarily is the minimum considered to be statistically significant. At that level, the particular distribution would be expected to happen by chance no more than 1 out of 20 times. The largest P value normally reported is P < .0001, at which level the particular distribution would be expected to happen by chance fewer than 1 in 10,000 times. The third number noted, degrees of freedom (D.F.), is derived mechanically from the number of rows and columns in the table. D.F. are cited because they affect the P of a given X^2 value.

Only statistically significant P values are mentioned in the summary below. The complete statistical analysis may be obtained from Dr Ó Maolalaigh or from the author of this statistical appendix.

Table 7.2: The number of accents per syllable written by each individual hand is highly statistically significant ($X^2 = 41.636$, P $\leq$ .0001, D.F. $= 4$). The individual cell X^2s and expected values support the observation in the text that Hands B, D and E 'use accents roughly to the same degree', whilst Hand A uses them far more frequently and Hand C far less frequently than expected.

Table 7.3: There is no statistical significance to the marking of vowels by length for any one of the five hands. Further, there is no statistical significance to the marking of long vowels based on stress, either in the texts as a whole or by any one of the five hands.

Table 7.4: For the Gaelic Notes as a whole, marking i for length is statistically significant, ($X^2 = 9.820$, P $= .0017$, D.F. $= 1$). *But see* the caveats below concerning the analysis of Table 7.5, particularly since the distribution of marking by hand is highly statistically significant ($X^2 = 37.646$, P $< .0001$, D.F. $= 4$), even though the distribution of long and short i by hand is proportional. As noted in the text, Hand A's marking of short i is the main contributor to this. However, Hands C and D contribute by their disproportionate lack of marking.

Table 7.5: Concerning marking of i by length, Hand C's usage is statistically significant ($X^2 = 6.905$, P $= .0086$, D.F. $= 1$), primarily due to fewer examples of long i being marked than expected. Hand D's is even more strongly statistically significant ($X^2 = 11.613$, P $= .0007$, D.F. $= 1$) primarily due to fewer examples of long i being marked than expected. Given the small numbers of examples of long i by the two hands (7 and 10 respectively), these data may not be reliable.

Marking i by length in Hands A and E is not statistically significant. Marking by length in Hand B just misses the minimal statistically significant value of P $\leq$ .05, but this is effectively meaningless given the number of textual features that were analysed.

Table 7.6: Marking of i next to n and m is statistically significant by hand ($X^2 = 15.678$, P $= .0035$, D.F. $= 4$). As noted in the text, Hand A's propensity to mark i in this context is the main contributor to the significance. Hands C and D contribute by their disproportionate lack of marking but the small numbers of examples by all hands except A render the data somewhat unreliable.

Table 7.7: Marking of pretonic syllables and vowels by each individual hand is weakly statistically significant (X^2 = 11.065, P = .0258, D.F. = 4). Hands A and B mark effectively at random and, as noted in the text, 1 example in Hand E is of no predictive value. Accordingly, the significance comes from Hand C, who marked disproportionately few pretonics, and Hand D, with relatively few examples and those split effectively evenly between marked and unmarked.

Table 7.8: Marking of *do* by category is barely statistically significant for the Gaelic Notes as a whole (X^2 = 3.907, P = .0481, D.F. = 1). As surmised, this actually reflects that the contribution of Hand A is highly statistically significant, (X^2 = 11.792, P = .0006, D.F. = 1), since such marking as exists in the other hands is effectively identical in distribution.

Table 7.9: There is no statistically significant difference between the hands as to marking of all stressed syllables, both with and without excluding those syllables containing either a long vowel or *i*.

Table 7.10: The choice of final *e* or *i* by a given hand is highly statistically significant, (X^2 = 19.167, P = .0007, D.F. = 4). The discussion above correctly notes that Hands A and C are the outliers, using predominantly *e* and *i* respectively, as compared to the effectively even distribution in the other three hands.

The Scotticisation of Gaelic: a reassessment of the language and orthography of the Gaelic Notes in the Book of Deer

ROIBEARD Ó MAOLALAIGH

INTRODUCTION*

The significance of the twelfth-century property records, the 'Gaelic Notes', contained in the Book of Deer (Cambridge University Library MS Ii.6.32) as one of the most important historical and linguistic sources for the history of Scotland has been recognised by scholars since the 'rediscovery' of the manuscript in 1860. They represent now, as they did then, the earliest surviving specimens of original continuous texts in Gaelic known to have been written on Scottish soil.[1] There is a long history of commentary on the language and orthography of the Notes spanning more than a century, beginning in the late 1860s (e.g. Stokes 1872 [1866], MacBain 1885, Strachan 1895, Fraser 1942, Jackson 1952) and culminating in 1972 with Professor Kenneth Jackson's classic and masterly study, *The Gaelic Notes in the Book of Deer*. Leaving aside a number of reviews of that work (Greene 1972, Ó Cuív 1972, R. Black 1973, MacAulay 1975), Jackson's linguistic interpretation of the Notes has not been questioned or reassessed in over thirty years. Jackson's treatment represents the most thorough analysis and commentary on the language of the Notes to date, and it is not surprising that little has been published about the Notes since the early 1970s.[2] However, as we shall see,

* I am grateful to the trustees of the Neil Kerr Memorial Fund, administered by the British Academy, for the award of a scholarship, which enabled me to visit Cambridge University Library in December 1999 in order to study the Book of Deer manuscript. My thanks are also due to Dr Katherine Forsyth who lent me her microfilm copy of the Book of Deer, and to Professor William Gillies who lent me the photostats made for Professor Jackson, and with which he worked while preparing his book, *The Gaelic Notes in the Book of Deer* (1972). I am indebted to Drs Brian Ó Curnáin, Caoimhín Breatnach, Thomas Owen Clancy, Simon Taylor and Dauvit Broun for reading and providing useful comments on a draft of this paper, and to Professor Liam Breatnach for his comments on a final draft. For the discussion of palaeographical matters I am grateful to Mr Ronald Black, Professor Pádraig Ó Macháin and Dr Caoimhín Breatnach. The usual disclaimer applies.   1 The
second- or third-oldest surviving specimens of Gaelic written in Scotland, notes added to the Murthly Hours *c.*1370–*c.*1430, have been recently edited by R. Black (2000b). They are written in a form of orthography not dissimilar to that of the early sixteenth-century Book of the Dean of Lismore.   2 Ó Cuív (1972, 343) commented that 'Professor Jackson's

Jackson's linguistic interpretation of the Notes was clouded by certain
preconceptions about the linguistic milieu in which the Notes were written,
our understanding of which has changed considerably in the last thirty or so
years. The time is therefore ripe for a reassessment of Jackson's approach to
the language and orthography of the Notes.

The linguistic interpretation of the Notes has been controversial almost
from the outset when scholars first began to assess their significance in the
latter third of the nineteenth century. On the one hand there were those who
regarded the language as being similar to, and indistinguishable from,
contemporary 'Irish' sources. This is perhaps implicit in Stokes (1872 [1866]),
while Strachan (1895, 15) claims that the Notes show 'the practical identity of
Scotch with Irish Gaelic' at the time when they were written. Fraser (1942,
59) notes bluntly that 'the language of the documents is Middle Irish' and
makes the extraordinary claim that 'such interest as these documents have is
not linguistic' (1942, 52). On the other hand there was a school of thought,
represented by Stuart (1869) and MacBain (1885),[3] which believed that the
Notes reflected vernacular Scottish Gaelic. Stuart (1869, xlvii) refers to 'the
vernacular Gaelic of Alba, in the eleventh and twelfth centuries'. MacBain
(1885, 139) referred to the Notes as 'the only specimen of Old Scotch Gaelic
extant' and went on to conclude:

> On the whole, then, there is a modern air—an air of posterity—about
> the Gaelic of the Book of Deer, as compared with contemporary Irish,
> and certain tendencies are displayed which nowadays characterise the
> Scotch Gaelic only, as compared with the Irish; so that we are quite
> warranted in accepting the book as containing genuine Scotch Gaelic of
> the time. (MacBain 1885, 142)[4]

Jackson's interpretation of the Notes follows largely in the tradition of Stokes,
Strachan and particularly Fraser. He begins his discussion of the orthography
(and language) of the Gaelic Notes as follows:

> Essentially the spelling of the Gaelic notes in Deer is the same as that of
> the ordinary late Middle Irish to which they belong; but though there
> are inconsistencies in M. Ir., there are far more of such in Deer. Many
> of them can be paralleled in M. Ir., but one would not expect to find

treatment of linguistic matters is so thorough that there is little more to be added'.
3 Jackson (1972, 126) comments that 'a good many of MacBain's linguistic and orthographic notes are misconceived and quite untrustworthy'.   4 The view that the Notes
contained at least one north-eastern Scottish Gaelic feature was expressed by Francis C.
Diack in an unpublished letter to the Revd Charles M. Robertson, dated 5 December 1911
(NLS MS 425, 5 Dec. 1911, p. 10ʳ): see the discussion of eclipsis below (4.2).

them in such profusion in any one text. Moreover, in addition to gross inconsistencies there are sometimes wholly 'wrong' or even fantastic spellings. (Jackson 1972, 125)

Jackson offers one explanation for the differences between the Gaelic Notes and that which we might expect in an Irish text of the same period. He claims that the Scottish scribes—due to their remote existence at the periphery of the Gaelic world—were 'imperfectly trained', that 'their spelling was not very "good"', that they 'tended [...] to strange hesitations, pronunciation-spellings, or mere mistakes', and that they were 'out of touch and poorly qualified' (Jackson 1972, 126). The Deer scribes are castigated quite severely, being referred to on one occasion as 'fumbling and ill-educated', and on another are accused of 'carelessness and ignorance' (Jackson 1972, 140, 150).[5] We may compare Jackson's views on the standard and quality of the earlier Latin texts and illuminations which appear in the same manuscript.[6] He refers to the Latin texts as having been copied in an

> outrageously careless corrupt manner, with numerous omissions, transpositions, repetitions, interpolations, capricious spellings and violations of grammar. Some of the errors suggest carelessness rather than ignorance. (Jackson 1972, 9–10)[7]

Jackson's approach and interpretation of the Gaelic Notes is best explained in the context of his understanding of the Gaelic linguistic situation in the twelfth century, which was heavily dependent upon his own theory of 'Common Gaelic' as set down in his well-known 1951 Rhŷs lecture, '"Common Gaelic": The Evolution of the Gaelic Languages'. To Jackson

---

5 Many other instances of negative and subjectively loaded descriptive language could be quoted. In the following list all numerical references are to pages in Jackson (1972): 'numerous spelling "mistakes" and other peculiarities' (30), 'the name is wrongly spelt twice' (37), 'wrong spellings', 'a scribal mistake' (40), 'a scribal inadvertence' (41), 'omitted by error, probably either by failure to write, or failure to copy' (55), '"abnormal" spellings' (126), 'a mere error' (129), 'scribal carelessness' (129), 'careless spelling' (131), 'scribes struggled with a variety of spellings' (134), 'Deer is notably aberrant' (138), 'must be errors' (140), 'it is probably a mistake' (143), 'the numerous incorrect, and occasionally fantastic, spellings' (150), 'the carelessness and ignorance of the scribes of this remote monastery' (150), etc. Jackson's conclusions and tone are similar to those of Fraser, who regarded the language of the Notes as Middle Irish / Gaelic, and who refers to 'fairly numerous mistakes' and 'misspellings' (Fraser 1942, 59, 60).   6 Cf. Stuart's (1869: xxviii) discussion of the Latin text, referred to by Jackson (1972, 9, n. 4; 126–7). For other interpretations of their poor quality, see O'Loughlin, this volume.   7 Cf. his comments on the illuminations: 'One may compare the extraordinary corruption and provincialism of the illuminations in the MS, which may well be evidence that these, and also the exceedingly corrupt original text of the Gospels, were produced at Deer, some centuries earlier' (Jackson 1972, 127).

'Common Gaelic' referred to a homogeneous 'common' language spoken (and written) throughout Gaelic Ireland and Scotland, which did not diverge significantly until the thirteenth century. Jackson, as a subscriber to his own theory of Common Gaelic, naturally, would not have expected to find any significant linguistic, and by implication, orthographic, differences between Ireland and Scotland during the twelfth century, when the Gaelic Notes were apparently written. Furthermore, the imperfect training and the sub-standard spellings, according to Jackson, were 'not at all unnatural, considering that Deer is on the remotest edge of the Common Gaelic civilisation-area; its writing masters must have been out of touch and poorly qualified' (Jackson 1972, 126). Clearly, then, Jackson's interpretation of the Gaelic Notes could be seen as being somewhat prejudiced, being reliant on his own theory of 'Common Gaelic'—a stance which on more than one occasion influenced his interpretation of linguistic and orthographic features, as we shall see. Since 'Common Gaelic' was an important frame of reference which Jackson brought to bear on the Gaelic Notes, some discussion of the concept is necessary at this point.

COMMON GAELIC

Jackson did not coin the term 'Common Gaelic'. The term appears to be first used by Borgstrøm in 1937 but may ultimately be based on a collocation found in T.F. O'Rahilly's pioneering synthesis on Irish (including Scottish and Manx) dialects, published in 1932:

> If small things may be compared with great, an interesting parallel might be drawn between the emergence of the modern Irish and Scottish Gaelic dialects out of the ruins of the *common literary Gaelic* and the rise of the Romance languages out of Latin. (O'Rahilly 1932, 258) [italics mine]

However, the use of lower case in 'common' and also the word 'literary' serve to highlight differences in the use of the term 'common' between O'Rahilly and later scholars such as Borgstrøm and Jackson. Clearly, O'Rahilly did not intend or use 'common Gaelic' as a specific collocation or as a new theoretical concept—steps which were to be taken by others after him. That is not to say that O'Rahilly did not believe that a period of unity existed in the history of the Gaelic languages as is clear from the following extract:

> In fact, the spoken Gaelic of Scotland and Man must have been substantially identical down to a comparatively late period; and there seems little doubt that, between *the original Gaelic unity* and the triple

division which is familiar to us to-day, there intervened a time (say, about seven centuries ago [i.e. thirteenth century]) when Gaelic might have been divided into two slightly differentiated branches, viz. the Gaelic spoken in Ireland, and that spoken in Scotland and the Isle of Man. (O'Rahilly 1932, 140) [italics mine]

The first scholar to use 'Common Gaelic' as a specific theoretical term appears to be Carl Hj. Borgstrøm. It is first attested in his monograph study of the dialect of Barra (1937), then in his 1938 article on 'Scottish Gaelic as a Source of Information about the Early History of Irish', and later in his monograph study of the dialects of the Outer Hebrides (1940). It does not appear in his 1934 article on 'The Expression of Person and Number in Gaelic', where older stages of the language are referred to as Old and Middle Irish.[8] The term is used without definition in Borgstrøm's monograph studies and usually occurs in the collocation 'Common Gaelic period' (1937, 75, 128; 1940, 221), although he also uses it to refer to 'the Common Gaelic system' (1940, 219). The term is interchangeable with 'Old Irish' and 'Early Gaelic'. He refers to 'hiatus due to the loss of spirants before the Old Irish or Common Gaelic period' (1940, 221) and 'the corresponding phenomena in Common Gaelic or Early Irish' (1938, 36); cf. (1940, 215). Borgstrøm defines quite clearly what he means by 'Common Gaelic' in his 1938 article. The passage is worth quoting in full:

> Let us suppose for a moment that no Old or Middle Irish manuscripts were known to us, that we possessed only the modern dialects in Ireland, Scotland and the Isle of Man. Having recognised the close relationship between these three groups, we should then at once have applied the comparative method to them in order to trace their origin back to *a 'Common Gaelic' language*. We should have been able to reconstruct some of the system of this *unknown source* by investigating what were the archaisms and what were the independent or common innovations in each of the three groups.
>
> It is obvious that the comparative method can, and must, be used to complete our knowledge about the older language which we now derive from older manuscripts. There is no doubt that Scottish Gaelic, and perhaps also Manx, can help us to understand points of pronunciation and grammar in *common Gaelic* [*sic*, lower case *c*], and even in Old and

---

8 It may be significant that Borgstrøm (1934) contains no references to O'Rahilly's *Irish Dialects Past and Present* (1932). On the other hand, Borgstrøm (1938, 37) does refer to O'Rahilly (1932). It is reasonable to conclude that Borgstrøm adopted the phrase 'Common Gaelic' some time during the period 1934–8 and that it may represent an adaptation of terminology used by O'Rahilly (1932).

Middle Irish where the information afforded us by Modern Irish is incomplete or faulty.

As *Common Gaelic* we may regard the language during the emigration from Ireland to Scotland, which, according to Irish annals, began round about 500 AD. Since the separation of Scottish Gaelic from the mother tongue began so early, its further development is to a great extent different from that of Irish, and its testimony about *Common Gaelic* to a similar extent independent of the Irish testimony. On the other hand, intimate relations were kept up between the people of Ireland and the Scottish colony through the ages; linguistic developments in the two groups must, therefore, have influenced each other to a certain extent; by this and by their *common starting-point* we can explain how the development of the two branches in other regards is closely parallel.

The object of the following lines is to call attention to some archaic features in Scottish Gaelic which can give us a better understanding of the corresponding phenomena in *Common Gaelic or Early Irish.* (Borgstrøm 1938, 35–36) [italics mine]

Borgstrøm uses 'Common Gaelic' in two different senses here—in both a theoretical and in a practical sense. It is a theoretical construct (based on the comparative method of reconstructing earlier forms of language from modern dialects) to which the modern Gaelic languages can be traced back. We may note in passing here the careful distinction which Borgstrøm makes between this hypothetical construction and the written language of 'older manuscripts', both of which are independent witnesses which can be used to inform us about aspects of 'the older language'. That Borgstrøm viewed his theoretical construct as having a basis in reality is also evident from his statement that Common Gaelic was the actual form of language used by Gaels 'during the emigration from Ireland to Scotland, which, according to Irish annals, began round about 500 A.D.' What is noteworthy for present purposes is that Borgstrøm believed that the 'period' of Common Gaelic ended 'early' on—almost as soon as Gaelic was introduced to Scotland. This was also the view of the mid-nineteenth-century Irish grammarian, John O'Donovan, who stated that:

> The Highland Gaelic is essentially the same as the Irish, having branched off from it in the sixth century; but there are peculiarities which strongly distinguish it, though the spoken Irish of the north-east of Ulster bears a close resemblance to it in pronunciation and grammatical inflections. (O'Donovan 1845, lxxviii)

We may note in passing here that the traditional fifth-century Dál Riadic migration paradigm has been recently discounted by some historians and archaeologists. Dumville (2002), for instance, argues that stories of Dalriadic origins as they survive in annals and other so-called historical texts bear no relevance whatsoever to historical reality in the period before the tenth century. E. Campbell (2001, 291) concludes that 'the people inhabiting Argyll maintained a regional identity from at least the Iron Age through to the medieval period and that throughout this period they were Gaelic speakers.' Similarly, Dumville suggests that 'the Gaelic culture of Argyll, Arran, Bute, and the Inner Hebrides [...] represents the northernmost extension—the high-water mark, as it were—of the gaelicisation (however achieved) of Ireland in the first millennium B.C.' (2002, 195). This new historical thinking has important implications and ramifications for our approach to, and our understanding of, the history of Gaelic in Scotland, although it does not mean that we should revive older notions of Scottish Gaelic deriving from a branch of Goedelic in Scotland distinct from that in Ireland: see Jackson (1951, 72). Recent developments in historical thinking serve to highlight the fact that AD 500 is an arbitrary date, which is almost certainly too late for the emergence of Gaelic / Goedelic in Scotland. When one considers this and the contact with other linguistic groups (e.g. varieties of British, Pictish, and Norse languages) which we know prevailed before and during the Old and Middle Gaelic periods, one sees that the potential for the emergence of dialectal divergences in the pan-Goedelic area must have existed for centuries before the Early Modern era, i.e. well before 1200.

It will be readily noted that Borgstrøm's (and O'Donovan's) model is quite different to O'Rahilly's (1932, 140) view which would date the significant divergence of Irish and Scottish Gaelic (including Manx) to the thirteenth century, and the emergence of modern Gaelic dialects in the thirteenth and fourteenth: 'It is probably during the thirteenth and fourteenth centuries that the formative period of our modern dialects is to be placed.'[9] (O'Rahilly 1932, 248) Ignoring the hypothesis that Scottish Gaelic was the modern reflex of Pictish, put forward most recently by F.C. Diack (1944, 82),[10] and which was

9 It is important to note that O'Rahilly was willing to accept that dialectal differences existed in the Old and Middle Gaelic periods. However, it was his opinion that 'there can be no doubt that such local differences as then existed were trivial in comparison with those of later times.' (O'Rahilly 1932, 248) O'Rahilly's dating of the formative period of Modern Irish dialects is to a large extent based on dialectal features which come increasingly to the fore in certain fourteenth- and especially fifteenth-century Gaelic manuscrips: see O'Rahilly (1932, 16–17). Annalistic, medical and religious texts are fruitful sources for the study of dialect features: for general comment, see, for instance, Ó Cuív (1980 [1951], 40–1). The systematic study of the language of prose texts from the period 1200–1600 remains a desideratum. For some examples, see Ó hInnse (1947, 214–17); Skerrett (1963, 115–17; 1966a, 186–7; 1966b, 189, 202–4); Ó Súilleabháin (1976, 203–6); Ó Laoghaire (1990, 491–4); C. Breatnach (2001). For a discussion of differences between the language of prose and (Classical Gaelic) poetry in the Early Modern period (c.1200–1650), see McManus (1994b). 10 William M. Alexander, in his preface to Diack (1944: x–xix), gives

refuted by Jackson (1951, 93–7), it is clear that before Jackson came to write his paper on Common Gaelic there were essentially two fundamentally different views on the early history of Scottish Gaelic: one which claimed that Irish and Scottish Gaelic diverged at an early date (Borgstrøm, O'Donovan), and another, which claimed that their divergence was quite late.[11] Jackson claimed that his reformulation of the theory of Common Gaelic was 'a considerable modification' of the former stance, although nowhere does he give credit to Borgstrøm's work.

Jackson's main modification to Borgstrøm's model of Common Gaelic was that Irish and Scottish Gaelic did not begin to diverge at the end of the fifth century (1951, 74), but rather that 'the two remained substantially identical, in fact a single language, until at least the tenth century, and in most respects the thirteenth' (1951, 74–5).[12] In other words, the period of Common Gaelic, according to Jackson, lasted much longer—in effect up until the thirteenth century. There can be little doubt that Jackson was heavily influenced by O'Rahilly's views on the subject, who as we have already noted, traced the origin of modern dialects to the thirteenth and fourteenth centuries.[13] The main difference between Borgstrøm's theory of Common Gaelic and Jackson's is that Jackson further developed what are essentially O'Rahilly's views and superimposed these on Borgstrøm's theory, borrowing Borgstrøm's term in the process. However, the differences between both theories are not just chronological. Literary sources receive different emphases in both. We have

a useful overview of earlier scholarly views on the origin of Scottish Gaelic: these include the views of George Buchanan (*Rerum Scoticarum Historia* 1582), James MacPherson (*Temora* 1763) and William F. Skene (*Four Ancient Books of Wales* 1868), all of whom believed that the Picts spoke a form of Gaelic. Cf. also Skene (1836, 44–57). **11** The bibliographer, John Reid, in his book, *Bibliotheca Scoto-Celtica* (1832: ix), was of the view that 'the Scotch Gaelic […] is without doubt derived from the Irish Gaelic' and 'that not more than 350 years ago [i.e. c.1480s] they [i.e. Irish and Scottish Gaelic] must have been not only the same language but identically the same dialect'. The unidentified 'gentleman in the Highlands', whose letter to Reid is reproduced verbatim in Reid (1832: xl–xlv), and who claims that Scottish Gaelic 'is not *derived* from its sister dialect [i.e. Irish], but is the simpler and *more* primitive of the two' (Reid 1832: xli), makes the important point that the Scottish Gaels' use of Irish orthography does not mean that their language was the same (ibid.). The view that Scottish Gaelic reflected more closely the 'original' Gaelic because of its simpler inflectional system was earlier stated by William Shaw in his *An Analysis of the Gaelic Language*, published in 1778 (Shaw 1778: xiii). **12** Cf. 'the oldest traceable divergence is not older than the tenth century, and that we cannot really speak of a separation until about the thirteenth century' (Jackson 1951, 79). **13** Notwithstanding the fact that O'Rahilly never refers to Irish as 'a homogeneous language', Jackson's reliance on O'Rahilly is evident in the statement: 'O'Rahilly has made it clear that the modern Irish dialects did not really begin to come into existence before the thirteenth or fourteenth century at earliest; until that time we must suppose Irish to have been a homogeneous language throughout the island except for such small local differences and incipient nuances of dialect as are bound to occur over such a comparatively large area' (Jackson 1951, 79). We may also note that Jackson sent an early draft of his Common Gaelic lecture to O'Rahilly, and that already noted Borgstrøm's careful distinction between the evidence of the written language of Old Irish / Gaelic and that of comparative reconstruction based on the modern dialects—both of which contribute independently to our knowledge of the older language. Jackson, on the other hand, did not draw a distinction between literary and vernacular language, and in this he differed from O'Rahilly. Furthermore, Jackson described the literary language of Classical Irish / Gaelic of the Early Modern period as 'an artificial survival of what had been about the twelfth or thirteenth century the everyday speech, at least among the educated, in Ireland and [...] in Scotland' (Jackson 1951, 75). He goes on to say that the Gaelic Notes in the Book of Deer are 'written in the language of the upper classes of Buchan in the middle of the twelfth century' and that 'their language is identical with contemporary Middle Irish, that is to say, it is the ordinary spoken Common Gaelic of the time; and they form a valuable proof that as yet Common Gaelic was a substantial unity.' (Jackson 1951, 88) However, it is clear from O'Rahilly's endorsement (1932, 259) of the views of Swiss linguist Charles Bally that he understood well the distinction between literary and vernacular forms of language. Jackson's untenable equation of literary and vernacular forms of language therefore represents a significant departure in his adoption and adaptation of O'Rahilly's views.[14] While Jackson's 1951 article shows no awareness of the important distinction between language registers, it is interesting to note that he was well aware of the distinction some thirty years later when he addressed the International Congress of Celtic Studies in Galway in 1979:

> [W]e cannot really say that at such and such a period the language had reached such and such a stage in respect of some linguistic feature (Jackson 1983, 2).

> We must always remember that we are dealing not with a spoken language but with a written one, in which deliberate archaisation could become a matter of pride to composers or scribes, to a greater or lesser degree according to period, type and 'level' of literary pretension, and style (Jackson 1983, 10).

These 'modern' insights have obvious implications for an assessment of Jackson's work on the Gaelic Notes as we shall see. However, before we reassess the value of the Gaelic Notes, it is important to consider briefly another tenet of Jackson's theory, namely the perceived historical and social context within which he believed the Gaelic Notes were written. This context,

O'Rahilly 'made a number of valuable suggestions' (Jackson 1951, 71, n. 1).   14 Ó Buachalla reminds us of 'the inherent methodological flaw in assuming that a literary norm or any one linguistic register is synonymous with "the language" of any specific era' (1997, 180).

according to Jackson, was one of a homogeneous Gaelic culture-province, taking in much of Ireland and Scotland during the Middle Ages and continuing down to the modern period. Jackson notes:

> The reason for the persistence of Common Gaelic in this form in Scotland is quite simply that until at least the end of the sixteenth century *Ireland and the Highlands formed a single culture-province*. The '*sea-divided Gael*', as they were called, were *closely linked not only by their language but also by their civilization, their customs and traditions*, by intermarriage between their noble kindreds, and by their aristocratic social system which fostered the hereditary bardic families who practised and preserved the Classical Common Gaelic. (Jackson 1951, 77) [italics mine]

In this we can discern the tangible influence of O'Rahilly who noted:

> To the Gaelic-speaking Scotsman of the past Ireland was the mother-country, whose culture and whose traditions belonged no less to himself than to his kinsmen in Ireland. This feeling of racial unity among the sea-divided *Gaoidhil* was so deeply rooted that, in despite of all obstacles, the same literary language as passed current in Ireland continued to be employed by Scottish writers down to comparatively recent times. (O'Rahilly 1932, 123)

The common global culture model for the Classical or Early Modern period is too simplistic. The complexity of socio-cultural relations between Gaelic Ireland and Scotland has been discussed recently by Ó Mainnín (1999) and MacLeod (2004). Ironically, and importantly, the existence of a common underlying Gaelic civilisation, set of customs and traditions, seems to be directly contradicted by the social and cultural matrices—substantially different to that which obtained in contemporary Ireland—which the Gaelic Notes in the Book of Deer imply existed in pre-twelfth-century eastern Scotland.[15]

We have seen that Jackson's theory of Common Gaelic represents a conciliation, with some reformulation, of the views of scholars such as Borgstrøm and O'Rahilly. The reformulation has resulted in an untenable model for the discussion of the historical development of the Gaelic languages. Nevertheless, it was accepted for almost twenty years, before criticisms began to be aired, although it is still occasionally adhered to by some.[16] The first real signs of

---

15 See particularly Jackson's discussion of titles such as the *toísech* and *mormaer*, and land-holding terms such as *pett* and *dabhach* (Jackson 1972, 102–24).   16 The hypothesis was accepted by R.B. Breatnach (1954) in his review of Jackson (1951). Compare Brian Ó Cuív's review of Jackson (1972), which accepted that the Gaelic Notes represented

criticism of Jackson's theory of Common Gaelic surfaced in reviews of Jackson (1972), most notably in Greene (1972) and MacAulay (1975).[17] Both drew attention to the verbal system of Scottish Gaelic, which they claimed (a) owed its characteristics to contact with a British language, and (b) must have come into existence prior to the eleventh and twelfth centuries, i.e. *before* the Gaelic Notes were written: see Greene (1972, 168); MacAulay (1975, 86). Greene and MacAulay also refer to differences in treatment of hiatus words in Irish and Scottish Gaelic, the contraction of which in Irish Greene (1972, 168) would place earlier than Jackson's tenth century date.[18] MacAulay, referring to Jackson's theory of Common Gaelic, notes that it implies 'an unparalleled sociolinguistic phenomenon considering the situation of contact and admixture that we know obtained' (1975, 86).[19] Both he and Greene refer to the considerable societal differences which obtained in medieval Scotland as noted above. Greene notes:

> The Irish reader cannot fail to be struck by the considerable differences in social organisation of two countries united by a common cultural heritage; it is made abundantly clear that Scotland and Ireland were quite distinct societies long before the Norman invasions began to erode both systems. (1972, 167)

'specimens of the Gaelic language in common use put in written form at that time' (Ó Cuív 1972, 341). More recently we might compare Ahlqvist (1988, 31), R.A. Breatnach (1993, 1–2; 1998, 4) and S. Watson's (1994, 661) acceptance of Jackson's hypothesis of Common Gaelic. On the use of 'Old Gaelic' for 'Old Common Gaelic', see Howells (1971, 90), who also uses the term 'Middle Gaelic' in order to differentiate between the varieties of language spoken in Ireland and Scotland during the so-called 'Middle Irish' period. 17 Cf. Ó Murchú (1997, 191). Since this paper was written, Professor Breandán Ó Buachalla delivered a plenary lecture at the first Rannsachadh na Gàidhlig / Scottish Gaelic Studies conference (held in the University of Aberdeen, 2–4 August 2000), entitled 'Common Gaelic Revisited'; see now Ó Buachalla (2002), which covers similar ground to that covered above. 18 The contraction of hiatus also made some inroads into Scottish Gaelic as is clear from words such as *còir < coäir*, *òg < óäc*, but the development never established itself universally there; however, the loss of hiatus in cases like *còir* and *òg* can be explained as backformations based on syncopated forms: see Ó Murchú (1997, 178). The retention of hiatus may have been reinforced by the loss of intervocalic fricatives, which dramatically increased the membership of the hiatus word class: cf. [Ó Murchú] (1996, 146). It is suggested below (220) that the existence of a rich system of short clear unstressed vowels in earlier forms of Scottish Gaelic may also have been a factor. 19 Cf. the following statements: 'It is not rash to assume that the Irish spoken in those times [i.e. during the Old and Middle Gaelic periods] by the common people was not quite uniform in every part of the country.' (O'Rahilly 1932, 248); 'It is in the highest degree improbable that the ordinary speech of the people [during the period of Old Gaelic] showed no dialect variations whatsoever; that is not the normal state of affairs in any linguistic community' (Greene 1969, 16); 'Now in principle, once a language has for some generations been spoken over a wide area by physically separate communities, regional variation can be expected in it. Regional variation must, therefore, have been established by the Old Irish period' (Ó Murchú 1985, 47); 'Naturally it seems unreasonable to assume that there were

Linguistic differences greater than 'local differences and incipient nuances of dialect' (Jackson 1951, 79) might well be expected in such circumstances, a fact which is implicit in Greene (1972), but made explicit in MacAulay (1975).[20] Furthermore, despite O'Rahilly's rightly cautious claim that 'of dialects in the Old Irish period nothing tangible is known' (1932, 17), some advances in knowledge about variation in earlier stages of the language have been made in the interim, many of which point towards an early northern–southern dialectal split in the pan-Goedelic world of Ireland and Scotland, with innovative features frequently, though not always, originating in northern areas.[21]

EARLY DIFFERENTIATION FEATURES IN GAELIC

Jackson (1951, 86) claimed that contraction of hiatus in certain Irish dialects had occurred by the end of the tenth century, no doubt based on evidence from *Saltair na Rann* (*SR*), although he notes that 'there are traces of its beginning even earlier', referring to some examples from the St Gall (mid ninth century) and Milan Glosses (first half of ninth century) discussed by Thurneysen (*GOI* 72). Cf. Bergin's (1907, 84) note on the possible contraction of hiatus in *cóir* in the St Gall Glosses. Carney (1964, xxix) claimed that contraction of hiatus had taken place 'in certain dialects of Old Irish' 'before the middle of the eight[h] century'; cf. Carney (1983, 194–9). Greene (1976, 43) accepted Carney's conclusions though he viewed them as 'conservative'. Carney's view is substantiated by McCone's study of the Würzburg Glosses (mid eighth century), where contraction is also attested, e.g. *mó* < *moö* (McCone 1985, 88). The contraction of hiatus in Gaelic dialects and earlier sources remains to be fully investigated. It is worth noting in passing that some of the examples which are quoted as early instances of contraction are open to other interpretations, and may not be indicative of a more general loss of hiatus. For instance, contracted *cóir* occurs in the Würzburg and St Gall Glosses, and in the *Calendar of Oengus* (Bergin 1907, 84; Carney 1964, xxix; 1983, 195). However, contraction in this case may be due to backformation or levelling with syncopated forms ending in vowels (e.g. *córai* Ml. 51d3, *córu* Wb. 5d37, Ml. 45b14) where contraction of hiatus is expected: see Ó Murchú (1997, 178). Leaving aside such cases, there are nevertheless sufficient examples to indicate that contraction of hiatus was a feature of certain varieties of Gaelic by the end of the eighth century.

no dialect divisions of any kind in Old Irish' (Ahlqvist 1988, 24). **20** 'It is surprising in those circumstances that Jackson should hold to his theory expressed in the Rhys Memorial Lecture [...] that Scottish and Irish remained the same language until the tenth century and in most respects until the thirteenth century' (MacAulay 1975, 86). **21** Cf. Ó Buachalla (2002, 7–9), who argues that the primary dialect split was between Northern and Southern Gaelic.

The simplest interpretation of the contrast between words such as *triúr* and *siúr*, deriving from earlier hiatus forms *triür* and *siür* respectively, and *triar* < *triär*, etc. is that contraction of hiatus occurred at a stage when there was still a contrast between *u* and *a* in closed unstressed syllables, i.e. some time before the Middle Gaelic period. L. Breatnach (1994, 231) implies this as a possibility although he sees the development of *í* / *i* in hiatus before originally unstressed *u* as problematic since we might expect disyllabic *iä* and *iü* to have merged as monosyllabic *ia* as a result of the merger of unstressed short vowels (and the contraction of hiatus). One possible explanation of the contrast between *triúr* / *siúr* and *triar*, and between the likes of *bídh* 'is' (< *büd*) and *biadh* 'food' (< *biäd*) is that the contrast between short clear vowels in unstressed position may have been retained longer in the environment of hiatus. Such a contrast or partial contrast may have been sustained by the operation of vowel harmony between stressed and unstressed syllables in hiatus (particularly in the case of the high vowels *i* and *u*?).

Vowel harmony between stressed and unstressed syllables is a well-known feature of hiatus words in Scottish Gaelic. We may note the following examples, where the unstressed vowel harmonises with the stressed vowel in words containing original hiatus: *leatha* [lʹɛ-ɛ], *rithe* [rʹi-ɪ] (Borgstrøm 1941, 90); *latha* [lʹa-a] (*SGDS* 564); *ogha* [ɔ-ɔ] (*SGDS* 667), etc. Cf. also Oftedal (1956, 146–47) and S. Watson (1999, 351–54). Instances where the unstressed vowel has affected the stressed vowel in hiatus words are naturally harder to come by in the modern dialects. However, *teotha* [tʃɔi-i] < [tʃɔ-i] (with analogical -[i]) (*SGDS* 840, points 191, 193, 202–04) provides a clear example. The following examples with round vowels in the stressed position must ultimately derive from vowel harmony with original unstressed round vowels: *giuthas* [g̊ʹu-us] < * *giüs* (*SGDS* 474); *teotha* [tʹɔ-ɔ] < *teü* (*SGDS* 840); *piuthar* ([pʰ[iu]-ur], [pʰʲu-ur], [pʰ[iu]-ər], etc.; *SGDS* 679), *leotha* < *leü* [lʹ[ɛɔ]-ɔ] (Borgstrøm 1941, 90); cf. Gillies (2004, 255). On the leftward spread of liprounding from unstressed into stressed syllables across velar fricatives, note, for instance, Scottish Gaelic *bleogha(i)n* from earlier *mlegon*; for other instances, see Gillies (2004, 255–6) and Ó Maolalaigh (2006, 68).

It is worth noting that of all co-articulatory settings, the labial setting has one of the longest segmental spans and can spread large distances within the word from right to left: see Laver (1994, 381). Scottish Gaelic *giuthas* and *piuthar* must in origin represent instances of such anticipatory co-articulation, in which the labial setting of the original unstressed vowel *u* spread leftwards to affect the stressed vowel, i.e. [i-ur] > [iu-ur] > ['u-ur], ['u-ər].[22] This provides an alternative model for the development of *triúr* in Irish, i.e.

---

22 It is unclear whether instances of [pʰ[iu]-ur], with unstressed [u], represent the retention of Old Gaelic unstressed *u* or a secondary development of schwa in forms such as [pʰ[iu]-ər].

[i(:)-ur] > [i-ur] > [iu-ur] > ['u-ur] (> ['u-ər]?) > ['u:r]. If correct, this would cast some doubt on the use of *triúr*, *siúr*, etc. as evidence for the early reduction of hiatus in such words, when *u* was still generally realised as a round vowel in unstressed syllables.

Wagner (1982, 98–109 (104)) argues that the variants *taigh* (northern) ~ *tigh* (southern) reflect 'a dialect division which was already in existence' in Old Gaelic.[23] P. Kelly (1982), considering lexical variation in the names of certain animals in some early sources, suggests that some of this variation may be indicative of dialect rather than high register. McCone (1985, 96–7) sees variant uses in relative clauses in the Old Gaelic Glosses as reflecting regional dialectal patterns, the preposition plus *-s(a)* type reflecting northern usage and the 'conjugated' preposition type reflecting southern usage. Wagner (1986, 1–2) argues that the negative particle *nícon* (later *cha*) was a northern innovation (possibly of the Old Gaelic period), which in time partially or totally supplanted older *ní*.[24] Ahlqvist (1988, 31) provides a summary of the main possible dialectal features which had been posited for Old Gaelic by scholars up to the year 1986, referring, however, to these in Jackson's words, as mere 'incipient nuances of dialect'. Ó Buachalla (1988) puts forward an explanation of the Scottish Gaelic plural ending *-an*, which argues for an early innovation in the matter of plural noun formation in Scotland and possibly Ulster.[25] I have argued for an early divergence between Irish and Scottish Gaelic in the development of the initial mutation of eclipsis: see Ó Maolalaigh (1995–96; 1998, 22–30) and further discussion below (4.2). R.A. Breatnach (1997) suggests that the Scottish Gaelic comparative particle *nas* is different in origin, though similar in function to, Irish *níos*. Furthermore, I have suggested the possible early development of a diminutive suffix *-éin* / *-ein* in Scottish Gaelic (Ó Maolalaigh 2001, 28–9); discussed a possibly early phonetico-lexical feature of dialectal differentiation in Gaelic dialects, namely *leaghmhan* (southern dialects) ~ *leaghmann* (northern dialects) ('moth') (Ó Maolalaigh 2007); and sought to trace the seeds of the Scottish Gaelic imperative plural *-ibh* to Old Gaelic (Ó Maolalaigh 2003c). Other features which require further historical analysis could be added to the list, e.g. the elaborate vowel system of Scottish Gaelic (Ó Maolalaigh 1997, 18–25); the

---

23 The modern contrasting forms *taigh* and *tigh* represent the results of two different outcomes of a process of levelling applied to the Old Gaelic pattern of dat. sg. *taig*, gen. sg. *tige*, pl. *tig-*, with northern varieties opting for *taigh(-)* and southern varieties opting for *tigh(-)*: see McCone (1994, 79, 103).   24 On the distribution and function of *ní* and *cha* in Ulster Irish and its relation to the use of present for future, see Ó Buachalla (1977). See also Ó Dochartaigh (1976).   25 See Ó Buachalla (1988) for a discussion of previous explanations. For an alternative explanation, which stresses internal Scottish Gaelic phonological and morphological factors, see Ó Maolalaigh (2003c). I hope to discuss the broader development of plural nominal inflexion in Scottish Gaelic elsewhere; cf. Ó Maolalaigh (1999a).

Scottish Gaelic pronominal system (*e, i, iad*) (see O Sé 1996); final *-ich*, which I hope to deal with elsewhere; the spread of adjectival *-aidh* (from Old Gaelic *aide*) to replace *-d(a)e*, which I intend to deal with elsewhere;[26] the classificatory type phrase *Éireannach atá ann*;[27] the change *o* > *a* (e.g. *cloch* > *clach*, *cos* > *cas*, *focal* > *facal*, *folt* > *falt*, etc. (see O'Rahilly 1932, 192–3); the merger of Old Gaelic leniting *ar* and nonleniting *for* as leniting *ar* in Irish but as nonleniting *air* in Scottish Gaelic; *cóig* (Scottish Gaelic) ~ *cúig* (Irish);[28] the rise of analytic forms in northern Gaelic;[29] possibly the use of *-(e)ar* in Scottish Gaelic as opposed to Irish *-t(e)ar* in (original) present passive forms (see Ó Baoill 1988, 127); the demonstrative relative *na* in Scottish Gaelic as opposed to a^N in Irish (see Ó Baoill 1988, 128);[30] lenition following the 'dative' / post-prepositional article, on which see further below; the reduction of unstressed long vowels—the latter two features probably representing Scottish innovations (see further discussion below). Finally, it may be noted that Scottish Gaelic nominative sg. *piuthar* (with original hiatus), not attested in Irish sources, represents quite an archaic conservative feature of Scottish

---

26 Cf. W.J. Watson (1926, 440). **27** The 'primary' type *tá sé ina fhear* has been dated in written sources by Dillon (1928) to *c*.1100. Dillon notes that 'in the spoken dialects it is of everyday use' (1928, 326). However, the type *Éireannach atá ann*, which may represent a secondary development of the 'primary' type, is restricted in Southern dialects to negatives such as *níl ann ach* [...] (see Dillon and Ó Cróinín 1961, 53); Ó Siadhail (1989, 225–7). This would seem to suggest that the predicative construction, (*Is é*) *Éireannach atá ann*, may have a northern locus of origin. **28** L. Breatnach (1994, 233) identifies the minor phonological rule of raising of *ó* following *c-* and preceding a palatal(ised) consonant, which is attested in the three words: *cóig* > *cúig*, *cóis* > *cúis*, *cóich* > *cúich*. Raising in Scottish Gaelic is attested only in *cùis*. The contrast between Scottish Gaelic *cóig* (always with high-mid [o:], see *SGDS* 219) and Irish *cúig* must be of old standing. The raising of *ó* to *ú* in the numeral *cóig* may be an Irish innovation, which can be dated in written sources to the early eleventh century. L. Breatnach (1994, 233) notes the form *cúig* from Rawlinson B 502 in the poem 'Temair Breg, baile na fian', ascribed in the Book of Leinster to Cúán Ua Lothcháin (d. 1024): see Joynt (1910, 108). On palaeographical and linguistic grounds Ó Cuív (2001, 174–5) would date Rawlinson B 502 to some time between the end of the eleventh century or the beginning of the twelfth, although he notes that the evidence of some of the versified king-lists suggest 'a date well into the twelfth century' for this manuscript; based on the content of these king-lists, Dr Dauid Broun (personal communication) would date the manuscript to the second quarter of the twelfth century, i.e. *c*.1130. On *cóig* / *cúig*, see also Uhlich (1995, 28) and Ó Murchú (1997, 182). **29** The development of analytic verbal forms is far more advanced in northern than in southern varieties of Gaelic, and is probably a Scottish innovation; cf. [Ó Murchú] (1996, 147). The acceptance of certain analytic forms in the prescriptive norm of Classical Gaelic from the early thirteenth century implies that the development was well under way before 1200. See Greene (1969, 20) and L. Breatnach (1994, 272–3, 290). **30** L. Breatnach (1994, 276–7) discusses the use of a^N, *an, ana* / *ina*, etc. in Middle Gaelic sources, and the change to conjunct verbal forms following this particle in Middle Gaelic. Modern Irish dialects use dependent verbal forms following a^N, whereas Scottish Gaelic dialects normally use independent / relative forms following *na* (although there variation occurs in some cases, notably with the substantive verb, e.g. *na tha* / *na bheil, na bha* / *na robh*), thus continuing the Old Gaelic usage.

Gaelic. The initial *p-* represents a back-formation based on the lenition of original *sw-*, which regularly yielded *f-* < **hw-* (see *DIL* s.v. *siur* and *GOI* 84–85 for instances of *ph-* and *f-* in literary sources).[31] It is interesting to speculate whether or not initial *p-* in this word may have been adopted from an early date in northern rather than southern varieties of Gaelic, due to contact or familiarity with a P-Celtic language, where initial *p-* was naturally a well-established feature.

Although there is a growing body of evidence which points towards early divergences between varieties of Gaelic in Ireland and Scotland, it is also clear that both regions continued to develop in tandem in many respects, although some shared developments are no doubt independent in both countries, such as diphthongisation before originally long or tense sonorants (see Jackson 1951, 85); compensatory lengthening of vowels resulting from the vocalisation of preconsonantal fricatives (Ó Maolalaigh 1997: *passim*); the merger of lenited *l* and non-lenited 'broad' *ll*; the breaking of *é* in 'central' Scottish Gaelic dialects, in Manx and in Munster dialects, and to a lesser extent in Ulster dialects (O'Rahilly 1932, 194; Jackson 1968); and the development of final unstressed *-agh* (< *-adh*). On the other hand, some demonstrably 'later' developments (i.e. post-twelfth and -thirteenth centuries) in one region may have penetrated the other. For instance, the loss of intervocalic *h* (< *th*) is a feature of Scottish Gaelic, ranging from Caithness in the north to Kintyre in the south (see *athair* (*SGDS* 63)), but it extends into east Ulster. [Ó Murchú] (1996, 147) concludes:

> The geographical distribution of this dialectal feature may be taken as clear evidence that even areas isolated from the heartlands of Gaeldom, such as eastern Perthshire, continued until modern times to share with the rest in changing linguistic fashion. Until a few centuries ago, a dialect continuum, with no formidable barriers to the dissemination of language change, continued to exist.[32]

The change *cn-* > *cr-*, *gn-* > *gr-*, *mn-* > *mr-*, *tn-* > *tr-*, common throughout Scotland and Man, Ulster and Connacht, may represent another example: see O'Rahilly (1932, 22–3), who claims, based on written sources, that 'this change of *n* to *r* is undoubtedly a comparatively late one'.

Equally, however, there are clearly developments attested in one region only. In Scotland, for instance, one thinks of the phonological development of preaspiration, *-chd* > *-chg* (e.g. *ochd SGDS* 666), the development of *s* in *rt-*

---

31 Irish *petta* 'pet' may represent a similar example: see Isaac (2003, 151–2); cf. Schrijver (2000, 197). On the early date of the change **hw-* > *f-*, see McCone (1996b, 46).
32 Ó Murchú includes 'parts of south Connacht' in this 'geographical distribution'. However, the development in south Connacht may be an independent development.

and *rd*-clusters (e.g. *ceart*, *àrd* (*SGDS* 174–5, 55)), epenthetic *t* in initial *sr*-clusters (e.g. *sròn* (*SGDS* 800)), and so on. The innovative present tense marker *-ann*, while productive in Ireland and attested in high register literary texts in Scotland, is not a feature of modern vernacular Scottish Gaelic, and may never have been (Ó Buachalla 1988, 56–8 (esp. 58)). The development of Gaelic in both countries requires a historical model which allows, and accounts for, divergence in some features and convergence in others at any given period—both processes being dependent to some degree on socio-cultural and socio-political factors. It is easy to envisage an early period where divergence may have been to the fore, due to interference resulting from bi- and multilingualism, as Gaelic spread northwards and eastwards, and came into contact with different linguistic communities. On the other hand, it seems quite probable that the establishment of the Gaelic Lordship of the Isles with its Irish connections, and reliance on 'common' conservative Gaelic cultural and political institutions, may have led to a certain amount of linguistic levelling and convergence in the Western Isles, especially in higher registers of the language, and this in some cases perhaps filtering down to lower registers; cf. Gillies (1994, 145).

If we abandon the strait-jacket of Common Gaelic and the idea of a strict homogeneous culture province—and by implication a homogeneous language province—it seems perfectly reasonable to expect a certain amount of linguistic variation and divergence by the time we come to the twelfth century, when the Gaelic Notes were written. In this respect, we may note C. Breatnach's (1990a, 486) conclusion, based on the evidence of contemporary scribes of the Annals of Inisfallen, that some Munster dialectal features can be traced back to the end of the eleventh century. Indeed, it might be argued that linguistic and orthographic divergence from what is perceived as an Irish 'norm' might be all the more expected in the north-eastern 'periphery' of the Gaelic-speaking world. In fact, this is demonstrably what we find in the Gaelic Notes. Jackson claimed that the Deer scribes tended to spell more by 'ear' than by tradition.[33] There is indeed a relatively high number of what may justly be described as 'pronunciation' as opposed to traditional spellings in the Gaelic Notes. But rather than dismissing them out of hand, it seems to me that they raise a number of interesting questions, which encourage us to look afresh at the data. Could we be dealing with an established, though flexible, norm, which was once more widespread in parts of peripheral Scotland? In other words, could the Gaelic Notes reflect a 'Scottish' or Scotticised orthographic system which represented merely one end of a linguistic continuum, which, orthographically speaking, was never terribly consistent or standard? There is

---

33 By tradition, of course, he means 'Irish tradition'. Similar 'ear' or pronunciation spellings are of course to be found in Irish manuscripts, an outstanding example of which is the fourteenth-century Book of Magauran (see McKenna 1947).

also the possibility that the orthography taught in eastern 'Scottish' schools differed from that of their Irish counterparts for good reasons, among which may have been a need to represent more satisfactorily a form of language which had diverged somewhat from its Irish relation and, moreover, from the inherited literary 'Irish' language.[34] Rather than reflecting the mistakes of ignorant scribes, it is possible that the orthography of the Deer Notes reflects the practice of the Gaelic literary élite in twelfth-century north-eastern Scotland.[35] Since we do not have any comparable contemporary Gaelic texts from Scotland, it is of course difficult to assess what writing traditions prevailed in eleventh- and twelfth-century eastern Scotland. However, Dauvit Broun has made some fruitful inroads into this area, based on his studies of Gaelic personal names in Latin texts of the royal genealogy and the Scottish king list, all with demonstrable links to twelfth- and thirteenth-century sources, and perhaps traceable to important Gaelic churches in eastern Scotland (Broun 1998, 1999). We shall see below that some orthographical features of the Notes are shared with such sources. Further analysis in this area will no doubt teach us more about earlier Gaelic orthographic practices in medieval Scotland.

The important question of the function of the Gaelic Notes also needs to be referred to as it may bear some relevance to the register and style in which they were written. The intended purpose of these texts may have encouraged a form of Gaelic which was less formal, and perhaps closer to the vernacular than to an inherited literary norm. In this context, we might refer to Jackson's suggestion that the Gaelic Notes may have formed part of evidence for presentation at legal courts in eastern Scotland (1971, 94); cf. MacBain's view that 'the literature of the Book of Deer is of a thoroughly practical kind', that 'it is for business purposes, and the Gaelic of the district must have been used'; also 'the circumstances which produced the book were [...] such as favoured, nay, necessitated, native Scotch Gaelic' (1885, 141). It is conceivable that such an important function may have required a form of language and orthography which was easily intelligible to as wide an audience or readership as possible: it is worth pointing out that pronunciation (vernacular) spellings (to be discussed presently) would also be compatible with the texts having been written for the purpose of being read aloud, perhaps in a court as Jackson suggests.[36] Whether or not the Gaelic Notes were ever used in such a

<hr/>

34 Possible Scottish orthographic practices may be reflected in the frequent use of *g(g)* in the Gaelic Notes to represent voiced *g*, an eclipsed form of radical *c*; the frequent use of *c >> cc* to represent *ch* in certain positions (see Jackson 1972, 138, n. 1); cf. also the use of *-ech / -eg* instead of *-ich / -igh* in final unstressed syllables.   35 Picard (1982, 217) puts forward a similar interpretation of the (Hiberno-)Latin spellings found in the Schaffhausen manuscript copy of Adomnán's *Vita Columbae*, written by Dorbene (d. 713), bishop of Iona.   36 See Ó Maolalaigh 'On the possible functions of the accents', this volume, for a discussion of how such a function provides a possible explanation for a

practical way as suggested by Jackson, it is important to stress the importance of the recording of land-acquisition in written form in the early medieval and medieval periods (F. Kelly 1997, 411; Davies 1982), particularly in *senscriband deoda* 'ancient holy writing', i.e. sacred books, see Davies (1982, 268) and F. Kelly (1988, 204).

An open-minded approach to the Gaelic Notes which is not reliant on Jackson's theory of Common Gaelic can, as we shall see, shed new light on some of Jackson's proposed 'errors', 'slips' and 'mistakes' especially if we admit the possibility of early dialect differences.[37] See, for instance, the new interpretations of the forms **íbbidbín** (AIII2), **helaín** (CVI32), and **donnac̲h̲ac** (CVI7) which are offered below.[38]

THE GAELIC NOTES

CONTENTS

1 PRONUNCIATION SPELLINGS
   1.1 **Significance**
   1.2 **Dropping of quiescent consonants (and vowels)**
2 PHONOLOGY: VOCALIC FEATURES
   2.1 **Raising**
      2.1.1 Raising of *ó / o*: *pústa*; *dochuíd*
      2.1.2 *ae, e* for *ai*: *Caerill, Caennaig, clenni, ele*; *ie, iai* for *ia*: *blienec, ienasi, iaidnaisse*
      2.1.3 *ae* for *ai?*: *araes*
      2.1.4 Unstressed *e* for *(a)i*
   2.2 **Lowering / breaking**
      2.2.1 Lowering of *u*: *Moridac*
      2.2.2 Lowering/breaking of short *e*: *mandaidib*
      2.2.3 *Deár* ('Deer')

hitherto unexplained aspect of the Gaelic Notes, namely the numerous suprasegmental accents or strokes which are peppered throughout the Notes, but which were ignored by Jackson. **37** Cf. Greene's comment that 'it might be expected that scribes at the periphery of the [Gaelic] culture area would make some 'mistakes' which would give us a glimpse of their vernacular' (1972, 169). **38** Manuscript forms from the Notes (and occasionally other manuscript sources) are printed here in Arial font. Bold type in the Deer manuscript forms is used to represent the coverage of suprasegmental accents; where two successive accents cover contiguous segments, italic font is used in addition to bold in order to illustrate the coverage of a second accent and to avoid ambiguity: see, for example, **as***áath*le (AI6) and Ó Maolalaigh, 'On the possible functions of the accents', this volume, for further discussion. Underlining has been used to indicate the expansion of manuscript contractions. References in round brackets following Deer forms are to the texts of the Gaelic Notes in the Diplomatic Edition (this volume): capital letters refer to the Hands, small capital roman numerals to the text, and arabic numerals to the line number.

  2.3 Smoothing
      2.3.1 *toísech* or *tóisech?*
  2.4 Svarabhakti / epenthesis
      2.4.1 General
      2.4.2 *Mareb, anim*
      2.4.3 *Donnachac*
  2.5 Reduction of long unstressed vowels:
      2.5.1 General
      2.5.2 *Mormar, Cinatha*
      2.5.3 *helain* ('Ellon')

3 PHONOLOGY: CONSONANTAL FEATURES
  3.1 Dental fricatives: *th (dh)*: *ahule, bead*
  3.2 Reduction of consonant groups
  3.3 Merger
      3.3.1 Merger of lenited and unlenited *l*: *Collum*
      3.3.2 Merger of palatal and non-palatal *n*; *m?*
      3.3.3 Merger of palatal and non-palatal *rr?*: The case of *Márr* (genitive)
      3.3.4 Merger of *dh* and *gh*: *cuitid*
      3.3.5 Merger of final unstressed palatal *gh* and *ch*: *Cannech*

4 MORPHO-PHONOLOGICAL FEATURES
  4.1 Sandhi
  4.2 Eclipsis
      4.2.1 Introduction
      4.2.2 The Scottish system of 'eclipsis'
      4.2.3 The historical development of eclipsis
      4.2.4 Eclipsis: The evidence from the Gaelic Notes
      4.2.5 Accusative singular

5 MORPHOLOGY: SPECIFIC FORMS: *BENACT, SEN, SÍ*
  5.1 *ros-benact*
  5.2 *sen*
  5.3 Pronoun *sí*

1 PRONUNCIATION SPELLINGS

1.1 Significance

It has long been recognised that the Gaelic Notes of Deer contain many so-called pronunciation spellings. Windisch, quoted by MacBain (1885, 143), refers to the 'pronunciation of the time' being represented in the Notes.

MacBain himself noted that the form of Gaelic used was 'not weighted by precedent and literary forms of bygone times; it consequently adapted itself to the time and locality in which it was produced'; there was 'a modern air' about the Gaelic Notes (MacBain 1885, 142). Fraser (1942, 60) refers to 'phonetic spellings'. Those who take a more negative view of certain 'deviant' forms in the Notes tend to dismiss them as mere errors or misspellings (Fraser 1942, 59, 60; Jackson 1972: *passim*). However, for the historical linguist, such apparent 'errors' are of primary rather than secondary importance, although the existence of technical lapses with no relevance or significance for the philologist must also be acknowledged. Indeed, as we shall see, an examination of many of what Jackson describes as 'errors' or 'fantastic spellings', may in fact be explained as pronunciation spellings with phonetic significance, although in many cases this is of course difficult to prove conclusively. Furthermore, many of what can be viewed as spelling pronunciations or phonetically-based features appear to give us a glimpse of a variety or varieties of language which in some cases are similar to that which we might expect in Ireland, but which in other instances may be distinctively local, i.e. Scottish, and eastern Scottish at that. We may compare MacBain's comment that 'the departure from all Irish lines are the most important and most remarkable facts. The spelling, though it is on the whole cast in the same moulds [as Irish], has some local peculiarities' (1885, 142).

The phonetic significance of orthographical anomalies has long been recognised. Indeed, the defining characteristics of Hiberno-Latin have been successfully established by examining such anomalies in Latin sources: see, for instance, Bieler (1954), Löfstedt (1965, 86–107; 1979), Picard (1982), and for the later medieval period, P. A. Breatnach (1988). Picard (1982, 248) notes that 'so-called spelling mistakes help us to determine what kind of Latin was taught in Irish schools and what may have been its pronunciation' and furthermore that 'plain spelling mistakes' are 'the most likely to provide information about local pronunciation and spelling'. We may compare O'Rahilly's (1932, 4) use of 'the "bad" spellings of the less learned or less archaistic scribes' of Gaelic Ireland from which dialectal information could be gleaned. Skerrett (1963, 115) extracts dialect information from 'deviations of spelling' in a text from the Liber Flavus Fergusiorum manuscript; cf. Skerrett (1966a, 163), who, in reference to another text from the same manuscript also containing dialect features, comments that it is 'rather carelessly written' and contains 'a number of mistakes and omissions'. Cf. Skerrett (1966b, 189, 202–4), Ó hInnse (1947, 214–17); Ó Súilleabháin (1976, 203–6); Ó Laoghaire (1990, 491–4); C. Breatnach (2001). R.L. Thomson (1977, 129) notes the fundamental importance and relevance of 'departures from tradition and normality' in Gaelic texts:

As with the elucidation of the history of the development of English
from Middle to early Modern, where there is little in orthographic
change to mirror the widespread phonetic changes we believe took
place, the work is one of detection and the picking up of hints rather
than simply observation, and instead of a balanced description of the
usage of a particular text *it is only what is a departure from tradition and
normality, however rare and untypical it may seem in its context, that is of
interest or value to this enquiry.* [italics mine]

Jackson (1972, 141) lists as 'fairly certain errors' the following forms:

> **braíth** (A16), choír (A1118), Moridac (A112), ardmandaidib (Cv122–23),
> blienec (A117), **éré** (A110), derad (C1126), Buchan (Cv133), morcúnn
> (A112) and morcunt (A118), colum (A1110, 13), colou̱m (A1111), thabárt
> (A1117), madchór (Bv4), **cá**ennaig (Bv16–17), íenasi (Bv10),
> iaidnaisse (Cv133), tu̱rbrud (Ev1112), culeón (A110), máledo̱mni
> (D1117), rosbenact (A116), hule (A1117), collum (A115, 18), **iar** (A17).

As 'possible' mistakes he notes **má**rr (D1118) and cannech (D1111). Many of
these and other forms are discussed in what follows.

1.2 Dropping of quiescent consonants (and vowels)

Evidence for pronunciation spellings frequently includes instances of the dropping of quiescent or redundant consonants and vowels. In some cases such
spelling forms can be viewed as simplifications of the inherited orthographic
system. For instance, the grapheme *f* is never written in lenition environments
in the Gaelic Notes: instead the silent *fh* is dropped:[39] roalseg < *rofhalseg*
(A12), malechí < *malfhechi* (Bv7–8), innaíenasi < *innafhienasi* (Bv10),
malæchín < *malfhæchin* (Cv132), dathótla < *dathfhótla* (Ev1110–11).[40] The

39 This is a frequent feature of the Annals of Inisfallen: see C. Breatnach (1990a, 426).
The fourteenth-century Magauran manuscript has a good deal of phonetic spellings
similar in nature, e.g. *leg* (*fhleidh* 335), *thearg* (*th'fhearg* 1260), *dhilidh* (*dh'fhilidh* 2585), *sann
idh* (*san fhiodh* 3928), *arta* (*fhearta* 4277); cf. *do namh* (*do shnámh* 2097). Other
pronunciation spellings from this source include: *g-* for traditional *gc-*: *gain* (*gcaoin* 1568), *is
a griaidh* (*isan gcriaidh* 1777), *ar gul* (*ar gcúl* 4279); *m-* for *mb-*: *mind* (*mbinn* 4286); *n-* for *nd-*
: *gu neachaidh* (*go ndeachaidh* 4215); note also *taibsi* (*taidhbhse* 796); *ubhdar* (*ughdar* 3368);
inin (*inghin* 3509); *abhran* (3663, 3664, 3667, 3670, 3681); *ceiri* (*ceithre* p. 437), etc.
References to Magauran forms are to line numbers in McKenna (1947) unless otherwise
stated. Note also the dropping of *fh* in *Casiaclaig* (for *Casfhiaclaig*) in the early thirteenth-
century Poppleton Manuscript text of the royal genealogy of the kings of Scots, whose
archetype is datable to the reign of David I (1124–53) (Broun 1999, 179, l. 67).   **40** The
genitive mec hídid (Bv2) (Jackson 1972, 70) with unidentified nominative may perhaps
represent another example (representing a possible *mec [f]hídid) with initial superfluous
h as in huli and helaín (Cv133). (For a recent discussion of word-initial *h-* in the older
language, see Schrijver 1997.) Cf. *'Fidaid?'* in W.J. Watson (1926, 107). On the use of *h* for

eleventh-century Gaelic marginalia in Codex Palatino-Vaticanus 830 provides similar examples: *huil* for *fhuil*, *ichit* for *fhichit*, *trener* for *trénfher* (Ó Cuív 1990, 49). The spelling **óhúnń** for *óshúnń* (AII9) may be another instance where the minimum is written in order to represent the required sound(s), i.e. *h* for *sh*, pronounced /h/.[41] We may compare also *f* for *ph* in **frís** < *phrís* (BV24); on the consistent use of *f* for Φ and *ph*, mostly in words of Greek origin, in Dorbéne's copy of *Vita Columbae*, see Picard (1982, 240). We may also note here *u* for lenited *bh* in **uéthé** (AII21), which derives from Latin usage: see Picard (1982, 238–39) for discussion and further references. The use of *u* in the Deer examples just quoted reminds us that the orthography of the Notes, like early Gaelic orthography in general, was open to influence from Latin orthography: for some possible instances, see below. On the elision of vowels, note **áńím** (AII9) < *a áńím*; **gillendrias** (EVII13) < *gille andrias* (cf. Ó Cuív 1972, 343); **go nic abbordobóir** (AI2–3) for *go nice*; cf. also **arhardchellaib** (CVI25–26) < *ar a hardchellaib*.

2 PHONOLOGY: VOCALIC FEATURES

2.1 Raising

2.1.1 Raising of *ó* / *o*: *pústa*; *dochuíd*

A number of other spellings, which Jackson (1972, 141) regarded as almost certainly errors can be interpreted as pronunciation spellings, perhaps even indicative of dialect forms. Before we discuss some of these, we may note the form **phústa** (CVI6) for 'normal' *pósta*, where Jackson's commentary is illustrative of his general cautious reluctance to admit dialectisms in the Notes. Jackson notes that the root is *pùs-* in some modern Scottish Gaelic dialects[42] and *poos-* in Manx, and comments that 'the development is likely to be quite old'. Despite such compelling evidence for an almost certain dialectism in the Notes, Jackson concludes that this 'may well be genuine

---

fh by an Anglo-Norman hand in the Annals of Inisfallen, see *heil* (for *fhéil*), *hod* (for *fhod*) (Mac Airt 374, 1280.2; 378, 1281.7); I am grateful to Caoimhín Breatnach for these references. It is perhaps possible that **hídid** represents [F]*híd*[*a*]*ig*, a genitive of *Fidach*, with confusion of final slender *d*[*h*] and *g*[*h*]; for *Fidach*, see O'Brien (1962, 149a34, 129a3, etc.); cf. discussion of **cuidíd** (AII18) below at 3.3.4.   **41** L. Breatnach (1994, 229) notes some examples from Middle Gaelic sources. Cf. *do hamrud* (1204 for *do shamrud*) and *o hen* (1206 for *o shen*) from the Annals of Inisfallen (C. Breatnach 1990a, 432). Cf. *do hil* for *do shíl* (Ó Cuív 1990, 49).   **42** Jackson cites no evidence from modern Scottish Gaelic dialects. However, Robertson (1907a, 232) notes *pùs* for the North of Sutherland in the Reay Country. Dwelly also notes the variants *pùs*, *pùsadh*, *pùsda* (*Dwelly* s.v.). The form *ri mhnaoi-phùisde* (MS ri **vreyh fūist**) occurs in the late seventeenth-century Fernaig manuscript (Mac Phàrlain [1923], 264, 265, §5d).

here' (1972, 76). He does not refer to the occasional attestation of *pūsta* in Irish annals, e.g. *do ferand phūsta* (*Annals of Connacht* s.a. 1239.7); *a sētid pūsta* (*Annals of Connacht* s.a.1314.6): see Ó Cuív (1972, 344) and *DIL* s.v. *pósad*. *Pós* has been posited as a loan from Latin *spons-* (MacBain 1896 s.v. *pòs*) or from Romance (Pedersen 1909, 206; *DIL* s.v. *pósaid*; *LEIA* s.v. *pósad*). O'Rahilly's (1932, 138, n. 1) suggestion that *ú* for *ó* is due to Old Norse *púsa* is rejected by Jackson (1972, 76).[43]

If Moridac (AII2) is a hypercorrection as tentatively suggested earlier, it may also be indicative of raising following a labial consonant.[44] The past tense of the verb *téit* ('goes'), dochuíd (AII1), may be another instance of raising, this time before historical hiatus (cf. Old Gaelic *do-coïd*).[45]

2.1.2 *ae, e* for *ai: Caerill, Caennaig, clenni, ele; ie, iai for ia: blienec, ienasi, iaidnaisse*

In stressed syllables *ae* is written on two occasions before palatal(ised) consonants where we might expect *ai*: caerill (AII5) and cáennaig (BV16–17) for expected *Cairill* and *Cainnig* respectively.[46] Jackson notes somewhat cautiously that this may represent 'a genuine phonetic development', whereby original *a* was raised 'in circumstances which are not perfectly clear'.[47] Despite citing evidence that this raising has resulted in *e*-like vowels in modern Gaelic dialects nearest to Buchan,[48] Jackson concludes that 'in view of its entirely isolated character, little stress should be laid on it' (1972, 128). Jackson's conclusion here may be too cautious, and as we shall see there is further corroborative evidence for the raising of *a* before palatal(ised) consonants in the Notes. There can be little doubt that the spelling clenni

---

43 Forms with *ú* may represent raised *ó*, perhaps due to the preceding labial. On the other hand, it is possible that perseveratory nasal spread from *bean* and *fearann* in collocations such as *bean phósta*, *fearann phósta* may have led to the nasalisation of *ó* in *phósta*, which in turn may have led to the raising of *ó* to *ú*. It is worth noting that lenited *phósta* contains one of the most conducive environments (i.e. high airflow voiceless fricatives) for the retention and / or development of nasalisation: see Ó Maolalaigh (2003a). However, against this, I have not noted any instances of nasalised vowels in reflexes of *pós-* in the modern dialects; similarly, instances of nasal spread from noun to following adjective are not at all common in modern Gaelic dialects.   **44** Jackson (1972, 69) deems it unlikely that *ú* in púir (DIV1) represents an instance of raised *ó*.   **45** It is perhaps possible that it reflects a hypercorrection or mixed form based on the Middle Gaelic form *do-chúaidh*. On the raising of stressed *o* in hiatus words, compare Scottish Gaelic *todhar* (with ahistorical *-dh-*) 'manure' with Irish *tuar*, and Scottish Gaelic *omhan* / *othan* 'froth' (with ahistorical *-mh-* and *-th-*) with Irish *uan*; cf. MacBain (1896, 268 s.v. *omhan*), Greene (1976, 29), Uhlich (1995, 12, 41).   **46** Cf. *GOI* 56 §86.1(b). If such instances do not represent the raising of //a//, then the question arises whether or not *ae* for *ai* might have been a northern (perhaps even Scottish) scribal practice.   **47** But see now Ó Maolalaigh (1997, 151–63, 202–15, 231–7), where it is illustrated that such raising of //a// is particularly common in the environment k __ r'. That it also occurred in the environment k __ N' is witnessed by modern realisations of the proper name *Coinneach* (< *Cainnech*).   **48** See Jackson (1952, 90), but note *cloinn* with [o] in Braemar (*SGDS* 197, point 189).

(CVI9) for *cla[i]nni* signalled a raised pronunciation of the stressed vowel;[49] cf. ele (AI7) < *aile* 'other'. Similar instances can be quoted from non-Gaelic sources, which may be indicative of the raising of original *a* in Gaelic speech, e.g. the texts of the royal genealogy of the kings of Scots, the archetypes of which can be traced to the reign of David I (1124–53). The Poppleton Manuscript text, though written in York *c.*1360, can be traced to a compilation which was originally compiled 1202x14, and probably based on a twelfth-century Gaelic genealogy of David I. We may note *Elela* (for *Ailella*, ll. 46, 58, 67) (Broun 1999, 174–180); similarly, the Poppleton text of the 'Pictish Chronicle' has *Elig* for *Ailig* (Hudson 1988, 145). Ralph of Diss' text, begun in 1188, and whose archetype also probably belongs to 1124x53, has the following forms: *Elpini* (a Latinised form for *Ailpini*), *Ellela* (for *Ailella* twice), *Elela* (for *Ailella*) (Broun 1999, 184–86). Forms with *ae* for *ai* are also found in the *Annals of Inisfallen* from the early twelfth century onwards,[50] e.g. *Aeilich* (1114 *Ailich*), *Aelig* (1129 *Ailig*), *Aergiallaib* (1125 *Airgiallaib*), *Aelbi* (1173 *Ailbi*). That such spellings had phonetic significance and indicated raising of original *a* would seem to be supported by forms with *e* for *ai*, e.g. *Elbi* (1163 *Ailbi*), *la hErgillaib* (1166 *la hAirgillaib*), *heli* (1191 *haili*) (C. Breatnach 1990a, 420). Raising of *a* to *e* before palatalised *l* accounts neatly for the place-name Rathelpie (NO500165), now a suburb of St Andrews, which derives from *Ráth Ailpín* (Watson 1926, 237; Taylor 1995, 419). Raising in this name is attested from the late twelfth century: Rathelpin (1173x78 *St A Lib* 141); Rathelpin (1183 *St A Lib* 58); Rathelpyn (1290 *St A Lib* 378); Rahelpy (1513 *RMS* ii, no. 3812);[51] on the variation between final *-ie*, *-y*, *-in*, *-yn*, see Ó Maolalaigh (1998, 30–38). Brian Ó Cuív (1990, 49) notes instances of *ae* for expected *ai* in the eleventh-century marginalia in Codex Palatino-Vaticanus 830, both in stressed (*glaen* for *glain*, *claenn* for *clainn*, *claenne* for *clainne*) and unstressed positions (*alaenn* for *álainn*, *Ádaem* for *Ádaim*, *coicaet* for *coícait*, *sechtmogaet* for *sechtmogait*, *Patráec* for *Pátraic*).[52] L. Breatnach (1994, 232) adds some examples form other sources.

Further supportive evidence for this raising in stressed syllables in the Notes is found in the spelling *ie* for the diphthong *ia* in the following two examples, the diphthong being followed by a nasal consonant in each case: blienec (AI17), íenasi (BVI0). Such raising before *n* might explain *iai* for *ia* in iaidnaisse (CVI33), which may be a hypercorrection, whereby *ai* in the

---

[49] However, it is perhaps possible that clenni may be a mistake for **claenni*. [50] All examples quoted from the Annals of Inisfallen are by contemporary hands. [51] I am grateful to Simon Taylor for references to these early forms. For other names containing *Ailpín*, see Watson (1926, 237, 409). It is possible that instances of *e* in non-Gaelic sources for underlying Gaelic *ai*, may represent the perception by non-Gaelic speakers of a Gaelic front *a*-vowel. [52] Ó Cuív (1990, 49) also refers to the similar forms *Leogaere*, *Lugaed* and (*Aed*) *Alaeinn* in the Latin Chronicle itself. Ó Cuív implies that *e* in the digraph *ae* functioned as a 'palatalization marker'.

stressed syllable is used to represent an *e*-like vowel. Here we might also
compare gillendrias (EVIII3), which Jackson edits as *Gille-'ndrias* (1972, 32).
However, if we read *Gill'-Endrias*, as Ó Cuív (1972, 343) suggests, we would
have yet another instance from the Notes of the raising of *a* to *e* before
palatals.

We may also note the frequent use of *ae* in the Annals of Ulster,
particularly in unstresssed syllables containing oblique forms of the
diminutive suffix *-án*, e.g. *Coelaen* (*Coeláin*), *Ronaen* (*Rónáin*), *Dubaen* (*Dubáin*),
Tommaen (*Tommáin*); cf. *Mac Aedhaein* (*Aedáin*). Instances in stressed syllables
containing original short *a* include *Maeni* (*Maini*), *Aerdd Machae* (*Aird
Machae*), *Laegen* (*Laighen*), *Aenmire* (*Ainmire*). Ó Máille (1910, 21–2) explains
these in purely orthographic terms and suggests that they may be mistakes.
They may, for instance, reflect the variation between *ae* and *e* in Latin, which
is typical of Hiberno-Latin: see Picard (1982, 231–330) for discussion and
references. An alternative explanation would be to see them as phonetic
spellings indicating raised vowels in the range of [ɛ:] or [ɛ]. (We may compare
Bieler's (1963, 30) suggestion that 'the frequent substitution of *ae* for *e* [in the
Irish Latin Penitentials] seems to indicate an open pronunciation of Latin *e*'.)
In support of this interpretation we may note the use of *ae* for expected *é* and
e, e.g. *Libraen* (*Librén*), *mac Acithaen* (*Acithé(i)n?*), *Laithgnaen* (*Laithgné(i)n?*);
indraedh (*indred*), *Bairdaeni* (*Bairdene?*) (Ó Máille 1910, 22, 24, 29). The
spellings *uae*, *ue* for expected *uai* may also indicate the raising of the final part
of the *ua*-diphthong before a palatal consonant (i.e. [uɛ]), e.g. *Chuaer*, *Chuer*
(*Chuair*), *Cluaen*, *Cluen* (*Cluain*) (Ó Máille 1910, 29); cf. *huaere* (*GOI* 56
86.1(b)).[53] However, the use of *oe* for *oi* in genitive forms of the adjective *mór*,
e.g. *moer* (Ó Máille 1910, 22), might indicate that the use of *e* in place of *i* may
have been purely orthographic. On the other hand, it could conceivably
represent a raised form of *á* in the variant form *már*, i.e. [mʷɛ:r]. We conclude
that there is some supportive evidence for the claim that *ae* in the Notes may
have signalled a vowel raised from the low position of *a*, and also that there is
some evidence to suggest that *e* may have functioned as an alternative spelling
convention for *i* following certain vowels, e.g. *á*, *a*, *ua*, and to a lesser extent, *ó*.

Ó Baoill (1988, 123) notes the form amaelanach ōg from the Scottish
scribe of a manuscript (NLS MS Adv. 72.1.1), written in Ireland in the year
1467 by Dubhghall Albanach mac mhic Cathail, whom Ó Baoill identifies as a
MacMhuirich (1988, 123–24); cf. also MacGregor (2000, 135–36). Ó Baoill
interprets this form as *am ſhoghlanach* (lit. 'in my learner, student'),
suggesting that *ae* represents a long centralised monophthongal vowel,
common in reflexes of the word *foghlaim* in Scottish Gaelic. This interpretation is problematic in that the form **foghlanach* is otherwise unattested.
Furthermore, it is important to note that lengthening to *ò* in reflexes of

---

53 Cf. *Guaere* for *Guaire* cited by L. Breatnach (1994, 232).

foghlaim is characteristic of a good deal of south-western Scottish Gaelic dialects, including Arran, Kintyre, Jura, Colonsay, Cowal, Mid Argyll, Mull, Tiree, Coll, etc.: see *SGDS* 437. If Dubhghall were a native of one of these southern dialects, *fòghlaim* with back round vowel may have been his vernacular form, thus arguing against **foghlanach*. I would suggest as a preferable interpretation of the manuscript form a reflex of the word *aileamhnach*, which in modern Scottish Gaelic is spelled as *oileanach*—the generic word for 'student'—i.e. for amaelanach we might read *am aelanach* (< **am aileamhnach*).[54] This reading has the obvious advantage of referring to a well-attested word, and moreover, it makes perfect sense in the context in which it appears. If correct it represents an instance of the raising of original *a* to a mid vowel (probably in the range of [e] to [ɤ]) which contrasts with original *o*.[55] The use of *ae* to represent this raised vowel can be compared with similar examples from the Book of Deer. The use of the digraph *ae* to represent varieties of raised original *a* can be seen to be a useful orthographic device, signalling simultaneously the raised vowel, and the non-palatal and palatal character of the preceding and following consonants respectively.

2.1.3 *ae* for ai?: *araes*

The phrase araes (Cv26) occurs appended to Text Bv, by Hand C (according to Jackson 1972, 13–14). Its fuller context is as follows: issaeri othesseach cubráth₇abennacht arcachhén chomallfas araes cubrath₇amallact arcachén ticfa ris (Cv25–26), which is edited and translated by Jackson as follows: *i ssaeri ó thésseach cu bráth; ₇ a bennacht ar cach hén chomallfas ar a és cu bráth, ₇ a mallacht ar cach én ticfa ris* ('free of toísech till Doomsday; and his curse on everyone who shall come against it'), (1972, 32, 35). The phrase *a bennacht ar cach hén chomhallfas ar a és cu bráth* is not translated by Jackson, his eye no doubt having jumped accidentally from the first *cu bráth* to the second, thus omitting the intervening phrase; nor is it discussed in the notes following his edition. However, a glossary entry s.v. *éis* (1972, 156) translates *ar a és* as 'after him, afterwards', thus establishing Jackson's interpretation of the phrase as containing the word *éis* 'trace, track' (*DIL* s.v.). Following Jackson's interpretation of *ar a és*, the phrase may be translated as follows: 'and his blessing on everyone who shall comply with it after him / afterwards'. Given, however, the possibility of *e* being used in place of *i*, four other possible interpretations of araes emerge. These are (A) *ar ais* with *ae*

---

54 Alternatively, it might be suggested that the MS form represents **maelánach*, meaning something like 'adherent, follower', based on *mael* (see *DIL* s.v.). However, such a form is not otherwise attested.   **55** The Scottish Gaelic word *oileanach* (with raising of original //a// to /ɤ/ rather than /ɔ/; cf. *coire* < *caire*, *coileach* < *caileach*, *goirid* < *gairid*, etc.; see Ó Maolalaigh 1997, 212–16) represents a substantival use of the original adjective *aileamhnach* (see *DIL* s.v. *ailemnach*).

for *ai*; (B) *ar* [*a*] *ais* with *ae* for *ai* and *a* elided, (C) *ar a ais* with *e* for *ai*; (D) *ar áis*. The first three options might be translated adverbially as 'afterwards' or more vaguely as 'similarly, in the same fashion'.[56] Any of options A–C might argue for an *e*-like pronunciation of the stressed vowel, similar to those instances discussed above. The fourth option (D) would involve the use of *e* for *i* following a long vowel, interpreting the phrase as *ar áis* 'willingly' (see *DIL* s.v. *áis*, l. 85). This, however, seems unlikely.

2.1.4 Unstressed *e* for (*a*)*i*

Hand A often writes *e* in unstressed syllables where we might expect *i* or *ai* (which he also uses).[57] Examples of *e* for *i* between palatal(ised) consonants include: roalseg (A12), doráten (A17), imbrether (A116), toíség (A116), inmulenn (A117), cannech (DIII1, genitive); we may also note proclitic *e* for *i* in essé (A14) for *issé*; cf. *es* for *is* (Ó Cuív 1990, 49).[58] Examples of *e* for *ai* between non-palatal(ised) and palatal(ised) consonants include: cósgreg (A11), dabég (AIII2).[59] Fraser (1942, 60), normally dismissive of deviant forms, states that 'the frequent substitution of *e* for *a* before "slender" consonants [...] may have more significance', although he does not elucidate any further. The fact that this comment appears in a section which mentions 'phonetic spellings' would suggest that he was willing to entertain the possibility that *e* in unstressed syllables in the likes of dabég (AIII2) may have indicated a phonetic spelling rather than being a purely orthographic device without phonetic significance. In other words, such instances may indicate that these unstressed vowels could have been realised as mid vowels in the region of [e] or [ɛ]. As it happens, we have corroborative evidence for similar spellings from other sources. The text of the eleventh-century Gaelic marginalia in Codex Palatino-Vaticanus 830 provides a number of examples: *obenn* for *oíbinn*, *manestrech* for *manistrech*, *coittcenn* for *coitchinn*, *ingen* for *ingin*, *munter* for *muntir*, *Déseb* for *Désib*, *chrédem* for *chrédim*, *Érenn* for *Érinn* (Ó Cuív 1990, 49). The text of the royal genealogy of the kings of Scots contained in the early thirteenth-century Poppleton Manuscript has two instances of unstressed *ei* for expected *ai*: *Tollgreich* (for *Tollgraich*) and *Bollgreich* (for *Bollgraich*) (Broun 1999, 179), although *ai* also occurs, e.g. *Ruamnaich, Feradaig, Casiaclaig, Buadaig, Tigernaig* (Broun 1999, 177–80).[60] Ralph of Diss's late twelfth-century text has the following forms: *Conere*

---

56 On the elision of the possessive in the second option, see [a]áńím (AI19) and ar[a]hardchellaib (CVI 25–26) referred to earlier.   **57** We may compare the occasional use of *ae* and *e* for *ai* in stressed syllables, discussed above.   **58** For the use of *i*, note thóisíg (AIII8).   **59** Cf. also dorodloeg (A18). Instances with (*a*)*i* include: rothidńaíg (A14), ingathraíg (A15), incathŕaig (A16); cóbrig (DIII2), petir (DIII3, 9), etc. See Jackson (1972, 132).   **60** It may be significant, as we shall see later, that these forms occur only before the palatal velar fricative in this source.

(twice for *Conaire*), *Faleg* (corresponding to *Fallaig* in Poppleton); cf. also *Ewein* (for *Eoghain*) (Broun 1999, 185–6). We may also compare the occasional use of *ei* for *i* and *ae* for *ai* in the unstressed position from the Annals of Inisfallen, e.g. *Murcherteig* (1200 for *Murchertig*), *Fathleinn* (1204 for *Fathlinn*), *Faitleinn* (1208 for *Faitlinn*), *Ciarraegi* (1128 for *Ciarraigi*) (C. Breatnach 1990a, 420).

Such spellings may have phonetic significance, perhaps representing the existence of clear *e*-quality vowels (rather than [I] or an obscure [ə]) in unstressed syllables following (or preceding) palatal(ised) consonants. We might compare the use of *ea* in thesseach (Cv25), which may be indicative of a clear unstresed vowel. Such a feature would provide a satisfactory explanation for the unstressed -*ai*- in cáennaig (Bv16–17), which, rather than being 'a slip' as Jackson suggested (1972, 133), may in fact be a hypercorrection for an *e*-like realisation.[61] Similarly, *saín* in the phrase ingathraíg saín (A15)—where broad *s* seems unusual following the palatal *gh*—may represent a hypercorrection for *sen*, which is the usual form for Hand A (see further below). For further corroborative evidence for clear vowels in unstressed position, see discussion of accents in Ó Maolalaigh 'On the possible functions of the accents', this volume.[62] On the other hand, the variant use of *e* for *i* in such instances may be purely orthographic, reflecting the merger of short unstressed vowels. Note *i* for *e* in Moridac (A112) for *Muredac*. We may note the occasional use of *i* for *e* in Middle Gaelic sources, e.g. *taitnimach* for expected *taitnemach*, *claidib* for expected *claideb*, etc.), (L. Breatnach 1994, 229).[63]

2.2 Lowering / breaking

2.2.1 Lowering of *u*: *Moridac*

Hand A also writes Moridac (A112)—with *o* rather than *u* in the stressed syllable, and *i* rather than *e* in the first unstressed syllable—for expected *Muredach* (cf. muredig Dᴵᴵᴵ10). Since this is unlikely to be an archaic spelling (with archaic *o* and *i*), it is possible that we are dealing with a variant

61 With this compare also helaín (Cv133)—perhaps for underlying [elɛ(:)n(´)]—discussed below (2.5.3). A similar instance can be quoted from the Annals of Inisfallen, where the same scribe writes *Aelaig* (1127) and *Aelig* (1129), (C. Breatnach 1990a, 420). However, this same scribe uses *ai* hypercorrectly for *e* in the second (unstressed) syllable of *Mairaithac* (1123), (C. Breatnach 1990a, 419). 62 That clear *e*-like vowels occur frequently in the unstressed position for the more usual -(*a*)*igh* / -(*a*)*ich* may bear relevance for the peculiarly Scottish development of these syllables (i.e. -*igh* → -*ich*), the significance of which I hope to discuss elsewhere. 63 Latin influence may be an additional factor in the Deer examples, and also perhaps in Moridac (A112) for *Muredac*. Forms with *e* for *i* are found in continental Latin sources, which may have directly and indirectly influenced Hiberno-Latin orthography, although the latter may also have been influenced by the

pronunciation here with lowering of *u* to *o*. The phenomenon of *r*-lowering is found in a variety of languages, including English and Latin sources (Picard 1982, 221; Hickey 1986, 217; P. A. Breatnach 1988, 63), and is of course well-attested in Gaelic dialects (Hickey 1986, 217; Ó Maolalaigh 1997, 454 *et passim*). Original *u* is lowered to *o* in the name *Murchadh* in some Scottish Gaelic dialects: see *SGDS* 641; Gunn (1890, 36); Robertson (1907b, 106).[64] Alternatively, the form may be hypercorrect and may imply the usual raising of //o// either following a nasal //m// and / or preceding a palatalised //rʹ//. We may compare the use of *o* for *u* by one of the early scribes of the Annals of Inisfallen in the name *Morchertach* for *Murchertach* (three times 1101, 1102) (C. Breatnach 1990a, 421). We may also compare *Moriuht*, the apparently Irish name of the protagonist of Warner of Rouen's early eleventh-century Norman-Latin satire dedicated to Archbishop Robert of Rouen; the name may be based on Gaelic *Muireadhach* or *Muircheartach*, possibly even *Murchadh*.[65]

2.2.2 Lowering / breaking of short *e*: *mandaidib*

As Jackson notes short stressed original *e* before non-palatals is consistently written as *e*, never as *ea* in the Notes (1972, 129). However, mandaidib (CVI22–23) for expected *mendaidib* (see *DIL* s.v. *mennat*) may be an exception. Jackson argues that mandaidib 'is hardly to be taken as an instance of breaking [i.e. *e* > *ea*]' and concludes that 'it is more likely due to scribal carelessness, perhaps under the influence of the flanking *a*'s' (1972, 129). Jackson's reasons for rejecting this example are 'the lateness (and, in Scotland, the incompleteness) of the development [i.e. *e* > *ea*], and the fact that this is unique in Deer' (ibid.). While the conclusion may be the right one, the reasons given in support of this conclusion may be questioned. It is assumed that the development in question is a late one in Irish and probably later in Scottish Gaelic because of the 'incompleteness' of the development in Scotland. Referring to O'Rahilly (1930, 162), Jackson notes that in Irish *e* had 'broken' 'already to some degree by the early thirteenth century'—the suggestion being that it cannot have been much earlier. However, the development may have occurred much earlier in certain phonological environments.

---

phonology of vernacular Gaelic (see Picard 1982, 223–8; P.A. Breatnach 1988, 63–4). 64 We may note the Braemar form *cuiridh* [cɔr] (*SGDS* 278, point 189). This future form could, however, be based on a verbal noun form *cor*. Note also the lowering to *o* before the lateral sonorant in *ullamh* in Braemar Gaelic also (*SGDS* 891, point 189). 65 For an edition and discussion of the poem, see McDonough (1995). On the name *Moriuht*, see Lapidge and Sharp (1985, 195) and McDonough (1995, 121–2). I am grateful to Thomas Owen Clancy for directing my attention to McDonough's edition. Fluctuation between *o* and *u*, which is typical of Hiberno-Latin, is a possible factor here; on this fluctuation, see Löfstedt (1965, 99–102; 1979, 167), Picard (1982, 220–3), P.A. Breatnach (1988, 62–3).

There is one apparent instance in the ninth-century Milan Glosses: *con-ru·sleachta* (Ml. 53d11; see *GOI* 57), and a small handful in the late twelfth-century Book of Leinster: *ro chrean* (*LL* 4368), *co mear* (*LL* 4370), *ba-cear* (*LL* 10898) (L. Breatnach 1994, 230).[66] In considering these materials and the development under consideration here, we should be mindful of the possibility of 'time-lag between linguistic innovations and their first attestation' in our sources (Ó Buachalla 1982, 425). Moreover, it is dangerous in the Scottish context especially to draw firm conclusions in the absence of comparable contemporary source materials.

The 'incompleteness' (Jackson 1972, 129) of the development in Scottish Gaelic refers to the fact that the phonological environments in which the change has occurred are quite restricted in comparison with Irish, where the change is practically universal.[67] However, it does not follow that the development in Scottish Gaelic is necessarily any later. Lowering of original *e*, or 'breaking' as Jackson refers to it, is mostly restricted in Scottish Gaelic to the position immediately preceding the original 'broad' tense sonorants *nn*, *ll*, *rr*, the lenited lateral *l* (which has in most dialects merged with *ll*) and the velar fricative *ch*. As it happens a following broad *nn* is a very conducive environment for the lowering of *e*.[68] This fact alone bestows a certain significance on the Deer example mandaidib (Cv122–23) for expected *mendaidib*, which, given the environment of *nd* (for *nn*), increases its chances of being a *bona fide* example of the lowering of *e* to *a* (possibly [ᵉa]). There are difficulties in accepting the spelling at face value since a lowered *e* following a labial might be expected to leave some trace, e.g. a palatal glide /j/. However, mandaidib may represent a hypercorrect spelling of expected *mendaidib*, with implied raising of *a* to *e* in the nasal environment: cf. Moridac (A112), discussed above. If so, the spelling with initial *ma-* rather than *me-* might be taken as evidence for the phonological non-palatalisation of labials in an earlier stage of Scottish Gaelic.[69]

Jackson's rejection of this example due to its uniqueness in the Gaelic Notes is misleading because his statement is not accompanied by a description

66 Carney (1964: xxxii, 159) cites some metrical evidence for the development.   67 The main exceptions being the adjective *beag* and certain forms of the verb 'to be', e.g. *bheadh*, *bheas*. The change is less universal in Ulster dialects (and perhaps even reversed in some instances where original //e// may have been lowered to /a/ and raised again to /e/; see Ó Dochartaigh 1987a, 78).   68 See Ó Maolalaigh (1997, 282–4). Although in certain western dialects a preceding labial can apparently block the development (Ó Maolalaigh 1997, 282 nn. 17, 18). Cf. *ceannach* /a/ but *feannag* /ɛ/ for the dialects of the Outer Hebrides, and *ceannach* /a/ but *feannadh* /ɛ/ for certain Skye dialects (Ó Maolalaigh 1997, 554–6). This constraint does not appear to operate in eastern dialects (although further research is needed to test this), e.g. *beann* /bjan:/, *feannag* /fjanag/ in East Perthshire dialects (Ó Murchú 1989a s.v. *beann*, *fionnag*).   69 We have cast some doubt on the use of *Col(u)im* in the Notes as evidence for the merger of palatal and non-palatal labials in earlier forms of Scottish Gaelic; see section 3.3.1 below.

of the phonological facts relevant to the development *e* > *ea*. There are twenty-two instances in the Gaelic Notes of original (stressed) *e* occurring before non-palatal consonants.[70] These occur before the following consonantal segments with frequencies given in brackets:[71] *r* (4), *d*[*h*] (3), *d* (MS *t*) (3), *s* (3), *g* (MS *c*) (2), *n* (1), *ll* (1), *nn* (3),[72] *rn* (1), *ch* (MS *c* before *t*) (2). Lowering of *e* in Scottish Gaelic does not usually occur in the majority of Scottish Gaelic dialects before *dh*, *d*, *s*, *r*, *g*, *n*—accounting for 68% (15/22) of the Deer examples containing stressed *e* before non-palatals. Lowering does, however, occur before *ll*, *nn*, *rn*, *ch*. The Deer examples of *e* occurring before these segments accounts for only 27% (6/22) of our examples. In other words, we could only reasonably expect the development to occur in six (as opposed to twenty-two) of the Deer examples. There is a considerable difference in referring to a single instance as 'unique' when it is considered as a single example out of a total number of six potential instances as opposed to twenty-two.

2.2.3 *Deár* ('Deer')

In the context of possible pronunciation spellings, mention should be made of the two instances of *ea* for apparently original long *é* in the stressed position, occurring before non-palatalised *r* in the Gaelic word for 'Deer' itself and in the noun *déara* 'tears': **deara** (A118), **deár** (A119); with these, contrast **dér** in the Latin text (EVII2).[73] Given that Hand A wrote *a* on both occasions it might be argued that some type of vocalic segment was audible to him following the *e* and preceding the *r*.[74] Jackson interprets *ea* in these two

---

70 These are: bec (A110), edba**írt** (A113), ernacde (A114), benact (A116), snecte (A114), edbarta (A116, 25), bennact (A1127), petir (DIII3, 9), **écl**asi (DIII2), **éscob** (DIII5), escob (DIII6), **néct**an (DIII6), fer (DIII10), feradac (DIV2), nesu (BV24), ben (CV15), benna**cht** (CV25), chellaib (CV125–26), petair (CV132), ferdomnac (EVIII3).   **71** Using modern spelling for the consonant segments for clarity. Note that multiple occurrences of individual words are counted individually.   **72** Including benact (A116) here.   **73** The Notes offer one further certain instance of original *é* before a non-palatal: **dénd**aes (A111). In Text 1 iar**néré** (A110)—if for *iarnéra* (Jackson 1972, 131)—may be another example. Similarly, if **éte** (DIII1) represents **éta* this would provide a further example but these two examples are uncertain.   **74** The *i*-glide, which is relatively uncommon in the Gaelic Notes (Jackson 1972, 127), appears to occur mostly before *th* (5) >> *t* = *d* (4) >> *nn* (2), presumably the environments where the glide was most audible. (On the insertion of *i*-glides before consonantal codas in stressed syllables in Old Gaelic, Thurneysen notes that 'it must have been quite audible, since it is rarely omitted in writing', although it is less common in stressed syllables when the following consonant represents the onset of the second syllable (*GOI* 55–7)). It may be no coincidence that the consonants involved form a natural class in that they may all be classified broadly as front consonantal. The frequent occurrence of the *i*-glide with segments from this 'front' class would seem to support a phonetic explanation for its occurrence. (The occurrence of *i* in forms of *toísech*, to be discussed below (2.3.1), are not included here since it is not certain whether the *i* is part of an *i*-gliding diphthong or a true on-glide, although it should be noted that palatalised *s* also

instances as containing *a*-glides (1972, 130) rather than instances of the breaking of long *é* to a true diphthong—the implicit reason being that a twelfth-century date for the breaking would be too early.[75] A diphthongal realisation similar to [ɛ·a] / [e·a] or [ɛ·ə] / [e·ə] is a further possibility to Jackson's suggested [eᵃ].[76] Such diphthongal realisations could represent an intermediate stage in the development *é* > *ia*.[77] Breaking of long *é* is, however, less common in modern peripheral eastern dialects, thus suggesting that breaking may not have been a common feature of older more eastern varieties; see Jackson (1968) and *SGDS* 416, which illustrates that breaking does not normally occur in eastern dialects in the phonologically similar word *feur*. Although the *SGDS* return for Braemar (point 189) was [fɛːr] without breaking, the return for Moray, [fɛ̣:ar], shows that breaking of the type suggested here may have been a sporadic feature of certain north-eastern twelfth-century Scottish Gaelic dialects.

That the *a* may have been more prominent than Jackson was prepared to believe is suggested by two factors: (a) the marking of *a* in the place-name by an accent (**deár**): see discussion of accents in Ó Maolalaigh 'on the possible functions of the accents', this volume; (b) the fact that in the case of the noun *déra* ('tears'), *dara* was written first and the *e* later inserted (see Jackson 1972, 19).

The presence of *a* in the place-name may, however, be of greater significance than has hitherto been realised. Rather than belonging to the coda of a stressed syllable (i.e. an *a*-glide ([ᵃ] or [ᵊ]) or the second element of a diphthong, [a] or [ə]), one wonders if the *a* in the place-name may represent the unstressed vowel of a disyllabic word containing hiatus, i.e. **Deär* [d′e-ar][78] or [d′e-ər]. With this we might compare the use of *ea* to represent the apparent

belongs to the coronal anterior class.) The glide never occurs before other segments such as single *l*, *n*, where the glide (if present) may have been relatively inaudible—perhaps suggesting (as we suggest tentatively below) in the case of *n* that lenited palatalised and non-palatalised *n* (i.e. //n′// and //n//) had merged, or were in the process of merging, in some eastern dialects by the time of the Gaelic Notes. (However, the forms *gaineamh* [gani] and *leanabh* [L′ɛnu], recorded from Braemar, may suggest the merger of //n′// and //n// occurred after the vocalisation of the final unstressed labial fricatives: see Ó Maolalaigh 2003e.) It may be significant that *i*-glides are marked with accents in stressed syllables 55% (11/20) of the time; see Ó Maolalaigh, 'On the possible functions of the accents', this volume, for a discussion of MS accents.   **75** Note his use of 'subsequent "breaking"' (1972, 130, n. 1). See Jackson (1968) for a discussion of the breaking of *é* to *ia* in modern Scottish Gaelic dialects, who does not, however, offer a date for the development.   **76** In support of Jackson's interpretation, it might be added that schwa on-glides were recorded in the phonologically similar word *feur* in the *SGDS* (416) returns for the peripheral points 194, 196, 197 (all East Perthshire), 199, 200 (both North West Perthshire) and 206 (South West Perthshire).   **77** On the earlier development of Early Old Gaelic *é* > *ia*, and its representation in Old Gaelic by the 'intermediate form' *ea* / *éa*, see *GOI* 36–7.   **78** On the occurrence of clear *a* in the unstressed position in eastern dialects, especially before *r*, see discussion of *galar* in Ó Maolalaigh 'On the possible functions of the accents', this volume.

hiatus forms m**ẹ**cbead (DIII7) and mec bead (BVI–2), both presumably representing *Beäd* [b´e-að] or [b´e-əð].[79] A possible disyllabic form **Deär* for the place-name may have influenced Hand A when he came to spell the noun *déara* ('tears'), which in the context has an obvious pivotal role to play in the origin legend of Deer, and as such could have been made to resemble as far as possible the form of the place-name.

Jackson (1972, 42) notes that the etymology of 'Deer' is unknown.[80] Taylor (this volume) suggests that the name may derive from the Pictish word for an oak-tree or oak-grove, cognate with Old Gaelic *dair*, *daire* and Welsh *derwen*, *derw*. To this I cautiously add the very tentative alternative suggestion that Deer may in origin be a river name. If de**á**r (AII9) represents a disyllabic hiatus form (which in Modern Gaelic might be written as **Deathar*), one could speculate that the word **Deär* contains the two elements **Dēw-* 'goddess' (as in *Deathan* of *Obar Dheathain*) and the ending *-ar*, found in stream-names, e.g. *Naver*, *Tamar*, *Calar*, *Gamhar*,[81] *Bruar*, *Labhar*, *Lugar* (see Diack 1920–1, 116–18; W.J. Watson 1926, 431–3; Rivet and Smith 1979, 422; but cf. Hamp 1993, 179). This derivation would support the suggestion that Deer may in origin have referred to a stream or river. Johnston and Johnston's *Gazetteer of Scotland* (1937, 100) gives 'Deer' as an alternative name of the South Ugie Water. However, it is unclear how reliable Johnston and Johnston's testimony may be here.[82] My tentative interpretation would suggest that the district of Deer received its name originally from a river. W.J. Watson (1926, 432) makes a similar suggestion in the case of *Labhar*, as does Jackson in the case of *Banbh* (1972, 80). The identification of the name 'Deer' as the Ugie river is admittedly difficult, though perhaps not impossible, to reconcile with the

---

79 Compare also the Gaelic name for Aberdeen contained in the Gaelic Notes: abberd**é**on (EVII5), abberdeon (EVIII4), with the main stress on *deon* in both cases, which may also represent a disyllabic form *Deön* [d´e-ɔn] / [d´e-on], which would regularly yield the modern form *Deathan* in *Obar Dheathain* [e-an] (with 'silent' *th* used to indicate the hiatus); see Diack (1920–1, 119–20), W.J. Watson (1926, 211–12), Jackson (1972, 60–1). It is impossible to know whether or not the 2pl. prepositional pronoun *doib* is monosyllabic or disyllabic: do**í**b (AI2), do**í**b (AI4), do**í**b (AII3). We have already alluded to the possible instances of hiatus in dochu**í**d (AII1) see section 2.1.1. **80** Jackson (1972, 6) refers with approval to O'Rahilly's (1946, 373–74) equation of *Ne(i)r* (Annals of Ulster s.a. 623, 679) with *Dér* (deriving from a locative phrase *i nDér*). If correct this might provide some early evidence for *Dér* being monosyllabic. However, O'Rahilly's suggestion has been questioned by me (Ó Maolalaigh 1998, 27; 49, n. 44) and, more importantly, by Clancy (2002, 414–15; also *infra*), who plausibly identifies *Ne(i)r* with the second element in the name of the medieval parish of Fetternear (Fethirneir 1157, 1163). **81** For the stream-name *Gamhar* in Ireland, see Mac Cárthaigh (1964–5, 43). **82** Dauvit Broun suggests to me that the origin of their statement regarding Deer as an alternative name to the South Ugie Water may come from Francis H. Groome's *Ordnance Gazetteer of Scotland* (1882–5, vol. 6, 464: 'its [the river Ugie's] chief tributary, the Water of Deer or South Ugie'. The use of 'the Water of Deer or South Ugie' is ambiguous here as it is unclear whether or not Deer and South Ugie apply to the surrounding area or the river itself. If 'the Water of Deer' is a genuine name it is most likely a late, secondary formation based on the place-name 'Deer'.

presence of the name Ugie, which Taylor (this volume) sees in the form dubucí (BV24), i.e. *Dub* 'black' + *Uci*.

2.3 Smoothing

2.3.1 *toísech* or *tóisech?*

Jackson (1972, 134) is cautious in his treatment of *o* and *oi* spellings of the Old Gaelic word *toísech*, which contained an original [oi]-like diphthong. He concludes on the overall evidence of the Notes that this word was most likely pronounced as a diphthong, rather than a long monophthong, which we find in modern Scottish Gaelic dialects (*tòiseach* usually with [ɔ:]). This is at variance with the conclusion reached in his earlier paper on the Notes, that Old Gaelic *áe* and *óe* 'had already fallen together, perhaps recently, or were now in the process of falling together, in some sort of weakly rounded $\bar{\bar{o}}$ and $\bar{\bar{o}}$'' (Jackson 1952, 91). However, Hand A is pretty consistent in his spelling of the word (each of the five times he uses it): with *o* (three times) and *oi* (twice). His forms are as follows: thóséc (A16), thoséc (A114), toíség (A116), thóisíg (A1118), tosech (A1128). It may be significant that *oi* occurs only in genitive forms, where the final syllable contains palatal *g*[*h*], and where the 'onglide' (if that is what it is) before the palatal *s* may have been more prominent. In non-genitive forms he consistently uses *o*. If *o(i)* represented an *i*-gliding diphthong in all of these examples, it is perhaps difficult to reconcile the use of the *i*-glide only in oblique forms. The use of *i* in oblique forms is perhaps more compatible with the preceding *o* representing a long monophthong.[83] Hand A never writes this word with *ae*, *æ* or *e*, unlike the other scribes (táesec BV17, tœsech CVI8–9, thesech C1126), although he uses *ae* and *e* in other words such as saere (A15), éda (A111). Although it might be claimed that Hand A consistently uses the historical form (albeit without the *i* in three instances), it must remain a distinct possibility that his vernacular form may have been long monophthongal *ó* rather than an *i*-gliding diphthong in this word.[84] Hand C's spelling of this word is also consistent with a monoph-thongal realisation: he uses *e* on two occasions and *æ* on another (thesech C1126, thesseach CV25, tœsech CVI8–9).[85] It is clear from literary sources that the word *taoiseach* (< *toísech*) had developed a number of variants by the

---

83 In support of this, we may note that the occurrence of *i* before palatal *s* in some of these forms concurs with the general occurrence of *i*-glides before certain coronals in the Gaelic Notes (see above), thus providing some admittedly very flimsy evidence for our interpretation. 84 It is difficult to know what to make of Hand B's sóre (BV7), which could indicate a diphthongal realisation or conceivably a long monophthongal vowel. 85 Forms of *toíseach* contained in Latin and Scots statutes and charters suggest that the original diphthong in *toísech* had been monophthongised by the fifteenth century in Scotland (Gillies 1996, 131–3, 134; Ó Maolalaigh 2003d, 324). Examples include: *tosheagor-, tochdore-, Tossichdoir, Tosichdore, Tosachdera, toschodera-, tosordereh,* etc. (Gillies 1996,

end of the Middle Gaelic period: *taoiseach*, *túiseach* and *tóiseach* are all accepted variants in Classical verse: see McManus (1994, 349). It is thus possible that the Deer forms reflect such dialectal (possibly even register) variation with Hand A perhaps exhibiting an early instance of what was to become the norm in modern Scottish Gaelic.[86]

Other 'pronunciation' spellings provide important evidence for three important vernacular features of Scottish Gaelic, which shall be discussed presently, namely svarabhakti, reduction of long unstressed vowels and eclipsis.[87]

2.4 Svarabhakti / epenthesis

2.4.1 General

Borgstrøm (1938, 41) stated that svarabhakti existed in Irish before the year 1100 but was prepared to believe that 'it may have begun several centuries later' (1938, 42). His conclusion is based on the use of accents in *Lebor na hUidre* to mark 'heavy' syllables, some of which later developed svarabhakti vowels. However, such accents may have indicated only that such syllables were longer or of 'middle length': see Greene's (1952) discussion of *síneadh meadhónach* ('middle length'). Jackson (1951, 84) concurs with O'Rahilly's view that svarabhakti is unlikely to be much older than the thirteenth century.[88] *Cathair Leamhnach* appears as *Catherlauenoch* in a charter dated to 1223 x 34 (W.J. Watson 1926, 223), where *-e-* before *n* may be indicative of an epenthetic vowel having developed in the Gaelic form.[89] C. Breatnach claims on the basis of spellings from contemporary hands in the Annals of Inisfallen that epenthesis may have developed in certain southern Irish dialects before the end of the eleventh century. He cites the following examples: *teidim* (1093 for *teidm*), *madmim* (1124 for *maidm*), *madim* (1129 for *maidm*), *Tadig* (1127 gen. for *Taidg*), *Ua Ruaric* (1122 for *Ua Ruairc*), *Arid Maca* (1122 gen. for *Aird Maca*), *arichinnich* (1204) for *airchinnich*; he also suggests that *Ciaargi* (1175) may be a hypercorrection for *Ciarraigi* (C. Breatnach 1989, 184). A

131–2). **86** For other instances of variation in the reflexes of *ao(i)*, see McManus (1994, 349). Cf. the variation between *fàilte* /ɑ:/ and *faoilte* /ə:/, /ɯ:/ in modern East Perthshire (Ó Murchú 1989a, 339). **87** Svarabhakti / epenthesis is of course found also in Irish and Manx. The reduction of long unstressed vowels is also a feature of certain northern Irish and Manx dialects, but is more advanced in Scottish Gaelic. **88** It seems clear enough that epenthesis must have developed, at least in southern Irish dialects, before *dh* merged with *gh*. Otherwise the name *Tadhg* might be expected to have yielded *Taghg* > **Tág* or possibly **Tag*: see Ó Maolalaigh (1997, 184; 2006, 59). O'Rahilly (1932, 171) provides possible evidence for epenthesis in *Tadhg* from sources dated to the end of the thirteenth century, e.g. *Tatheg, Tadheg, Tadhog*. Cf. O'Rahilly's (1932, 202) assertion that epenthesis must have developed in *colbtha(ch)* [koləpə(x)] before *th* ceased to be a dental frivative. **89** I am grateful to Dauvit Broun for providing me with the date of this charter. It is possible in such instances that the epenthesis represents the perception or pronunciation of non-Gaelic speakers, however.

number of these spellings are, however, problematical. Leaving aside the alleged hypercorrection, *Ciaargi*, it may be significant that the supposed epenthetic vowel in the remaining 7 examples is spelled as *i* and that it occurs in the environment of palatal(ised) consonants. It may also be significant that 5 of these 7 examples were written by the same scribe (Hand 20). One wonders whether *aCi* may be a scribal transpositional error for *aiC* in some of these examples (where *C* stands for a consonant or consonant cluster). Similarly, *Ciaargi* may represent a transpositional error for *Ciaragi*. As far as *Arid* is concerned, it should be noted that epenthesis is not attested in the cluster *rd* in vernacular speech, but see Greene (1952, 217, n. 1), who notes the variant *arad-* for *árd-* in Munster verse. L. Breatnach (1994, 234) refers to the two forms, *recaras* (= *fhrecras*) and *garú* (= *garbh*), from the Harleian 1802 manuscript (dated to 1138), which he suggests may indicate the development of epenthesis in vernacular speech in the first half of the twelfth century. However, both forms are problematic since *recaras* may represent a back-formation based on the unsyncopated stem *frecair*; *ú* in *garú* may be purely orthographical for *bh*. Furthermore, *recaras* rhymes with a disyllable and *garú* with a monosyllable as L. Breatnach himself points out.

2.4.2 *mareb, anim*

There are instances in Deer of what appear at first sight to be svarabhakti or epenthetic vowels—not normally shown in traditional orthography (see Jackson 1972, 135 for discussion). These are **maréb** (A110) and **áním** (A119) for traditional *marb* and *ainm* respectively. In the case of **maréb** (A110), the scribe appears to have written by ear and upon realising his mistake placed cancellations points above and below the *e* (Jackson 1972, 135). The form *ainim* occurs in the Milan Glosses (Ml. 30ª9: see *DIL* s.v *ainmm*), and, interestingly, also in the 1408 MacDonald charter: *ainim* (Munro and Munro 1986, 21). It is possible that spellings such as *a(i)inim* ('name') may have been influenced by *ainim(m)* ('soul'). It is also possible that **áním** (A119) represents a scribal transpositional error similar to the examples referred to above from the Annals of Inisfallen. However, if the Deer forms do represent the existence of epenthetic vowels in such environments at this period, the use of *e* and *i* rather than *a* in both could be significant in that it might suggest that the epenthetic vowel was not an exact copy of the original stressed vowel as typifies svarabhakti in many modern western Scottish Gaelic dialects. In modern Aberdeenshire dialects the epenthetic vowel tends to be a variety of schwa as in Irish (see A. Watson and Clement 1983, 401; and *ainm, dorcha, marbh*, etc. *SGDS* 17, 332, 600). The Deer forms may represent epenthetic vowels of this eastern type, and if so, they may represent an eastern Gaelic feature. The fact that both svarabhakti vowels are marked with accents may also be significant. The personal name donna<u>ch</u>ac (Cv17) may be another instance but see Jackson (1972, 76–77) and further discussion below.[90]

Ralph of Diss's late twelfth-century royal genealogy of the kings of Scots has the form *Enegussa* twice, for historical *Óengusa* (Broun 1999, 185, 186; cf. Broun 1998, 190). The *e* which occurs before *g* may be indicative of the development of an epenthetic vowel in this word in the Gaelic form, in which case it would also imply the shortening of the original long vowel since epenthesis does not generally develop following stressed long vowels (O'Rahilly 1932, 199; Jackson 1972, 108). The initial vowel of the name *Aonghas* is invariably short in modern Scottish Gaelic dialects, and all modern forms can be satisfactorily derived from a svarbhakti form $[_{\lceil}ɣnɣ_{\rceil}ɣəs]$ or $[_{\lceil}ɰnɰ_{\rceil}ɣəs]$; for modern realisations of the name, see *SGDS* 50. The shortening of the vowel in this case may represent one strategy for the resolution of overly long syllables containing a long vowel followed by certain heavy clusters containing sonorants;[91] other strategies include epenthesis (e.g. *iarann* < *íarn* < *iärn*; *lárag* < **lárg* < *laärg*) and devoicing (*Rúa(i)rc* < *Rúa(i)rg*; *cúairt* < *cúaird*): see O'Rahilly (1942).

2.4.3 *Donnachac*

The name *Donnchad* occurs four times in the Notes: Donchad (Bv1), m<u>ac</u> donnchid (Cv131–32), m<u>ac</u> donn<u>ch</u>aid (Cv132), doncado (EvIII0). The curious form donna<u>ch</u>ac (Cv17) also occurs. In what follows I shall assume that *Donnachac* is not a mistake for *Donnachat*[*h*] with -*c* for -*t*.[92] Jackson (1972, 76–77) has a full discussion of the form but ultimately rejects the possibility that it illustrates the development of epenthesis between *nn* and *ch*, even though it is a feature of *all* modern Scottish Gaelic dialects in this word: see *SGDS* 330–31. The grounds for rejection are that 'there is no really clear evidence that epenthesis can have been as old as the earlier twelfth century' (1972, 76). Jackson prefers to interpret *Donnachac* as a hypocoristic form of the name *Donn-* or *Donnchadh*, representing an original unattested **Donnacóc* (comparable to attested *Donnacán*), with *ch* as 'a misspelling' for *c*, and -*ac* representing -*ác* (1972, 77). This involves a good deal of special pleading. Jackson dismisses the possibility that *Donnachac* might represent a form like [doNəxək] or [duNəxək], which is actually attested for *Donnchadh* in eastern Scottish Gaelic dialects in Easter Ross, North East and North West Inverness-shire, and Moray (*SGDS* 330, 331). However, in the majority of the eastern dialects of North East Inverness-shire, Moray, Speyside, Badenoch, Braemar

---

90 The manuscript form banb (EvII5) is unlikely to mark a svarabhakti syllable, although it might conceivably mark 'middle length' as in the examples discussed by Greene (1952). 91 Alternatively, it is possible that the long vowel in *Óengus* was reduced in patronymic collocations such as *Óengus Iain*, where the main stress occurred on the defining element *Iain*. 92 For Latin forms such as *Dunckach, Dunekach*, see Broun (1999, 158).

and Perthshire final *-adh* in this and other nominal forms has been lost. This might argue against the development of *-adh* > [ək] in earlier stages of eastern Scottish Gaelic. Jackson also rejected interpreting the Deer form as representing modern [doNəxək] / [duNəxək] on the grounds that it 'presupposes the prior change of /ð/ to /ɣ/ (of which there is no other trace in Deer)' (1972, 76). It is curious that Jackson did not mention the possibility that donnachac could have represented *Donnachac[h]*, with final *-ac* for *-ach*, especially since *c* occurs so commonly for *ch* in the Notes, e.g.

> cruthnec (A13), **thóséc** (A16), gleréc (A110), dattác (A111), glerec
> (A111), ernacde (A112), **c!**loic (A113), chloíc (A113), ernacde (A114),
> benact (A116), blienec (A117), (cf. buadacc (A117), **ímácc** (A119)),
> Moridac (A112), thoséc (A114), glerec (A119), Málsnecte (A114),
> acuitíd (A118), cec (A119, 27, 28), cainnéc (A124), bennact (A127);
> **óc**mad (D1115), **néc**tan (D1116), **b**recini (D1116), mic<u>ae</u>l (D1v1), docrist
> ₇docolimcilli (D1v1), feradac (D1v2), doc<u>ris</u>t (Bv4), merlec (Bv15),
> táesec (Bv17), do c<u>ris</u>t (Bv19), mallact (Cv26), ferdomnac (Eviii13).[93]

Although Hand C normally writes *ch* or *c͟h* (in 16 cases out of 17), he does have mallact (Cv26), assuming that Jackson is correct in attributing this portion of Text v (i.e. Cv25–26) to Hand C (Jackson 1972, 13–14). There is some basis, therefore, for interpreting donnachac (Cv17) as *Donnachach*. This would strongly support the interpretation that this word represents the name *Donnchadh*. If correct, it is important in a number of respects. It shows clearly the development of epenthesis where it would be expected. More importantly, it could also suggest that the dental fricative *dh* had already become a guttural spirant in this word by the early twelfth century, where *c* (= *ch*) represented [ɣ], possibly devoiced [ɣ̊] in final unstressed position.[94] If this analysis is correct this particular 'departure from tradition and normality' is a salutary reminder of the highly literate and conservative linguistic nature of the Notes in other respects, and particularly in the representation of original dental fricatives as *th* and *d*[*h*]. In an extraordinary coincidence, the name *Donnchadh* appears in a similar form, *Don(n)c(h)ach*, twice in the Annals

93 The frequent occurrence of *c* for *ch* in the Notes suggests that it may have been a widespread Scottish scribal feature, although it is, of course, also attested in Irish sources; Ó Máille (1910, 39) suggests that Irish *ct* for *cht* may be due to Latin influence. (Though not representing a fricative, *c* for *ch* has also been noted in Hiberno-Latin (Picard 1982, 240).) However, it is worth noting that the addition of *h* in the cluster *cht* is redundant as an orthographic form in the absence of a stop cluster *ct*. 94 Perhaps by backformation based on the development *Donnchaidh* > *Donnchaigh* through the merger of palatal(ised) *dh* and *gh*. Alternatively, donnachac (Cv17) could have developed from *Donn(a)chagh* with assimilation between *ch* and *gh*. Other possible instances of the confusion of unstressed broad *ch* and *gh* can be cited from texts whose originals can be traced to twelfth- and thirteenth-century sources, e.g. *Lugthag* (for *Lugdach*), *Cailbrech* (for *Coelbreg*), (Broun 1999, 186).

of Inisfallen: *Donnchach* under the year 1101 by Hand 6 and *Doncach* under
the year 1270 by contemporary Anglo-Norman Hand 34. We may also note
the verbal form *gu dicfac* for *gu dicfach* (= *go dtiocfadh*) under the year 1195
(Hand 26), (C. Breatnach 1990a, 432, 457), which may reflect modern
southern Irish realisations of verbal -*adh* as [əx]. R.A. Breatnach suggested
that final *dh* may not in all cases have merged with *gh*, and put forward the
hypothesis that unstressed *dh* may have been devoiced to *th*, which
subsequently was reduced to *h* and eventually lost. He claimed that this could
explain the development -*adh* > -*a* in nouns in Munster dialects (R.A.
Breatnach 1952, 51–52). C. Breatnach (1990a, 476) expands on this hypothesis
and suggests that in some instances a weakened form of unstressed *th* may
have been associated with a weakened form of *ch*, and that this could account
for the -*ch* spellings in the name of *Donnchadh* in the Annals of Inisfallen. He
puts forward a similar explanation in the case of verbal *ticfac* for *ticfad*,
although in this case he is willing to accept that final -*th* may have developed
into -*ch* (citing in support the change -*th* > -*ch* in monosyllables, also attested
in the Annals of Inisfallen and in some modern Gaelic dialects). A similar
explanation involving -*dh* > -*th* > -*ch* could conceivably account for the Deer
form donnachac (Cv17).

2.5 Reduction of long unstressed vowels

2.5.1 General

The reduction of long unstressed vowels is one of the most salient
phonological features differentiating Scottish Gaelic, and to a certain degree,
Manx, from the majority of Irish dialects. O'Rahilly noted that 'this vowel-
shortening of Scottish Gaelic probably constitutes the most important single
difference between it and Irish' (1932, 127). Though shortening also occurs in
Ulster Irish dialects (see Ó Dochartaigh 1987a, 19–62) and in Manx, it is more
developed and widespread in Scottish Gaelic. The weight of the modern
dialectal evidence suggests strongly that this prosodic innovation first
occurred in Scotland and spread to Ulster and Man.[95] It was O'Rahilly's view
that this may have occurred 'as far back as, say, the twelfth century' (1932,
126) and that it could have been due to the influence of Old Norse, although
he was prepared to believe that it could have come about 'without any external
stimulus' (1932, 127–8). O'Rahilly subsequently revised this view in a letter to
Kenneth Jackson, dated 27 September 1948, in which he claimed that a
twelfth-century date was too early (Jackson 1951, 87, n. 4). The basis for this
revision rested on the hypothesis that the shortening of unstressed syllables

95 Cf. 'The development in question was essentially a Scottish one' (O'Rahilly 1932, 128).
Ó Dochartaigh concludes based on modern dialectal evidence that this change spread from
north-east Ulster to south-west Ulster (1987a, 34).

(at least in Manx) occurred later than the development of forward stress in words such as *faasaag* (= *féasóg*), which O'Rahilly explained as being due to the influence of Norman French. In other words, according to O'Rahilly, the shortening of unstressed long vowels could not be much older than the beginning of the fourteenth century. This is based on the assumption that forward stress in Manx developed before the reduction of unstressed long vowels. Ó Sé (1991), however, argues that the shortening of long unstressed vowels was the earlier of the two developments in Manx. He claims that the shortening was well-advanced in Manx at the time of 'the collapse of the Kingdom of Man and the Isles in 1266 A.D.' (1991, 170). If he is correct, and if we can assume that the centre of diffusion for the shortening lay in Scotland, it follows that shortening in Scotland is almost certainly older than the thirteenth century, although just how early remains one of the most crucial questions to be answered satisfactorily by Gaelic linguistic historians. Ó Sé puts forward the hypothesis that 'the northern vowel shortening is very likely coeval with the reduction of short [unstressed] vowels at the beginning of the Middle Irish period' (1989, 169, 175–6). The hypothesis is attractive in that it suggests a possible structural relationship between the reduction of long and short unstressed vowels in northern varieties of Gaelic, one possibly having induced the other by a chain effect. Given the apparently universal reduction of unstressed short vowels throughout the Gaelic-speaking area, it might reasonably be concluded that this was the primary change, and that the reduction of long vowels occurred secondarily to fill the gap, as it were, 'vacated' by originally short clear vowels. (See, however, below for an alternative explanation.) According to this interpretation, the potential for the reduction of unstressed long vowels may have existed from the beginning of the Middle Gaelic period, i.e. from approximately the tenth century onwards, and possibly even earlier in certain varieties of Gaelic (see further comments below). Substratum or adstratum influence from Pictish (or Norse as O'Rahilly initially suggested) may have been a contributory factor, which would also place the reduction in a period anterior to the twelfth century.

It is generally accepted that all Old Gaelic short unstressed vowels merged as the phoneme /ə/ during the Middle Gaelic period, although it is possible that the reduction may have occurred in certain colloquial registers by the eighth century (McCone 1985, 87). Indeed, this phonemic reduction has recently been described as 'by far the most important phonological development in Middle Irish' (McCone 1996a, 142). This interpretation is generally supported by modern dialectal evidence, and is certainly the most economic way to describe orthographic forms and variation from the Middle Gaelic period onwards: see McCone (1985, 87–8). However, this is not to say that all Old Gaelic short unstressed vowels were realised phonetically as [ə] during the Middle Gaelic period or subsequently. Note that McCone (1996a, 135) is prepared to believe that in Old Gaelic the phoneme /ə/ in unstressed closed syllables may have had the following allophonic variation: [a] before non-palatal consonants when preceded by non-palatal consonants or *i* in hiatus; [i] between palatal consonants; [e] between palatal and non-palatal consonants; [e] or [i] after *i* in hiatus before palatal consonants. There is good evidence to suggest, for instance, that [a] in *-ach* syllables reflects a relict feature of certain Gaelic dialects rather than an innovation.[96] It is possible, as we have suggested above, that clear vowels may have been retained in some hiatus words, partly perhaps due to the operation of vowel harmony. It is also possible that clear vowels may have been retained in certain sonorant environments, rather than representing later lowerings of schwa, e.g. *galar* -/ar/ (discussed further in Ó Maolalaigh 'On the possible functions of the accents', this volume). In other words, the subphonemic, possibly also the phonemic, situation may have been a good deal more complicated in some dialects than has been previously thought.[97] The possible existence of unstressed clear non-schwa-like vowels (i.e at least [a], [ɛ]), whether subphonemic or phonemic, in the Middle Gaelic period and subsequently in earlier varieties of Scottish Gaelic suggests another structural explanation for the reduction of unstressed long vowels in northern Gaelic. The distinction of length between long and short unstressed vowels may have been neutralised in favour of the short series, perhaps because the functional load of the opposition was relatively low. In other words, the reduction of unstressed long vowels in northern Gaelic may in origin have come about due to the prior existence of a system of unstressed short vowels.[98]

2.5.2 *mormar, Cinatha*

Jackson (1972, 135) notes three possible examples of the reduction of unstressed long vowels in the Notes, namely, mormar (AII27), mórmar (DIII8) for *mormaer*; and cinathá (AIII1; first *a*) for possible *Cinaetha / Cinaeda* (1972, 135). To these, turbrud (EVIII2) (if for *Turbruad*) may be tentatively added.[99] *Cinada* also occurs in the Poppleton Manuscript text of the royal genealogy of

---

96 O'Rahilly claims that *-ach* was in Old Gaelic pronounced with a clear [a], and that this pronunciation continued into the Middle Gaelic period 'as English and French spellings of Irish names in the thirteenth century make abundantly clear' (1932, 109–12, at 110). 97 Cf. 'In the Middle Irish period, when nearly all short unstressed vowels had become *obscured*' and 'A clear unstressed short vowel being something of an *anomaly* in Irish after the Old-Irish period' (O'Rahilly 1932, 110) [italics mine].   98 The retention of certain unstressed short vowels in earlier varieties of Gaelic posited here would suggest that the phonology of unstressed syllables in northern Gaelic was conservative. A parallel conservative feature in the vowel phonology of Scottish Gaelic might be seen in the phonemic contrast between low and high mid long vowels (back and front), which could represent to some degree vestiges of the earlier contrast between /eː/ ~ /ɛː/ and /oː/ ~ /ɔː/ in Early Old Gaelic, said to have been lost by the Old Gaelic period according to McCone (1996a, 138).   99 On the reduction of long unstressed *ú* to /u/, see, for example,

kings of Scots (Diss's manuscript has Kinath (Broun 1999, 176, 184)), and in the Annals of Inisfallen (*Úa Cinada* 1178; C. Breatnach 1990a, 424). If Jackson's (1972, 77) interpretation of donna<u>ch</u>ac (CVI7) as *Donnacóc is correct, it possible that -*ac* may present a reduced clear *a*-vowel. It is possible, however, that unstressed *a* in these examples may represent long *á*.[1] It may be significant that both instances of *mormar* in the Notes are followed by the sequence (-)*ar*(-), and it is therefore possible that both scribes inadvertently anticipated this syllable when writing *mormar*: ar cecmormar ₇ar cectosech (AII27–28); m**ó**rmar m**á**rr (DIII8).

2.5.3 *helaín* ('Ellon')

The dative place-name helaín (CVI33) has long been identified with modern Ellon, the chief town of Buchan: see MacBain (1885, 149), Fraser (1942, 64), Alexander (1952, 53), Jackson (1972, 79). Alexander (1952, 53) tentatively suggested a derivation from Gaelic *ailén* (or dative / locative *aileón* 'island').[2] However, he ultimately dismissed this etymology because the Deer form occurs without the article. This is not a strong argument against a derivation from *ailén* since the article can be dropped or may not occur in some place-names. Jackson's (1972, 79) rejection of this etymology may have been based on the supposition that long *é* (or *eó*) could not have been reduced to a short vowel by the end of the twelfth century, and that -*én* would not have been spelt as -*ain*: cf. his comments on Alexander's derivation from *àilean* (1972, 79).[3] Jackson's suggested derivation from 'an [unattested] *n*-stem, nominative *Ela' with dative *Elain* does not inspire confidence; significantly, it does not account for the various twelfth-century spellings in non-Gaelic sources with *o* in the final syllable (e.g. Ellon 1157, 1165, 1493; Elone 1328), which strongly suggest that we are not dealing with an original short unclear vowel (i.e. schwa) but rather a representation of dative singular *aileón*.[4]

There are, however, good reasons for accepting *ailén* ('island') as the underlying etymon in the name Ellon. There is wider evidence to support *ailén* as an inland topographical feature. On the use of *oileán* (< *ailén*) in Irish place-names to signify 'an area of raised, and therefore, dry land surrounded by what is, or was bog', see Flanagan and Flanagan (1994, 127 s.v. *oileán*). A.

---

mórchuis (< *mórchùis*) /moːrxuʃ/ (Oftedal 1956, 352).   **1** Cf. Ó Buachalla (2000, 11, n. 11). **2** MacBain (1896, 154) derived Gaelic *ailén* from Norse *eyland*. This is not generally accepted. It seems more likely that the word represents a formation containing *ail* ('rock') + diminutive -*én*. See, for example, *LEIA* s.v. *ailén*. In any case, it is clear from its first attestations that the last syllable was interpreted as containing the suffix -*én*.   **3** Jackson (1972, 79), following Alexander, is willing to accept the derivation from *ailén* in the case of Ellon in Strathspey—presumably because 'its Gaelic form is still extant' (Alexander 1952, 53).   **4** Cited in Alexander (1952, 53). The date 1165 may appear in the wrong place in Jackson (1972, 79). Simon Taylor kindly provides the following additional early references: Elon (1274 *Bagimond's Roll* 43); Elone (1314x18 *RRS* v, no. 484).

Watson and Allan's (1984, 77–8) *Place Names of Upper Deeside* lists almost
thirty place-names containing the element *Eilean*, which they translate as
'riverside-field', e.g. *An t-Eilean, Eilean Aitinn, Eilean Dubh, Eilean Mór*, etc.
'Island' names in East Ulster, which can be topographically described as
isolated or 'insular' hillocks usually meared by rivers or surrounded by
swampy or marshy land on one or more sides are discussed by Ó Mainnín
(1990, 200, 204), who suggests that *inis* 'a river holm or meadow' may have
been the underlying Irish form in many of these names, although he notes
that Magill (1937, 86) would trace many of the townland names now containing
the element 'island' to an original *oileán* 'island' (the Modern Irish form of
earlier *ailén*).[5] Ó Mainnín's (1990, 204, n. 16) preference for *inis* rather than
oileán seems to be based on the fact that Irish *oileán* and Scottish Gaelic *eilean*
are not attested in modern lexicographical sources with the meaning of a river
holm or similar. This is, of course, not a serious objection given the possible
figurative use of *ailén* in describing the topographical features concerned. One
wonders if Dwelly's *eilean lòn* [*sic*], which he noted from an Arran source and
which he glosses as 'a mud island', might provide a possible instance of *eilean*
as an inland 'insular' topographical feature.[6] We may note here that Tara is
described as *ailénchnocc* ('island-hill') and *ailénphort* ('island-fort') in the
poem, 'Temair Breg, baile na fían',[7] which is ascribed in the Book of Leinster
to Cúan Ua Lothcháin (†1024); see Joynt (1910, 92 §4cd) and Ó Mainnín
(1990, 203). Dauvit Broun, who is familiar with the Aberdeenshire Ellon area,
informs me that the topography of Ellon itself supports the derivation from
ailén suggested above. It also suits the Strathspey Ellon in the Braes of
Abernethy (NJo62175).

    There may be good Scottish linguistic reasons for accepting *ailén* as the
original form of Ellon. Original *a* in this word is invariably raised to the mid
position in Scottish Gaelic dialects, and is usually realised as /e/; this is
reflected in the modern spelling, which is *eilean* or *eilein*.[8] Furthermore, a
derivation from *ailén* accounts satisfactorily for earlier forms with unstressed *o*
such as Ellon, Ellone in non-Gaelic sources, which can be plausibly derived
from *aileón*, the dative / locative form of *ailén* (see *DIL* s.v. *ailén*). If this

---

5 He quotes an unpublished source which shows that Deirdre Flanagan derived the
townland name Islanbane from *Oileán Bán* (Ó Mainnín 1990, 204, n. 16).   6 See *Dwelly*
(s.v. *eilean*). *Dwelly* (s.v. *lón*) notes the obsolete meanings of 'marsh, morass' and 'pond,
lakelet, water, mud' for *lón*, which usually means 'meadow' in modern Scottish Gaelic,
although he also notes from the Revd Charles M. Robertson for the island of Skye the
meaning of a 'small brook, especially with marshy banks'.   7 In line c of the fourth stanza
ailénchnocc appears in both Rawlinson B 502 and in the Book of Leinster; in line d,
however, Rawl. has *ailénphort* and *LL* has *ailénchnocc*.   8 Note, however, that /ɛ/ and /e/
occur in East Sutherland; see Dorian (1978, 154). For early instances in Scottish sources of
the development of initial *ai-* > *e-*, see the forms discussed above, including *Elig* for *Ailig*
in the Poppleton 'Pictish Chronicle', which contains the same underlying root as *ailén*
('island'); cf. also W.J. Watson's (1926, 81) discussion of *na h-Eileacha Naomha*.

derivation is correct it remains to account for the spelling of the final syllable in Deer helaín (Cvi33), apparently with palatalised *n*, which is highly reminiscent of the modern diminutive *-ein* / *-ain* which usually occurs following palatal consonants. A comparative reconstruction of realisations of modern Scottish Gaelic *eilean* / *eilein* (realised variously in modern dialects as -[ɛn], -[ɛN´], -[aN´], -[an]) illustrates that these forms can be traced back to a form *eilein* or *eiléin* with final palatalised *n*.[9] This provides further corroborative evidence for the equation of helaín (Cvi33) with a reflex of Old Gaelic *ailén*. It remains to offer an interpretation of *aí* in the unstressed syllable. There are four possibilities:[10] (A) *aí* = [a:], (B) *aí* = [ɛ:], (C) *aí* = /a/, (D) *aí* = /ɛ/, the latter being the case if *aí* is taken as a hypercorrection for an *e*-like vowel similar to *ai* in cáennaig (Bv16–17) discussed earlier; possibility (B) would suggest a hypercorrect spelling indicative of the raising of *á* (cf. my comment on gobraíth (AI5) for *go bráth* in n. 13 below). If possibility (C) or (D) is correct, then we would have a spectacular example of the reduction of an original long vowel in the unstressed position, and its lowering to a clear vowel /a/ or /ɛ/ before the end of the twelfth century; we would also have evidence for the early development of the Scottish Gaelic diminutive *-ein*. However, possibility (A) or (B) cannot be dismissed. Irrespective of the quantity of the unstressed vowel in helaín (Cvi33), a derivation from *ailén* would suggest that the form represents an early stage in the development of the Scottish Gaelic diminutive ending *-ein*.[11] The personal name colbain (Cvii–2) may also contain the Scottish Gaelic diminutive *-ein*: see Diplomatic Edition (notes on Text vi) for the form *Colbain* in preference to Jackson's *Colban* (1972, 21). If so, the name, which appears to have been borrowed from Old Norse *Kolbeinn* (Marstrander 1915, 49; Jackson 1972, 75), may have been borrowed into Scottish Gaelic as *Coilbein*, in which case the Deer form with *-ain* would provide a further parallel for helaín representing an underlying *helein* or *heléin*.

It remains to discuss the two early instances of *Helin* (representing the place-name Ellon) attested in the years 1183 and 1328 (Alexander 1952, 53). Although these forms appear on the surface to corroborate Jackson's derivation from a dative *n*-stem noun *Elain*, one can suggest a number of other interpretations: (a) *Helin* may represent a corruption of Gaelic *ailén*; (b) *Helin* might be taken as possible evidence for the confusion of the two diminutive endings *-ín* and *-én* at an earlier stage in Scottish Gaelic, or

9 On the development of the Scottish Gaelic diminutive *-ein* and earlier *-én* in Scottish Gaelic, see O'Rahilly (1932, 126) and Ó Maolalaigh (2001). 10 Note the accent over the *i* is likely to be a feature used to mark the *i*-grapheme: see Ó Maolalaigh, 'On the possible functions of the accents', this volume. 11 Alexander's (1952, 53) phonetic transcription of the name Ellon with clear unstressed [a] provides some (admittedly flimsy) support for an original *-én* ending rather than a dative *n*-stem ending (containing an original short unclear vowel [ə], although phonetic or analogical lowering of schwa is a possibility).

substitution of -*ín* for Scottish -*éin* as occurs in the Early Modern period; (c) *Helin* may be purely scribal and influenced by the 'locational' suffix -*in*, which is very common in the early period; see Ó Maolalaigh (1998, 30–8) for discussion. In support of the latter interpretation, Simon Taylor suggests Kilgour (old name of Falkland parish, Fife) as a possible parallel. Early forms of the name include: *Kilgouerin* (1224 *St A Lib* 327); *Kilgoueri* (*c.*1250 *St And Lib* 33); *Kilgoueryn'* (*c.*1250 *Dunf Reg*, no. 313); *Kylgouerin* (1274 *Bagimond's Roll*, p. 37); *Kylgouery* (1274 *Bagimond's Roll*, p. 60); *Kylgouerȳ* (1316 NLS Adv. MS 15.1.18, no. 58); *Kilgoveri* (1329 *Cal. Papal Letters* ii, 304); *Kylgoure* (1418 x 1443 *St A. Cop.*, no. 65); *Kilgour* (1510 *RMS* ii, no. 3427). W.J. Watson (1926, 323, 519) suggests that this place-name contains the name of the early Celtic saint Gabréin, possibly identical with Gabrán, a contemporary of Columba. If correct, we would seem to have another instance of the confusion of a Gaelic diminutive suffix with the locational suffix -*in* (possibly also confusion between the Gaelic diminutive suffixes -*éin* and -*ín*). The form Kilgour for expected *Kilgourie may have arisen in order to clearly distinguish it from Gowrie, the name of the territory immediately north of Fife.[12]

We may here anticipate some of the results of our investigation in Ó Maolalaigh 'On the possible functions of the accents', this volume, of the use of suprasegmental accents in the Notes. It is argued that Hand A's marking of certain unstressed syllables by accents may be indicative of clear vowels, e.g. **thóséc** (A16), **gleréc** (A110), **dattác** (A111), **thoséc** (A114), **toíség** (A116), **dabég** (A112), **Cainnéch** (A1120), **cainnéc** (A1124), **galár** (A19), **thabárt** (A1117), **cathál** (A1117), **cathál** (A1121), **cathál** (A1123), **cathál** (A1125). In the case of syllables containing original non-oblique -*ach* / -*ech*, the existence of clear vowels is attested in Gaelic dialects and appears to be a relict feature; a clear vowel may also be indicated by *ea* in **thesseach** (Cv25). Clear vowels may also have characterised oblique forms of such words in earlier stages of Scottish Gaelic, perhaps through analogy. In the case of sonorants, we may note that the second syllable of *galar* and similar words are frequently realised with clear vowels in Modern Scottish Gaelic; a clear vowel may be indicated by *ea* in **Cómgeall** (A111). Hand A marks originally long unstressed vowels more consistently than any other hand: he marks these 61% of the time. It seems likely that the name *Drostán* contains the Gaelic diminutive -*án*; Hand A marks its final syllable with an accent 11 times out of 12. If Hand A's use of the accent in the case of originally long unstressed vowels (such as -*án*) is similar in function to the marking of the unstressed (clear?) vowels in -*ach* / *ech*, and possibly also in **galár** (A19), **thabárt** (A1117), **cathál** (A1117), **cathál** (A1121, 23, 25), one could conclude that both types of syllables were phonetically similar. If correct, this would suggest that originally long

12 I am grateful to Simon Taylor for this suggestion and for providing references to older forms of the name Kilgour.

unstressed vowels were realised as short clear vowels—the normal reflex of long unstressed vowels in all modern Scottish Gaelic dialects. This interpretation would add some support to the claim that the reduction of long unstressed vowels was older than the twelfth century, which is not impossible given the geographical distribution of the feature in Scottish Gaelic, Manx and Ulster Irish. If accepted, it also provides further evidence for a Scotticism in the Notes. Furthermore, it provides some tentative support for interpretations (c) and (d) above of the form helaín (C VI 33).

3 PHONOLOGY: CONSONANTAL FEATURES

3.1 Dental fricatives: *th* (*dh*): *ahule, bead*

Jackson thought it unlikely that **áhule** for *á thule* (AIII7) should be classified as a pronunciation spelling since he judged a twelfth-century date for the reduction of the dental fricative *th* to *h* to be too early,[13] and the form could be explained as 'a mere inadvertent omission of the *t*' (Jackson 1972, 55).[14] It is possible that **áhule** for *á thule* (AIII7) may have been influenced by **nahúle** (AIII6) of the previous line. Nevertheless, the development *th* > *h* requires further comment. Jackson's dating for the development *th* > *h* is based on 'Irish' literary evidence discussed by O'Rahilly (1930) and R.A. Breatnach (1952, 51–52), which suggests that *th* was reduced to *h* mainly during the thirteenth century.[15] Taylor (1995, 43) concludes on the basis of certain Fife

13 One wonders if the apparent confusion of broad and slender *th* in the phrase gobraíth (AI5) for *go bráth* might also imply the reduction of the dental fricative *th* to *h* in vernacular speech. Cf. *maithir* (1095 for *máthair*) (C. Breatnach 1990a, 437). (However, *aí* in gobraíth may indicate a raised vowel in the region of [ɛ:], perhaps representing a hypercorrection indicative of raising of *á* before palatals.) Similarly, the use of *-d* for original *-th* in gobrád (BV7) may also indicate that *th* had been reduced to *h*, the scribe being uncertain how to spell the historical dental fricative in this case. We may compare R.A. Breatnach's comment on 'the confusion in *Átha Cliad*, 36ª7 (1126) [in the *Annals of Inisfallen*], and the hesitation between *d*(*h*) and *th* in *Cadthal*, 40ᶜ12 (1192), which may mean that *th* was equivalent to *h* at this time' (1952, 51–2, n. 4); on the other hand, such variation may represent an archaising orthographic feature originating from environments where such variation was common in the earlier language; see *GOI* 77–8, 80–3; we may compare chadraíg (AII6) with *adramail* (representing *athir* + *amail*), discussed by Thurneysen (*GOI* 80). On the use of *d* for *th* in Middle Gaelic, see L. Breatnach (1994, 229). On the possible development *d*[*h*] > *g*[*h*], see discussion of donnachac (CVI7) and cuidíd (AIII8) below (3.3.4); cf. also tentative discussion of hídid (BV2) above (n.39).   **14** This stance contrasts with the views expressed in Jackson (1952, 93; cf. Jackson 1951, 83), where áhule (for *á thule* AIII7) is cited as evidence for 'the beginning of the change to *h*, perhaps slightly earlier than in Ireland'.   **15** C. O'Rahilly (1973, 4 n. 11) suggests that a number of instances of initial *h-* in the Book of Leinster represent *th-* and as such illustrate 'the pronunciation of *th* as *h*': *hopair* (for *th'opair* LL 8783), *a hús* (for *a thús* LL 12413), *hām* (for *thám* LL 34840). However, the interpretation of *h-* in some of these examples is uncertain. For instance, *hopair* may represent *opair*; *hús* may represent *aus* 'adventures, story, tidings' (see *DIL* s.v. *aus*). I am grateful to Professor Liam Breatnach for discussing these examples with me.

place-names that the dental fricative *th* retained its dental articulation during
the twelfth century in Fife and 'that its loss occurred sometime between the
early years of the 13th c[entury] and the demise of G[aelic] in the St Andrews
area towards the end of that same century'. If the form *Karnebehyn* for *Carn
Beithe* is reliable, we may have evidence for the reduction of *th* to *h* in early
thirteenth-century Fife (1235x1239 *St A. Lib.* 277; Taylor forthcoming).
[Ó Murchú] (1996, 147) claims that intervocalic *th* was pronounced as a dental
fricative in the Strathord district of Perthshire in the thirteenth century. Gaelic
words in Scottish non-Gaelic sources from the twelfth and early thirteenth
century consistently retain the dental fricative in the likes of *conveth* <
coinnmheadh (*cunevethe* 1127; *conueth* 1164; *cuneueth c.*1190); *month* < *monadh*
(*muneth* 1198–99; *moneth* 1241); *ogthiern* < *ógthighearn(a)* (*oghtierne* 1220;
*ogthiern c.*1300); see *DOST* s.v. conveth, month², ogthiern; see also Pödör
(1995–96, 175–82).

The change *th* > *h* is characteristic of all varieties of Gaelic, and it is clearly
an old development. As O'Rahilly himself remarked the change 'was naturally
a slow one, and probably extended over two or three centuries' and furthermore that 'it was doubtless accomplished sooner in the speech of the common
people than in that of the learned' (1930, 194). If we take this into account
and the time-lag which often occurs between the development of a linguistic
feature and its first attestation in literary sources (Ó Buachalla 1977, 136;
1982, 425), this would suggest that the reduction of *th* to *h* may well have
been a feature of some varieties of vernacular twelfth-century Gaelic. Certain
registers may have been impervious to the change *th* > *h* for quite some time,
especially during the initial stages of the change; for instance, we may have to
deal with a degree of conservatism in the pronunciation and spelling of certain
place-names, even in those which were lexically transparent to Gaelic speakers.

It seems likely that the reduction of *th* occurred in conditioned stages, and
that it occurred earlier in particular phonological environments than others,
e.g. in certain consonantal clusters, and in words containing other dental fricatives by a process of dissimilation. O'Rahilly (1930, 186–7) cites Old Gaelic
aithgne > *aichnem* (LU), *aichne* (LL) as evidence of the development *th* > *h* in
the cluster -*thg*[*h*]*n*- > -*chn*-; however, the development *th* > *h* is not necessary
to account for the development -*thg*[*h*]*n*- > -*chn*- as cluster coalescence is
sufficient to explain it; note also that Classical Gaelic retains *th* in this word:
aithne < Old Gaelic *aithgne* (McManus 1994a, 353); compare, however,
Classical Gaelic *friochnamh* < *frithgnam*, *suaichnidh* < *suaithgnid*, where the
dental fricative *th* has been lost in similar clusters (O'Rahilly 1930, 187;
McManus 1994, 353). We may also compare the apparent loss of *d*[*h*] in
clusters in the Deer forms: blienec (A117) for *bliednec, íenasi (Bv10) for
*fhiednasi. The presence of another dental fricative (in this case *s*) appears to
have led to the early loss of *th* by a form of dissimilation in the Old Gaelic

adverb *af(h)rithissi*, thus giving rise to a new hiatus form **af(h)riïssi*.[16] All modern forms of the adverb *arís(t)* (Irish) / *a-rithis(t)*[17] (Scottish Gaelic) derive from an underlying hiatus form, which most likely developed at a time when the phoneme *th* was still realised as a dental fricative. The form *arīsse* is attested in the late tenth-century (*Saltair na Rann*; see O'Rahilly 1930, 187) and *a-rís(i)* is the form always used in Classical Gaelic (McManus 1994, 353). The two instances of **mec̲bead** (DIII7) and **mec bead** (BVI–2) in the Notes, representing an underlying genitive form *Mec Bethad*, most likely represent a similar instance of dissimilation between dental fricatives.[18] It is perhaps possible that such dissimilation may have in some instances operated across word boundaries in commonly occurring collocations, perhaps even in **arthabárt áhule dó** (AII17), in which the second *th* may have been phonetically reduced. On the other hand, it is possible that a following high back round vowel may have been an early conducive environment for the reduction of *th* > *h*.[19] The case of **cuidíd** (AII18) (discussed further below), with possible confusion of final *d[h]* for *g[h]*, suggests that the palatalised dental fricative *d[h]* may have lost its dental articulation in some environments by the twelfth century in eastern Scotland. There is some evidence to suggest that the merger between palatal(ised) *dh* and *gh* may have occurred earlier than the merger between non-palatal(ised) *dh* and *gh*: see Ó Maolalaigh (2006, 42). Although it is unclear whether the loss of dental articulation in *th* and *dh* occurred at the same time (as is sometimes implied), the evidence of **cuidíd** (AII18), coupled with **áhule** (AII17) and **mec̲bead** (DIII7), **mec bead** (BVI–2), suggests that the dental articulation of the older fricatives *th* and *dh* was in the process of being lost in some environments at least at the time of writing of the Gaelic Notes.[20] See also the discussion of **donnac̲hac** (CVI7)

16 The loss of intervocalic *h* (< *th*) in Scottish Gaelic is marginally more common in words containing initial *s* (e.g. *saothair* and *soitheach*), where the fricative *s* appears to be a relevant factor in the reduction; cf. Ó Maolalaigh (2003d, 316). O'Rahilly (193, 187, n. 82) refers to a similar example from English: *since* < Middle English *siðenes*.   17 *th* in Scottish Gaelic *a-rithis(t)* is not a survival of Old Gaelic *th*; it represents a relatively recent orthographic development in Scotland as a marker of hiatus, and is based on the common loss of intervocalic *th* in southern and eastern dialects.   18 Cf. Jackson (1972, 63) who refers to 'a haplology of the two dental spirants, so that the first disappeared under the influence of the second.'   19 The place-name Romanno < *Rath Manach* in Peebles occurs without *th* from the latter half of the twelfth century: *Rumanach* (1165x70; *RRS* ii no. 39), *Rumanach* (1179xc.1189; *RRS* ii no. 243), *Rumanach* (1179x89; *RMN* no. 125); cf. *Rothmaneic* with *th* (1165; *RRS* i no. 261). See W.J. Watson (1926, 153) for some of these forms. I am grateful to Dauvit Broun for providing the dates and references to *RRS* and *RMN*. If these forms are reliable for Gaelic speakers' pronunciation of this name, it would suggest that the unstressed position may have been a conducive environment in the twelfth century for the loss or reduction of *th*, although in the present case dissimilation with the voiceless fricative *ch*, and / or cluster reduction, may also have been factors.   20 W.J. Watson (1926, 115–16) derives the name *Muireb* ('Moray') from *moirthreabh* < **mori-treb-* ('sea-settlement'), and quotes the following forms from the Annals of Ulster: *Murebe* (gen. 1032), *Muireb* (1085), *Moreb* (1130), *Moriab* (1116). He also quotes the form *Muref* from

above (2.4.3). Future investigations of the historical development of the dental fricatives will need to pay close attention to macro- and micro-phonological environments.

3.2 Reduction of consonant groups

There is some evidence for the reduction of certain consonant groups or clusters: *dhn > n*: blienec (AII7) < *bliednec*, íenasi (BV10) < *iednasi*; *ght > t*: brite (EVIII1) < *brigte*;[21] *psc > sc*: éscob (DIII5) < *épscop*; *rtn > rn*: garnaít (AII4, AII3) < *gartnaít* (for which compare Gartnait DIII1, gartnait DIV1);[22] *chtmh > chmh*: ócmad (DIII5) < *óctmad* (cf. Jackson 1972, 136).

3.3 Merger

3.3.1 Merger of lenited and unlenited l: *Collum*

The appearance of *ll* for original *l* twice in Hand A (collum AII5,18) for the name *Colum* may well be evidence for the beginning of the merger between lenited (*l*) and unlenited broad (*ll*), which is a characteristic feature of the majority of modern Gaelic (both Irish and Scottish) dialects, including eastern Scottish Gaelic dialects (Ó Maolalaigh 1997, 32, 41–43, 59). The merger is more common in certain northern and eastern Scottish Gaelic dialects, although it is of course impossible to say how early the merger may have been. For a discussion of the contrast in Scottish Gaelic and the recent merger in a modern north-western Scottish Gaelic dialect, see Wentworth (2002). If we are correct in interpreting this variation as evidence for the seeds

the twelfth-century (1165x84) tract, *De Situ Albanie* (W.J. Watson 1926, 107–8) and the Norse forms *Mærhafi >> Morhæfi* (cf. Craigie 1897, 451) as evidence for the stage *h < th* (W.J. Watson 1926, 115). To these we may add the form *Muriam* from the Annals of Inisfallen (Mac Airt 1988, 292, 1130.5). If W. J. Watson's derivation is correct and if we can take the above forms as contemporary or near-contemporary, it would imply the loss of *th* in the vicinity of *r* in this word at an early date. However, the loss of *th* might be expected to have yielded **Muirreb* with *rr* (cf. Wyntoun's form *Murrave* quoted in W.J. Watson (1926, 115)) rather than *r*. The forms *Moriab* and *Muriam* suggest, however, that the second syllable was long, which argues against Watson's derivation. 21 Cf. Gilla Bridi (for *Gilla Brighdi*) MS RIA D ii 1 (Book of Uí Mhaine, dated to end of fourteenth century) 58v7: see http://www.isos.dias.ie/. 22 David Sellar points out to me that the *-t-* survives in the place-name *Pitgartney* (a farm in the Black Isle) and in the personal name *Gratney*, borne by at least one of the medieval earls of Mar. The *t* appears to have been lost in the name *Gairnieston* (NJ748555), which is about 4 miles NNE of Turriff. I am grateful to Dauvit Broun for the latter example. Simon Taylor suggest to me that Pittengardner (Fordoun parish, Kincardineshire, NO74 76) may contain the personal name *Gartnait*. He kindly provides the following early forms: Petme[n]gartenach (1219x1242 *Arb Lib* i, no. 290; 1265 *Arb Lib* i, no. 247); Petinagartenach *or* Pet[m]agartenach (1315 *RRS* v, no. 49); Petyngartnay (1442 *Arb Lib* ii, no. 85); Pettygartnar (1462 *Arb Lib* ii, no. 138). The epenthetic vowel between the *t* and *n* in early forms seems to represent a development of the cluster *-rtn-*, although it is unclear to which language this development should be

of the merger, it could imply that the environment of rounded (back) vowels may have been one of the most favourable environments for the merger of the original phonemes //l// and //L//.[23] As well as differing in places of articulation, it seems reasonable to assume that the degree of velarisation may have been a further differentiating factor between both phonemes //l// and //L//, with velarisation possibly being weaker in //l// than in //L//. It is conceivable that the degree of velarisation may have been blurred in the environment of back rounded vowels, whose tongue positions resemble that for velarisation. In this context we may note the following three instances of *ll* for *l* from the Annals of Inisfallen, all of which occur following a back rounded vowel: *Ullad* (1101), *Ullthu* (1101),[24] *Collmáin* (1208) (C. Breatnach 1990a, 433). Alternatively, it is possible that double *ll* in *Colum* may have been influenced by the following *Cille*; or that *ll* derives from a hypocoristic variant.

3.3.2 Merger of palatal and non-palatal *n; m?*: Nominative for genitive*(?)*

Jackson refers to a number of instances 'which look at first sight as if the nominative is being used for the genitive', all of them lacking the required genitive (palatalisation) marker *i*. Leaving aside the troublesome **rósábard** (AII3) (see Jackson 1972, 51), ambiguous **toíség** (AII6), **mulenn** (AII7), **cannech** (DIII1),[25] **arthabart** (AII7) possibly for *arthabairt* (Jackson 1972, 132), the words in question are: **búchan** (AI4), **búchan** (CVI3), **buchan** (CVI33), **drostán** (AII8), **morcúnn** (AII2), **morcunt** (AII8), **malcolum** (AII10, 13), **malcoloum** (AIII1), **márr** (DIII8), **madchór** (BV4), all of which are proper names; see Jackson (1972, 145).[26] On the omission of the palatalisation marker particularly following *e, é* in some eleventh-century texts, see Ó Cuív (1990, 49). Rather than seeing them as evidence for the 'breakdown of the case-system' (a familiar feature of modern eastern Scottish Gaelic dialects),[27] he concludes that 'these things are probably instances of the carelessness of the scribes of Deer' (Jackson 1972, 145). Other explanations are possible, however, in individual cases.[28] It is possible that some of these examples may have linguistic significance. Jackson himself refers to the non-marking of palatal *m* (in **Malcolum** AII10, 13 and **Malcoloum** AIII1), as

---

assigned.   **23** Double solidi are used here to denote (theoretical reconstructed) phonemes in 'Common Gaelic' (in Borgstrøm's sense of the term).   **24** Double *ll* in *Ullad* (1101) may, however, be an analogical form based on syncopated forms containing *-lt-*: cf. *Ullthu* (1101).   **25** On the possible use of *e* as a palatalisation marker, see discussion above. **26** Though clearly not nominative, compare **culeón** (AII10) possibly for *culeóin*.   **27** For a rebuttal of Jackson's evidence for the early break-down of the inflected nominal system in eastern Scotland, see Ó Maolalaigh (1998, 20–1).   **28** For instance, scribal practices might account for the lack of *i* before *n* and *m* in some cases: it may be significant that *i* is absent before *n* in 6 of these examples, and before *m* in 3 examples. Although minims are generally clearly distinguished in the Notes, it is perhaps possible that the practice of not writing *i* before *n* and *m* may have first arisen as a way of avoiding a potential for ambiguity which a

conceivably being 'due to the beginnings of the depalatalisation of labials which is characteristic of Sc. G.' (1972, 132).[29] Jackson (1972, 42), in the case of genitive **drostán** (AII8), rightly notes the lack of genitive forms in the *-án* diminutive in Irish sources from the Old and Middle Gaelic periods,[30] and it may be that such uninflected forms were intended by the scribes in the case of **drostán** (AII8) and possibly **búchan** AI4, **búchan** CVI3, **buchan** CVI33. Indeed, Ó Cuív (1972, 343) suggests that non-palatal *n* may have been intended by the scribes in the case of **drostán** and **cuileón**. However, we know that genitive forms did subsequently develop in both Irish and Scottish Gaelic, and it is thus possible that a genitive *drostáin* was intended or was 'underlyingly' present. The forms in genitive contexts (**búchan** AI4, **búchan** CVI3, **buchan** CVI33, **drostán** AII8, **culeón** AIIIo), taken together, might then suggest that original broad and slender lenited *n* may have merged or were in the process of merging by the twelfth century in certain eastern Scottish Gaelic dialects and in certain phonological environments.[31] This merger is particularly characteristic of modern eastern Scottish Gaelic (see Ó Maolalaigh 2001), although we cannot at present date this merger.[32] Ultimately, of course, it is difficult to decide between scribal and phonological factors in such cases. Similarly, evidence suggestive of a weakening of the contrast between lenited and unlenited broad *n* can also be explained in scribal terms.[33]

---

cluster of minims might introduce. **29** This might also be suggested by the forms **choluim** (BV6,21) and **colim** (DIVI), which Jackson (1972, 132–3) suggested might represent 'hypercorrections'. However, the use of palatal *m* in these three examples, if they do not represent instances of sandhi (on which see below 4.1), may conceivably represent feminine dative singular forms; note that the preposition *do* precedes in each example. We may compare *do Cholaim Chille* in the Gaelic Life of Adomnán, which, however, the editors' suggest may 'reflect a local pronunciation or an Ó Cléirigh idiosyncrasy' (Herbert and Ó Riain 1988, 70). See also C. Breatnach's (1992, 184) comments on this form. **30** See also *GOI* 178. Carney (1964, 155) quotes a number of nom. pl. forms in *-án* from early sources, e.g. *ind énán, maccán, in rannán*. I am grateful to Professor Liam Breatnach for these examples. **31** The etymology of *Buchan* is unclear; we cannot be certain if the final syllable was originally long or short although Alexander (1952, 26) recorded it short in modern Scottish Gaelic. Thomas Owen Clancy has suggested to me (personal communication) that Mar and Buchan may conceivably be Pictish cognates of Welsh *mawr* 'large' and *bychan* 'small', the implication being that both areas were once contiguous and paired together (cf. Cantref Mawr and Cantref Bychan in Dyfed). This hypothesis is attractive but it does not account for the phonological difficulty of deriving Gaelic *Marr* (with unlenited *rr*) from an underlying single *r*. See further discussion in Ó Maolalaigh, 'On the possible functions of the accents', this volume. **32** The possible relevance of this merger for the development of the Scottish Gaelic plural allomorph *-an* is discussed in Ó Maolalaigh (2003b). **33** Single *n* occurs on four occasions for expected double *nn*: **benact** (AII6), **blienec** (AII7), **íenasi** (BVIo), **donchad** (BVI). Cf. *griana, Conachtu* (Ó Cuív 1990, 50).

3.3.3 Merger of palatal and non-palatal *rr?:* The case of *Márr* (genitive)

Jackson thought the genitive form **márr** (D8) was probably a mistake for intended *Mairr* (1972, 141), and tentatively suggested that the lack of 'expected' *i* might just indicate the merger of palatal *rr* //ʀ´// with non-palatal *rr* //ʀ// (1972, 128), which is a relatively old development given that it has occurred throughout the Gaelic-speaking area (see Ó Murchú 1989b; cf. Ó Murchú 1986). However, Ó Baoill (2000) establishes that the earliest form of the word (in the genitive), occurring in the *Annals of Ulster* under the year 1014 was *Marr*.[34] Ó Baoill (2000, 165) quotes the rhyming pair *crann: Mharr* from 'a pre-sixteenth-century syllabic couplet' listed in the *Irish Grammatical Tracts*. To this may be added the *deibhidhe* rhyme *Marr* (gen. sg.): *Domhnall*, from a poem which Ó Cuív (1972, 344) suggested could date to the twelfth century.

3.3.4 Merger of *dh* and *gh: cuitid*

The word *cuitid* occurs in the sentence robaíth cathál árachoír chetna acuitíd thóisíg in Text II (AII17–18), and is translated by Jackson as 'Cathal "quenched" his toísech's dues on the same terms' (1972, 34), thus equating *cuitid* with *cuit*, which he consistently translated as 'dues'[35] in the phrases cuit mormoir (AII5), cuít toíség (AII6), cuít rííg (AIII11–12), ar chuit cetri dabach (CVII19–20).[36] Jackson in his notes to Text II states that *cuitid* 'is a derivative of *cuid*', though he does not explain what type of derivative it might be (1972, 55). Note that *cuitid* is not included in his discussion of inflected forms (1972, 145–46). In the glossarial index, *cuitid* appears as a separate head-word and is glossed 'same as *cuit*' (1972, 155, s.v. *cuitid*). Jackson (1972, 141, 27(c)) seems to imply that *cuitid* is a nominative for accusative form, presumably because it is followed by lenition rather than eclipsis.[37]

Two different lexical forms rarely 'mean' or 'refer to' exactly the same thing, though semantic differences may be relatively minor. If *cuitid* represents a

34 Ó Baoill (2000) illustrates that the genitive form of the name, *Mair*, occurring in nineteenth-century editions of the *Annals of Ulster*, and accepted by W.J. Watson (1926, 115) and Jackson (1972, 128), is incorrect and based on a transcription error. **35** See translations in Jackson (1972, 34, 35) and his discussion (1972, 119). **36** Dauvit Broun argues elsewhere in this volume that the final example may not actually be an example of *cuit* in its technical sense of 'dues', and may represent a use of the prepositional phrase *ar chuit*, meaning 'as regards'; see *DIL* s.v. *cuit* §10. Similarly, *cuit* could have its generic meaning of 'portion' in this example. It may be worth noting that *cuit*, when used in its technical sense of 'dues', seems always to occur with a following specific in the genitive. Cf. *cuid oidhche*, which occurs in non-Gaelic sources as *cuddy* (*DIL* s.v. *cuit* §5) and *cudeigh* (*CSD* s.v. *cudeigh*; *DOST* s.v. *cuddeich*). **37** In his support we may note that the use of nominative for oblique forms (whether dative, genitive or accusative) at various periods in the history of the Gaelic languages seems to be particularly common with nouns which are qualified by noun modifiers or epithets. See McKenna (1941) for the rules in Classical Gaelic. This is largely true of the modern languages also.

separate lexical item,[38] we might expect it to have a rather more specialised meaning than *cuit* since it is the marked congener in the pair *cuit ~ cuitid*. Dauvit Broun suggests elsewhere in this volume, based on the occasional use of *cuitig* for *cuit* in the sense of 'portion of food' in Irish sources, that *cuitid* (for *cuitig*) may refer specifically to the farming produce due to a *toísech*, thereby emphasising the edible nature of the dues expected by him, which, he argues, makes sense in the context of extinguishing land dues as opposed to simple grants of land. This argument relies on Jackson's interpretation that '*cuit* was the dues and services liable to be rendered by the tenants of the estates named, to the king, and also to the mormaer and the toísech [...] in virtue of their office' (1972, 119), rather than the more straightforward interpretation of *cuit* as being a portion of land (granted by a king, *mormaer* or *toísech*). This suggestion is presumably based on the comment made by the editors of *DIL* that *cuitig* occurs 'frequ[ently]' in the sense of 'portion of food, meal, evening meal' (*DIL* s.v. *cuit* §5). The examples cited from Irish sources in *DIL*, however, do not readily support a semantic difference between *cuit* and *cuitig*.

Linguistically, *cuitid* must be in origin an inflectional rather than a lexical derivative of *cuit / cuid*, i.e. an oblique case form (dative or accusative), possibly adopted as a new nominative here as Jackson suggests. However, it is quite possible that *cuitid* functions as the accusative sg. of *cuit* here even though the following *thoísig* is lenited. (With this we might compare the accusative form ịnchadraíg (A116), where the accusative noun is lenited rather than eclipsed by the preceding article (cf. Jackson 1972, 146); contrast accusative ịngathraíg (A15) eclipsed by the preceding article.) If correct, the lenition of following *thoísig* may be significant and could suggest that eclipsis of nominal modifiers (possibly also adjectives) following accusative sg. nouns was not the norm in certain varieties of Gaelic in twelfth-century eastern Scotland; note also the lack of eclipsis of *ele* in ịncathŕaig ele (A16–7).

There is no compelling evidence to suggest that *cuit* joined the ranks of a dental declension. However, the available evidence argues strongly that *cuit*—originally an *i*-stem—became a guttural stem with oblique *cuitig* some time before or during the Middle Gaelic period (*c*.900–1200 AD).[39] However, the

---

38 For an example of lexically differentiated forms deriving from morphophonemic variants of a single underlying stem, see Jasanoff's (1989) discussion of Old Gaelic *ben* and *bé*.   39 See *DIL* s.v. *cuit*. This change in declension is also supported by the 'variant' forms *cuid* and *cuidigh* (both feminine nouns) in the *Irish Grammatical Tracts* (also *DIL* s.v. *cuit*). See also Thurneysen (1936). (Note that the guttural declension of *cuit* is also attested in Scottish Gaelic *codach* (genitive singular) and *codaichean* (plural); see *Dwelly* s.v. *cuid*.) It is possible that the southern Connacht variant *cuide* (de Bhaldraithe 1977, 148) may be a reflex of the variant *cuidigh*, although it may contain epenthetic final *-e*, or be a backformation based on the nexus *cuid* + *de* (cf. *leithéide* < ? *leithéid de*). Liam Breatnach provides the following late example from the Law commentaries: *cuite geill righ* (Binchy

by-form *cuitid* also occurs occasionally in Irish sources, which Thurneysen (1936, 367) takes to be a secondary form of *cuidig*. The most simple and straightforward explanation of the Deer form cuitíd (AIII8) for *cuitig* is that it implies the merger or partial merger of the palatalised dental and velar fricatives (in final unstressed position), as is attested occasionally in contemporary Irish sources in other words from the eleventh and twelfth centuries.[40] This is the conclusion favoured by Ó Cuív (1972, 344). The collective evidence from the Gaelic Notes would seem to suggest that the merger between palatalised *d*[*h*] and *g*[*h*] was not general by the time of the writing of the Notes, but this could be attributed to orthographic conservatism.[41] As noted above, it is quite likely that the merger of the two spirants proceeded in stages, beginning in specific phonological environments, and then later spreading to others. We have also suggested that the merger may have occurred or begun earlier with the palatal(ised) pair *dh* / *gh*, and the evidence of *cuitid* for *cuitig* may well support this. Moreover, it is possible that the final unstressed position may have been a favourable environment for the initial stages of the merger of palatal(ised) *dh* and *gh*, as indeed is suggested by the Middle Gaelic evidence; see Ó Maolalaigh (2006, 42). Alternatively, sporadic instances of variation between both fricatives (*dh* and *gh*) can be seen as part of the almost universal tendency for the interchange of accoustically similar fricatives. In other words, *cuitid* for *cuitig* can be accounted for on phonetic and phonological grounds. On the other hand, *cuitid* could be a hyper-correction of one sort or another—either purely orthographic (i.e. *-id* for *-ig*) in nature or, possibly representing actual pronunciation at a time when there was variation in the vernacular between [ð´] and [ɣ´]; cf. the possible borrowing of *seagh* (with variant *seadh*) as *shayth* into Scots (Breeze 2003).

3.3.5 Merger of final unstressed palatal *gh* and *ch: Cannech*

The almost categorical use in the Gaelic Notes of final *-g* rather than *-c*(*h*) to represent the palatal fricative in final unstressed position, which is written *-igh* in Irish and *-ich* in Scottish Gaelic, is noteworthy. Examples include:

cósgreg (AII), roalseg (AI2), rothidńaíg (AI4), gathraíg (AI5), cathŕaig (AI6), dorodloeg (AI8), chadraíg (AII6), toíség (gen. sg. AII6), dabég (dual, AIII2), luloíg (AIII4), thóisíg (AIII8), cóbrig

---

1978, 1402.10). **40** Confusion of dental and velar fricatives, particularly when palatalised and in final unstressed position, is evidenced from the eleventh and twelfth centuries in manuscripts such as Lebor na hUidre, the Annals of Inisfallen, Rawlinson B502, and the Book of Leinster: see L. Breatnach (1994, 234–5) and Ó Maolalaigh (2006, 42). **41** See Jackson (1972, 138–40). Jackson suggests that the loss of dental articulation in the voiceless dental fricative *th* was only beginning by the end of the twelfth century (1972, 55). See, however, our discussion above for a more nuanced view of the historical development.

(DIII2), muredig (DIII10), cennedig (BV13), cáennaig (BV16–17),
sithig (CVI8).

Against these 16 examples, there is one case of the apparent use of *ch*, i.e.
cannech (gen. sg. D1); cf. also máledo͟mni m͟ac m͟ecbead (D7), which, if
it is not a scribal error, may represent the loss of the palatal fricative in sandhi.
If rosbenact (A116) is a mistake for *rosbenac* (i.e. *rosbennaich*), the use of *-ac*
(for *-aich*) rather than *-ig* / *-eg* may provide another example (but for another
interpretation, see discussion above and Jackson 1972, 41). Given the phonetic
nature of some spellings in the Notes one obvious conclusion to draw from
forms in *-g* is that these forms were pronounced as voiced rather than
voiceless fricatives. The single instance of cannech (possibly for *canne[i]ch*),
if not nominative for genitive in error, could suggest that such fricatives were
pronounced as voiceless, in which case spellings with *-g* could represent
literary 'Irish' forms.[42] Diack notes that *-ig* spellings in Deer 'by themselves
will not prove that the sounds were voiced in S[cottish] Gaelic at the period',
noting the the 'absolute dominance of Irish influence in all early documents of
Scottish provenance must be taken into account' (1922, 150).[43] That such
conservative spellings were used by learned Scottish Gaels in later periods is
shown by forms found in the 1408 MacDonald charter (e.g. *riabhoige* for
vernacular *riabhaiche* (Munro and Munro 1986, 22)); the 1467 manuscript
(e.g. *rochuibrighedh* Ó Baoill 1988, 126); the mid-sixteenth-century treaty
between Argyll and O'Donnell (e.g. *d(h)uthaig(h)* for vernacular *d(h)ùthaich*
MacKechnie 1953, 97, 98); the Books of Clanranald (e.g. *Laighnigh*,
Roithechtaigh, *Chobhuigh* (cf. *Chobhaidh*), etc. (A. Cameron 1894, 148); the
1614 Charter of Fosterage (where the genitive form *cainnigh* occurs 9 times;
cf. also *muiredhaigh* (J. Cameron 1937, 222)); the mid-seventeenth-century
Scottish Gaelic grammatical tract (e.g. *tealuigh* for vernacular *-aich*: R. Black
1990, 9). However, *-ich* also occurs occasionally, e.g. *gruamaich* (A. Cameron
1894, 212). John Carswell in his Gaelic translation of the Book of Common
Order, published in Edinburgh in 1567, has numerous examples of *idh* and *igh*
for what is normally *ich* in modern Scottish Gaelic (see R.L. Thomson 1970:
xii *et passim*); so also in the Gaelic translation of Calvin's Catechism,
published *c*.1631, and notably also in the Shorter Catechism, published in
1659, which shows a large number of Scotticisms.[44] In the first fifty metrical

42 Jackson (1972, 139) notes cautiously that this single example may 'represent the
beginning of what became later the normal development in Scotland of Common Gaelic -
/ɣ'/, namely -/x'/; but on the other hand it could well be a "wrong spelling"'.   43 The
highland gentleman, quoted by Reid (1832: xli–xlii (xli)), makes a similar point about the
adoption by Scottish Gaels of Irish orthography 'in latter times' and that consequently 'the
Scottish Gaelic, through time, became in a degree Iricised'.   44 Cf. 'Now it is clear from
the description of the language of *SC* [Shorter Catechism] that it represents the spoken
language of Scotland with some rather half-hearted attempt at keeping up the fiction of a

psalms published by the Synod of Argyll, genitive *-igh* is common but *-ich* also occurs; see R.L. Thomson (1976, 152). Edward Lhuyd's 'phonetic' transcription (*c*.1700) of the Revd John Beaton's reading of the first two chapters of Genesis from Robert Kirk's 'Irish' Bible (published in 1690) provides an extraordinary and unique insight into the pronunciation of literary (classical) Irish by a literate Scottish Gael. It is clear from Lhuyd's forms that Beaton consistently pronounced these with final unstressed [i], even though his vernacular form was almost certainly *-ich* [ix´]. We may also note Lhuyd's transcription of the form *Neialih* from the Revd Beaton, which may point to *Naoi-ghiallaich* with voiceless *-ich* [ix´] (J.L. Campbell and D. Thomson 1963, 40–1). Instances where Lhuyd transcribes with *i* or *í* include: *bheannaigh* (§§1.22, 1.28, 2.3), *chomhnaigh* (§2.2), *chruthaidh* (§§1.1, 1.21, 1.27, 2.4), *chorraigh* (§1.2), *phlanndaigh* (§2.8), *geinealaigh* (§2.4);[45] cf. also *inghean Chuinn Chéad-chathaigh* (*Chàhi*), *Eachtrin Chonaill Cheárnaigh* (*Chairni*), (J.L. Campbell and D. Thomson 1963, 38–9).

It is unlikely that an opposition existed between a voiced and voiceless palatal fricative in the unstressed position (leaving aside epenthetic clusters) during the twelfth century in Ireland or in Scotland, in which case final unstressed *-gh* (or *-ch* for that matter) could represent either /ɣ´/ or /x´/. Ó Maolalaigh (forthcoming), based on a paper delivered in Galway in 1998, argues that the merger of final unstressed voiceless palatal *ch* and voiced palatal *gh* in earlier forms of Gaelic in Scotland during the Old Gaelic period may have occurred in the opposite direction to Irish, i.e. that merger resulted in *ch* rather than *gh* in Scotland. The different outcome of the merger in Scotland may have been partly due to analogical pressure of nominative *-ach* / *-ech*,[46] and possibly also the clear nature of the unstressed vowel in *-ach* / *-ech* syllables. It is interesting to note that Diack expressed a similar view as far back as the year 1922, though this is not acknowledged by scholars such as W.J. Watson (1926) or Jackson (1951; 1972). Diack claimed that 'the change of voiceless to voiced did not take place' in Scotland, noting the influence of Irish orthography on that of Scottish Gaelic (Diack 1922, 149, 150).

The Poppleton text of the Scottish royal genealogy, whose archetype dates from 1124 x 53, shows evidence of both final *-g* and *-ch*, although the former is more common: compare *Aislingig* (27), *Ellatig* (39), *Feradaig* (58), *Aibrig* (for *Almaig* 64), *Casiaclaig* (67), *Cobthaig* (71), *Buadaig* (73), *Tigernaig* (92), *Fallaig* (93) with *Ruamnaich* (29), *Tollgreich* (75), *Muredaich Bollgreich* (76) (Broun

standard literary language different from the spoken one' (R.L. Thomson 1962: xxxix). The regular use of unstressed *igh* and *idh* for modern Scottish Gaelic *ich* in the Gaelic translations of the *Book of Common Order*, Calvin's Catechism and the Shorter Catechism may not be straightforward Irish literary forms. It is perhaps possible that these spellings reflect a south-western dialect feature of Scottish Gaelic whereby such syllables are realised as /i/; see O'Rahilly (1932, 57) and Ó Maolalaigh (1999b, 221). **45** All examples from J.L. Campbell and D. Thomson (1963, 77–87). **46** Cf. now Ó Buachalla (2002, 3).

1999, 176–80).[47] The text of the genealogy which survives in Ralph of Diss'
late twelfth-century manuscript frequently departs from conventional Gaelic
orthography and as such is of interest to our enquiries; see Broun (1998,
190–1). Diss has the following forms: *Aslingich, Romaich, Etholach, Feredach*
(presumably genitive), *Firalmai, Cassieclai,*[48] *Cobthai, Lotherai, Bolgai, Thiernai*
but *Faleg* (Broun 1999, 184–6; cf. 1998, 190–1). These sources suggest
strongly that there was orthographic variation between *-ch* and *-gh* in Gaelic
sources whose originals can be dated to twelfth-century eastern Scotland.
Although such variation is ambiguous with regard to the pronunciation of the
velar fricative in unstressed syllables in twelfth-century eastern Scottish
Gaelic,[49] it does illustrate that the Deer evidence may be somewhat conservative. In a Latin charter datable to *c.*1200, and probably written by a canon of
the Augustinian priory at Inchaffray, the genitive form *Lonseg / Longsig*
appears as *longsih* (Broun 1998, 188). Broun notes a tendency towards 'actual
pronunciation' in the Gaelic forms of names in this charter and one wonders
if the spelling *longsih* is an attempt to represent voiceless *-ich*, i.e. [x´]. We
might compare Edward Lhuyd's transcription (*c.*1700) of the Revd John
Beaton's pronunciation of the title *Konnal Gyllybwyn mac Neal Neialih*,
which J.L. Campbell and D. Thomson (1963, 40–41) transliterate as *Conall
Gulban mac Néill Naoi-ghiallaich*, where *-ich* may be signalled by *-ih*. This
contrasts with *-i* for *-igh* in other titles (e.g. *inghean Chuinn Chéad-chathaigh*
(*Chàhi*), *Eachtrin Chonaill Cheárnaigh* (*Chairni*), J.L. Campbell and D. Thomson
1963, 38–39) and in Beaton's reading of parts of Kirk's 'Irish' Bible.

3.3.6 Merger of final unstressed palatal *gh* and *ch*: Onomastic evidence

Certain place-names have often been quoted as evidence for the development
-ich > *-igh* in Scottish Gaelic. W.J. Watson (1904: xxxiv–xxxv) states: 'In old
Gaelic, as is still the case in Irish, the dative or locative, and also the genitive
case of nouns ending in *-ach* was formed in *-aigh* (pronounced nearly *-ie*), and
this old formation survives in a considerable number of names'. Hence his
derivation of modern Scottish Gaelic names such as Logie, Dornie, Duchary,
Arriecheirie, etc. as oblique forms *-igh* of underlying *-ach* names. He
interprets variation between English *-ie / -y* and Scottish Gaelic *-ich* (e.g. in
Pitglassie ~ Bad a' Ghlasaich, Glen Docharty ~ Gleann Dochartaich) as 'a
process of levelling up to the modern *-aich* formation' (W.J. Watson 1904:
xxxv), thus implying that Scottish Gaelic *-ich* is a secondary development.
MacBain was of the same view. He writes *Cruaidhlaigh* [*sic*] as a locative of

---

47 References in parentheses refer to line numbers.   48 Broun (1998, 190; 1999, 186, n.
197).   49 Given the variation between *-igh* and *-ich* in Poppleton, it is tempting to
interpret variation between *-ai* and *-ich*, *-ach* in Diss as reflecting variation between *-igh*
and *-ich* respectively in the source used by Diss. However, on the representation of *-igh / -ich*
by final *-i*, *-ie*, *-y* in non-Gaelic sources, see further below (3.3.6).

Crua(i)lach and derives Pitourie from 'an old genitive *odharaigh*' (MacBain 1891, 187, 189). Similarly, he derives Cluny from 'Cluanaigh, a locative of "cluanach"' (MacBain 1907, 78).[50] G.F. Black (1993 [1946]): s.v. Mackenzie) also notes that 'the English form of the name [i.e. Mackenzie] is interesting as preserving the mediæval Gaelic pronunciation of the genitive, which in early Irish is *Cainnigh* [*sic*], pronounced "cainny"'. More recently, Cox (2002, 56, 60) suggests that 'the archaic oblique case form [i.e. *-aigh*] of nouns in *-ach* survives in [i], e.g. *Lagaidh, Ceann Loch Shlodhaidh*', which he derives from **lagach* and **slodhach* respectively. Many other instances can be quoted from W.J. Watson's *The history of the Celtic place-names of Scotland* (1926):

> Altan Albany (Allt an Albanaigh, Ayrshire, 12), Ferincoskry (Fearann Coscraigh, south-east Sutherland, 117), Belhelvie (Baile Shealbhaigh, Aberdeenshire, 137), Cockenzie (Cùil C(h)oinnigh?, 141), Deuchrie (Dubhchàthraigh, 141; cf. Cnoc Dubhcharaigh, Ross-shire, 141), Glenbirnie (Gleann Braonaigh, 141; cf. Birnie, Moray, 142), Culbirnie / Kilbirnie (Cùil-bhraonaigh, near Beauly, 189), Craigentinnie (Creag an t-Sionnaigh, Edinburgh; cf. Ardentinny, 144), Currie (dat. of Currach, 144), Dunsappie (gen. of Sopach, Edinburgh; cf. Torsappie < Torsoppie, 144), Leny (Lànaigh, 145), Binny (dat. of Binneach, 146), Glenpuitty (Gleann Puitigh, near Dalmeny, 147), Logie (Logaigh, dat. of Logach, 147), Kilkenzie (Cill Chainnigh, Carrick; but Kilmechannache in a charter of Robert I, 188); Drumranny (Druim Raithnigh, near Girvan; cf. Kilranny, 199), Bardrainney (Barr Draighnigh, 200); 'Draighnigh, Drynie, in the Black Isle, is locative' (200), Kilnotrie (Coille an Otraigh, Kirkcudbright, 201), Talnotry (Talamh an Otraigh, Kirkcudbright, 201), Gartsherrie (Gart Searraigh, Lanarkshire, 203), Roshearty (earlier Rossawarty) (Ros Àbhartaigh, near Fraserburgh, 236–37), Dunaverty (Dùn Àbhartaigh, 237), Ramornie, Ramorgany (RMS 1512 for Rath Morganaigh, Fife, 239), Kilberry (Cill Bhearaigh, Argyll, 301), Carpullie (contains pollaigh, 371), Kenandheni (from source dated 1226–34, Cenn ind Enaig[h], 417), Dulschangy (RMS 1345) (Dul-seangaigh, 419), Inverebrie (Inbhir-eabraigh, Aberdeenshire, 438), Invernenty (in Gaelic Inbhir-leanntaigh < Inbhirneanntaigh, 438), etc.

Before we proceed it is important to note that Watson's derivation from *-igh* may be incorrect in some instances. MacDonald (1941, 49) dismisses Watson's (1926, 146) derivation of the West Lothian place-name Binny, and cites the early form *Bennyn* (*c.*1200). This form may contain a Gaelic diminutive suffix

---

50 MacBain does not suggest *-igh* in the case of Kingussie, presumably because the Gaelic form is *Cinn [a']* Ghiuthsaich; see MacBain (1891, 175), where the name is spelt as *Cinn-ghiubhsaich.*

(Ó Maolalaigh 1998, 36) or the locational suffix *-in*. Similarly, Logie (Fife) is attested as Logine (*c*.1260); see Taylor (1995, 489–90) and Ó Maolalaigh (1998, 31). Birnie (Moray) is problematic since early forms of the name suggest an original underlying final dental fricative *-th*: *Brennath* (1210); *Brennath* (1239); *Birneth* (1421); *Byrneth* (1451); *Birneth* (1543); *Birnet* (1554); *Birnet* (1571) (all from *Moray Registrum*); *Birney* (1596); *Birney* (1651); *Birnie* (1695); *Birnay* (1718); *Birnie* (1732) (all from Records of Elgin); see Keillar (1993, 21–22) for references. More investigation of late medieval and early modern forms is required in some instances before an acceptable derivation can be established.

Diack (1922, 148–51) discusses Scottish Gaelic place-names with expected final *-ich*. He criticises W.J. Watson's and MacBain's use of *-igh* rather than *-ich* to represent oblique forms of names in *-ach*. He has three objections: (a) 'some explanation is wanted of how it comes that *-aigh* has survived only in place-names and in them only sporadically'; (b) 'to write [*-aigh* ...] without accounting for the existence in the same area and at the same time of [*-aich* ...] is hardly satisfactory'; (c) 'in Scotland the change of voiceless [*-ich*] to voiced [*-igh*] did not take place' (Diack 1922, 150). As far as (a) is concerned, it should be noted that *-i*, *-ie*, *-y* spellings are in fact also found in early and modern forms of many Scottish surnames, which can be associated with oblique *-igh* / *-ich*, e.g.

> MacAughtrie (Mac Uchtraigh), MacBratney (Mac Breatnaigh), MacCoskrie (Mac Coscraigh), MacCullony (Mac'Ill Domhnaich), MacHarrie (Mac Fhearadhaigh), MacKelvie (Mac Shealbhaigh), MacKenzie (Mac C(h)oinnich), MacKerley (Mac Thearlaich), MacKirdie (Mac Mhuircheartaigh), MacLaverty (Mac Fhlaithbheartaich), MacMurray (Mac Muireadhaigh), etc. (G.F. Black 1993 [1946] s.v.).

Diack's last objection, though perhaps correct, is nevertheless based on unsound reasoning. He claims that *-ich* could not have been voiced to *-igh* in Scottish Gaelic since 'otherwise we should have to hold that in Scottish Gaeldom *ch* universally became *gh* and *finally silent*, as in Irish, and that at a later period the original *ch* was (except in the southern fringe [of Arran, etc.]) universally restored' (Diack 1922, 150 [italics mine]). The assumption that the final syllable *-igh* would have been pronounced in earlier forms of Scottish Gaelic as [i] with silent *gh* is objectionable since the argument for deriving modern Scottish Gaelic *-ich* from earlier *-igh* rests on the necessity of *gh* being pronounced (either as a velar fricative or possibly a glide). In other words, the proposed change *-igh* > *-ich* must have occurred when *gh* was still realised as a consonant.

Although more research remains to be done on the subject, it seems to be generally true that *-i*, *-ie*, *-y* spellings occur earlier than *-ich*, *-ych* spellings in

PLATES

I 1st opening IV

Liber g̅n̅iationis ihu
x̅p̅i fili dauid fili abra
cham · abracham g̅h̅uic mac
Issác h̅ g̅h̅uic iacob · iacob h̅
g̅h̅uic iudam · iudam ⁊ p̅r̅is̅ h̅z
sudar h̅ g̅h̅uic phares ⁊ zana
oththaman · phares h̅ g̅h̅uic es̅
rom · esrrom h̅ g̅h̅uic aram ··
Aram h̅ g̅h̅uic aminadab · am
nadab h̅ g̅h̅uic naaron · naaron
h̅ g̅h̅uic solmon · solmon h̅ g̅h̅uic·
boos othachab · boos h̅ g̅h̅uic
obeth exuich · obeth h̅ g̅h̅uic ihse
ihse h̅ g̅h̅uic dauid nigun · dauid
h̅ nex g̅h̅uic salmonon exea q̅
puic uriae · salamon h̅ g̅h̅uic
roboam · roboar h̅ g̅h̅uic abina
abina h̅ g̅h̅uic — asaph ·····

Omnes igitur generationes ab Abraham usque ad Dauid generationes ·xiiii· et a Dauid usque ad
transmigrationem babilonis generationes ·xiiii· et a transmigra-
tione babilonis usque ad xp̄m
generationes ·xiiii· ⁊

Finit prologus. Incipit nunc
euangelium secundum matheum ⁊

Columcille ⁊ Drostán mc Coscreg a dalta
tángator a hÍ mar ro falseg Día dóib go
nic̄ Abbordoboir ⁊ Bede cruthnec ro bo mormær
Buchan aragginn ⁊ ise ro thidnaig dóib
in cathraig sin i saere go bráith ó mormaer
⁊ ó thosec. Tángator as a athle sen i cathraig
ele ⁊ do raits ri Colum Cille si ⁊ ro falseg do Bede
⁊ do ro lóeg a immorbus i bede go n-dár
tabrad dó ⁊ ni thanic ⁊ ro gab mc dó galar
iar nimmbie na-gcleirec ⁊ ro bo marb acht mad beca
iar sin do chuid in mormaer da attac na-gcleirec gon-díguith

binnacde leʒ inic ʒondipad planice do ꝛdopiac
īfobahiʒ uaclore ītppiac ʒonice ehlore pēcc
ine ʒaynaic dopompac īnbinnaede ꝛtaine
planice do ꝛ aynnen dopiac collūcille do nop
can īchadpiaiʒ pōn īnopbchacc ꝛpoyiacaib ꝛbpie
thiʒi ʒebe cypio pipinabao blisinec buaoacc can
ʒac dayia dpiopican aypicayichain ppi collūcille
pilabopi colūcille bedeiqi aninj ohunn iniacc;
Comʒeall inc boa dopiac uaopici nice pupuine
docolūcille ꝛdo dpiopican . Mopuoac nēe mopicupip
dopiac pēcc ine ʒaynnac ꝛachao coche cnīnj
ꝛbahe pobomopiniapi ꝛpiobochopiē . Pacaiqi
ine cathull dopiac cuic inopinopicialci ꝛculi inc
baciqi dopiac cuic coipeʒ . Domnall inc ʒipie
ꝛinallbpiʒce inc chachal dopiac pēcc īinulenn
do dpiopican . Cathal inc mopicucic dopiac achao
naʒliʒiē do dpiopican . Domnall inic puiadiii ꝛ
malcolū inc culéon dopiacpiac biobin do dia ꝛdo
dpiopican . Malcolou inic einacha dopiac cuic
piiiʒ ibbiobin ꝛīpēc inc ʒobnioiʒ ꝛda dabeʒ
uaccaiin piopiabaio . Malcolū inc moilbpiʒce
dopiac ꝛdelsic . Malpinēce inc luloiʒ dopiac

pēt malduib do drostan; Donall mc meic
dubbacin robarth nahule ebarta rodror
tan ayrthabacut ahule do; robaith cathal
ayachorn cētna acuizio tonrig 7 dorac
prorin chē cecnolloce 7eccaipe do dia
7do drostan. Catinnech mc meic dobarreon
7cathal donarrac altin alla ucthe
necā 7egonice 7berth toarooa altin
donac donmall 7cathal erdanin
do dia 7do drostan. Robaith Catinnec
7donall 7cathal nahule eobarta in
dia 7in drostan otorac gouenao mene omor iocerec
gart nar mc cannech 7ece igeugillemichel
donarput petmec cobrig ricorerrao eclar
cmpt 7petin abrtoil 7oocolucille 7oodnorta
ren onahulib doloorib conanarcao docormc
epcob duim callein. inoemao bliaoi rrgroo
Cerab; rrair nerran epcob abb; 7leot ab brecani
7maledoni mc meb eao; 7algune mc apcill; 7ruao
in mormar marn 7 macan brrcēm; 7gillecrrpt
mc conmaic; 7malpetin mc donaill; 7oo ongart
rerlegin cunbruad; 7gillecolai mc muneois; 7oub
ni mc mal colai ss docrrpt 7oocolicilli 7oodnorta
Donat ganr . . . 7igeugillemied ball dōm rpet rpan
Cerre gillecallme racam 7renaoac mc mal brrci 7 mal
gme mc rralin

5 Property records 4r

6 2nd opening 4v

Xρι autem gene
ratio sic erat
cum ħrs disponsata ma
ter eius maria ioseph
antequam ... uirtute
in utero habens
r̄ oħpu r̄co Ioseph autem
uir eius cum ħrs homo ius
tus et nollet eam traducere
uoluit occulte dimittere
eam hec autem eo cogitante
ecce angelus dm̄i in somnis
apparuit ei dicens ioseph
fili dauid noli timere acci
pere mariam coniugem tuā
quod enim ex ea nascetur de spu
r̄co et pariet autem filium et uoca
bit no ħi ihm ipse ħ saluum facit

Robard collt
in monney
buchan fe
ua ī gen ga
rnat aben
phurta

⁊ donnachac
mc gilli to
rech clenn
morganni
malnih edba
ita in choc
mdnortan
⁊ macolui
cilli ny pe
tair cap teī
malnil ib
balabih en
chnt cenn
dabach do
mdnypad
gagiomand
cichib alba
eucagcenn
tayeanodel
laib der bi
braccenny
mc abb tri
bruaidy
morganni
mc donnel

10 ⁊ gilli petair mc donncaid ⁊ malechin ⁊ da mc matni
⁊ matne buchan inili maradnarte in he laiu⁚

7 2nd opening 5r

8 3rd opening 16v

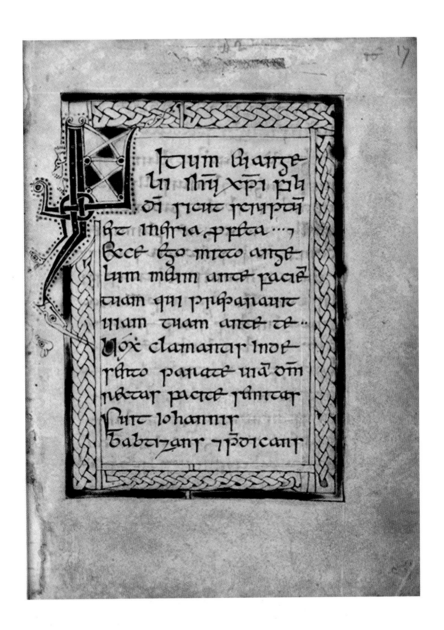

11 The Office for the Visitation of the Sick 29r

12 4th opening 29v

13 4th opening 30r

qui : fuit noe   qui . fuit . thor

qui : fuit lameh   qui . fuit . adam

qui : fuit mthusla qui : fuit : cainan

qui : fuit : enoc   qui : fuit : seth

qui : fuit : iared   qui : fuit : di ·····⁊·⁊

qui : fuit : malael   ·············

Fuit autem pleluur iphu reo resnssur

⁊ cum abiondane ⁊ascebacur impiu

In mostheu ⁊cumptabacur adiabulo····⁊

Dauid · rex scortoz oib; plus hoib; ff · salutes ·

Sciatis qd clerici · dedbr · se dea ⁊i munes

aboi laicoru officio · ⁊exactione idebita

sic ilibro eorum scribtu est · ⁊dirago

nauert ap · banb · ⁊iurauert ap · abbdon ·

quapp firmitr pcipio ut nullus eis aut

psumat · T · aquo · epo · deduncallden · T ·

andrea epo · decat · T · samsone epo · dbre ·

T · doncado comite · desib · ⁊ malmori · dau

norla · ⁊gillebrite · comite · deng · ⁊ggil

lecoded · me as · ⁊broci · ⁊cormac · dethbrud ·

⁊ada · me ferdomnac · ⁊gillendrias · me ·

matni · ap · abbdeon ·

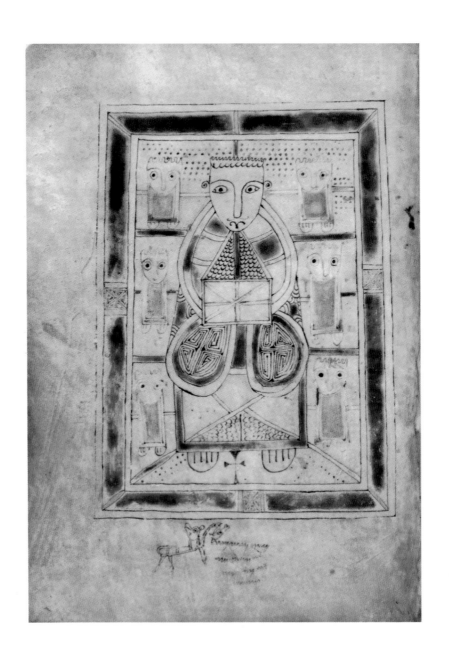

15 5th opening 41v

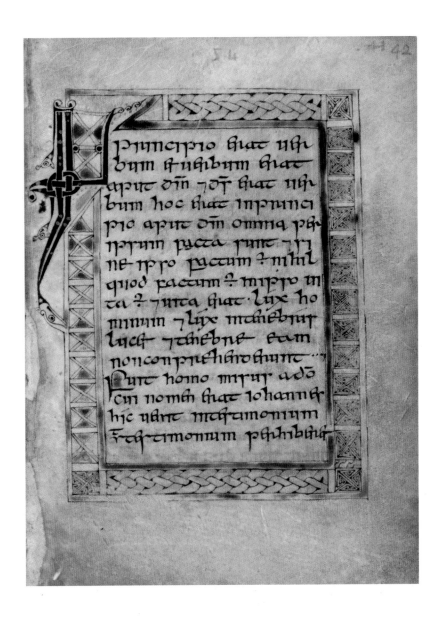

16 5th opening 42r

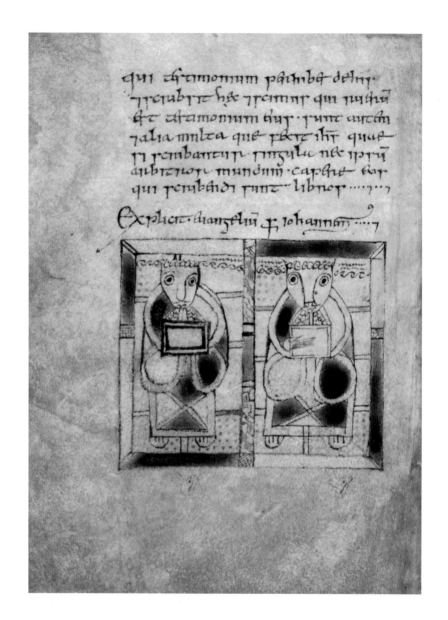

17 6th opening 84v

19 7th opening 85v

20 7th opening 86r

21 Sample text and marginalia (detail) 54v

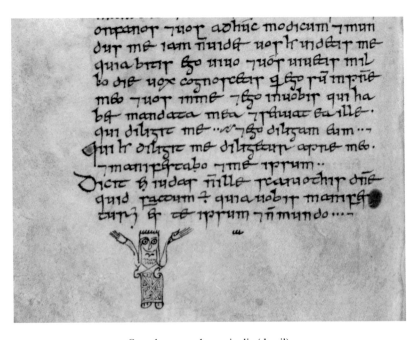

22 Sample text and marginalia (detail) 71v

non-Gaelic sources for personal names and for place-names,[51] a fact which might seem to provide corroborative evidence for the existence of *-igh* in earlier strata of the language and for *-ich* in later strata. Such an interpretation is based on the equation of *-i, -ie, -y* with Gaelic *-igh*. However, early spellings with *-i, -ie, -y* need not necessarily imply an underlying voiced *-igh* in Gaelic as has been previously assumed by scholars such as MacBain (1891; 1907), W.J. Watson (1904; 1926) and G.F. Black (1993 [1946]). In fact, *-i, -ie, -y* spellings in non-Gaelic sources may tell us little at all about how Gaelic speakers pronounced these names, and in all likelihood tell us more about the phonology of the borrowing language, English or Scots. Such spellings are in fact ambiguous, since it is possible that Gaelic *-igh* [iɣ´] or *-ich* [ix´] could have 'sounded like' [i] to non-Gaelic speakers whose phonology did not permit such sounds in final unstressed position. A cursory survey of Scots word phonology suggests that final unstressed velar fricatives did not (normally) occur in the native lexicon of Scots (Dieth 1932, 112–13; Zai 1942, 216–18), and were relatively rare in earlier stages of other Germanic languages (Jordan 1974, 178–83; Prokosch 1939, 82–4). In such a scenario it is conceivable that Gaelic names ending in either *-igh* or *-ich* could have been interpreted by non-Gaelic speakers as containing final -[i].[52] A similar hypothesis has been postulated for the borrowing of Gaelic final unstressed *-ach* into Scots as -[o]; see Ó Maolalaigh (1998, 38–44; 2003d, 325–28). We

---

51 Early forms of personal names with final [i] are attested from the twelfth and thirteenth centuries onwards and include: MacKelli (*Mac Ceallaigh/ch* c.1150), Macsalny (for *Macsalui*), Make Salui (*Mac Shealbhaigh/ch* 1296, 1300 resp.), Make Gille Reue, M'Gilrewy (*Mac Gille Riabhaigh/ch* 1300, 1376 resp.), Mac Lulli (*Mac Lulaigh/ch* 1350), MacM'Cleri (*Mac Cléirigh/ch* 1376) (see G.F. Black 1993 [1946] s.v. MacKelly, MacKelvie, Macilriach, MacLulich, MacChlery). Forms with *-ich* are attested from the end of the fifteenth century onwards and include: M'Cleriche (*Mac An Chléirigh/ch* 1461), M'Murghaich (*Mac Mhuireadhaigh/ch* 1485), M'Yldonich (*Mac Gill'Domhnaigh/ch* 1504), Makgylquhinnych (*Mac Gille Choinnigh/ch* 1506), Maklafferdich (*Mac Fhlaithbheartaigh/ch* 1524), Makarlich (*Mac Thearlaigh/ch* 1535), Makmuldonych (*Mac Maoldomhnaigh/ch* 1540) (see G.F. Black 1993 [1946] s.v. MacChlery, MacVurich, Macaldonich, Macgillwhinnich, MacLaverty, MaccCarlich, Macaldonich). These lists are based on a cursory reading of *Mac*-surnames in G.F. Black (1993 [1946]). Further in-depth research will no doubt provide earlier examples of *-ich* spellings. **52** We may also note the following forms from twelfth-century sources: *Villa mineschedin* (for *Villa inineschedin* 1172) and *villa Inienschedin* (1174). W.J. Watson (1926, 204) cites these as evidence for 'lightly sounded *gh* being disregarded in […] phonetic spelling'. The former seems to contain the genitive *inghine*; the latter may contain the nom. *inghean*, although W.J. Watson thought that genitive *inghine* was present in both. The point may not be that *gh* was 'lightly sounded' but rather that the spelling represents an approximation of the Gaelic word or pronunciation. We may compare O'Rahilly's (1930, 167) comments on the dropping of *dh* in early thirteenth-century French forms of Irish names: 'Its omission in the French forms is, of course, to be interpreted, not as meaning that the *dh* was silent, but rather that, being a weak spirant, the nearest approximation the French writer could give was simply to omit it'. Cf. also C. Breatnach's (1990b, 144–5) comments on the form *blein* by an Anglo-Norman hand for *bliadhain*.

conclude then that spellings with *-i*, *-ie*, *-y* in place-names and in personal names do not preclude the possibility of underlying *-ich* in such names.

If, however, spellings with *-i*, *-ie*, *-y* represent underlying *-ich* in the corresponding Gaelic forms, we are left with the problem of accounting for instances of final unstressed -[i] in modern Gaelic place-names where *-ich* [ix´] might be expected. In some cases it is possible that [i]-forms do not derive from original velar fricatives. For instance, Cluny, which MacBain derived from 'Cluanaigh a locative of Cluanach', may derive from *Cluainidh* with dental inflection,[53] or possibly from *Cluana* (the genitive of *Cluain*), both of which would regularly yield Cluny in Scots or English. In other cases, it is possible that the Scots or English form with final [i] has been adopted by Gaelic speakers. This would also account for the variation between final [i] (from Scots *-ie*) and [ix´] (from Gaelic *-ich* / *-igh*) in certain Gaelic place-names, which Diack reports. However, this subject requires further detailed study.

In summary, then, we find ourselves agreeing with Diack that the Deer *-g* forms may tell us nothing at all about vernacular Scottish Gaelic, and that such forms may represent conservative literary forms, a view which is perhaps strengthened by the solitary genitive form cannech (DIII1).[54]

4 MORPHO-PHONOLOGICAL FEATURES

4.1 Sandhi

The final nasal of the article is sometimes dropped before the fricatives *ch* and *p*[*h*]: árachoír (AIII8) < *ár an choír*; ipúir (DIV1) < *in p*[*h*]*úir*;[55] cf. also imbrether (AII6–17) possibly for *in mbrether*. Elision of unstressed vowels occurs in: áńím (AII9) < *a áńím*; gillendrias (EVIII3) < *gille andrias* (cf. Ó Cuív 1972, 343); go nic abbordoboír (AI2–3) for *go nice*; cf. also arhardchellaib (CVI25–26) < *ar a hardchellaib*; we may also note níce (AIII) for *gonice*. Jackson (1972, 140) drew attention to two possible instances of sandhi: bedéar (AII9) < *bed déar*, mec cóbrig (DIII2) < *mec góbrig*. The dropping of *g*[*h*] in máledomni (< *máledomnig*) mac mecbead (DIII7) may

---

53 *Cluain*, originally a masculine *i*-stem, is attested in the *Irish Grammatical Tracts* with dental inflection; see *DIL* s.v. *clúain*.   **54** A modern parallel from Scottish Gaelic would include the use of *tigh* instead of vernacular *taigh*, the former being more common in modern Scottish Gaelic prose literature. We may also note the categorical use of the spelling *-chd* rather than *-chg* in modern Scottish Gaelic to represent -/xg/, e.g. *seachd* /ʃɛxg/ ~ /ʃaxg/, *ochd* /ɔxg/, *bochd* /bɔxg/, etc.; Scottish Gaels use the conservative spelling although for them it signifies an entirely different form than that implied by the orthography. The use of *-g* in the Gaelic Notes of Deer may represent a similar example, whereby *-g* represents the received literary orthographic form but which signified -/x´/ rather than -/ɣ´/ for native speakers.   **55** Possibly also rósábard < *Ros a*[*n*] *Bard* (AIII3) but see Jackson (1972, 51–2).

be a further instance, although Jackson (1972, 141) viewed it as 'a fairly certain' error.[56] If we accept Jackson's (1972, 55) interpretation of *choir* in árachoír chetna (AIII8), it might be argued that the palatal (second) *r* anticipates the following palatal *ch*. However, it seems more likely that *choir* here represents an idiomatic use of *cóir*; we may compare *fon cōir cētna* 'in the same way' in Rawlinson B 502 (see *DIL* s.v. *cóir*, ll. 55–56). Palatal *m*, which occurs three times in the nexus *do Chol(u)im Cille* (DIV1, BV6, 21), may represent a further instance of sandhi where the palatal *m* anticipates the following palatal *c / ch*.[57]

4.2 Eclipsis

4.2.1 Introduction

It is impossible to know for certain when exactly the Scottish systems of 'eclipsis' (also called 'nasalisation', 'nasal mutation' or 'prenasalisation') developed. Jackson's view was that 'such evidence as is available on the date of the rise of this new system in Scotland suggests that it was late, probably distinctly later than the time of the notes in Deer' (1972, 143). In his 'Common Gaelic' paper he suggested that the Scottish Gaelic type of nasalisation 'probably dates from about the fourteenth or fifteenth century' (1951, 95). A Scottish type had certainly been in existence at least in Perthshire since the beginning of the sixteenth century as the Book of Dean of Lismore testifies, and more universally in Scotland since the seventeenth as a number of disparate sources imply, and it is perhaps difficult to accept that the Scottish type(s) could have developed and spread so rapidly throughout Scotland within a period of two or three hundred years. Jackson concluded, on the evidence for eclipsis in the Gaelic Notes, that the Scottish system had not fully developed by the twelfth century although he conceded on the basis of 'four[58] cases where the spelling is such as to suit the later, Sc. G. treatment of nasalisation' that the Scottish system may have been 'just faintly beginning, in the north-east'.[59] He claimed that the more numerous instances 'which prove

---

56 In the context of máledomni, we may note that *-i* for *-ig* (*-ich?*) is also evidenced in texts of the royal genealogy of kings of Scots traceable to the twelfth century: *Firalmai, Cassieclai, Cobthai, Lotherai, Bolgai, Thiernai* (Broun 1999, 184–6; cf. 1998, 190–1). 57 See, however, 230 n.29 for another interpretation of these forms. 58 Using Jackson's own criteria this should be altered to five, since Jackson omitted the example insaere (preposition, A15). 59 He also includes the case of cetri dabach (CVII9–20), where eclipsis of *dabach* might be expected following *ar chuit* (see Jackson 1972, 143). On the lack of eclipsis following the numeral *deich* (*dech bliadna*) in an eleventh-century (Irish?) source, see Ó Cuív (1990, 50); the same scribe writes *nan n-ingen* ('of the daughters'); the lack of eclipsis following *deich* and the form *nan* are both reminiscent of the Scottish Gaelic type of eclipsis. The form *nan* (genitive plural article) also occurs in *Lebor na hUidre* in M's hand; the manuscript reads lóeg nan teóra mbó (see www.isos.dias.ie) but the Diplomatic Edition reads *lóeg na teóra mbó* (Best and Bergin 1929, 283 l. 9411); I am grateful to Dr

the Irish type or prove neither' argue more strongly in favour of the Irish system existing in twelfth-century eastern Scotland than the handful of examples, which, though they may imply the beginnings of the Scottish system, 'can hardly have much weight' (Jackson 1972, 143–44). This kind of reasoning cannot stand. As we have remarked earlier, it is the departures from tradition rather than conservative features of the tradition which are significant and of relevance to the present enquiry. Furthermore, we know from the Early Modern and Modern periods that literate Scottish Gaels were well capable of reproducing the correct 'Irish' form of eclipsis in their writings or texts. This is abundantly clear from texts such as the 1408 MacDonald charter (J. Cameron 1937, 216; Munro and Munro 1986, 21–22); the text, *Fiarfaidhi San Anselmuis*, contained in the 1467 Manuscript (Ó Baoill 1988); the late sixteenth-century treaty between Argyll and O'Donnell (MacKechnie 1953); the 1614 Contract of Fosterage written by Toirdhealbhach Ó Muirgheasáin for Sir Roderick MacLeod (J. Cameron 1937, 222); the (*c*.1603x16) Gaelic contract of lease written by Hugh MacPhail (R. Black 1984); the later Books of Clanranald (A. Cameron 1894, 138–309); and the mid seventeenth-century Scottish Grammatical Tract recently edited by R. Black (1990). Medical manuscripts written by Scottish Gaels reveal many instances of the Irish type of eclipsis; see, for instance, Bannerman (1998 [1986], 98, n. 2; 101, n. 26; 102, n. 28; 103, n. 37; 104, n. 41; 107, n. 63). In many of these sources the Irish type of eclipsis is the norm although, interestingly, the Scottish type 'breaks through' on a number of occasions:[60] *dandiubersa* (*dán dtiubersa*), *dancrochad* (*dán crochad*), *an craidhib, aganfuaighel* (*agán fuaighel*), *an roibe, nampiasd* (*nam piasd*), *nambiast* (*nam b*[*p*?]*iast*) (Ó Baoill 1988, 129); *go ndainic,*

Feargal Ó Béarra for drawing this example to my attention.   **60** The Book of the Dean of Lismore is different in this respect, where the Scottish type seems to be by far the more common (Ó Maolalaigh 1998, 24), i.e. *c, t, f* are voiced but *b, d, g* tend on the whole to be uneclipsed by the preceding nasal. The following random examples have been taken from W.J. Watson (1937): ni gran (*na gcrann* VI, 12b), ni goych (*na gcuach* VI, 18b), ni gwrri (*na gcuradh* VI, 19c), nyn geyvin (*na gcéibheann* VI, 24c); dasky (*i dtaisgidh* IX, 7c), ir dy (*ar dtoigh* IX, 21a), an deiss (*dá dtíosadh* IX, 27a), ni dromzav (*na dtromdhámh* XIV, 16d); ny voynni (*na bhfonn* VII, 24c), ni wyagh (*na bhfaighdheach* IX, 1a), ni waa raan (*na bhfaireann* IX, 6a); in druim (*in druim* VI, 16c), nin dawe (*nan dámh* VI, 23b), in dyffris (*in daidhbhreas* IX, 2c), ny drocht charit (*na*(*n*) *drochcarad* IX, 7c), da dernit (*dá dearnsad*(?) IX, 29a), lane dargkyr (*lé ndeargthar* XIV, 12a); ni ban (*na*(*m*) *ban* VI, 4d), er boyin (*ar* (*m*)*buain* VI, 7d), in boltew (*in buailtibh* VI, 10a), nym bass (*nam bas* VI, 25b), nym broyve (*nam brodh* VII, 22c); in gness (*i ngreis* IX, 32c), ni gawle (*na*(*n*) *nGall* XIV, 1c), in gloet (*in gliaidh* XIV, 11b), ni gawle (*na*(*n*) *Gall* XIV, 14d); note, however, nerg (*ndearg*) where the 'Irish' eclipsis of *d*- is clearly shown (Meek 1986, 54, 55 §2b); see also Meek (1986, 51–2) for a discussion of eclipsis forms in the poem *Naoinear a chuadhmar fá choill*. Note also ide possibly for *i dtigh* or *i dtaigh* ('in house') alongside in balle (in valle?), possibly for *in bhfeil* ('in which is' — a possible Scotticism), in one of the second- or third-oldest surviving Gaelic texts in Scotland (*c*.1370–*c*.1430), (R. Black 200b, 341–2); cf. ? bell (vell?), possibly for *bhfeil* (R. Black 2000b, 338).

an Temhruigh, an dechuidh, an roibh, an derna, don daobhsa, na mbiningedh, na mpicedh (also *na bpiced*), *da ndainic, an gcuidecht* (A. Cameron 1894, 150, 152, 154, 164, 184, 188, 190, 198, 212); *ann cceill* (R. Black 1990, 16).[61] 'Irish' forms of eclipsis are the norm in the Gaelic translation of the *Book of Common Order*, published in Edinburgh in 1567 (see R.L. Thomson 1970: xl–xli) and in the translation of Calvin's Catechism, published *c*.1631 (see R.L. Thomson 1962: xxix–xxxii). However, in the Shorter Catechism, published in 1659, although the 'Irish' form of eclipsis occurs, the Scottish type is very much in evidence (see R.L. Thomson 1962: xxxvi). The first fifty metrical psalms, published by the Synod of Argyll in 1659, has both traditional 'Irish' literary forms and vernacular Scottish Gaelic forms; see R.L. Thomson (1976, 169–70). Edward Lhuyd's 'phonetic' transcription of the Revd John Beaton's reading of the first two chapters of Genesis from Robert Kirk's 'Irish' Bible shows that Beaton could pronounce Irish literary 'eclipsis' forms,[62] e.g. *mar an cceadna* (*myr yn gêadna* §1.16; cf. §2.9), *a ccinéil* (*y genèl* §1.21), *ar ccosamhlachda* (*er gossavlachdy* §1.26), *a bhfiormament* (*y Virmament* §1.14; cf. §§1.7, 1.17, 1.20), *a bhfuil* (*y vwil* §1.20; cf. §1.30), *dá bhfuil* (*da vwyl* §1.29), *as an bhfear* (*as yn veaŕr* [*sic*] §2.23), *ar ndeilbh* (*er niêlyv* §1.26), *dá ndearna* (*da nearny* §1.31); note also *ar an ttalamh* (*er yn dàlyv* §§1.15, 1.17, 1.25; cf. §2.6) but also *ar an talamh* (*er yn talav* §§1.11, 1.22, 1.26, 1.28, 1.30, 2.5, 2.9). However, the single form *ym bî* for *a mbí* (§1.11) seems to betray his normal vernacular Scottish usage where *b* is not eclipsed in the Irish fashion.[63] Indeed, this particular source highlights spectacularly the significance and value of a solitary 'deviant' example against the almost categorical use of the inherited literary 'Irish' norm, and serves to justify the view that 'it is only what is a departure from tradition and normality, however rare and untypical it may seem in its context, that is of interest or value' (R.L. Thomson 1977:129) to the linguistic historian.

MacBain (1894, 88) remarked of eclipsis that 'Scottish Gaelic never got further than the Old Irish stage', thus implying that Scottish Gaelic differed from Irish in the matter of eclipsis since the period of Old Gaelic although he did not provide convincing evidence for this. It was Diack's view that 'Scottish eclipsis is not identical with Irish, and probably never was, at least

---

61 The early seventeenth-century Gaelic contract of lease has the 'Irish' type of eclipsis in da mb<u>eith</u> and a gcuid oidhchi (R. Black 1984, 134, ll. 7, 8; however, MS '[...]cht butalla' may represent *ocht butalla* ('eight bottles'), in which case the lack of eclipsis following the numeral *ocht* would represent a Scotticism (R. Black 1984, 134, l. 11; 137–8); cf. agentive *-air* in fiac[h]adair and perhaps preaspiration in vich (for *mhic*) as further instances of Scotticisms in this text (R. Black 1984, 134, ll. 9, 11; 137, 138). Note also *an thempall na ccaillech dubh* ('in the church of the Black Nuns') (A. Cameron 1894, 158), where *an th-* may perhaps indicate Outer Hebridean [əN dʰ-] or [əN tʰ-].   62 All examples from J.L. Campbell and D. Thomson (1963, 77–87).   63 Cf. *aity* (= Scottish Gaelic *áite*) for Irish *áit* (§2.21), which may represent another vernacular form.

within historical times. [...] the whole subject of eclipsis in the two languages will probably be found to be of importance for the question of their historical relationship' (Diack 1922, 128). Because of the potential importance of eclipsis as a possible early differentiating feature between Scottish Gaelic and Irish, and the existence of a new theory of its development, particularly in Scotland (Ó Maolalaigh 1995–96), the evidence for eclipsis in the Notes deserves to be discussed afresh. Our discussion will shed a slightly different light on the evidence and will provide a plausible explanation for one potentially significant example which Jackson could not explain and which he concluded was 'probably a mistake' (1972, 143).

4.2.2 The Scottish system of 'eclipsis'

Before we turn to the Deer evidence, it will be necessary to describe the Scottish systems of 'eclipsis' / 'nasalisation'. The differences between the Irish and Scottish systems of eclipsis relate to (a) eclipsing particles themselves, which in Scottish Gaelic all have nasal codas,[64] and (b) the effects of eclipsis on radical initial consonants. The picture is less uniform in Scotland than in Ireland in that there are three different main types of eclipsis in Scottish Gaelic. Irish orthography reflects the initial mutation by prefixing consonants to the initial of words (e.g. *i gcoill*) whereas in Scottish Gaelic the initial mutations are not represented. The different systems may be summarised as follows:

Table 1: Eclipsis in Irish and Scottish Gaelic

	IRISH ORTHOGRAPHY		SCOTTISH GAELIC ORTHOGRAPHY	TYPE A	TYPE B	TYPE C
p	*bp-*	[b]	*-m + p-*	[b^h]	[m^h]	[b]
t	*dt-*	[d]	*-n + t-*	[d^h]	[N^h]	[d]
c	*gc-*	[g]	*-n + c-*	[g^h]	[ŋ^h]	[g]
b	*mb-*	[m]	*-m + b-*	[b]	[m]	[b]
d	*nd-*	[N]	*-n + d-*	[d]	[N]	[d]
g	*ng-*	[N]	*-n + g-*	[g]	[ŋ]	[g]
f	*bhf-*	v	*-m + f-*	f	f	f >> v, b, p
s	*s-*	s >> z	*-n + s-*	s	s	s >> z

Type B is marginal and occurs, for instance, in Lewis, certain northern Skye dialects, and the Isle of Raasay. Type A is fairly typical of other Outer Hebridean dialects and western mainland dialects. Type C, however, typifies

---

64 Leaving aside the first and second person plural possessive pronuns *ar*, *(bh)ur*, which prefix *n-* to vowels.

the peripheral dialects of eastern and south-western dialects, including the dialects of Aberdeen.[65] Diack (1922, 127) referred to the area in which Type C occurred as 'the east central', extending from the northern limit of the Spey valley southwards to Perthshire, and he suggested, based on place-name evidence, that this 'dialectal unity extended in pre-English days to the [eastern] seaboard'. Modern dialectal evidence, unavailable to Diack, shows that this type was also a feature of certain south-western dialects (see Holmer 1938, 64; 1957, 94; 1962, 64). The Irish and Scottish Gaelic systems agree in the sense that voiceless stops are voiced (always in Irish, but in Scottish Gaelic also with aspiration in Type A, and with aspiration and nasalisation in Type B). The main difference in the effects of 'eclipsis' between Irish and the majority of Scottish Gaelic dialects (Types A and C) is the treatment of original *b*, *d*, *g*. These are replaced by their nasal counterparts in Irish. However, in Scottish Gaelic, radical *b*, *d*, *g* are generally voiceless (i.e. [b̥], [d̥], [g̊]) and are voiced in 'eclipsis' environments; nasalisation and aspiration in Type B is a secondary development of Type A, and does *not* represent the 'Irish' type. Such subtle phonetic changes are not easily represented in orthography. The occasional voicing of voiceless fricatives *f* and *s* may be noted in passing in dialects of Type C; see further below.

Ó Murchú (1989a, 115) illustrates the different degrees of phonetic eclipsis (which he refers to as 'prenasalization') in Type C by considering the variable realisations of the noun phrase *am pùd* ('the small bird'), which is phonologically transcribed as /mbu:d/. There are two main phonetic realisations, namely (a) [ᵐbu:d̥], where the nasal is realised as a short nasal segment and is followed by a voiced stop; and (b) [m̩ 'b̥u:d̥] or less frequently [ᵊm 'b̥u:d̥], where the nasal is realised usually as a syllabic nasal segment, and is followed by a voiceless stop. In other words, the stop is voiced only when the preceding nasal is expressed weakly. This may have implications for some of the Deer forms. Ó Murchú (1989a, 115) further adds that the nasalising segment is sometimes omitted in highly frequent forms such as /bals/ for /mbals/ *am pailteas* ('plenty') or /vɛr/ for /mvɛr/ *am fear* ('the man') or fossilised phrases such as /pàr nə záɬ·m/ for /pàr nə nzáɬ·m/ / *Pàra nan Salm* (a nickname). The presence and strength of the nasalising segment appears to depend on the speech tempo: the faster or more casual the speech, the more likely the nasal is to be weakened or lost altogether. We shall refer further to this in our discussion below.

---

65 Cf. A. Watson and Clement (1983, 401). Jackson (1972, 142) curiously does not refer to Type C in his description of the Scottish system of eclipsis, which is odd given the existence of this type in eastern dialects such as Aberdeen. Perhaps he thought this type was a later development; cf. his statement that Type B 'is a secondary development' (1972, 142 n. 1).

4.2.3 The historical development of eclipsis

In papers presented at the Fourth International Conference on the Languages
of Scotland and Ulster in 1994 and the 10th International Congress of Celtic
Studies in 1995—now published in Ó Maolalaigh (1995–6; cf. also Ó
Maolalaigh 1998, 23–30; 1999a)—I presented the hypothesis that 'eclipsis'
developed differently in Irish and Scottish Gaelic, and that 'Irish eclipsis'
developed in two stages: (1) the earliest and first stage affected the voiceless
stops *c*, *t* (later *p*) and was common to all varieties of Gaelic (in Ireland and
Scotland); (2) the later second stage which involved the assimilation of nasal
+ voiced stop clusters to nasals at word boundaries affected only southern, i.e.
Irish, dialects. It is claimed that the second stage did not develop in certain
northern varieties, where original voiced stops were not 'eclipsed' to
homorganic nasals at word boundaries.[66] The subsequent development of
eclipsis in northern varieties can be explained as a process of levelling which
sought to reconcile (a) the earlier system of the voicing of voiceless stops
(*c*, *p*, *t*) and the non-'eclipsing' of the originally voiced series (*b*, *d*, *g*), and (b)
the varying forms of certain 'eclipsing' particles, which had vocalic codas
before *c*, *p*, *t* and nasal codas before *g*, *b*, *d*.[67] Evidence for the assimilation or
coalescence of nasal + homorganic voiced stop begins to appear in written
sources towards the end of the Old Gaelic period, notably in the early ninth-
century Milan Glosses (Strachan 1903, 55–6). This assimilation no doubt
proceeded in different stages; it seems, for instance, to have occurred sooner
in certain unstressed environments (*GOI* 93–4; McCone 1985, 86). The
evidence of Modern Irish, Manx and Scottish Gaelic illustrates that this
assimilation occurred word finally and word internally in all varieties, e.g.
clann < *cland*, *cam* < *camb*, *cime* (cf. Scottish Gaelic *ciomach*) < *cimbid*. My

---

66 The only contrary evidence which I have consists of *go mba* /gəmə/ from Modern
Scottish Gaelic dialects and the complicated *gonice* (< *gondice* < *co ttice*) from the Gaelic
Notes themselves. However, both examples consist of unstressed functors, which are liable
to develop differently from full lexemes. Note that the development *nd* > *nn* and *mb* > *mm*
occurs earlier in pretonic words (*GOI* 93–94; McCone 1985, 86); Thurneysen also notes
that 'initial *b* in pretonic forms of the copula is often assimilated to a preceding nasal' (*GOI*
94). We may also compare Ó Murchú's statement about East Perthshire Gaelic (a Type A
dialect): 'Infrequently, in rapid speech, prenasalised clusters may be replaced by the
affinitive simple nasal, e.g. /gə mîx/ for /gə mbîx/ *gum biodh* or /ŋɔu/ for /ŋgɔu/ *an
gabh thu*' (1989a, 115).   67 Compare MacBain's comment that 'Irish has an elaborate
system of initial changes caused by this *n*, but Scottish Gaelic never got further than the
Old Gaelic stage in respect to this matter, and eventually it lost the influence of *n* with the
loss of inflections and the consequent levelling up of forms and sounds' (MacBain 1894,
88). Cf. 'For Scottish Gaelic we must recognize a different treatment in which the fusion of
closing nasal and initial obstruent did not take place (or ceased to take place).' (Gillies 1993,
168). A similar view may be inferred from [Ó Murchú's] (1996, 147) recent statement that
'*mb*, *nd* become *m(m)*, *nn*, e.g. *camb* ('crooked') > *cam(m)*, but not in word-initial position in
Scotland, thus making possible an eventual restructuring of the system of nasal mutation
there'; cf. also Ó Murchú (1997, 186).

contention is that this assimilation did not extend across the word boundary in the precursor of Scottish Gaelic, although it clearly did in Irish (and Manx); one possible reason for the difference in development between Scottish Gaelic and Irish may be that radical *b*, *d*, *g* were already devoiced in some Scottish Gaelic dialects. Strachan (1903, 55–6) notes *debe mec* (= *debe mbec* 'a little difference' Ml. 40a2) from the early ninth-century Milan Glosses and claims that it represents coalescence of the nasal-plosive cluster, and if his interpretation is correct, it would suggest that the second 'Irish' stage of eclipsis could be as old as the late Old Gaelic period, i.e. the ninth century. Feuth (1982, 91), however, expresses the view that *mec* is 'a writing error'. In any case, it is clear from a number of late Middle Gaelic sources that the 'Irish' second stage of eclipsis had developed by the twelfth century; see L. Breatnach (1994, 238).

It is clear, especially from the use of the *punctum delens* above the nasal element in certain nasal-plosive clusters in Old Gaelic sources (at word boundaries in positions of 'eclipsis', and word internally), that coalescence was not a general feature of Old Gaelic; see Feuth (1982) for strong and convincing arguments for *mb*, *nd*, *ng* in Old Gaelic representing nasal-plosive clusters rather than coalesced nasals *m*, *n*, ŋ in eclipsis and some other environments.[68] It would appear, therefore, that the potential for the development of the original Scottish Gaelic type existed from the time of the Old Gaelic period. In other words, eclipsis may well have been one of the earliest differentiating features between Gaelic dialects. For an alternative interpretation of W.J. Watson's (1926, 240–43) evidence for the 'Irish' type of eclipsis in Scottish place-names, see Ó Maolalaigh (1998, 26–30).

Although we have no means of dating the rise of each of the subtypes A, B, C in Scottish Gaelic, the different stages of development are relatively clear. From all three types, we can suggest a common underlying system of eclipsis of stops for Scottish Gaelic which consisted of eclipsing particle / word ending in a nasal followed by a voiced stop, although Types A and B would suggest that in the case of voiceless aspirated stops that postaspiration was also a feature of the system. This can be expressed as follows (E = eclipsis; –VN = an eclipsing word ending in a vowel + a nasal consonant):[69]

---

68 I was unaware of Feuth's (1982) article when I presented similar arguments for the interpretation of Old Gaelic *mb*, *nd*, *ng* as nasal-plosive clusters in a paper delivered in 1994 at the Fourth International Conference on the Languages of Scotland and Ulster. For reasons of space, the arguments for this interpretation (which lent heavily on the use of the *punctum delens* in nasal-plosive clusters as an orthographic device to represent clusters without coalescence) were not presented in the published version of that paper; see Ó Maolalaigh (1995–6, 170, n. 21). Feuth's (1982) interpretation of these Old Gaelic clusters is accepted by Grijzenhout (1995, 95).   69 In the following I ignore the development of original voiced stops to voiceless stops in non-eclipsis environments.

Old Gaelic
E + c, p, t; g, b, d → g, b, d; ŋg, mb, nd

$$\left\{ \begin{array}{l} \text{Modern Irish} \\ \rightarrow\text{g, b, d; ŋ, m, N} \\[1em] \text{Scottish Gaelic} \\ \rightarrow \text{-VN + g}^h\text{, b}^h\text{, d}^h\text{; g, b, d} \end{array} \right.$$

This comparative reconstruction illustrates that Type A reflects closely the stage from which all modern types may be derived:

$$-VN + g^h, b^h, d^h; g, b, d \ (= \text{Type A}) \rightarrow \left\{ \begin{array}{l} -VN + \eta^h, m^h, N^h; \eta, m, N \ (= \text{Type B}) \\[1em] -VN + g, b, d; g, b, d \ (= \text{Type C}) \end{array} \right.$$

This reconstruction suggests that the stage immediately preceding this 'common' stage, the proto-'common' stage, consisted of eclipsing particle / word with nasal coda followed by radical c, p, t, g, b, d, i.e.

$$E + c, p, t; g, b, d \qquad = \qquad -VN + c, p, t; g, b, d$$

This, at least, is the most straightforward reconstruction for Scottish Gaelic dialects. This reconstruction rests on the assumption that the voicing of voiceless unaspirated stops in Scottish Gaelic eclipsis is the result of a natural phonetic development of assimilation between the nasal and following voiceless stop, whereby the feature of voicing spreads progressively to the stop. Type A can be seen as an early stage in the development of such assimilation, and Type C as a later stage whereby the assimilation is complete with the total loss of postaspiration.[70] The development of Type C from Type A can be compared with the merger of original voiced and voiceless stops in postvocalic position in some eastern Scottish Gaelic dialects (see Ó Murchú 1985, 196–7). Type B is similar although here there is assimilation based on the feature of nasalisation rather than just voicing.[71] Finally, we note that the potential for the development of the Scottish Gaelic prototype existed from

70 MacBain (1894, 88) notes for the Gaelic dialect of Badenoch the pronunciation of *an cù* as 'an gu or an gcu', which seems to imply variation between Types A and C.
71 However, the voicing of voiceless stops in theory can be explained differently. It is just possible that this voicing reflects a vestige of the original voicing of stage 1 in the development of eclipsis in all varieties of Gaelic. The process of levelling which must have occurred may have led to variation between -VN + g, b, d (i.e. with voicing) ~ -VN c, p, t. This may be illustrated with *a gcú* ('their dog'). Stage 1 in the development of eclipsis in all varieties of eclipsis resulted in *a gcú* /gu:/ in all dialects. The process of levelling may have led to variation between *a gcú* /gu:/ and *an cú* /kʰu:/, which in turn may have led to the mixed form *an gcú* /gu:/, the latter representing a mixed form 'half-way' between original *a gcú* /gu:/ and innovative *an cú* /kʰu:/. This in turn may have led to mixed forms such as [-ŋg ku:] or [-ŋ gʰu:]. This interpretation would suggest that Type C may be more conservative than Types A and B. This latter interpretation of the facts is less straightforward than that presented above, and therefore seems less probable.

the Old Gaelic period. The presence of the Irish system of eclipsis in earlier forms of Manx (Kelly 1870 [1804], 6–8; Rhŷs 1894, 80–1; Kneen 1931, 41, 44; Jackson 1955, 133; Broderick 1984–6, I, 20–1; III, 64, 66)[72] and possibly in Galloway (Ó Maolalaigh 1998, 29–30) might be taken as evidence against the very early development of the Scottish type of eclipsis since if it were early we might expect it to have affected Manx also. However, the differences

Table 2: The representation of eclipsis in the Gaelic Notes

i(n) preposition	article acc. sg.	article gen. pl.	poss. 3 pl.	*go(n)*
igginn (Bᴠ23) incathŕaig? (A16)[73]	ingathŕaíg (A15) incathŕaig? (A16) inchadraíg (A116) ingorthe (Bᴠ22–23)	na gleréc (AI10) naglerec (A111) naglerec (A119)	aragínn (A14)	
inpett (A1112)[74] ipet (Dɪᴠ1)				
intestus (Bᴠ10)	[75]			
íbbidbín (A1112)	imbrether (A117)[76] in• béíŧh (A1122)[77]			
				gondas (A18–9) góndéndaes (A111) gondisád (A112)
insaere (A15) issaére (A1126) insóre (Bᴠ7) issaeri (Cᴠ25)			dansíl (A1128)	
[77a] inálteri (A115) in helaín (Cᴠɪ33)	inedbaírt (A113) innernacde (A114) indelerc (A1114) innócmad (Dɪɪɪ5)		daneis (A1128)	

72 I am grateful to R.L. Thomson who discussed with me by letter (20 July 1994) the subject of eclipsis in literary and vernacular Manx. **73** It is unclear whether incathŕaig? (A16) contains the preposition *i(n)* or the article. **74** Following Jackson's reading 'in Pett Meic-Gobroig' (1972, 34). **75** Possibly indelerc (A1114) if this is underlying nominative singular article for accusative (**intelerc*) although this seems unlikely: cf. gen. sg. art. in intiprat (A113), where no 'Scottish' eclipsis of *t* is implied. **76** Taking im to represent the accusative article rather than the simple preposition *i(n)*. The formula *forácaib bréthir* is common without the article / preposition: see *DIL* s.v. *briathar* (b). **77** Possibly for *in b[h]eith*. **77a** Cf. also iarnéré (AI10) and cónánascad (DIII4). Variation between *n* and *nn* in forms of the accusative singular article and in prevocalic forms of the preposition *i(n)* may suggest that by the period of the Gaelic Notes there may have been no difference in realisation between prevocalic forms of the nominative and accusative singular article and the simple preposition *i(n)*. However, against this it should be noted that the use of *nn* between Manx and Scottish Gaelic can be explained in a number of other ways: (A) the existence in Manx of the Irish type at an early stage; (B) the Scottish type once existed in Manx but was later replaced by the Irish type (here we might compare the existence in Manx of both 'northern' reduction of unstressed long vowels and 'southern' forward stress); (C) the Manx system represents a development of the original Scottish Gaelic type. It is important to note that though Manx agrees with Scottish Gaelic against Irish with respect to a number of characteristics, the development of some features in Manx parallels Irish rather than Scottish Gaelic developments: see, for instance, the development *gh* > [j] discussed in Ó Maolalaigh (2006, 54–56)

4.2.4 Eclipsis: The evidence from the Gaelic Notes

We turn now to the evidence of the Notes in the Book of Deer for the eclipsis of the segments *c*, *p*, *t*, *b*, *d*; initial vowels and also the segment *s* in eclipsis environments. This is presented in Table 2, where the occurrence of eclipsis (or expected eclipsis) in traditional environments is divided into five main categories: the preposition *i(n)*, the accusative singular article, the genitive plural article, the possessive third plural adjective and the conjunction *go(n)*.

It appears to be significant, as Jackson pointed out, that the preposition *i(n)* and the possessive pronoun show signs of having developed forms with final nasals in the preconsonantal position by the time of the Gaelic Notes. These suggest that a Scottish system of eclipsis may have already developed by the twelfth century, although it is perhaps possible in the case of the preposition *in* that the development of such forms was independent of the development of the Scottish Gaelic system of eclipsis. Forms of the accusative article and the conjunction *go(n)* are of course ambiguous in this respect. The genitive plural article shows no overt signs of having developed a final nasal coda. However, in light of Ó Murchú's comments on the various realisations of the nasal segment in eclipsis, these three examples should not perhaps be dismissed totally out of hand. The occurrence of nasal codas in two of the three categories where we might expect them in a Scottish context requires further comment.

The five examples which seem to have developed nasal codas in the Scottish fashion are not without their problems of interpretation. Jackson refers to 'four cases where the spelling is such as to suit the later, Sc. G. treatment of nasalisation' (1972, 143). These are: dansíl (third plural possessive, AII28), inpett (preposition, AII12), intestus (preposition, Bv10), insóre (preposition, Bv7), to which insaere (preposition, AI5) should be added, which Jackson apparently overlooked.

(including in indelerc (AII14) if *nd* is for *nn*) is more consistent in prevocalic forms of the accusative singular article. The example inedbaírt (AII3), may represent an example of nominative sg. for accusative sg. These prevocalic forms do not, however, tell us much, if

Jackson concluded that forms dansíl (AII28), inpett (AIII2), intestus (BVIO), insóre (BV7) (presumably also insaere (AI5)) 'are probably merely analogical spellings under the influence of cases like *iar n-ére*, from which analogies indeed the Sc. G. type itself arose' (1972, 144). The only serious case for 'analogical spelling' is dansíl which could conceivably have been affected through anticipation of daneis (AII28), which immediately follows it. While dansíl provides very good evidence for the development of the third person plural possessive pronoun *an*, which is compatible with the development of the Scottish type of eclipsis, its occurrence next to daneis nevertheless casts some suspicion on it. Similarly, if incathŕaig ele (AI6–7) contains the preposition *i(n)*—discussed further below—it might be argued that the spelling has been influenced by the article in ingathraíg saín (AI5) of the preceding line. However, other instances of the prepositon *in* are unlikely to be analogical spellings. Certainly, they could represent analogical forms based on bound allomorphs occurring before vowels, and, if the arguments presented in Ó Maolalaigh (1995–6) are accepted, also the allomorphs occurring before the stops /b d g/. It is important to note that the development of analogical back-formations of this sort may have developed independently of the development of the Scottish type of eclipsis,[78] and it is therefore questionable whether or not these forms can with confidence be cited as evidence for the existence of the Scottish system of eclipsis. We note that the two instances where *in* occurs before underlying voiceless stops, namely, inpett (AIII2), intestus (BVIO), show no overt signs of voicing. A possible similar instance of the preposition *in* (for original *i*[N]) functioning as relative 'in which' may occur in one of the second- or third-oldest surviving Gaelic texts in Scotland (*c*.1370–*c*.1430), if *in balle* (*in valle*?) represents *in bhfeil* ('in which is'): see R. Black (2000b, 341–42); on the similar form *ann bfuil* in the Gaelic translation of the Shorter Catechism, published in 1659, see R.L. Thomson (1962, 246 §96). Having considered what is generally considered to be the strongest evidence for the early existence of the Scottish Gaelic type of eclipsis, we now turn our attention to the remaining evidence for 'eclipsis' in the Notes.

In our discussion of possible Scotticisms it may be instructive to take a fresh look at the form incathŕaig (AI6) and the context in which it appears. The origin legend set out in Text I tells us that Colum Cille and Drostán left Iona and came to Aberdour, where Bede the Pict bestowed upon them 'that *cathair*', usually translated as 'monastery'. We are told that they set off from there and arrived at the *cathair*, which was 'later' to be known as Deer. The text reads: tangator asááthle sen incathŕaig ele ₇doráten ricolumcille sí (AI6–7). Most commentators have interpeted in of incathŕaig ele as the

anything, about the Irish or Scottish system of eclispsis. 78 Cf. the development of *nyn* ('our, your, their') in Manx, which had the 'Irish' system of eclipsis.

(accusative sg.) article and translated: 'They came after that to the other monastery (or town), and it pleased Colum Cille'; see, for instance, Stokes (1872 [1866], 108), MacBain (1885, 145), Strachan (1895, 17) and Jackson (1972, 33, 40). However, this is not the only interpretation. It seems quite possible that in here may represent another instance of the preposition *in* occurring in preconsonantal position and if so we might translate the sentence as follows: 'They came after that (in)to *another* monastery (or town), and it pleased Colum Cille'.[79] In fact, this is how Fraser (1942, 60) chose to translate the phrase incathraig ele ('to another monastery'); unfortunately, he has no linguistic discussion of the phrase. That the later ecclesiastical foundations of Aberdour and Deer were firmly in the mind of the narrator is clear from his references to each as a *cathair* (see Jackson 1972, 40; Fraser 1942, 60, n. 2); while this would account for the use of the article in the phrase incathraig ele in reference to *the* (later) monastery of Deer, it could be argued that 'another monastery' makes better textual sense. It is after all the first reference to a monastery at 'Deer', and we might arguably expect the reference to be indefinite. (The article is certainly used in ingathraíg saín (AI5) ('that monastery') to refer to Aberdour but the context is unambiguous in this case as Aberdour (abbordoboír AI3) has already been introduced into the discourse two lines earlier.) In support of this alternative interpretation, we note that Hand A uses the *in*-form of the preposition preconsonantally in the preceding line: insaere (preposition, AI5), and also later in inpett (preposition, AII12); he also writes dansíl (third plural possessive, AII28).

Simon Taylor suggests elsewhere in this volume that pette mec garnaít (AII3–14), pett mec garnaít (AII3) may contain gen. pl. rather the gen. sg. of *mac*, in which case we should expand the manuscript contraction as mac rather than mec, and translate as 'farm / estate of the sons of *Gartnait*'. If gen. pl. *mac* were present in this appellation we might expect *mac* to be followed by a nasalising *n*, i.e. *pett mac nGarnaít, and its absence here could be significant. One of the main structural differences between eclipsis in Scottish Gaelic and Irish is that eclipsing nasal segments were lost in the former in the interconsonantal position.[80] Eclipsis is absent in many Scottish place-names which apparently contain gen. pl. *mac*, some of which are attested from the twelfth century: *Ledmacdungal* ('the hill-side of the sons of Dúngal'), near Dunfermline, Fife (Taylor 1995, 180–1); *Petmacdufgille* ('farm / estate of the sons of Dougal', *c*.1189, *Dunf Reg*, no. 147; cf. also W.J. Watson

---

79 While the accusative of destination is common with verbs of motion in the earlier language (see Mac Cana 1990), instances of the preposition *i* are also attested. See, for instance, *DIL* s.v. *téit* §10; *do-roich* §II; *i* §B.1. I am grateful to Caoimhín Breatnach for discussing this feature with me and for providing the following example from *Scéla Cano Meic Gartnáin*: 'Tecaid ind fhir na ndiaid ind aigi isin gleann' (Binchy 1963, 10, ll. 269–70).
80 See Ó Maolalaigh (1995–6, 160–1, 164–6) for discussion. On the frequent omission of eclipsing nasals in interconsonantal position in Old Gaelic, see Thurneysen (1905), Quin (1979–80) and L. Breatnach (1989, 28).

1926, 409);[81] *Kirkma(k)brick* ('church of the sons of *Breac*'; *Baile mac Eoghain* ('stead of the sons of *Eoghan*'); *Sìthean Druim Mhac Bhranduibh* ('fairy knoll of the ridge of the sons of Brandubh'); *Dùn Mac Tuathail* ('fort of the sons of Tuathal'); *Dùn Mac Glais* ('fort of the sons of Glas'); *Beinn Mac Duibh* ('hill of the sons of Dubh'); *Baile Mac Cathain* ('stead of the sons of Cathan') (W.J. Watson 1926, 166–67, 220, 237–8).[82] Twelfth-century attestations would seem to indicate that nasalising segments following gen. pl. *mac* were already lost in certain varieties of eastern Scottish Gaelic by the early part of the twelfth century. The gen. pl. interpretation may cast some new light on the variation between **gobróig** and **cóbrig**, found in **pett mec gobróig** (AIII2) and **petmec cóbrig** (DIII2). If the manuscript contraction were expanded as **ma͜c** (i.e. gen. pl.) in the former it could be argued that the following *g*- represents eclipsed *c*- rather than radical *g*-. However, the spelling **mec** in the latter seems to argue against a gen. pl. interpretation in this case. On the other hand, **petmec cóbrig** may conceivably represent a corruption of, or a backformation based on, *mac Gobroig*, with devoicing of *g*- following *mac*, and / or with re-analysis of gen. pl. *mac* as *mec*.[83] The variation between *g*- and *c*- may indicate that variation existed between eclipsis and non-eclipsis of voiceless stops following eclipsing words with consonantal codas. Jackson (1972, 51) explains the variation in purely phonetic terms, arguing that *Gobroig* was the underlying name (based on *gabor* 'goat' or 'horse')[84] 'since -*c* + *g*- giving -*c* + *c*- is more likely than the reverse'. Our alternative interpretation would suggest *Cobrach (possibly *Cabrach) as the underlying name, perhaps related to *cobur* ('desiring, desirer')[85] or *cobrae* ('speech, conversation').

Jackson refers to 'the curious *i bbidbin* [**íbbidbín** (AIII2)]', which he claims 'cannot be explained on either Irish or Sc. G. lines'; he concludes that 'it is probably a mistake' (1972, 143).[86] On the contrary, this form has its parallels in other Gaelic sources, and, moreover, can be explained in purely Scottish terms. Indeed, I would claim that it could be highly significant for our discussion of the Scottish type of nasalisation. The 'gemination' of original voiced stops in eclipsis environments is attested occasionally in Irish sources.

---

81 See Taylor (*infra*) for further discussion of these two names.   82 Cf. *Cell mac nÉnáin*, *Cell mac nEogain*, *Cell mac nEoin*, *Cell mac nOdhráin*, *Ess mac nEirc*, *Ráith mac nAeda*—all with eclipsis (Hogan 1993 [1910], 197–8, 402, 574) and *Árd mac Bren*, *Baile mac Colgain* (Hogan 1993 [1910], 43, 82) apparently without eclipsis. Cf. *Maigh Ó gCanann* ('Plain of the O'Cannons') (Toner and Ó Mainnín 1992, 150–1), *Carraig Ó gCaoindealbháin* ('Ó Caoindealbháins' rock') (Hughes and Hannan 1992, 226–27).   83 Cf. *Cill mac nÉnáin* > *Cill mic nÉnáin / Nénáin* (Hogan 1993 [1910], 198 s.v. *c[ell] mac n-énáin*).   84 The change *gabhar* > *gobhar* was well established in the Early Modern period, a fact which is reflected in the permitted variants *gabhar*, *gobhar* in the *Irish Grammatical Tracts*; see *DIL* s.v. *gabor*; cf. *SGDS* 488.   85 See Watkins (1962, 116), however, who notes that *cobur* 'does not appear as a free form, but only as the second element of a compound'.   86 Jackson (1952, 94) had earlier suggested that *bb* was 'presumably a slip for *mB*-'. I confess that I do not fully understand MacBain's (1885, 153–4) statement that the Book of Deer 'preserves it [i.e. *n*] by the Irish method of eclipsis in *i b-bidbin*, *i g-ginn*'.

Greene (1972, 169) cites the similar Irish example *co bba* (for expected *co mba*) from *Togail Bruidne Da Derga* (Knott 1963 [1936], 1.12) and refers to it as 'a curious representation of nasalisation by gemination'. We may also note *coggabsat* (for expected *co ngabsat*) in the Rawlinson B 512 version of *Bethu Phátraic* (Mulchrone 1939, 9, l. 198).[87] Liam Breatnach suggests to me that the use of double *gg* in examples like *coggabsat* may ultimately be based on Greek Agma (with the sound [ŋ]) which is spelt γγ; see, for instance, McManus (1991, 29–30). It is possible that *bb* in the Deer and *Togail Bruidne Da Derga* examples may represent an extension of the use of *gg* for *ng*, in which case *bb* could be intended for *mb*. However, other intepretations are possible. Geminate *gg* and *bb* may represent an extension of the practice of doubling initial voiceless stops and sonorants in eclipsis environments, e.g. *tt*, *cc*, *ll*, *nn*, *rr*, *mm*; for examples of some of these from Middle Gaelic sources, see L. Breatnach (1994, 228–9); on the use of *dd-* to indicate eclipsed *t-*, note *a ddonich(h)as* (L. Breatnach 1990, 139). Alternatively, the doubling of voiced stops in initial position is attested occasionally in Irish sources to represent voiced stops, this device perhaps emphasising that such forms were not lenited, e.g. *a ggnūis* (*Saltair na Rann*), *a bbās* (*Liber Hymnorum*, glosses) (L. Breatnach 1994, 228); *la gglais*, *cu bbrath* (*Book of Armagh*), *robbadhadh* (*Annals of Ulster*) (Ó Máille 1910, 38, 41). We may also note the occasional use of the doubling of voiceless consonants in initial position to represent voiceless (non-lenited) consonants, e.g. *a ccomairle* (*LL*), *a ttír* (*Saltair na Rann*) (L. Breatnach 1994, 228).[88] The evidence just quoted suggests that the gemination of *bb* in **íbbidbín** (AII12) may have been intended to indicate (voiced) *b*. If this is correct, the occurrence of voiced *b* following the preposition *i* is highly significant in a Scottish context. Indeed, our form can be interpreted as the result of a Scottish Type A or C nasalisation of *b*, where the nasal segment was so weak as not to warrant being written. With it we may compare the realisation of *am poll* /əᵐ boL/ in modern dialects not too far removed from the district of Deer.[89] In other words, the 'curious spelling' may reflect an actual eastern Scottish Gaelic linguistic phenomenon, namely the Scottish (as opposed to the Irish type) of nasalisation of *b*.[90] The lack of the nasal may not be a slip and could conceivably reflect the historical form *i*, or, as we have suggested, that the nasal component was weak. Our interpretation of *bb* casts a somewhat different light on the geminate *gg* in **igginn** (BV23) which could also betray the Scottish type of nasalisation. Eclipsed initial *c* is fairly

---

87 Such examples may provide further evidence for the non-assimilation of *mb* and *ng* clusters in an earlier stage of the language.   88 It is not clear whether *na ggiallne* in the *Annals of Ulster* (s.a. 720) represents a gen. sg. or gen. pl. form: see Ó Máille (1910, 38). 89 See A. Watson and Clement (1983, 401). 90 It is worth mentioning as an outside possibility also the form **indelerc** (AII14), which might, though perhaps unlikely so, represent underlying (*intelerc*), with nominative (Scottish) eclipsing article for accusative. Against this, compare genitive article **intiprat** (AII3); cf. also **intestus** (BV10).

consistently written as *g* (or *gg* in one instance) by Hands A and B.[91] Although this is attested occasionally in Irish sources from the Middle Gaelic period (see L. Breatnach 1994, 238), it is not to my knowledge so consistently written in any single text.[92] If our interpretation of geminate *bb* and *gg* in the Notes (perhaps representing voiced *b* and *g* respectively in 'eclipsis' environments) is correct, it represents a canny and shrewd adaptation of the inherited orthographic system. Given the consistency of practice coupled with other similarities between Hands A and B (see discussion of accents in Ó Maolalaigh 'On the possible functions of the accents', this volume), it might even represent a Scottish scribal development of the inherited orthographic system, in order to represent a peculiarly Scottish linguistic feature (perhaps even indicating the voicing of all stops in eclipsis environments). However, the possibility that *bb* may represent *mb* based on the equation of *gg* = *ng* cannot be ruled out, and our suggestion that *bb* may represent voiced *b* must therefore remain conjectural.

Our tentative interpretation of geminate *bb*, *gg* as representing *b* and *g* respectively in the Notes leads us to reconsider the two instances of the phrase issa**é**re (CII26), issaeri (Cv25), both written by Hand C, with double geminate *ss* in an 'eclipsis' environment. Though geminate *ss* is common in Irish sources to mark 'eclipsed' *s*, the question arises whether or not *ss* could in these cases represent a voiced /z/ sound. The eclipsis or nasalisation of *s* as *z* is attested in some eastern Scottish Gaelic dialects,[93] including Speyside, East Perthshire, North West Perthshire (see *an saoghal SGDS* 738), Braemar (Aberdeenshire) (A. Watson and Clement 1983, 401) and Banffshire (Grant 2002, 81). Voicing of *s* as a result of eclipsis has also been reported in some Irish dialects; see Ó Dochartaigh (1987b, 26–27) for discussion and references. Ó Dochartaigh refers to this development in Irish as 'a secondary analogical extension of nasalisation to /s/' (1987b, 26). It is unclear how old this feature is in Irish and Scottish Gaelic dialects. One interpretation of the areal distribution might be that it reflects a relict feature, and that it may be old. However, the interpretation of Deer *ss-* as /z/ is of course purely conjectural but is mentioned in passing here in the context of possible Scotticisms, or more specifically, local dialectisms.

Jackson (1972, 143) and W.J. Watson (1926, 239–43) consistently refer to the voicing of *c* in Scottish Gaelic as an instance of the 'Irish type of nasalisation'. However, as we have noted above, the voicing of voiceless stops is not at all inconsistent with the Scottish type of nasalisation witnessed in

---

91 If incath**r**aig (AI6) contains the article, it could conceivably represent the accusative sg. 'eclipsing' article *in* + *cathr̄aig*, where *c* = [k] or [g]. However, little can be made of this as the leniting article may have been intended (i.e. inc[h]athr̄aig) as in the case of inchadraíg (AII6).   92 However, it occurs frequently enough in the Annals of Inisfallen (C. Breatnach 1990a, 436) and in the fourteenth-century Magauran manuscript (see 200 n.39 above). 93 Also in parts of Mid-Argyll (*SGDS* 738).

Types A and C, and must also have typified earlier stages of Type B. As we have argued above, a comparative reconstruction of all Scottish Gaelic types shows that voicing must have been a feature of an earlier proto-type; see also Ó Maolalaigh (1998, 23–30, esp. 25, 27). Similarly, there is good evidence to suggest that eclipsis developed in two stages, the first stage of which occurred in all varieties of Gaelic and resulted in the voicing of voiceless stops. It follows that it is misleading to refer to the voicing of voiceless stops in Scottish Gaelic as being of an 'Irish' type. The lack of a nasal before the *g* in examples such as aragínn (A14), igginn (BV23) and before *p* (= [b]?) in ipet (DIV1) can be explained in a number of different ways: (A) the orthography is conservative and reflects inherited 'Irish' literary usage; (B) the orthography reflects an intermediate stage between the first 'common' stage of eclipsis in which voiceless stops were voiced but in which eclipsing particles ending in vocalic codas had not yet developed nasal codas; (C) the Scottish type of eclipsis had developed but the nasal component was expressed so weakly that it was not deemed necessary to represent it in writing; a weak nasal articulation with a 'stronger' (i.e. voiced) stop articulation may perhaps be implied by the geminate *gg*, and similarly, as we have argued, in the case of *bb*.[94]

The Deer forms representing the 'eclipsis' of originally voiced *b* and *d* are ambiguous (cf. Jackson 1972, 143). We cannot be certain whether *mb* and *nd* in the Notes represent *m* and *n* (i.e. with Irish type of eclipsis) or *m-b* and *n-d* (with Scottish type of nasalisation) respectively; there is no word division in the four examples concerned to help us decide.[95] There are, however, a number of arguments for interpreting *mb* and *nd* as unassimilated clusters in the Deer Notes. The general phonetic nature of the Notes might suggest that when *mb* and *nd* clusters were written that phonological clusters were intended. In other words, in light of *g(g)* for eclipsed *c*, and the tendency towards phonetic spellings in the Notes, we might expect *n(n)* for eclipsed *d*, and *m(m)* for eclipsed *b*,[96] although admittedly this is not a particularly persuasive argument, especially given the relatively small number of examples involved, and the influence of the inherited orthographic tradition.

Jackson, curiously, lists imbrether (A117), which he interprets as containing the accusative singular article, as an instance 'where the Irish type

94 Francis C. Diack, in a letter to the Revd Charles M. Robertson, dated 5 December 1911, expressed the view that the voicing of voiceless stops was 'long established' in eastern Scottish Gaelic dialects. (NLS MS 425, p. 7ᵛ). He goes on to say 'I notice that it is already in evidence in the Bk. of Deer. This peculiarity, if it *is* a peculiarity and not normal in other parts of the Highlands, must have been a north-eastern feature in very early times. I have a vague recollection that this infection is one of the arguments used by those who w[oul]d fain show that the Gael[ic] of the Bk. of Deer is not native north-eastern but must have been written by Irishmen. This clearly won't hold' (ibid., p. 10ʳ).   95 Leaving aside in béíth (AII22), which may, however, be for in b[h]éíth, with nominative article for accusative.   96 Such examples occur very occasionally in Middle Gaelic sources; see L. Breatnach (1994, 238).

of nasalisation is clearly shown' (1972, 143). However, this example is just as ambiguous as the examples of *nd* which he quotes later in the same passage. On the other hand *imbrether* rather than *inmbrether* has a modern Scottish feel to it. It is unclear if gonice in béíth (AII22) represents a nominative article *in b[h]éíth* or an accusative *in [m]béíth* as already noted.[97] Jackson opts for the former (1972, 143), although the accusative is attested following *gonige* elsewhere in the Notes, e.g. gonige ingorthe (BV22–23). It is possible, however, that in béíth contains the eclipsing accusative article, but that the nasalising *m* has been elided; the lack of nasalising *m* in the cluster *n+m+b* is a feature which is attested in Old Gaelic sources (see Quin 1979–80, 256–7)—a feature incidentally that argues further for the non-assimilation of nasal-voiced stop clusters in earlier stages of the language.

Jackson notes that gondisád (AII2) for *gondísad* 'need not be a Sc. G. type of case [...] since the new *dísad* could still be nasalised as *ndísad* [i.e. as *n-*]' (1972, 143).[98] However, *nd* is ambiguous here as it is not clear whether we should pronounce *nd* as *n(n)-* or *n-d*. Although it is possible to argue that the *d* in this case represents a nasalised or eclipsed *t* (thus representing an underlying *tísad*), caused by the preceding *gon*, it seems just as likely that we are dealing with a new underlying form *dísad* (itself most likely the result of a nasalised or eclipsed *tísad*, resulting from the 'common' stage 1 of eclipsis in Gaelic generally). The fossilisation, through eclipsis, of initial *d-* forms from original *t-* forms occurs in a small set of 'irregular' verbs (including the verbs of motion 'come' and 'go') in both (northern) Ireland and Scotland; see O'Rahilly (1931, 116–17). Such fossilised forms occur in Irish sources occasionally, as early as the eighth-century Würzburg and the ninth-century Milan Glosses. The form <u>condísed</u> occurs in Wb. 25a6; cf. <u>condanicc</u> Wb. 3c27, etc. (cited in Strachan 1903, 55); cf. also *nicon dét* Ml. 53a17 (*DIL* s.v. *téit* 124.70).[99] In Old Gaelic such forms tend to occur following a preceding *n* (*GOI* 147). In these examples it is uncertain whether or not *nd* in such cases is to be interpreted as *n(n)* (i.e. eclipsed *d*) or as a cluster *nd*.[1] It can be readily seen that our interpretation of cases of the 'eclipsis' of *b* and *d* in the Notes depends to a large degree on our view of the history of eclipsis. If we accept O'Rahilly's (1932, 155–6) and Jackson's (1951, 95; 1972, 143) view that

---

97 Cf. tangator [...] incathŕaig (AI6) which is also ambiguous in this respect (Jackson 1972, 143); cf. lenition in the 'accusative' form inchadraíg (AII6). 98 In this he has moved somewhat from his stated earlier position: '*Gon disad* [note word separation] in I [...] appears to represent exactly the stage described by O'Rahilly when the stem *tig-* in dependent position had become stereotyped *dig-* in Sc. G. owing to the frequence of nasalization (of the Irish type), and then was further prefixed by the '*n* of the new type in nasalizing position' (Jackson 1952, 94–5). 99 For other instances, see Strachan (1903, 55). 1 An underlying 'Irish' eclipsed *d-* form is implied by the Middle Gaelic form *co n-igsed* [= *co ndigsed*, by Mael Muire (d. 1106)] (L. Breatnach 1994, 238) in the eleventh–twelfth-century *Lebor na hUidre* l. 2251.

eclipsis developed in Scottish Gaelic as in Irish, that the Scottish Gaelic type is later than the twelfth century and represents a development of the 'Irish type', then we will naturally interpret *mb* and *nd* as assimilated clusters, i.e. as *m* and *n(n)*. If, however, we accept the hypothesis put forward in Ó Maolalaigh (1995–6), then we will interpret *mb* and *nd* as unassimilated clusters as occurs in the majority of modern Scottish Gaelic dialects. Finally, the placement of accents in the form **góndé**nd**aes** (AIII) may be significant in this context. Two accents occur, the first spanning *gon*, and the second spanning *dé-* of the verbal form. If these accents were intended to function as differentiating markers (see Ó Maolalaigh 'On the possible functions of the accents', this volume) they could imply that the scribe intended *gon* to be pronounced as a separate word, thus perhaps suggesting that the cluster *nd* was unassimilated. We may compare the frequent use of the *punctum delens* above the 'eclipsing' nasal in Old Gaelic, which appears to have had a similar function; see Feuth (1982, 94–5).

A cautious conclusion with regard to the evidence of eclipsis might be that the Notes may provide evidence of the initial stages of a Scottish system of eclipsis.[2] A less cautious conclusion might be that there are signs of a more advanced stage of development, similar to that of Type C (or A), which is commensurate with the system found in modern eastern Scottish Gaelic dialects.

4.2.5 Accusative singular

Finally, before we leave the subject of eclipsis, I would like to comment briefly on a feature whose historical development may be related to the history and nature of eclipsis in Scotland. The feature in question is the universal adoption of leniting forms of the singular article following prepositions in Scottish Gaelic—also a feature of Manx and Ulster Irish. In southern Gaelic dialects in Munster and Connacht, however, eclipsis is the norm following the singular article preceded by a preposition (see O'Rahilly 1932, 169, 213–14). For the boundary between Ulster and southern dialects in relation to this feature, see Ó Baoill (1978, 255–6). The merger of dative and accusative forms of the article has had different results in northern and southern varieties of the language: in effect the singular dative article survives in northern dialects and the singular accusative article survives in southern dialects. It may be no coincidence that the pattern of lenition following preposition + article developed in Scotland (possibly spreading southwards into Ulster) where the Scottish type of 'eclipsis' or nasalisation developed, and that eclipsis following preposition + article became the predominant

---

2 Cf. Jackson's (1972, 144) conclusion that 'the possibility that the new development was just faintly beginning, in the north-east, should perhaps not be totally excluded'.

pattern in southern dialects where the full system of 'Irish' eclipsis developed. In other words the Scottish type of 'eclipsis' may have been a possible contributory factor in the direction and ultimate outcome of the merger between dative and accusative forms of the article. If the development of eclipsis in Scottish Gaelic outlined above and in Ó Maolalaigh (1994–5) is correct, in earlier forms of Scottish Gaelic, it would have been difficult to differentiate between nominative and accusative forms of article + noun (beginning with *f, b, d, g* and with no inflected accusative form—including all masculine nouns), e.g. *an/m bard beag* (nominative) ~ *leis an/m bard beag* (accusative). The resulting homophony which left many nouns unmarked following accusative-inducing prepositions may have been resolved by the adoption of dative lenition; note the use of lenition in the Notes with the accusative form: in̲chadraíg (A116), which seems to represent an early example of dative for accusative singular in Scottish Gaelic. While the adoption of nominative singular for accusative singular in the direct objects of verbs may be due to the general simplification of the case system in the direction of the nominative, it is interesting to speculate whether or not the adoption of the nominative singular may in part have been due to the homophony which must have existed in earlier forms of Scottish Gaelic between nominative and accusative in certain contexts containing the article. Could the variation in Classical Gaelic between nominative and accusative in the likes of *mol an mbard mbeag* ~ *mol an bard beag* ('praise the small bard'; see McManus 1994a, 359) reflect southern-northern dialectal traits? Could it be that the accusative was lost earlier in Scottish Gaelic dialects than in southern Irish dialects perhaps partially as a result of the quite different system of eclipsis which developed in Scotland? The adoption of eclipsis following preposition + article in southern Irish dialects may suggest that the accusative may have been retained longer in southern dialects, although this is of course unnecessary.

The geographical distribution of the leniting article following prepositions suggests that it is not a recent but an old development. If the choice and adoption of lenition following prepositional forms of the article in northern dialects was influenced by forms of eclipsis which prevailed in these areas in earlier times, it would follow that the northern forms of nasalisation / eclipsis (i.e. without nasal assimilation in the initial clusters *m-b, n-d, n-g*) must predate the merger of dative and accusative articles in these dialects. If Scottish Gaelic *sam bith* derives from the old accusative *isin m-bith* (rather than a development of a dative form *insan bhith* > *sam bhith* > *sam bith* with delenition), we have a unique relict survival of the Scottish Gaelic type of nasalisation in the accusative without assimilation of the *m-b* cluster.[3]

3 Although I would disagree with McCaughey's (1971, 30) contention that *sa m(b)ith* with Irish type of eclipsis once existed in an earlier stage of Scottish Gaelic, he is clearly correct in maintaining that Scottish Gaelic *sam bith* 'must belong to the period *after* the

5 MORPHOLOGY: SPECIFIC FORMS: BENACT, SEN, SÍ

5.1 *ros-benact*

Jackson suggested that the use of *-t* in rosbenact (A116) is 'a scribal inadvertence' (1972, 41) and he lists it as one of his suggested 'fairly certain errors' (1972, 141),⁴ thus dismissing his earlier suggestion that it could represent the adoption of the verbal noun root *bennacht* as finite verbal stem (1972, 41).⁵

5.2 *sen*

Jackson does not attach any particular importance to the fact that Hand A spells the demonstrative (adjective and pronoun) as *sen / sén* four times out of five and *saín* only once (asáá*th*le sen (A16), iarsén (A111), iarsén (A115), inchadraíg sén (A116), ingathraíg saín (A15)). Although *sen, sein* and *saín* occur in contemporary Irish sources (see *DIL* s.v. *sin*), it is possible that *sen* may have been a feature of certain eastern Scottish Gaelic dialects in the early twelfth century, and that this is what is reflected in the Deer forms.⁶

5.3 Pronoun *sí*

As further evidence of a possible (local) Scotticism, we may note the use of the disjunctive pronoun sí (A17) in doráten ricolumcille sí ('it (fem.) pleased Colum Cille') (A17), which Jackson curiously does not comment on although the use of *sí* here may be quite significant if only from an attestational point of view. This was noted by David Greene who added that 'a discussion of the one occurrence of the independent pronoun as subject would have been helpful' (1972, 169). No instances of *s*-initial disjunctive pronouns (nominative or accusative) have been noted in Irish sources from the

introduction of the new eclipsis into Scottish Gaelic'. However, if the Scottish Gaelic type of eclipsis of voiced stops can be traced back to Old or Middle Gaelic, as I have claimed, it follows that *sam bith* (if it derives from an accusative rather than a dative form) also continues the Old Gaelic usage. **4** A further possible instance may occur in the Yellow Book of Lecan version of *Immram Snédgusa 7 Mac Riagla*, i.e. beannachtsadar (Atkinson 1896: fol. 87r 41). Stokes (1905, 136, n. 3) cautions that this may be a mistake for *beannachsadar*. Against this, however, we may note that the same manuscript contraction for *acht* is used in the preceding line in leamnachta (Atkinson 1896: fol. 87r 41). It has recently been argued by Thomas Owen Clancy (2000, 217–21) that this text is a Derry composition, which suggests as a possibility that this verbal form in *-acht* may represent a northern dialectal form. **5** I have noted the use of *faighneachd* in place of *faighnich* in the speech of a speaker from Glenuig; see also *Dwelly* s.v. *faighneachd¹*. **6** John MacInnes (formerly of the School of Scottish Studies) informs me that he heard [ʃɛn] from Aberdeenshire speakers. Note also his comment in MacInnes (1977, 433–4). Borgstrøm (1940, 188) notes [ʃɛn] for Harris. Ó Murchú (1989a, 397 s.v. *sein*) notes /šɛn/ for East Perthshire, although there it varies with /šin/ (and infrequently with /šen/). *Sin* is the form found in most Irish dialects although *san* is also found in Munster in certain contexts.

early period with the exception of one example of the 3rd person plural *siad*: *bas-rópart Cū Chulaind síat* ('Cú Chulainn attacked them') (LL, *TBC*; L. Breatnach 1994, 272), and vowel-initial forms (*é, í, íat*) are what we would expect—in an Irish context at any rate.[7] Greene (1972, 169) cautiously suggests that our instance of *sí* might represent 'a piece of hypercorrection by a writer to whom *sí* was not a familiar form';[8] see also 'The disjunctive *sí* of the Book of Deer [...] is unparalleled in Irish and looks like a hypercorrection' (Greene 1973, 123).[9] If correct this could imply a date as early as the 12th century for the modern system of vowel-initial pronouns in Scottish Gaelic, which is not inconceivable. In support of this claim it is interesting to note the hypercorrection made by no less a scholar than Professor William J. Watson, who citing 'Irish' usage, produces the phrase '*níor marbhadh sé*' (for expected *níor marbhadh é* 'he was not killed') in his introduction to the *Scottish Verse from the Book of the Dean of Lismore* (W. J. Watson 1937: xxiii). We may also note the use of *sí* for expected *í* in a later Scottish source, namely, in the late seventeenth–early eighteenth-century Black Book of Clanranald: [*agus*] *h-aghnaiceadh si aní* ('and she was buried in Iona') (A. Cameron 1894, 158).[10] The Black Book also has: *fa nám ar marbhadh se* ('at the time he was killed'), which occurs in the line preceding the more 'correct' usage seen in: *no gur tuismedh í* ('until she was confined') (A. Cameron 1894, 162).[11]

If on the other hand we accept the Deer form *sí* at face value what are we to make of it? Are we to conclude that Old Gaelic *sí* survived intact in twelfth-century eastern Scottish Gaelic (cf. Ó Sé 1996, 23)? And if so, did the Old Gaelic system of *sí, é, iad* survive intact? Cf. Ahlqvist (1976, 174). Alternatively, did a dual system *sí, sé, siad ~ í, é, iad* develop as in Irish and if so did s-forms

---

7 The example *ni faicfe tu siad* ('they will not see you') from *Aisling Tundail* is cited in Ahlqvist (1976, 174). For a recent discussion of the spread of subject pronouns in Irish, see Roma (2000: esp. 128 on the use of disjunctive subject pronouns). 8 Alternatively, *sí* may represent the analogical use of 'nominative' based on the use of disjunctive nominative noun phrases with this intransitive verb when it means 'pleases, is congenial to', e.g. 'rothaitne frisin Coimdid an itche sin' (taking *itche* to be feminine here: see *DIL* s.v. *itge, itche*); 'rotaitin co mor fria Poimp int inad sin' (*DIL* s.v. *do-aitni* (c)). 9 For a further possible hypercorrection in the Notes, we may perhaps compare iar (A17), which Jackson (1972, 40, 141) interprets as a scribal mistake for *air* ('because'). However, it is possible that iar (A17) represents a hypercorrection based on the merger of the preposition *iar* with *air*: cf. L. Breatnach (1994, 328). 10 This and similar examples are not to be confused with the occasional use of *inn* and *ibh* (for *sinn* and *sibh* respectively) as subjects in Classical Gaelic (see McManus 1994a, 429), which are (always?) used for alliterative purposes, e.g. *do-éid inn, tharla ibh ag ól, do bhean inn ón fhior* (McKenna 1947: ll. 1012, 3872, 3930). We may note the following instance of disjunctive *sí*, also from a Classical Gaelic poem: *ní fhéad bean a seachna acht sí*, where, significantly, *sí* alliterates with *seachna* (McKenna 1947: l. 1518; underlining in the examples just quoted illustrates the alliterating pairs); we may compare McManus's (1994, 429) comment: 'Mar dheighiltigh agus leis an mbriathar *is* nó *tarla*, úsáidtear foirmeacha le s- nó gan s- sna forainmneacha ar fad ina bhfuil siad inmhalartaithe.' 11 Cf. also *do marbhadh é fein*, 'he was killed' (A. Cameron 1894, 164).

function as subjects and vowel-initial forms disjunctively, including as objects? In the Deer example *sí* is the logical subject of the verb, and analogy with post-verbal subjective *sí* may explain the use of subjective *sí* rather than disjunctive *í*. On the other hand, it is interesting to speculate whether certain varieties of Scottish Gaelic may have developed in the opposite mirror-image direction to Irish,[12] using vowel-initial forms conjunctionally, and *s*-initial forms disjunctively and with the copula.[13] However, all of this is purely conjectural and it is impossible, based on the Deer evidence alone, to know how *sí* functioned, if at all, in eastern twelfth-century vernacular Scottish Gaelic.

Judging from contemporary Irish sources Irish had diverged from the Old / Middle Gaelic system (*sí, é, é* > *iat / iad*) by the twelfth century. The Deer example, if genuine, could suggest that the modern system (*i, e, iad*) may not have developed or may not have been acceptable as literary forms in the twelfth century. The existence of *sí* in an Aberdeenshire dialect in the twelfth century, however, provides grist for the mill of those who would argue that the independent future -*as* forms (which are found in many northern and eastern peripheral Scottish Gaelic dialects, including Braemar and Lewis, most commonly with pronouns) derive ultimately from the historical future -*idh* + *sé, sí, siad*, although the Deer form has not generally been cited in that particular context (but see now Ó Sé 1996, 24). This theory was first proposed by MacBain (1894, 92) and later by O'Rahilly (1932, 133), who added that *molai sé* (< *molaidh sé*) became *mol(a)s é* 'under the influence of the relative form in -*as* or -*s*'. Others have claimed that the independent future -*as* in Scottish Gaelic represents an extension of the relative -*as*; see Fraser (1914, 280), Greene (1973, 123) and Gleasure (1986). John Reid, author of *Bibliotheca Scoto-Celtica*, published in Glasgow in the year 1832, makes an interesting comment on this feature. Of Northern [Scottish] Gaelic, which he deemed to be further removed from Irish, he notes:

---

12 For other evidence of mirror-image or opposite developments in Scottish Gaelic and Irish we may note the differences in the leniting aspect of the preposition *a(i)r* in both languages. The merger of Old Gaelic leniting *ar* and nonleniting *for* has resulted in leniting *ar* and nonleniting *air* in Irish and Scottish Gaelic respectively, except for fossilised collocations (such as *ar buile, ar crith* (Irish) vs. *air bhoil, air chrith* (Scottish Gaelic)), in which the opposite pattern prevails, i.e. nonleniting *ar* and leniting *air* in Irish and Scottish Gaelic respectively. We may also note the differences: *a dó, dhá* ('two', Irish) and *a dhà, dà* ('two', Scottish Gaelic); see Borgstrøm (1938, 42–4). The merger of dative and accusative articles has resulted generally in the adoption of the dative in Scottish Gaelic and the accusative in southern Irish dialects as discussed above. Original unstressed //ɣ′// and //x′// merged as /ɣ′/ in most Irish dialects but as /x′/ is most Scottish Gaelic dialects. We may also note that the Middle Gaelic system of *sí, é, iad* has resulted in *sí, sé, siad* ~ *í, é, iad* in Irish but as *i, e, iad* in Scottish Gaelic.   **13** It is impossible to know whether *é* or *sé* is underlyingly present in the copula form **essé** (A14).

> In Ross-shire, and other northern counties, they have flexions of the verb 'to be', which are not known in Cantyre nor the mid-Highlands; they make the future indicative end in *eas*, instead of *idh*, they say *bitheas, tu, e, i, &c.*, and they always use the pronoun *se*, instead of *e*. (Reid 1832: xxxix)

It is difficult to know what to make of this latter statement on the use of *se* especially when he lists the form *bitheas e* immediately before it. One wonders if he was thinking of copula forms such as *'s e*. This evidence requires further study as indeed does the form [bu·əl´iʃ e:], quoted in the recently published *SGDS* materials for North Sutherland (*SGDS* 131, point 137).[14] We conclude then that the attestation of *sí* here may be more significant than Jackson apparently believed, although its precise significance is far from clear.

CONCLUSIONS

Jackson concludes that the language of the Gaelic Notes does not provide evidence for earlier forms of Scottish Gaelic. Indeed he claims that the language is 'virtually indistinguishable from contemporary Irish' (1972: vii); cf. L. Breatnach (1994, 225). Despite many similarities with contemporary Irish forms, some of the forms discussed above seem nevertheless to point towards a number of Scotticisms, some of which may betray local eastern Scottish Gaelic dialect forms. Our conclusion is reminiscent of that of MacBain (1885, 142):

> The Scotch Gaelic, while keeping to the general style of spelling and writing which the Irish had, was not weighted by precedent and literary forms of bygone times; it consequently adapted itself to the time and locality in which it was produced. [...] The departure from all Irish lines are the most important and most remarkable facts. The spelling, though it is on the whole cast in the same moulds, has some local peculiarities.

It is also in keeping with Derick Thomson's (1994 [1983], 99) statement with regard to the general historical development of Scottish Gaelic orthography:

---

14 This form (i.e. *buailis* [bu·əl´iʃ]) does not occur in the transcript which Jackson made of Eric Hamp's original field notes. Jackson's copy has [bu·əl´i̯] and has no note indicating that he has changed Hamp's recorded form. Hamp's original field copy has [bu·əli̯(ʃe:)]

> Our earliest Scottish sources are in the literary language we describe as
> Classical Common Gaelic, but at all times this language is open to
> modification in the direction of spoken Scottish Gaelic, just as in
> Ireland there is modification in the direction of spoken Irish Gaelic.

It is a matter for speculation how we regard the profusion of such localisms.
Jackson would put them down to ignorance of the Irish tradition. However, it
is possible to view these in a more positive light. They suggest a drift towards
orthographic forms which perhaps better and more clearly represented the
form of Gaelic, which was used in eastern Scotland during the twelfth
century—a drift which represents a gradual movement within the confines of
the inherited orthographic system which better served Scottish Gaelic literati.
Rather than unveiling a coterie of ill-educated and incompetent scribes, our
interpretation of the Notes points towards a high degree of linguistic
awareness and sophistication, which we know Gaelic *fir léighinn* were well
capable of achieving; furthermore, the fact that some of the orthographic-
linguistic features discussed are attributable to more than one scribe is suggestive of an established tradition or 'school', in some cases slightly different
from that pertaining in contemporary Ireland.[15] It is important to note that
some of the scribal practices discussed can be discerned in near-contemporary
Scottish texts written in eastern Scotland (see Broun 1998). We have also
suggested that the orthography of the Notes may in certain cases have been
influenced by Latin orthography. Further study of the orthography of Latin
and Gaelic sources in medieval Scotland will no doubt shed more light on
orthographic practices during the period, and, in particular, on the ways in
which both systems of orthography interacted and influenced each other.

In summary, our reassessment of the language and orthography of the
Gaelic Notes suggests that we have a good deal of evidence for a drift towards
a slightly differentiated system (or systems) which was perhaps better suited
to represent the emergent variety of Gaelic used in twelfth-century eastern
Scotland. In this sense I would suggest that the Gaelic Notes represent an
early example of the Scotticisation of Gaelic.

SYMBOLS

/ / / /	hypothetical 'Common Gaelic' phonemes
E	eclipsis
-VN	an eclipsing word ending in a vowel + a nasal consonant

---

15 It is in this context and against this background that the neglected acute-like accents,
which are peppered through the Gaelic Notes, are tentatively analysed in Ó Maolalaigh,
'On the possible functions of the accents', this volume.

ABBREVIATIONS

Arb Lib	*Liber S. Thome de Aberbrothoc*, ed. C. Innes and P. Chalmers (Edinburgh: Bannatyne Club, 1848–56).
Bagimond's Roll	'Bagimond's Roll: statement of the tenths of the kingdom of Scotland', ed. A. I. Dunlop, in *Miscellany of the Scottish History Society* (3rd ser., vol. vi (114), (Edinburgh, 1939).
Cal. Papal Letters	*Calendar of entries in the papal registers relating to Great Britain and Ireland: papal letters*, ed. W.H. Bliss et al. (London: HMSO, etc., 1893–).
CSD	*The Concise Scots dictionary*, ed. M. Robinson (Aberdeen, 1987 [1985]).
DIL	*Dictionary of the Irish language* (compact edition), ed. E.G. Quin (Dublin, 1983). Repr. 1990.
Dunf Reg	*Registrum de Dunfermelyn*, ed. C. Innes (Edinburgh: Bannatyne Club, 1842).
Dwelly	*The illustrated Gaelic-English dictionary*, by E. Dwelly (Glasgow, 1901–11). Repr. 1977.
DOST	*A dictionary of the older Scottish tongue*, ed. W.A. Craigie et al. (1931–2002).
LEIA	*Lexique étymologique de l'irlandais ancien*, by J. Vendryes (Dublin, 1959–).
GOI	*A grammar of Old Irish*, by R. Thurneysen (Dublin, 1946). Repr. 1993.
RMN	*Registrum S. Marie de Neubotle*, ed. C. Innes (Edinburgh: Bannatyne Club, 1849).
RMS	*Registrum Magni Sigilli Regum Scotorum*, 9 vols, ed. J.M. Thomson et al. (Edinburgh: General Register House, 1882–97, 1912).
RRS	*Regesta Regum Scottorum*, 4 vols (Edinburgh: Edinburgh University Press), vol. I (1960) ed. G.W.S. Barrow; vol. II (1971) ed. G.W.S. Barrow and W.W. Scott; vol. V (1988) ed. Archibald A.M. Duncan; vol. VI (1982) ed. Bruce Webster.
SGDS	*Survey of the Gaelic dialects of Scotland*, 5 vols, ed. C. Ó Dochartaigh (Dublin, 1994–7).
St A. Cop.	*Copiale prioratus Sanctiandree: the letter-book of James Haldenstone, Prior of St Andrews (1418–1443)*, ed. J.H. Baxter (St Andrews: St Andrews University Publications 19.4, 1930).
St A. Lib	*Liber Cartarum Prioratus S. Andree in Scotia*, ed. Thomas Thomson (Edinburgh: Bannatyne Club, 1841).

REFERENCES

Ahlqvist, A. (1976) 'On the position of pronouns in Irish', *Éigse* 16.3, 171–6.

—— (1988) 'Remarks on the question of dialects in Old Irish', in *Historical Dialectology*, Trends in Linguistics: Studies and Monographs, 37, ed. J. Fisiak, (Berlin: Mouton de Gruyter), 23–38.

Atkinson, R. (1896) *The Yellow Book of Lecan* [...]. Facsimile edition, Dublin.

Bannerman, J. (1998 [1986]) *The Beatons: a medical kindred in the classical Gaelic tradition* Edinburgh. Repr.

Bergin, O.J. (1907) 'Palatalization', *Ériu* 3, 50–91.

Best, R.I. (1933) 'The manuscript', in *The Annals of Inisfallen: reproduced in facsimile from the original manuscript (Rawlinson B 503) in the Bodleian Library*, ed. R.I. Best and E. Mac Neill, Dublin, 1–25.

Bieler, L. (1954) 'Hibernian Latin', *Studies: An Irish Quarterly Review of Letters, Philosophy & Science* 43, 92–95.

—— (ed.) (1963) *The Irish Penitentials*. Scriptores Latini Hiberniae 5, Dublin.

Binchy, D.A. (1963) *Scéla Cano Meic Gartnáin*, Dublin.

—— (1978) *Corpus Iuris Hibernici*, Dublin.

Bischoff, B. (1990) *Latin palaeography: antiquity & the Middle Ages*, translated by Dáibhí O Cróinín and David Ganz, Cambridge.

Black, G.F. (1993 [1946]) *The surnames of Scotland: their origin, meaning, and history*, Edinburgh.

Black, R. (1973) Review of Jackson (1972), *Celtica* 10, 264–7.

—— (1984) 'A Gaelic contract of lease, c.1603 x 1616', *Stair Society: Miscellany II*, 132–43.

—— (1990) 'A Scottish grammatical tract, c.1640', *Celtica* 21, 3–16.

—— I. M. (2000a) 'Scottish fairs and fair-names', *Scottish Studies* 33, 1–75.

—— (2000b) 'Appendix 6: Later Additions in Gaelic', in John Higgitt, *The Murthly Hours: devotion, literacy and luxury in Paris, England and the Gaelic West*, London and Toronto, 336–45.

Borgstrøm, C.Hj. (1934) 'The expression of person and number in Gaelic', *Norsk Tidsskrift for Sprogvidenskap* 7, 129–40.

—— (1938) 'Scottish Gaelic as a source of information about the early history of Irish', *Scottish Gaelic Studies*, 5, 35–44.

—— (1940) *The dialects of the Outer Hebrides*, Oslo.

—— (1941) *The dialects of Skye and Ross-shire*, Oslo.

Breatnach, C. (1989) 'Varia IV', *Ériu* 40, 184–6.

—— (1990a) 'Teanga na Tréimhse 1050–1321 in *Annála Inse Faithlinn*—Léargas ar an Nua-Ghaeilge' (unpublished PhD thesis, University College Dublin).

—— (1990b) 'Varia VI: *Blein* for *Bliadhain* in the *Annals of Inisfallen*', *Ériu* 41, 143–46.

—— (1992) Review of Herbert and Ó Riain (1988), in *Éigse* 26, 177–87.

—— (2001) 'Language and orthography', in *Apocrypha Hiberniae: I. Evangelia Infantiae*. Corpvs Christianorvm, Series Apocryphorum 13, ed. M. McNamara et al., Turnhout, 139–41.

Breatnach, L. (1989) 'The first third of *Bretha Nemed Toísech*', *Ériu* 40, 1–40.

—— (1990) 'Varia V, 1. On the nasalization of the preverb *to*', *Ériu* 41, 139–40.

—— (1994) 'An Mheán-Ghaeilge', in *Stair na Gaeilge in Ómós do P[h]ádraig Ó Fiannachta*, ed. K. McCone et al., Maigh Nuad, 221–333.

Breatnach, P.A. (1988) 'The pronunciation of Latin in medieval Ireland', in *Scire litteras: Forschungen zum mittelalterlichen Geistesleben* (= Bayerische Akademie der Wissenschaften Philosophisch-Historische Klasse, Abhandlungen, Neue Folge, Heft 99, Sonderdruck), ed. S. Krämer and M. Bernhard, München, 59–72.

Breatnach, R.A. (1952) 'The origin of the 2pl. Ipv. in Northern Irish', *Ériu* 16, 49–60.

—— (1993) 'Cregeen's Manx proverbs and familiar phrases', *Éigse* 27, 1–34.

—— (1997) 'The periphrastic comparative in Eastern Gaelic', *Éigse* 30, 1–6.

Breatnach, R.B. (1954) Review of Jackson (1951), *Éigse* 7.3, 210–12.

Breeze, A. (2003) 'Scots *Shayth* "reason" and Gaelic *Seadh* "esteem"', *Scottish Gaelic Studies* 21, 251–2.

Broderick, G. (1984–86) *A handbook of late spoken Manx*, 3 vols, Tübingen.

Broun, D. (1998) 'Gaelic literacy in Eastern Scotland between 1124 and 1249', in *Literacy in medieval Celtic societies*, ed. Huw Price, Cambridge, 183–201.

—— (1999) *The Irish identity of the kingdom of the Scots in the twelfth and thirteenth centuries*, Woodbridge.

Cameron, A. (1894) *Reliquiæ Celticæ: texts, papers, and studies in Gaelic literature and philology* […], ed. A. MacBain and J. Kennedy, vol. 2, Inverness.

Cameron, J. (1937) *Celtic law: the 'Senchus Mór' and 'The Book of Aicill,' and the traces of an early Gaelic system of law in Scotland*, London etc.

Campbell, E. (2001) 'Were the Scots Irish?', *Antiquity* 75, 285–92.

Campbell, J.L. and D. Thomson (1963) *Edward Lhuyd in the Scottish Highlands 1699–1700*, Oxford.

Carney, J. (1964) *The poems of Blathmhac Son of Cú Brettan together with the Irish Gospel of Thomas and a poem on the Virgin Mary*. Irish Texts Society, vol. 47, Dublin.

—— (1983) 'The dating of Early Irish verse texts, 500–1100', *Éigse* 19.2, 177–216.

Clancy, T.O. (2000) 'Subversion at sea: structure, style and intent in the *Immrama*', in *The otherworld voyage in early Irish literature: an anthology of criticism*, ed. Jonathan Wooding, Dublin, 194–225.

—— (2002) 'Scottish saints and national identities in the early Middle Ages', in *Local saints and local churches in the early medieval West*, ed. R. Sharpe and A. Thacker, Oxford, 397–421.

Cox, R.A.V. (2002) *The Gaelic place-names of Carloway, Isle of Lewis: their structure and significance*, Dublin.

Craigie, W.A. (1897) 'Gaelic words and names in the Icelandic Sagas', *Zeitschrift für celtische Philologie* 1, 439–54.

de Bhaldraithe, T. (1977) *Gaeilge Chois Fhairrge: An Deilbhíocht*, Dublin.

Diack, F.C. (1920–21) 'Place-names of Pictland [I]', *Revue celtique* 38, 109–32.

—— (1922) 'Place-names of Pictland [II]', *Revue celtique* 39, 125–74.

—— (1944) *The inscriptions of Pictland: an essay on the sculptured and inscribed stones of the North-East and North of Scotland: with other writings and collections*, ed. W.M. Alexander and J. MacDonald, Aberdeen (Third Spalding Club).

Dieckhoff, C. (1932) *A pronouncing dictionary of Scottish Gaelic*, Edinburgh and London.

Dieth, E. (1932) *A grammar of the Buchan dialect*, Cambridge.

Dillon, M. (1928) 'Nominal predicates in Irish: [Part 2]', *Zeitschrift für celtische Philologie* 17, 307–46.

—— and D. Ó Cróinín (1961) *Teach yourself Irish*, London.

Dumville, D.N. (2002) 'Ireland and North Britain in the earlier Middle Ages: contexts for *Míniugud Senchusa Fher nAlban*', in *Rannsachadh na Gàidhlig 2000: Papers read at the Conference* Scottish Gaelic Studies 2000 *held at the University of Aberdeen 2–4 August 2000*, ed. C. Ó Baoill and N.R. McGuire, Obar Dheathain, 185–211.

Feuth, E. (1982) 'Two segments or one?: Nasalized voiced plosives in Old Irish', *Zeitschrift für celtische Philologie* 39, 88–95.

Flanagan, D., and L. Flanagan (1994) *Irish place names*, Dublin.

Fraser, J. (1914) 'The tenses of the verb in modern Scottish Gaelic', *Transactions of the Gaelic Society of Inverness* 28 (1912–14), 269–84.

—— (1942) 'The Gaelic *Notitiae* in the Book of Deer', *Scottish Gaelic Studies* 5, 51–66.

Gillies, W. (1993) 'Scottish Gaelic', in *The Celtic languages*, ed. Martin J. Ball with James Fife, London and New York, 145–227.

—— (1994) 'The Celtic languages: some current and some neglected questions', in *Speaking in our tongues*, ed. Margaret Laing and Keith Williamson, Cambridge, 139–47.

—— (1996) 'Some thoughts on the *Toschederach*', *Scottish Gaelic Studies*, 17, 128–42.

—— (2004) 'Varia II: Early Irish *lía*, Scottish Gaelic *liutha*', *Ériu* 54, 253–56.

Gleasure, J. (1986) 'Synthetic and analytic: some comments on the Irish/Gaelic present/future', *Scottish Gaelic Studies* 14.2 (Winter), 94–101.

Grant, S. (2002) 'Gaelic in western Banffshire: the extent of Gaelic speech in 1881 and the nature of the Gaelic dialect spoken', in *Rannsachadh na Gàidhlig 2000: Papers read at the Conference* Scottish Gaelic Studies 2000 *held at the University of Aberdeen 2–4 August 2000*, ed. C. Ó Baoill and N.R. McGuire, Obar Dheathain, 75–90.

Greene, D. (1952) 'Middle quantity in Irish', *Ériu* 16, 212–8.

—— (1969) 'Irish as a vernacular before the Norman invasion', in *A view of the Irish language*, ed. B. Ó Cuív, Dublin, 11–21.

—— (1972) Review of Jackson (1972), *Studia Hibernica* 12, 167–70.

—— (1973) 'Synthetic and analytic: a reconsideration', *Ériu* 24, 121–33.

—— (1976) 'The diphthongs of Old Irish', *Ériu* 27, 26–45.

Grijzenhout, J. (1995) *Irish consonant mutation and phonological theory*, Utrecht.

Groome, F.H. (1882–5) *Ordnance Gazetteer of Scotland: a survey of Scottish topography, statistical, biographical, and historical*, 6 vols. 2nd ed. [no date].

Gunn, A. (1890) 'The dialect of the Reay Country', *Transactions of the Gaelic Society of Inverness* 15 (1888–89), 35–46.

Hamp, E.P. (1993) 'Varia III, 2. Morphological criteria and evidence in Roman British', *Ériu* 44, 177–80.

Herbert, M, and P. Ó Riain (1988) *Betha Adamnáin: the Irish Life of Adamnán*, Irish Texts Society, 54, Dublin.

Hickey, R. (1986) 'Issues in the vowel phoneme inventory of Western Irish', *Éigse* 21, 214–26

Hogan, E. (1993 [1910]) *Onomasticon Goedelicum: Locorum et Tribuum Hiberniae et Scotiae*, Dublin.

Holmer, N.M. (1938) *Studies on Argyllshire Gaelic*, Uppsala.

—— (1957) *The Gaelic of Arran*, Dublin.

—— (1962) *The Gaelic of Kintyre*, Dublin. Repr. 1981.

Howells, D. (1971) 'Miscellanea, 1. The nominative plural of the noun in the Gaelic of the Isle of Lewis', *Studia Celtica* 6, 90–97.

Hudson, B.T. (1988) '*Elech* and the Scots in Strathclyde', *Scottish Gaelic Studies* 15, 145–49.

Hughes, A.J. and R.J. Hannan (1992) *Place-names of Northern Ireland. Volume Two. County Down II: The Ards*, Belfast.

Isaac, G.R. (2003) 'Some Old Irish etymologies, and some conclusions drawn from them', *Ériu* 53, 151–55.

Jackson, K.H. (1951) '*Common Gaelic': the evolution of the Gaelic languages*, London. Also published in *Proceedings of the British Academy* 37.

—— (1952) 'Some remarks on the Gaelic Notitiae in the Book of Deer', *Ériu* 16, 86–98.

—— (1955) *Contributions to the study of Manx phonology*, Edinburgh.

—— (1968) 'The breaking of original long é in Scottish Gaelic', in *Celtic studies: essays in memory of Angus Matheson 1912–1962*, ed. J. Carney and D. Greene, London, 65–71.

—— (1972) *The Gaelic Notes in the Book of Deer*, Cambridge.

—— (1983) 'The historical grammar of Irish: some actualities and some desiderata', in *Proceedings of the Sixth International Congress of Celtic Studies, held in University College, Galway, 6–13 July, 1979*, ed. G. Mac Eoin et al., Dublin, 1–18.

Jasanoff, J.H. (1989) 'Old Irish *bé* "woman"', *Ériu* 40, 135–41.

Johnston, W., and A.K. Johnston (1937) *Gazetteer of Scotland: including a glossary of the most common Gaelic and Norse names*, Edinburgh and London.

Jordan, R. (1974) *Handbook of Middle English grammar: phonology*, The Hague.

Joynt, M. (1910) 'Echtra Mac Echdach Mugmedóin', *Ériu* 4, 91–111.

Keillar, I. (1993) 'The place-name Birnie', *Moray Field Club Bulletin* 21 (December 1993), 21–2.

Kelly, F. (1988) *A guide to early Irish law*, Dublin.

—— (1997) *Early Irish farming: a study based mainly on the law-texts of the 7th and 8th centuries AD*, Dublin.

Kelly, J. (1870 [1804]) *A practical grammar of the antient Gaelic or language of the Isle of Man usually called Manks*, ed. W. Gill, Douglas.

Kelly, P. (1982) 'Dialekte im Altirischen?', in *Sprachwissenschaft in Innsbruck*, ed. W. Meid, H. Ölberg, H. Schmeja (Innsbruck: Institut für Vergleichende Sprachwissenschaft der Universität Innsbruck) (= Innsbrucker Beiträge zur Kulturwissenschaft, Sonderheft 50), 85–9.

Kneen, J.J. (1931) *A grammar of the Manx language*, Oxford and London.

Knott, E. (ed.), (1963 [1936]) *Togail Bruidne Da Derga*, Dublin.

Laver, J. (1994) *Principles of phonetics*, Cambridge.

Lapidge, M., and R. Sharpe (1985) *A bibliography of Celtic-Latin literature 400–1200*, Dublin.

Löfstedt, B. (1965) *Der hibernolateinische Grammatiker Malsachanus*. Acta Universitatis Upsaliensis, Studia Latina Upsaliensia 3, Uppsala.

—— (1979) 'Some linguistic remarks on Hiberno-Latin', *Studia Hibernica* 19, 161–69.

Mac Airt, S. *The Annals of Inisfallen (MS Rawlinson B. 503)*, Dublin.

MacAulay, D. (1975) Review of Jackson (1972) *Scottish Historical Review* 54, 84–87.

MacBain, A. (1885) 'The Book of Deer', *Transactions of the Gaelic Society of Inverness* 11 (1884–5), 137–66.

—— (1891) 'Badenoch: its history, clans, and place names', *Transactions of the Gaelic Society of Inverness* 16 (1889–90), 148–97.

—— (1894) 'The Gaelic dialect of Badenoch', *Transactions of the Gaelic Society of Inverness* 18 (1891–92), 79–96.

—— (1896) *An etymological dictionary of the Gaelic language*, Glasgow. Repr. 1982.

—— (1907) 'Place-names of Inverness-shire', *Transactions of the Gaelic Society of Inverness* 25 (1901–3), 55–84.

Mac Cana, P. (1990) 'On the accusative of destination', *Ériu* 41, 27–36.

Mac Cárthaigh, M. (1964–65) 'Gamhar—a "Winter" stream', *Dinnseanchas* 1, 43.

MacDonald, A. (1941) *The place-names of West Lothian* (Edinburgh: Oliver & Boyd).

MacGregor, M. (2000) 'Genealogies of the clans: contributions to the study of MS 1467', *Innes Review* 51.2 (Autumn 2000), 131–46.

MacInnes, J. (1977) 'Some Gaelic Words and Usages', *Transactions of the Gaelic Society of Inverness* 49 (1974–6), 428–55.

McCaughey, T.P. (1971) 'Scottish Gaelic "*sam bith*"', *Scottish Gaelic Studies* 12.1, 30–3.

McCone, K. (1985) 'The Würzburg and Milan glosses: our earliest sources of "Middle Irish"', *Ériu* 36, 85–106.

—— (1994) 'An tSean-Ghaeilge agus a réamhstair', in *Stair na Gaeilge in ómós do P[h]ádraig Ó Fiannachta*, ed. by K. McCone et al., Maigh Nuad, 61–219.

—— (1996a) *Towards a relative chronology of ancient and medieval Celtic sound change*, Maynooth.

—— (1996b) 'Prehistoric, Old and Middle Irish', *Progress in Medieval Irish Studies*, ed. Kim McCone and Katharine Simms, Maynooth, 7–53.

McDonough, C.J. (1995) *Warner of Rouen: Moriuht: a Norman Latin poem from the early eleventh century*, Studies and Texts 121, Toronto.

MacKechnie, J. (1953) 'Treaty between Argyll and O'Donnell', *Scottish Gaelic Studies* 7, 94–102.

McKenna, L. (1941) 'Initial eclipsis and lenition, use of nominative for accusative in Early Modern Irish (based mainly on Magauran MS and Duanaire of Y.B.L.', *Éigse* 3, 52–66.

McKenna, L. (1947) *The Book of Magauran: Leabhar Méig Shamhradháin*, Dublin.

McLeod, W. (2004) *Divided Gaels: Gaelic cultural identities in Scotland and Ireland c.1200–c.1650*, Oxford.

McManus, D. (1991) *A guide to Ogam*, Maynooth.

—— (1994a) 'An Ghaeilge Chlasaiceach', in *Stair na Gaeilge in ómós do P[h]ádraig Ó Fiannachta*, ed. K. McCone et al., Maigh Nuad, 335–445.

—— (1994b) 'Teanga an Dána agus Teanga an Phróis', *Léachtaí Cholm Cille* 24, 114–35.

Mac Phàrlain, C. ([1923]) *Dorlach laoidhean do sgrìobhadh le Donnchadh Mac Rath, 1688 / A handful of lays written by Duncan Mac Rae, 1688*, Dùn Dé.

Magill, P. (1937) 'Irish place names in County Antrim [part 3]', *Down and Connor Historical Society's Journal* 8, 82–9.

Meek, D.E. (1986) 'The banners of the Fian in Gaelic Ballad tradition', *Cambridge Medieval Celtic Studies* 11 (Summer 1986), 29–69.

Mulchrone (1939) *Bethu Phátraic: The tripartite Life of Patrick*, Dublin.

Munro, J. and R.W. Munro (eds), (1986) *Acts of the Lords of the Isles 1336–1493*, Edinburgh.

Ó Baoill, C. (1978) *Contributions to a comparative study of Ulster Irish and Scottish Gaelic.* Studies in Irish Language and Literature, 4, Belfast.

—— (1988) 'Scotticisms in a manuscript of 1467', *Scottish Gaelic Studies* 15 (Spring 1988), 122–39.

—— (2000) 'Of Mar', *Scottish Gaelic Studies* 20, 165–9.

O'Brien, M.A. (1962) *Corpus Genealogiarum Hiberniae*, vol. 1, Dublin.

Ó Buachalla, B. (1977) '*Ní* and *Cha* in Ulster Irish', *Ériu* 28, 92–141.

—— (1982) 'Scribal practice, philology and historical linguistics', in *Papers from the 5th International Conference on Historical Linguistics*, ed. A. Ahlqvist (Current Issues in Linguistic Theory, 21), 425–32.

—— (1988) 'MacNeill's Law and the plural marker -(e)an', *Proc. RIA* 88 C 3, 39–60.

—— (1997) 'Synthetic and analytic: addendum', in *Miscellanea Celtica in Memoriam Heinrich Wagner*, ed. S. Mac Mathúna and A. Ó Corráin, Uppsala, 175–81.

—— (2002) '"Common Gaelic" revisited', in *Rannsachadh na Gàidhlig 2000: Papers read at the Conference Scottish Gaelic Studies 2000 held at the University of Aberdeen 2–4 August 2000*, ed. C. Ó Baoill and N.R. McGuire, Obar Dheathain, 1–12.

Ó Cuív, B. (1972) Review of Jackson (1972), *Éigse* 14.4, 341–6.

—— (1973) 'A typographical casualty', *Éigse* 15.1, 66.

—— (1980 [1951]) *Irish dialects and Irish-speaking districts*, Dublin.

—— (1990) 'The Irish marginalia in Codex Palatino-Vaticanus No. 830', *Eigse* 24, 45–67.

—— (2001) *Catalogue of Irish language manuscripts in the Bodleian Library at Oxford and Oxford College Libraries. Part 1: Descriptions*, Dublin.

Ó Dochartaigh, C. (1976) '"Cha" and "Ní" in the Irish of Ulster', *Éigse* 16.4, 317–36.

—— (1987a) *Dialects of Ulster Irish*. Studies in Irish Language and Literature, 7, Belfast.

—— (1987b) 'Mutation of *s*-Clusters in Gaelic', *Scottish Language*, 7, 22–30.

O'Donovan, J. (1845) *A grammar of the Irish language*, Dublin.

Oftedal, M. (1956) *The Gaelic of Leurbost Isle of Lewis*, Oslo.

Ó hInnse, S. (1947) *Miscellaneous Irish Annals (AD 1114–1437)*, Dublin.

Ó Laoghaire, D. (1990) '*Beatha Eustasius* agus *Beatha Mhuire Éigiptí*', *Celtica* 21, 489–522.

Ó Máille, T. (1910) *The language of the Annals of Ulster*. University of Manchester Publications 53, Manchester.

Ó Mainnín, M. (1990) 'The element *Island* in Ulster place-names', *Ainm* 4 (1989–90), 200–10.

—— (1999) '"The same in origin and in blood": bardic windows on the relationship between Irish and Scottish Gaels, *c*.1200–1650', *Cambrian Medieval Celtic Studies* (Winter 1999), 1–51.

Ó Maolalaigh, R. (1995–96) 'The development of eclipsis in Gaelic', *Scottish Language* 14–15, 158–73.

—— (1997) 'The historical short vowel phonology of Gaelic', 2 vols (unpublished PhD thesis, University of Edinburgh).

—— (1998) 'Place-names as a resource for the historical linguist', *The uses of place-names*. St John's House Papers 7, St Andrews, Edinburgh, 12–53.

—— (1999a) 'The development of eclipsis and common Gaelic', in *Celtic connections: Proceedings of the Tenth International Congress of Celtic Studies. Vol.1: Language, literature, history, culture*, ed. R. Black et al., East Linton, 539.

—— (1999b) 'Transition zones, hyperdialectisms and historical change: the case of final unstressed -*igh*/-*ich* and -*idh* in Scottish Gaelic', *Scottish Gaelic Studies* 19, 195–233.

—— (2001) 'Forás na nDeirí Díspeagtha -*ean* agus -*ein* i nGaeilge na hAlban', in *Béalra: Aistí ar Theangeolaíocht na Gaeilge*, ed. B. Ó Catháin and R. Ó hUiginn, Maigh Nuad, 1–43.

—— (2003a) 'Processes in nasalisation and related issues', *Ériu* 53, 109–32.

—— (2003b) 'Varia II: A possible internal source for Scottish Gaelic plural -*an*', *Ériu* 53, 157–61.

—— (2003c) 'Varia IV, 2. On the 2pl. imperative in Scottish Gaelic', *Ériu* 53, 174–78.

—— (2003d) Review of *Festschrift for Professor D S Thomson*, ed. D. MacAulay et al. (= *Scottish Gaelic Studies* 17 (1996)), *Celtica* 24, 306–30.

—— (2003e) '"Siubhadaibh a Bhalachaibh, Tha an Suirbhidh a-nis ullamh agaibh": Mar a dh'Éirich do *bh* agus *mh* gun chudrom ann an Gàidhlig Alba', *Scottish Gaelic Studies* 21, 163–219.

—— (2006) 'Coibhneas idir consan (*dh / gh*) agus Guta i Stair na Gaeilge', in *Aistí in Ómós do Bhreandán Ó Buachalla*, ed. A. Doyle and S. Ní Laoire, 41–78.

—— (2007) '*Péisteoigín itheas éadach*: the significance of *leaghmhan* "moth"', in *'Fil Súil nGlais'. A grey eye looks back: a Festschrift in honour of Colm Ó Baoill*, Ceann Drochaid, 213–40.

—— (forthcoming) 'Forás -*ich* agus impleachtaí do Stair na Gaeilge', *Éigse*.

Ó Murchú, M. (1985) *The Irish language*, Dublin.

—— (1986) '*R* Caol i dtús focal: blúire canúineolaochta', in *Féilscríbhinn Thomáis de Bhaldraithe*, ed. S. Watson, Baile Átha Cliath, 19–26.

——— (1989a) *East Perthshire Gaelic: social history, phonology, texts, and lexicon*, Dublin.

——— (1989b) 'Some Irish phonological rules and their chronological order', *Ériu* 40, 143–46.

——— (1996) 'Dialects of Irish', in *The Oxford companion to Irish literature*, ed. R. Welch and B. Stewart, Oxford, 145–48.

——— (1997) Review of *Stair na Gaeilge in Ómós do P[h]ádraig Ó Fiannachta*, ed. K. McCone et al., in *Éigse* 30, 171–95.

O'Rahilly, C. (1967) *Táin Bó Cúalnge from the Book of Leinster*, et al., Dublin.

O'Rahilly, C. (1973) 'Teacht tuidecht', *Éigse* 15.1, 1–6.

O'Rahilly, T.F. (1930) 'Notes on Middle Irish pronunciation', *Hermathena* 20, 152–95.

——— (1931) 'Some verbal forms in Scottish Gaelic, Manx and Ulster Irish', *Scottish Gaelic Studies* 3, 111–32.

——— (1932) *Irish dialects past and present*, Dublin.

——— (1942) '*Iarann, lárag*, etc.', *Ériu* 13, 119–27.

——— (1946) *Early Irish history and mythology*, Dublin.

Ó Sé, D. (1989) 'Contributions to the study of word stress in Irish', *Ériu* 40, 147–78.

——— (1991) 'Prosodic change in Manx and lexical diffusion', in *Language contact in the British Isles: Proceedings of the Eighth International Symposium on Language Contact in Europe, Douglas, Isle of Man, 1988*, ed. P. S. Ureland and G. Broderick, Tübingen, 157–180.

——— (1996) 'The forms of the personal pronouns in Gaelic dialects', *Éigse* 29, 19–50.

Ó Siadhail, M. (1989) *Modern Irish: grammatical structure and dialectal variation*, Cambridge.

Ó Súilleabháin, P. (1976) 'Beatha Cholaim Chille: an chóip atá i LS. A 8', *Celtica* 11, 203–13.

Pedersen, H. (1909) *Vergleichende Grammatik der keltischen Sprachen*, vol. 1, Götingen.

Picard, J.M. (1982) 'The Schaffhausen Adomnán—a unique witness to Hiberno-Latin', *Peritia* 1, 216–49.

Pödör, D. (1995–96) 'The phonology of Scottish Gaelic loanwords in Lowland Scots', *Scottish Language* 14–15, 174–89.

Prokosch, E. (1939) *A comparative Germanic grammar*, Philadelphia.

Quin, E.G. (1979–80) 'Nasalization of *g- b- d-* in Early Irish', *Studia Celtica* 14–15, 255–59.

Reid, J. (1832) *Bibliotheca Scoto-Celtica: or An account of all the books which have been printed in the Gaelic language with bibliographical and biographical notices*, Glasgow.

Rhŷs, J. (1894) *The outlines of the phonology of Manx Gaelic*, Douglas.

Rivet, A.L.F. and C. Smith (1979) *The place-names of Roman Britain*, London.

Roberston, C.M. (1907a) 'Scottish Gaelic dialects [III]', *The Celtic Review* 3, 223–39.

——— (1907b) 'Sutherland Gaelic', *Transactions of the Gaelic Society of Inverness* 25 (1901–3), 84–125.

Roma, E. (2000) 'How subject pronouns spread in Irish: a diachronic study and synchronic account of the third person+pronoun pattern', *Ériu* 51, 107–57.

Schrijver, P. (1997) 'On the nature and origin of word-initial *h-* in the Würzburg Glosses', *Ériu* 48, 205–27.

——— (2000) 'Varia V: Non-Indo-European surviving in Ireland in the first millenium AD', *Ériu* 51, 195–99.

Shaw, W. (1778) *An analysis of the Gaelic language*, Edinburgh.

Skene (1836) *The Highlanders of Scotland: their origin, history, and antiquities* [...], London. 2nd ed., ed. Alexander MacBain, 1902.

Skerrett, R.A.Q. (1963) 'Two Irish translations of the Liber de Passione Christi', *Celtica* 6, 82–117.

—— (1966a) 'Fiarfaidhi San Anselmuis', *Celtica* 7, 163–87.

—— (1966b) 'Two Irish verbal systems of the fifteenth century', *Celtica* 7, 189–204.

Stokes, W. (1872 [1866]) *Goidelica: Old and Early-Middle-Irish glosses, prose and verse*, 2nd ed., London.

—— (1905) 'The adventure of St. Columba's clerics', *Revue celtique* 26, 130–70.

Strachan, J. (1895) 'The importance of Irish for the study of Scottish Gaelic', *Transactions of the Gaelic Society of Inverness* 19 (1893–94), 13–25.

—— (1903) 'On the language of the Milan Glosses', *Zeitschrift für celtische Philologie* 4, 48–71.

Stuart, J. (1869) *The Book of Deer*, edited for the Spalding Club, Edinburgh.

Taylor, S. (1995) 'Settlement names in Fife' (unpublished PhD thesis, University of Edinburgh).

—— (forthcoming) *The place-names of Fife*, vol. 2., Stamford.

Thomson, D.S. (1994 [1983]) 'Gaelic: orthography', *The companion to Gaelic Scotland*, Glasgow, 99–101. 2nd ed.

Thomson, R.L. (1962) *Adtimchiol an chreidimh: the Gaelic version of John Calvin's Catechismus Ecclesiae Genevensis […]*. Scottish Gaelic Texts 7, Edinburgh.

—— (1970) *Foirm na n-urrnuidheadh: John Carswell's Gaelic translation of the Book of Common Order*. Scottish Gaelic Texts 11, Edinburgh.

—— (1976) 'The language of the *Caogad* (1659)', *Scottish Gaelic Studies* 12.2, 143–82.

—— (1977) 'The emergence of Scottish Gaelic', in *Bards and makars: Scottish language and literature: medieval and renaissance*, ed. A. J. Aitken et al., Glasgow, 127–35.

Thurneysen, R. (1905) 'Miscellen zur altirischen Grammatik: I. Die Nasalierung des Anlauts nach deklinierten Wörten im Altirischen', *Zeitschrift für celtische Philologie* 5, 1–19.

—— (1936) 'Zur Seitenfüllung', *Zeitschrift für celtische Philologie* 20, 367.

Toner, G., and M.B. Ó Mainnín (1992) *Place-names of Northern Ireland. Volume One. County Down I: Newry and South-West Down*, Belfast.

Uhlich, J. (1995) 'On the fate of intervocalic *-u̯- in Old Irish, especially between neutral vowels', *Ériu* 46, 11–48.

Wagner, H. (1982) 'Studies in the history of Gaelic dialects, Part 1', *Zeitschrift für celtische Philologie* 39, 96–116.

—— (1986) 'Iarfhocal ar *Ní* agus *Cha* sa Ghaeilge', in *Féilscríbhinn Thomáis de Bhaldraithe*, ed. S. Watson, Baile Átha Cliath, 1–10.

Watkins, C. (1962) 'Varia II, 1. Irish *milchobur*', *Ériu* 19, 114–16.

Watson, A., and R.D. Clement (1983) 'Aberdeenshire Gaelic', *Transactions of the Gaelic Society of Inverness*, 52 (1980–2), 373–401 (esp. 400–2).

Watson, A., and E. Allan (1984) *The place names of Upper Deeside*, Aberdeen.

Watson, S. (1986) 'The sounds of Easter Ross Gaelic: historical development', *Scottish Gaelic Studies* 14.2, 51–93.

—— (1994) 'Gaeilge na hAlban', in *Stair na Gaeilge in Ómós do P[h]ádraig Ó Fiannachta*, ed. K. McCone et al., Maigh Nuad, 661–702.

—— (1999) 'Aspects of some Nova Scotian Gaelic dialects', in *Celtic connections: Proceedings of the Tenth International Congress of Celtic Studies. Vol 1. Language, Literature, History, Culture*, ed. R. Black et al., East Linton, 347–59.

Watson, W.J. (1904) *Place-names of Ross and Cromarty*, Inverness etc.

—— (1926) *The history of the Celtic place-names of Scotland*, Edinburgh.

—— (1937) *Scottish verse from the Book of the Dean of Lismore*, Edinburgh.

Wentworth, R. (2002) 'Na Bolaichean aig na Geàrrlaich 's an Loch Làn Diubh: Fòineimean Taobhach ann an Dualchainnt Ghàidhlig an Ros an Iar', in *Rannsachadh na Gàidhlig 2000: Papers read at the Conference* Scottish Gaelic Studies 2000 *Held at the University of Aberdeen 2–4 August 2000*, ed. C. Ó Baoill and N.R. McGuire, Obar Dheathain, 91–99.

Zai, R. (1942) *The phonology of the Morebattle dialect*, Lucerne.

The toponymic landscape of the Gaelic Notes in the Book of Deer

SIMON TAYLOR

THE PARISH OF DEER AND ITS NEIGHBOURS

Before examining the names contained in the property-records of the Book of Deer in detail, we begin with an exploration of the parochial structure of medieval Buchan. In Scotland the medieval parish in the sense of the area within the jurisdiction of a baptismal church evolved mainly (but not exclusively) during the reign of David I (1124–53),[1] that is around the time when the Deer records were being written down. However, the work of historians such as Geoffrey Barrow and John Rogers has shown that the units which gained parochial status in this period were in fact much older, secular units, often to be equated with the secular unit known by the late eleventh century as 'shire', probably an Old English (Northumbrian) loan-word into Scottish Gaelic.[2] It can therefore be assumed that the medieval parochial structure of Buchan represents an administrative frame-work in place when many, if not all, of the grants recorded in the Book of Deer were made.

The current parishes of Old and New Deer are seventeenth-century creations from a single medieval parish of Deer.[3] As a lowland Scottish medieval parish that of Deer was very large indeed, constituting a rough square c.16km by 16km, one of the largest lowland parishes in the diocese of Aberdeen (see fig. 9.1). The place-name 'Deer' occurs only once in the Deer property-records, in the context of the foundation-legend of the monastery (I).[4] This also offers by far the earliest explanation of the place-name, and is a good example of the kind of onomastic legend—known by the Irish term *dindshenchas* 'lore of famous places'—which abound, and which, indeed, are still being invented to explain obscure or opaque place-names. The Deer foundation-legend tells us that Drostán's tears (*déara*) fell as he was parting from Columba, so Columba said, 'Let *déar* (Gaelic 'tear') be its name from now on'. A much more likely derivation is the one which was first suggested by John Stuart in his 1869 edition of the Book of Deer.[5] Here he proposes

---

1 See Cowan 1961.   2 See for example Barrow 1973, chapter 1, and Rogers 1997.   3 New Deer was first called Auchreddie 'from the field on which the church is situated' (*OSA*). 4 Note that the two early occurrences in the Annals of Ulster under the years 623 and 679 of the name *Nér* may not in fact refer to Deer, as suggested by O'Rahilly in 1946 (see Jackson 1972, 6), but to Fetternear, a medieval parish now forming the south part of Chapel of Garioch ABD. See Clancy, this volume.   5 Stuart 1869, xlviii.

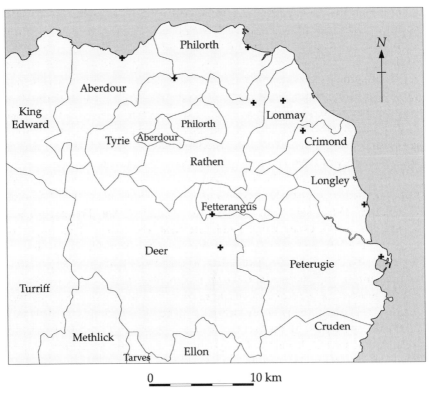

9.1 The medieval parish of Deer and its contiguous parishes
(sites of medieval parish churches marked +).

that it is connected with a word meaning 'oak', which in Old and Middle Irish
was *dair* (gen. *daro/darach*); or *daire/doire* 'oak-grove'.[6] Several important
monasteries in Ireland contain *daire* 'oak', such as Durrow, Derry and
Kildare, while the old name for Holywood Abbey in Dumfriesshire is
Dercongal or Darcongal, '(St) Congall's oak or oakwood'. It comes from the
Early Celtic root **derv-*, which has yielded Welsh *derw* 'oak', and the Pictish
word would no doubt have been similar. A superficial resemblance to Gaelic
déar 'tear' will have contributed to the development of the story of Drostán's
tears. It is probably coincidence that one of the most important markets in the
North-East was held on the slopes opposite the Cistercian abbey of Deer at a
place called 'Aikie Brae', which contains the Scots word *aikie* 'oak-covered'.
Apart from the early occurrences of the place-name Deer noted in the
Appendix, it seems also to occur in or shortly before 1214 as the first element
of *Derevan* (thrice), the name of a hill (*mons*) in the north-western corner of
the medieval parish of Deer.[7]

6 In modern Scottish Gaelic *darach* is 'oak', while *doire* has developed a more general
meaning of 'grove, small wood'.   7 *A.B. Coll.* 407–9. From the places associated with

In the north-east corner of the medieval parish of Deer there was a small separate parish called Fetterangus. This appears first, in the early thirteenth century, as the name of a chapel in a detached part of the parish of Inverugie or Longley, now St Fergus.[8] However, the chapel of Fetterangus later achieved parochial status, and was united to Deer before 1618 (*Fasti* 6, 225). Jurisdictionally, from at least as early as *c*.1400, St Fergus and Fetterangus both lay within the sheriffdom of Banff, and it was not until the rationalisation of boundaries in Scotland in 1891 that they became part of Aberdeenshire. It is significant that none of the identifiable lands of both the earlier and the later monastery of Deer lay within the parish of Fetterangus.

The generic element *Fetter-* is common in names of parishes and high-status settlements in eastern Scotland such as Fetternear ABD, Dunottar, Fettercairn, Fetteresso, KCD, Ferness NAI, Forteviot PER, Fodderty ROS. It occurs also in the estate name Fedderate NDR, the centre of an important barony in the Middle Ages.[9] Although Watson suggests that it means 'terraced slope' (1926, 509), it is more likely that, in eastern Scotland at least, it was an early administrative term adopted into Scottish Gaelic from Pictish **uotir*. It is thus more closely related in meaning to its Welsh cognate *godir* 'district, region'.[10] The argument for an ultimately Pictish origin of this element is further strengthened by the fact that it does not occur in any place-names in Ireland. The second element in Fetterangus may be the personal name 'Angus'. If so, it is the only *Fetter*-name to have survived with a personal name as a specific. Fedderate (*Fedreth* × 1214) consists simply of *foithir* with a locational ending meaning 'place of the *foithir*'. Its importance as an administrative or territorial unit suggested by its meaning is borne out by its continued importance as the centre of a barony in the later Middle Ages. As a territorial unit it occupied all of the north-west corner of the medieval parish of Deer,

'*mons de Derevan*' in this charter, it would seem to refer to the whole upland area of what is now the parish of New Deer, between Balthangie NJ83 51 on the west and Grassiehill NJ91 52 on the east. It is possible that the medial *v* in *Derevan* is a remnant of the labial fricative or semi-vowel in the Celtic root, which might well have survived in Pictish, and which has become vocalised in Welsh *derw*. A similar development can be seen in the French place-name Derval (Loire-Atlantique), containing Gaulish **dervos* 'oak' with a suffix *–alis* (Dauzat and Rostaing 1978 *s.n.*). The final syllable in *Derevan* is probably also some kind of locational suffix. The Derran Burn, which for part of its length forms the parish boundary between Deer and Longside *c*.2.5 kilometres south of Mintlaw, probably contains the Celtic 'oak' word, or alternatively 'Deer' as an existing territorial name. It could in fact be the modern reflex of *Derevan*. As it lies at the opposite end of the medieval parish from 'hill of *Derevan*', this latter might rather be interpreted as 'hill or upland of the territory of *Derevan*', implying that this territory was much more extensive than its *mons*. *Derevan* may therefore have been roughly co-extensive with the parish of Deer.   8 The church of *Inuirhugin* with the chapel of *Fetheranus*, granted to the abbey of Arbroath 1208x26 *Arb. Lib.* i, no.199. 9 For the detailed marches of three contiguous davochs within Fedderate, *viz.* Easter Aucheoch, Atherb and Affath, before 1214, see *A.B. Coll.* 407–9. See also below, 297–8 and n. 2.   10 See *Geiriadur Prifysgol Cymru* (Cardiff 1950–) s.v.

and it may well have been the secular centre of the Deer area, head-quarters of at least some of the *toísig* mentioned in the Deer records. Kingedward, the parish which marches with Deer on the north-west (Fedderate) side, also contains the *foithir*-element, meaning 'end of the *foithir*', and probably refers to the same administrative entity represented by Fedderate.[11]

The medieval and modern parish of Lonmay borders with Fetterangus on the north-east, separating it from St Fergus. Both Lonmay, and the earlier name for St Fergus parish, Lonley †, contain Gaelic *lann* 'enclosure, field', perhaps, in a religious context, 'church'. This is certainly the development of this word in eastern Ireland, as well as in Wales, where its Brittonic cognate has supplied the common ecclesiastical place-name element *llan* 'church'.[12]

Immediately east of Deer lay the medieval parish of Inverugie Petri or Peterugie.[13] The Book of Deer contains a record (III) of the grant, made in 1131 or 1132 by Gartnait son of Cainnech and Éte daughter of Gille-Míchél, of *pet mec cóbrig* for the consecration of a church of Christ and of Peter. This is our first reference to the church at a place which by the late thirteenth century was being referred to as the parish kirk of *Inverugy Petri* (1274), the settlement at the mouth of the river Ugie under the protection of St Peter. By the late fifteenth century this appears as *Pettirugy*, while the town which grew up on the headland to the south of the river-mouth, and east of the old kirk, became known as Peterhead, first mentioned as such in 1544. It is indicative of the continuity of rights and possessions from the old ecclesiastical community at Deer to the new Cistercian monastery that the church of Peterugie was under the patronage of the latter, evidently from an early date (Cowan 1967, 164), and the monastery held lands there. It is also probable that *pet mec cóbrig*, given to Deer in conjunction with the consecration of the church of St Peter, was somewhere near that church, the most likely candidate being the estate which later became known as Grange (of Rawhill), just west of Peterhead. Grange is a Norman-French word meaning 'barn', and in Scotland almost always refers to an outlying monastic estate. As would be expected from the name, Grange by Peterhead belonged to the Cistercian abbey of Deer.[14] In the early seventeenth century the parish of Peterugie was split in two, with the western part, that contiguous with Deer, being called first *Over Peterheid*, later Longside, which was the site of the new kirk.

From this early twelfth-century mention of the church of St Peter at Peterhead in the Deer property-records, it would appear that the monastery at

---

11 Some early forms of Kingedward are: *Kynedor* 1178, *Kenedward c.*1250, *Kyneduart* and *Kennedor* 1273. See Alexander 1952, 76. It consists of the same elements as the medieval parish of Kinneddar MOR, as well as the farm-name Kinneddar, Saline FIF.   12 For a fuller discussion of this element in an eastern Scottish context, see Taylor 1998, 8–10, 16–22. 13 For early forms of this name, see Alexander 1952, 99, under 'Peterhead'.   14 *lie Grange de Rawhill* 1587 *RMS* v no.1309, formerly belonging to Deer abbey.

Deer was the mother church for an area even larger than the medieval parish of Deer.[15] If medieval Peterugie (modern Longside and Peterhead) is included in the area of Deer's *parochia*,[16], then the position of Deer parish kirk on the very eastern edge of Deer parish becomes more understandable, since, although geographically peripheral in relation to Deer parish, it is central to the combined area of Peterugie and Deer. All except one of the identifiable lands granted to the early monastery lie within this territory of Deer/Peterugie. The one exception is *Etdanin* (II.13), usually identified with Ednie, St Fergus parish.[17] However, the fact that it lies outwith the above-defined *parochia*, as well as the fact that it is not included amongst the later possessions of the Cistercian abbey of Deer, should make us wary of accepting this identification.

The parish bordering Deer to the south-east is Cruden. This was originally Invercrudan,[18] '(at the) mouth of the Cruden', the name of the burn now known as the Water of Cruden. As a place-name it is therefore structurally identical with the names of the settlements on the river- or burn-mouths directly to the north, viz Invernettie (Peterhead parish) and Inverugie, which as we have seen spawned the parish-names of Inverugie Petri (Peterugie later Peterhead) and Inverugie (St Fergus).

Also bordering Deer parish on the south-east is Ellon, a large parish straddling the Ythan, and containing the later *caput* of the earldom of Buchan. Ellon first appears as the place-date of property-record VI (1131×32) (*i nhelain* 'in Ellon'), and is discussed by Jackson, who concludes that 'no etymology suggests itself' (1972, 79). However, Roibeard Ó Maolalaigh (*infra* 221–2) suggests that it derives from Gaelic *eilean* 'island'.

Continuing around the boundary of Deer parish in a clockwise direction, a thin sliver of Tarves parish crosses the Ythan and touches Deer,[19] followed to the south-west by a wider swathe of Methlick parish. Along most of the west side of Deer is the medieval parish of Turriff, now represented by the parish of Monquhitter, which was created out of the eastern part of Turriff in 1649 (*Fasti* 6, 268), and named after the farm where the new kirk was built. While Deer, and all its contiguous parishes to the north-east, east and south, lay in the Aberdeen deanery of Buchan, the medieval parishes to the west and north-west, namely Turriff, Kingedward, Aberdour and Tyrie, lay in the Aberdeen deanery of Boyne.

---

15 The existence at Deer of an early pastoral centre or minster with responsibility for a larger area than that of the later medieval parish of Deer is posited by I.B. Cowan, who prefers to see Deer as such a centre rather than as a Celtic (*sic*) monastery (1961, 46). **16** i.e. pastoral sphere of influence in the pre-parochial period. **17** See, for example, Jackson 1972, 57. **18** *Innercroudan* 1163 *RRS* i, no.237. **19** The lands which occupy this sliver of Tarves parish are those of Schivas (*Scheves* 1437 *ER* v, 8). This name is probably made up of G *sèimh* 'smooth, mild', but which in Old and Middle Irish (*séim*) means 'slender, narrow' + locational suffix *-es*. It is likely therefore that it is this administrative

Turriff appears in the Deer property-record thrice: in the witness-lists of III, VI, and VII (1131×32, ?1140s, 1150). Jackson suggests a nominative form *Turbruad*.[20] Neither Jackson nor Alexander (1952, 129–30) suggests an etymology. As it stands it shows a strong similarity to Old Irish *turbród/turbrúd* 'penalty, violation, infringement',[21] a highly unlikely place-name. The site of Turriff old kirk is remarkable, perched as it is on a headland which falls steeply down to the haughs of the River Deveron. It is more likely that this conspicuous topographical situation lies behind the name. I would tentatively suggest an originally Pictish name consisting of cognates of Gaelic *tòrr* 'steep hill(ock)' + *bràighe* (gen. *bràghad*) 'neck, throat; upper part (of places)'[22] or *bruach* 'slope, bank', assimilated at a later date to *turbród/turbrúd*, in a similar fashion to which the place-name 'Deer' was assimilated to the Gaelic *déar* 'tear'. Like Deer, Turriff was the site of an early monastery,[23] and, if the speculation about its name is correct, there was probably a now lost piece of *dindshenchas* to explain the spurious idea of penalty, violation or infringement.

Adjacent to the north-west (Fedderate) corner of Deer is the parish of Kingedward, which contains the same *foithir*-element as Fedderate, discussed above. Next is Aberdour parish, sharing a common march with Deer of *c*.2km., despite the fact that Deer and Aberdour old parish kirks lie 20km apart.[24] Aberdour is closely linked to the foundation legend of Deer, as recounted in the first record. This name, probably completely Pictish, despite a Gaelicised second element, is fully discussed by Jackson (1972, 38). It is identical to the place-name Aberdour FIF.[25] The meaning of both is 'mouth of the Dour' with the river-name deriving from a Pictish **duvr* 'water'.

Tyrie, the next parish, contains Gaelic *tìr* 'land', more specifically 'arable land', with what is probably a locational suffix, most likely –*in*, 'place of or at the (good) arable land'. The final parish in this circuit of medieval Deer is Rathen parish, which formed much of the northern boundary of Deer. This is today represented by Strichen, a parish created in 1633 out of a part of Rathen (along with a small part of Philorth/Fraserburgh).[26] Rathen itself contains either Gaelic *ràth*, or its Pictish cognate, 'fort', with what is probably a diminutive suffix, thus 'little *ràth*'.[27]

anomaly which is being referred to in the place-name 'narrow land' or 'narrow place'. **20** Jackson 1972, 67–8, 133 (15) and index.   **21** I am grateful to Thomas Clancy for bringing this to my attention.   **22** This is simplifying a more complex development of this word, Old Irish *braga*. See MacBain 1911 s.v.   **23** See Jackson 1972, 67–8.   **24** *c*.12 miles. Jackson's siting of Old Aberdour 'about 6 miles north-west of Deer' is wrong (1972, 38). **25** See Taylor with Márkus 2006, 56–7.   **26** See *A.B Ill.* ii, 391–2.   **27** (church of) *Rathyn* 1270x79 *Abdn. Reg.* ii, 53, (church of) *Rathyn* 1328 *RRS* v no. 348, *Rathine* 1510 *Abdn. Brev.* pth f.vii. For a detailed discussion of *ràth* in Scottish place-names, see MacDonald 1982; for a recent thorough reassessment of the evidence relating to *ráth* as a place-name element in Ireland, see Toner 2000.

THE LANDS OF DEER

Introduction

Any analysis of the place-names contained in the property-records in the Book of Deer must begin with an attempt to define what is meant by a place-name. In eastern Scotland place-names occur frequently in documents written in Latin from the twelfth century onwards. A place-name is usually treated by the scribe or compiler of the document as an untranslatable item. This might be because he does not understand what it means, or because its meaning is unimportant as far as its function is concerned.[28] This principal function is not to describe the place in question, with words taken from the lexicon, or stock of common nouns, adjectives, and the like; but rather its function is to denote the place by a name from the nomenclature, or stock of proper nouns— also known as the onomasticon—which does not need to 'mean' anything in lexical terms. Most place-names, however, start life as part of everyday language.[29] Furthermore, most eastern Scottish place-names are derived from Scottish Gaelic. Since our text is written in Gaelic, it is not always possible to distinguish whether a noun phrase is functioning primarily as a name (part of the onomasticon) or as a descriptive phrase (part of the lexicon), which might or might not develop into a name.

The first property-record in the Book of Deer (I) contains a good illustration of this problem. It states that Bede *mormaer* of Buchan gave to Columba and Drostán land '*ua cloic in tiprat gonice chloic pette mec-garnait*'.[30] How is this to be translated? *Cloch in tiprat* has the perfectly transparent meaning '(the) stone of the well or spring'. Since twelfth-century scribal conventions did not use capitals in the way in which many modern languages, including English, do to signal a proper noun, there can be no definitive translation of this phrase. There is nothing in the transmitted text which tells the reader whether *cloch in tiprat*, for example, is functioning primarily as a name or as a descriptive phrase. Should it be translated as K.H. Jackson did: 'from Cloch

---

28 An illuminating exception to this is the place-name 'Inchaffrey' PER, Gaelic *Innis Aifreann* 'island of the offerings [to God] i.e. masses'. In many of the early documents relating to its establishment as an Augustinian house in 1200 it is referred to by the Gaelic form of the name (e.g. *Inchaffren*) as well as translated into Latin as *Insula Missarum* 'island of masses'. The name no doubt refers to the religious community which existed there before the Augustinians, and it has been translated because its place-name expressed so well its continuing religious function under a new régime.   29 It should be borne in mind, however, that this stock of everyday language can contain existing names, both personal and place, and so cannot be designated purely as lexicon. Take for example Auchtydonald, Longside ABD (*Achidonald* 1378), which contains the personal name 'Dòmhnall/Donald'. 30 I use a semi-diplomatic form of the text based on Ó Maolalaigh's edition (this volume), in order not to pre-empt any discussion of proper or common nouns. Except where otherwise stated, name forms are referred to by text and grant number (see Text and translation, this volume).

in Tiprat as far as Cloch Peitte Meic-Garnait' (1972, 33);[31] or as A.O. Anderson did: 'from the [boundary-] stone of the well to the [boundary-] stone of Gartnait's son's[32] farm' (1922 ii, 175); or as a compromise between these two: 'from the stone of (*or* by) the well as far as Pitmacgartnaid's Stone *or* the stone of MacGartnait's farm'? In fact a noun or noun phrase can exist as part both of the lexicon and of the onomasticon, and it may well be that this is the situation here, a subtlety which a modern English translation cannot convey. It is thus with many of the 'place-names' in this text. Anderson sums up the problem in a footnote to the second occurrence of *pett m͞c garnait*: 'I translate these names because they seem to be descriptive, and not yet entirely proper names' (1922 ii, 176 n.2).

Pett

The consideration of this problem leads on to some wider toponymic issues in Jackson's 1972 edition. Record II.2 states that Muiredach son of Morgann gave to Columba and Drostán *achad toche temni* along with *pett m͞c garnait*. Jackson translates *achad toche temni* as 'the field of Toiche Teimni'. *Pett m͞c garnait* on the other hand he writes 'Pett Meic-Garnait'. He justifies this, at least partly, by stating in the historical commentary to his edition that the Pictish word *pett* was not borrowed into Gaelic as a common noun 'any more than *ville*, so common in forming American village names, has really been borrowed into American as such, though the *meaning* is known' (1972, 115 n.3). In other words it remained simply part of the onomastic language, a term whose meaning was understood, but which occurred only in place-names. I have argued elsewhere (Taylor 1997) that *pett* was indeed a loan-word in Scottish Gaelic during the first centuries of the kingdom of Alba, i.e. from the late ninth century onwards, even if it became generally obsolete in the later medieval or early modern period.[33] It can therefore be classed alongside Scottish Gaelic words such as *dail* 'haughland, water-meadow' and *monadh* 'hill, hill-pasture', both of which were also borrowed from Pictish.[34] The only difference is that *dail* and *monadh* are still part of most Scottish Gaelic dialects.[35] *Pett* no doubt had a well-defined function as a term describing a land-holding unit within the Pictish kingdom, and was adopted into Scottish Gaelic as part of the administrative system inherited by Alba from its Pictish predecessor.

If we accept that *pett* was part of the lexicon of north-east Scotland in the early centuries of Scottish Gaelic, then we must seriously consider the possibility that it is being used as a common noun in the property-records in

---

31 With the translations in footnotes, *viz.* 'The Rock of the Spring' and 'The Rock of the Holding of Mac-Garnait'.   32 Or 'sons' farm'; see below 286–8.   33 See also Cox 1997, 51–3, where a similar conclusion is reached using different evidence.   34 For *dail* see Watson 1926, 414–19; for *monadh* see ibid., 391–407 (where for 'British' north of Forth read 'Pictish'); for *monadh* see also Barrow 1998, 62–6.

the Book of Deer. It occurs there seven times, with five different specific or qualifying nouns. Three of these are personal names: *pett malduib* (II.9) 'estate or holding of Maelduib (Malduff)'; *pett<e> m̄c garnait* (I, II.2) 'holding of a man called Mac-Gartnait'; or conceivably, reading *mac* instead of *mec*, 'holding of the sons of Gartnait'; and *pett mec gobroig/pet mec cobrig* (II.7, III) 'holding of a man called Mac-Gobraig'.[36] Compared with the other personal names in the Deer records, there is nothing to suggest that these are particularly archaic, and could therefore simply contain the names of the last laymen to hold these lands before they were granted to the monastery of Deer. The fact that none of these names containing *pett* plus a personal name occurs again in the later medieval record, and only one can be identified with any confidence, also suggests that the name may have changed as a result of ownership-change, and therefore that they may be functioning in the notes as a noun phrase descriptive of ownership or control. This could certainly be the case for *pett m̄c garnait*, which appears to have been one of the first lands to be given to the monastery; as well as for *pett malduib*, granted by Mael-snechta son of Lulach in the late eleventh century.[37] The case of *pett mec gobroig/pet mec cobrig* is more complex. It occurs twice in the property-records, firstly during the reign of Mael-Coluim II (1005–34), and secondly in 1131 or 1132 (Jackson 1972, 58).[38] By the time of its second appearance it would seem, therefore, to have developed into a fully-fledged place-name. However, as the set of property records which includes Mael-Coluim II's grant of a 'king's share in *pett mec gobroig*' has been shown to be retrospective,[39] it is conceivable that an early twelfth-century name has been projected back 100 years, and is in fact describing tenure or occupation of the later period.

Achad

Achad is a difficult word to translate. Modern Gaelic *achadh* means 'field' or, as in Wester Ross, 'field on hill'.[40] It is used in the Deer records once unequivocally as an appellative or common noun (V.3), when it is contrasted to *sliab* 'upland, moorland, open, unenclosed land'.[41] Jackson translates it 'pasture' or

---

35 For the possible survival of a modern Gaelic reflex of *pett* in Lewis Gaelic meaning 'small piece of land', see Cox 1997.   **36** Jackson suggests that the personal name which it contains is 'Gobrach', cognate with Gaelic *gabhar/gobhar* 'goat', though not otherwise attested (1972, 51). Compare Gabhran (earlier Gabrán), 'little goat', the name of the sixth-century king of Dál Riata and eponym of the royal kindred Cenél nGabráin. However, see Ó Maolalaigh, *infra*, 253, for the suggestion that the underlying name is Cobrach. **37** Died 1085; see Jackson 1972, 52–3.   **38** For the suggestion that it is now Grange by Peterhead, see below, 278.   **39** See Broun, this volume.   **40** See Wentworth 1996, under *field* ('field on hill, outside township, formerly – in pre-crofting times – cultivated in some years'). This is similar to its use in the Ochil Hills in southern Perthshire, where it seems also to have the meaning 'hill-field' or 'piece of ground cleared for grazing or cultivation', occuring between *c*.50 and *c*.500 metres (Watson 1995, 155).   **41** For a re-assessment of *sliabh* in Scottish place-names, see Taylor 2007.

'pasture-field'; however, there is nothing conclusive in its early usage to say that it was pasture rather than arable, and the contrast which is being set up in the phrase *etar sliab acus achad* 'both upland and *achad*' would in fact suggest arable. It is probably best seen as being as unspecific as English 'field', meaning enclosed land for both arable and pastoral activities.

It is clear from the present status of many *A(u)ch*-place-names that it came to represent a viable agricultural unit. An in-depth study of the distribution of this element in Scotland between the Moray Firth and the Firth of Tay concluded that places with *A(u)ch*- names tend to be on higher ground and poorer soils than those with *Bal*- and *Pit*-names. Buchan, which has a relatively high density of *A(u)ch*- names, seems to present something of an anomaly, since here they are mainly on the better soils in the lower part of the Buchan plateau. However, when compared to the *Bal*- and *Pit*-names of the same region, they are still on poorer soils, so that the general pattern is affirmed (Fraser 1998, 113, 125–6). They appear to represent secondary settlement from an existing settlement pattern (ibid. 131), thus confirming the conclusion reached by W.F.H. Nicolaisen from his work in the 1960s and 70s on the distribution of this element throughout Scotland.[42]

Achad occurs thrice in the Deer records denoting a particular place: *Achad na Glérec* 'field of the clerics' (II.5); *Achad Toche Temni* (II.2); and *Achad Madchor* (Auchmachar) (V.1). The specific elements of these names, and their locations, are discussed below. There are ten place-names still surviving in the parishes of ODR and NDR alone which contain *achadh* as a generic. These are Affath NDR, Affleck NDR,[43] Atherb NDR, Aucheoch NDR, Auchmachar ODR, Auchmaliddie NDR, Auchmunziel NDR, Auchnavaird ODR, Auchreddie NDR and Auchrynie ODR (formerly Fetterangus).[44] Of these Affleck, Auchmachar, Auchmunziel and Auchreddie belonged to the Cistercian monastery of Deer (see fig. 9.2).

Identifying the properties

The Deer property-records contain 32 units which can loosely be described as place-names or place-descriptive phrases and which refer to the places in and around the parish of Deer. Of these only about one half can be identified with

42 See Nicolaisen 1976, 125–8, 140–3 [2001, 161–4, 180–3]. When the Scotland-wide distribution of this element is considered, there remain some unanswered questions. On map 15 in Nicolaisen (1976, 140 [2001, 181], reproduced in McNeill and MacQueen 1996, 60) a cluster of three dots is shown representing *achadh*-place-names in central Fife. None of them is a genuine *achadh*-name, with two containing Gaelic *àth* 'ford', and one *Auchter*-. There are in fact no certain *achadh*-names in Fife (see Taylor 2000, 209). It is also almost completely absent from the Outer Hebrides.   43 Both of which show the later Scots development of the unvoiced palatal fricative *ch* to unvoiced labio-dental fricative *f*.   44 Note that Auchnagatt NDR first appears as [land of] *Aldyngat*' (1328 *RRS* v no. 347), containing Gaelic *allt* 'burn'. It had been assimilated to *Auch* by 1544 (*Achnagat* in *A.B. Ill.* iv, 22).

a reasonable degree of certainty with places which have survived into the early modern period. Compared with the place-names contained in Scottish property records which begin with a vengeance in the later twelfth century, this is a low rate of survival. It is probably due to two factors: firstly, to the fact, already discussed above, that many may not be functioning as fully fledged place-names at all, but rather as descriptive phrases; secondly, to the fact that the later twelfth and thirteenth centuries in the eastern lowlands of Scotland were a time of a certain amount of re-naming. A new language was rapidly spreading throughout eastern Scotland, a Germanic language, descended from Northern Old English, with a strong admixture of Scandinavian, more accurately described as 'Older Scots', but which I will refer to simply as Scots.[45] Although often the case, it cannot always be assumed that a Scots settlement-name means that that settlement was first created in the Scots-speaking period. We are sometimes fortunate enough to get a glimpse of an earlier nomenclature, as for example *Lethmacdungal near Dunfermline FIF 'the half or hill-sideof the sons of Dúngal', which belonged to Dunfermline Abbey, and was held by Master Aelric the mason in the mid-twelfth century. By the early thirteenth century this land was called *Maistertun*, after its twelfth-century tenant, and it is still known as such locally, while its Scottish Standard English form is Mastertown (Taylor with Márkus 2006, 331, 337–8).[46]

As Jackson has pointed out, there is a degree of continuity between the identifiable possessions of the older monastery of Deer, probably on the site of the parish kirk of Old Deer, and those of the Cistercian abbey of Deer, founded one km to the west in 1219. He adds: 'it is reasonable – but alas, virtually entirely unprofitable – to look for [the unidentified names] in the general region which belonged to the later abbey; mainly the parishes of Old and New Deer' (1972, 2). I will leave the reader to judge how profitable or otherwise are the following attempts at identification!

When the Cistercian abbey of Deer ceased to exist as a legal corporate institution in 1587, its lands were resigned to James VI, who erected them to a temporal lordship, the 'Lordship of Altrie', in favour of Robert Keith, Commendator of the abbey of Deer and his nephew George Keith, fifth Earl Marischal.[47] In

---

45 For a full definition of 'Older Scots', see *Concise Dictionary of Scots*, (Robinson 1985) xiii–xvi. The more modern variety of this language is known variously as Lallans, Scots, or, especially in the North-East, 'The Doric'.   46 Such re-naming was not just a feature of the linguistic change-over from Gaelic to Scots; the same must have happened in the transition from Pictish to Gaelic in the ninth and tenth centuries. We have in fact a glimpse of this in the St Andrews Foundation Legend B, where two names are given for several places mentioned in the text, an earlier one and a 'modern' (i.e. twelfth-century) one. Although heavily worked over in the mid-twelfth century, this text does seem to contain genuine early material. For example, for the place known today as Braemar, formerly Gaelic *Kindrochit* (*Ceann Drochaid*), it gives the earlier (Pictish) name *Doldauha*, adding '*nunc autem dictus chendrohed*' (see Skene 1867, 185; Anderson 1974, 12; Taylor with Márkus, forthcoming 3).   47 See Dilworth, this volume.

the absence of a Deer cartulary, the abbey's possessions at the Reformation can be mapped on the evidence of the royal charter erecting this lordship,[48] supplemented by that of a decree of 1574, detailing the teinds due to the Earl Marischal from the parishes of Deer, Peterhead and Foveran,[49] and a 1638 contract between the Earl Marischal and the king.[50] As already noted, most of the abbey's possessions lay within the medieval parish of Deer, and these are indicated in fig. 9.2. This map reflects the earliest determinable boundaries of the relevant farms and distinguishes clearly between those lands mentioned in the Deer property-records which are later held by the Cistercian abbey, and those which were in the possession of the Cistercian abbey, but which cannot be linked to the earlier holdings with any certainty. Excluded entirely are those monastic lands outwith the parish of Deer which are known to have come to the monastery after 1219: Fechil, Ellon parish, granted to the monastery by its founder, William Comyn earl of Buchan 1219×33;[51] also the parish kirks of Foveran ABD, granted by Robert I,[52] and Kingedward ABD granted by John Comyn earl of Buchan (1290×1308) and confirmed by Robert I.[53]

The earliest grant is that mentioned in the foundation legend (I) by the mormaer Bede *Cruithnech* of the land 'from *cloic in tiprat* as far as *chloic pette m̄c garnait*'. This must represent either the land on which the monastery was built (i.e. the peninsula surrounded on three sides by the South Ugie, now the site of the parish kirk of Old Deer), or land immediately adjacent to it. There are several wells marked on the First Edition of the OS 6 inch map in this area, the most notable being 'Grian's Well', on the southern edge of the modern village of Old Deer (NJ977474).[54] The stone of *pette m̄c garnait* must be a boundary stone marking the limit of this holding which was later given to the

---

48 *RMS* v no. 1309.   **49** *A.B. Ill.* ii, 431; see also Jackson 1972, 1 and Lawson 1896, 81 ff. **50** *A.B. Ill.* ii, 439   **51** *A.B. Ill.* ii, 427–8, in which detailed marches are given.   **52** See Cowan 1967, 70.   **53** See Cowan 1967, 111.   **54** There is a remarkable set of correspondence about this name accompanying its entry in the Ordnance Survey Object Name Book (Aberdeenshire, Book 68, p.89). The original surveyor (a Sergeant Bracken) in 1870 recorded it as 'St Drostane's Well', on the authority of two local people. This was challenged by Mr Ranken the dean of Aberdeen and Episcopalian minister of Old Deer, who insists, in a letter dated 25 Sept. 1881, that 'the well is, and always has been, "Grians Well", i.e. "the well of the sun-worship". ... There are many Grians in the North. I know at least half a dozen; Another of them in this Parish close by another Druidical stone circle three miles to the North.' The Ordnance Survey, despite a degree of scepticism, consented to the change, and on the 1884 reprint of the 1873 OS 1st edition 6 inch map it appears as 'Grians Well'. The correspondence is revealing of a number of things, such as the intellectual snobbery, as well as the antiquarian romanticism, of Dean Ranken, and the scrupulous, intelligent and well-informed attitude of a Major J.S. White of the Royal Engineers, one of the officials charged with overseeing the Ordnance Survey in Scotland. At the end of the day he was unable to gainsay the authority of a dean, but subtly implies that he does not approve of the change. Not having to take into consideration social hierarchies in late nineteenth century Deer, unlike Major White, I would say that the name 'Grians Well' is probably spurious, and certainly less likely than the St Drostane's Well originally recorded by Sergeant Bracken.

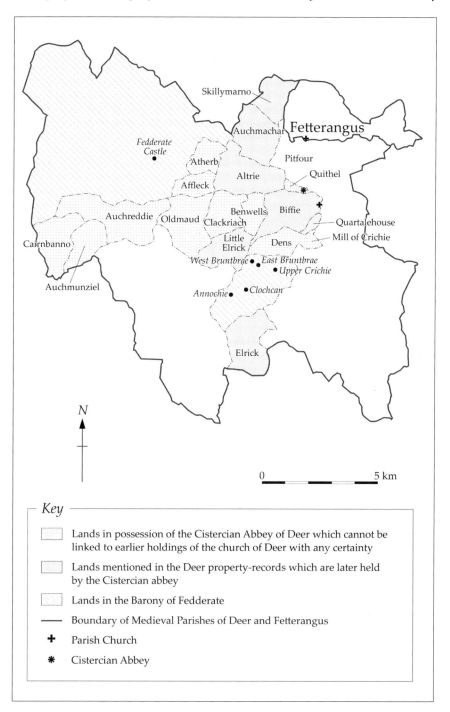

9.2 Land-holding within the medieval parish of Deer.

monastery.[55] The fact that the lands of Aden on the east side of the South Ugie (opposite the site of the parish kirk) were not in the hands of the Cistercian monastery, and that all the identifiable lands in Deer parish mentioned in the property records lay on the west side of the river, strongly suggests that *Pitm̄cgarnait, too, lay to the west of the monastery, perhaps a holding within what is now part of the large holding of Biffie (for which see below).

*Pitm̄cgarnait itself was subsequently granted to the monastery (II.2), by Muiredach son of Morgann, *mormaer*, presumably of Buchan, as well as *toísech* of Clann Morgann. This is one of several grants by members of this family. There remains the question as to whether the name of this holding should be restored as *pett meic garnait*, i.e. 'holding of the son of Gartnait (*or* of a man called Mac-Gartnait)', or *pett mac garnait*, 'holding of the sons of Gartnait'. The manuscript's abbreviated form of *mc* with a stroke here and in I (Diplomatic Edition AI.14 and AII.3) would suggest *mac* rather than *me[i]c*, were it not for the one occurrence of *pet mec cobrig* in III (Diplomatic edition DIII.2). Jackson assumes the latter, pointing out that it does not mean 'holding of the son of Gartnait', but 'holding of [a man called] Mac-Gartnait', the personal name being a 'true first name' equivalent to Gartnaitson or Gartnait's-son (1972, 41). In other words it does not mean that the eponymous holder of *Pitm̄cgartnait was the son of a man called Gartnait.[56] Generally speaking, place-names composed of *pett* + personal name are associated with a single individual, one exception being *Pitmacdougal, Moulin PER (*Petmacdufgille* c.1189 *Dunf. Reg.* no.147) 'holding of the sons of Dougal'.[57] *Baile*, on the other hand, combines with the genitive plural *mac* several times e.g. Balmule, Aberdour FIF; and Balcanquhal, Strathmiglo FIF.[58]

The other property which Muiredach son of Morgann gave to Deer, along with *Pitm̄cgarnait, was *achad toche temni* (II.2).[59] Again it can be assumed that this lay close to the site of the monastery, perhaps contiguous with *Pitm̄cgarnait. Jackson translates this 'the field of *Toiche Teimne*' (1972, 33), and discusses possible meanings in his notes (ibid. 45–6). Here he points out

---

55 For more on standing stones in the vicinity of Old Deer, see below, oo and n.oo. 56 For a further illuminating discussion of early Scottish *mac*-names, see Bannerman 1993, 20–2. 57 Examples of *pett* + individual personal names are Pitblain (Blán), Daviot; Pitandlich (Fionnlagh), Towie; Pitmachie (Mal(e)chi), Oyne; ABD (see Alexander 1952 *s.n.*); Pitconochie, Pitconmark FIF, Pitoutie † FIF (and PER) (Ultán); Pittargus † (Fergus) KCD; *Pitmaldoc, Pitaldonich (Mael-Domnig), Pitkeathly PER. The personal name Gartnait is apparently contained in Pittengardner, Fordoun KCD ('that davoch in Mearns called *Petme[n]gartenach*' 1219×42 *Arb. Lib.* i, no. 290). It is not clear what the middle element is: a Pictish cognate of Welsh *maen* 'stone'? See Watson 1926, 375, 387. For a full list of *Pit-*, *Bal-* and *Auch*-names in eastern Scotland (between the Firth of Tay and the Moray Firth) containing possible personal names, see Fraser 1998, 190–1. 58 'Holding of the sons of Mael' (Taylor with Márkus 2006, 57–9) and 'Anacol' (Taylor 1995, 324) respectively. This is also the pattern in Ireland up until *c.*1200; see Price 1963. 59 For a discussion of the generic element *achad*, see above page 283–4.

that the first element looks like Middle Irish *toiche* 'propriety, due order', but admits that if this is indeed the word involved, it is not clear what it might mean in this context. It is much more likely to be related to *toich*, Old Irish 'inheritance, property' (*DIL*).[60] As regards the second element Jackson suggests *teimne* 'darkness', or the genitive feminine of the adjective *teimen* 'dark'. Alternatively he suggests (with A.O. Anderson 1922 ii, 176, n.3) that it derives from Middle Irish *timna* (Old Irish *timn(a)e*) 'bequest'). None of this is very satisfactory. I would suggest that *temni* may rather represent the genitive of the personal name Temne (regular masculine *io*-stem).[61] It would thus mean 'field or farm of Temne's inheritance or property'.

Cathall son of Morgann was probably the brother of the above-mentioned Muiredach son of Morgann. If Cathall was not one of the founders of the monastery of Deer, perhaps instrumental in moving it from Aberdour to Deer, he certainly emerges as its chief benefactor. However, he cannot even be assigned to a century with any certainty.[62] He is associated with the following lands: *achad na glerec* (II.5); *alterin alla uethe na camsse gonice in beith edar da alterin*; (II.12); and *etdanin* (II.13).

achad na glérec: 'field of the clerics' (II.5).[63] This is almost certainly a retrospective name, in that it would have become known as the field of the clerics as a result of Cathall's grant. According to Jackson, the place cannot be identified (1972, 49). Lawson, however, points out the resemblance between this name and the Scots place-name 'Clerkhill', which latter he describes as

> a small pendicle of land which lay between the village of Deir and the Wuddy Hill,[64] if the Wuddy Hill be not part of the pendicle itself ... The name remained until the middle of the eighteenth century, when it is mentioned in a disposition of lands of Aden, Deir and Biffie by the laird of Kinmundy to the laird of Moncoffer.

He goes on to suggest that *achad na glérec* is in fact the Glebe of Deer, 'the stretch of land by the waterside, of most unusual extent for a glebe', which seems to have always been church property (Lawson 1896, 103). The Glebe in fact stretches along the south side of the South Ugie westwards from the

60 Note that *Toichi* appears as a place-name in Ossory, Leinster (Hogan 1910, 641). **61** The genitive of this personal name is *Temne* in the Book of Leinster, 351c; see Stokes 1905, 79 note 2 and personal name index. There is also the name *Teimen*: AU 732 *Teimen Cille Garadh relegiosus clericus* [Teimen of Kingarth, Bute], cf. St Tevanan of Burghill (*Buthirkill' c.*1250 *Arb. Lib.* i p. 241), now part of Brechin parish, for which see *CSSR* iv no. 1290 and Cowan 1967, erroneously under Unthiekil. **62** The late ninth or tenth century would seem most likely. See Forsyth, this volume. **63** For a discussion of the generic element *achad*, see above 283–4. **64** A prominent hill now crowned with a mature beech wood 700m west of Old Deer parish kirk (NJ972475).

parish kirk to a point almost opposite the Cistercian abbey of Deer, which lies on the north bank of the river, a distance of 1km. The pendicle of Clerkhill would have abutted this land on the south. In fact, it is likely that Clerkhill was the former name of Wuddy Hill, while Lawson is probably correct in his identification of *achad na glérec* with the glebelands of Old Deer.

Watson (1926, 267) cites some other examples of place-names which contain the element which in modern Gaelic is *cléireach*. His *Pettincleroch* in the earldom of Strathearn is modern Pittencleroch, Fowlis Wester PER. To his list can be added Arnclerich, Port of Menteith PER, Auchenclery, Colmonell AYR, the now obsolete Bancliro, Leslie FIF,[65] Ballencleroch, Campsie STL[66] and Tarrieclerach, Rathven BNF; also Rossie, formerly Rossieclerach, a medieval parish now part of Inchture parish PER.

Alterin: Altrie (II.12, II.3). A now obsolete name which has been superseded by the place-name 'Bruxie', Altrie survived as the name of the barony which was created out of the Deer Abbey lands after the Reformation in favour of the Keith Marischal family. It is mentioned twice in the Deer records: in II.12, when the above-mentioned Cathall along with Cainnech grandson of Dobarchú (or the son of MacDobarchon) grants lands in Altrie, and again in II.3, which records Matain son of Caerell's gift of a *mormaer*'s dues in Altrie and Cú Lí son of Baíthín's gift of the dues of a *toíseach*. The latter record does not help us with identification and the former is problematic as Scribe A has partially erased the end of one line and erased and corrected part of the beginning of the next (II.12 = fol. 4r l.7), rendering the correct reading far from certain.[67] Jackson read '*alterin alla uethe na camsse gonice in beith edar da alterin*', which he translated as 'the Altrie of the cliff of the birch tree of the river-bend as far as the birch tree between the two Altries'. If this is correct, there is one place which is most immediately suggested by the juxtaposition of cliff and river-bend. The South Ugie runs through gently undulating countryside for most of its course. However, in one place the river-bank rises steeply to about 15[!]m in height, with rocky outcrops.[68] This is also where the river makes a dramatic loop, immediately east of the assumed site of the early monastery. Leaving to one side palaeographical arguments, there are two problems with this reading. Firstly, if the birch tree has to be identified as the one 'of the river bend', why use it (rather than the bend alone) to distinguish the cliff. Surely it could only be superfluous. A more serious objection is that

---

65 For which see Taylor with Márkus, forthcoming 2, *s.n.*   **66** The nasalisation of the *c* after the genitive plural article, found in the Deer record's *Achad na Glérec*, is evident also in an early form of Ballencleroch, *viz. Balneglerauch c.*1200 *Glasg. Reg.* i, no. 103.   **67** This palaeographical conundrum is discussed in detail by Jackson 1972, 24–6 and Ó Maolalaigh, *infra* 128. See also Cox, *infra*, 311–2.   **68** This feature lies on the lands of Aden, for which see below, 294.

there can be no doubt that the lands known in the late medieval and early modern period as Altrie lay at least 2km to the west of this site, west even of the Cistercian abbey of Deer, and this is confirmed in the first cartographic representation of the area in the 1590s.[69]

An alternative explanation is proposed by Richard Cox (this volume), which removes the cliff and replaces one of the birch-trees with a well. He suggests: ... *uethe[prat] | na camsse gonice in beith edarda alterin*, which he translates as: 'the Altrie on this side [i.e.] from the well of the bend as far as the birch between the two Altries'. Although it depends on some bold textual emendations, Cox's interpretation could more easily be transferred to the lands of Altrie, along the course of either the South Ugie or the Bruxie Burn, the former of which forms an approximate southern march, the latter a north-eastern march, of the lands of Altrie. The same name is found near Crathie on Deeside ABD, in Monaltrie, and the Altrie Burn, a former name of the Coldrach Burn.[70] Watson & Allen (1984, 117) suggest that it may be based on *ail* 'rock or stone'.[71]

Etdanin: unidentified (II.13). The third land-grant associated with Cathall son of Morgann was identified by Diack as Ednie, St Fergus parish, (Alexander 1952, 52), an identification endorsed by Jackson (1972, 57). However, as discussed above, this identification is highly problematical due to the fact that the lands of Ednie lack any later connection with the lands of the Cistercian monastery,[72] and lie outwith the territory defined by the medieval parishes of Deer and Peterugie, which contain all the other identifiable early grants to Deer.

Pett in Mulenn: 'holding of the mill' (II.4). If, as seems likely, the father of Mael-Brigte son of Cathall is the Cathall son of Morgann, then the next Clann Morgann grant is that of *Pett in Mulenn* (II.4). Clearly meaning 'holding of the mill', it is impossible to say whether this is functioning primarily as a place-name or as an appellative description. Either way, it is referring to a place which certainly had had a mill at some point, and which probably still had the mill when the grant was made to the monastery. The mill itself may well have been the reason for the grant, adding a valuable

69 Pont MS 10 (see Stone 1989, 75). Both Pont (less precisely) and John Thomson's 1826 map of Aberdeenshire show *Altrye* and *Altree* respectively where Overton of Bruxie is today (NJ933488). **70** *Altry* 1755×69 *Reports on Annexed Estates*, 55 [described as a rivulet]; *Altrie Burn* 1788 RHP; Mains of Monaltrie NJ243953. The earliest record of Monaltrie is given by Watson & Allen (1984, 117) as *Monaltrie* 1702 Invercauld papers. For a full discussion, see loc.cit.. **71** See also the discussion of Quartalehouse below. **72** This problem is also alluded to by Jackson (1972, 57). The first certain reference to Ednie is 'villam et terras de *Ednye*' 1609 *RMS* vii no.204 (in the barony of Inverugie, belonging to Keith Marshall). See also above, 279.

industrial facility to the property of the monastery. John Stuart identifies this
with the old mill on the South Ugie which had stood 'a short way to the north
of the church, with a "sheelin'-hill" [73] beside it' (1869, l). This is much more
likely to be the site of *pett in mulenn* than Pitmillan, Foveran ABD,[74] since the
other identifiable place-names associated with the early church of Deer all lie
much nearer that church. Furthermore, Pitmillan, Foveran, has no connections
with the later abbey of Deer. That the teinds of Pitmillan, Foveran, are due to
the Earl Marischal in 1574 by tack from the Commendator of the abbey of
Deer (as noted by Jackson 1972, 49) is simply by virtue of the fact that the
monastery held the parish kirk of Foveran, and therefore had a claim on the
teinds of all the lands in its parish.

   The name may be compared also to Pitmullen, St Andrews and St Leonards
FIF, and Pitmilly, Kingsbarns FIF which may refer to the same mill (see Taylor
with Márkus, forthcoming 3, *s.n.*). Early forms are *Pethmulin* 1165×72 *St A.
Lib.* 179 and *Pethmolin* 1165×72 *RRS* ii no.13. Note however, that, unlike the
Book of Deer form, these show no trace of the definite article.

Another kindred emerges as major benefactors of the monastery of Deer:
Clann Channan, represented by Cainnech son of Mac-Dobarchon (II.12,
II.14), and his sons Comgell, *toísech* of Clann Channan (V.3), and Gartnait
together with his wife Éte daughter of Gille-Míchél (III, IV). This latter pair
made a grant recorded in 1131×1132, perhaps implying a floruit for Cainnech
of *c.*1100.

Ball domin i pet i[n] puir: 'the deep spot in Pitfour' (IV). This early
twelfth-century grant of a piece of land within a larger estate is the sole
subject of IV. Gartnait, one of the donors, is probably *mormaer* of Buchan,[75]
while the other donor, the daughter of Gille-Míchél, is no doubt his wife Éte,
who occurs with Gartnait also in record III in connection with the conse-
crating and endowing of the church of St Peter at Peterhead (see above, 278).

   Ball domin, which Jackson translates 'deep spot', i.e. 'hollow' (Jackson 1972,
35 n.2; 68), remains unidentified, although it evidently lay within the lands of
Pitfour. The bulk of these lands seem never to have been in ecclesiastical
hands. It might be reasonably assumed therefore that *Ball domin* lay on the
edge of Pitfour, a possible candidate being the land around the Mill of Bruxie,
which makes a slight indentation into the Pitfour estate on the north side of
the Bruxie Burn. The second element of 'Pitfour' is discussed in detail by
Jackson (1972, 68–9), elaborating and refining Watson's discussion (1926,

73 'a piece of rising ground where grain was winnowed by the wind' (*Concise Scots
Dictionary*). The only mill on the OS 6 inch 1st edition map of 1873 fitting this description is
'Waulkmill' (now Mavisbank). What is probably the mill-lade still exists, joining the South
Ugie where it meets the B9030.   **74** A name which contains the same elements, *pett* and
muileann.   **75** For a full discussion of this identification see Jackson 1972, 58.

376–7). It is related to Gaelic *pòr* (m), genitive *pòir*, 'seed, grain, crops', and would appear to be a loan-word from Pictish. An important difference in Jackson's and Watson's interpretation is that the latter suggests that it means 'pasture', while the former suggests 'crop-land'. It is remarkably common in eastern Scottish place-names, best known in Balfour (ABD, ANG, FIF, KCD). Pitfour is found in Perthshire and Ross (thrice), besides here in Old Deer. A cursory study of the positions of these place-names, often at or near the centre of lowland parishes, on good, well-drained soil, suggests that Jackson's interpretation as 'crop-land' is the more likely, although further investigation of all the places containing this element would be necessary before anything conclusive can be said. Besides combining chiefly with *achadh*, *pett*, *baile*, *dabhach* and *tulach* 'hillock', it is also found as a simplex in Purin, Falkland FIF (with diminutive ending) and Pourie ANG a few km north of Dundee. The diminutive ending is found also in Pitfirrane by Dunfermline FIF (see Taylor with Márkus 2006, 351–2), and, of course, in the Deer records (II.1) as the unidentified (*'nice*) *Fúrené*.

The analysis of *Ball domin* has some consequences for Scottish toponymics which have not previously been fully recognised, especially if Jackson is correct in seeing Baldovan near Dundee as the same name (1972, 68). The first element *ball* 'spot, place', although in Gaelic phonologically quite distinct from *baile* 'farm, estate', loses this distinction when borrowed into Older Scots as an unstressed generic element in place-names. This means that some at least of the *Bal*-names in eastern Scotland might well derive from *ball* rather than *baile*. Perhaps we should re-examine early forms of these names, recorded when Gaelic was still being widely spoken in the eastern Lowlands (i.e. before *c*.1200), and distinguish between those written as *Bale-* (from *baile*) and those written as *Bal-* (perhaps from *ball*).[76] The earliest recorded *baile*-name in Scotland is Balchrystie, Newburn FIF, appearing as 'villa de *Ballecristyn*' in a charter of Mael-Coluim III and Margaret 1070×93 (*St A. Lib.* 115), which clearly shows the unstressed final *e* of *baile*. Also the description of this holding as *villa* ('vill') further strengthens the case for *baile* as opposed to *ball* here, since it is likely that *baile* was the Gaelic term used for this tenurial unit.[77]

Domin 'deep' (modern Gaelic *domhain*) is also found in the simplex place-name Devon, Kettle FIF (*Dovyn* c.1320 *SHS Misc.* v, 13), 'deep place, i.e. place in a hollow'.

For *Pett Meic-Gobraig* (II.7, III) see above under *Pett* and under discussion of Inverugie.

---

76 The earliest form of Baldovan by Dundee (Mains and Strathmartine ANG) which I have found is *Baldovyn* 1466 (*Yester Writs*, no. 130). This is far too late to be able to distinguish between *ball* and *baile*. *Ball* would appear to be very rare in Irish place-names from early sources: there is only one certain example in Hogan 1910 (*ball áluinn*).   77 See Taylor 1994, 107–8 and n. 12; also Taylor with Márkus, forthcoming 2, *s.n.*

gonige in gorthe mor i gginn in fris is nesu daldín alenn o dubuci go lurchari etar sliab acus achad (V.3): This is translated by Jackson: 'as far as the great pillar-stone [i.e. standing stone, Gaelic *coirthe*] at the end of the thicket nearest to *Ailldín Ailenn*, from *Dubuice* to *Lurchaire*, both rough-grazing and pasture'[78] (1972, 35).

This is one of the more difficult grants to interpret, a fact reflected in the long note on it in Jackson 1972 (73–4). Amidst Jackson's complex phonological arguments there is not a single certain geographical co-ordinate, since he rejects, with perhaps too much casuistry, the most obvious identification of *aldin* with Aden ODR (for the early forms of which see Appendix I *s.n.*). Despite Jackson's misgivings, I would argue that *aldin* is indeed an early form of Aden, the large estate which lies immediately east of the site of the parish kirk and village of Old Deer. No part of Aden belonged to the Cistercian monastery, and therefore it is reasonable to assume that this was the case with regard to its predecessor. *Aldin alenn* is no exception to this, as it is simply defining that part of Aden which lies near to the march of the land granted by Comgell son of Cainnech. Jackson convincingly derives *aldin* from *ailltín*, 'little gully', perhaps referring to the rocky heights at Aden past which the South Ugie flows at the great bend in the river immediately east of Old Deer parish kirk. As to the meaning of *alenn*, Jackson (loc. cit.) discusses this at length and inconclusively. I would suggest that it contains Gaelic *ail* 'rock, cliff' with an adjectival or locational extension, and refers to that part of Aden (already being used as a place-name in the property-records) nearest to the same rocky heights that, as suggested above, gave rise to the name Aden itself.

The large standing-stone mentioned in this grant is, as Jackson rightly says, no longer identifiable, but must have stood much nearer the old church than those he suggests (1972, 72). The NMRS shows nothing of note, except perhaps the Tow Stone at NGR NJ97804768.[79] However, there are remains of what may well have been one or more large standing-stones on the Aden estate at NJ98104748, as well as the conspicuous outcrop of what is probably bedrock overlooking the South Ugie at NJ9794715. There were no doubt several more in the area: the intensive period of agricultural change in the eighteenth and early nineteenth century will have swept away many archaic features such as standing-stones. One such stone has left an onomastic trace behind it in the place-name Quartalehouse, and estate immediately south of the South Ugie opposite Aden, and marching with Biffie to the west (see fig. 10.2). Its earliest form is *Cortailhows* (1544; see Appendix I for more details). This name may be analysed as *coirthe* 'standing-stone'[80] + an existing place-

78 An alternative translation of both *sliab* and *achad* here are suggested above, 283–4.
79 Containing Scots *tow* 'toll', from the fact that tolls were collected and market disputes settled at it (NMRS NJ94NE no. 20).   80 Although *coirthe*, the word used in record V.3 in

name *Aileas or *Alas, which appears also in a now lost place-name *Knokailhous* (1544 *Aberdeen-Banff Illustrations* iv, 21), associated with the adjacent lands of Knock ODR.[81] Quartalehouse thus means '*Aileas* of the standing-stone'. *Aileas* etc. itself would seem to contain the common place-name element *ail* 'rock, cliff' with the locational suffix *-as* or *-us*.[82] The lands of Quartalehouse belonged to Deer Abbey, and it is quite possible that they represent the grant under discussion made by Comgell son of Cainnech. The case for this identification is strengthened by the second part of the grant, 'from Dubuice to Lurchaire'. This may be defining the limits of the grant in a different direction, or it may be repeating the first part using different co-ordinates. Either way, *Dubuice* (ms *dubuci*) must be the South Ugie.[83] The first element *dub* (modern Gaelic *dubh*) 'black' is common as an affix to distinguish a river which runs close to another, or which forms two branches, with the other river called contrastively 'white'. Examples of this are found both in Scots and Gaelic hydronyms, e.g. Findhorn and Deveron; Devon and Black Devon; Whiteadder and Blackadder; Black Cart and White Cart.[84] The North Ugie, which meets the South Ugie *c.*2km north-east of the village of Longside, between Peterhead and Old Deer, would no doubt have been known as *Finnuci 'the White Ugie'.[85] The spelling of /g/ as *c* in *uci* is a perfectly regular feature of Middle Irish orthography, and is found elsewhere in the Deer records.[86] The suggestion that Comgell's grant centred around the lands of Quartalehouse is further strengthened by the identification of *dubuci*, since the South Ugie forms the northern march of these lands. *Lurchari*, which is given as the other limit, may lie somewhere on the southern march of the lands of Quartalehouse. It has been suggested (Lawson 1896, 104) that it is represented by Pitlurg, the name of a cottage or small-holding on the lands of Knock, on the south side of the South Ugie *c.*1km east of the northern march of Quartalehouse. The house has gone, but the name remains in the nearby river-feature 'Pots of Pitlurg' (see Appendix for details). There are certain phonological objections to *Lurchari* becoming *lurg*, although these could be overridden by arguing for assimilation to the fairly common place-name element *lurg* 'shank', often used to refer to an elongated piece of land.[87] A

its nasalised form *gorthe*, often retains its dental fricative /θ/ in place-names in eastern Scotland (e.g. Pitcorthie (thrice) FIF, Pitforthie ANG, and various Aquhorthies etc. ABD), there are several examples of /θ/ becoming a dental stop /t/; e.g. in the nearby Cortiecram ODR (*Cortycrum* c.1446 *Abdn. Reg.* i, 247; *Corticrom* 1544 *A.B. Ill.* iv, 22 'bent or crooked standing stone'). In some examples this change can be seen taking place relatively late, e.g. Cortiebrae RHN appears as *Corthebray* in 1592 (*RMS* v no. 2176). **81** I am grateful to Mrs C. Penny of Quartalehouse Mill for drawing this to my attention. **82** For *ail* see Watson 1926, 33, 502–3; see also above, 290–1 under Altrie; for locational suffixes in Gaelic place-names, see Ó Máille 1990. **83** I am grateful to Thomas Clancy and Katherine Forsyth for this important insight. **84** See Nicolaisen 1976, 184 [2001, 237]. **85** The affixes 'South' and 'North' appear to be very late. See Appendix under 'Ugie'. **86** See Jackson 1972, 136. **87** See for example Watson 1926, 412, 510.

more cogent objection is that the nearby lands of Kinmundy ODR belonged to
the Gordons of Pitlurg (in Keith BNF) in the sixteenth century, and it is likely
that we are dealing with a transferred name here.[88]

Two grants (II.8, II.9) are made by members of Clann Ruaidrí, Mael-Coluim
son of Mael-Brigte (king of Alba 1020–1029) and Mael-Snechta son of
Lulach (king of Moray 1058?–1085).[89]

ind elerc: Elrick (II.8).[90] The grant of *ind elerc* by Mael-Coluim mac Mael-
Brigte is one of only three grants in the retrospective section II which can be
dated, and even then, not with any precision. This record provides another
good example of the blurring between common and proper noun, especially as
the noun appears here with the definite article *ind*. It means literally 'the deer-
trapping enclosure', a constructed feature, but one which used the shape of
the local landscape. It was usually constructed, presumably of stone-walling
or pallisading, in relatively low ground, into which deer were driven often
from a large swathe of the surrounding area.[91] *Ind elerc* exists today as the
large estate of Elrick in the south of Old Deer parish. We cannot say for
certain whether this estate still had a deer-trapping enclosure at the time of
the grant, however it is not as unlikely as Jackson suggests; nor can we point
with any confidence to the exact location of the *elerc*.

Jackson, following Watson, connects the word *elerc* (later *eileirig/iolairig*)
found only in Scottish Gaelic, with an Old Irish *erelc*, found only twice, both
times in the Milan Glosses.[92] It does not appear in any Irish place-names, and in
Scotland it is found mainly in the east, as well as the south-west. There are
around sixty extant place-names containing this element in Scotland, with
highest concentrations in Galloway and Aberdeenshire, but with none in Argyll
or north of Inverness.[93] This southerly and easterly distribution points in fact to
a Pictish and British provenance for this word, and, rather than the derivation
proposed by Watson, it may share the same origin as the unidentified place-name
Eleirch Fre in the *Gododdin*,[94] as well Eleirch in Ceridigion, Wales.

88 Note that Pitlurg, Slains ABD was originally called Leask, and changed to Pitlurg when it
was acquired by a Gordon of Pitlurg (Alexander 1952, 102). 89 See Woolf 2000. 90 I am
grateful to Thomas Clancy for his valuable contribution to this section. 91 Definition
from Watson 1914, 163. It is interesting to note that a few km east of Meikle Elrick, in the
Moss of Auquharney, Cruden, a wooden deer-trap was dug up in 1921, which has recently
been dated to around AD 600. It is now in the Marischal Museum, Aberdeen, and can be
viewed also at http://www.abdn.ac.uk/virtualmuseum (navigate via Index to 'Deer'). It is
unlikely that such deer-traps were used in deer-trap enclosures described above, but this
find does underline the importance of deer to the economy of Pictish Buchan. I am
grateful to Alex Woolf for bringing this to my attention. 92 Kelly (1997, 277) derives the
Milan gloss forms differently (from *air/ar/er* + *selg* 'hunting'), but also connects it with
the Scottish element. 93 These are 'root names', i.e. Meikle and Little Elrick are counted
as one, as are Eilrig and Allt na h-Eilrig INV. They are taken mainly from Hooker's OS
Pathfinder Gazetteer. See also Watson 1914, 16, who seems, however, not to have been
aware of the large number in the south-west (17 in KCB and WIG alone). 94 Koch (1997,

The extent of the original lands given by Mael-Coluim mac Mael-Brigte is difficult to assess, since by the later Middle Ages there are two distinct estates bearing this name, both of them belonging to the Cistercian monastery. These are Meikle Elrick (now Mains of Elrick) and Little Elrick, and they are separated by the lands of Annochie and Clochcan, both of which lay within a completely different lordship, that of the secular barony of Fedderate[95] (see fig.10.2).

For *Pett Malduib* (II.9) see above, discussion of *Pett*.

Another grant by a king is that of Mael-Coluim son of Cinaed (king of Alba 1005–34) recorded in II.7.

uactair ros abard: Auchnavaird (II.7): Jackson translates this 'upper *Ros abard*', treating *Ros abard* as an existing place-name,[96] with the addition of the noun which in modern Gaelic is *uachdar* 'upper part, upland', and which appears in many lowland place-names Anglicised as 'Auchter'. It is thus possible that the whole noun phrase is functioning as a place-name, which, had it survived, would have become locally something like '*Auchterros(a)vaird'.[97] *Ros abard* can be further analysed as **ros in baird* 'promontory of the poet'.[98] Jackson (1972, 52) tentatively suggests that this name is linked to Auchnavaird ODR, which contains the same specific *bard* 'poet' (modern Gaelic *bàrd*). This is very likely for several reasons. Firstly, Auchnavaird sits on a low but conspicuous promontory which runs south from Logan Hill beside Mains of Elrick and whose southern limit is the Burn of Fortree, the march-burn between Old Deer and Ellon parishes. Auchnavaird appears late in the record,[99] but would seem to form part of the monastery's lands of Meikle Elrick, which may have been given to Deer at about the same time (see above, 296–7). The biggest problem with this identification is the fact that two davochs were given 'of the upland of *Ros abard' or 'of *Auchterros(a)vaird'. A davoch is a large unit of land, very variable at different periods, and in different areas, but estimated at around 240 Imperial acres of arable with a tract of grazing land attached sufficient for its needs.[1] Its size in thirteenth-century Buchan can be well judged from a charter relating to the lands of Fedderate NDR. It was

80–1) translates it 'Hill of Swans' (Old Welsh *älärch*). There may in fact be a connection between the shape of the deer-trapping enclosure and the swan's neck. **95** The earliest records of both these names are as part of the barony of Fedderate, *viz. Annochy* 1507 *RMS* ii no.3127 and *Clochcan* 1573 *RMS* iv no.2158. For early forms of Elrick, see Appendix. **96** See also Cox , this volume, 310. **97** It is found locally in Auchterellon, Ellon and Auchterlownie, Slains. **98** See Jackson 1972, 51 and Cox, this volume, 310. For a discussion of *bard* 'poet' as a place-name element, see Bannerman 1996. **99** As *Auchnaverd* 1696. See Appendix *s.n.*. **1** This is the figure arrived at for northern Scotland by G.W.S. Barrow, based on Pennant, and calculating on the basis of 1 Scotch acre = 1.26 Imperial acres. For a full discussion of this unit, see Jackson 1972, 116–17 and Barrow 1973, 265–74. Note that the Barrow *Scottish Studies* vi (1962) article which was heavily used by Jackson *loc. cit.* was reprinted as Barrow 1973, 257–78 [2003, 233–49]. See also

issued by Fergus, earl of Buchan, before 1214, whereby he grants to John son of Uchtred three davochs of Fedderate in exchange for the lands of Slains and Crudan. These three davochs are named as Easter Aucheoch, Atherb, Auchquhath and Conwiltes †, and from the detailed marches given they would seem together to occupy much of the north-western corner of NDR, covering an area of approximately 12 square kilometres (almost 3,000 acres).[2] In short, two davochs must have been considerably larger than the modern farm of Auchnavaird, and it may well have included the adjacent monastic estate of Meikle, now Mains of, Elrick. Even then the area is small when compared to the three early thirteenth-century davochs of Fedderate, and in fact an area stretching from (and including) Little Elrick to Auchnavaird would be more comparable. It may be that this whole tract is meant by *ind elerc* and *da dabeg uactair ros abard*,[3] including Annochie and Clochcan, which only later came into the hands of the lairds of Fedderate (see above, under *ind elerc*).

The remaining grants were made by people for whom there is insufficient evidence to assign them to any of the kindreds already mentioned.

(Ua) orti (nice) furene: '(from) *Oirte (as far as) *Púiréne'(II.1). As neither of these nouns is preceded by the definite article, we can assume that they are functioning as place-names, and they are treated as such by Jackson in his translation (1972, 33). *Oirte (fem. *iá* stem) is, as Jackson points out in his notes (1972, 44), probably related to Old Irish *ord* (m. *o*-stem) 'hammer' a common place-name element in the North-East, referring to low, rounded hills (see also Watson 1926, 140). *Púiréne, a diminutive of *púr*, is discussed above, 292–3. Neither place can be identified today.

Bidbín: Biffie (II.6). A large, well-drained estate *c*.2.5km square, it lay contiguous with the core land around the original monastery on the west and the south-west. By the sixteenth century it consisted of at least three subdivisions: the Raw of Biffie (NJ966478), Parkhouse of Biffie (NJ955469), and Biffie itself, probably at Mains of Biffie (NJ965471). Today there are the farms of Biffie (NJ972472), Brae of Biffie, Wester Biffie, Mains of Biffie, Parkhouse, North Parkhouse and Windhill. The original estate probably also included some if not all of Bridgend.

No satisfactory explanation of the name, which would have been pronounced something like /'biðvin/ or /'biðvin/ in the eleventh century, has appeared in print. Following a suggestion by Professor John Koch (pers. comm.)

Broun, this volume. **2** *A.B. Coll.* 407–9. It is also discussed briefly by A. Young (1993, 179, 184). It contains a wealth of details about the early thirteenth-century Buchan landscape, such as a physician's cross (*crux medici*), sheepfolds, and carefully dug ditches. See also above, n. 276 n. 7 and n. 277 n. 9, also Forsyth, *infra* 413–7. **3** The fact that both these grants are mentioned consecutively in record II may also suggest contiguity.

it may represent a Pictish reflex of the Celtic word which appears in Gaelic as *beith* and in Welsh as *bedw* 'birch', thus 'place of the birch or birches'. As we have already seen (above p. 290–1) birches were scarce enough in this area in the early medieval period to be used as boundary markers, and so it is perfectly plausible to find them being used to distinguish what was already in the early eleventh century an important place. The second element must be the locational ending *-in* or *ín*, so common in the forms of Celtic place-names in eastern Scotland recorded before *c.*1300, which after that date is regularly reduced to *-ie*. This ending is found elsewhere in the Deer records in *alterin* (Altrie) twice (II.3, II.12). For a discussion of this phenomenon, see Ó Maolalaigh 1998, 30–8.

acchad madchor: Auchmachar (V.1): This represents the lands occupied today by North Auchmachar, South Auchmachar, Braeside of Auchmachar and Knapperty, a good tract of land which lies immediately north of Altrie † (now Bruxie). The first element has been discussed above (283–4). The second element Jackson would interpret as a male personal name, Madchar[4] (1972, 70) or Madchor (ibid. 161, index). As far as I am aware this name occurs nowhere else in Ireland or Scotland. It is also worth pointing out that in eastern Scotland, at least, the combination *achadh* + a personal name is very rare.[5] It might rather be a descriptive term derived from Gaelic *math* 'good' + *cor*, a word with a wide variety of meanings, the basic one being 'act of putting or placing',[6] in the sense 'good piece of (allotted) land'.

(gonige) Scali merlec: Skillymarno (V.2). Cormac son of Cennédig gave as far as Scáli Merlec, with *gonige* probably being used inclusively here. Despite Alexander's misgivings (1952, 115), which have more validity than Jackson allowed,[7] there can be little doubt that this is Skillymarno, which lies about 5km north of Old Deer. Skillymarno appears amongst the lands of the Cistercian monastery in the later Middle Ages and, furthermore, it is contiguous with Auchmachar. Its possession thus gave the monastery a continuous swathe of land from its core holdings to the northern edge of the parish (see fig. 10.2). The development of the specific element *merlec* 'thieves' to the saint's name Mo Ernoc or the like can be explained in two ways: either by deliberate re-interpretation of the second element in a Gaelic-speaking context, and under the influence of its ecclesiastical owners; or by purely phonological process, through the dissimilation of l + rl to l + rn. The first of

---

4 Apparently an error for 'Madchor'.   **5** See Fraser 1998, 190–1.   **6** See *DIL* under *cor*.
7 Jackson states (1972, 71) that Alexander's proposed '*mo Ernoc* would not give *-marno*', but does not explain why. Elsewhere, *mo Ern-* gives such place-names as Kilmarnock, Marnoch; and the final voiceless velar consonant of this name is clearly seen in the early forms (see Appendix under Skillymarno).

these processes would have been further encouraged by the existence of a cult of Marnock in the North-East.[8]

However, the nearby place-names Skilmafilly NDR and the two Skelmonae's (MET and TYR) are best interpreted as containing saints' names, with the first probably representing a hypocoristic form of Palladius, whose cult was established at Fordoun in the Mearns (KCD) at the very latest by the eleventh century.[9] This raises the possibility that *Scali Merlec* might be a re-interpretation or re-formation of an earlier *Scali Mo-Ernoc, and that *scali* was being used locally with specifically ecclesiastical overtones. This is further suggested by one of the applications of Middle Irish *scál* 'hut' (but not found as a place-name element in Ireland), referring to a humble hut dwelt in by the early fathers of the church (*DIL*). According to Marstrander (1915), it is a loan-word from Norse *skáli*, which also originally meant 'hut or shed put up for temporary use'; interestingly, but no doubt coincidentally, the Old Icelandic *skála búi*, literally 'hut-dweller', can mean 'robber'![10] It is unique to find a Norse loan-word in Scottish Gaelic generating place-names in eastern Scotland at this early date. A plausible context for such an early borrowing might be that of trading, with the *skálar* referring to the temporary trading booths. Its distribution as a Gaelic place-name element in eastern Scotland is, however, extremely restricted, being found only in the area in and around Deer, in the place-names Skilmafilly NDR, Skelmonae MET and TYR, and probably Skellmuir ODR.[11]

However, another derivation unconnected with Norse suggests itself, from Gaelic *sgàil* (MIr *scáile*, 'shadow, shade' (m. or f.; from Common Celtic *skâlî, 'shade, shadow'). Amongst the various meanings for this word given by Dwelly (1901) are 1) 'shade, shadow, 2) veil, curtain, covering, mask, 6) bower'. Thus the Deer records' *scali* might well represent accusative singular or plural of feminine *iá*-stem *scáile* with the meaning 'simple place which affords shade or protection', i.e. 'hut'.[12]

8 See Thomas Clancy, this volume. 9 That the medial ma/mo represents Gaelic *mo* 'my', 'saint', is confirmed by the local pronunciation of Skilmafilly and Skelmonae, with the stress on the first and final elements (the *i* of *filly* and the *ae* respectively). See Alexander 1952, 115. For the cult of Palladius, see Clancy, this volume. 10 Geddes' statement that *skáli* means 'hut-dweller or robber' is based on a misreading of this sentence (1998, 547). W.J. Watson certainly seemed to think that *scali* was from Norse *skáli* as he gives a modern rendering of *scalí merlec* as *Sgalan Mhèirleach* (1929, 189–91). 11 Note Skellybogs NDR does not belong to this group, as it is a Scots place-name containing Scots *skelly* 'wild mustard'. 12 I am grateful to Peadar Morgan for this suggestion. In any final assessment of this element, place-names such as Cnoc na Sgàile, Kiltarlity and Convinth parish INV (NH619457), with its nearby hut-circles, will have to be taken into consideration. Whatever the ultimate origin of *scali* etc., I would be much more cautious than Jane Geddes when she writes that the place-names Skillymarno, Skilmafilly, Skelmonae and Skelmuir 'may indicate traces of temporary Viking settlement, either for trading or raiding, near to Deer' (Geddes 1998, 547).

The Gaelic Notes in the Book of Deer are vitally important for many aspects of Scottish history and language, and are no less important as a toponymic text. Their close study increases our understanding of the place-names not only of Aberdeenshire but of the whole of Scotland, giving us a unique glimpse into place-name formation. On the other hand, our growing and developing understanding of the toponymy of Scotland as a whole informs, and will continue to inform, our interpretation of the place-names and place-descriptions in the Deer text.

APPENDIX

Early forms of place-names discussed in the text

Where possible a six-figure NGR is given, which is of the modern farm-steading. The names as they appear in the property-records in the Book of Deer are given following Ó Maolalaigh's diplomatic text (this volume), however, modern word division has been introduced. The conventions are those used by Richard Cox (this volume).

ADEN   ODR NJ981479
   (*d*)*aldín alenn* V.3
   Alnedene in *Bouchane* cum nova foresta 1324 *RRS* v no.261 [From a copy made in 1430; Robert I grants to Keith Marischal Aden in Buchan, with the new forest]
   (barony of) *Alden* 1378 *Abdn. Reg.* i 121ff
   (barony of) *Aldene* et foreste de *Kyntor* 1407 *RMS* i no.884 [Keith Marischal]
   (barony of) *Aldane* 1427 *A.B. Ill.* iv 33
   (lands & barony of) *Auden* 1592 *RMS* v no.2176 [Keith Marischal; all its constituent lands listed cols. 2–3.]
   (barony of) *Alden* 1609 *RMS* vii no.204
   /ˈadən/

NGR is of Aden steading, now the Heritage Centre of Aden Country Park. For a discussion of this name, see above, 294.

ALTRIE †   ODR c.NJ937498
   (*in*) *álteri* II.3
   alterín II.12
   Altry 1544 *A.B. Ill.* iv, 20 [assedation of lands of monastery of Deer]
   Altrie 1587 *RMS* v no.1309 [part of lands of monastery of Deer, now in the hands of the Keiths]
   Alterye 1590×99 Pont MS 10

(lands, lordship and barony of) *Altrie* 1612 *RMS* vii no.758 [comprehending the lands once belonging to the monastery of *Deir*]

town and lands of *Over Altries* 1776 Alexander 1952, 5 [town and lands of *Over*, *Nether* & *Middle Altries* 'with the croft of *Stockbridge* & ... old miln of *Bruxie*']

Altree 1826 Thomson [on site of present-day Overton of Bruxie NJ933488]

The NGR is that of present-day Brownhill, following Lawson, who states that 'the mansion house of Altrie stood where is now the steading of the farm of Brownhill' (1896, 101). For a full discussion of this name and its original site, see above, 290–1.

AUCHMACHAR ODR NJ947499
  acchad | madchór V.1
  Ardmauchter 1539 *A.B. Ill.* iv, 551–2
  Achmachqwhan 1544 *A.B. Ill.* iv, 20 [assedation of lands of monastery of Deer]
  Achmachhar 1544 *A.B. Ill.* iv, 23 [assedation of lands of monastery of Deer]
  Auchmachir 1554 *A.B. Ill.* iv, 28
  Auchmacher 1587 *RMS* v no.1309 [part of lands of monastery of New Deer, now in hands of Keiths]

NGR is of OS Pathfinder 'Braeside [of] Auchmachar', which on OS 6 inch 1st edition is given simply as 'Auchmachar'. For the discussion of this name, see 299 above.
  /ax'maxər/

AUCHNAVAIRD   ODR NJ944404
  Auchnaverd 1696 *Pollable Persons* i, 614

See Ros abard below.

BALL DOMIN
  báll dómin IV

See Pitfour below; also main discussion above, 292–3.

BIFFIE   ODR NJ965471
  bidbín II.6
  (i) *bbidbín* 1005×32 II.7
  Biffy 1544 *A.B. Ill.* iv, 20 [assedation of lands of monastery of Deer]
  Rytre of Biffye 1544 *A.B. Ill.* iv, 23 [in list of rental of garbal teinds of parish of Deer belonging to monastery of Deer; immediately precedes *The Raw of Biffe* and *Perkhows*]

The Raw of Biffe 1544 *A.B. Ill.* iv, 23 [in list of rental of garbal teinds of parish of Deer belonging to monastery of Deer]

Biffy 1554 *A.B. Ill.* iv, 28 [in rental of lands of monastery]

Byffie 1587 *RMS* v no.1309 [part of lands of monastery of Deer, now in hands of Keiths; immediately precedes *lie Raw de Byffie* & *Parkhous* de *Byffie*]

lie Raw de Byffie 1587 *RMS* v no.1309 [part of lands of monastery of Deer, now in hands of Keiths]

NGR is of modern Mains of Biffie. See main discussion 298–9.

DEER   NJ979477

deár ×1130s I

(*clerici de*) *der* 1150 VII

Dere 13th c *Abdn. Reg.* ii 53

NGR is of the Old Deer parish kirk.

ELRICK   ODR NJ943410

ind Elerc 1020 ×1029 II.8

Mekil Elryk & *Litil Elryk* 1544 *A.B. Ill.* iv, 19 [assedation of lands of monastery of Deer; note that rent more than twice as high for M.E. as for L.E.]

(lands of *Glakreoch* &) *Litill Elraik* (in lordship of *Deir*) 1554 *RMS* iv no.1145 [part of lands of monastery of Deer, now in hands of Keiths]

Lyttill Elrig 1587 *RMS* v no.1309 [part of lands of monastery of New Deer, now in hands of Keiths]

Mekill Elrik (with mill) 1587 *RMS* v no.1309 [part of lands of monastery of Deer, now in hands of Keiths]

NGR is of Mains of Elrick. Note also Elrick Moss, Mill of Elrick, Milton of Elrick; all on lands of Mains of Elrick, formerly Meikle Elrick. Little Elrick NJ926448 lies *c.*4km to the north. See main discussion 296–7; also main discussion of Auchnavaird and Ros abard, 297–8.

PITFOUR   ODR NJ988494

(*i*) *pet i[n] puir* c.1130s IV

terras nostras de Petfoure 1383 *RMS* i no.731 [royal lands; Robert II grants 'our lands' of Pitfour to his son Alexander Stewart]

Pettfovre 1443 *A.B. Coll.* iv, 43–4

terras de Petfour 1476 *RMS* ii no. 1253 [Egidia Stewart of Lunan (*Lownane*) ANG grants to her eldest son Walter Tiry various lands throughout Scotland including the lands of Pitfour]

terras dimedietatis de Petfour 1477 *RMS* ii no. 1295

terras dimedietatis de Petfoure 1506 *RMS* ii no. 2978

dimedietatem de *Petfour* 1507 *RMS* ii no.3166 [to Walter Innes, to be held
of the king, the lands of Toux (*Touchis*) and half of Pitfour (*Petfour*), united
into barony of Toux ODR]

NGR is of Mains of Pitfour. The core of the estate was probably further west,
and nearer the site of the now demolished Big House (NJ978491). See main
discussion, 292–3.
/pit'fuːr/

PITLURG   ODR NJ988466
Pitlurg 1874 OS 1st edn 6 inch
Pots of Pitlurg 1874 OS 6 inch 1st edn [in the South Ugie, immediately
north-east of Pitlurg]
Pots of Pitlurg OS Pathfinder

NGR is of the house, now gone. See main discussion, 295–6.

QUARTALEHOUSE   ODR NJ975464
Cortailhows 1544 *A.B. Ill.* iv, 19 [assedation of lands of monastery of Deer]
Quartailhous 1554 *A.B. Ill.* iv, 27 [in rental of lands of monastery]
(lands of) *Quartailhous* (& their waulkmill) 1587 *RMS* v no.1309 [part of
lands of monastery of New Deer, now in hands of Keiths]
/kər'taləs/
/kər'teləs/

See main discussion, 294–5

ROS ABARD
(*da dabeg*) *uactair ros abard* 1005×34 II.7

See Auchnavaird above; also main discussion, 297–8.

SKILLYMARNO   ODR[13] NJ958527
(*gonige*) *sca | li merlec* V.2
Skelemerno 1544 20 *A.B. Ill.* iv, [assedation of lands of monastery of Deer]
Skillemarnocht 1554 *A.B. Ill.* iv [from Alexander 1952, 115]
Skalymarnoth 1558 Sheriff Court Records ABD [from Alexander 1952, 115]
Skillemarno 1587 *RMS* v no.1309 [part of lands of monastery of New
Deer, now in hands of Keiths]
(hill of) *Skillimarnock* 1723 *A.B. Ill.* i, 410

See main discussion, 299–300.

---

13 Alexander (1952, 115) wrongly places it in STR, no doubt because the ODR/STR parish
boundary runs through Little Skillymarno.

UGIE

(*ó*) *dubuci* V.3 [South Ugie]
watter of *Ugy* 1495 *ADC* [reference from Alexander 1952, 130]
/ˈjugi/

See main discussion, 295. Note also the following description from *c*.1680: 'Its head is divided into two branches, ordinarily called The Fore and Back water of Ugy' (*A.B. Coll.* 95).

ACKNOWLEDGMENTS

Many individuals and groups have contributed to this chapter. Firstly I am pleased to thank the Society of Antiquaries of Scotland for a grant to carry out field-work in Buchan, to familiarise myself with both the physical and the toponymic landscape of Deer and to prepare a first draft of fig. 10.1. I would also like to thank Celia (Bunty) Penny and the Friends of the Book of Deer for their information, interest, kindness and support over the years. Thanks are also due to the many individuals in and around Deer who took the time to tell me about their names and places, especially to the Rhind family of the Old Bank House, Old Deer, where I was so well and hospitably lodged during my visits. And finally I would like to thank my friends and colleagues, many of whom are contributors to this book, who have read various drafts of some or all of this chapter, and from whose comments and suggestions I have greatly benefitted, above all Dauvit Broun, Thomas Clancy, Richard Cox, Stephen Driscoll, Katherine Forsyth, Gilbert Márkus, Roibeard Ó Maolalaigh and Alex Woolf. Needless to say, all mistakes are my own.

COUNTY AND PARISH ABBREVIATIONS

ABD	Aberdeenshire	ODR	Old Deer ABD
ANG	Angus	PER	Perthshire
AYR	Ayrshire	RHN	Rathen ABD
BNF	Banffshire	ROS	Ross-shire
FIF	Fife	STF	St Fergus ABD
INV	Inverness-shire	STL	Stirlingshire
KCB	Kirkcudbrightshire	STR	Strichen ABD
KCD	Kincardineshire	TYR	Tyrie ABD
MET	Methlick ABD	WIG	Wigtownshire
NDR	New Deer ABD		

PRIMARY SOURCES

A. B. Coll. *Collections for a history of the shires of Aberdeen and Banff*, ed. J. Robertson
and G. Grub (1843), 5 vols (Spalding Club 69), Edinburgh.

A. B. Ill. *Illustrations of the topography and antiquities of the shires of Aberdeen and
Banff*, ed. J. Robertson and G. Grub (1847–69), 4 vols (Spalding Club),
Edinburgh.

Abdn. Reg. *Registrum Episcopatus Aberdonensis*, ed. C. Innes (1845), (Spalding Club
13–14, Maitland Club 63), Edinburgh.

ADC *The acts of the Lords of Council in civil causes*, ed. T. Thomson et al. (1839,
1918–), Edinburgh.

Arb.Lib. *Liber S. Thome de Aberbrothoc*, ed. C. Innes (1848–56), (Bannatyne Club
86), Edinburgh.

CPS *Chronicles of the Picts: Chronicles of the Scots*, ed. W.F Skene (1867),
Edinburgh.

CSSR *Calendar of Scottish Supplications to Rome*, ed. E.R. Lindsay et al.
(1934–1997) (Scot. Hist. Soc.), Edinburgh.

Dunf. Reg. *Registrum de Dunfermelyn*, ed. C. Innes (1842) (Bannatyne Club 74),
Edinburgh.

ER *The Exchequer Rolls of Scotland*, ed. J. Stuart et al. (1878–1908), Edinburgh.

Fasti *Fasti Ecclesiae Scoticanae (Synods of Aberdeen and of Moray)*, vol. 6, new
edition, H. Scott (1926), Edinburgh.

OSA *Old Statistical Account of Scotland.* = Cruden (1799)

Pollable *List of Pollable Persons in the Shires of Aberdeen, 1696*,
  Persons i, transcribed and published 'by the Gentlemen of the County',
  614 2 vols, Aberdeen 1844 (Parishes of Old Deer and Longside published as
The people of Old Deer and Longside 1696, with an index by Bruce
Henderson, by Aberdeen & North-East Scotland Family History Society
1989, reprinted 1996.

RHP (West) Register House Plan.

RMS *Registrum Magni Sigilli Regum Scottorum*, ed. J.M. Thomson et al.
(1882–1914), Edinburgh.

RRS v *Regesta Regum Scottorum* vol. v (*Acts of Robert I*), ed. A.A.M. Duncan
(1988), Edinburgh.

SHS Misc. *The Miscellany of the Scottish History Society*, SHS 1893– .

St A. Lib. *Liber Cartarum Prioratus Sancti Andree in Scotia*, ed.
T. Thomson (1841), (Bannatyne Club 69), Edinburgh.

Yester Writs *Calendar of writs preserved at Yester House 1166–1503*,
ed. C.C.H. Harvey & J. Macleod, SRS 1930.

REFERENCES

Alexander, W.M. (1952), *The place-names of Aberdeenshire* (Third Spalding Club).

Anderson, A.O. (ed.), (1922), *Early sources of Scottish history 500 to 1286*, 2 vols, Edinburgh
(reprinted with preface, bibliographical supplement and corrections by M.O.
Anderson, Stamford, 1990).

Anderson, M.O. (1974), 'St Andrews before Alexander I', *The Scottish tradition: essays in honour of Ronald Gordon Cant*, ed. G.W.S. Barrow, Edinburgh, 1–13.

Bannerman, J. (1993), 'MacDuff of Fife', in *Medieval Scotland: crown, lordship and community*, ed. A. Grant & K.J. Stringer, Edinburgh, 20–38.

—— (1996), 'The residence of the King's poet', *Scottish Gaelic Studies* 17, 24–35.

Barrow, G.W.S. (1973), *Kingdom of the Scots*, London (2nd ed. Edinburgh, 2003).

—— (1998), 'The uses of place-names and Scottish history: pointers and pitfalls', in *The uses of place-names*, ed. S. Taylor, Edinburgh, 54–74.

Robinson, M. (ed.), (1985), *Concise Scots dictionary*, Aberdeen.

Cowan, I.B. (1961), 'The development of the parochial system in medieval Scotland', *Scot.Hist.Rev.* 40, 43–55 [re-published in Cowan 1995, 1–11].

—— (1967), *The parishes of medieval Scotland* (Scottish Record Society vol. 93), Edinburgh.

—— (1995), *The medieval church in Scotland*, ed. James Kirk (Edinburgh).

Cox, R.A.V. (1997), 'Modern Scottish Gaelic reflexes of two Pictish words: **pett* and **lannerc*', *Nomina* 20, 47–58.

Cruden, G. (1799), 'Parish of Deer', in *The statistical account of Scotland. Drawn up from the communication of the ministers of the different parishes by Sir John Sinclair* (1791–9, 21 vols), Edinburgh, vol. xvi, 469–83.

Dauzat, A., and Ch. Rostaing (1978), *Dictionnaire étymologique des noms de lieux en France*, (2nd ed.) Paris. (1st ed., 1963).

DIL Dictionary of the Irish language (based mainly on Old and Middle Irish materials), compact edition, ed. E.G. Quin, Dublin (1983, repr.1990).

Dwelly, E. (1901), *The illustrated Gaelic-English dictionary*, E. Dwelly 1901–11 (9th edition 1977).

Fraser, D.M. (1998), 'An investigation into distributions of *ach-*, *bal-* and *pit-* place-names in North East Scotland' [Scotland north and east of a line joining Perth and Inverness], unpublished M. Litt thesis, University of Aberdeen.

Geddes, J. (1998), 'The art of the Book of Deer', *Proc. Soc. Antiq. Scot.* 128, 537–49.

Hogan, E. (1910), *Onomasticon Goedelicum*, Dublin.

Jackson, K.H. (1972), *The Gaelic Notes in the Book of Deer*, Cambridge.

Kelly, F. (1997), *Early Irish farming* (Early Irish Law Series 4), Dublin.

Koch, J. T. (ed.), (1997), *The Gododdin of Aneirin: text and context from Dark-Age North Britain*, Cardiff.

Lawson, A., (1896), *A book of the parish of Deer*, Aberdeen.

MacBain, A. (1911), *An etymological dictionary of the Gaelic language*, Stirling (reprinted by Gairm Publications 1982).

MacDonald, A. (1982), '*Ràth* in Scotland', *Bulletin of the Ulster Place-name Society*, series 2, vol. 4, 32–57.

McNeill, P.G.B., and H.L. MacQueen (eds) (1996) *Atlas of Scottish history to 1707* Edinburgh.

Marstrander, C. (1915), *Bidrag til det norske sprogs historie i Irland*, Kristiana.

Nicolaisen, W.F.H. (1976), *Scottish place-names*, London (second imp. with additional information 1979; second ed. Edinburgh, 2001).

Ó Máille, T.S. (1990), 'Irish place-names in *-as, -es, -os, -us*', *Ainm* 4, 125–43.

Ó Maolalaigh, R. (1998), 'Place-names as a resource for the historical linguist', in *The uses of place-names*, ed. S. Taylor, Edinburgh, 12–53.

Price, L. (1963), 'A note on the use of the word *baile* in place-names [in Ireland]', *Celtica* 6, 119–26.

Rogers, J. M. (1997), 'The formation of parishes in twelfth-century Perthshire', *Records of Scottish Church History Society* 27, 68–96.

Stokes, W. (ed.), (1905), *The Martyrology of Oengus* (Henry Bradshaw Society 29), London (repr. Dublin 1984).

Stone, J.C. (1989), *The Pont Manuscript maps of Scotland: sixteenth century origins of a Blaeu atlas*, Tring.

Stuart, J. (ed.), (1869), *The Book of Deer* (Spalding Club 36), Edinburgh.

Taylor, S. (1994), 'Babbet and Bridin Pudding or Polyglot Fife in the Middle Ages', *Nomina* 17, 99–118.

—— (1995), 'Settlement-names in Fife', unpublished PhD, University of Edinburgh.

—— (1997), 'Generic-element variation, with special reference to Eastern Scotland', *Nomina* 20, 5–22.

—— (1998), 'Place-names and the early church in Scotland', *Records of Scottish Church History Society* 28, 1–22.

—— (2000) 'Place-names of Fife', in *The Fife Book*, ed. D. Omand (Edinburgh), 205–20.

—— (2007) '*Sliabh* in Scottish place-names: its meaning and chronology', *Journal of Scottish Name Studies* 1, 99–136.

Taylor, S., with G. Márkus (2006), *Place-names of Fife* vol. 1 (West Fife between Leven and Forth), (Donington) [volume 1 of a 5-volume series].

—— (forthcoming 2) *Place-names of Fife* vol. 2 (Central Fife between the Rivers Leven and Eden) (Donnington) [volume 2 of a 5-volume series].

—— (forthcoming) *Place-names of Fife* vol. 3 (St Andrews and the East Neuk) (Donnington) [volume 3 of a 5-volume series].

Toner, G. (2000), 'Settlement and settlement terms in medieval Ireland: *ráth* and *lios*', *Ainm* 8 (1998–2000), 1–40.

Watson, A., & E. Allan (1984), *The place-names of Upper Deeside*, Aberdeen.

Watson, A. (1995), *The Ochils: placenames, history, tradition*, Perth.

Watson, W.J. (1914), 'Aoibhinn an Obair an t-Sealg', *Celtic Review* ix, 156–68.

—— (1926), *The history of the Celtic place-names of Scotland*, Edinburgh.

—— (1929), *Rosg Gaidhlig: specimens of Gaelic prose*, Glasgow, 2nd ed. (1st edition 1915).

Wentworth, R. (1996), *Gaelic words and phrases from Wester Ross/Faclan is Abairtean à Ros an Iar* (Gairloch, Feb. 1996 version).

Woolf, A. (2000), 'The "Moray Question" and the kingship of Alba in the tenth and eleventh centuries', *Scottish Historical Review* 79 (2), 145–64.

Young, A. (1993), 'The earls and earldom of Buchan in the thirteenth century', *Medieval Scotland: crown, lordship and community*, ed. A. Grant & K.J. Stringer, 174–202.

The syntax of the place-names

RICHARD A.V. COX

The aim of this article[1] is firstly to look at the range of structures found in place-names cited in the property records in the Book of Deer, taking those names that are in or within the immediate orbit of Old Deer, and excluding the forms for Aberdour, Buchan, Aberdeen, Turriff and Brechin, which also occur; and secondly to consider the range of formulae that are used for identifying locations in the records whether for reasons of granting land or granting dues in connection with land.

The forms of names used are from Roibeard Ó Maolalaigh's diplomatic edition of the property records (this volume) with numbering indicating record number and line; accompanying prepositions, while not acknowledged in translations below, are shown in round brackets, otherwise the relevant case is noted; line breaks within words are shown by a vertical bar.

THE STRUCTURES

From a syntactical point of view a simple structure consists of a noun with or without an adjective, with or without the article (a simplex). There are six examples of names consisting of NOUN only: *deár* I.19, *(úa)orti* II.1, *(níce) fúrené* II.1, *bidbín* acc. II.10, *étdanin* acc. II.23, and *álterin* acc. II.22. There is also one example where the article *(ind)* occurs: *in̲delerc* acc. II.14.

There is at least one, possibly two examples, of a structure (ARTICLE +) NOUN + ADJECTIVE: *báll dómin* acc. 'deep place' IV.1, and *(gonige) ingort|he mór* 'the large stone' V.22. The latter example may have no onomastic value. It is difficult to be certain either way, but it is probably unlikely, since without the further directions to the stone—'at the end of the thicket nearest to ...'— one would, it seems, be none the wiser as to the location in question, although this is not a necessary criterion in the definition of a place-name as many names will attest.

The river name *(ó)dubucí* V.24 is structurally different to the foregoing both syntactically and onomastically: on the one hand, the adjective *dub* 'black' and its following noun form a close grammatical compound with initial-element stress; on the other, *dub* qualifies the name form *ucí* contrastively.[2]

---

1 I am grateful to Professor Colm Ó Baoill for his helpful comments on an earlier draft of this article. 2 After Taylor, this volume, *s.n. dubuci*. The current Scots name is the *South Ugie*, as opposed to the *North Ugie*.

Of complex names (i.e. names with structures consisting of two or more simplexes, each in genitival relationship to the preceding one), there are four examples of a noun followed by a personal name (NOUN x PERSONAL NAME): *acchad madchór* acc. V.3,[3] *pett mec garnaít* acc. II.3, *pett malduíb* acc. II.15, *petmec cóbrig* acc. III.2 (which is also cited in the prepositional phrase *inpett mec gobróig* II.12).

There is one example of a noun followed by an appellative in the genitive (NOUN x NOUN): *(gonige) sca | li merlec* 'shelter of thieves' V.14.

There are four examples of a noun followed by a (genitive) simplex consisting of article + noun (NOUN x ART. + NOUN): *áchád naglerec* acc. 'the holding of the clerics' II.8,[4] *(i)pet ipúir* 'the holding of the crop-land' IV.1, *pett inmulenn* acc. 'the holding of the mill' II.7, and *(úa)cloic intiprat* 'the stone of the well' I.13. It may be that the last two examples consist of an onomastic structure generic + (specific), where the specific is an erstwhile name or *ex nomine* unit; but there is no way of being certain.

There is one example of NOUN x NOUN x PERSONAL NAME: *(gonice) chloic pette mec garnaít* I.13; and in this instance *pette mec garnaít* certainly constitutes an *ex nomine* unit as the form *pett mec garnaít* acc. occurs independently elsewhere (II.3).

There may possibly also be one example of NOUN x NOUN + ADJECTIVE: *áchád toche temní* acc. II.3, which may contain an *ex nomine* unit (i.e. *toche temní*), but the specific remains obscure for the time being.[5]

Finally, a structure NOUN x NOUN x ARTICLE + NOUN occurs: *uactaír rósábard* gen. III.13, which I take to be for **uactair ros in baird*, literally 'the upland of the promontory of the poet'. Here one might hazard a guess and say—assuming the interpretation of the specific (**ros in baird*) is accepted—that this name also contains an *ex nomine* unit, and therefore that it has an onomastic meaning 'the upland of **ros in baird*'. Jackson suggests that here *ros* probably stands for genitive *rois*, however it may be that in this instance the name form **ros in baird* has simply retained its radical form in composition as specific in the dependent name **uactair ros in baird*.[6]

The name forms *(gó)lurchárí* V.24 and *(d)aldín alenn* V.24 remain obscure, or at least partially obscure.[7] For *alterín alla uéthé* etc. II.21, see below.

This range of possibly nine different types of structure, then, amply demonstrates how diverse and varied the structure of Gaelic place-names had already become by the first half of the twelfth century, and is obviously significant for the chronology of Gaelic place-names.

---

3 Following Jackson's view of *Madchor* as a masc. personal name, here in the genitive (1972, 132, 141, 145). **4** The term 'holding' is used neutrally. **5** Jackson (1972, 33) translates this name as 'the field of *Toiche Teimne*'. **6** Jackson (1972, 34) translates 'and two davochs of upper *Ros abard*', as though 'upper' had a contrastive function similar to the post-positional adjective *úachtarach* 'upper'; *rósábard* is in genitival relationship to the noun *uactaír*. **7** For *aldín alenn*, see Taylor, this volume.

THE FORMULAE

Two main formulae are used to identify the location of grants of land or grants of dues in connection with land. The first is where named features are used to demarcate the intended area in a phrase 'from *x* up to *y*' or 'from *x* as far as *y*' with the prepositions *ua* and *gonice*. This formula is used in the case of the first two grants mentioned: *úaćloic intiprat gonice chloic pette mec garnaít* I.13; and *úaorti níce fúrené* II.1.

The second and commoner formula then follows. Here the name of the place granted is cited directly and occurs in accusative position as direct object of a finite verb (which is invariably the 3rd person singular or 3rd person plural of the perfect, as preterite, of *do-beir* 'gives'): *dorat pett mec garnaít 7áchád toche temní* II.3; *dorat pett inmulenn* II.7; *dorat áchád naglerec* II.8; *doratsat bidbín* II.10; *dorat indelerc* II.14; *dorat pett malduíb* II.14; *dorat ... étdanin* II.23; *dóratsat petmec cóbrig* III.2; and *dorat acchad madchór* V.3. In one instance two davochs' worth are specified and the place-name therefore follows in the genitive: *dorat ... dá dabég uactaír rósábard* II.11. In another instance, the location (*ipet ipúir*) of the place granted (*báll dómin*) is also given: *Dorat ... báll dómin ipet ipúir* IV.1.

Towards the end of the property records, the formula with *gonice* is again used, but here the point of departure is implied, not stated: *do|rat goníge sća|li merlec* V.13, presumably from the starting point of the boundary of Auchmachar, the contiguous property granted in the previous record (*acchad madchór* V.3); and, with the only logical point of reference being the monastery itself, *dó|rat ... gonige ingort|he mór* V.18.

alterín alla uéthé na [?][8]

This forms part of an intriguing passage: *doratsator alterín alla uéthé | na [?] gonice in• béith edarda álterin* (II.21). Jackson (1972, 34.18–20) translates as follows (the forms in parentheses are my additions): '[they] gave Altrie (using the later form of the name) of the cliff (*alla*) of the birch-tree (*uéthé*) of the river-bend? (*na [?]*) as far as the birch-tree (*gonice in• béith*) between the two Altries (*edarda álterin*)'. In his own notes on the text, Jackson apparently looks upon '*Alla Uethe na Camss*[?]*e*' as a name (in the genitive) in its own right (1972, 56).

Jackson's translation hinges to a large extent upon the interpretation of *uéthé* at the end of the first line. It seems to me, however, that the inherent difficulties in the logic of the passage as translated here—there is one birch-tree too many—demand that we try to find a more satisfactory interpretation. Unless, that is, one allows for *ex nomine* units, by translating for example 'Altrie of (genitive) *alla uéthé* of the [?]' or 'Altrie of (genitive) *alla* of (genitive) *uéthé*

8 For a discussion of the possible readings here, see Ó Maolalaigh, this volume. Jackson's reading (1972, 24–6, 56–7) is a tentative *camsse*, taken as genitive singular of *camus* 'bend in

na [?]'. The latter attempt in fact makes more sense of the lenition in *uéthé* (i.e. a lenited genitive of *beith*) although it would be a very early example of the lenition of a place-name in the genitive in this way.

There is perhaps an alternative solution. In the MS, at the end of the line (fol.4r line 7), Jackson says that 'five letters (or perhaps four arranged in two twos with a gap between) seem to have been written and then rubbed out; they are extremely faint and are not now legible' (1972, 24).[9] Assuming that these letters were originally significant, the suggested alternative involves the following reconstruction: ... *uéthé*[*prat*] | *na* [?] *gonice in• béith edarda álterin*, with a prepositional phrase *ua thiprat, literally 'from the well of the ? up to or as far as the birch between the two Altries'.

Although there are difficulties with regard to the orthography, notwithstanding variation in the text, this reading shows a correspondence with the first of the formulae described above, as in the example *úaćloic intiprat gonice chloíc pette mec garnaít* 'from the stone of the well up to or as far as **cloc pette mec garnaít*' I.13.

The question of *alla*, Jackson's 'of the cliff', remains. It is evident that there were two Altries and, given the demarcation (from the monastery's perspective) of 'from *tiprat na [?] up to or as far as the birch between the two Altries', the land in fact granted would seem to be *this* Altrie, the Altrie *on this side*, i.e. the one on this side of the birch-tree. *Alla*, then, would be in error for *alle*, variant of *ille illei* 'over here, on this side; hither' (Thurneysen 1946, §§483, 845), which is also attested in 16th century name-forms from Lewis: for example *Pabble illé* beside *Pabble*; *Knockillé* beside *Knock* (Stone 1991, 45). The restored text, then (*doratsator alterín alla uéthé*[*prat*] | *na* [?] *gonice in• béith edarda álterin*), would translate as '[they] gave *this* Altrie from the well of the ? up to the birch-tree between the two Altries'.[10]

In conclusion, there seems nothing remarkable about the use of the formulae found in the property records in the Book of Deer, unless it is their consistency. They are appropriate attempts to define real spaces—real places—either by using an existing place-name whose onomastic meaning corresponds to the given area, or by delimiting that area within the bounds of other locations which are defined either by name or by appellative.

REFERENCES

Jackson, K. H., (1972) *The Gaelic Notes in the Book of Deer*, Cambridge.
Stone, J., (1991) *Illustrated maps of Scotland from Blaeu's Altas Novus of the 17th Century*, London.
Thurneysen, R., (1946) *A grammar of Old Irish*, Dublin (rev. ed. 1975).

a river'.   9 Only the rubbing out, not the number of letters, seems to be discernible from the image of the MS at my disposal.   10 *Tiprat na [?] may have been a place-name in its own right, of course.

The property records in the Book of Deer as a source for early Scottish society[1]

DAUVIT BROUN

It is a familiar irony that our written sources for society before the onset of 'Europeanisation' in the twelfth century are preponderantly Latin charters which were themselves an important dimension of the process of Europeanisation (Bartlett 1993, 283–8; Broun 1995, 46–7). The principal exception to this is the property records which were written onto blank pages and margins in the Book of Deer sometime between c.1130 and c.1150. They are unique in Scotland in the central Middle Ages in that all but one of them are wholly in Gaelic (bar the odd snippet of Latin). They include, moreover, the only intact examples of Scottish property-records written in a form which precedes the adoption of charters.[2] The later records in the Book of Deer, in fact, belong to a transitional phase, betraying a growing consciousness of Latin charters, with scribes C and D incorporating witness lists introduced by the Latin phrase *testibus istis*, and scribe E writing a Latin charter itself (albeit with some unusual features) (Broun 2000, 117–18). A few of the transactions documented in the Deer records, however, occurred much earlier:[3] there are grants by Mael

1 I am very grateful to Dr John Bannerman, Professor G.W.S. Barrow, Dr Stephen Boardman, Professor Thomas Owen Clancy, Prof. A.A.M. Duncan, David Sellar, Dr Simon Taylor and Alex Woolf for reading earlier (much longer!) drafts of this piece and offering very helpful comment and criticism. Any errors of fact or judgement are, of course, my own. I am also very grateful to Dr Nerys Ann Jones for her constant support and encouragement.   2 Some 'pre-charter' property-records exist relating to the Céli Dé of Loch Leven, but these survive only as a Latin translation of Gaelic originals (Broun 1995, 32).   3 It has been suggested (Barrow 1997, 131 n. 3) that the pre-twelfth-century transactions (no.II) must have been copied from contemporary notes. If a collection of such notes ever existed, it might be compared with *codices traditionum* (or *Traditionsbücher*, as defined in Geary 1994, 82). It has been argued convincingly that *Traditionsbücher* had a historical and sacred role as well as the more obvious function of securing property rights in a legal or administrative sense (Geary 1994, 86, citing Molitor 1990: for a discussion in English of a particular example, see Hecht 2000). The small scale of II (compared to *Traditionsbücher*) and the limited nature of its items does not, however, necessarily require the existence of texts in order to explain the source of scribe A's information; the names of the donors and their donations could have been remembered by oral means, reinforced in a liturgical context. Nonetheless, it might be useful to see scribe A's work (I and II) as belonging in general terms to the genre of *Traditionsbücher* (there are *Traditionsbücher* and early cartularies which include accounts of origins: see Geary 1994, 92). The immediate inspiration for the Deer records could perhaps also be compared with those early cartularies produced in response to the transfer of Bavaria to Carolingian rule (Geary 1994, 90–3): the parallel here with Deer would include not only a dramatic change in the political

Coluim mac Cinaeda (d. 1034) and Mael Coluim mac Maíl Brigte (d. 1029), and the possibility cannot be ruled out that other transactions are older still.[4]

It is no surprise that, since the rediscovery of the Book of Deer in 1860, these property-records have attracted the attention of scholars as a source for Scottish society before the twelfth century. It might be wondered, more than 140 years later, whether anything of significance could possibly be added to what has already been said. The texts, moreover, are brief: the records fill a mere three pages in Jackson's edition, and there are less than 150 entries in Jackson's glossarial index (Jackson 1972, 30–2, 153–62). There is, however, a methodological problem which has never been addressed. No study, to date, has examined the records without being strongly influenced by ideas about early Scottish society conceived by scholars unaware of the Book of Deer itself. Because the records are without parallel as an historical source in a Scottish context, it was quite natural that the first full-scale analysis of the information on social organisation that may be gleaned from the Deer records (Stuart 1869) looked to the most recent work on early Scottish society for guidance; it was also natural that this in turn should have influenced the only other detailed examination of this aspect of the records (Jackson 1972). It is, however, precisely because the Deer records are so exceptional that, to maximise their potential as a source for Scottish society, they need initially to be studied free from any preconceptions about the structure of that society.

The idea which has exerted the greatest influence on the way the Deer records have been interpreted as evidence for early Scottish society is that there was a hierarchy of local and regional officials under the king. In the first part of this paper the history of this idea and its relationship with the Deer records will be traced, beginning with the generation of scholars whose work spanned the period before and after the rediscovery of the Book of Deer. It will be argued that a pivotal role was played by Jackson's study, published in 1972, which put the notion of a royal administrative hierarchy on a new footing with the Deer records at centre stage. This means that the core business of this paper—a fresh examination of the Deer records, free from existing notions about the nature of Scottish society—has the potential not only to open up new ways of interpreting the texts, but also to undermine a key element in the current consensus about the organisation of the Scottish

---

landscape (the fall of the ruling order of Moray following the defeat and death of Oengus mac ingen Lulaig in 1130) but also the effort to obtain confirmation of previous grants by the new secular power (VII: the charter of David I). For a more detailed (and different) assessment of what inspired the records, however, see below. 4 It has been suggested (Jackson 1972, 47–8) that Domnall son of Giric in record no. II could, because of the rarity of the name *Giric*, be a son of King Giric who succeeded Aed, king of the Picts, in 878. Unfortunately, named individuals from Gaelic Scotland in this period are themselves rare in extant records, so it is impossible to say with any conviction whether a name would have been particularly unusual.

kingdom before Europeanisation. Although a key conclusion of this paper is that Jackson's reading of the records is unsustainable, it will need to be left to another occasion before it can be seen how this might relate to social organisation on a broader front than the area of central Buchan with which the Deer records are immediately concerned.

THE DEER RECORDS AND THE CONSTRUCTION OF THE EARLY SCOTTISH STATE, 1860–2000

The administrative system envisaged by Jackson is most clearly revealed in his account of the technical term *cuit* in the Deer records (which can be translated 'portion' or 'share', although there are other possibilities, discussed below, 350). He explained this as referring to 'the dues and services liable to be rendered by the tenants of the estates named, to the king, and also to the mormaer and the toísech under whose authority they were, not as landlord but in virtue of their office' (Jackson 1972, 119). One of the official tasks of *mormaer* and *toísech*, according to Jackson, was the collection of royal revenue (Jackson 1972, 109, 113). The 'portion' (*cuit*) respectively of king, *mormaer* and *toísech* was therefore taken by him to mean that 'each of these ranks and officers was entitled to his own 'cut' from the estates concerned, in the form of taxes and services; and every piece of land was liable to these payments unless remitted' (Jackson 1972, 119). He made a case for seeing *mormaer* and *toísech* as 'inherited from the Pictish system of administration' (Jackson 1972, 108: see also 113–14, 117), and so made it possible to see this system as much older than the Deer records, and to regard it as a peculiar feature of Scottish society north of the Forth.[5]

Jackson presented this hierarchy of royal officials as based firmly on the evidence of the Deer records. Its roots, however, lie in scholarship conducted in ignorance of the Book of Deer itself. An important preliminary was the early work of W.F. Skene (1809–92) in which he referred to 'maormors' (*sic*) as both 'leaders of great tribes' and regional 'governors'; he also saw the *toísech* (whom he identified as the oldest cadet of a chiefly kindred) as typically the 'maor or steward' collecting the revenues due to the chief (Skene 1837 i, 79–83, 174–6). This was followed by the comprehensive account by E. William Robertson (1815–74) of the 'consolidation and compactness' of Scottish government before the twelfth century (Robertson 1862: quotation from i, 106). Although Robertson's *magnum opus* was published shortly after the Book of Deer had come to light, he only became aware of its existence very late in the day, too late for it to have any influence on the ideas about the

---

5 Jackson was not, however, the first to regard the Deer records as evidence for Pictish social organisation: see, for example, Mackie 1964, 34.

organisation of early Scottish society he articulated in his book. His discussion of the Deer records was therefore limited to a long footnote (Robertson 1862 ii, 499–501). At the heart of Robertson's conception of royal administration was the *mormaer*, who in his eyes was 'no other than a greater thane' (Robertson 1862 ii, 467–8). Robertson regarded the *mormaer* as responsible for collecting royal dues in a province, retaining a portion for himself, while 'maors or thanes' collected these dues within their thanages (Robertson 1862 i, 103–6). His principal evidence was not only his interpretation of *mormaer* as consisting of two elements, *mór* ('great') and *maer* ('steward') (hence 'Lord High Steward': Robertson 1862 i, 104), but his keen awareness of Continental and English parallels, such as the *ealdormenn* in England who administered the king's dues and services in the shires, retaining a third for themselves.

Robertson's model exercised a profound influence on how the Deer records were interpreted in the first extensive historical commentary on them, which appeared as part of the first edition of the Book of Deer, published in 1869 by John Stuart (1813–77). For example, when Stuart came to interpret the *cuit* of the *mormaer*, he described this as the 'interest of the mormaer in the lands ... ; probably consisting of that part of the royal returns which fell to him', having already explained that the mormaer possessed 'an official title ... to a share of the royal dues, for which, as steward, he accounted to the King of Alba' (Stuart 1869, lxxix). Stuart made no bones about his debt to Robertson, especially in his discussion of *mormaer* and *toísech* (Stuart 1869, lxxvi–lxxxi), in which he often quoted Robertson at length (e.g. Stuart 1869, lxxvi, lxxviii, lxxxi n.1, which have substantial quotations from Robertson 1862 i, 107, ii 469, and i, 104n respectively).

Robertson's model does not offer a completely satisfactory guide to the Deer records, however. A particular problem is how to interpret *toísech*. This term appears in the Deer records in the context of the *cuit* of a *toísech* and in *toísech clainne* 'head of a (noble) kindred': no mention is made of a *maer* or thane. There is no tidy way of reconciling this with Robertson's administrative hierarchy. Two possible approaches to Deer's *toísech* immediately come to mind. First, it might seem logical, if *cuit* was taken to represent a portion of royal revenue retained by the *mormaer* as a regional royal official, to explain the *cuit* of a *toísech* in the Deer records as evidence that *toísech* was a term for the local royal official (Robertson's *maer* or thane); but this would leave *toísech clainne* unexplained. Alternatively, the *toísech* who received *cuit* could be identified with *toísech clainne* (head of a noble kindred)—which would, ostensibly, suggest that whatever was meant by the term *cuit*, it would have to have been a function of lordship appropriate to the head of a kindred. It would follow from this that *cuit* would no longer have the potential on its own to conjure up visions of a hierarchy of royal officials: it would merely signify some aspect of lordship which could be exercised by the king and *mormaer* as well as a *toísech* in a kin-based society.

The first historians to be confronted by the Book of Deer did not draw attention to this problem in the records. They were already embroiled in a dispute about the nature of *toísech* and thane which they had inherited from an earlier generation of scholars.[6] By 1860 all were generally agreed that *toísech* was in some sense the 'Celtic' precursor of the 'Saxon' thane. But that was as far as consensus went. Every logical possibility of the relationship between *toísech* and thane was advocated by one of the key figures in the world of Scottish history from the late 1850s to the 1870s. Was *toísech* a 'tribal chief' who, with the increase in royal authority and onset of 'Saxon' influence from the late eleventh century, became a royal official, called a thane? Or was *toísech* already the Gaelic term for a royal official, who under 'Saxon' influence became known as a thane, holding his position heritably by charter? Alternatively, were thanes royal officials at all? Was 'thane' simply the *toísech*, as 'tribal chief', in a new guise, placed on a new legal footing under 'Saxon' influence? The debate was fuelled by different approaches to the evidence of legal texts and charters, and by drawing different comparisons with similar social structures furth of Scotland. The Deer records, once they became available, were largely treated as a small additional element to the established range of sources, serving chiefly to increase the supply of named individuals who were known to have been *mormaer* or *toísech*.[7] Scholars otherwise tended to see the appearance of *toísech* in the Deer records only in the light of their own view on this issue, which (with the notable exception of W.F. Skene) remained unchanged in its essentials throughout their careers. It is perhaps not surprising, therefore, that no detailed examination of *toísech* in the Deer records was undertaken by the leading historians of the day in the 1860s and 1870s as part of the wider debate.

Robertson himself rejected the possibility that *toísech* was simply the thane-as-royal-official in an earlier Gaelic guise. Before he was aware of the Book of Deer, he saw the *toísech* as leader of the tribal host, a separate function of government from the tribe's hereditary head which could be traced back to the Gauls (Robertson 1862 i, 26–7). He recognised that there were circumstances in which a thane might also be a *toísech*, but he was careful to explain (in a passage reminiscent of Skene 1837, i, 174–5) that, 'though the oldest cadet, and the thane in his military capacity, were known as *Toshachs*, it

---

6 Innes referred for support of his definition of thane to Thomas Thomson (1768–1852) (Innes 1872, 83), and Skene, preferring a different interpretation, quoted James Macpherson (1736–96) for a definition of *toísech* (Skene. 1837 i, 175). Lord Hailes (1726–92) regarded it as probable that some thanes became earls in the reign of Mael Coluim III (1058–93) (Dalrymple 1776 (1819), 28); George Chalmers (1742–1825), however, declared that it was impossible for 'the Saxon policy of Thanes to have existed, during the Celtic government of North Britain' (Chalmers 1810, 456, 716). 7 There was a tendency, indeed, to regard every donor in the Deer records (apart from Mael Coluim mac Cinaeda, king of Alba) as either a *mormaer* or *toísech*: e.g. Skene 1880, 55–8.

by no means follows that a *Toshach* was necessarily either one or the other'
(Robertson 1862, i, 104n). When confronted at the eleventh hour with *toísech*
in the Deer records, he regarded it as standing on a par with the *mormaer* as an
example of 'divided, or double, authority so observable amongst the Celts'
(Robertson 1862, ii, 499). Stuart offered nothing new: his dependence on
Robertson was such that he simply repeated Robertson's words in denying any
necessary link between *toísech* and the office of thane (Stuart 1869, lxxxi, n.1).
When Robertson himself returned to this issue in an essay published in 1872,
he elaborated on his previous discussion, focusing more on the central and
later middle ages. He explained how the *toísech* developed into the thane, but
still preserved his original position that the two were not strictly identical,
even though he regarded it as common for the headship of a kindred and the
office of thane to have been held by the same person. He proposed that the
thane, 'essentially a royal official', belonged to a 'somewhat different state of
society' to the *toísech*, whom he described as 'resembling the Irish captain, or
the Elect of the kindred confirmed in his authority by the sovereign' (Robertson
1872, 162). He envisaged that, when 'tenure by charter superseded the earlier
system in Scotland … so may the Toshach have been converted into a thane
by resigning his elective seniority, and accepting it from the sovereign as a gift
by charter of the Crown' (Robertson, 1872, 162–3). He was careful to point
out, however, that not all thanes were necessarily converted *toísig* (Robertson
1872, 165).

It was left to Cosmo Innes (1798–1874) to champion the proposition that
toísech was originally an administrative post. To begin with he was slightly
hesitant. He noticed a reference to a 'Fionnlagh Tòiseach thane of Glentilt'
(*Finlayus Toschoch thanus de Glentelt*) in a charter of the earl of Atholl in 1502
(Paul 1882, no. 2655), and suggested (albeit tentatively) that Fionnlagh's
surname was due to his position as thane, and was therefore evidence that
tòiseach was Gaelic for thane (Innes 1837a, xxviii n.a). The year before the
rediscovery of the Book of Deer, however, he gave a much more confident
account of his understanding of *toísech* and its relationship to the Scottish
thane, declaring that 'the inquirer into the history of Scotch Thanes must
begin with discharging from his mind everything that has been written on the
subject' (Innes 1859, x, n.1). As far as he was concerned, the change from
toísech to thane was simply the formalisation of an existing position coupled
with a change in language. 'The administrator of the Crown lands, the
collector of rents, the magistrate and head man of a little district, known
among his Celtic neighbours as the "Toshach", took a charter of the whole
district from the Sovereign, whereby he became, under the Saxon name of
Thane, hereditary tenant … preserving all his ancient authority now
strengthened and legalized' (Innes 1859, x). Innes republished this discussion
of *toísech* and thane within a year of first learning of the Book of Deer (Innes

1861, 396–7). His view was not apparently informed in any way by more prolonged acquaintance with the Deer records, however. It is true that, in his introduction to the first publication of facsimiles of the Book of Deer, he referred briefly to *toísech* as an official who became known as a thane (Innes 1867, viii). But in his most extended discussion of the topic, published in 1872, he confined himself to late-medieval evidence (Innes 1872, 79–84), repeating his conviction that 'the Gaelic toschach is equivalent to our Scotch thane', who he described as an 'administrator or steward' (Innes 1872, 80–1).

When Innes instructed his readers to delete from their memory everything written hitherto on the subject of thanes, he referred in particular to 'the foolish fictions of lawyers like Skene and historians like Boece'. The Skene he referred to here was Sir John Skene (1543–1617); and, although Innes did not identify what it was that Skene had written which merited such disdain, a contrary view to Innes's can be found, for example, in Skene's commentary on the oldest Scottish legal texts. Here Skene explained that thane is a title (*nomen dignitatis*) equivalent to son of an earl, and that thane is 'Tosche' in Gaelic, as in 'Maktosche', 'who today is ruler of the tribe or family of Clanchattan'[8] (Skene, J. 1609, 102). The inference that a thane was essentially a 'tribal chief' rather than a royal official was not confined to writers in the sixteenth century.[9] Sir John Skene's statement was partially quoted as an authority by his descendant, W.F. Skene, in his first discussion of thanes and *toísig* since the rediscovery of the Book of Deer (Skene 1872, 447), and again when W.F. Skene adapted this material in the final volume of his *Celtic Scotland* published in 1880 (Skene 1880, 216 n.12).[10] W.F. Skene was aware that the idea that thanes 'were merely crown officers or stewards appointed to levy the crown dues' was generally accepted by scholars of his day, but declared that he had 'never been able to accept the theory' (Skene 1880, 239 n.62). His own position on *toísech* had, however, changed significantly from his earlier conviction that the term denoted the eldest cadet in a chiefly family (Skene 1837 i, 175; see also Macbain 1897, 197–8, 200). His new ideas about *toísech* do not appear, however, to have been provoked by any familiarity with the Deer records, but seem to have emerged from his more all-embracing work on thanes and thanages in which Sir John Skene was his guiding light (see e.g. Skene 1880, 239 n.62). W.F. Skene now maintained that *toísech* was essentially the leader of a 'tribe' (which he equated with the Irish *túath*), but explained that, under the increasing influence and power of the Crown from the late eleventh century, the *toísech* was transformed into the thane, and the

---

8 *Qui hodie est Princeps tribus, seu familiæ Catanæorum (Clanchattan).* 9 Although Skene's work was not published until 1609, he had been working on this material since the mid-1570s: see MacQueen 1995, 16. 10 The part quoted was where 'Tosche' was identified as Gaelic for thane: it is clear from the context of these quotations that W.F. Skene understood this to refer to a 'tribal chief'.

tribe (or *túath*) into a thanage (Skene 1872, 446–9; Skene 1880, 215–16, 238–9, 281–2).[11] The *mormaer*, 'the head of the aggregate of tribes forming a province', likewise became an earl (Skene 1872, 446–7; see also Skene 1880, 215–16). He was happy to recognise that thane and *toísech* were equivalent terms (referring to the same family of Tòiseach, thanes of Glentilt, as did Innes: Skene 1872, 447; see also Skene 1880, 272–4), but took this as evidence that the thane was not an administrative official of the Crown. Indeed, he regarded the root meaning of thane (Old English *thegn*, from *thegnian* 'to serve') as a salutory example of how 'the etymology of a word which has come to be used in a technical sense, is a very unsafe guide to its subsequent application' (Skene 1872, 457). He approached the etymology of *mormaer* in similar vein, acknowledging that *mormaer* represented *mór maer* (which he translated as 'great Maer or steward'), but without reading anything particular into this, insisting merely that the 'office, whatever it was', was hereditary according to the custom of tanistry (Skene 1880, 49–56).

Because Skene refused to regard *toísech* and *mormaer* as part of an administrative structure under the king, he alone was able to provide an interpretation of the Deer records which had the merit of being internally consistent. He achieved this because he was prepared to regard *cuit* (as in the *cuit* 'portion', of *toísech*, *mormaer* and king) in a different light from Stuart. He recognised *cuit* as the 'share in definite proportions' of all common burdens (food renders, hospitality and military service) due to *toísech*, *mormaer* and king (Skene 1872, 456; Skene 1880, 236),[12] but did not understand this as forming an administrative hierarchy, with *toísech* acting as collector for *mormaer* and *mormaer* for king.[13] Rather, he envisaged the *toísech*, leader of the 'tribe or clan' in his territory, as the bottom rung in 'a gradation of persons possessing territorial rights' (Skene 1880, 57–8; see also generally Skene 1872, 458). To his mind *toísech* and *mormaer* formed a social hierarchy which only fell directly under royal power at the onset of 'feudalism'.[14]

It is little wonder, given that Skene's understanding of *toísech* was the only one on offer which sat easily with the evidence of the Deer records, that his interpretation was favoured by Alexander Macbain (1855–1907), the next

11 Note, however, that Skene did not apparently regard every thane as necessarily the successors of a *toísech* (Skene 1872, 418; and, with a different explanation of Fordun's *principes* who held thanages, Skene 1880, 239–40). 12 Skene was aware of the term *cuid oidhche* (referring to a night's hospitality owed to a lord), but associated it with the common burden of obligatory hospitality (known in medieval Gaelic as *coinnmed*, Scots *conveth*, and English 'waiting'): Skene 1872, 453–4, Skene 1880, 232–4. 13 He understood that every thanage had a *maer* (Skene 1880, 279–81). 14 When, according to his scheme, thanages became crown land, the *toísech*/thane began to contribute a share of the produce in the form of *cáin* to the king—a situation which Skene saw as readily capable of assimilation to feudal tenure, with the *cáin* regarded as annual feu-duty (Skene 1880, 238–9). As for the *mormaer*, when his territory became crown land, it was held on the same terms as barons held baronies, without paying *cáin* or feu-duty (Skene 1880, 63–4).

scholar who focused specifically on the records as a source for early Scottish society. Macbain followed Skene in all essentials when he came to describe the social hierarchy of king, *mormaer* and *toísech*, and repeated Skene's view that thane was an equivalent term for *toísech* meaning 'a tribal or district chieftain' (Macbain 1885, 140, 151).[15] Skene's theory of the relationship between *toísech* and thane did not, however, gain general acceptance. Indeed, as far as subsequent generations of historians were concerned, the cumulative legacy of Innes, Robertson, Skene and Stuart on the structure of early Scottish society was one of confusion and uncertainty. Hume Brown (1850–1918),[16] for example, favoured a combination of Innes and Robertson, but without showing much confidence in the matter (Brown 1899 i, 45–6). After describing *mormaír* as originally 'representing the authority of the king in the respective provinces assigned to them', he went on to note that 'under the mormaers were certain officials known as *toisechs*, of whose precise character we know even less', whose duties may have been 'chiefly military; though at a later period he appears to have been a kind of "ground-officer" and "sheriff-officer" in one'. His final comment was that 'by analogy and conjecture we may fill up this general framework; but of the precise conditions, political and social, under which king and mormaer discharged their respective functions, no contemporary authority enables us to speak with any certainty'. James Mackinnon (1860–1945)[17] shared this gloomy conclusion about the state of knowledge on this issue, but in his discussion produced a slightly different cocktail of earlier scholarship by juxtaposing Skene and Robertson (confused partly with Innes) (Mackinnon 1924, 70–1). He noted initially that *mormaer* and *toísech* in the Book of Deer referred respectively to 'ancient territorial rulers' and 'the head of the tribe or district', but commented that 'we know … nothing very definite as to the function of either'. He then referred to the possibility that these represented an administrative hierarchy, attributing this to Robertson (but, in fact, merging Robertson's general idea with Innes's specific argument that *toísech* was an official).

By the 1960s the leading Scottish historians of the day had continued the process of merging Skene, Robertson and Innes into an indistinguishable brew—served (as ever) in an atmosphere of doubt and apprehension. W. Croft Dickinson (1897–1963)[18] suggested that the *toísech* was 'possibly the head of a family group, though later identified with the thane' who, in the reign of David I had certainly become a royal official, commenting that 'there is not sufficient evidence to prove that these thanes were the old Celtic toisechs with

15 The next discussion of social structure which focused specifically on the Deer records was also simply a summary of Skene's views, but did not look wider to consider thanes: Kemp 1927, 172. 16 Professor of Scottish History at Edinburgh University from 1901, and Historiographer Royal from 1908. 17 Professor of Ecclesiastical History at Edinburgh University, 1908–30. 18 Professor of Scottish History at Edinburgh University, 1944–63.

their rights and duties more clearly defined, though such a theory has much to commend it'; he was more certain, however, that the *mormaer* was probably 'the head of a province' (Dickinson 1963, 61, 67). J.D. Mackie (1887–1978),[19] for his part, attempted a curious amalgam of earlier hypotheses by proposing that 'possibly the 'thane', though he later developed into a laird, was at first an officer, half royal servant and half landowner, who looked after a portion of the king's land', and that thanages 'may, though not certainly, represent the holdings of the old toiseachs' (Mackie 1964, 55–6, 67). He also commented that in the Deer records, which he regarded as 'a good piece of evidence as to the land system of ancient Pictland', there were gifts given by 'a Mormaer (earl) who may represent the old provincial chief and by a 'Toiseach' who may be equated with the later 'Thane'' (Mackie 1964, 34).[20] An important exception to this climate of uncertainty tinged with confusion was an elegant reformulation of Innes's position by Geoffrey Barrow in his *Feudal Britain*. He argued that the likely introduction of thanes 'managing the estates of the king or some other great lord', which he dated to no later than the eleventh century, 'was made easy by the presence north of the Forth of a Celtic officer, the *toisech* (literally "first" or "chief"), not dissimilar to the thane in function' (Barrow 1956, 133, 232).

The idea of an administrative hierarchy seemed to recede even further, moreover, when the etymology of *mormaer* as 'great steward' was undermined. This was especially unsettling because the etymology of *mormaer* was one of the few key details apon which Innes, Robertson and Skene were agreed (even if they did not all attach the same significance to this). It was noticed that Modern Gaelic *morair*, 'lord', which derives from *mormaer*, was unlikely to have assumed this form if the first syllable had been long, as in *mór maer* (Matheson 1948, 67; and Anderson 1948, 40). If the first syllable had been short, then *mormaer* would be analysed as *mor maer*, 'sea steward'.[21] Whereas 'Great Steward' had the potential to conjure up a vision of a high-ranking official with subordinates, 'Sea Steward' was an altogether less certain prospect.

It was to this scene of deepening uncertainty that Jackson turned his attention in his seminal study. He performed a remarkable intellectual feat, taking hold of the disparate strands bequeathed by Robertson/Stuart and

---

19 Professor of Scottish History at Glasgow University, 1930–57. **20** Perhaps such confusion and uncertainty was partly because the discussion of *toísech* and *mormaer* in the most recent detailed treatment of the Deer records available to Dickinson and Mackie (Cameron 1937, esp. 230–3) was itself an uncritical blend of Skene, Robertson and Innes, garnished with some curious misconceptions. **21** This was first suggested in Watson 1915, index, s.v. *morbhair* (whence Mackinnon 1924, 70 n.35). For *mor* as a compositional form of *muir*, 'sea', compare *Moireabh*, Moray, where *mor* is combined with *treabh*, 'settlement' and *A' Mhorbhairn*, Morvern, with *bearn*, 'gap' as the second element: Watson 1926, 115, 123; instances of *mor*, rather than *muir* or *mur*, as the compositional form of *muir* were brusquely dismissed by Jackson (1972, 107) as 'secondary Sc.G. deformations'.

Innes and working these into a compelling synthesis which, for the first time, had the Deer records themselves standing firmly in the foreground. His achievement was based on new explanations of *toísech* and *mormaer*. For *toísech* he advocated a daring solution. He adopted Innes's understanding that both *toísech* and thane were officials (Jackson 1972, 112–13),[22] but at the same time accepted the idea (favoured by Robertson and Stuart) that *toísech* represented the head of an aristocratic kindred. He brought off this mix of seemingly incompatible positions by arguing that two kinds of *toísech* are witnessed in the Deer records: the thane[23] and the head of a kindred. For *mormaer* Jackson worked out an ingenious alternative progression to *morair* (Jackson 1972, 108) which made it possible, again, to translate this term as 'great steward'. With the credibility of *mór maer*, 'great steward', restored, Jackson (and others) have, like Robertson and Stuart before them, regarded this etymology as sufficient evidence that the *mormaer* was a high-ranking administrative agent of the Crown (Jackson 1972, 109; see also Bannerman 1993, 38; Barrow 1973, 67–8; Grant 2000, 65).

Jackson did not present his analysis as indebted to Robertson or Stuart, and in only one instance did he explicitly acknowledge Innes (when he required a brief account of the functions of a thane: Jackson 1972, 113 n.1). Nevertheless, it must be doubted whether he would have expended so much effort on denying the derivation of *morair* from *mor maer* ('sea steward') if he had not been aware both of the earlier suggestion that *mormaer* signified 'great steward', and of the way this had been used by Stuart to explain the otherwise unique references to the *cuit* of the *mormaer* in the Deer records. With ruthless logic, Jackson insisted that if *cuit* denoted the share of royal dues when it was used of a king or *mormaer*, then it must mean the same thing when applied to a *toísech* who must, therefore, in this context represent a royal official, not the leader of a kindred. As a result, the Deer records were, at last, fully integrated into Robertson's model of a hierarchical administrative structure under the king. There is no indication, however, that Jackson was aware of Skene's views. None of Skene's works are referred to by him, and none appear in his bibliography of previous work on the Deer records (which includes discussions as well as editions and translations) (Jackson 1972, viii–xi).[24]

22 Although Jackson did not refer to Innes directly for the equation of *toísech* and thane, he did refer to Innes 1872, 80, for his description of thane, which is immediately preceded by Innes's assertion that *toísech* was the Gaelic term for thane.   23 Jackson was undecided about how to explain the correspondence between *toísech* and thane. He considered it possible either that *toísech* 'was really the Anglo-Saxon thane borrowed and accommodated with a vaguely appropriate Gaelic title', or that *toísech* was identified with thane as part of a process of Anglicisation, 'whether the correspondence was exact or only partial' (Jackson 1972, 113–14).   24 The early part of the bibliography is, in fact, based on Fraser 1938, 51–2. In Jackson's defence it might be pointed out that he would have gained little idea of the significance of Skene's treatment of *toísech* or the Deer records themselves if he went no further than consulting the inadequate indices in Skene 1872 and Skene 1880. Also, he

Jackson's study has been enormously influential, featuring regularly in accounts of society in pre-twelfth century eastern Scotland (e.g. Duncan 1975, 109–10; Driscoll 1988, 221; Whyte 1995, 10–11, 15; Hudson 1996, 153). Key elements, moreover, have been approved by subsequent scholars. His proposal that there are two different kinds of *toísech* in the Deer records—an administrative *toísech* as well as a *toísech clainne*, head of a kindred—has been endorsed and elaborated by Grant (Grant 1993, 42). His involved explanation of how *morair* could have developed from *mór maer* has been greeted as 'very persuasive indeed' by Hamp (who removed any latent objection to the 'adjective + noun' word order: Hamp 1986, 138–40). Despite its elements of daring originality, however, Jackson's study is essentially the apogee of a tradition of historical scholarship which has its origins in an intellectual world innocent of the Book of Deer. Jackson put their house in order; but he did not examine the Deer records outside the confines of that house. As a result, recent scholarship on Scottish society before the onset of Europeanisation has continued to inhabit this refurbished mid-nineteenth-century structure—although not exclusively as mediated by Jackson. The other mainstay of the current consensus on the nature of early Scottish government is Barrow's seminal study of shires and thanes published the year after Jackson's work. Barrow fully acknowledged that his approach to this topic was shaped by the views of previous generations of scholars, with E. William Robertson among them. His own contribution, nonetheless, was immense, presenting a coherent picture based on fresh research which has (along with the studies of 'multiple estates' by Glanville Jones: e.g. Jones 1963, Jones 1979, Jones 1989) played a central part in modern scholarship's understanding of the operation of early forms of lordship throughout Britain (see e.g. Faith 1997, 1–14, esp. 4 and 10). Fortified by Jackson's defence of *mormaer* as 'great steward', Barrow observed at the end of his essay that 'the gradation mormaer: maer would have been formally equivalent to earl: thane, but appropriate to the period before English terms had been fully adopted', and suggested that the earlier Gaelic word for thane would thus have been *maer* (Barrow 1973, 67–8). This is, strikingly, a purer statement of Robertson's administrative hierarchy than Jackson's proposal that *toísech* was the Gaelic term for thane. It is not clear whether Barrow meant thereby to question Jackson's analysis: this has not been discussed further, by Barrow or anyone else, despite the potential here for doubt about a key element in Jackson's exposition of *toísech* in the Deer records.[25]

would not have been alerted to Skene's contribution through reading Cameron because, unfortunately, Cameron made no reference to Skene in his treatment of *toísech* and *mormaer* in the Deer records (Cameron 1937, esp. 230–3: his discussion is indebted chiefly to Innes, Robertson and Stuart, but without discussing their differences).   **25** It will be recalled that, long before Jackson, Barrow had regarded *toísech* as the most likely nearest equivalent official to the thane of later record (Barrow 1956, 133). At that stage Barrow followed the prevailing consensus that the etymology of *mormaer* was 'sea officer' (Barrow

Robertson's template for a precociously consolidated kingdom has also had 'new blood' injected into it by scholars with both an intimate knowledge of the archaeological evidence for early Scottish society and a familiarity with more general models of state formation. Some of these contributions have taken as their starting-point that Scotland was 'the only Celtic realm with well formed and independent political institutions' (Driscoll 1988, 218 and Driscoll 1991, 81, quoting Duncan 1975, 110). It has been argued that the structure of regional and local officials, as outlined by Jackson, and the nature of local lordship detailed in Barrow's work on thanages (Barrow 1973), can be matched with the tangible legacy of developing social relationships furnished by the archaeological record; looked at from this perspective, the early Scottish state (if not necessarily the terminology of *mormaer* and thane) has acquired a significantly more visible Pictish character than even Jackson supposed (Driscoll 1988, esp. 221; Foster 1996, 36, 108–9; see also Driscoll 1991). It hardly needs to be said that an archaeological perspective on early Scottish society can exist quite independently of the Deer records, or Jackson's conclusions, and that its potential should not be underestimated (Driscoll 1992).

The most significant recent discussion of the 'Robertson-Jackson' model of regional and local officials collecting royal dues, as applied to the property-records of the Book of Deer, is Grant's paper on the 'construction of the early Scottish state' (Grant 2000). This is a *tour de force* of synthesis, combining insights from Barrow's work on thanages and Jackson's analysis of the Deer records together with Benjamin Hudson's recent account of Scottish politics (Hudson 1996: but see now Woolf 2000). The result is the most original explanation of Scottish political development from the late Pictish era through to the thirteenth century since the great works of Robertson and Skene (albeit on a much smaller scale). At the heart of Grant's discussion is a realisation that the logical outcomes of Barrow's and Jackson's portrayals of the structure of early Scottish society do not fit together comfortably unless Jackson's administrative hierarchy is understood to relate to a period before any of the transactions in the Deer records had taken place. Grant, however, did not discuss a nagging doubt which naturally arises from this: to what extent can any conclusions about society be sustained by the Deer records if their evidence is significantly later?

The chief element that Grant took from Jackson was the administrative hierarchy of *mormaír* and *toísig* under the king. Grant saw this as implying 'a simple model for the local and regional structure of the early Scottish state' consisting of a 'network of multiple estates … grouped into provinces under mormaers' in which 'the main functions of government, justice and defence,

1956, 126 n. 1). His later preference for *maer* rather than *toísech* as the Gaelic equivalent of thane would appear, therefore, to represent a considered change of view on the basis of Jackson's etymology of *mormaer*.

would have operated' (Grant 2000, 55). He recognised, however, that the landscape of lordship revealed by charters and other novel kinds of document in the twelfth and thirteenth centuries showed that a *mormaer* typically held only some estates in his province, and that most of the rest were in the king's hands. This situation, he argued, probably pertained from the tenth century onwards. By that time the 'provincial model' had given way to a 'dual territorial structure' in which the king possessed estates throughout Alba, each managed by a thane, with *mormaír* retaining the remaining estates in their regions (Grant 2000, 57–63). The key underlying factor was the monopolisation of the kingship, from 900 to 1034, by Clann Chinaeda meic Ailpín, the male descendants of Cinaed mac Ailpín (d.858). Other provincial rulers were no longer in the running for the top prize: their aspirations were now confined to supporting one or other rival member of the royal dynasty in an increasingly violent (if spasmodic) competition for the throne (especially in the period 965–1005), with the result that, if they backed an unsuccessful candidate, they could lose lands to the victor, or be displaced by a supporter of the new king. In this way, in Grant's view, the Scottish kingship of the twelfth and thirteenth centuries inherited estates in provinces throughout their realm, and even some provinces in their entirety (Grant 2000, 66–70).

For Grant 'the crucial stage in the construction of the early Scottish state' was the transition to a system 'in which the land of the provinces was only partly held by the provincial rulers': the very beginning of this change may even coincide with the coining of *Alba* as the kingdom's name in (or around) 900 (Grant 2000, 65; Broun 1999a, 99–108). Grant's extrapolation from Jackson of a provincial structure undisturbed by the intrusion of royal estates is essential to his argument: without it the political development he outlined would lose its trajectory. His account of social structure as evidenced in the Deer records is, however, clearly dependent on Jackson's (Grant 2000, 54). A radical re-reading of the Deer records free from the influence of Robertson's model of the early Scottish 'state' is therefore bound to have serious implications for this most recent and impressive manifestation of Robertson's legacy.

THE NEED FOR A FRESH LOOK AT THE DEER RECORDS AS EVIDENCE FOR EARLY SCOTTISH SOCIETY

In the earliest published comments on the Deer records, Cosmo Innes declared that 'the discovery of this book sets the whole discussion which excited the Scotch antiquaries of the last century on an entirely new footing' (Innes 1860, 325). As we have seen, however, the natural response of scholars at the time was to interpret the evidence of the Deer records according to ideas they had already formulated. As a result, although the Deer records ostensibly have played a key part in sustaining a particular vision of the early

Scottish state, this owes much ultimately to Robertson (particularly through Stuart's discussion of the records), and in one key respect to Cosmo Innes. No attempt has so far been made to provide a comprehensive examination of Deer records in their own right, without any interference from Robertson's legacy. Such an attempt is the chief objective of this paper. In one respect this is long overdue. In the century preceding Jackson's study the only internally consistent interpretation of *toísech*, *mormaer*, and *cuit* in the Deer records was Skene's, based on a rejection of any notion that these terms related to an administrative hierarchy. Yet Skene's analysis has been largely forgotten by modern scholarship, and the latent challenge posed by Skene to the Jacksonian edifice has never been addressed.

The key to unlocking new perspectives on the Deer records is not, however, simply about trying, crudely and directly, to liberate our interpretation of them from the influence of nineteenth-century scholarship. Neither should it be about advancing another model of society as more appropriate than Robertson's. It is chiefly about how the Deer records themselves should be treated as evidence for property-transactions. To date there has been an unspoken assumption that they could be read as matter-of-fact statements of equal value. This may seem a perfectly reasonable supposition, particularly to the modern mind; we are so accustomed to the use of writing to describe and convey property-rights that any document which records information of this kind is almost instinctively regarded as a sufficient and transparent statement of the social realities with which it is immediately concerned. Since the publication of Michael Clanchy's seminal *From Memory to Written Record* (1979; 1993), however, it has potentially been much easier to appreciate that the Deer records are fundamentally different. This is because they are the products of a society in which writing had only a limited role in establishing property-rights. Property-transactions were expressed symbolically in public rituals, such as the handing over of earth and stone. Clanchy has commented how 'writings seem to have been thought of at first as subsidiary aids to transitional memorizing procedures and not as replacements of them', until 'by the thirteenth century documentary proof had become more familar and routine' (Clanchy 1993, 327).[26] He has summed this up as 'the gradual acceptance of literate ways of doing business' (Clanchy 1979, 232; 1993, 295). The same can be said of Scotland, where the emergence of 'literate ways of doing business' with regard to property-transactions may, in one key respect, be dated to the mid-thirteenth century: the date of the first known example of a charter preceding the transaction which it records is 1271 (Broun 1995, 13–16; Donaldson

---

26 Clanchy acknowledges that this is not an original point: see especially the comment by V.H. Galbraith: 'As late as the twelfth century the charter is a record of an oral transaction of which it formed no part … charters were still the exception, though fast becoming the rule. For by the next century the importance of ceremony and procedure waned …'

1985, 170).[27] It should not be a surprise, therefore, that early generations of charters, not produced in established writing-offices, are characterised by the 'amateur effort' of draftsmen and scribes 'to master the complexities of documentary proof for the first time' (Clanchy 1979, 231; 1993, 294). The Deer records stand only at the dawn half-light of the process of using writing in any systematic way to guarantee property-rights; indeed, had a specialised form of writing existed for this purpose, the *clerici* of Deer would not have had to resort to recording these property-transactions in a rather homespun fashion in their gospel book (Broun 2000). As Stuart so strikingly put it, 'they are destitute of the formality of charters' (Stuart 1869, lxviii).

It is not uncommon to find that property-records, written before 'literate ways of doing business' had begun to take hold, are effectively useless on their own as enduring or sufficient statements of the transaction to which they refer. This is chiefly because they have been drafted on the unconscious assumption that any point at issue could be tested and established by other, non-literate, means. A celebrated example is the charter (very likely produced on the occasion of David I's inauguration in April 1124) recording David's grant of Annandale to Robert Brus. Here we are told that Robert was to hold Annandale 'with all those customs which Ranulf Meschin ever had in Carlisle and in his land of Cumberland on that day when he had them most fully and freely' (Barrow 1999, no.16).[28] Nothing more is added to explain what these customs were. The lack of intelligible detail for anyone depending on the written word alone is noteworthy. Even more striking, however, is the reference to Ranulf Meschin, whose lordship was already a thing of the past: he had ceased to hold Carlisle and Cumberland in 1120 (Kapelle 1979, 206). This statement had no prospect of retaining its meaning for future

(Galbraith 1948, 27). **27** This is not to say that charters could not be regarded as sufficient evidence of a transaction (particularly by those responsible for their production). The point is the extent to which this had become sufficiently systematic to be a commonplace in the initiation and defence of property-rights. I am grateful to Professor Barrow for drawing to my attention the following early examples of the high value placed in charters. In one instance David I declares that 'I have seen the charter and gift of my brother King Edgar which I now send you; whatever that charter bears witness to I will that they shall have' (Barrow 1999, no.11); Baldwin lord of Biggar, sheriff of Lanark, draws the text of one of his charters to a close by declaring that 'I cause this charter to be written in the presence of responsible men. I confirm it by affixing my seal which I desire to come to the notice of all who come after. Of this charter these are the witnesses ...' (Innes 1832, 112); another example from the mid-twelfth century is when Robert Avenel is said to have 'given and chartered this land to the monks [of Melrose]' (Innes 1837b i, 30–2; see also Barrow 1995, 15). **28** It has been argued that the reference to Ranulf Meschin was because he had previously controlled Annandale when he was lord of Carlisle. The wording of the charter, though, merely requires that Ranulf's lordship was taken as a model (Scott 1997, 31). This does not detract from the important suggestion (Scott 1997, 15–24) that Carlisle should be likened to an intrusive lordship like those on the Welsh border, and that at some stage (probably in the 1090s) lower Annandale fell under its power.

generations. The nature of Robert's lordship would, we may presume, have been understood by David I and Robert Brus and those who were present at the ceremony in which Robert was established as lord of Annandale (a ceremony which, it may be inferred, had been performed when Ranulf was still in possession of Carlisle and Cumberland). Any dispute about this could have been settled by referring to the testimony of men of standing who would have had first-hand experience of the customs exercised by the lord of Annandale.

An appreciation that the Gaelic property-records in the Book of Deer are potentially ambiguous, imprecise and incomplete as explanations of the transactions they purport to describe, does not mean that they should be dismissed as a fruitlessly elusive source for the realities of lordship. The way the records are examined as evidence, however, has to be different from what would seem natural if they were regarded as straightforward statements of equal value. As a result of adopting this fresh approach, a new understanding of a range of issues will become possible, such as the 'portion' (*cuit*) of *mormaer* and *toísech*, the 'extinguishing' of church-lands, 'joint grants', and grants of settlements and of 'portions'.

RE-READING GRANTS OF PROPERTY-RIGHTS

The nature of the Deer records as an example of writing concerning property can begin to be gauged from an obvious instance of their insufficiency.[29] There are a few occasions where the bounds of a piece of land are described in some detail: 'from the stone of the well as far as the stone of the holding of the sons of Gartnait' (I), 'from the well of the bend as far as the birch tree between the two Altries' (II.12, accepting the emendations proposed by Cox elsewhere in this volume), 'as far as the large standing stone at the end of the thicket nearest *Ailldín Ailenn*, from the Black Ugie to *Lurchaire*, both enclosed and unenclosed land' (V.3). The birch-tree between the two Altries and the thicket nearest *Ailldín Ailenn* may have been well known landmarks at the time, but were unlikely to endure for generations. It is also assumed that the reader will know some of the bounds already: *gonice*, 'as far as', appears five times, but 'from where' we are meant to go 'as far as' is never explained. The scribes obviously knew what was meant by what they wrote, but they frequently did not provide enough information to allows us, centuries later, to see with any precision what they intended.

A crucial example of (slightly) imprecise drafting, it must be suspected, is the statement (II.3) that 'Matain son of Cairell gave a *mormaer*'s *cuit* in Altrie, and Culi son of Baíthín gave a *toísech*'s *cuit*'. This has been taken as evidence

29 See 136–43 for Text and translation.

that dues and services were rendered to the local *toísech* and the *mormaer* from a single settlement (Stuart 1869, lxxx–lxxxi; Jackson 1972, 119; Grant 2000, 54 and n.39). Such an interpretation rests chiefly on the assumption that *cuit* denoted the shares of general dues which were retained by *toísech* and *mormaer*. This is not immediately apparent from the records themselves. The key here is in a passage which has just been quoted (II.12), from which it is apparent that there were 'two Altries'. It would be rash on this evidence to insist that all the inhabitants of Altrie owed *cuit* to both *toísech* and *mormaer*. The existence of 'two Altries' could be explained where one part rendered *cuit* to the local *toísech* while the other part rendered *cuit* to the *mormaer*. This could readily be described as grants of a *mormaer*'s *cuit* and a *toísech*'s *cuit* 'in Altrie'.

The example of II.3 suggests that another key passage can be read differently with similar results. This is the statement (II.2) that Muiredach son of Morgann, when he gave the holding of the sons of Gartnait and the field of Teimen's inheritance/lawsuit, 'was *mormaer* and *toísech*'. This has been taken to imply that Muiredach was granting both his *mormaer*'s and his *toísech*'s 'shares' (Stuart 1869, lxxxi; see also Grant 2000, 54: Jackson 1972, 118, saw this as a simple grant of land, but did not discuss why Muiredach was described here as *mormaer* and *toísech*). But there is no immediate reason to assume that Muiredach's lordship in these two places was on the same basis, as both *mormaer* and *toísech*; he could very well have exercised lordship as *mormaer* in one of these places, and as *toísech* in the other, without any overlap 'on the ground' at all. A further point of specifying that he was *mormaer* and *toísech* may have been to emphasise that Muiredach's patronage affected his successor in each of these two capacities: at the time of writing these may not have been the same person.

There are other instances where a literal reading of the text may conceal a more complex reality. These are what seem on the face of it to have been 'joint grants'. There are Domnall son of Giric and Mael Brigte son of Cathal, who gave the *pett* of the mill (II.4); Domnall son of Ruaidrí and Mael Coluim son of Cuilén, who gave Biffie (II.6); Cainnech son of the son of Dobarchú and Cathal (son of Morgann), who gave a piece of Altrie (II.12); and Domnall and Cathal who gave *Etdane (II.13). There are also instances where a *mormaer* and his wife are both named as making a grant (III, IV). (Instances where more than one person is named as enacting an 'extinction' will be discussed in the next section.)

Jackson (1972, 118) viewed the formula 'A and B gave X' as possible evidence of joint-ownership of land. Grant (2000, 54) has been more forthright; by taking these together with grants of *cuit*, he has concluded that 'in about half the grants … the same pieces of land appear to have been given to Deer Abbey jointly by local toiseachs and mormaers'.[30] Stuart also saw a

30 This possibility was rejected by Jackson 1972, 118 n. 1. Grant appears to have assumed that all donors were either *mormair* or *toísig*.

link with *cuit* by suggesting that these should be interpreted as *mormaer* and *toísech* granting their 'shares' (Stuart 1869, li; see also Robertson 1862 ii, 499n). A more likely scenario, however, is that in each case the farmland was divided, so that there was no joint-ownership (or co-lordship) as such. Perhaps the division was into two consolidated units; or the holdings of each lord consisted of strips mixed with strips belonging to another lord within a single field. A parallel would be the grant of half of *Balegallin* (possibly Gaston in Crail parish: Taylor 1995, 158) by David I to May priory, probably in 1148×50 (Barrow 1999, no.165). To take one of the examples from the Deer records: in II.12 the bounds are given in some detail of the land granted in Altrie by Cainnech son of the son of Dobarchú and by Cathal. Instead of supposing that Cainnech and Cathal held this patch jointly, we could envisage that some strips of arable were held by one of them, while the remaining strips were held by the other. Did they, however, grant their respective parts on the same occasion? In the case of *Balegallin*, for example, it is known that the other 'half' was granted to the priory of May about twenty years later (1165×71) by William I, David I's grandson (Barrow 1971, 195–6).

It is striking that all these apparent joint grants appear in no. II, the only record which takes the form of a summary of transactions stretching over a century or more of Deer's existence.[31] The formula 'Cainnech and Cathal gave X' could be used quite naturally by a scribe looking back over the entire history of Deer's landholdings: even if Cainnech and Cathal had been generations apart, it would be perfectly accurate to say that that piece of land had been given by them both. Jackson's assumption that the use of this formula indicated that the persons named were contemporaries (see e.g. his discussion of II.6, and the persons named in II.14: Jackson 1972, 43 and 49–50) should therefore be resisted.

This leads to another possible explanation of the use of the 'joint grant' formula. Conceivably there was no division of land, and the formula merely signified that a grant had later been 'confirmed' by someone else. Biffie (to take an example at random) may have been granted originally by Domnall son of Ruaidrí, and at some later stage this may have been repeated by Mael Coluim son of Cuilén. If this is true, then the second grant would have been made by someone who was, in some sense, the successor of the person who made the first grant. Perhaps the second donor was the first's heir, but had been unwilling to recognise his predecessor's generosity, a problem which could have been resolved by a fresh statement of the original grant. The successor may, however, have taken violent possession of the lands concerned, and been pursuaded at some point to recognise the original grant.

31 This contrasts with VI, an 'extinction' enacted by a *mormaer*, his wife, and a *toísech*, where witnesses and a place-date are given. (This transaction will be discussed further in the next section.) In this case there is no reason to doubt that the parties involved arranged to come together to announce the enactment which is the subject of that record.

A different problem is posed by instances in which a husband and wife are named as the grantors. There is no reason to doubt that both made the gift at the same time. Should they, however, be regarded in some sense as joint owners (e.g. if the property was part of the wife's tocher)? Apart from the act of 'extinction' in VI (which will be discussed in due course), there are the grants in III and IV by a man—who, from other evidence (discussed by Jackson 1972, 58), can be identified as *mormaer* of Buchan—and his wife. Jackson was justifiably wary of seeing this as evidence that the *mormaer* held these lands in right of his wife. It is possible that the wife's inclusion was designed to add significance to the act without necessarily implying that she was regarded as joint-owner of what was being granted. Perhaps naming her may have served to associate her family with the deed. A more straightforward explanation would be that it was more natural to think of husband and wife together where ostensible acts of piety were involved: certainly there are instances of this in charters to religious houses.[32] In the other instance (VI) where a *mormaer* and his spouse are named together it is more likely that the *mormaer*, Colbain, did indeed hold his position in right of his wife, who was Eva daughter of Gartnait (presumably Gartnait son of Cainnech, *mormaer* of Buchan in III and IV). It has been suggested that Colbain himself originated in Fife, and had a son who was lord of Kennoway (Young 1993, 179–80).

RE-READING INSTANCES OF 'EXTINGUISHING' (BÁDUD)

Another feature which needs to be reconsidered is where a donor 'extinguished' *edbarta*. Some explanation of terms is required. *Edbarta* literally means 'offerings' or 'alms', and refers in this context to settlements/land granted to Deer. In the translation of the records given in this volume it has been rendered as 'offerings'. In this discussion I will take this one stage further and refer to *edbarta* as 'church-lands'. The term translated as 'extinguished' is *ro báid* (preterite of *bádud*). Jackson preferred 'quenched', but he commented that 'the meaning in the passages in Deer is probably literally 'extinguished, exterminated' (Jackson 1972, 120). *Bádud* is not encountered anywhere else in the context of property-rights.[33] It can be found in literature, conveying a sense of erasing all prior claims. In the poem, 'The Harrowing of Hell', it is described (in verse 31) how

---

32 Note also the observation that 'a glance at any Mediterranean cartulary will show this common role of women as co-donors and cosignatories to property alienation, even when their dowry lands were not directly involved' (Cheyette 1988, 843 n. 58).   33 The only examples cited in Quin 1983 come from the Deer records.

Sínus Adam in láim luinn / gur báidh álad in ubhuill
Adam stretched out his eager hand and extinguished the crime of the apple (Bergin 1910, 119)[34]

In what follows I shall render *ro báid* as 'extinguished' in order to express the sense of finality that was evidently intended by the use of this term in the context of the Deer records.

All-in-all, *ro báid* 'extinguished' appears four times. On three occasions (II.10; II.14; VI) it is said that one or more individuals extinguished all *edbarta* 'church-lands'. The summary nature of II means that no more details are forthcoming about what was intended by this. In VI, however, we are told that 'Colbain, *mormaer* of Buchan, and Eva, daughter of Gartnait his wedded wife, and Donnachach son of Síthech, *toísech* of Clann Morgainn, extinguished all offerings [i.e. church-lands], in favour of God and of Drostán and of Columba and of Peter the apostle, from all burdens ...'.[35] From this Jackson reasonably concluded that extinguishing 'is defined as bringing freedom from all imposts' to Deer's lands (Jackson 1972, 121), releasing them from general dues and services. The evidence provided by VI that these burdens were, indeed, general dues and services will be examined in more detail later.

Jackson was inclined to take a literal view of these statements that *all* Deer's lands thereby obtained immunity. He understood this to mean that the donor 'undertook himself to render in future all taxes, services, etc., due from the monastery to toísech, mormaer, and perhaps king from all the estates hitherto granted to it' (Jackson 1972, 122). This is unconvincing on a number of counts. Jackson regarded such arrangements as a 'known feature in feudal land-granting' (Jackson 1972, 122 n.1). The known feature of land-granting to which he referred, however, was significantly different. What he evidently had in mind were the numerous instances recorded in Latin charters where a donor of land to a church establishment undertook to perform all services owed from that land (typically these were owed to the king).[36] A donor did not have to be particularly prominent, or the land involved especially large. For example, when (sometime in the thirteenth century, probably mid-thirteenth) Aed Ruad[37] and his wife granted a nameless stretch of land adjacent to Lingo (Carnbee parish, Fife), he declared in his charter that he and his heirs 'warrant and acquit' the land in question 'in perpetuity from army, hosting

---

34 I am very grateful to Thomas Owen Clancy for providing me with this passage. 35 The rest of VI poses serious problems of translation and interpretation discussed below, 339–40. 36 He cited (Jackson 1972 122 n. 1), by way of a reference, the brief discussion of this phenomenon in Shead 1970, 8, in which an example is given of one individual's undertaking to be responsible to the king for all services and exactions due from the land he was granting to Glasgow cathedral. 37 'Eggou Ruffus': note that 'Egu' and 'Eggu' is found for *Aed* in Barrow 1971, 138, 424 (see also Bannerman 1993, 32). There is a formal possibility, however, that 'Eggou' is a mistranscription of 'Eggon' (*Aedán*).

and multure, and all service and exaction' (Thomson 1841, 382–3; Stuart 1868, 18). This kind of arrangement does not, however, match Jackson's idea of releasing all Deer's lands from all burdens. Jackson's explanation of extinguishing *all* Deer's lands actually requires that a donor undertook not only to perform the services owed from any lands he himself may have granted, but also to perform services due from lands which must have been granted to Deer by other donors. This is a very different proposition from what Aed Ruad and countless others in Latin charters were prepared to accept. Indeed, it would be extraordinary for anyone to undertake such burdens for lands with which they had no prior connection.[38] Yet this is clearly what Jackson envisaged.

Jackson was aware that there are other difficulties with his explanation of what was meant by extinguishing 'all' Deer's lands. Why, if Deer was thus freed from all burdens, was there more than one extinction of 'all church-lands'? He suggested that these arrangements may have lapsed so that 'fresh acts of 'quenching' became necessary from time to time' (Jackson 1972, 122). This is not inconceivable. Nonetheless, an explanation of extinguishing 'all church-lands' would obviously be more convincing if it did not require such a sequence of lapses to be envisaged. Jackson's awareness of another, more serious, difficulty may be inferred from the awkward 'perhaps king' which appears in his list of those to whom all the dues and services, once owed by Deer, were to be rendered on their behalf by the individual(s) who enacted an extinction. He did not discuss why there should be any hesitation about the king's exaction of dues and services. Had he done so, he would have had to confront a potential contradiction between the evidence relating to extinctions and his understanding of the hierarchy of officials under the king who administered the dues and services that were the specific target of the process of 'extinguishing' Deer's lands. The extinction of 'all church-lands' by three individuals recorded in II.14 has been completed in hand C with the statement that the lands involved are, as a result, 'free from *mormaer* and *toísech* till Judgement'. If an extinction meant that *all* dues and services owed by Deer were to be rendered on Deer's behalf, why did scribe C not specify that, in his view, II.14 made Deer's lands free from the king, as well as from *mormaer* and *toísech*? Presumably the scribe intended here to 'improve' his predecessor's account of this extinction, not to diminish it. Moreover, although scribe C should not be regarded as a contemporary witness to the deed recorded in II.14, he was responsible for documenting the act of extinction recorded in VI (which he probably entered into the Book of Deer only shortly after it had

38 It could not be argued that a donor who extinguished all Deer's lands might have been undertaking services due from lands granted by earlier generations of his family: there can be no doubt that more than one family made donations to Deer at an early stage (including the ruling family of Moray).

taken place).[39] There can be no doubt that he knew what was meant by the 'extinguishing of all church-lands'. Also, he was not alone in aspiring to freedom from *mormaer* and *toísech* till Judgement: the same phrase was used by the scribe of records I and II in relation to the (alleged) earlier foundation at Aberdour. Again, it is striking that 'freedom from king' is not mentioned.

There is no apparent way of reconciling this with Jackson's suggestion that whoever enacted an extinction undertook to acquit Deer of all its burdens. It will be recalled that he saw *mormaer* and *toísech* as royal officials who retained a share, *cuit*, of the king's revenues, and that every piece of land was liable to the *cuit* of *toísech* and *mormaer*, as well as the portion retained by the king (the king's *cuit*) 'unless remitted' (Jackson 1972, 109, 113, 119). It should follow from this that the king's share of the dues and services rendered by Deer was a burden too, not just the shares of *toísech* and *mormaer*: indeed, according to Jackson's scenario, the dues and services from which the *clerici* of Deer sought immunity were regarded, first-and-foremost, as pertaining to the king, and collected by his officials, the *toísech* and *mormaer*. There can be no doubt, however, that as far as the *clerici* of Deer themselves were concerned, what mattered to them was the burden of dues and services which they owed to *toísech* and *mormaer*.

In fact, it may be inferred from this that Deer's lands were not generally liable to render dues and services to the king at all. This would seem to be supported by VII, where we are told that David I confirmed that the *clerici* of Deer 'are quit and immune from all lay service and undue exaction, as has been written in their book, and they have upheld at Banff and sworn at Aberdeen'. Strictly speaking, this should mean that the freedom from *mormaer* or *toísech* 'written in their book' amounted to complete immunity from lay service (at least in the eyes of whoever drafted VII).[40] Is it conceivable, however, that no dues and services (including the widespread obligation to contribute to the king's army) were owed routinely by Deer to the king from its lands? This would have been remarkable in the kingdom's core area south of the Mounth (at least from the point when documentary evidence comes 'on tap'). The *mormaer* of Strathearn, for example, was unable to grant land immune from any secular exaction to his foundation at Inchaffray without stipulating that he and his hiers would perform the king's service which was owed from that land (see, e.g., Lindsay, Dowden and Thomson, 1908, 45, 194–5). If the king in general terms only demanded military service and aids, however, then conceivably this limited (and probably only occasional) burden may have been less keenly felt north of the Mounth.[41] Be this as it may, there

---

39 Certainly sometime between III and VII, i.e. sometime during the 1130s and 1140s.
40 Remembering that VII could have been inscribed directly into the Book of Deer, and need not be a copy of a text written originally on a single sheet with seal appended. As it stands, therefore, it cannot certainly be regarded as a royal statement. See below, 343.
41 Note that there is a hint elsewhere north of the Mounth that royal burdens were not

is certainly no better evidence for Buchan than the Deer records themselves. From this it appears that, at the time the property-records were written in the gospel book between *c.*1130 and *c.*1150, the scribes' idea of gaining immunity seemed to relate only to the demands of *mormaer* and *toísech*.[42]

Is there a more satisfactory way of explaining what was meant by extinguishing 'all church-lands'? The individuals who can most readily grant immunity from lay services are those to whom the exactions are owed. For example, when King William sometime in the late 1160s confirmed the grant of Kinclaith to Glasgow Cathedral by his brother, Mael Coluim IV, in 1165, he specified that this settlement (along with others confirmed in the charter) was to be 'free, quit, and absolved from every service and custom and secular exaction', as well as from any claim (Barrow 1971, 194; Shead 1970, 7). It is clear that the 'service, custom and secular exaction' mentioned here had been owed from Kinclaith to the king because in the charter recording Mael Coluim's gift (Barrow 1960, 276–7) it is specified that Kinclaith was to be held as freely as any other land was held by a church in Mael Coluim's *regnum* 'saving, however, my armies' (Shead 1970, 8). The release from dues and services in King William's confirmation thus embraced all that had been excused originally by Mael Coluim as a normal feature of church-lands granted by the king as well as the remaining obligation to perform military service which had been specifically reserved in Mael Coluim's charter.

In the case of Deer's lands, it is explicitly stated in VI that the extinction was conferred by a *mormaer* and a *toísech*. It may be inferred from this that all those who extinguished Deer's lands in II were also either *mormaer* or *toísech* (or both). When Domnall son of the son of Dubaicín 'extinguished all church-lands' (II.10), this would mean that he renounced the dues and services that he exacted from Deer's lands. The statement that 'all' church-lands were extinguished could have been perfectly logical, insofar as it was understood that none of Deer's lands would be subject to exactions from

---

universal. Alexander II stipulated in a charter for Kinloss that 'our service' was to be retained 'from lands from which we ought to have service' (Innes 1837a, 459), from which it can be inferred that there were lands exempt from such service.   **42** Perhaps the king's regular enjoyment of general dues and services was limited to his thanages, and was extended as a matter of course only later (in the case of military service and associated 'aids'). The king's insistence on reserving his service when land was granted by one subject to another only becomes commonplace during the reign of William I (1165–1214). It is impossible to be sure whether this signifies a real change in attitude and expectations, or simply reflects the growing sophistication of charters. Finally, if *cuit* was not a function of the levying of general dues and services (which may only be a formal possibility: see below, 353–3), then it would be easier to imagine that the royal levying of these exactions was originally limited before the strengthening of the kingship in the twelfth century. It is possible, however, that the profile of royalty had once been greater in Buchan, recalling that a king of Alba in the early eleventh century was able to grant land and *cuit* from two named settlements, and that rulers of Moray were able to grant lands in the early eleventh century and sometime in the 1060s or 1070s.

Domnall (or, presumably, from his successors).[43] This would also make better sense of *bádud*, 'extinguish', because the exactions referred to would be permanently eliminated. This contrasts with Jackson's scenario, in which they would still have been imposed, although acquitted by someone on behalf of Deer. The elimination of Domnall's exactions would not, of course, have meant that Deer's lands would have been freed from exactions levied by others. If the Deer records are taken as a whole, it may be surmised that, in the period between *c.*1130 and *c.*1150, Deer's lands lay (in whole or part) within the ambit of the *toísech* of Clann Morgainn and the *toísech* of Clann Chanann, as well as the *mormaer* of Buchan. Perhaps this situation was of longer standing. If this assumption is made, then Domnall could have represented one of three local powers who were accustomed to levy exactions from Deer's lands. What of the other two?

One's eye turns immediately to II.14, where we are told that 'Cainnech and Domnall and Cathal extinguished all *edbarta* (church-lands)'. This evidently represents a cumulative statement in which new and previously recorded extinctions have been brought together.[44] Domnall and Cathal are mentioned earlier in II in connection with extinctions.[45] It will be recalled that 'Domnall son of the son of Dubaicín extinguished all *edbarta* (church-lands)' (II.10). Cathal's act of extinction, recorded in II.11, is the only one which is not expressed as applying to 'all church-lands': we are told simply that he extinguished the *cuit* due to him as *toísech*. (This will be discussed further in due course.) Cainnech's extinction in II.14 is, therefore, the only one which is certainly made for the first time at that point. The reason for combining new and old extinctions in a single statement, it may be surmised, was that it represented the abolition of exactions on Deer's lands by all three local powers: it was the moment when Deer achieved the complete immunity from secular burdens which it craved.[46]

---

43 It is not possible to gauge what proportion of the exactions enjoyed by Domnall and his successors were being alienated by granting immunity to Deer's lands. Domnall and his successors would have continued to enjoy them elsewhere in Buchan, of course.   **44** There is a formal possibility that II.14 records an actual ceremony in which Domnall and Cathal repeated their earlier acts of extinction. In the light of what has been said above about the use of the 'joint-grant formula' in II (see below, 374–5), the most natural reading of II.14 is that the earlier acts of extinction have simply been restated by scribe A without any implication that Cainnech, Domnall and Cathal performed a joint act of extinction, or that they were necessarily even contemporaries.   **45** Jackson assumed that these were different individuals, and that the extinction of all church-lands by Cainnech, Cathal and Domnall in II.14 represented a fresh act following the possible repudiation of the extinction of all church-lands by Domnall son of the son of Dubacán by his heirs (Jackson 1972, 122). For the identity of Domnall and Cathal in II.14 with Domnall and Cathal in II.10 and II.11 respectively, see below, 338.   **46** The possible identifications of Cathal, Domnall and Cainnech with the positions of *mormaer* of Buchan, *toísech* of Clann Chanann, and *toísech* of Clann Morgainn, are discussed below, 351–2.

The reading of II.14 as a scribal reiteration of earlier extinctions is not mere supposition. It can be shown that we are dealing with the same Domnall in II.10 and II.14 and a single person named Cathal in II.11 and II.14 (a possibility that Jackson did not consider: Jackson 1972, 42–3). Throughout the whole text of II (which, it will be recalled, summarises at least a century of transactions), there are only three names which appear without a patronymic: Cainnech (in II.14), Domnall (in II.13 and II.14) and Cathal (in II.11, II.13 and II.14). It is striking, therefore, that on their first mention in II, these forenames appear with patronymics in the usual way: there is Cainnech son of the son of Dobarchú (II.12), Domnall son of the son of Dubaicín (who has already been met in II.10) and Cathal son of Morgann (II.5). It would be too much of a coincidence if these were not the same three individuals throughout. Presumably it was possible to name all three in II.14 without patronymics because this information had already been provided.

It may be noted in passing that this has implications for the view that the transactions listed in II may have been arranged in chronological order (see, most recently, Woolf 2000, 160). Cathal son of Morgann is unlikely to have been a contemporary of both Mael Snechta mac Lulaig (d. 1085; his father was killed in 1058) and Mael Coluim son of Cuilén, if Mael Coluim is regarded as son of Cuilén mac Illuilb (king of Scots 966–71) and brother of Custantín (king of Scots 995–7) (as suggested in Jackson 1972, 42–3): Mael Coluim was probably dead by 995 (Woolf 2000, 158). Other indications that the order of II is not chronological will come to light later.

The final notice of 'extinguishing' is in VI: the last of Jackson's suggested three general quenchings of all *edbarta* 'church-lands'. Again, this can be interpreted less problematically if 'all' is not taken quite so literally. Logically, the earlier instances of extinguishing 'church-lands' represented in II.14 would have applied to what Deer possessed at that time, and not to lands which it acquired subsequently: the 'deep place' in Pitfour (IV), 'as far as Skillymarno' (V.2), and the land delimited in V.3. (The *pett* of Mac Gobraig granted in III is specified to be free of all burdens, while Auchmachar (V.1) is stated to have been given 'in freedom till Judgement'.) On the face of it, then, the extinguishing of 'church-lands' in VI was presumably intended to apply specifically to these acquisitions recorded in IV and V (all datable to sometime after 1131/2, the date of III: see Jackson 1972, 14–15, 94).

This could help to clarify a key point. So far it has been inferred that extinguishing church-lands 'from all burdens' in VI meant a grant of immunity from general dues and services which were owed to the donor. In VI, however, this statement is only part of a sentence; the significance of the whole sentence relating to the extinction of Deer's lands remains to be explored. At the very least it offers a unique opportunity to gain some detailed insights into what was meant when church-lands were 'extinguished'.

Unfortunately, the passage in question is very difficult to interpret, and different translations have been suggested. The text reads:

> *Ro báid Colbain mormér Buchan ₇ Éua ingen Garnait a ben phústa ₇*
> *Donnachac mac Síthig tœsech Clenni Morgainn na h-uli edbarta ri Dia ₇ ri*
> *Drostán ₇ ria Colum Cilli ₇ ri Petar apstal, ó na h-ulib dolaidib ar chuit cetri*
> *dabach don-í thíssad ar ard-mandaidib Alban cu cotchenn ₇ ar [a] h-ard*
> *chellaib. Testibus his: Bróccín ₇ Cormac abb Turbruaid ₇ Morgunn mac*
> *Donnchid ₇ Gilli-Petair mac Donnchaid ₇ Mal-[F]œchín ₇ dá mac Matni, ₇*
> *mathe Buchan huli 'na [f]iaidnaisse i nHelain.*

Which Jackson translated (1972, 35–6):

> Colbain, mormaer of Buchan, and Eva, daughter of Garnait his wedded
> wife, and Donnchad son of Síthech, toísech of Clann Morgainn,
> 'quenched' all the grants from all imposts, in favour of God and of
> Drostán and of Columba and of Peter the apostle, in return for the dues
> on four davochs'[-worth] of that which should devolve on the chief
> religious houses of Scotland in general and on its chief churches. These
> being witnesses: Bróiccín, and Cormac abbot of Turriff, and Morgann
> son of Donnchad, and Gille-Petair son of Donnchad, and Mal-
> Fhéichín, and the two sons of Maitne, and all the 'good men' of Buchan
> in witness of it, at Ellon.

The crux here is how to interpret … *ó na h-ulib dolaidib ar chuit cetri dabach*
don-í thíssad ar … . Jackson saw this in terms of a *quid pro quo*: the price of
extinguishing all church-lands was liability to a set quantity of dues such as
devolved on chief religious houses and chief churches (Jackson 1972, 77;
similarly Stuart 1869, ciii, and Fraser 1938, 64 n.1). Among the many other
attempts to render this (discussed in Jackson 1972, 77–8), a quite different
understanding of this passage may be noted in A.O. Anderson's translation:
'… [freeing them] from all exactions, upon the extent of four dabachs, of
[taxes] that would be owing upon …'; Anderson commented that 'it seems to
me that the monks were immune from taxation upon four dabachs only'
(Anderson 1922 ii, 180 and n.5).

In terms of language alone, the problem is the first *ar*, which can yield
either Jackson's or Anderson's translations. Jackson was presumably persuaded that his choice was correct because he took the extinguishing of all
grants to refer literally to *all* Deer's possessions. If, however, the extinguishing
was specifically intended to cover only those lands granted in IV and V
(because they were the only ones which, at that time, could have owed dues
and services to *mormaer* or *toísech*), then Anderson's sense that the rescinding

of burdens related only to four davochs would be preferable. The whole passage might therefore be translated:

> Colbain, *mormaer* of Buchan, and Eva, daughter of Gartnait his wedded wife, and Donnachach son of Síthech, *toísech* of Clann Morgainn, extinguished all church-lands, in favour of God and of Drostán and of Columba and of Peter the apostle, from all burdens relating to the portion of four davochs, of that which would apply to the chief districts[47] of *Alba* in general and on its chief churches ...

It is difficult to envisage what might be intended by 'all burdens relating to the portion of four davochs': what could be meant by *cuit* 'portion' in this context? There is a way of cutting this Gordian knot. It is possible that *ar chuit* has been used here as an idiomatic phrase, so that *ar chuit cetri dabach* might mean something like 'as regards four davochs', 'in terms of four davochs', 'so far as concerns four davochs'. The passage could then be translated:

> extinguished all church-lands, in favour of God and of Drostán and of Columba and of Peter the apostle, from all burdens of that which would apply to the chief districts of *Alba* in general and on its chief churches so far as concerns four davochs ...

Arriving at a plausible translation, however, is only half way towards achieving an understanding of the text. How is it to be interpreted? The key is the term *dabach* (davoch). There is general agreement that *dabach* (literally 'vat') was essentially related to arable capacity (Barrow 1962, 129–36; Duncan 1975, 168, 380–1; Easson 1986, 54–89). This is how it appears to have been used in II.7 where Mael Coluim son of Cinaed gave two *dabach*. There is less agreement, however, about whether this is how *dabach* originated. According to Barrow, 'there is little doubt that the davoch, whenever it began to be used of land, was a strictly agricultural unit, a measure of arable capacity', rather than 'originally and essentially a large fiscal unit' (Barrow 1962, 133, 132). Alternatively, it has been suggested that it 'expressed the amount of food payable as a food render' (Dodgshon 1981, 76), so that 'it may be that the word was applied to land as a measure of the tribute or render which would arise from it' (Duncan 1975, 318). Easson, in the most detailed study yet to be undertaken, regarded it as probable that the *dabach* was the basis for levying universal tribute, although she observed that there is no direct evidence for this (Easson 1986, 90, 93).

There is abundant evidence, however, that 'forinsec' service was assessed by the *dabach*. 'Forinsec' has been aptly described as a general term for what is

---

47 Literally 'inhabited places'. The precise meaning is obscure. (Jackson 1972, 78, suggested 'house', meaning here 'religious house'.) Perhaps Buchan was intended (see below).

'outside (*forein*) or additional to whatever is due to the immediate lord' (Duncan 1975, 380). This is usually equated with the universal requirement to serve in the 'common' or 'Scottish' army in defence of the realm: there are examples where army service alone was intended (Barrow 1980, 164–6). There were other general burdens which are also likely to have been levied in relation to davochs. On one occasion the king reserved 'common works' and 'common aid' as well as 'common army'[48] (Barrow 1971, 222); on another occasion exemption was granted from army service, works, and all secular burdens, but not 'from the royal geld which is taken generally from the lands and alms throughout the kingdom of Scotland'[49] (Barrow 1971, 232). 'Common works' could have taken a variety of forms: in one of the Loch Leven records immunity is claimed from bridge-building, hosting or hunting (Thomson 1841, 115); there is also evidence for carriage service which was assessed by the *dabach* (Easson 1986, 93).[50] As far as 'common aid' is concerned, the earliest reference to 'aids' is in a brieve of Mael Coluim IV datable to 1162×4 (Barrow 1960, 269). It has been suggested that this may have been in connection with royal marriages which were celebrated at that time (Barrow 1960, 54); it has also been suggested that although 'the word 'aid' [*auxilium*] may suggest an innovation of Anglo-Norman origin … it is likely that only the word was new' (Duncan 1975, 389). If 'aid' had a longer Scottish pedigree than might at first be assumed, then perhaps it could refer to the provision of supplies for a military campaign. When, for example, Alexander II exempted those north of the Forth from serving in the army which he led into England in July 1216, he took 'supplies' (*expensas*) in lieu (Stevenson 1835, 123):[51] in a royal charter shortly afterwards this was referred to as *auxilium* (Barrow 1990, 136; Innes and Chalmers 1848, 79). Taken as a whole, therefore, the indications are that, regardless of its precise origins, the *dabach* was the unit of assessment for 'public' obligations north of the Forth, performing a similar function to the *hide* in England (with which it was equated: Duncan 1975, 380–1, citing Skene 1871, 302). The potential range of these obligations may also be gauged by comparison with Ireland: in one of the Kells property-records a church and its estate was granted *cen cis cen chobach cen fecht cen shluagad cen choinnim ríg na toisig* 'without tribute, without dues, without expedition, without hosting, without billetting of king or toisech' (Mac Niocaill 1990, 157–8).

---

48 *excepto comuni auxilio, comuni exercitu, comuni operatione*: the charter survives as an original single sheet in the hand of the royal scribe, Richard of Lincoln.   **49** *de geldo regio quod communiter capietur de terris et de elemosinis per regnum Scocie.* Barrow's initial interpretation of this was as a reference to extraordinary taxation (*auxilium* 'aid'): Barrow 1971, 53. More recently he has suggested that 'royal geld' here means *cáin*: Barrow 1985, 14 and 23 n.81. I would regard his first interpretation as preferable.   **50** A wide-ranging discussion of common burdens and immunity from them is given in Stuart 1869, lxxxviii–xcix.   **51** *Scoti* referring here to those living north of the Forth, see Broun 1999b, 142 n.32.

The mention of davochs in VI, when combined with the reference to *Alba*, the kingdom as a whole, is a clear indication that general dues and services were what was meant by the burdens that 'would apply to the chief districts of *Alba* in general and on its chief churches'. The most obvious explanation of the reference to 'chief districts' and 'chief churches' would be that these exactions were of a different kind and degree for the lands of a place like Deer than for less important churches and districts. This is not certain, however. The expression of free possession in these terms may be compared with statements found frequently in Latin charters—such as the following (selected at random)—in which land was declared to be held by the beneficiary 'as freely and honourably as other barons', 'as freely and peaceably as other knights' (Barrow 1971, 128, 151), 'as freely and peaceably, fully and honourably as any earl or baron in the kingdom of *Scotia*' (Barrow 1960, 224); or in which the donation itself (in the following examples it was a church) was said to be held and possessed 'as freely and peaceably as any church in my kingdom', or 'as freely and peaceably as any churches of my demesnes in *Scotia*' (Barrow 1960, 246, 272) (for other examples see Barrow 1980, 154 n.52). In all these cases the beneficiary is granted possession in the fullest sense which was conceivable at that time (usually for a specified return). The mention of different kinds of lay lord—knights, barons and earls—and the distinction between a church of the royal demesne and any other church has no necessary significance in terms of free possession of land: it is essentially a reference to the status of the donee or of the donation. The mention in VI of freedom from burdens applicable to the chief districts of *Alba* in general and on its chief churches could conceivably have had a similar significance: a general statement of Deer's standing as a 'chief church' and Buchan as a 'chief district', rather than a specific reference to a differential tariff of services. The end result, after all, was the same regardless of any differentiation: immunity from general dues and services.

So far this discussion of the records has been rather dry and technical. It should not be forgotten, however, that they were written by real flesh-and-blood people. Writing property-records into a gospel book was not a routine occurrence. It was a dramatic gesture. What could have provoked the *clerici* of Deer in the 1130s and 1140s to assert their property-rights with the greatest spiritual force at their disposal? It is tempting to suppose that this was a response in some way to the defeat and death of the king of Moray in 1130 at the battle of Stracathro. Could Buchan have become unsettled at this time, threatening Deer's peaceful enjoyment of its property-rights (Broun 2000, 126)? It may seem more likely, however, that the subsequent consolidation of David's authority in the North East meant greater security in the region, rather than the reverse (see Oram 1999). Too little is known about Buchan's politics in this period to discern with any certainty whether the 1130s and 1140s was a time of growing stability or increasing instability. There is no need, however, to resort to open speculation in an attempt to explain why the Deer records were written. The records themselves are a potent witness, not just in what is said in them, but also in how they have been written. Our attention is thus drawn from the hazy vista of the wider political landscape towards a close-up appreciation of the physical evidence of the records in the manuscript itself.

Jackson has pointed out that the later scribes (C, D, and E) showed a particular concern for Deer's immunity from secular exactions (Jackson 1972, 88–97). He saw E's Latin charter as the culmination of a process whereby C and D, anticipating the legal hearings held in front of David I at Banff and Aberdeen, attempted to emend earlier records in order to meet the standards of what he described as 'the new Norman type of court which the Celtic monks had to face' (Jackson 1972, 88–91). This 'Norman court' is, however, a fantasy. There is no indication that the proceedings were conducted in a manner that scribes A and B would have found foreign. The initiative for producing the gospel-book in evidence was presumably Deer's, using the records to defend its rights in a legal forum in a way which scribes A and B would presumably have contemplated when they wrote them. Also, the Latin charter (VII) is likely to have been produced by a Deer scribe, probably writing directly into the gospel-book (Barrow 1999, 119).[52] Finally, there can be little doubt that the proceedings were conducted in Gaelic, given that all the eleven witnesses cited in VII were Gaelic-speakers.[53]

The reason why some—if not all—of the records were written only emerges from closer scrutiny of the scribal activity noted by Jackson. The key here is that the heightened efforts to insist on immunity from lay exactions follow immediately from the attainment of blanket immunity affirmed by scribe A in II.14 (according to how this was interpreted, above). The last part of II.14 itself has been rewritten and expanded by scribe C so that the extinctions were stipulated as representing 'freedom from *mormaer* and *toísech* till Judgement' (Jackson 1972, 13–14). Scribe C also added a statement in the same vein to scribe B's text at the end of V.3, declaring that the land (which had been granted by the *toísech* of Clann Chanann) was 'free of *toísech* until Judgement'. The most remarkable property-record is III, which apparently documented the first significant grant since Cainnech's extinction noted in II.14. (Cainnech, who was presumably a *toísech* and maybe also *mormaer*, was probably the father of Gartnait son of Cainnech, *mormaer* of Buchan, the

---

52 There are highly unusual diplomatic features (*salutes* rather than *salutem* in the greeting, and the repeated appearance of *teste* in the witness list) which make it inconceivable that VII is a copy of an original single-sheet charter produced by a royal scribe (Barrow 1999, 119, who now sees no need to consider that it might be a forgery: Barrow 1991, 29). An alternative, that there was originally a single sheet produced by a Deer scribe which could have been sealed (Broun 2000, 118) is unnecessarily fussy.   **53** For David I as a Gaelic speaker, see for example MacQueen, MacQueen and Watt 1995, 149, 266.

donor of III.) A striking feature is the pledge given by Gartnait and his wife to Cormac, bishop of Dunkeld (presumably in his capacity as 'head', in some sense, of Columban churches in Scotland). Writing this into the record was a highly unusual step; the giving of a pledge to someone was itself untypical, contrasting with the more regular guaranteeing of a transaction by a number of significant people as witnesses or sureties (Broun 1995, 35–6). Another curiosity is that the transaction has been dated according to the king's regnal year. The main purpose of this—in the absence of any established archival practice that would have required the deed to be fixed in time—was presumably to make the record seem more weighty.

The most extraordinary feature of all, however, is that III (along with IV) has been erased and rewritten. Jackson argued persuasively that III and IV were originally written by scribe A (Jackson 1972, 14–15). He suggested that A's text had come to be regarded as unsatisfactory—for example, by perhaps failing to mention that the grant had been made 'free of all imposts', or by recording the witnesses 'inadequately'—prompting the desperate measure of scraping A's work away and writing the records again (Jackson 1972, 90). A fair amount of material must have been added to the original text of III, because the scribe has run out of room for IV (Jackson 1972, 14–15). The additional elements, it may be assumed, would have included the regnal year and the statement about the pledge. Jackson was convinced that the scribe responsible for this rewriting was later than scribe C, and consequently dubbed him 'D'. There is, however, no obvious reason why scribe C could not have been later than 'D'. The fact that 'D' consists of the rewriting of III and IV would, on its own, explain why this hand is found over an erased section of scribe A's work: it has nothing to do with a lack of space in folios nearby because of B's writing of V and C's writing of VI.[54]

The point at issue in rewriting III and IV is unlikely to have been possession of the lands concerned. Scribe A's original record would at least have identified what had been granted to Deer. Given the amount of space involved, moreover, it is probable that scribe A gave more information than the bare mention of donor and benefaction which characterises II. For once he would presumably have been recording a transaction soon after it had occurred (in 1131/2 in the case of III), rather than simply continuing his summary of earlier grants. The most likely extra information he would have provided in his version of III and IV is the list of witnesses. If so, then IV may not be much different from what scribe A originally wrote: it may have been rewritten simply because room had to be made for the expanded version of III. The key to this remarkable process of erasure and rewriting is likely,

---

54 It may also be noted that C's addition to II.14 is cramped, apparently by III. Jackson observed, however, that this does not necessarily mean that C's interpolation was not already there when III was rewritten: C's addition here could have been cramped by A's original version of III (Jackson 1972, 15).

therefore, to be found in III. If mere possession of the settlement noted in III was not the problem, then what was presumably at stake was the settlement's 'freedom from all burdens'. In fact, it may have been anticipated at the outset that the settlement's immunity was at risk, hence the requirement to give the pledge to the bishop of Dunkeld.

Why should Deer's claim to immunity for lands granted after II.14 have been so contentious? The answer can be deduced from a curious feature of VI (the only record written in its entirety by scribe C). On the face of it Deer achieved in VI a renewal of the blanket immunity of their lands from secular exactions. Why, then, is the extinction in VI explicitly quantified as relating to four davochs—that is, to lands granted after II.14? If the intention was to grant complete immunity, why has this been spelt out so specifically?[55] It has been assumed (above, 338) that the acts of extinction noted in II.14 would not have applied to lands acquired by Deer subsequently, hence the need for the later extinction of 'all church-lands' recorded in VI. It is unlikely, however, that this was plain sailing. It would appear from the subsequent interpolations and rewriting (and particularly the addition by scribe C to II.14) that the *clerici* of Deer claimed that all its lands for all time were covered by the extinctions in II.14—that is, not only those it possessed at that time, but also any lands it might acquire in the future. The *mormaer* and *toísig* evidently did not agree. Seen in this context, the stipulation in VI that the grant of immunity related to four davochs can be seen as something of a compromise. The *clerici* of Deer, as a result of VI, achieved complete immunity for all their lands once again; but it may be inferred that, at the same time, they had to abandon their claim that a grant of immunity applied equally to future grants. Not only would the specification of four davochs (referring to lands granted after II.14) have conceded the point that the immunity represented by II.14 applied only to lands held by Deer at the time of Cainnech's act of extinction, but it would also have made it clear that the immunity enshrined in VI was not open-ended.

This reading of VI might also explain why the *clerici* of Deer decided that VI should not be the last word on the matter. They may have hoped that David I would declare in favour of the limitless immunity which they had failed to secure from *mormaer* and *toísech* in Buchan. David I's judgement was that Deer should enjoy 'immunity from all lay service ... as is written in their book', and that no-one henceforth should harm them or their property. This all-embracing statement may have been regarded by Deer as an endorsement of their reading of grants of extinction (notwithstanding the apparent concession in VI, although this was only implicit in the record). The most striking aspect of VII, however, is its position in the Book of Deer: it occupies

55 Deer's lands as a whole were presumably much more than four davochs in total. It will be recalled that two *dabach* were granted by Mael Coluim mac Cinaeda (II.7).

the last significant blank space. This could be seen as an attempt to present VII as the final statement on the subject of immunity. It would, equally, have allowed any future grants of land to be recorded earlier in the book, perhaps to avoid any ambiguity that David's instruction to leave the *clerici* and their possessions alone would apply to any further acquisitions. Again, the most curious feature of a property-record can be explained in the context of an ongoing dispute about whether extinctions automatically embraced the future as well as the past.

Can knowledge of this dispute shed any light on the earlier records? Jackson maintained that scribe A was not concerned with the issue of immunity at all (Jackson 1972, 93). The very first donation noted by scribe A, however, is stated to have been in 'freedom till Judgement from *mormaer* and *toísech*' (I). This is in A's account of the gift of the *cathair*[56] of Aberdour, which is presented as the forerunner of Deer itself. Jackson may have dismissed this automatically as of no relevance to Deer's landholdings described by scribe A in II. As fiction, however, it can at least be accepted as indicating what scribe A regarded as an ideal arrangement which he may have hoped that donors would emulate. The most significant statement made by scribe A on the subject of immunity, however, is II.14. It will be recalled that two of the three acts of extinction appear to be repetitions of earlier acts restated by scribe A when he recorded the only fresh extinction in II.14, that of Cainnech (probably the father of Gartnait son of Cainnech, *mormaer* of Buchan, donor in III and IV). It was argued that the reason for recalling the earlier extinctions could have been that Cainnech's extinction represented the final stage in Deer's attainment of complete immunity: all its lands were now free from the burdens of *mormaer* and *toísig*. This can now be seen as consistent with Deer's interpretation of extinctions: if the earlier extinctions were understood to apply to future grants, then it would make sense to recall them when immunity was finally recognised by all parties involved in levying general services from Deer's lands.

It is likely, indeed, that freedom from *mormaer* and *toísech* was the central theme in scribe A's work. His summary record of Deer's property-rights begins with the initial statement of the freedom of the very first land-grant, and ends with the achievement of comprehensive immunity for Deer's lands celebrated in II.14. It is true that scribe A did not finish at II.14. The original versions of III and IV which he penned must, however, have been of a different character to the summary records of II.1 to II.14 if they filled the half page which separates II.14 from scribe A's final exhortation to *mormaír* and *toísig* on the top of the following page: it will be recalled that A's putative version of III and IV probably included witnesses. This change in character from II to A's presumed versions III and IV would suggest that scribe A did

56 On this term see above, 133.

not write these all on the same occasion. It would appear that he initially wrote from I to II.14, and then added his versions of III and IV when these grants were made.[57] His final comment, bestowing 'the blessing of the Lord on every *mormaer* and on every *toísech* who shall comply with this, and to their descendants after them', was evidently written at the same time as III and IV; it is unlikely, however, to have referred only to these two grants (both made by a *mormaer* and his wife). The emphasis on *mormaír* and *toísig* in general and in the future suggests that, here again, the immunity of all Deer's lands for all time to come has been assumed. It was presumably because of this assumption that scribe A did not spell out specifically that the settlement granted in III was free from all burdens: it was only once this came to be disputed openly that A's record of III was rewritten.

It is possible that scribe B shared the assumption that Deer's lands were automatically exempt from exactions. Such an assumption may be all that lies behind his statement that the first land-grant he recorded was 'in freedom till Judgement' (V.1). He may not have stipulated this in the following cases (V.2 and V.3) because he took it as read. In the case of V.3, however, this apparently came to be disputed, causing scribe C to add his statement that the land was free from *toísech* for ever. C's further statement at this point, offering 'his blessing on everyone who shall comply with this thereafter for ever, and his curse on everyone who shall come against it', may on the face of it relate only to the freedom from *toísech* claimed for V.3. Given that this sanction appears after the final land-grant in the book, however, it may be read as having the same import as the similar statement by scribe A after III and IV: namely, that compliance was sought not so much for immunity for what was granted in the transaction(s) immediately preceeding, but for fulfilment of the principle that Deer's lands should be free of all burdens for ever.

The pieces of this argument can now be assembled into a possible narrative of how and why the Deer property-records came into existence.

(i) Scribe A writes as far as II.14 to mark the final stage in securing freedom from all secular exactions when Cainnech, the last of the local powers, renounces his rights to general services from Deer's lands. This historic moment inspires scribe A to summarise all previous benefactions, and gives him an opportunity to list the lands that are now released from all burdens imposed by *mormaer* and *toísech*. Cainnech was probably the father of Gartnait, *mormaer* of Buchan. If so, then his act of extinction may be dated to sometime before 1120, when Gartnait is attested as *mormaer* (Lawrie 1905, 30) (by which time he would presumably have also been *toísech*).

(ii) Deer is granted lands by Gartnait, *mormaer* of Buchan, and his wife. One of these grants occurs in 1131/2. These are recorded by scribe A (i.e., the

---

57 The appearance of witnesses could readily be explained if the transactions recorded in III and IV were written contemporaneously by A.

erased versions of III and IV). Scribe A assumes that these lands are covered by the blanket exemption from exactions recorded in II.14, and exhorts all *mormaír* and *toísig* to comply in the future with the comprehensive immunity for Deer's lands.

(iii) Further grants are recorded by scribe B, who also assumes that these are covered by Deer's immunity. The last of these grants is made by Comgell son of Cainnech, *toísech* of Clann Chanann: if he is the brother of Gartnait, then presumably he would have succeeded Gartnait as *toísech*, while someone else may have become *mormaer*.[58]

(iv) The immunity of the settlement granted in III by Gartnait and his wife comes to be disputed. As a result, the record of their grant is expanded in such a way that the settlement's freedom from all burdens is emphasised, and the document itself made to seem more imposing. This is achieved by erasing scribe A's version of the grant, and also scribe A's version of IV, in order to make enough room for scribe 'D' to write the enlarged record of III. The record of IV is squeezed into the space that remains. The dispute may have been initiated by the putative successor of Gartnait as *mormaer*, and seems to have hinged on whether the immunity commemorated in II.14 applied to lands granted subsequently to Deer. This question may, indeed, have arisen at the time Gartnait made this grant (the first, apparently, since complete immunity had been attained); on that occasion it was resolved when Gartnait gave a pledge to Cormac, bishop of Dunkeld, guaranteeing that the subject of the grant would be free of all burdens.

(v) The dispute rumbled on about the immunity of lands acquired since Cainnech's act of extinction in II.14. It seems to have flared up specifically in relation to the land granted in V.3 (initiated by Comgell's successor as *toísech* of Clann Chanann?), causing scribe C to add to scribe B's record. Deer's claim that all its lands were immune from lay exactions as a result of the extinctions noted in II.14 may have been more generally contested, provoking scribe C to 'clarify' II.14 and perhaps add the sanction to V.3.

(vi) A resolution of this dispute was proclaimed at Ellon, witnessed by 'all the good men of Buchan', by Colbain, *mormaer* of Buchan (who was probably also Comgell's successor as *toísech* of Clann Chanann),[59] and by the *toísech* of Clann Morgainn. They recognised the immunity of lands acquired by Deer since the extinction by Cainnech in II.14, but did so in such a way that Deer

---

58 Although it is possible that, as far as the lands grant in V.3 were concerned, Comgell's position as *toísech* may have been all that was relevant: if so, he may (for all we know) have been *mormaer*. It will be recalled that the grants by Muiredach son of Morgann (II.2) may have been for land in his capacity as *mormaer* and different land in his capacity as *toísech* (see above, 330). **59** Colbain may have been *mormaer* and *toísech* in right of his wife, Eva, daughter of Gartnait. For Colbain's Fife connections, see Young 1993, 179–80. Presumably Eva's father was Gartnait son of Cainnech, *mormaer* of Buchan in the 1130s (see III); her uncle was probably Comgell son of Cainnech, *toísech* of Clann Chanann (V.3).

had to concede that grants of immunity were not eternally open-ended, but were restricted to whatever lands were held by the *clerici* at that time. This was all recorded by scribe C in VI. It is likely that the limited extinction in VI was enacted soon after Colbain became *mormaer* of Buchan:[60] conceivably it was on the occasion of his inauguration, which was probably celebrated at the ceremonial mound at Ellon known as the 'Earl's Hill' (see Robertson, J. 1862, 3 n.2 at p.5).

(vii) VI represented as much as Deer could gain from the leading men of Buchan, but it was not satisfied with the concession they had made in the process. The appearance of David I in the region towards the end of his reign gave them the opportunity to re-establish the principle that immunity from secular exactions was unlimited. The case was heard initially at Banff, and finally settled at Aberdeen. David's instruction that the *clerici* and their possessions should not be molested may have been taken by Deer to have been unlimited.[61] The record of David I's judgement (VII) was inserted into the gospel-book in such a way that it could have been read as applying to any grants that might in the future have been recorded in the blank spaces in earlier folios. This may have been an attempt by the *clerici* of Deer to dispell any ambiguity about what they evidently felt was a vindication of their claim that immunity from lay services applied to their lands in total, including whatever may be granted to them in the future.

THE PROBLEM OF 'CUIT'

At the heart of Jackson's understanding of extinguishing was his conviction that *cuit* referred to the share of general dues and services which was retained by the *toísech* and then the *mormaer* who collected them for the king. The way his argument unfolded logically from this premiss can be seen in his treatment of the one instance when an extinction was *not* expressed as extinguishing all church-lands: Cathal's extinction of his *toísech*'s *cuit* in II.11. Jackson maintained that 'extinguishing all church-lands' (II.10, II.14, and VI) must be different from a *toísech* extinguishing his *cuit* (II.11) because 'if it meant the donor remitting all the dues on all the monastic estates to which he himself was entitled, this would be the same as the above-described 'quenching' [of the *cuit* of a *toísech*] ... and would surely therefore be phrased in the same

---

60 Perhaps *c.*1150? Colbain was *mormaer* as late as 1178 (Barrow 1971, 252, 257); Fergus, the next known *mormaer* of Buchan, is attested in 1193×5 and was dead by 1214 (Barrow 1971, 317, 471–2). It is likely, but incapable of proof, that Colbain had not long been *mormaer* when the hearings were held before David I *c.*1150 which resulted in VII.   61 It was, however, witnessed by three of those named as witnesses in VI; there may, therefore, have been some ambiguity about whether David's judgement differed materially from what had been achieved in VI.

way' (Jackson 1972, 121–2). As we have seen, however, Jackson's alternative explanation of extinguishing 'all church-lands' is not only inherently improbable, but fails to account for the clear indications in the Deer records themselves that extinguishing all church-lands meant freedom from *mormaer* and *toísech*, without ever mentioning the king. If Jackson's argument is unsustainable, then this calls into question his initial premiss about the meaning of *cuit* in the Deer records.

The term *cuit* has a wide range of meanings.[62] It can be translated not just as 'share' or 'portion', but as 'portion of food, meal'; it can also be translated 'goods' or 'property', and in a legal context as 'due, proportion, fixed amount' (see Quin 1983 under *cuit*, sections 1, 3, 5 and 8). There is, however, no other instance apart from the Deer records (as far as I am aware) of *cuit* being extinguished or granted. Any conclusions about the meaning of *cuit* in the context of lordship in Buchan must be based first-and-foremost on an analysis of its appearances in the Deer records themselves.

Three points may be noted at the outset. First, if acts of extinction amounted to the renunciation of the dues and services concerned, then presumably a grant of *cuit* (II.3 and II.7) must have meant the transfer to Deer of what was exacted as *cuit* from a particular settlement, rather than its abolition.[63] Secondly, if the interpretation of *ar chuit* in VI advanced here is accepted, our knowledge of *cuit* in the Deer records is confined solely to what was written by scribe A. It is impossible to be sure, therefore, whether *cuit* in this context was a term in widespread use, or whether there were alternatives. The final point is that *cuit* does not appear on its own, but is qualified as the *cuit* of a *toísech*, *mormaer* or king. Given that these positions were particularly distinguished by their regular enjoyment of common dues and services, this might suggest that *cuit*, whatever it was exactly, was related in some way to the general burdens imposed by king, *mormaer* and *toísech* on settlements within the areas they controlled.

This would seem to take us back to Jackson's initial premiss about the nature of *cuit*. It will be recalled, however, that Skene envisaged *cuit* in the

---

62 Note that *cuit* in II.11 (the extinction of his *toísech*'s *cuit* by Cathal) appears with accusative singular *cuitid* rather than *cuit* (as elsewhere in the Deer records). I am grateful to Dr Seán Duffy and Professor Breandán Ó Buachalla for pointing out to me that this could be an early example of *cuit* with velar inflexion (on which see Quin 1983 s.v. *cuit*) rather than an instance of *cuitig*, a by-form of *cuit* (suggested in Jackson 1975, 55: he nevertheless treated this as if it were synonymous with *cuit*). This would still require *cuitig* to have been rendered *cuitid* by the Deer scribe. It is not obvious how lenited *-g* could have become lenited *-d* by the second quarter of the twelfth century. For discussion of this problem, see the chapter by Roibeart Ó Maolalaigh. **63** Because Jackson saw acts of extinction as acquitting rather than abolishing dues and services, he argued (rather uncomfortably) that granting *cuit* could mean its abolition or its transfer, depending on whether the settlement concerned was already in Deer's possession or not (Jackson 1972, 119). The relationship of *cuit* to possession of a settlement is discussed below, 353 n.65.

Deer records as the 'share in definite proportions' of general dues and services without any suggestion thereby that *toísech* acted as collector for *mormaer* and *mormaer* for king; instead, he saw these ranks as constituting 'a gradation of persons possessing territorial rights' (Skene 1872, 456, 458; Skene 1880, 57–8, 236). *Cuit* could therefore be likened to the payments and services imposed on their territories by local rulers in medieval Ireland, summarised in legal texts as *sloiged*, *cís* and *congbáil*, 'hosting, tribute and maintenance' (Simms 1987, 130–3); parallels can be found for the situation where a *mormaer* as overlord levied exactions from settlements which were also burdened with dues and services to a *toísech* as their local lord (Simms 1987, 92, 145). Jackson was surely justified, however, in insisting that Cathal's extinction of his *toísech*'s *cuit* denoted something different from 'extinguishing all church-lands'. How might this be explained?

It has been argued above that when a *mormaer* or *toísech* 'extinguished all church-lands' he rescinded his claim to general dues and services from Deer's lands. It was suggested that the statement that 'all' Deer's lands were thereby freed did not necessarily imply that the donor (if he was a *toísech*) was accustomed to enjoy these dues and services from each and every one of Deer's settlements; it may simply have meant that he undertook not to levy these burdens on any of Deer's lands in the future (or, to be more precise, on any of the lands held at that time by Deer). An alternative reading of 'all' is possible, however. For this we need to retrace our steps to where it was argued that the extinctions recorded in II represented the gradual attainment of a comprehensive immunity from these exactions, with Cainnech's act of extinction in II.14 as the last stage in this process. The significance of Cainnech's extinction was indicated by restating the earlier extinctions along side it: the three individuals thus brought together in II.14 as responsible for Deer's comprehensive immunity from lay burdens represented the three 'powers' with authority over settlements in Deer's possession—the *mormaer* of Buchan, the *toísech* of Clann Chanann and the *toísech* of Clann Morgainn. There are some assumptions in this scenario which now need to be examined more closely. One of two options must be envisaged: (i) that neither of the two individuals who enacted the earlier extinctions—Domnall son of the son of Dubaicín (II.10) and Cathal of Morgann (II.11)—was *mormaer*; or (ii) that both of them were *toísech* of Clann Morgainn and one was *mormaer*. Cainnech (who, it will be recalled, was probably father of Gartnait *mormaer* of Buchan and Comgell *toísech* of Clann Chanann) could therefore have completed the process by rescinding the exactions owed to the *mormaer* (according to option (i)) or those owed to the *toísech* of Clann Chanann (according to option (ii)).

A different scenario can be suggested. It was argued that Deer's blanket immunity was 'updated' in VI by the *mormaer* of Buchan and the *toísech* of

Clann Morgainn, with the *mormaer* acting also as *toísech* of Clann Chanann. The three 'powers' could, therefore, be represented by two individuals. This makes it possible to see the earlier extinctions in II in a slightly different light. We are told in II.11 that Cathal enacted his extinction in his capacity as *toísech*. Domnall, however, could have done so as both *toísech* and *mormaer*. If, therefore, Cathal's extinction was the first in the series, it could quite naturally have been described as the extinction of the dues and services owed to him as *toísech*—his *cuit toísig*; when Domnall subsequently rescinded the dues and services owed to him, then if he was *mormaer* as well as *toísech* of the other *clann*, this would have amounted to complete freedom from lay exactions. 'Extinguishing all church-lands' could, therefore, have meant the achievement of blanket immunity. According to this scenario, Cainnech's later act of extinction (II.14) would have to be seen as an 'updating' of Deer's immunity. To take this line of argument a step further, it is possible that Deer only acquired lands within the territory of Clann Chanann after Domnall and Cathal's acts of extinction (which would require that at the time of Domnall's act Deer's lands all lay within the control of Clann Morgainn, and that Domnall acted as *mormaer* alone).

It is possible, therefore, to explain the difference between extinguishing *cuit toísig* and extinguishing 'all church-lands' in a way which would allow *cuit* to refer to a *toísech* or *mormaer*'s entitlement to general dues and services. There is no suggestion thereby that *cuit* was necessarily a function of a royal administrative hierarchy. Some collateral points should be noted. Cathal's extinction of his *cuit toísig* appears *after* Domnall's extinction of 'all church-lands'. This scenario therefore requires that the transactions in II have not been given in chronological order. This is not a serious difficulty: there are other indications that the items in II have not been arranged chronologically.[64] No chronological conclusions can be drawn, either, from the appearance of Cathal and Cainnech as donors of land within one of the Altries (II.12), or of Cathal and Domnall's grant of **Etdane* (II.13). Another point is that, if *cuit* referred to an entitlement to general dues and services, then these must have been levied by Mael Coluim mac Cinaeda (1005–34) as king of Alba. It has been suggested above, however, that by the first half of the twelfth century the *clerici* of Deer suffered lay exactions from *mormaer* and *toísig*, not the king. It would appear, then, that (according to this scenario) the effective lordship wielded by the king over settlements in central Buchan had disappeared within the space of a century.

The most serious problem with all this is simply that an explanation of *cuit toísig* along these lines is based ultimately on an *a priori* assumption that *cuit* refers to an entitlement to general dues and services. Alternative approaches are possible. If Jackson, for instance, had not started from this assumption,

64 See 331 and 338.

but had begun his analysis with the evidence that extinctions of 'all church-lands' meant freedom from general dues and services, his ruthless logic could have led to a wholly different interpretation of *cuit*. His point that extin-guishing *cuit toísig* and extinguishing 'all church-lands' must be different would thus surely have led him to conclude that—whatever else might be said about *cuit*—it had to be quite distinct from the regular imposition of common dues and services. It might therefore relate to some other type of exaction.[65] Alternatively, the implied distinction between *cuit* and general dues and services may be explained in a less radical way by supposing that it denoted only one element (for example, the payment of tribute in kind), or a particular genre of exaction (say, all those involving the render of edible goods, such as tribute and obligatory hospitality). The difference between this and extin-guishing 'all church-lands' may thus be interpreted as the difference between a limited and a comprehensive cancellation of general dues and services.

Unfortunately no obvious preference for any of these options emerges from a detailed examination of all the instances of *cuit* in the Deer records (although the easiest choice, given the weight of previous assumptions about *cuit*, would be to accept a scenario based on *cuit* as a function of general dues and services). For further progress to be made in understanding the peculiar use of this term in the Deer records an examination of charter evidence for lordship in eastern Scotland north of the Forth is required, keeping all the possibilities which have been generated from the Deer records in mind.

CONCLUSION

One conclusion which has emerged as a result of this re-reading of the Deer records is that they should not be seen as offering evidence for the administrative hierarchy under the king envisaged by Robertson and Jackson. There is no need, of course, to doubt that *mormaer* and *toísech* controlled common obligations and imposed tribute. But this is less impressive as evidence of a precociously consolidated kingdom than would be true if *cuit* represented shares in a regular levy retained respectively by *toísech* and *mormaer* as royal agents. *Mormaer* and *toísech* controlled general dues and

65 It has often been maintained that the grant of the *cuit* of a *toísech* and the *cuit* of a *mormaer* from Altrie (II.3) is an example of *cuit* owed to *mormaer* and *toísech* from the same settlement. It will be recalled, however, that this should be read alongside the statement that there were two Altries. It was argued that this can be read to mean that *cuit* was rendered to the *mormaer* from one Altrie and to a *toísech* from the other Altrie. If this interpretation of II.3 is accepted, then *cuit* could conceivably be seen as a burden rendered from a named settlement (rather than a piece of land within a settlement) to a single beneficiary: the king, the *mormaer*, or a *toísech* (or, of course, an ecclesiastical establishment like Deer).

services in their own right: as leading lords, not as officials. Indeed, it is surely significant that Deer sought immunity from secular exactions first of all from *toísech* and *mormaer*, and only latterly sought confirmation of this from the king. If *mormaer* and *toísech* functioned first-and-foremost as royal officials, then immunity would presumably have been sought initially from the king, followed up with royal instructions to *mormaer* and *toísech*.

What of the proposal that *toísech* in the Deer records in some cases meant 'thane' in the sense of an overlord's agent? This has to be based principally on the evidence of the Deer records themselves. Two aspects of the texts have been cited in particular. One is the reference to the *cuit* of the *toísech*: this has been discussed above, with different results from Jackson. The other is the statement in record II.2 that a donor 'was *mormaer* and *toísech*'. Jackson argued that *toísech* here 'can hardly be being used in the sense of 'chief of a kindred', since anyone who was *mormaer* of, e.g. Moray would surely also ... be chief of the ruling family of Moray' (Jackson 1972, 112). Jackson's choice of Moray as an example is not obviously apposite for record II.2, where the donor (Muiredach son of Morgann) was presumably *mormaer* of Buchan. As such, Muiredach would have exercised lordship in the environs of Deer both in his capacity as *mormaer* and also in the area dominated by his kindred, whose head he was. It was argued above that, in view of the fact that two grants by Muiredach are recorded in II.2, he may have exercised lordship over one as *toísech clainne* and over the other as *mormaer*.[66] The most natural reading of the Deer records, therefore, is that *toísech* and *toísech Clainne X* referred to the same position—literally the leader of a kindred.[67] It should be noted that *toísech*, as a leader or chief of a kindred or people, is not unique to Deer in the twelfth century: it is attested, for example, in the Kells records (Mac Niocaill 1990, 156–7, 161–2).[68]

Was this the kind of person who was intended by the term 'thane' in some contexts in the twelfth and thirteenth centuries? One instance might be in the social hierarchy of *rex-comes-thanus-ogthiern-rusticus* (king-*mormaer*-'thane'-*ócthigern*-peasant) sketched out in a tract on compensation for killing and injury.[69] The provisions detailed in this tract may still have had some legal relevance into the thirteenth century (MacQueen 1990, 87–93). Here *mormaer*

---

66 It is likely, moreover, that some lands were attached to the positions of *mormaer* and *toísech*: note, for example, an Irish reference to *ferann taisigechta* (Kelly 1998, 403). I am grateful to Thomas Clancy for this reference.   67 As implied by Duncan 1975, 108–11, who is nowhere tempted into making the link between *toísech* and thane.   68 *toísech tuaithi Cnogba* and *lantoísech Síl Tuathail*, 'chief/leader of the people of Knowth' and 'full chief/leader of Síl Tuathail'.   69 The tract is preserved in material known as *leges Scocie* in the earliest manuscript (MacQueen 1990, 86–93), and is found attached to *Regiam Majestatem* (Thomson and Innes 1844, 640–1), as well as in a French version known to scholarship as *leges inter Brettos et Scottos* (Thomson and Innes 1844, 663–5: the title was first used of this tract in Skene 1609, 103, although something going by this name was known in 1305: see MacQueen 1990, 91 and 101 n.119).

and 'thane' are treated as equivalent to a king's son and *mormaer*'s son respectively; the *ócthigern*, however, is not equivalent to the thane's son (who stands alone in the list of tariffs), but to the thane's *nepos*. This could be an important clue to the identity of 'thane' in this context. *Nepos* can be translated as 'grandson' or 'nephew' or simply 'kinsman'. If 'grandson' was intended then it is hard to imagine how this would have had much practical force; it could only be explained as a rather contrived attempt to create extra distance between the thane and the *ócthigern*. If 'thane' stood for *toísech clainne*, however, and his status therefore depended uniquely on being head of a kindred (as the status of the other ranks did not), then the reference here to 'kinsman' could be perfectly natural. There might have been some sense in regarding the bottom rank above peasant as equivalent to an ordinary member of a noble kindred. Be this as it may, the extent to which this might lead to a re-opening of Grant's discussion of thanes (Grant 1993) will have to be kept for another occasion. The Deer records themselves offer a window into Buchan only. All that can be said at this stage is that all sightings of *toísig* there can readily be identified with the *toísech clainne*.

Once the Deer records are allowed to 'speak for themselves' (as it were), particularly in the light of the most recent understanding of early property-records, a different view of society emerges from the one constructed by Jackson. The most prominent lords were the head of a noble kindred, *toísech clainne*, and the *mormaer* of Buchan (the predominant *toísech* in the region). Both *mormaer* and *toísech* enjoyed general dues and services throughout the areas they controlled, as well as possessing specific lands (such as the lands granted by the *toísech*, Cathal son of Morgann, in II.5, II.12, and II.13, or granted by the *mormaer*, Gartnait son of Cainnech, in III and IV).[70] It should not be assumed, however, that all donors were of the rank of *toísech* or *mormaer*. There were, presumably, many landowning kindreds other than those few whose heads were recognised as a *toísech*. What presumably distinguished a *toísech* and *mormaer* from other landholders was the right (or claim) to levy general dues and services. A few donors of settlements—such as Mael Snechta son of Lulach, king of Moray (II.9)—were even more powerful than the *mormaer* of Buchan.

In all this the king of Scots seems but a shadowy figure. General dues and services were possibly levied by Mael Coluim mac Cinaeda (1005–34), but this depends on how the *cuit* is interpreted which he gifted to Deer from two named settlements in II.7. Mael Coluim mac Cinaeda also owned two *dabach*

---

70 They may also have received (according to the most radical interpretation of *cuit*) a levy from settlements possessed by other lords: for example, each of the 'two Altries' may have yielded this levy, one to the *mormaer* Matain son of Cairell and the other to the *toísech* Culi son of Báithín (II.3), while one of the Altries was possessed by the *toísech* Cathal son of Morgann and by Cainnech son of the son of Dobarchú (who was probably *mormaer* as well as *toísech* of Clann Chanann) (II.12).

of land (II.7). Others who may have been descendants of Cinaed mac Ailpín (d.858), the definitive ancestor of the kingship of Alba, include Mael Coluim son of Cuilén, donor of (at least) part of Biffie (II.6), who may have been son and brother of two kings of Scots (Cuilén 966–71 and Custantín 995–7); and Mael Coluim mac Maíl Brigte (d.1029), who possessed the Elrick (II.8), and is likely to have been a successor to Custantín's claim to the kingship, perhaps through his mother or grandmother (Woolf 2000, 155).[71] It is only at the very end, with the assertion by David I of Deer's immunities, that the king of Scots appears as a particularly prominent power in the records—at the point when the *clerici* of Deer, by writing a document approximating closely in form to a Latin charter, displayed their growing consciousness of Europeanisation.

The records only testify indirectly, however, to the balance of political and institutional authority wielded by local, regional and regnal power in Buchan. The core concern which inspired the creation, continuation, interpolation and rewriting of the records themselves over a period of twenty or thirty years was evidently immunity from general obligations such as 'hosting, tribute, and maintenance' (see above, 343–7). In an Irish context it has been suggested that such immunities for church-lands became a particular priority of reformed ecclesiastics in the twelfth century (Simms 1987, 130). The progressive achievement and assertion of freedom from all secular burdens which (it has been suggested) is the central feature of the Deer records may, therefore, be seen as a witness to the participation of local secular powers and the *clerici* of Deer, no later than the second decade of the twelfth century, in a fundamental aspect of Europeanisation: a new recognition of the special place of the Church in society.

REFERENCES

Anderson, A.O. (1908) *Scottish annals from English chronicles, AD 500 to 1286* London (facsimile reprint, with corrections and foreward by M.O. Anderson, Stamford, 1991).
—— (1922) *Early sources of Scottish history, AD 500–1286*, 2 vols, Edinburgh.
—— (1948) 'Ninian and the Southern Picts', *Scot. Hist. Rev.* 27, 25–47
Bannerman, John (1990) 'The Scots language and the kin-based society', in Derick S. Thomson (ed.), *Gaelic and Scots in harmony together: Proceedings of the Second International Conference on the Languages of Scotland, University of Glasgow 1988* (Glasgow, Dept of Celtic, University of Glasgow), 1–19.

71 Domnall son of Ruaidrí, who also possessed Biffie (II.6) may have been brother of Mael Brigte son of Ruaidrí, father of Mael Coluim (d. 1029), and may thus also have been deemed a successor to the agnatic line which evidently died out with Custantín mac Cuiléin (d.997). If so, it is conceivable that the explanation of the 'joint-grant formula' in II.6 is that Biffie was originally held in its entirety by Mael Coluim son of Cuilén and that Domnall succeeded to Mael Coluim's property and confirmed Mael Coluim's gift of Biffie in a separate ceremony. (Domnall, indeed, may have been seen as an appropriate successor to Mael Coluim if he, like Mael Coluim, was a less prominent but closely connected member of the leading dynasty north of the Mounth.)

—— (1993) 'MacDuff of Fife', in Grant and Stringer, 1993, 20–38.

Barrow, G.W.S. (1956) *Feudal Britain: the completion of the medieval kingdoms, 1066–1314*, London.

—— (ed.), (1960) *Regesta Regum Scottorum*, vol. i, *The acts of Malcolm IV, king of Scots 1153–65*, Edinburgh.

—— (1962) 'Rural settlement in central and eastern Scotland: the medieval evidence', *Scottish Studies* 6, 123–44.

—— (1969) 'Northern English society in the twelfth and thirteenth centuries', *Northern History* 4, 1–28 (republished in Barrow 1992, 127–53).

—— (ed.) (1971), in collaboration with W.W. Scott, *Regesta Regum Scottorum* vol. ii, *The acts of William I, king of Scots 1165–1214*, Edinburgh.

—— (1973) 'Pre-feudal Scotland: shires and thanes', in G.W.S. Barrow, *The kingdom of the Scots: government, church and society from the eleventh to the fourteenth century*, London, 7–68.

—— (1980) *The Anglo-Norman era in Scottish history*, Oxford.

—— (1985) *David I of Scotland (1124–1153): the balance of old and new* (Stenton Lecture 1984), Reading (republished in Barrow 1992, 45–65).

—— (1990) 'The army of Alexander III's Scotland', in Reid (1990), 132–47.

—— (1991) 'The charters of David I', in *Anglo-Norman Studies* 14, 25–37.

—— (1992) *Scotland and its neighbours in the Middle Ages*, London.

—— (1995) 'Witnesses and the attestation of formal documents in Scotland, twelfth-thirteenth centuries', *Legal History* 16, 1–20.

—— (1997) 'The pattern of non-literary manuscript production and survival in Scotland, 1200–1330', in Richard Britnell (ed.), *Pragmatic literacy, East and West 1200–1330*, Woodbridge.

—— (1999) *The charters of King David I: the written acts of David I king of Scots, 1124–53 and of his son Henry earl of Northumberland, 1139–52*, Woodbridge.

Bartlett, Robert (1993) *The making of Europe: conquest, colonization and cultural change 950–1350*, London.

Bergin, Osbern (1910) 'The harrowing of hell', *Ériu* 6 (1908–10), 112–19.

Broun, Dauvit (1995) *The charters of Gaelic Scotland and Ireland in the early and central Middle Ages* (Quiggin Pamphlets on the Sources of Mediaeval Gaelic History, 2), (Dept. of Anglo-Saxon, Norse, and Celtic, Univ. of Cambridge), Cambridge.

—— (1999a) 'Dunkeld and the origin of Scottish identity', in Dauvit Broun and Thomas Owen Clancy (eds), *Spes Scotorum: Hope of Scots: Saint Columba, Iona and Scotland*, Edinburgh, 95–111.

—— (1999b) 'Anglo-French acculturation and the Irish element in Scottish identity', in Brendan Smith (ed.), *Britain and Ireland 900–1300: insular responses to medieval European change*, Cambridge, 135–53.

—— (2000) 'The writing of charters in Scotland and Ireland in the twelfth century' in Heidecker 2000, 113–132.

Brown, P. Hume (1899) *History of Scotland*, vol. 1 (3 vols, 1899–1911), Cambridge.

Cameron, John (1937) *Celtic law: The 'Senchus Mór' and 'The Book of Aicill', and the traces of an early Gaelic system of law in Scotland*, London.

Chalmers, George (1810) *Caledonia, or An account, historical and topographic of North Britain, from the most ancient to the present times*, vol. 1, London (3 vols, 1810–24).

Cheyette, Frederic L. (1988) 'The "sale" of Carcassonne to the counts of Barcelona (1067–70) and the rise of the Trencavels', *Speculum* 63, 826–64.

Clanchy, Michael (1979) *From memory to written record: England 1066–1307*, London.

—— (1993) *From memory to written record: England 1066–1307*, 2nd edn, Oxford.

Dalrymple of Hailes, Sir David (1776 (1819)) *Annals of Scotland from the accession of Malcolm III in the year M.LVII...*, 2 vols (1776, 1779); 3rd ed. 1819, Edinburgh.

Dickinson, W. Croft (1961) *Scotland from earliest times to 1603*, London.

Dodgshon, Robert A. (1981) *Land and society in early Scotland*, Oxford,

Donaldson, G. (1985) 'Aspects of early Scottish conveyancing', *apud* Peter Goldesbrough, *Formulary of Old Scots legal documents* (Stair Society), Edinburgh, 153–86.

Driscoll, Stephen T. (1988) 'Power and authority in Early Historic Scotland: Pictish symbol stones and other documents', in J. Gledhill, et al. (eds), *State and society: the emergence and development of social hierarchy and political centralization*, London, 215–36.

—— (1991) 'The archaeology of state formation in Scotland', in W.S. Hanson and E.A. Slater (eds), *Scottish archaeology: new perceptions*, Aberdeen, 81–111.

—— (1992) 'Discourse on the frontiers of history: material culture and social reproduction in early Scotland', *Historical Archaeology* 26.4, 12–25.

Duncan, A.A.M. (1975) *Scotland: the making of the kingdom* (Edinburgh History of Scotland vol. i), Edinburgh.

Easson, Alexis (1986) 'Systems of land assessment in Scotland before 1400', unpublished PhD dissertation (University of Edinburgh).

Faith, Rosamond (1997) *The English peasantry and the growth of lordship*, London.

Foster, Sally M. (1996) *Picts, Gaels and Scots: early historic Scotland*, London.

Fraser, J. (1938) 'The Gaelic *notitiae* in the Book of Deer', *Scottish Gaelic Studies* 5.1, 51–66.

Galbraith, V.H. (1948) *Studies in public records*, London.

Geary, P.J. (1994) *Phantoms of remembrance: memory and oblivion at the end of the first millennium*, Princeton NJ.

Grant, Alexander (1993) 'Thanes and thanages, from the eleventh to the fourteenth centuries', in Grant and Stringer 1993, 39–81.

—— (2000) 'Constructing the early Scottish state', in J.R. Maddicott and D.M. Palliser (eds), *The medieval state: essays presented to James Campbell*, London, 47–71.

—— and Keith J. Stringer (eds) (1993) *Medieval Scotland: crown, lordship and community: essays presented to G.W.S. Barrow*, Edinburgh.

Hamp, Eric P. (1986) 'Scottish Gaelic morair', *Scottish Gaelic Studies* 14.2, 138–41.

Hecht, Alexander (2000) 'Between *memoria*, historiography, and pragmatic literacy: the *Liber Delegacionum* of Reichersberg', in Heidecker 2000, 205–11.

Heidecker, Karl (ed.), (2000) *Charters and the use of the written word in medieval society* (Utrecht Studies in Medieval Literacy, 5).

Hudson, Benjamin T. (1996) *Kings of Celtic Scotland*, Westport CT.

Innes, Cosmo (ed.) (1832) *Registrum Monasterii de Passelet* (Maitland Club), Edinburgh.

—— (ed.) (1837a) *Registrum Episcopatus Moraviensis, e pluribus codicibus consarcinatum circa AD MCCCC* (Bannatyne Club), Edinburgh.

—— (ed.) (1837b) *Liber Sancte Marie de Melros. Munimenta Vetustiora Monasterii Cisterciensis de Melros* (Bannatyne Club), Edinburgh.

—— (ed.) (1845) *Registrum Episcopatus Aberdonensis*, 2 vols (Spalding and Maitland Clubs), Aberdeen and Edinburgh.

—— (ed.) (1859) *The Book of the Thanes of Cawdor: a series of papers selected from the Charter Room at Cawdor, 1236–1742* (Spalding Club), Edinburgh.

—— (1860) *Scotland in the Middle Ages: sketches of early Scotch history and social progress*, Edinburgh.

—— (1861) *Sketches of early Scottish history and social progress*, Edinburgh.

—— (ed.) (1867) *Facsimiles of national manuscripts of Scotland*, vol. 1 (3 vols 1867–1871), Southampton.

—— (1872) *Lectures on Scotch legal antiquities*, Edinburgh.

—— and Patrick Chalmers (eds) (1848, 1856) *Liber S. Thome de Aberbrothoc*, 2 vols (Bannatyne Club), Edinburgh.

Jackson, Kenneth H. (1972) *The Gaelic Notes in the Book of Deer*, Cambridge.

James, Edward (1982) *The origins of France: from Clovis to the Capetians 500–1000*, Basingstoke.

Jones, G.R.J. (1963) 'The tribal system in Wales: a re-assessment in the light of settlement studies', *Welsh Historical Review* 1 (1960–3), 111–32.

—— (1979) 'Multiple estates and early settlement', in P.H. Sawyer (ed.), *English medieval settlement*, London, 9–34.

—— (1989) 'The dark ages', in D. Huw Owen (ed.), *Settlement and society in Wales*, Cardiff, 177–97.

Kapelle, William E. (1979) *The Norman conquest of the North: the region and its transformation*, London.

Kelly, Fergus (1998) *Early Irish farming: a study based mainly on the law-texts of the seventh and eighth centuries AD*, Dublin.

Kemp, R.S. (1927) 'The Book of Deer', *Transactions of the Scottish Ecclesiological Society* 8.3 (1926–7), 164–74.

Lawrie, Sir Archibald C. (1905) *Early Scottish charters prior to AD 1153* (Glasgow,

Lindsay, William A., John Dowden, and J. Maitland Thomson (1908), (eds), *Charters, bulls and other documents relating to the abbey of Inchaffray* (Scottish History Society), Edinburgh.

Macbain, Alexander (1885) 'The Book of Deer', *Transactions of the Gaelic Society of Inverness* 6 (1884–5), 137–66.

—— (1897) 'Mr Skene *versus* Dr Skene', *Transactions of the Gaelic Society of Inverness* 21 (1896–7), 191–214.

Mackie, James D. (1964) *A history of Scotland*, London.

Mackinnon, James (1924) *The constitutional history of Scotland from earliest times to the Reformation*, London.

Mac Niocaill, G. (ed. and trans.) (1990) 'The Irish "charters"', in Peter Fox (ed.), *The Book of Kells, MS 58, Trinity College Library, Dublin: commentary*, Luzern, 153–65.

MacQueen, Hector L. (1995) '*Regiam Majestatem*, Scots law, and national identity', *Scot. Hist. Rev.* 74, 1–25.

MacQueen, John, Winifred MacQueen, and D.E.R. Watt, (1995), (eds), *Scotichronicon by Walter Bower in Latin and English*, gen. ed. D.E.R. Watt, vol. iii, *Books V and VI*, Edinburgh.

Matheson, Angus (1948) 'Varia', *Éigse* 6.1, 59–69.

Molitor, Stephan (1990) 'Das Traditionsbuch: Zur Forschungsgeschichte einer Qullengattung und zu einem Beispiel aus Südwestdeutschland', *Archiv für Diplomatik* 36, 61–92.

Oram, Richard D. (1999) 'David I and the Scottish conquest and colonisation of Moray', *Northern Scotland* 19, 1–19.

Paul, James Balfour (ed.) (1882) *Registrum Magni Sigilli Regum Scotorum. The Register of the Great Seal of Scotland, AD 1424–1513*, Edinburgh.

Quin, E.G. (ed.) (1983) *Dictionary of the Irish language, based mainly on Old and Middle Irish Materials. Compact edition*, Dublin.

Reid, Norman H. (ed.) (1990) *Scotland in the reign of Alexander III*, Edinburgh.

Robertson, Joseph (ed.) (1847) *Illustrations of the topography and antiquities of the shires of Aberdeen and Banff*, vol. ii (3 vols, numbered ii–iv 1847–62), (Spalding Club), Aberdeen.

Robertson, E. William (1862) *Scotland under her early kings: a history of the kingdom to the close of the thirteenth century*, 2 vols, Edinburgh.

—— (1872) *Historical essays in connexion with land, the church etc.*, Edinburgh.

Scott, J.G. (1997) 'The partition of a kingdom: Strathclyde 1092–1153', *Transactions of the Dumfriesshire and Galloway Natural History and Antiquarian Society*, 3rd series, 72, 11–40.

Shead, Norman F. (1970) 'Benefactions to the medieval cathedral and see of Glasgow', *Innes Review* 21, 3–16.

Simms, Katharine (1987) *From kings to warlords: the changing political structure of Gaelic Ireland in the later Middle Ages*, Woodbridge.

Skene, Sir John (ed.) (1609) *Regiam Majestatem Scotiæ Veteres Leges et Constitutiones*, Edinburgh.

Skene, William F. (1837) *The Highlanders of Scotland: their origin, history, and antiquities*, 2 vols, London.

—— (1871) *Johannis de Fordun Chronica Gentis Scotorum*, ed. William F. Skene (Historians of Scotland vol. i), Edinburgh.

—— (1872) 'Tribe communities in Scotland', in *John of Fordun's Chronicle of the Scottish Nation*, trans. Felix J.H. Skene, ed. Willaim F. Skene (Historians of Scotland vol. iv), Edinburgh, 441–60

—— (1880) *Celtic Scotland: a history of Ancient Alban*, vol. 3 (3 vols 1876–80), Edinburgh.

Stevenson, Joseph (ed.), (1835) *Chronica de Mailros* (Bannatyne Club), Edinburgh.

Stuart, John (ed.) (1852) 'Decreet of the Synod of Perth, AD MCCVI', *Miscellany of the Spalding Club* 5, ed. John Stuart (Spalding Club), Aberdeen, 209–13.

—— (ed.) (1868) *Records of the priory of the Isle of May* (Society of Antiquaries of Scotland), Edinburgh.

—— (ed.) (1869) *The Book of Deer* (Spalding Club), Edinburgh.

Taylor, Simon (1995) 'The Scandinavians in Fife and Kinross: the onomastic evidence', in B.E. Crawford (ed.) *Scandinavian settlement in Northern Britain: thirteen studies of place-names in their historical context*, London, 141–67.

Thomson, Thomas (ed.) (1841) *Liber Cartarum Prioratus Sancti Andree in Scotia. E registro ipso in archivis baronum de Panmure hodie asservato* (Bannatyne Club), Edinburgh.

Watson, W.J. (1915) *Rosg Ghàidhlig: specimens of Gaelic prose*, Inverness.

—— (1926) *The history of the Celtic place-names of Scotland*, Edinburgh.

Whyte, Ian D. (1995) *Scotland before the Industrial Revolution: an economic and social history*, London.

Woolf, Alex (2000) 'The "Moray question" and the kingship of Alba in the tenth and eleventh centuries', *Scot. Hist. Rev.* 79, 145–64.

Young, Alan (1993) 'The earls and earldom of Buchan in the thirteenth century', in Grant and Stringer 1993, 174–202.

DEER IN CONTEXT

Deer and the early church in North-Eastern Scotland

THOMAS OWEN CLANCY

The first Gaelic entry in the Book of Deer describes the foundation of Deer by its patron saint, Drostan (Text I, 158, 159). This short foundation-legend promises, as such narratives often do, a vision of the earliest seeds of Christianity, in this case in Buchan, and thus in the North-East more generally.[1] The presence of Columba suggests either a link with Iona in the foundation of Aberdour and Deer, or, as the tradition in the Aberdeen Breviary records, a familial connection. Columba is there cast as Drostan's uncle (Brev. Abd. vol. 2, pars hyemalis, fol. xix). Equally, the connection with Columba seems to situate the foundation of Deer during his lifetime; and the donation of Deer by the *mormaer* suggests a close relationship from its inception between the *mormaír* of Buchan and the church.

It is a fine foundation legend, and many parallels can be drawn with legends of saints elsewhere. Analysis of such foundation legends, however, has often shown that we should distrust these as historical records, and should instead approach them as related to the political and ecclesiastical aspirations of the time of their composition or recording. Suggestive of contemporary concerns in this tale are details such as the relationship with the *mormaer*, and especially the granting of the monastery 'in freedom from *mormaer* and *toísech*', since this is an apparent preoccupation of the property records which follow. Given that the foundation legend appears to be a 'preface' to the property records, we should see it as a text of the period when those records were written, and likely even a new composition of that period, albeit perhaps based on older folklore. Approaching the text in this way, we must then call into doubt the historical basis of the tradition of a relationship between Drostan and Columba.

It seems unlikely that this tradition was terribly ancient at the time of the writing of the Gaelic notes. Although Columba's name is prominent in some of the property records as a co-recipient of grants to Deer, examination of the long entry (II), written by the same scribe, 'A', who wrote the foundation legend, reveals a more complex picture. Columba is mentioned alongside Drostan only in the first grant, which immediately follows the foundation legend and was perhaps influenced by its vision of the past. After that, II

---

1 I use 'North-East' in this article to indicate, roughly, the corner of Scotland delimited by the Moray Firth on the one hand and the Mounth on the other. This is for convenience in the present context, and not through lack of awareness that there is more of both north and east in Scotland that is in need of discussion.

contains grants which are described only as being to Drostan, or to God and
Drostan (Jackson 1972, 30–1). What this may suggest is that devotion to
Columba was a later development in Deer, perhaps in an attempt to attract
patronage from Gaelic nobility who may have been less interested in cultivating a
local, probably Pictish, saint like Drostan. The success of the connection with
Columba may, perhaps, be seen in the property records themselves.

A parallel for this can be seen in the twelfth-century foundation of a
subsidiary church of Christ and Peter the Apostle, probably at Peterugie, later
Peterhead, as recorded in Text III (see Taylor, this volume). Here, the new
patronage of Peter reflects 'Europeanising' tendencies within twelfth-century
Scotland, just as, it may be suggested, devotion to Columba at some earlier
period reflected Gaelicising tendencies.[2]

Far from a straightforward story then, the foundation legend in Text I
presents the more recent history of cult in Buchan and the North-East, as
much as the early history of the Church (for reflections on this tendency
elsewhere, see e.g., Cubbitt 2002, Padel 2002 and Blair 2002). At some point
in Deer's history—perhaps as late as the twelfth century, though perhaps
more likely sometime in the tenth or eleventh century—the church at Deer
acquired the royal, Gaelic saint Columba as an adjunct to its local saint,
Drostan.[3] This strategy was then repeated by the church and its patrons in
the twelfth century with regard to a subsidiary foundation, in the adoption of
a universal saint, St Peter. This provides us with a model through which we
may approach the question of the early church in Deer and the North-East of
Scotland. By interrogating progressively the different layers in this model of
successive cults—Drostan's, Columba's, Peter's—we may be able to contex-
tualise ecclesiastical change in this most poorly documented area of Scotland.

The first Gaelic entry provides other clues, however, to the state of the
Church in the North-East at the time that the Gaelic notes were entered, as
indeed do all the property records. The nature of the texts means that the

2 This is by no means to suggest that the cult of Peter in Scotland was exclusively a
phenomenon of the 'Europeanising' twelfth century. We know of dedications from the
eighth century in Pictland (cf. Bede, *HE* v.21), and on the Clyde from sometime in the
early middle ages (Kilpeter, now Houston), and the probably seventh-century stone from
Whithorn dedicating a *locus* to St Peter suggests that his cult there preceded the arrival of
Northumbrian influence (see Forsyth 2005). Raymond Lamb (1993, 1998) has suggested
early medieval dates for the Peterkirks of the Orkneys. Peterugie is, however, clearly a
twelfth-century dedication, and the saintly patron should thus be read in a twelfth-century
context.   3 That Columba was held in special regard by kings of Alba in the lines
descended from Cinaed mac Ailpín is evident from the devotional name *Mael Coluim* held
by three kings between 900 and 1093, and by a further king of Alba from the kindred
termed Clann Ruaidrí by Alex Woolf, in his recent discussion of the succession to the
kingship in the tenth and eleventh centuries (Woolf 2000, 146). It is uncertain precisely
how this kindred was tied in to the main branch of descendants of Cinaed. It is surely
significant that three kings of this name are found patronising the church at Deer in the
property records (II.10, II.11, II.13; Jackson 1972, 30–1; cf. Woolf 2000, 158).

information we may glean about the church in Deer in the early twelfth century also extends geographically to the surrounding locale, and chronologically to the century or so preceding their writing. Combined with the liturgy for the Visitation of the Sick, and the Gospel book itself, the Book of Deer, examined in the round and interrogated with care, is a varied and eloquent witness to Christianity in North-East Scotland from its earliest times to the twelfth century.

SAINTS' CULTS

Discussion of the early church among the Picts has traditionally been dominated by the question of the involvement of Columba and Iona in the Christianisation of Pictland. Partly this is dictated by the fact that so many of our surviving sources relating to the conversion of the Picts are drawn from Iona sources. Whether or not the journeys up the Great Glen recorded by Adomnán (*VC* ii.32–5, 42), were in fact part of a conversion effort by Columba (rather than, for instance, an attempt to secure safe passage and secure livings for his monks in Pictish territory); whether or not we should believe the testimony of the *Amra Choluimb Chille* concerning Columba's teaching 'the tribes of the Tay' (Clancy and Márkus 1995, 118–19); we can be fairly certain that he had nothing to do directly with the Christianisation of the north-eastern corner which later became the medieval dioceses of Moray and Aberdeen. That is not to say that its Christianity did not stem from Iona: this is something we cannot discount, and as we shall see there may be some evidence to suggest that it did in part. However, few if any dedications to Columba in the North-East need be of any great age (Taylor 2000) and, as we have seen, the one explicit literary connection of Columba with the North-East, the Deer foundation legend, has indications of being a later product.

If Drostan is, at least temporarily, detached from Columba, we have an opportunity to look in somewhat clearer light at the Pictish church in the North-East. This to an extent follows a line taken by the likes of, for instance, W. Douglas Simpson (1927, 1943), but in the past an 'anti-Columban' thesis has tended to produce unsound evidence for a Ninianic mission, or one by Kentigern, based on dubious late dedications, or impossibly early dates for Pictish churchmen without supporting evidence. Thus, the historiographical argument has had a tendency to be reduced to ingenious shufflings of the influences of saintly superpowers. Much of the main national influence of previously local or regional saints such as Kentigern or Ninian can, however, be shown to be products of the twelfth-century (Clancy 2002). On the whole, our chances for recovering much of the religious history of the North-East are slender, since documentation from this part of Scotland is so thin (thinner than usual), but one or two pieces of information are at hand with which to begin such a study.

The historical evidence for the early church in the North-East must rest heavily on the analysis of place-names, and especially dedications to saints, although the archaeological and art historical evidence tells its own, perhaps more eloquent story. We know now that the analysis of dedications as if they always unfailingly demonstrated the areas of operations of the living saints is flawed. Many dedications are later, and indeed, it is possible that in many cases the cult of certain saints, Ninian for instance, were imported only very late, well after 1100, into the North-East (Clancy 2001; 2002). The way in which a saint's cult with early beginnings could develop in new directions in the later Middle Ages, both geographically and iconographically, has been superbly demonstrated by Simon Taylor with regard to St Fillan (Taylor 2001).

Nonetheless, as Taylor himself has pointed out, where a fairly obscure saint with seemingly local or native pedigree displays only a very limited and local cult, we may well be dealing with that saint's original churches, or at the very least those of his followers (Taylor 2001, 176; Taylor 1999, 35; for similar comments anent the situation in Cornwall, see Padel 2002). This is especially true if other evidence may be adduced to lay alongside the dedication evidence. For instance, very limited cult-spreads and other circumstantial evidence would seem to support the hypothesis that those cult centres in Atholl and Easter Ross respectively relating to the bishops Cóeti and Curetán, who both lived around 700, owe something to the actual activities of these saints (see Taylor 1996, 101–3; 1999, 57–60). Likewise, Taylor (1996, 100) has suggested that the two isolated dedications in Fife to the otherwise uncommemorated abbot of Iona Dúnchad, who died in 717, are likely to testify to a historical connection between him and east Fife. Nonetheless, even in these instances, we must be cautious: the link between the saint commemorated and the place could be close (for instance, he could be the founding cleric); more distant (the church could be a daughter-church of a monastery or mother-church associated with that cleric); or yet more distant still (the church could contain a relic of that saint). In some cases, obscure individuals commemorated in the names of churches may not be 'saints' at all, but rather the secular landowners whose patronage founded a church, though this explanation has not been explored in the Scottish context (but see Padel 2002, 312 for Cornish and Welsh explorations).

In the first part of this contribution, I will be examining a series of cults of ostensibly Pictish saints who have a fairly restricted number of commemorations in the North-East. This is ground already covered to some extent by W.J. Watson (1926) and W. Douglas Simpson (1925, 1927, 1943), though to rather different effects and using rather different methodologies. What I hope such a study will provide is an understanding, even in a somewhat amorphous form, of some of the beginnings of the church in the North-East, and hence the religious context for the early monastery at Deer.

Nechtan and Uineus
Under the years 623 and 679 in the Annals of Ulster are recorded the deaths of two abbots of a place called *Nér* (or *Ner*, or *Neir*). The entries read:

> 623.2 *Quies M. Lasre abbatis Ard Machae 7 Uinei abbatis Neir.*
> 679.4 *Dormitatio Nectain Neir.*

The latter is also commemorated in the Martyrology of Óengus (Stokes 1905, 34) at Jan 8—*Nechtán Néir de Albae*—and likewise in the related Martyrology of Tallaght (Best and Lawlor 1931, 6). The Book of Leinster forms are difficult to read (cf. O'Sullivan 1983, p. 1599, l.49071), but later manuscripts provide variants *Nechtan an ner, Nechtan ner de Albae*.

Although Stokes emended the word *neir/ner* to the adjective *nár* 'noble', following the readings in two manuscripts, the reading in the majority, including the Book of Leinster and the Martyrology of Tallaght, and the *lectio difficilior*, is *Néir* (Stokes 1905, 34). This entry localises Nér in Britain, or more specifically in Scotland, since all the other instances of the use of the term *Alba* in the text of the Martyrology of Óengus clearly refer to Scotland.[4]

Hogan was the earliest author to note the possibility that *Nér* and Deer should be equated (Hogan 1910, 554). T.F. O'Rahilly had the ingenious idea that *Nér* was the original name for Deer, and that the form *Dér* arose by a back-formation from the dative following the nasalising preposition *i n-*, *i Nér* having been understood as representing *i nDér* (1946, 373–4n). This has since been cautiously accepted by various scholars, including Jackson (1972, 6; and cf. Hudson, 1994, 147), who misrepresented O'Rahilly's view whilst positing the more plausible development of *Nér* as 'a deformation of *Dér* ... arising from the common instances where the name stood in the "locative" after the preposition "in"; that is, *i nDér*, pronounced *i Nér*.'

I believe that neither explanation is entirely satisfactory. In neither the annal entries, nor the martyrologies, do we find the name in a dative/locative context; in all instances it appears to be in the genitive case. The annal entries do not really encourage emendation; and the phrasing of the 623 entry, with the parallelism between two abbots *of* places, not *in* them, seems to guarantee

---

4 *Pace* Lacey 1999, 130, who follows the Martyrology of Donegal in identifying Nechtan with the 'Neachtain of Dungiven in *Ciannachta Glinne Geimin*' (I thank Alex Woolf for this reference). This is one of a spate of saints with Scottish spheres of activity who are relocated by the Martyrology of Donegal among the Ciannachta Glinne Geimin; others include Finnlug(an) (see Lacey 1999, 130), and Cóeti (see Martyrology of Donegal, Oct. 24 and 25, and 284–5, n. 2). Of course, there may have been cults of these saints localised there at some stage in the Middle Ages.

a genitive form. The arguments of both O'Rahilly and Jackson seem to me to rest on an assumption that there is no place of the name *Nér*. If there is such a place, the arguments for identification between Deer and *Nér* must be discounted, and this would hold good even if we could not now identify that place.

I would suggest that Nér is a separate place altogether, and that it can be identified with the second element in Fetternear ABD (*Fethirneir* 1157; *Fethyrneir* 1241, PNA 276). The place-name element *fetter-* seems to be from a Gaelic term (*foithir*) formed on the basis of an earlier Pictish administrative or territorial term (**uotir*, cf. W. *godir* 'territory, district'), though its precise connotations have yet to be assessed (see Taylor, this volume; Clancy and Taylor, forthcoming). In at least one instance, the name comprises the element *fetter-* alongside a term used independently for a local name (Fetter*cairn*, < *cardden*, c.f. Kin*cardine* KCD). Perhaps the most interesting possible instance of the use of *fetter-* with an element denoting a larger contiguous region is Fothrif, which may derive from **foithir F(h)ibe*, 'the *fetter* of Fife' (Taylor 2000b: compare Rosyth < *ros F(h)ibe*). What precise derivation we should accord the second element of *Fetternear* I am unsure, but I would suggest that Nér here is a nearby place or region, and Fetternear is the *foithir* associated with it. The ecclesiastical foundation connected with the two names in *AU* may then be posited in the immediate vicinity of Fetternear, though arguably distinct from Fetternear and its medieval parish.

A saint whom we shall call Nechtan, variously realised as, for instance, Nathalan, Nachlan, Mo Nithoc, Mo Neittoc, has a strong but heavily localised cult nearby (Watson 1926, 329–30). The name is probably originally Pictish. Certainly *Naiton* (Bede's form) or *Nechtan* (the form in Gaelic sources) was a relatively common name among Pictish kings, and the first element in the name is frequently represented on Pictish ogham inscriptions.[5] Closest to

---

5 The Pictish version of the name is uncertain. Bede records as *Naiton* the early eighth-century Pictish king known in Gaelic sources as Nechtan. See Jackson 1955, 145 for discussion. Watson 1926, 329–30, discusses the form found in the saint's name, Nathalan, suggesting that the second element is *–launos* 'pure, clear'; Forsyth (1996, 281), suggests more probably that the common Celtic ending *–lano-* 'full, replete' is more to be expected (cf. Evans 1967, 215 for the ending). If this is the case, perhaps this is the original name of the saint, and the other forms, Nechtan, Mo Nithoc, etc., are hypocoristic forms. A parallel would be the range of names in Finnio, Finnian, Finnén; Uinniauus, Winnin, etc., all of which have their origin as hypocorisms for an original **Uindobarros*, Gaelic *Findbarr* (see Clancy 2001, 12–20; Dumville 1984, 209–10). However, the whole question of the name of this saint bears re-examination. A number of the forms, esp. in *Nechtan, Necton*, etc. may be influenced by Gaelic, but other forms such as that in **Eccles Mo Nethoc*, with forms in *Nythock* and *Neyttock* make the picture a good deal more complex. As noted, the forms in *-la-* have been explained by Watson as deriving from a suffix **-launos* or the like, but I am uncertain whether all the forms support this. Note in particular the forms in *Nathtlayk/ Nathelath* for Tullich, and the potential form *Nehtla* on the Formaston ogham inscription (Forsyth 1996, 280) . We may wish also to note the saintly bishop called *Nechtlaicc*, commemorated at 23 May in the Martyrology of Tallaght, which seems independently to

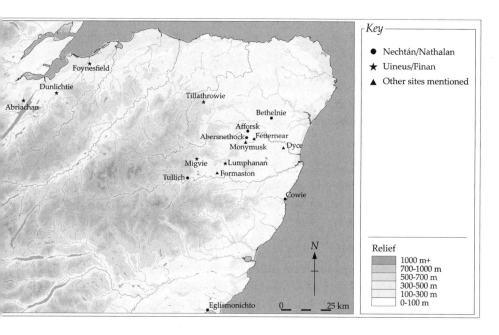

12.1 Sites associated with Nechtán/Nathalan and Uineus/Finan.

Fetternear (4.5km west) of dedications to a saint of this name is that of Abersnithock, originally Eglismonithoc, (*Eglismenythok* 1211, *Eglismeneyttock* 1245: Watson 1926, 331) for *Eccles Mo Nethoc, an early church name commemorating Nechtan (cf. Barrow 1983, 8,12). Now near Braehead farm (NGR NJ685172), it lies 2.5km north of Monymusk, to which it belonged in the twelfth century, and the ruins of a small chapel or oratory are still to be seen there (*A.B. Coll.*, 585; Alexander 1952, 136; Taylor 1998, 5–6). It is striking that in the 1211 document which settled the conventions of the *céli Dé* community in Monymusk, this is the only older property specifically associated with Monymusk and the *céli Dé* to be mentioned, suggesting a very close association with that monastery's past (Reeves 1864, 256; MacPherson 1895, 109–12; Clancy 1999b, 25–7). It is also apparently the most northerly of the place-names which employ the generic *eccles*, and the dedication to Nechtan provides something of a *terminus post quem* for some of them: they must continue to be productive in the nomenclature until at least after 679. It may be added that the presence of a fair number of apostolic or continental saints among the *eccles*- dedications has suggested to scholars that the early eighth

attest to the form found for the saint of Tullich. I wonder if the forms Nathalan/Nachlan are in fact Gaelic realisations (in a diminutive *-án*) of some Pictish name using a native diminutive (*-la/-lach/-lath?*).

century period of the influence of the Northumbrian church on Pictland is an appropriate time for some of these dedications (Taylor 1998, 5–6). Another form of the name Nechtan, presumably though not certainly this saint, is employed in one other *eccles-* name, the now lost *Eglismonichto* (thus in 1482) near Monifeith in Angus (Barrow 1983, 12). In the context it is worth emphasising that the *eccles-* names derive from a Brittonic word, loaned from Latin *ecclesia*, and presumably either independently loaned, or loaned through British, into Pictish (see in general Barrow 1983; Taylor 1998).

Curiously, according to traditions of, at the latest, the eighteenth century, the chapel at Abersnithock was dedicated to a St Fin(n)an (*A.B. Coll.*, 585). Although the tradition is late as it stands, there seems no obvious motivation for a late, spurious association with this name. Such double dedications, preserved on the one hand in the toponym itself, and on the other hand in the patron of a church or chapel, are known elsewhere, as for instance at Inchinnan in Renfrewshire, dedicated to St Conval, but incorporating the name of a saint called Finnan or Finnian. The overlaying of dedications is also notable at St Andrews, with its previous dedication to St Regulus (for Gaulish equivalents, see Pearce 2003, 64).

In these instances, the dedications seem to suggest different strata of cult. At Abersnithock, however, something else may be going on. Although the name Fin(n)an is a common one in dedications, and may stand for any number of persons, in this context, connected with a dedication to Nechtan, and in close proximity to a name containing the element Nér, the name of *Uineus*, the earlier abbot of Nér who died in 623, comes to mind. It may be that in this case Fin(n)an is a Gaelicisation and modernisation of a hypocoristic form of the name which *Uineus* represents[6] Strengthening such an identification for the Fin(n)an of Abersnithock is the entry for January 8 in the Martyrology of Tallaght, which commemorates a *Finanus episcopus* alongside Nechtan of Nér. Joint feast-days for successive saints associated with foundations are known elsewhere, most famously in the case of Columba and his cousin and successor

---

6 It is difficult to be certain what name might lie behind the form *Uineus*. Most plausibly, it should be the word which lies behind the OI diminutive *Fínán*, which is probably *fín*, 'wine' (note that Uineus looks like a masculine form of L. *uinea* 'wine'). We could posit instead Pictish **Uuin*, cf. W. *Gwyn*, OI *Finn* but these names seem not to be in common use in the early Middle Ages, being instead reserved for mythological figures, and in any case *Uineus* shows a different consonantal quality for the –n-. Ó Riain 1985 notes a bishop called *Fin* (§705.243). Finally, we should probably bear in mind the OE personal name *Wine*. Given that *Saxones* were monks in the monastery of Iona in Columba's day (VC iii.10, iii.22), and that Augustine's mission was a quarter of a century old in 623, it is not entirely impossible for *Uineus* to have been a Saxon named Wine (cf. the *Finanus saxo* commemorated in MT on 9 Jan.; for an historical Wine, the seventh-century bishop of Winchester, see *HE* iii.7). Whatever the underlying name might be, if the proposal made above is correct, it must have been conflated or confused at some stage (perhaps early?) with the names Fínán and Finnán.

Baithéne, both commemorated on 9 June. Although, as noted above, there are many saints called Finnan and Fínán, with variants, in Ireland and elsewhere, these more famous ones are not commemorated on January 8, and thus perhaps we are dealing here with Fin(n)an, alias Uineus of Nér.[7]

The cumulative evidence of a dedication to Nechtan of Nér, and possibly Uineus of Nér as well, at Abersnithock; and a name containing the element *Nér* at Fetternear is allied to the presence at Monymusk of a later important monastic site with early connections in the form of a *céli Dé* community, as well as Christian sculptured stones from nearby (on Monymusk generally, see Simpson 1924). All this is suggestive of the possibility that in the vicinity, perhaps even at Abersnithock or Monymusk, the monastery of Nér lay.

We may conjecture, then, that somewhere in this triangle formed by Bennachie, the Don and the Urie, lies Nér, the earliest historically documented ecclesiastical settlement in the North-East of Scotland. In terms of the history of the region, it is particularly important that both these saints, and their associated monastery, are noticed in Gaelic sources prior to 850. In addition, dedications in the region more widely to saints bearing variants of the names of the saints attached to Nér suggest that, although associated in the Gaelic sources with Nér, they were also influential elsewhere in the region, either whilst living, or posthumously in the form of local saints' cults.

Nechtan, in forms such as Nathalan and Nathlach, is commemorated in medieval parishes in the nearby vicinity: Tullich ABD and Bethelnie ABD (now Old Meldrum parish). There may also have been a dedication further south at Cowie KCD (Watson 1926, 329–31; MacKinlay 1914, 221–3). Tullich was known as *Tulynathtlayk* (*Abdn Reg.*, 1275) and *Tulynathelath* (ibid., 1366), and in modern times at least seems to have been known by the Gaelic name of *Cill Nachlan* (Redford 1988, 89; Watson and Allan 1984, 42). That this saint is the same as Nechtan of Nér seems to be supported by the fair celebrated on 8 January at Tullich, confirmed by James V in 1541 (MacKinlay 1914, 222).

Bethelnie certainly had Nathalan as its patron, celebrating his feast of 8 Jan. as a holiday into the eighteenth century, but it is less clear whether the place-name contains the saint's name. Earlier suggestions that the name comes from *baile-* followed by the saint's name have been rightly dismissed, but it seems to me to be plausible for the name to contain a metathesised form of Nathalan or some variant (cf. Forsyth 1996, 281–2, on *Nehtla-* in the

---

7 It may be that the *Finanus episcopus* commemorated on 8 January, and the *Finanus saxo* commemorated on Jan. 9th are the same. Clare Stancliffe (in an unpublished paper) has also postulated that this is the same as Finan of Lindisfarne, and has pointed to the ascription in other martyrologies of the epithet *Rímid* to the Finan on Jan. 8th as possibly indicating a relationship between Colmán Rímid and bishop Finan of Lindisfarne, and hence also a relationship with Oswiu, king of Bernicia. AU 660.1 backs up this equation describing the bishop of Lindisfarne as *Finnanus episcopus filius Rimedo*. Finan of Lindisfarne was, however, commemorated on 17 February (Farmer 1992, 178).

Formaston ogham inscription) after a generic *both-* originally 'hut'. *Both-* names have been shown (Taylor 1996, 96–8) to belong to early Scottish ecclesiastical nomenclature, with a fair number which became medieval parishes containing a saint's name as the specific. As **Both Nethlaicc / *Both Nechtla* or similar (recall here the form of the name in the early sources for Tullich, *-nathtlayk*, *-nathelath*), Bethelnie would join a small group of such *both-* names in the north east. (The others are Boharm BNF (*Bocharnye* 1426); Botriphnie BNF (*Buthrothyn*, *Buttruthin*, 1226); and Botary ABD, now Cairnie parish (*Butharryn* 1232; see Taylor 1996, 104). For the sort of confusion of the name in the second element being proposed here, one may compare Kilrennie (*Kilrethni* c.1170), which Taylor takes as representing St Ethernan 'in some mangled or hypocoristic form' (1996, 99).

The name Uineus, as suggested above, may have been realised in Gaelic in a form which came out in documents of the Scots period as Finan, Latinised Fin(n)anus. A saint of this name had a dedication in the medieval parish of Migvie ABD, and a well and probably chapel dedicated at Tillathrowie, now in the parish of Gartly in Strathbogie (MacDonald 1891, 81). At Migvie, the church was granted as '*ecclesia S. Finnani de Miggeveth*' by Agnes countess of Mar to St Andrews in the twelfth century (*St A. Lib.*, 249), and Forbes (1872, 347) notes 'In the beginning of the last century [i.e., the eighteenth] Finzean's fair, at the kirk of Migvie, was kept whiles in March, and whiles in April, on the Tuesday before Midlentron fair at Banchrie' (cf. *A.B. Ill.*, vol. ii, xlvi). These co-ordinates neither help nor hurt the case for association with *Uineus* of Nér, but they do further illustrate the potential confusion of names involved (here *Finnanus* and *Finzean*, which implies an underlying Finnian).

The associations of Lumphanan ABD with a saint Finan rest purely with the name, which has been derived from a Gaelic *lann-*, here with a meaning similar to its Welsh, Cornish and Breton cognates, combined with the saint's name. As Watson (1926, 286) notes, however, the early forms (*Lumfanan*, *Lonfanan*, c.1250) are problematic. Taylor (1998, 19) cautiously rejects the association with the saint, noting that 'the second element must remain obscure'.

As noted above, Finnan/Finnian and another name based on a different underlying element, Fínán, are both common in a variety of forms, and may also be confused in their resulting conversion into English/Scots orthography in modern place-names and records of fairs. Still, one or two very prominent saints may be behind a majority of the dedications to names like 'Finnan' in Scotland. This restricted north-eastern collection, however, with its proposed linkage to Uineus through the dedication at Abersnithock, argues for identification with the more local saint. We may in this case want to extend his cult slightly further west, and take in a number of other dedications. According to Watson, a Finan was commemorated at Foynesfield, Nairn at *Seipel Fhionain*, at Abriachan on Loch Ness at *Cill Fhionain*, and also at

Dunlichitie, as noted in the Presbytery records for Inverness in 1643: 'there was in the Paroch of Dunlichitie ane Idolatrous Image called St. Finane, keepit in a private house obscurely'. Said image was burned in Inverness at the Merkat Cross (Watson 1926, 286).

I want to focus briefly on the main centres associated with these two saints in the vicinity of Fetternear: Monymusk (because of the association with Abersnithock); Tullich; and Migvie. All three of these sites are identifiable by physical remains as important early Christian sites. There is an important series of early sculptures from Tullich, including a Pictish 'Class I' symbol stone (Allen and Anderson 1903, ii.187), and seventeen cross-incised slabs (five of which are noted by Allen and Anderson (1903, ii.196). One cross-slab, apparently destroyed in 1857 (Simpson 1925, 28) appears to have been of considerably antiquity, bearing close resemblance to the Skeith Stone in Kilrenny, Fife (Trench-Jellicoe 1998; cf. Gibb 1878, 196). Migvie has a plaited interlace cross-slab which is one of a series belonging to a clear local style, the others being at Kinnord, at Formaston, and in somewhat different fashion at Dyce (for a full discussion of these related crosses, see Forsyth 1996, 263–7, on which the following discussion draws). It may be noted that Migvie, Formaston, Dyce and Monymusk share the uncommon feature of representing symbols and crosses on the same face: in the case of Migvie and Monymusk, these are crosses in low relief on undressed pillar-stones, lending credence to the idea that these are, if not transitional forms between classical 'Class I' symbol stones and 'Class II' symbol-bearing cross-slabs, then certainly they are a local hybrid (see Henderson and Henderson 2004, 177–8). Moreover, Dyce and Migvie both exhibit multiple pairs of symbols as opposed to the usual single pair (with or without the additional mirror and comb). The Formaston cross-slab is fragmentary, the surviving piece bearing a mirror to the left of the cross-shaft.

Like Tullich, Monymusk too has one fine incised cross monument. One should note also the example of Dyce, connected in artistic terms with Migvie and Monymusk, where another good collection of early cross-carved stones exists alongside symbol stones. Finally, one may note that the fragmentary cross slab from Formaston (the kirkyard of the old parish church of Aboyne), part of this regional school of cross carving, displays a fine and probably complete ogham inscription. This has been read most recently[8] as

MAQQoiTALLUORRH | NeHHT[V]ROBBACCeNNEVV

---

8 Forsyth 1996, 267–72. Conventions: underline = character clear but appropriate transliteration uncertain, [ ] = character unclear. (Discounting the interpretations of Cox (1999), whose readings are, in most cases, not independent of Forsyth's or other earlier scholars, as he himself acknowledges. For criticism of Cox's central thesis, see Clancy 1999c; Barnes 1999.)

with subsequent discussion making a suggested interpretation of the first
element in the second line as *nehht* or *nehhtla* (Forsyth, 1996, lxxviii, 279–82).
Forsyth suggests connections both with St Nechtan/Nathalan and, on the
basis of the final letters in the inscription, perhaps with the parish of Kinneff
KCD.[9] Interesting in the context is the recently discovered cross-incised stone
from Mains of Afforsk on the lower south-east slopes of Bennachie, with its
cross and ogham inscription, where the name *Necton* is clearly readable (see
Forsyth 1997, pl.1, opposite p. 34, for illustration; also note that Afforsk
(*Achqwhorsk* 1391) is from *Achadh a' Chroisg*, 'field of the cross/crossing', cf.
Watson 1926, 486). We might add to this the fact that yet another ogham
inscription has been found at Dyce, though nothing in the inscription itself
connects it further into this cluster.

What these connections suggest is that all three, Monymusk, Migvie and
Tullich were important ecclesiastical sites in the early medieval period. The
putative dedications to *Uineus* and Nechtan in the vicinity of Monymusk, and
to Nechtan at Tullich, give them a seventh-century start date, but the important
crosses at Migvie and Monymusk, connected as they are to others such as
Dyce and Formaston, suggest continuity of culture and patronage into the
eighth and ninth century. Forsyth suggests the ninth century as a more likely
date for the ogham on Formaston, because of its employment of some of the
later 'scholastic' ogham letters (1996, 285, where she terms it 'one of the latest'
of the ogham inscriptions in Scotland), but it may in any case be secondary to
the sculpture. Continuity of a similar sort is evident at Monymusk, where we
may conjecture a seventh-century foundation at the roots of the ultimately
Augustinian priory, with a *céli Dé* community present from some time in the
period between 800 and 1200 (see Simpson 1924 for Monymusk's later history).

That we are dealing here with the *disjecta membra* of the North-East's
religious history should by now be obvious. The fragments of information
(chronicle references to Nér and its clerics; traces of local saints' cults of what
may be these clerics in church dedications; and physical evidence of these
churches' importance in the early Middle Ages) hardly add up to a readable
narrative or even a partial picture. Nonetheless, these are fragments to build
from, and importantly to build without invoking the super-narratives of
Adomnán or Bede. We may take these examples of early, historically attested
churchmen, putatively working in, and later culted in what were apparently
important Christian centres on the Dee and the Don, and look further at
other figures who may belong to the same sort of developing church. There
are a number of saints with Pictish names, and with rather limited cult

9 However, we might note the presence of a church of Kynnef Martin in Stratha'an
(Barrow 1989, 4, 12 n.31). Was there a term, derived perhaps from an oblique case of
Gaelic *cenn* (e.g., *cennaib*) which had ecclesiastical significance? In which case, was this the
original name of the church at Aboyne?

distributions, suggestive of a local evolution of churches. I want to look briefly at several saints, before returning at greater length to Drostan, the saint of Deer.

Ethernan and Corindu

Another historically attested saint with operations in the east is Ethernan, who died in 669 among the Picts, according to AU:

AU 669.2: *Itarnan 7 Corindu apud Pictores defuncti sunt.*[10]

His principle locale of commemoration is Fife, where he seems to have been active in the Isle of May and elsewhere (Kilrenny, Isle of May, Scoonie FIF, see Taylor, 1996, 99; Yeoman 1998), but he also had dedications at Madderty in Perthsire, possibly at Forfar in Angus, and in the North-East at Rathen, which the Aberdeen Breviary says was founded by him, and where there was a tradition of the saint's hermitage at 'St Eddran's Slack' (for discussion of name as well as dedications, see Forsyth, 1996, 486–91; Watson 1926, 321). As we shall see, Etharnan forms something of a mirror-image in cult to, for instance, Drostan and Fergus, whose main centres of cult are in the North-East, but who have outlying dedications in Angus and Fife. We may simply be seeing mobility of cults at a later stage of development, rather than evidence of spheres of activity. We might suggest that for instance Ethernan worked and established foundations in Fife, but owing to mobility of the worshipping aristocracy, and to the gradual uniting of the kingdom, the cult was transferred at some stage to the North-East. It may even be quite late. Forsyth (1996, 490), for instance, notes a grant by Alexander Comyn, earl of Buchan, to St Ethernan's on the Isle of May, suggesting a plausible and very late route for the commemoration in Rathen. On the other hand, the earl of Buchan's generosity to the Isle of May might have been prompted by already existing local associations with the same saint. In this context, the likelihood that the noble kindreds of Fife and Buchan were joined through marriage in the early twelfth century is borne witness to by the Deer property records themselves (III; see Jackson 1972, 58). Inscriptions bearing versions of the name Ethernan—

10 The use of *apud* here would suggest in fact that these men were slain by the Picts, judging by its use elsewhere in AU (I am grateful to disussions with Nicholas Evans and Alex Woolf for this point), though localising their activity amongst the Picts is still likely to be correct. Alex Woolf has further noted (pers. comm.) the odd form *Pictores* here, which, as he points out, would literally imply these men were 'slain by the painters'. I take it, nonetheless, as an anomalous form for the normal *Picti*. For discussion of the use of *apud* in AU, see Dumville, 'Latin and Irish in the *Annals of Ulster*, AD 431–1050', in *Ireland in Early Medieval Europe: Studies in Memory of Kathleen Hughes*, ed. D. Whitelock et al. (Cambridge 1982) [reprinted in D.N. Dumville 1990, at 324 n.11, and my discussion of an important Scottish entry in Clancy 2004.

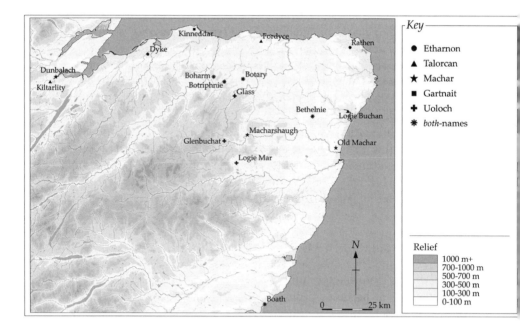

12.2 Sites associated with Ethernan/Etharnon, Talorcan, Machar, Gartnait and Uoloch.

Idarnoin at Fordoun in roman script (Okasha 1985, 51–3), *Eddarrnonn* in ogham at Brodie (as at Scoonie), (Forsyth 1996, 139–59, 480–94) and, perhaps, *Iddarrnnn* at Newton (Forsyth 1996, 435)—may, if these are linked to a saint's cult, suggest its presence in the North-East rather earlier.

Before leaving the subject of Ethernan, we should note his companion in the AU entry, Corindu. This name is unattested elsewhere, and there is no obvious way to emend it to a more common personal name. (*Cormdu* is a possible reading in one of the manuscripts (see *AU*, 138 n.669b), but equally unhelpful). One suggestion for Ethernan's companion might be his identity with the still mysterious Machar (earlier Machor) of Aberdeen (see Ó Baoill 1993 who, however, suggests a different identity). The earliest attestations of this name are as *Machorius* (?=*Mo Chor), *Mo Chumma* and *Mo Chonda*, two at least of which are plausible hypocoristics for the name Corindu. The shift of accent to the first syllable in Machorius>Machar may be explicable simply by reference to a re-analysis from the Latin version of the name (by analogy with, for instance, Gregorius> Gregor/Griogar).[11]

[11] It will be noted that I am unconvinced by the identification suggested by Ó Baoill 1993. In particular, the introduction of an -*r* into a name like Mo-Cha (< Mo-Thatha) is a bit perplexing, as is the idea of a pre-twelfth century importation of the cult of Kentigern into the area, for which I can find no convincing historical context. (On Kentigern's cult, see Clancy 2002.) On the other hand, there are unexplored possibilities, such as the name Mechar, cf. Ó Riain 1985, §§175, 364, 663.1.

It should be noted that though we have a dating reference for Ethernan and Corindu, it is uncertain whether we should regard them as Gaelic or Pictish in origin. The annal description of them as dying *apud Pictores*, might suggest that they were Gaels who died in foreign lands, but neither name is well known in Ireland, and both may rather be Pictish.

Uoloch, Talorcan, Gartnait

Three saints with Pictish names and very limited cults should be mentioned here: St Uoloch (and variants) has a small, localised set of dedications, at Glass in Strathbogie where there was the Walla Kirk and St Wallach's Well and Bath (Mackinlay 1914, 143; Watson 1926, 335 seems to imply that this was in the Middle Ages a separate parish from Glass, but without evidence), and in the medieval parish of Logie Mar, where there was a fair on Wallach's feast (Watson 1926, 335; on Wallach generally, see Mitchell 1874, 604–13). Most discussion of the name Uoloch/Wallach/Volocus, etc., has centred on its supposed similarity to the rare Gaelic names Úallach, Úallachán (Watson 1926, 336; in at least in one Irish example, *AI* 934, this is a female name) or implausibly to Fáelchú (MacKinlay 1914). A more likely explanation which fits the orthography better is a Pictish cognate of the Welsh name Gwallawg (indeed, a Pictish form *Uallauc*> Uoloch/Wallach seems extremely sensible). Of course, we know nothing about this saint (though he is perhaps also commemorated as Makkuoloch ?<Mo Uoloch, in the problematic 'Dunkeld Litany', Watson 1926, 336; for comment on the latter, see Clancy 2002).

A second such saint with Pictish name and localised cult is Talorcan. Here, with one of the most Pictish of names, is a saint with a wider spread of dedication, with two in the North-East, at Logie Buchan (*Logyn-talargy* 1275) and in BNF at Fordyce, with a 'St Tarkin's Well' and a fair held *in festo S. Tallericani* (Watson 1926, 298). His too was the parish of Kiltarlity (*Kyltalargy*, 1224) in Invernessshire just south of Beauly. A church in Skye, near Portree, is presumably dedicated to the same saint (Watson 1926, 298).

Of course with such saints we have no idea as to their floruits (though it is possible that Talorcan is the *Tolarggan Maphan* who died in 726 AU), but taken along with the evidence of a local church with a Pictish flavour in the second half of the seventh century, such saints could well belong to this period. Additionally, we may conjecture for such local dedications, once again, Pictish saints at work in the immediate vicinity of these locales, though we would be hard pressed to identify the main centre for either saint.

In that context, however, the generic element Logie (from Gaelic *locin* later *lagan*) which is allied to the territorial names in both Logie Mar and Logie Buchan, is interesting. Logierait, originally Logiemahedd < *Locin Mo Chedd*, in Atholl, probably dates from *c.*700 (see Taylor 1996; 1999). In a forthcoming study, I suggest that this place-name element is an ecclesiastical one, derived ultimately from L. *locus* in its Early Medieval meaning '(holy) place, place of burial, church'. It may be either Pictish in origin or loaned through OI *loc*, which can be shown to have had similar meanings. There were fourteen medieval parishes taking their name from some form of this element, distributed across eastern Scotland north of the Forth, and the parish names in Logie, taken as an ecclesiastical element, vastly increase the number of church sites in the east whose names can be shown to go back to Early Medieval ecclesiastical terms.

One other extremely obscure saint deserves to be mentioned here, and that is the patron of the parish of Kinneddar, now Drainie, known as *Gervadius* and variants, often anglicised as Gerardine (on this cult generally, and the connections with local sculpture, see Dransart 2003). Some of the forms of this names (i.e., Gernadius) make it plain that the underlying name is a Pictish one, Gartnait (see Forbes 1872, 354–5; Dransart 2003, 247 n.67 is unduly cautious). We should reject the tenor of the nineteenth-century scholarship on this saint, which saw in the legend in the Aberdeen Breviary (which sets the saint's career during an invasion of Scotland by an English king) the justification for dating this saint's career to the time of king Athelstan. Rather, we should see the legend found there as a reworking of traditions of the saint to coincide with the demands of a later period of invasion and warfare with England, more probably the period of the Wars of Independence. It is more likely that the saint culted here belongs, like the vast majority of others, to the earlier part of the early Middle Ages.

No saint of this name is known in early martyrologies or genealogies, enhancing the idea of this Gartnait as a very local saint. The name is a royal one in Pictish king-lists, and another possibility is that the name of a secular patron and founder has been adopted as that of the patron saint, due to some confusion in the church's origin legend. For what it is worth, Gartnait resurfaces as a name in the family of the *mormaír* of Buchan, as seen in the Book of Deer (III). The fine if fragmentary sculptural remains suggest that this was once a very important church (Allen and Anderson 1903, ii, 142–9; Dransart 2001; Henderson 1998, 130–1; (Henderson and Henderson 2004, 49, 130, 194, ill. *191, 298*).

Thus while the very obscurity of these saints seems to point towards local religious traditions, and a church in the North-East whose structure may have been based in part on the efforts of local churchmen, once again, the fragmentation of the record allows us to say very little about these men, their relationships to the churches that commemorated them, and their role in the overall development of the Pictish church. We are deprived in these three cases even of any sense of chronology.

Fergus

Fergus, however, provides another historical anchorage, but brings with him some caveats regarding our understanding of the workings of the Pictish church, dedications, and the early Insular churches in general. St Fergus is without doubt to be identified with the *Fergustus Episcopus Scotiae Pictus* who was signatory to a council in Rome in 721, alongside a Gaelic bishop 'of Britain', *Sedulius episcopus Britanniae de genere Scotorum*[12] (*Sac. Conc.* XII, 261–6). The ascription makes it clear that Fergus was a bishop in Ireland at the time, though he was perhaps, like many bishops of the time, of highest rank but without fixed see or jurisdiction (on bishops generally, see Etchingham 1994; also 1999, 177–94; though he champions the presence of bishops with territorial jurisdiction, this does not do away with the presence of bishops without fixed see in Ireland). He would certainly seem to be a representative of the Gaelic church at this council in Rome, and attempts to make him a 'romanising' Pictish bishop must take this into account. He was commemorated in Ireland as *Fergus Cruthnech* at 8 September in the Martyrology of Tallaght, of the early ninth century.

Thus Fergus appears to have been a bishop in Ireland, with a recognisable and early Irish cult. Despite this evident Irish slant to Fergus's career, any account of the saint should take into view the obvious fact that there is no trace of local cult in Ireland outwith the martyrologies, while in Scotland there is an abundant cult, prominent in the North-East, but with outliers elsewhere. Of the saints' cults we are examining here, his is the most problematic next to Drostan's in its widespread and diverse nature. There are two important centres in the North-East, at Longley (*Lungle* c.1250 < G. *lann*, here with ecclesiastical connotations (Taylor 1998, 18), with perhaps second element *glé* 'pure, clear, bright'), now St Fergus, and at Dyce, with its important collection of early sculpture (a 'Class I' symbol stone, an ogham-inscribed 'Class II' cross-slab and four so-called 'Class IV' simple, cross-marked stones). There was also a chapel at Fetterangus, formerly a detached part of Longley parish, where there is a symbol stone and 'bullaun'. His body, however, was held to have rested at Glamis, where his well still exists, and where there are four surviving pieces of sculpture, including two major symbol-inscribed cross-slabs . The neighbouring church of Eassie, also with a symbol-inscribed cross-slab, claimed Fergus as patron. There was evidently some movement of his relics in the later Middle Ages. His head was removed

12 There are various ways to interpret this ascription. The linkage with a Pictish bishop from Ireland might suggest that he is to be placed in the north of Britain, and hence he was perhaps bishop of the northern Britons in their kingdom of Dumbarton. But there is no reason why he could not have been a bishop in Wales. A riskier strategy might be to consider whether *Britannia* here masks an underlying word like *Prydyn* (= Pictland), or even *Alba* (which usually means northern Britain, in Irish usage). There are two good candidates for the identity of this Sedulius, *Sidal* of Druim Laidggin whose death is noted at *AU* 722.7, or *Siadhail mac Luaith, doctor*, whose death is noted at *AU* 759.1. Almost certainly he is the *Sital episcopus* commemorated in the Martyrology of Tallaght for 12 February. Gorman and Donegal identify that Siadal with Siadal mac Luaith, whom they associate with Áth Cliath (Dublin). There is one further Siadal commemorated in Tallaght, *Siadal Cinn Locha*, 8 March.

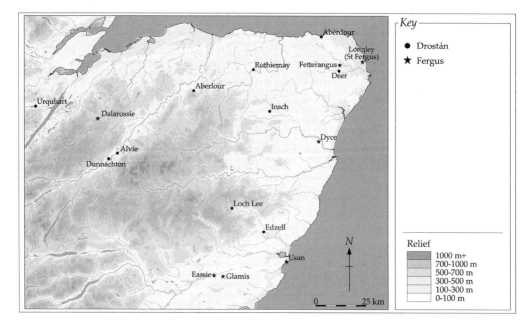

12.3 Sites associated with Drostán and Fergus.

to Scone, being enshrined in silver in 1504. However, an arm reliquary of the saint was in Aberdeen in 1464 (MacKinlay 1914, 210–13).

In addition to this southern group of dedications, there is a more northerly group as well, with Fergus commemorated in Wick and Halkirk in Caithness. There was also a dedication in Dalarossie (*Dulergussyn, Dulergussi* < **dal Fhergusa* / **dal Fherguis*) in Strathdearn in Invernessshire, a parish later united to Moy (Mackinlay 1914, 210–13; Barrow 1989, 2).

What then to make of St Fergus? We have a historically attested saint whose *floruit* coincides with a seemingly crucial period in the development of the Pictish church, overlapping as it must have with the decisions taken in the second decade of the eighth century by the Pictish king Nechtan on the dating of Easter and the tonsure, as well as the still enigmatic '*expulsio familiae Iae*' noted in *AU* 717.4 (for some thoughts on the latter, see Veitch 1997). Whether the Irish period of his career followed after this (and was precipitated by the *expulsio*), or had begun before this we cannot say, nor can we say adequately whether his activities in Scotland are earlier or later than 721.

It is also difficult to be sure what Fergus's presence in Rome in 721 signifies. He and Sedulius are quite isolated among the largely Italian bishops present at this council; there is otherwise only one bishop from Spain (called in the Preface *Sindered[us] archiepiscop[us] Hispaniae*, but in the list of subscriptions, *Sinderedus episcopus ex Hispaniae*). All the priests and deacons who subscribe to the decisions of the council are Roman, and that the primary target of the council's deliberations was 'the Italian province' and 'Romans and Lombards' seems implied in the Preface. This suggests strongly that Fergus and Sedulius were in Rome on other episcopal business, and were drawn into the council of Italian bishops simply because they were there. Some of the deliberations were, however, probably of interest: questions of celibacy and prohibitions of marriage and other sexual unions among the clergy and religious; a ban on divination and soothsayers; and perhaps most likely to spark interest to a Pictish churchman in 721, a resolution '*si quis ex clericis relaxaverit comam, anathema sit*' ('If there is anyone amongst the clergy who lets their hair grow, let them be anathema').

It is, of course, possible that the presence of these bishops in Rome does relate to the reform of the Pictish church under Nechtan as outlined by Bede, which saw follow-on reforms in Iona itself. Perhaps the changes in Pictland and Iona had repercussions with respect to questions of episcopal jurisdiction and royal prerogative. It is also quite possible that the tonsure issue had something to do with it, as it is not clear to what extent Ireland had adopted the Petrine tonsure along with the roman date of Easter in the seventh century, though by *c*.721 Irish churchmen were already beginning to be able to wash their hands of association with their old-style tonsure, as witness the *Collectio Canonum Hibernensis*, partly a product of Iona churchmen, which refers to that tonsure as a British one (Wasserschleben 1885). Bede on the other hand describes British clerics as having no tonsure. The resolution on clerical hair-cuts in the Roman council, although it resurrects earlier concilliar decrees, may well be directed towards Insular rather than Italian concerns; and this may be reflected in its placement as something of an add-on. But the descriptions of both Fergus and Sedulius prevent us from directly connecting their presence with ongoing church development in Pictland.

What we can perhaps conjecture, on the basis of the Irish activities of other Pictish and indeed English saints (such as Iogenan the Pict in the *Life of Columba*, who travelled in Leinster, *VC* ii.9 or Ecgberht, whom we find in England, Ireland, Pictland and Iona[13]), is that he was part of a mobile Insular church in the early eighth century, one which still looked to Ireland as intellectual home in many respects, but one with solidifying regional churches as well.

---

13 Ecgberht provides an interesting parallel for Fergus in that he, too, seems to have been a bishop (Bede calls him *sacerdos* twice, a term he elsewhere uses to mean bishop; and later writers thought of him as a bishop, see HE iii.4 and Colgrave and Mynors 1969, 225 n.3), but one whose ethnic background did not coincide with his place of residence. One wonders how he would have been described if he had been present in Rome in 721, living as he had for the past five or so years on Iona. Where, from a Roman point of view, was Iona? In 'Scotia'? In 'Britannia'?

Drostan

Fergus is thus a good case-study alongside which to re-introduce Drostan, because in so many respects their cults seem extremely similar. The main centre of Drostan's cult seems to be in the North-East, with Aberdour and Deer as apparent early centres (the Book of Deer being our earliest clear witness to both of these), to which might be added Insch ABD and Rothiemay BNF. There is a strong cult further west, however, with Sgìre Drostan, now Aberlour parish, Alvie and Dunnachton in Badenoch, as well as a dedication in the parish of Urquhart INV. Like Fergus there are southern traditions, with a cult in Glenesk, at Edzell and at Lochlee in Forfarshire, as well as Markinch in Fife. And also like Fergus, there is a northern extension, with dedications in Caithness in Canisbay and Westfield (Redford 1988, 189; Watson 1926, 318).

Another overlap with Fergus is an association with Ireland. There is a strong probability that Drostan is to be identified with a saint whose death was noted in the Irish annals. *AU* 719.2 notes:

> *Drostain Dairtaighe quieuiti /nArd Breccan/*

There are a number of points to note here. First, an identification with our Drostan has usually been dismissed (e.g., Jackson 1972, 5n.2), presumably on the basis that it is rather later than the date the foundation legend would imply for Deer. That legend has no real basis in fact, however, and we should be open-minded about Drostan's dates and connections. Second, Drostan is named in this annal entry as being 'of' an unknown *dairthech*, but only as dying 'in Ardbraccan', not being a cleric of that place. In other words, the Irish connection could be a tenuous one, potentially amounting to little more than a saint dying on pilgrimage.

The two places mentioned in the entry bear some discussion. *Dairthech* is a Gaelic term for an oratory, and these appear to be significant features of several early Irish monasteries, mentioned in the annals under circumstances when they are burned or looted (e.g., Manning 2002, 38, 42–6). It could be taken that the *dairthech* of this annal is the oratory of Ardbraccan itself. Drostan might thus be associated with it because he built it, or because he saw out his life in prayer there. It could, however, be a completely separate place.

It might be worth speculating, however, on some connection between the names of *Dér* (*Der, Deir*) and the *dairthech* to which this Drostan is attached. The etymology of Deer remains uncertain, but arguably has something to do with the Pictish word for an oak-tree or oak-grove (OI *dair; daire*; W. *derwen, derw*; see Taylor, this volume). The word *dairthech* itself derives from 'oak-house', and appears frequently in the form *derthech*. One might speculate that an annalist unfamiliar with the name *Dér (Der, Deir?*—we have no early form in the genitive), might take it as an abbeviation, and supply the better known word *derthech*, and that an otherwise mysterious Drostan Déir has been transformed (via a form **Drostan Deirthaige?*) into a more transparent *Drostan Dairthaige*.

Jackson noted the possibility of a Columban connection with Ardbraccan (1972, 5n2), but this must be dismissed. Ardbraccan only came fitfully into the Columban *familia* through the personal rulership of several Kells abbots over the monastery during the course of the tenth century, and the increasing involvement of the successors of Columba in Meath (Herbert 1988, 82). Any connection between Drostan and Ardbraccan does not relate to Columba.

One slight trace of Drostan's Irish cult seems to confirm that he was considered a saint from overseas. A poem found in the Book of Leinster version of the Martyrology of Tallaght, discussed by Watson, recounts the seven sons of Óengus m. Aeda m. Eirc m. Echach Munremuir, a piece of tradition also recorded in prose form (Watson 1926, 298; Ó Cróinín 1981, 104–8, 112–14; Ó Riain 1985, §§209, 701). The seven sons are described as having crossed the sea to Ireland, and are named as Mo Thrianóc, Itharnaisc, Eoganán, Torannán, Agatán, Mo Chuilli and Troscan.

It seems unlikely that these are all in fact sons of the said Óengus, progenitor of a by-line of the Scottish Dál Riata. Rather, like many similar antiquarian poems, this verse attempts to link individuals who share a common feature. In this case it seems likely that all seven founded or had dedicated to them churches in the Meath-Leinster area which were claimed by the poem as Uí Néill property (for identifications, see Ó Cróinín 1981), and that all share an origin in Scotland. Although the poem represents their Scottish origin as being from the Scottish Dál Riata, this is probably simply a convenient antiquarian device, since some of the saints have both Pictish names and predominantly eastern distributions of Scottish dedications. Certainly Torannán, known also as Mo Thoria and in Scotland as Ternan and variants, has a name more likely to be Pictish than Gaelic, and has dedications both in Ireland at Tulach Foirtchern and Drumcliff, and in Scotland in Banchory-Ternan (Ó Cróinín suggests that two individuals are simply confused by the tradition, but offers no persuasive argument). Óengus described him at 12 June in his Martyrology as having come across the sea. Itharnaisc would appear to be commemorated in Lathrisk in Fife, and may be the same as Ethernan, though the case is not good (Watson 1926, 324). It is very tempting in the circumstances to equate the Eoganan here mentioned with the Iogenan the Pict described by Adomnán (VC ii.9). This Iogenan was travelling in Leinster in the anecdote told by Adomnán, and in the poem on the seven sons Eoganán is described as having a foundation at Cenn Leccaig, which Ó Cróinín identifies with Leccach in Co. Kildare (1981, 114).

Whilst the remaining two are not identifiable, Troscan would appear to be. The crucial lines on him are:

Troscan tren tarrasair
i nArd Breccain co mbinni,

Mighty Troscan who remained
in Ardbraccan sweetly.

This must be the same as the Drostan of Ardbraccan who died in 719, the name originating in the known doublet of Trostan/Drostan, and the –st- becoming –sc- either by phonological change or scribal error. This is further evidence, based on his being grouped here with other seemingly Scottish saints, that this Drostan was at least traditionally from Scotland.

Be that as it may, to my mind the most persuasive arguments for accepting the identity of Drostan Dairthaige and Drostan of Deer are that there are virtually no other known saints called Drostan (though see Ó Riain 1985, §670.60), and that the comparison with the career of the better-documented Fergus makes it clear that Pictish churchmen of just this period were at least partly involved in Ireland. I would argue that unless there is persuasive evidence to the contrary, we should take it that Drostan of Deer died in Ardbraccan, in Ireland, in 719. That Aberdour later claimed his body is not very important: the mobility, multiplicability and flexibility of saints' bodies is well known.

It should be noted that this may suggest further lines of enquiry. The parallelism between the cults of Drostan and Fergus is extremely interesting, especially in their northern dedications. Why are both saints commemorated in Caithness? There would seem to me to be two main possibilities. The first is that these dedications belong to a period after the Norse political dominance of the area had ebbed, and when Gaelic recolonisation of Caithness, perhaps partly from the North East, might have led to the importation of cults from elsewhere. The cults of Fergus and Drostan may be the result of immigrants from Aberdeenshire, for instance, into twelfth- or thirteenth-century Caithness, and therefore be quite late. A second possibility is that in both cases the cults represent genuine early activity by these saints, or others connected with them. It might be plausible to see an extension of the church into Caithness in the early eighth century, perhaps from bases in the North-East. But this must remain extremely speculative.

Nonetheless, I would suggest that it is in the period around 700 that we should place Drostan's *floruit*, as we should place Fergus's as well. This ties in fairly well with the activities of other early saints whose names we know, and whose dates are comparatively more secure (e.g. Nechtan, Ethernan). We could see these North-Eastern cults at Dyce and Lungley, Aberdour and Deer as part of an expanding and consolidating church in Buchan.

This discussion began by noting that a Columban conversion model has excessively dominated discussions of the development of the Pictish church.

The evidence of dedications in the North East however suggests strongly that there was a local and prospering church there from the seventh century onwards, and that we can identify some of the centres of activity by reference to dated individuals and saints with localised cults and Pictish names. Centres like Abersnethock/Monymusk on the Don and Tullich on the Dee are important in this development, as well as perhaps later centres on the Ugie at Deer and further down the Don at Dyce, as well as Lungley and Aberdour elswhere in Buchan. The date-range for the individuals discussed here ranges from the early seventh to the early eighth century, and thus gives the Pictish church in the North-East a period of initial development roughly coterminous with that of Bernicia. This is unlikely to be the whole story, and archaeo-logical and art historical evidence may ultimately point to earlier roots, just as the excavations at Portmahomack now suggest for Easter Ross (Carver 2004).

GAELIC INFLUENCE ON THE PICTISH CHURCH IN THE NORTH-EAST

Despite the doubt cast on the Columban foundation story in the Book of Deer at the beginning of this article, and various other Columban links in stories in the Aberdeen Breviary, there are some hints of Columban or Iona influence in the North-East. Though there are no demonstrably early dedications to Columba, there are a few to Adomnán, such as the important dedication further west in Badenoch at Insh INV (Taylor 1999, 66–7, and generally, 62–70; Taylor 2000a). The Torannán of Banchory-Ternan, already discussed, seems to have strong traditional links with Columba. He is associated with the Columban monastery of Drumcliff, and the tradition in the twelfth-century Irish Life of Columba that he left *Mo Thoria* (i.e., Torannan) there (Herbert, 1988, 236, 283). It should be noted, however, that there is no early evidence that Drumcliff was part of the Columban *familia* (though the art historical evidence adduced in Hawkes 1997 is suggestive). It could easily have been drawn into association with Columba at a later date, much as we have seen happened to Ardbraccan, and it has been suggested here happened to Deer itself.

Iogenan the Pict, perhaps the Eogenán associated with Torannán and Drostan (as *Troscan*) in the Book of Leinster poem, is depicted by Adomnán as having been in contact with Iona, since he possessed a Book of Hymns written by Columba (*VC* ii.9). The miracle he tells appears to have happened after Columba's death (see the setting of ii.8), and thus may help to indicate when Iogenan worked; however, Pictland is a big place, and there is no guarantee that this Iogenan had anything to do with the part of Pictland in which we have interest. The link with Leinster is nonetheless interesting.

Even the Nechtan with which this discussion began may have associations with Iona, if it could be argued that the Nechtan to whom churches in Iona and Islay were dedicated is the same saint (*Cill Mo Neachdáin* in Iona;

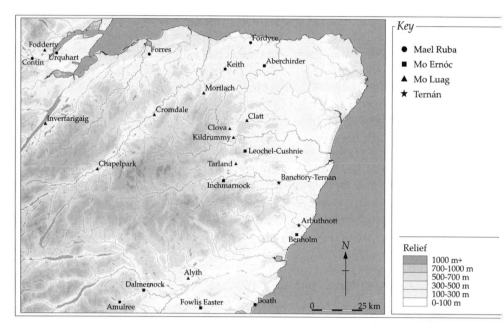

12.4 Sites associated with Gaelic influence: Mael Ruba, Mo Ernóc, Mo Luag and Ternán.

Kilnaughton in Islay: Watson 1926, 308). However, there is no concrete evidence at present to establish this link. What sort of connection might be implied by his culting in these two places would in any case be unclear.

Finally in this context, the North-Eastern dedications to a saint called Marnock are worth noting. This name is almost certainly based on a hypocoristic form of Ernán, as M'Ernóc and similar forms. There are significant dedications at Leochel ABD, at the chapel of Inchmarnoch in Glenmuick parish ABD (Cowan 1967, 85), and especially at Aberchirder BNF, which claimed the saint's head and relics in the fifteenth century (Mackinlay 1914, 74–6). One Ernán was the uncle of Columba, who was one of his original companions, but there are of course many others, and there is no possibility of proving a Columban link.

Thus, while we may trace several possible connections in tradition between churchmen in the North-East and Iona and its founder saint, these are hardly so compelling as to constitute the church in the North-East as 'Columban' in character, or as under the sway of Iona in any meaningful way. In this respect the short-hand of some scholars (e.g., Veitch 1997) and the generalisations of Bede must give way to the jejune but rather negative evidence for the development of the church in the North-East having taken place from other roots and having been open to other influences, including internal ones and ones from elsewhere in Ireland.

The textual evidence relating to Fergus and Drostan, inconclusive and elusive as it is, nonetheless shows that connections with Ireland were strong even in the early eighth century. They point, however, to a relationship with churches in Ireland, especially in midland and southern Ireland, that need not be mediated by Iona or any other Columban connection. We may speculate that it was always likely that some religious training for Pictish churchmen in the seventh and eighth century would have taken place in the west, especially when placed in the context of the English experience.

Ternan

Possibly the best example of these sort of connections relates to St Ternan, to whose cult there have been several references already, under his Irish name Torannán. In the 12th-century glosses to the Martyrology of Oengus, this Torranán is identified with St Palladius, the first bishop to the Irish. We know that Palladius was thought, as early as the 8th century, to have founded a church in the Mearns, at Fordun. This church is contiguous with the parish of Arbuthnott, dedicated from an early date to Ternan. There is a much more tangled web than there is time to treat here (but see Clancy 1999a; 2000, 95–6; and forthcoming a). A few general suggestions may be pertinent however. It looks likely that the cult of Palladius came to north-eastern Pictland from Armagh, it is unclear by what means. It may be at this time also that the cult of St Lawrence, whose relics Armagh had and whose cult they promoted, came to the church now called Lawrencekirk, formerly Conveth (see Clancy 1999a). Ternan is linked with Palladius in Scottish tradition also—is it possible that Ternan/Torannán was in some way involved in bringing the cults of these saints to the Mearns, perhaps with their relics also?

What is significant about the linkages in these parishes in the Mearns is the ostensible linkage to Ireland, and hence to the Gaelic church, through means involving neither Iona nor, as far as one can see, missionaries. Rather, if this scheme is plausible, we may be dealing with the transmission of information, cults, and relics due to forms of contact such as training and education.

Mo Luag and Mael Ruba

Without doubt the most impressive suggestions of Gaelic influence on the church in the North-East come, not in the form of Columban connections, but in ones to two prominent saints with centres elsewhere in Argyll, Mo Luag and Mael Ruba. The two saints are very different in date, Mo Luag having died in 592, with his base in Lismore, while Mael Ruba came to Scotland in 671, establishing his monastery at Applecross in 673, and dying at the age of 80 in 722 (see *AU* 592.1; 671.5; 673.5; 722.1).[14] Both have very

---

14 The Annals of Ulster dates for the 670s through to some point in the 690s seem to be awry—or rather, seem to be correct and should not be rectified by one year as is done for

strong western cults, especially in Argyll, and these deserve more thorough investigation than they have hitherto received.

However, what is interesting in the context of the present discussion is that both have an expanded eastern cult, with Mo Luag in particular present in the North-East (on this, see now the important article of Woolf 2007, the implications of which could not be incorporated in this paper). There are dedications to Mo Luag in Fodderty and to Mael Ruba in Contin ROS. There is a dedication to Mael Ruba at Keith (earlier *Kethmalruf* 1214), and there appear to have been fairs of Mael Ruba called *Samarive's Fair, Summaruff's Fair* in Keith, Forres and Fordyce, although, as Mackinlay notes, these latter parishes were dedicated to other saints (1914, 176). A dedication to Mo Luag at Inverfarigaig (*Cill Mo Luag* and *Croit Mo Luag*) stands on the east side of Loch Ness, 4 or 5km south of, and opposite, Urquhart. Mo Luag is prominent in Strathspey, at Cromdale, further south in Chapel Park, now in Kingussie parish, and slightly east at Mortlach. There is a cluster of churches dedicated to him at Clova, Kildrummy and Clatt, and a further dedication at Tarland (Watson 1926, 292–3; 287–9; Mackinlay 1914, 157–61, 172–5; Barrow 1989).

This is an impressive eastern spread, and I think there are three possible explanations. First, it may be that these dedications arise from separate causes, Mael Ruba's dedications being based on a later expansion of Gaels into the North-East. Mo Luag's on the other hand could derive from the early training of some of the Pictish clergy in Lismore, and the subsequent influence of Lismore in this region. This would account for the greater penetration of Mo Luag's cult into the straths of Spey, Dee and Don. There is, of course, no clear evidence in support of either of these proposals.

A second possibility is that both derive from Gaelic expansionism, and the bringing with it of Argyll-based cults. This must date to some time after 722, since Mael Ruba's cult is a feature of this expansion. Another feature of this expansion may be the replacement of earlier cults in some centres, as for instance, the tradition that Mo Luag's body was at Rosemarkie, surely more suggestive of a colonisation by cult than of a real early foundation at this site so strongly associated with Curetan.[15] A similar phenomenon perhaps lies behind the association of Mael Ruba with Urquhart in the Black Isle, where local tradition apparently held him to have been martyred, presumably by Vikings (Mackinlay 1914, 174).

But a third and to my mind the most likely solution is this. With Gaelic expansion came the culting of these two prominent Argyll saints, with 'colonisation' of sites along Loch Ness and into Strathpeffer and Contin, and

the rest of the annals. Mael Ruba's journey and foundation are thus probably AD 670 and 672 respectively.   15 On this, and Mo Luag generally, see Dransart 2003; Woolf 2007. It should be said that the sixth-century radiocarbon dates obtained from one grave in Portmahomack must make us hesitant to rule out early ecclesiastical settlements in this region (see Carver 2004).

further east still, into Strathspey, where dedications are strongly Gaelic and biblical/Continental in flavour, and as far as Keith and Mortlach. This may be coupled with the establishment of one new main eastern centre for each saint, as Alex Woolf has tentatively suggested in the case of Mo Luag and Rosemarkie (2007). At some point later, during a period of centralising control and church re-organisation, Mortlach became or was made the base for a bishop, from which the bishopric was transferred to Aberdeen in 1157. The traditions of three eleventh-century bishops there, Beyn (=Béán or Béoán) Denort (=?Domangart, or perhaps Dinertach) and Cormac need not be discounted. As a result of Mortlach's increasing influence, the cluster of churches in Clova, Kildrummy and Clatt, and also in Tarland, became Mo Luag dedications.

The dedications to these strongly Gaelic saints then are the result only of gradual expansion into the North-East. The cross-over between the different cults is marked most strongly by Drostan and Mo Luag, facing each other across Loch Ness at Urqhuart and Inverfarigaig, in Strathspey at Aberlour and Mortlach. Once again, however, it should be stressed that Gaelic influence through training in Ireland must have been a separate issue. The Pictish oghams of the North-East, some of which are clearly in Old Irish, and all of which are aware of the Irish ogham tradition, are nonetheless distinctly local and Pictish: a fitting mirror for our picture of Pictish saints training in Ireland, but active at home. One brief ninth-century account brings this home: the *Life of Fintan of Rheinau* depicts him escaping from slave-traders on an island in the Orkneys. He is brought to the local bishop, who though not a native Gaelic speaker, had been educated in Ireland and therefore knew Gaelic (Christiansen 1962, 151, 159). This bishop, almost certainly a Pict, is our last contact with such educational exchange before the gradual colonisation of Pictland by Gaels during the latter part of the ninth century. Education in Ireland would continue to be a habit for eastern Scots, as the *Life of Cadroe* demonstrates (Dumville 2001, 176).

WHAT KIND OF CHURCHES?

So far this discussion of the early Church in north-eastern Scotland has attempted to work outward from the historical data of the obits of churchmen, towards the chronologically more mobile data of the dedications of churches and other sites to saints bearing these names. Coincidentally, the discussion has brought in some evidence for the early medieval prominence of some the churches culting these saints, though here only to indicate that if these church-sites extend back into the early Middle Ages, the cults of their saints at these sites may do also.

Clearly, one could provide an entirely different approach to the early church in the North-East beginning from an archaeological angle. Equally, however, there are other historical approaches which could be taken. Aspects of the property records in the Book of Deer allow us to pose some questions about the nature of churches in the North-East in the eleventh and twelfth centuries, and these may allow us to interrogate further the ecclesiastical organisation of the early medieval North-East that Deer may be taken to have inherited. A thorough discussion is beyond the scope of this article, and would also involve more intensive investigation of the records of other churches in the North-East than I have been able to perform. Nonetheless, some preliminary 'boundary walking', along lines already pursued by Alan Macquarrie in two important essays (1992, 1999), may be helpful.

In respect of the influence of individuals, I have been seeking to get beyond the old orthodoxies involving Columba, Ninian and the like, towards a more complex if more fragmentary picture of how the Church might have developed in the North-East. Equally, in order to understand what we might call the church's institutional or organisational development, we should have our minds concentrated by the recent attention being paid to these problems in Ireland (see Sharpe 1983, Etchingham 1999) and in England (see Blair 1988, 1995; Blair and Sharpe 1992; Cambridge and Rollason 1995). These have sought to retrench from previous approaches to churches of the early Middle Ages which tended to see them as capable of description as 'monastic' or 'episcopal' in nature, especially in a Celtic context. Instead, we should allow for a more flexible system of organisation in respect of regions over time and in respect of individual churches. The early medieval church throughout Europe had a strong monastic impulse at every level, and this impulse waxed and waned, and took on different levels of standardisation. Because of this, even small churches may have had at times 'monastic' attributes (for instance, two or more clergy living in community, celibate clergy, clergy who had trained in monasteries, clergy who observed the canonical hours in liturgically structured prayer). Likewise, both smaller churches and large monasteries could at times be the residence of bishops in Ireland, where there are few signs of a strongly localised sense of episcopal sees, despite the importance of territorial bishops (on which see Etchingham 1994). Furthermore, ecclesiastical settlements once established as monasteries could evolve, or perhaps one might wish to say devolve, into local churches, or grow into ecclesiastical establishments housing little in the way of 'monasticism in its strict sense' (for some thoughts on which, see Etchingham 1999, esp. 319–62).

The fact that the bulk of our evidence for these churches and their relationship to a wider ecclesiastical organisation is twelfth-century and later makes this sort of investigation doubly problematic. The studies of Barrow (1989) and Rogers (1992, 1997) have revealed that there is no straightforward recipe for the evolution of those churches which would become the parishes of the central Middle Ages. Instead, we must envisage a patchwork of ecclesiastical sites existing in the eleventh and twelfth century, some of which became parish churches, some of which were transformed into reformed monasteries of varying types, and some of which remained merely chapels, once brought into the classificatory glare of the new order.

The Book of Deer and similar contemporary sources allow us to make some assessment of where some of the ecclesiastical establishments we have been looking at stood at the time of the writing of the property records. The references to Uineus and Nechtan as abbots of Nér in 623 and 679 implies, at this early date, a monastic establishment of some description, and this accords well with the suggestion I have put forward here that Nér ultimately underlies the *céli Dé* community, and later the Augustinian priory, in Monymusk (on its transformation, see Clancy 1999b). Of course, this need not be a straightforward instance of monastic continuity. There are signs in the twelfth-century sources that the *céli Dé* community in Monymusk may have been a comparatively late one. The nature of sites which employed the place-name element **egles* has yet to be established, but there have been suggestions that they were normally comparatively small or minor churches. If that be the case, what relationship would Abersnithock have to the establishment at Monymusk, and what relationship did it have to our conjectured earlier monastery of Nér?

The property records in the Book of Deer make clear that Turriff was a monastery, having both an abbot and a *fer leiginn* by the twelfth century, though it is uncertain how far back this would go. Ironically, the situation of Deer itself is less certain. In Text I both Deer and Aberdour are described as *cathraig*, which implies monastic establishments of a decent size. For Aberdour there is no clear evidence. However, scholars have noted the references in Deer only to *clerici*, and considered the possibility that Deer acted more as a pastoral centre and 'minster church', than as an actual monastery (Cowan 1974, Macquarrie 1992). This may be so at the point when the grant which uses the term *clerici* was instituted (*c*.1150), but the earlier entries contain indications to the contrary, not least the considerable amount of land granted by secular lords to Deer, an amount unlikely to have accrued to a minor church. Moreover, Text VI implies that Deer should be considered as among 'the chief religious houses' and one which has its own 'chief churches' (context is dative: *ar ard-mandaidib Alban ... ar [a] h-ard-chellaib*) (see Broun this volume).

One odd feature of the medieval parish of Deer is its great size (see Taylor, this volume), especially if we consider that originally it probably served also the parish of Peterugie. It also abuts Aberdour, which was, according to the Book of Deer, a monastery pertaining to Drostan, and therefore theoretically part of the same swathe of ecclesiastical territory, in which there are few signs of subsidiary churches or the like. This is in complete contrast to the situation elsewhere in North-East, for instance, in the straths of Dee, Don, Urie, Deveron and Spey, where instead we find networks of small churches with clear signs both of continuity of religious use from the pre-Christian past (symbol stones, stone circles, etc.), on into the twelfth century codification of the parish church structure (see Barrow 1989 on Strathspey). Although there is little sign of the sort of lavish involvement of secular patronage we find in Angus and Easter Ross, as evidenced by the wealth of ambitious sculpture there (though see Forsyth, 'Stones', this volume) there is an abundance of simple cross-marked stones (so-called 'Class IV') at sites like Clatt, Clova, Aboyne, Tullich, Banchory Ternan which seem to add additional testimony to the early establishment of local churches in these areas (see Henderson 1987; Henderson and Henderson 2004, 162–5). Even within the 'North-East' then, we can discern quite varied patterns of church organisation.

What I believe we can posit, very hesitantly, is the gradual establishment during the period from the seventh through the ninth century, of small local churches serving restricted territories defined by geography and secular structures, the siting of which was often determined by a tradition of sacred space in the region. We should neither imagine these as the efforts of Irish missionaries, nor as a wholly local development, but should perhaps consider the expansion of pastoral services out from mother churches or monastic centres like Deer and Tullich. Allegiances to particular saints may reflect the centres from which such local church foundations spread, as, for instance, the suggestion that the cluster of dedications to Mo Luag in the upper Don springs from a stronger centre at Mortlach. Taken in such terms, the role of Drostan and his monasteries appears pivotal across a wide range of territory.

What this discussion also suggests is that the key period in the formation of local churches, and for the church in the North-East generally, is roughly 670–720, during the floruits of Nechtan, Drostan and Fergus. That this is also a period which recent research has suggested brought new centres to East Fife, Fothrif, Atholl and Easter Ross, seems at first sight to tie in well with the notion of an expanding Gaelic church, largely under the patronage of Iona and Pictish kings linked to it. However, as we have seen, the North-East seems different both by virtue of its personnel and also the patterns of church establishment.

This of course does nothing to illuminate the life of this church. For that, in the North-East, we do not even have the sorts of evidence that can be extracted from sculptured stones in Angus or Easter Ross. All we have, really, is the Book of Deer, for which we must assume, rather than deduce a local origin. This portable gospel book, with its services for the sick, its creed and also its land grants is highly suggestive of a living, worshipping and functioning church in the North-East in the early Middle Ages. It is more challenging to build a coherent context for it from the other fragments of data at our disposal.

COUNTY ABBREVIATIONS

ABD Aberdeenshire
BNF Banffshire
INV Inverness-shire
KCD Kincardineshire
ROS Ross-shire

PRIMARY SOURCES

A. B. Coll   *Collections for a history of the shires of Aberdeen and Banff*, ed. J. Robertson (Spalding Club, 1843), Aberdeen.

Abdn. Reg.   *Registrum Episcopatus Aberdonensis* (Spalding and Maitland Clubs 1845), Aberdeen.

A. B. Ill.   Robertson, J. (1847–69) *Illustrations of the topography and antiquities of the shires of Aberdeen and Banff*, ed. J. Robertson, 4 vols (Spalding Club, 1847–69), Aberdeen.

AU   *The Annals of Ulster (to AD 1131)*, ed. S. MacAirt and G. Mac Niocaill (1983), Dublin.

AI   *Annals of Innisfallen*, ed. Seán Mac Airt (1951), Dublin.

Brev. Abd.   *Breviarium Aberdonense*, 2 vols (Bannatyne Club, 1854), London.

HE   Bede, *Historia ecclesiastica gentis Anglorum*, ed. B. Colgrave and R.A.B. Mynors (1969) *Bede's ecclesiastical history of the English* people, Oxford (rev. ed. 1991).

Mart. Donegal   *The Martyrology of Donegal: a calendar of the saints of Ireland*, (eds) J.H. Todd and W. Reeves (1864), Dublin.

Mart. Gorman   *Félire húi Gormáin: The Martyrology of Gorman*, ed. W. Stokes, (1895) London.

Mart. O *Félire*   *Óengusso: The Martyrology of Óengus*, ed. W. Stokes (1905), Henry Bradshaw Soc. 29, London (repr. Dublin, 1984).

Mart. Tallaght   *The Martyrology of Tallaght*, ed. R.I. Best and H. Lawlor (1931), London.

St A. Lib.   *Liber Cartarum Prioratus Sancti Andree in Scotia* (Bannatyne Club, 1841), London.

Sac.Conc.   *Sacrorum Conciliorum nova et amplissima Collectio*, ed. J.D. Mansi (repr. Graz, 1960–2).

VC   Adomnán, *Vita Sancti Columbae*, ed. A.O. and M.O. Anderson, *Adomnán's Life of Columba* (Oxford, 1961; rev. ed. 1991).

REFERENCES

Alexander, W.M. (1952) *The place-names of Aberdeenshire* (Third Spalding Club), Aberdeen.

Allen, J. Romilly, and Joseph Anderson (1903) *The early Christian monuments of Scotland*, 2 vols, Edinburgh (repr. 1993).

Anderson, A.O. (1922) *Early sources of Scottish history*, 2 vols, Edinburgh (repr. 1990).

Barnes, Michael P. (1999) Review of R.A.V. Cox, *The language of the ogam inscriptions of Scotland*, in *Northern Studies* 34, 129–39.

Barrow, G.W.S. (1983) 'The childhood of Scottish Christianity: a note on some place-name evidence', *Scottish Studies* 27, 1–15.

—— (1989) 'Badenoch and Strathspey, 1130–1312: 2. The church', *Northern Scotland* 9, 1–16.

Best, R.I., and H. Lawlor (1931) *The Martyrology of Tallaght*. London.

Blair, John (1988) *Minsters and parish churches: the local church in transition 950–1200*, Oxford.

—— (1995) 'Ecclesiastical organization and pastoral care', *Early Medieval Europe* 4, 193–212.

—— and Richard Sharpe (1992) *Pastoral care before the parish*. Leicester.

Caldwell, David (2001), 'The Monymusk Reliquary: the *Brecbennach* of Columba?', *Proc. Soc. Antiq. Scot.*, 131, 267–82.

Cambridge, Eric, and David Rollason (1995) 'The pastoral organization of the Anglo-Saxon church: a review of the "minster hypothesis"', *Early Medieval Europe* 4, 87–104.

Carver, Martin (2004) 'An Iona of the East: the early-medieval monastery at Portmahomach, Tarbat Ness', *Medieval Archaeology* 48, 1–30.

Christiansen, Reidar Th. (1962) 'The people of the North [including edition and translation of *Vita Findani*]', *Lochlann: A Review of Celtic Studies* 2, 137–64.

Clancy, Thomas Owen (1999a) 'The foundation legend of Laurencekirk revisited', *Innes Review* 50, 83–8.

—— (1999b) 'Reformers to conservatives: Céli Dé communities in the North East', in *After Columba, after Calvin: religious comunities in north-east Scotland*, (ed.) J. Porter, Aberdeen. 19–31.

—— (1999c) Review of R.A.V. Cox, *The language of the ogam inscriptions of Scotland*, *Peritia* 13, 332–41.

—— (2000) 'Scotland, the 'Nennian' recension of the *Historia Brittonum*, and the *Lebor Bretnach*', in *Kings, clerics and chronicles in Scotland, 500–1297: essays in honour of Marjorie Ogilvie Anderson on the occasion of her ninetieth birthday*, ed. Simon Taylor, Dublin, 87–107.

—— (2001) 'The real St Ninian', *Innes Review* 52, 1–28.

—— (2002) 'Local saints and national identities in early medieval Scotland', in *Local saints and local churches in the early medieval West*, (ed.) R. Sharpe and A. Thacker, Oxford. 397–421.

—— (2004) 'Philosopher-king: Nechtan mac Der-Ilei', *Scottish Historical Review* 83, 125–49.

—— (forthcoming a), 'The cults of Saints Patrick and Palladius in early medieval Scotland', in *Saints' cults in the Celtic world*, ed. Steve Boardman, Woodbridge.

—— (forthcoming b) 'Logie bared: an ecclesiastical place-name element in eastern Scotland'.

——, and Gilbert Márkus (1995) *Iona: the earliest poetry of a Celtic monastery*, Edinburgh.

Cowan, Ian B. (1967) *The medieval parishes of Scotland*, Edinburgh.

—— (1972) 'The medieval church in the diocese of Aberdeen', *Northern Scotland* 1, 19–48.

—— (1974) 'The post-Columban church', *Rec. Scot. Church Hist. Soc.* 18 (1972–4), 245–60.

Cox, R.A.V. (1999) *The language of the ogam Inscriptions of Scotland: contributions to the study of ogam, runic and Roman alphabet inscriptions in Scotland*, Aberdeen.

Dransart, Penelope (2001) 'Two shrine fragments from Kinneddar, Moray', in *Pattern and purpose in Insular art: Transactions of the Fourth International Conference on Insular Art*, ed. M. Redknap et al., Oxford, 233–40.

Dransart, Penelope (2003) 'Saints, stones and shrines: the cults of Sts Moluag and Gerardine in Pictland', in *Celtic hagiography and saints' cults*, ed. J. Cartwright, Cardiff, 232–48.

Dumville, David N. (1982) 'Latin and Irish in the *Annals of Ulster*, AD 431–1050', in *Ireland in early medieval Eruope: studies in memory of Kathleen Hughes*, ed. D. Whitelock et al. (Cambridge 1982) [reprinted in D.N. Dumville, *Histories and pseudo-histories of the Insular Middle Ages* (Aldershot 1990) XVII], 320–41

—— (1984) 'Gildas and Uinniau', in *Gildas: new approaches*, ed. M. Lapidge and D. Dumville, Woodbridge, 207–14.

—— (2001) 'St Cathroe of Metz and the hagiography of exoticism', in *Studies in Irish hagiography: saints and scholars*, ed. J. Carey, M. Herbert, and P. Ó Riain, Dublin, 172–88.

Etchingham, Colmán (1994) 'Bishops in the early Irish church: a reassessment', *Studia Hibernica* 28, 35–62.

—— (1999) *Church organisation in Ireland, AD 650 to 1000*. Maynooth.

Evans, D. Ellis (1967) *Gaulish personal-names: a study of some continental formations*, Oxford.

Farmer, David (1992) *The Oxford dictionary of saints* (3rd ed.), Oxford.

Forbes, A.P. (1872) *Kalendars of Scottish saints*, Edinburgh.

Forsyth, Katherine (1996) 'The ogham inscriptions of Scotland: an edited corpus' (PhD thesis, Harvard Univ.) Ann Arbor, Michigan.

Forsyth, Katherine (1997) *Language in Pictland: the case against 'Non-Indo-European Pictish'* (A.G. Van Hamel Lecture 1995), Munster.

—— (2005), '*HIC MEMORIA PERPETUA*: the inscribed stones of sub-Roman southern Scotland', in *'Able minds and practised hands': Scotland's early medieval sculpture in the 21st century*, ed. S. Foster and M. Cross (Society for Medieval Archaeology Monograph series), Oxford, 113–34.

Fraser, James (2004) 'Adomnán, Cumméne Ailbe and the Picts, *Peritia* 17–18 (2003–4), 183–98.

Gibb, A. (1878) 'Some suggestions as to our mural antiquities', *Proc. Soc. Antiq. Scot.* 12, 192–8.

Hawkes, Jane (1997) 'Columban virgins: iconic images of the Virgin and Child in insular sculpture' in *Studies in the cult of St Columba*, ed. C. Bourke, Dublin, 107–35.

Henderson, Isabel (1987) 'Early Christian monuments of Scotland displaying crosses but no other ornament', in *The Picts: a new look at old problems*, ed. A. Small, Dundee, 45–58.

—— (1998) '*Primus inter pares*: the St Andrews Sarcophagus and Pictish sculpture', in *The St Andrews Sarcophagus: a Pictish masterpiece and its international connections*, ed. S.M. Foster, Dublin, 97–167.

Herbert, Máire (1988) *Iona, Kells and Derry: the history and hagiography of the monastic Familia of Columba*, Oxford (repr. Dublin, 1996).

Hogan, Edmund (1910) *Onomasticon Goedelicum*, Dublin (repr. 1993).

Hudson, Benjamin T. (1994) 'Kings and church in early Scotland', *Scot. Hist. Rev.* 73, 145–70.

Jackson, K.H. (1955) 'The Pictish language', in *The problem of the Picts*, ed. F.T. Wainwright, Edinburgh, 129–160 (repr. Perth 1980, with appendix, 161–6).

Jackson, Kenneth H. (1972) *The Gaelic Notes in the Book of Deer*, Cambridge.

Lacey, Brian (1999) 'County Derry in the early historic period, in *Derry and Londonderry: history and society: interdisciplinary essays on the history of an Irish county*, ed. G. O'Brien, Dublin, 115–48.

Lamb, Raymond (1993) 'Carolingian Orkney and its transformation', in *The Viking Age in Caithness, Orkney and the North Atlantic*, ed. C. Batey, J. Jesch and C. Morris, Edinburgh. 260–71.

—— (1998) 'Pictland, Northumbria and Carolingian Europe', in *Conversion and Christianity in the North Sea World*, ed. B. Crawford, St Andrews. 41–56.

MacDonald, James (1891) *Place names in Strathbogie*, Aberdeen.

Mackinlay, J.M. (1914) *Ancient church dedications in Scotland*, Edinburgh.

MacPherson, William M. (1895) *Materials for a history of the church and priory of Monymusk*. Aberdeen.

Macquarrie, Alan (1992) 'Early Christian religious houses in Scotland: foundation and function', in *Pastoral care before the parish*, ed. J. Blair and R. Sharpe, Leicester, 110–33.

—— (1999) 'Early Christian communities in the North East: the evidence from Deer and from St Laurence's Kirk at Conveth', in *After Columba, after Calvin: religious comunities in north-east Scotland*, ed. J. Porter, Aberdeen. 13–18

Manning, Conleth (2000) 'References to church buildings in the Annals', in *Seanchas: studies in early medieval Irish archaeology, history and literature in honour of Francis J. Byrne*, ed. A.P. Smyth, Dublin, 37–52.

Mitchell, Arthur (1874) 'Vacation notes in Cromar, Burghead, and Strathspey', *Proc. Soc. Antiq. Scot.* 10, 603–89.

Ó Baoill, Colm (1993) 'St Machar—some linguistic light?', *Innes Review* 44, 1–13.

Ó Cróinín, Dáibhí (1981) 'The oldest Irish names for the days of the week?', *Ériu* 32, 99–114.

Okasha, Elisabeth (1985) 'The non-ogam inscriptions of Pictland', *Cambridge Medieval Studies* 9, 43–69.

O'Rahilly, T.F. (1946) *Early Irish history and mythology*, Dublin.

Ó Riain, P. (1985) *Corpus Genealogiarum Sanctorum Hiberniae*, Dublin.

O'Sullivan, Anne (ed.), (1983) *The Book of Leinster, formerly Lebar na Núachongbála*, vol. 6, Dublin.

Padel, O.J. (2002) 'Local saints and place-names in Cornwall', in *Local saints and local churches in the early medieval West*, ed. A. Thacker and R. Sharpe, Oxford, 303–60.

Pearce, Susan (2003) 'Process of conversion in north-west Roman Gaul', in *The cross goes north: processes of conversion in northern Europe, AD 300–1300*, ed. M. Carver, York, 61–78.

Redford, Morag (1988) 'Commemorations of saints of the Celtic church in Scotland', unpubl. M. Litt thesis, Univ. of Edinburgh.

Reeves, William (1864) *On the Céli-Dé, commonly called Culdees*, Edinburgh.

Rogers, J.M. (1992) 'The formation of the parish unit and community in Perthshire', unpubl. PhD thesis, Univ. of Edinburgh.

—— (1997) 'The formation of parishes in twelfth-century Perthshire', *Rec. Scot. Church Hist. Soc.* 27, 68–96.

Sharpe, Richard (1984) 'Some problems concerning the organization of the church in early medieval Ireland', *Peritia* 3, 230–70.

—— (1992) 'Churches and communities in early medieval Ireland: towards a pastoral model', in *Pastoral care before the parish*, ed. J. Blair and R. Sharpe, Leicester, 81–109.

Simpson, W. Douglas (1924) 'The Augustinian priory and parish church of Monymusk, Aberdeenshire', *Proc. Soc. Antiq. Scot.* 59, 34–71.

—— (1925) *The origins of Christianity in Aberdeenshire*, Aberdeen.

—— (1927) *The historical saints Columba*, Aberdeen.

—— (1943) *The province of Mar*, Aberdeen.

Stokes, Whitley (1905) *Félire Óengusso: The Martyrology of Óengus*, Henry Bradshaw Soc. 29, London (repr. Dublin, 1984).

Taylor, Simon (1996) 'Place-names and the early church in eastern Scotland', in *Scotland in Dark-Age Britain*, ed. B. Crawford, St Andrews, 93–110.

—— (1998) 'Place-names and the early church in Scotland', *Rec. Scot. Church Hist. Soc.* 28, 1–22.

—— (1999) 'Seventh-century Iona abbots in Scottish place-names', in *Spes Scotorum, Hope of Scots: St Columba, Iona and Scotland*, ed. D. Broun and T.O. Clancy, Edinburgh, 35–70.

—— (2000a) 'Columba east of Drumalban: some aspects of the cult of Columba in eastern Scotland', *Innes Review* 51, 109–28.

—— (2000b) 'Place-names of Fife', in *The Fife Book*, ed. D. Omand, Edinburgh, 205–20.

—— (2001) 'The cult of St Fillan in Scotland', in *The North Sea world in the Middle Ages: studies in the cultural history of north western Europe*, ed. T.R. Liszka and L.E.M. Walker, Dublin, 75–210.

Thacker, Alan, and Richard Sharpe (eds), (2002) *Local saints and local churches in the early medieval West*, Oxford.

Trench-Jellicoe, Ross (1998) 'The Skeith Stone, Upper Kilrenny, Fife in its context', *Proc. Soc. Antiq. Scot.* 128, 495–513.

Veitch, K. (1997) 'The Columban church in northern Britain, 664–717: a re-assesment', *Proc. Soc. Ant. Scot.* 127, 627–47

Wasserschleben, H. (ed.), (1885) *Die Irische Kanonensammlung*, Leipzig (repr. 1996, Leipzig).

Watson, A., and E. Allen (1984) *The place-names of Upper Deeside*, Aberdeen.

Watson, W.J. (1926) *The Celtic place names of Scotland*, Edinburgh.

Woolf, Alex (2000) 'The "Moray Question" and the kingship of Alba in the tenth and eleventh centuries', *Scot. Hist. Rev.* 79, 145–64.

—— (2007) 'The cult of Moluag, the see of Mortlach and Church organisation in northern Scotland in the eleventh and twelfth centuries', in *Fil súil nglais. A Grey Eye Looks Back: a Feschrift in honour of Colm Ó Baoill*, ed. S. Arbuthnott and K. Hollo, Brig o'Turk, 299–310.

Yeoman, Peter (1998) 'Pilgrims to St Ethernan: the archaeology of an early saint of the Picts and Scots', in *Conversion and Christianity in the North Sea world*, ed. B.E. Crawford, St Andrews, 75–91.

Youngs, Susan (ed.), (1989) *'The work of angels': masterpieces of Celtic metalwork, 6th–9th centuries AD*, London.

The stones of Deer

KATHERINE FORSYTH

STONES IN THE PROPERTY RECORDS IN THE BOOK OF DEER

To those in the south, Buchan may seem peripheral and remote, a modern perspective which, however skewed, appears to have coloured scholarly expectations of what the region was like in the Middle Ages.[1] In what follows I hope to show that a consideration of physical remains from Deer, in the form of early medieval carved stones, will go some way towards countering this prejudice by providing insight into the cultural context of the early church in Deer. In turn I hope to show how this may inform the debate about the Book of Deer's place of origin.

Central Buchan is 'White Stone Country'[2] and stones of one sort and another have been used to define and articulate its landscape since the Neolithic (Coles 1904). References to boundary markers are few in the property records in the Book of Deer. In most cases the land is simply named and its boundaries taken as understood, but in six instances landscape features are invoked to define the extent of grants. Of these features, half are stones.[3] In text V.3 the land given by Comgell son of Cainnech is stated to extend *gonige in gorthe mor i gginn in fris*, 'as far as the great *coirthe* at the end of the thicket'. The *coirthe* in question, a prominent 'pillar, standing-stone, menhir' (*DIL*) appears to be commemorated in the nearby name of Quartalehouse (*Cortailhows* 1544), which Taylor has explained as 'the standing-stone of **Aileas*' (*infra*, 294–5). Indeed Quartalehouse may be the very land granted by Comgell.

Corthe mor implies a particularly imposing pillar-stone and it is tempting to identify the one in question with the famous 'White Cow of Crichie', a huge block of quartz which formerly stood as a boundary marker at NGR NJ 9744 4504, due south of Quartalehouse (OS Name Book No. 68, 129). It had already been broken up and moved by the time of the Ordnance Survey mapping of the district in 1870, and by 1904 was lying on edge at the avenue at Crichie (NJ

---

1 See Jackson's comments about Deer being 'on the remotest edge of the Common Gaelic civilisation area; its writing-masters must have been out of touch and poorly qualified' (1972, 126), and Hughes comments about the Book of Deer being 'on the fringes' of Irish tradition, and the (unlocalised) scriptorium in which it was produced being 'a provincial one' which 'had little paint for the pictures' (1980, 37). 2 The title of David Ogston's autobiographical account of growing up in the area (1986). See also the place name Whitestones (*Quhitestanis* 1530 *RMS* iii no. 912) on the boundary of Deer parish and Monquitter. 3 The other features are: a tree (II.12) and a water-course (V), and possibly a well (II.12).

9758 4516). The stone then measured 5'6" x 3'4" x 2'7" (1.68 x 1.02 x 0.79m), but was thought by that stage to be only a fragment of the original White Cow (Coles 1904, 262). Thereafter it appears to have been broken up even further and has all but disappeared. The only remaining trace of the White Cow today is the notable run of white quartz in the dry-stone wall by the road opposite the farm. The near total disappearance of this monument in recent times is salutary and the *corthe mor* of V.3 must remain unidentified.

The prominence of prehistoric standing stones in the landscape of eastern Scotland—a prominence which would have been even greater in pre-Improvement times—is reflected in the frequency with which they are commemorated in place-names (see Taylor, *infra* 294). This is borne out by a glance at the Ordnance Survey map of the area around Deer which also shows that there is a notable correlation between such features and boundaries. There is a Cortiecram, 'bent or crooked pillar', at the southern boundary of Deer parish and another at the southern boundary of Lonmay parish. The eponym of the latter, the 'Gray Stone' was described in 1904 as 'lying half prostrate' (Coles 1904) but there is no trace of it today as it was destroyed in the 1940s (CANMORE: NK05 SW4). Cortiebrae in Strichen (formerly Rathen) parish lies near the boundary with Lonmay parish.[4] Immediately outside Deer parish, Auchorthie, 'field of the standing stone(s)', stands at the southern boundary of Rathen parish, and the similarly named Auchnagorth stands in Kingedward parish by the three-way parish boundary with Aberdour and Deer. The remains of the eponymous stone circle are still visible nearby (NJ 8390 5629, Coles 1904, 281–4).

A different kind of stone is indicated by the references in the Deer foundation legend (Text I) to the initial grant by Bede, Pictish mormaer of Buchan, as being '*ua cloic in tiprat gonice chloic pette m̄c̄ Garnait*', 'from the stone of the spring/well to the stone of **pett m̲a̲c̲ Garnait*' ('the holding of the sons of Gartnait'). Gaelic *cloch* has a wide semantic range very similar to the breadth of meanings covered by English 'stone' (*DIL*). It glosses Latin *lapis* 'stone' and can mean something as small as a little pebble or as large as a cross-slab. A number of inscribed Welsh monuments refer to themselves, in the accusative case, as *hunc lapidem* (Nash-Williams 1950, nos. 61, 101, 182, 253), including the Pillar of Eliseg (no.182), which is almost 2.5m tall. While the diminutive inscribed cross-slab from Iona which identifies itself as '*lapis Echodi*' is only 0.36 x 0.27m (Fisher 2001, 128; Charles-Edwards 2004). Recent work on the place-names of Fife suggests that there, at least, *cloch* in place-names referred to a carved stone, as opposed to *coirthe* an undecorated standing stone (Taylor with Márkus, forthcoming). In two of the Fife instances the *cloch* in question may be identified: Pitlochie, Kinglassie parish, where the eponymous stone is almost certainly the free-standing cross from

4 For forms see Taylor, *infra* 294–5 n.80.

Dogton, while Pitlochy, an obsolete name in Collessie parish, may refer to the Collessie Stone, a 2.7m tall prehistoric standing stone incised in the Pictish period with a human figure.[5]

The phrasing of the Deer grant echoes the description of the founding grant of land to the monastery of Abernethy by the Pictish king Nechtan. The Abernethy foundation legend is an addition to the Pictish king list and states that the king's initial grant extended *a lapide in Apurfeirt usque ad lapidem juxta Ceirfuill* (Skene 1867, 6) 'from the stone in Aberargie as far as the stone beside Carpow' (Anderson 1980, 93). As at Deer, only two points are mentioned, and both are marked by a stone. The conundrum of how an *area* of land can be delimited with reference to only two points may be solved at Deer if it is accepted that the remaining sides of the polygon were formed by a loop of the river South Ugie.[6]

The position of the Old Kirk of Deer, bounded on three sides by a great bend in the South Ugie, is strikingly reminiscent of Old Melrose, site of the early medieval predecessor of the Cistercian abbey of Melrose, which is situated within a similar, though larger, loop of the Tweed. Such positions, within the bend or at the confluence of a river, appear to have been frequently favoured as the location of Early Medieval churches in eastern Scotland and there is a strong suspicion that Old Deer is similarly early (Simpson 1952). Although the church is not documented before 1252 and there are no physical remains there older than the thirteenth century (Fawcett, *infra* 459), nevertheless the topography of the site points strongly towards this being an early medieval ecclesiastical site, specifically the sub-circular form of the churchyard, which is now recognised as a strong pointer towards pre-twelfth-century date in Western Britain and Ireland (Thomas 1971, 81–5; for Cornwall see Preston-Jones 1992, for Wales see Brook 1992, for Ireland see Swan 1993). The old shape of the kirkyard at Deer is reflected in the extant wall, in the layout of surrounding old buildings and lanes and in the curve of the road. Although the wall has been straightened in sections, the underlying shape is clearly curvilinear and ancient: there is considerable accumulation of soil within it. Local tradition maintains that when new gate pillars were built at the entrance to the churchyard it was found that burials had taken place outwith the churchyard wall suggesting the enclosure was formerly larger.[7] Indeed, traces of a second, outer enclosure appear to be preserved in the layout of the modern village. This is clearest in the route of a tree-lined lane which runs north-west in an arc from the vicinity of St Drostan's Well[8] at the southern approach to the village. Its course, including a possible continuation northwards looping back to rejoin the river near the modern Bridge of Deer,

5 I owe these references to Simon Taylor. 6 In the case of Abernethy, the stones presumably delimited a strip of land running between the Tay and the hills. 7 www.bookofdeer.co.uk 8 Marked 'Grian's Well' on OS 1st edition, see Taylor *infra* 286 n.54 for discussion of the name.

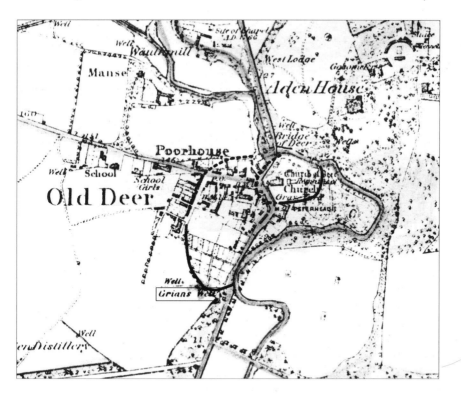

13.1 OS 6" map, 1st Edition (1874) Aberdeenshire and Banffshire, Sheet xxi. Detail showing proposed enclosures, Old Deer.

can be seen on the Ordnance Survey 1st edition map (fig. 13.1). A further indication of the nature of the ecclesiastical precinct is provided by accounts of 'the Minister's Mound', a small mound directly across from the church 'where the Minister stood, in all weathers, after the service, to bless his parishioners as they left the church'. It has been suggested that landscaping for a post-War development of sheltered housing in the vicinity accounts for the disappearance of the mound today.[9] Although some of the lower-lying ground between the churchyard and the river would have been prone to flooding, the area bounded by the outer enclosure and the river is substantial, an indication that this was a major church (Brook 1992, 85–7). This is consistent with the royal patronage indicated by the Deer property records.

If the shape of the possible *vallum* identified above is accepted then its terminus by St Drostan's Well assumes added interest. Might this be the *tiprat* mentioned in the original grant? If so, the 'stone of the well' which marked the boundary is long gone. The location of the other stone mentioned

9 www.bookofdeer.co.uk. The Minister's Mound at Deer recalls the small mound known as Queen Vanora's Grave, in the churchyard at Meigle, Perthshire.

in the initial grant, the 'stone of the holding of the sons of Gartnait', is not so readily identified. We are probably looking for a carved stone, such as a cross or Pictish symbol stone, but are we to envisage the initial grant as covering a relatively small area—the tight loop to the east of the village which encompasses the parish church—or a somewhat larger loop, say as far as the site of the later abbey on the opposite bank of the river a little over a km upstream? The two points mentioned in the Abernethy grant are about 4km apart, although it, of course, was a major royal foundation and thus might be expected to be endowed on a grander scale.

As the holding of the sons of Gartnait was itself subsequently given to the monastery (II.2) it appears that the aforementioned stone stood on the boundary of the estate in question, at least at the time the property record was written in the early twelfth century. The question is, were these two stones existing landmarks—like the prehistoric stones and cairns mentioned above, or like the Pictish symbol stones discussed below—or were they erected specially to mark the boundary of the grant? A distinction should be drawn between the land delimited by the *coirthe*—which was simply a possession of the monastery—and the land delimited by the two *clocha*—which was the extent of the monastery itself. The *clocha* therefore were marking sacred ground, perhaps the limit of the monastery's sanctuary (*termonn*) and as such, might be expected to be cross-marked.

Before turning to the surviving sculptured stones of Deer, mention should be made of a final place-name which may be connected to the Deer foundation legend as set out in Text I. The name 'Deer' is explained as deriving from the tears (*déara*) shed by Drostán following Colum Cille's valedictory blessing (see Clancy, this volume). Simon Taylor has suggested (pers. com.) that this foundational blessing may be commemorated in the place-name Cairnbanno (*Carnebennach* ×1214, *A. B. Coll.* 407; 'cairn of blessing'). The location of Cairnbanno, which belonged to the Cistercian abbey, lends credence to this theory for it stands on the boundary of the Medieval parish, at the point where the road south crosses the Little Water (fig. 9.2). This boundary would have marked a significant point on the journey to and from the south-west as the traveller entered or left the lands of Deer. It is natural that the parting of Colum Cille and Drostán would have been imagined to have taken place at such a point and that a fitting piece of *dindshenchas*, or 'place-name lore', would have evolved to link the physical landscape of prehistoric burial cairn, road and boundary with this, a defining moment in the origin legend of Deer.

CROSS-MARKED SYMBOL STONE, DEER ABBEY

The oldest Christian monument in the parish of Deer to survive into modern times is the cross-marked symbol stone which, up until the early 1850s, could

13.2 Cross-marked symbol stone, Deer Abbey (Stuart 1856, pl. 11).

be seen 'placed at the west end of the old [i.e. Cistercian] Abbey Church' (Pratt 1858, 106). Sadly, the stone disappeared in 1854 when the area, including much of what remained of the church, was cleared away by the proprietor, Admiral George Ferguson of Pitfour, to build a family mausoleum in Greek style, now itself removed (see Fawcett, *infra* 444–6). Romilly Allen records that it was 'believed that the stone was taken away ... and used to build the foundations of a lodge near the monastery'; an act of wanton destruction which moved him to comment: 'This is one of the few instances of the deliberate desecration of an ancient monument that have to be recorded in this volume' (Allen and Anderson 1903, 162 n.2).

No trace of the Deer stone remains today. It is known only from the lithographic sketch (fig. 13.2) taken 'from nature' by P.A. Jastrzębski, the Polish painter and draughtsman employed by the Aberdeen lithographic firm of Keith and Gibb to work on the plates for Stuart's *Sculptured Stones of Scotland*, 1856 (McEwan 1994, 299). Jastrzębski had considerable experience of drawing Early Medieval sculptured stones, having been engaged by Patrick Chalmers of Aldbar to produce the plates for *Ancient Sculptured Monuments of the County of Angus* (Chalmers 1848), nonetheless, the reliability of his drawings came to be

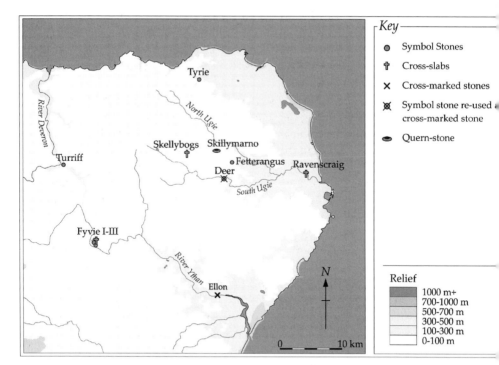

13.3 Early medieval carved stones from Buchan.

impugned. A colleague recalled that following the discovery of 'inaccuracies' in the drawings for Stuart's volume 'a good many of the plates ... were condemned as worthless, and the work was taken out of Jastrzçbski's hands and entrusted to Mr Gibb' (George Reid, quoted by Ritchie, 1997, 123). Yet the fact that Jastrzçbski's sketch of the Deer stone was among those not scrapped presumably indicates that it was considered sufficiently accurate to stand (Stuart 1856, pl. 11; fig. 13.2). It is, in any case, all that we have to go on.

Stuart (1856, 6) states the stone to have stood 6' tall and to have been 2'6" across (*c.*1.83 x 0.76m). The sketch shows a typical Pictish symbol stone—which may, or may not, have been a re-used prehistoric standing-stone[10]—incised with the standard pair of symbols: in this case a 'rectangle' above a 'crescent-and-V-rod'. Both have typical curvilinear internal ornamentation. The (original) right–hand edge of both is missing. On the reverse is a simple Latin cross in outline. The upper arm is slightly wedge-shaped and reaches the upper edge, the side arms are straight with curved terminals and stop short of the edge. There is no elaboration of the arm-pits and the bottom of the straight shaft is gently curving. The cross is inverted relative to the

---

10 Clarke includes it on his 'Provisional check-list of prehistoric standing stones re-used as Pictish symbol stones' on the grounds of size (2007, 38–9).

symbols and the taper on the stone indicates that it would have first stood with symbols upright, narrow end at the top, and, therefore, that the carving of the cross is secondary. Pictish symbol stones are conventionally dated between the fifth and seventh centuries, the difficulty lies in attempting to date the carving of the cross.

The Deer cross-marked stone bears some similarities, of both form and scale, to examples from among the collection of fifteen cross-marked stones at Tullich, by Ballater (Henderson and Henderson 2004, 163, fig. 239), although it lacks the distinctive point to the end of the shaft which is such a feature of some of the Tullich crosses (Henderson and Henderson 2004, 165). Cross-marked stones are common on Deeside (8 examples) and Donside (10 examples) but are rare in northern Aberdeenshire (Henderson and Henderson 2004, 158, map 5). The only other cross-marked stone known from Buchan is the incised fragment, 0.76 x 0.31m, found reused as a window jamb of the parish church of Ellon, which features an outline Latin cross with expanded, bar, terminals (Ritchie 1915, 43; fig. 13.5).[11] Although 'simple and undatable', incised cross-marked stones such as these are part of a 'monumental tradition datable to the 6th to 9th centuries' (Henderson and Henderson 2004, 163, 159). If the Deer stone is to be bracketed with them, then—in its cross-marked phase—it would likely pre-date the Book of Deer and be the oldest Christian relic associated with the parish. According to this scenario the interval between the two uses of the Deer stone could have been as little as a generation, or as long as a couple of centuries.

There are, however, reasons to believe the Deer cross may belong to a later tradition and date instead to the period thirteenth-fifteenth century. In Jastrzçbski's sketch the interior of the cross is shown lighter in colour, with hints of damage indicating, it seems, that it was carved in relief. There is a plastic, gently swelling quality to Jastrzçbski's representation but note, in particular, indications that a small area has broken away half way down the left side of the shaft. This is consistent with local damage of a relief edge.[12] A relief cross, though far from unprecedented, would be highly unusual in an early medieval context. The form of the cross—with curved terminals stopping short of the edge while the upper arm touches it and, especially, with curved shaft terminal and no hint of a skeumorph base—also sits more happily in the central Middle Ages. If this were the case the stone could have been either a recumbent grave-cover or an upright cross, perhaps a *termonn* marker, like the four large free-standing crosses which marked the extent of the sanctuary at Dull, Perthshire (Allen and Anderson 1903, 342). Depending on which date is favoured for the cross we have two very different scenarios of

11 The Latin cross incised on a rock at Cross-stone, Ellon (NJ 473 486), appears to be a boundary marker of later medieval date (Gordon 1956, pl. LXIV). 12 I owe this insight to Ross Trench-Jellicoe.

reuse: an earlier one, dating to some time in the sixth-ninth century when the import of the symbols may still have been understood and the cross a possible response to them, and a much later one (thirteenth-fifteenth century) when the symbols were probably virtually invisible and certainly meaningless.

The meaning and function of Pictish symbol stones continues to provoke debate (most recently Forsyth 1997, Mack 1998, Clarke 2007) despite the fact that 'modern excavation is beginning to confirm that one of their functions was to mark the sites of burials, either individually or in cemeteries' (RCAHMS 2007a, 122). Clarke argues that Pictish symbol stones are unlikely to be grave-stones on the grounds that the appropriation of a person's burial marker to mark the grave of another would have been intolerable (2007, 29). Examination of cognate 'individual inscribed memorials' from elsewhere in Britain and Ireland—including the sub-Roman inscriptions of western Britain and the ogham stones of Ireland—indicates, however, that, even if erected as part of funerary ritual, these monuments are not personal grave-stones of the kind one would find in a modern cemetery, nor indeed a Roman one. Rather, if Handley is to be believed, they are better thought of as 'charters' asserting a kin-group's right to landownership at a boundary location, a right also asserted by the burial of kin-group members at that location (1998). Far from there being a conflict between the functions of boundary-marking and memorial-stone, given what we know about boundary associations in early Irish law and literature (Ó Riáin 1972, Charles-Edwards 1976), we should expect the two functions to be combined. The likelihood that the lost Deer symbol stone served as an estate-boundary marker raises the distinct possibility that it is to be identified as the *cloch pette mac Garnait* mentioned in Text I as marking the extent of the original endowment.

The near contemporary re-use of symbol stones which troubles Clarke (2007)[13] can be paralleled among the aforementioned contemporary cognate inscribed memorials: both western British memorials and Irish ogham stones are occasionally found with secondary inscriptions or crosses[14] and ogham stones are found quite frequently built into souterrains of early medieval date (Moore 1998, 29–31). Both forms of re-use are more readily interpreted as arising from the re-cycling of available stone following the redundancy of the original monument—because the kin-group had died out, or the land changed hands, or simply because the right no longer needed to be asserted in this manner—rather than some more symbolically-loaded gesture of denigration.

---

13 To his list of symbol stones with multiple lives could be added the Fetterangus symbol stone and, of course, the Deer stone itself. 14 For instance, Ballynahunt, Co. Kerry (Macalister 1945 no. 171). The converse, an ogham inscription added in the seventh century to a cross-marked stone, is seen at Church Island, Iveragh (O'Sullivan and Sheehan 1996, 258; Swift 1997, 76–7). See also the apparently unrelated ogham on seventh-century inscribed cross-marked pillar, at Kilfountan, Co. Kerry (Okasha and Forsyth 2001, 161–5).

The evolution of pre-Christian burial grounds into Christian cemeteries is well known (Thomas 1971, 52–8) and the desire to mark these grounds as Christian is the likely explanation of the re-use of ogham stones as cross-marked stones. In these cases, as at Deer, we should not rush to interpret the re-use of the stone as a gesture of Christian triumphalism over a toppled paganism. Having said that, the inversion and re-erection of so massive a stone is not a trivial undertaking. It must have accomplished something more than would have been achieved by simply inscribing a cross on the back of a standing monument. Of course, if, as seems possible, the cross was not carved until much later in the Middle Ages, then the chances are increased that the stone had simply already fallen over.

Mack has argued that symbol stones are typically found at burial sites, many, though by no means all of which, later became church sites (1998, but see Clarke 2007). The frequent collocation with early church sites is true of Pictish symbol stones in general but is particularly true in northern Aberdeenshire. The Deer stone is one of six Pictish symbol stones from Buchan (see fig. 13.4 a–e). All of the remaining five were found in or near their parish churches. The stone from Tyrie was found in the foundations of the old parish church (Stuart 1856, 7; Allen and Anderson 1903, 187–8; Shepherd and Ralston 1979, 28) and that from Turriff was found in use as a lintel in the church (Allen and Anderson 1903, 187). The Fetterangus stone was 'found near the church' (Gibb 1878, 196–7; Allen and Anderson 1903, 164) and at least one of the two stones from Fyvie ('2') seems to be original to the kirkyard. The other ('Fyvie 1') was found a few hundred metres away built into the wall of a tailor's shop in the village (Allen and Anderson 1903) and may also have come originally from the church, or its *termonn* (Stuart 1867, 8; Allen and Anderson 1903, 164–5; Shepherd and Ralston 1979, 28).[15] Fyvie 2 and Turriff have been carefully trimmed to form neat, rectangular building blocks. Thus with at least four, and perhaps five, out of the six Buchan symbol stones coming from churches or churchyards, this corner of the North-East stands out against the national figure of 28% of all 'Class I' symbol stones (Mack 1998). It also begs the question: how many more early medieval sculptured stones are still built into church buildings in Buchan?

A key to understanding the link between symbol stones and early churches is the tendency of both to occupy boundary locations (RCAHMS 2007a, 124). This is in keeping with the more general pattern seen in western Britain and Ireland where churches of all sizes are commonly found, not at the centre of their parishes but in traditional boundary areas (Ó Riáin 1972, 18). The parish church at Tyrie sits beside the stream which forms the boundary with Aberdour parish where it abuts the medieval parish of Philorth, and at Fetterangus the medieval parish boundary—also, in this case, a former county

---

15 A third symbol stone higher up in this wall came from Rothiebrisbane.

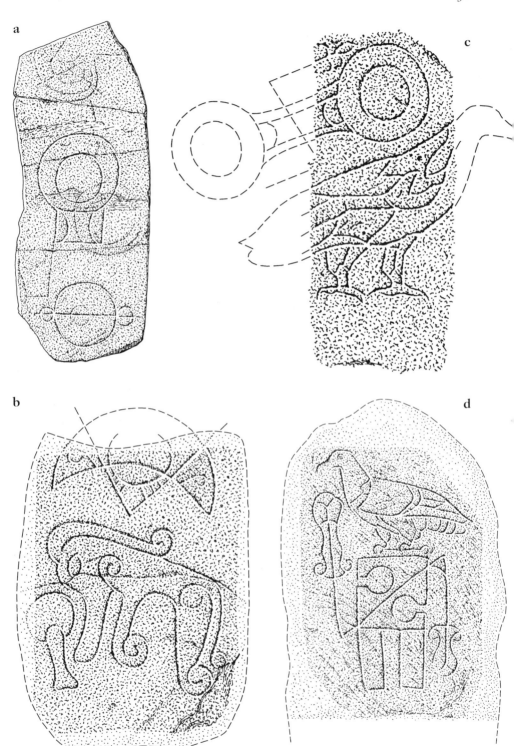

13.4 Symbol stones from
Buchan:
a) Fetterangus Height 1.1 m
(SC1081353),
(b) Fyvie I Height 0.71 m
(SC 1081334),
(c) Fyvie II Height 0.68 m
(SC 1081329),
(d) Tyrie Height 1.1 m
(SC 1081266),
(e) Turriff Height 0.5 m
(SC 1081271)
(all Crown Copyright:
RCAHMS);
(drawings: John Borland).

Not to scale

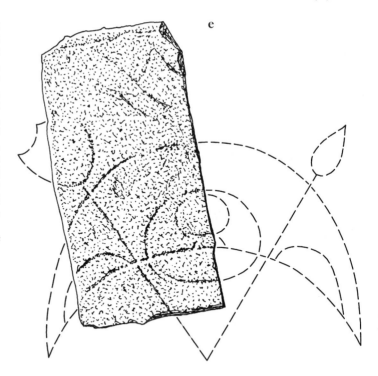

e

boundary—is deflected around the kirkyard wall itself. The other three churches to have produced early medieval sculpture—Turriff, Ellon and Fyvie—may have been more substantial foundations. The Deer property records provide evidence that there was a monastery at Turriff in the early twelfth century large enough to support a scriptorium or school (III is witnessed by the *fer léginn* and VI and VII by the abbot of Turriff). Sculptural evidence discussed below points to a wealthy establishment at Fyvie, and Ellon was the *caput* of Buchan, site of the court of mormaer and earl (text VI) All three of these churches stand on the outer edge of the later medieval earldom of Buchan: Ellon and Fyvie on the north bank of the Ythan and Turriff on the east bank of the Deveron (see fig. 9.1). Again, this fits the pattern seen in Ireland where major monasteries frequently occupy the border-lands between polities (Ó Riáin 1972).

Writing within a few years of the stone's disappearance, Pratt states that 'Nothing is known as to the precise original locality of the stone' (1858, 106), implying that it was known *not* to have been in its original position. It is not clear whether the uncertainty concerned simply whereabouts in the abbey precinct it had been found, or reflected the belief that it had come from somewhere else entirely. The latter cannot be ruled out. There are certainly numerous examples from elsewhere in Scotland of sculptured stones larger than this being moved quite considerable distances by antiquarian-minded

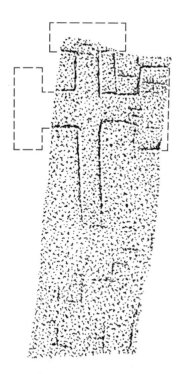

13.5 Cross-marked stone, Ellon
(Crown Copyright: RCAHMS; SC
1090350; drawing: John Borland).

proprietors of the eighteenth and ninteenth centuries.[16] By and large,
however, these are ornate cross-slabs moved to the policies or gardens of the
'big house'; simpler cross-marked stones do not seem to have attracted the
same kind of attention. On balance, it seems more likely that the Deer stone
originated in or near the abbey precinct. It is not, however, marked on the
1789 plan of the abbey (fig. 14.1) nor is it mentioned in the Old Statistical
Account of the parish (Cruden 1799). The latter refers to the abbey as 'now
very much in ruins' and records the recent discovery of a semicircular Doric
column from the abbey church and notes: 'Were more of the rubbish cleared
away, it is probable similar pillars might be found in other parts of the
building' (483). It is possible the stone came to light during the programme of
landscaping and preservation instigated at the abbey in 1809 by the then
proprietor James Ferguson of Pitfour. This involved large-scale clearance of
accumulated ruins and the lowering of the ground level within the church to
reveal its plan (Fawcett, *infra* 444), processes likely to lead to the recovery of
the stone if it had been built into the walls of the abbey.[17]

16 E.g. Monreith, Woodwray, Hilton of Cadboll, Dupplin 'Hanging Stone', Jordanhill.
17 Jastrzębski's sketch of the Deer stone depicts some loss of carving on the left-hand edge
of the upside-down symbols. The somewhat straight edge here may reflect deliberate
trimming for re-use as a building block, but more radical re-sizing might be expected if
this were the case.

The incorporation of early medieval sculptured stones into the walls of later medieval churches is widely attested throughout Scotland and accounts for the preservation of a high proportion, perhaps even a majority, of the early medieval cross-slabs which survive to the present. Examples are numerous and include major churches, such as St Andrews and Whithorn, as well as more minor parish churches (Allen and Anderson 1903, *passim*). While the primary motivation for this widespread phenomenon may have been simply the practical advantages of reutilising a convenient source of building material, there remains the strong suspicion of a symbolic component to this incorporation of the old in the new. Where stones have been found built into post-twelfth-century parish churches these are generally known, or thought to be, on the site of their early medieval predecessors. Clearly this has implications for our understanding of the pre-thirteenth-century history of the site of the Cistercian abbey. Although it has been touted as the location of the original church of Deer, this has generally been deemed unlikely on the grounds of the Cistercian order's known preference for 'green-field' sites (Jackson 1972, 2). Certainly, Cistercian foundations in Scotland do appear to have been typically on new sites—as noted above, the Cistercian abbey of Melrose lies about 4km up-stream from the site of its early medieval predecessor at Old Melrose—but this was not always the case. The collection of early medieval sculpture in the churchyard of the Cistercian abbey of Culross implies that it occupied the site of an eighth- or ninth-century monastery (RCAHMS 1933, 74 no.150; Hall 2004). Since the foundation of Culross Abbey was roughly contemporary with that of Deer and the two are the only daughter-houses of Kinloss in Scotland (Fawcett, *infra* 440), this parallel carries particular weight. Nonetheless, the topographic evidence, outlined above, for two curvilinear enclosures at Old Deer, constitutes positive evidence in favour of the kirkyard as the site of the pre-Cistercian foundation.

To summarize, then, the Deer stone has indeed experienced 'multiple lives', to use Clarke's phrase (2007). As many as six identities can be deduced: possible prehistoric standing-stone, Pictish symbol-stone, cross-marked stone (whether early or later medieval), possible medieval building-stone, nineteenth-century picturesque antiquity, nineteenth-century building-stone. If we decide to reject the possibility that the stone was brought to the abbey site only in the eighteenth or nineteenth century, in favour of its having had a genuinely ancient association with the site, then this physical location becomes the key to unlocking its history. The frequent use of prehistoric standing-stones as boundary markers in the historic period has already been noted. A pre-existing boundary function may be the reason the Deer stone attracted use as a symbol-stone, in, say, the sixth or seventh century, marking the extent of land-ownership by a kin-group and possibly the grave of one of its members. If we are to imagine that the cross was upended and carved with a cross at an early period then that act may mark the transition from pre-Christian family burial ground to Christian family burial ground in the era before the Church was able to assert a monopoly on burial at churchyards, something it was increasingly able to do in Ireland from the early eighth century (O'Brien 1992). This begs the question of the relation between a possible Christian cemetery here and the early church or monastery on the site of the parish church.

Sticking with the 'early re-use' scenario for now, we may be mistaken, of course, in presuming that it was the burial function of the site which continued into the stone's cross-marked phase. Instead it could have been its boundary association which persisted.[18] While the majority of cross-marked stones in eastern Scotland come from church sites—of which some, at least, would have originated as cemeteries—there are a few which appear to have stood in the landscape at boundaries and on routeways. Two Aberdeenshire examples are the cross-marked, ogham-inscribed stone from Afforsk on the slopes of Bennachie which stands in the vicinity of several important boundaries, including that of the medieval bounds of the lands of Monymusk (RCAHMS 2007a, 127); and St Machar's (*recte* 'St Muchrieha's') Cross which stood on a mound beside a well at a boundary location above Aboyne (Ogston 1912; Simpson 1935, fig. 13). Thus the sacred space labelled by the Deer cross need not have been a cemetery. Alternatives include a stage on the pilgrimage route to the church site, the limit of the church's sanctuary (*termonn*), or a small oratory dependent on it. Indeed these three examples are not mutually exclusive. A North-East comparison for the latter, a small oratory, may be found in the chapel of Abersnithock, 2.5km north of Monymusk, which Clancy identifies as, in origin, a dependency of the important nearby monastery (this volume). The distance between Deer abbey and the church is short, a little over one kilometre. This, however, is similar to the distance between the church of Whithorn and the seventh-century inscribed cross-slab known as the 'Peter Stone' which stood beside an important routeway from Whithorn to the coast marking the '*locus* of the Apostle Peter', either a separate cemetery, or the boundary of the monastery itself (Forsyth 2004).

This bears particular consideration in the light of evidence from tenth/ eleventh century Uppland, Sweden regarding the location of Christian rune-stones at parish churches. What appears to have happened is that these rune-stones first stood out in the landscape or in secular settlements, marking ownership of the land on which they stood. They belonged to the very first phases of Christianisation and the families who erected them were among the first to convert. In time communities of Christians banded together to erect church buildings, and endowed them with lands. As the rune-stones were, in effect, 'charters' of land-ownership, when the land was transferred to the

---

18 Note also the proximity of a Medieval court-site, as evidenced by the place-name Quithel (*Cwthyll* 1544, *A. B. Ill.* iv, 20; Gaelic *comhdháil* 'court', 'meeting place').

Church, the rune-stones were physically transferred to the churchyard, frequently indeed being incorporated in the fabric of the church (Anders Andrén pers. com.; see also Gustavsson 1986 and Johansen 1997). Such a mechanism has not been invoked to account for the many Pictish symbol stones found at churches in Scotland but it is worth considering.

It has been suggested that the remaining community of *clerici* at Deer in the early thirteenth century were absorbed into the new Cistercian community (Fawcett, this volume), just as the land-holdings of the old foundation passed to the new. We can assume that the continuing relevance of the property records in the Book of Deer would have caused the mansucript to have been physically re-housed in the Cistercian abbey. Might anything else have been brought from the old site? To take the stone and build it into the fabric of the new church would have been a fitting gesture of incorporation and make the stone of Deer, in some sense, a monumental counterpart to the Book itself, whose chance survival is the result of its having served a practical function throughout the later Middle Ages, as a building block in the Cistercian monks' legal defense of land-title.

CROSS(-SLAB) FRAGMENT, SKELLYBOGS/'CRUX MEDICI'

A second lost item of early medieval sculpture from Deer is what appears to have been a fragment of a cross or cross-slab from Skellybogs on the northern limit of the parish. It was discovered about 1848 during renovation of the bridge which carried the old road from New Deer to Strichen between the farms of Grassiehill and Skellybogs[19] (NJ 9111 5201). The piece was described as 'a stone sculptured with the likeness of a man and a book', but no indication is given regarding dimensions or whether or not it was thought to be complete. It was given to the tenant of Skellybogs (NJ 908 519) 'who took it home', but by 1898 it had been lost sight of and was 'probably built into some wall or dyke on the farm' (Milne 1898). A search by Ordnance Survey archaeologists in April 1968 found no trace of it. The road is an old one, and leads north from Fedderate Castle to Strichen, skirting an extensive area of bog which formed the southern limit of the parish of Strichen. In the late twelfth or early thirteenth century there stood in this vicinity a cross known as the *crux medici*, mentioned as a boundary point in a charter of Fergus, earl of Buchan, to John son of Uchtred, ×1214 (text: *A.B. Coll.* 407–8; translation: Paterson 1895, quoted in Tocher 1910, 135–7).

It was the Revd James Paterson who first suggested this cross and the Skellybogs fragment were one and the same (Paterson 1895), a suggestion which seems highly plausible. Fergus was the grandson of Colbain and Eva,

---

19 Then spelled Greaciehill and Skillybogs.

the patrons of Deer in Text VI, and the father of Marjorie, who married William Comyn *c.*1212, and with him, founded the Cistercian abbey of Deer. The charter concerns the exchange of 'the three davochs of Fedderate' for the lands of Slains and Cruden and incorporates a detailed perambulation of the march of the lands of Fedderate (Young 1993, 179, 184). Various landscape features are used as boundary points, principally streams, roads, and large ditches, but the charter also twice mentions a 'crux medici' (*usque ad crucem medici*) standing in the vicinity of Grassiehill. Latin *crux* 'cross' could mean a free-standing cross, or, more likely in this case, 'cross-slab'.[20] Free-standing crosses are rare in eastern Scotland, and the only certain examples north of the Mounth are fragments of two examples from Kinneddar (Henderson and Henderson 2004, 194). The designation *medici* could be an epithet, 'of the doctor'—as appears on a sixth-century inscribed stone from Llangian, Caernarfonshire (Nash-Williams 1950, No. 92)—or a personal name 'of *Medicus*'. The very similar personal name appears on the ninth-century inscribed cross-fragment from Lethnot, Angus, which commemorates [-] FILII MEDICII 'of [-] the son of Medicius' (Okasha 1985, 53–4). Latin *medicus* 'doctor, physician', is used to gloss Gaelic *líaig* and is the source of the loan-word *midach* 'physician' (*DIL*). Irish legal and other evidence points to the relatively high status and hereditary nature of the role of physician in Medieval Gaelic society (Kelly 1988, 57–9; see also Bannerman 1986). Although primarily meaning a medical healer, the word *líaig* comes, by extension, to mean also a spiritual advisor (*DIL*). Colum Cille himself is described as *líaig* in *Amra Columcille*.[21] It is intriguing to know what could have given rise to the name *crux medici* in the late twelfth or early thirteenth century: perhaps an interpretation of a figure depicted on the stone, or the reading of an inscription, or some contemporary association such as proximity to the dwelling of a *medicus*. Perhaps it stood on land which belonged to a *medicus*.[22] A local example of a place-name commemorating a social status is *Rosabard* (Deer records, II.7), which is *ros in baird* 'promontory of the poet' (Taylor, *infra*, 297–8).

The statement that the carving depicted 'a man and a book' brackets the Skellybogs cross with a small group of major Scottish cross-slabs which feature a variety of Biblical and ecclesiastical figures with books (Henderson

20 The ninth-century inscribed cross-slab from Llanddetty, Brecknockshire, refers to itself as *crux* (Nash-Williams 1950 no. 46).   **21** I owe this observation to Gilbert Márkus.   **22** It is a curious coincidence that the nearby estate of Auchmachar was given to Deer by one Donnchad son of MacBethad (V.1) as it was a family of the name MacBethad (Beaton) who were to become the most prominent of Gaelic medical families in the later Middle Ages. There is unlikely, however, to be a connection as this family was thought to have come from Ireland *c.*1300 and settled first in Islay (Bannerman 1986). The forename MacBethad is not common but occurs elsewhere in the Deer records as the name of the father of a witness of III, Mael-Domnaig son of MacBethad, who may or may not be related to this Donnchad. Of course, the grandfather of Mael-Snechta son of Lulach (II.9) was also a MacBethad, the famous king of Alba.

and Henderson 2004, 146–52). The great cross-slab from Nigg, Easter Ross, is topped by a depiction of Sts Paul and Anthony bowed over books. Nearby at Portmahomack (Tarbat), one of the figures on the so-called 'Apostle's Stone' holds a book (Henderson and Henderson 2004, 146–7). The Hendersons interpret the figures on the Lethendy, Perthshire (fig. 2.9), slab as a depiction of the Trinity, which would make the figure displaying the book Christ himself (2004, 143). According to them the book-holding cleric beside an angel on St Vigean's 11, could be Zacharias (2004, 220). Angels themselves hold books on the great road-side cross-slab from Aberlemno and at Brechin books are held by evangelist symbols. Nigg, Tarbat, Brechin and Aberlemno: these are all large and ambitious monuments. Lethendy, although of cruder workmanship, is nonetheless a substantial piece, derived from a 'good early pictorial model' (Henderson and Henderson 2004, 144). Given these comparanda it is likely that the lost stone from Skellybogs came from a similarly sophisticated piece of sculpture. Comparison with Tarbat, Brechin, St Vigeans and Lethendy, puts Skellybogs, with them, in the later phases of early medieval sculpture (ninth and tenth centuries). In the light of the recent discovery at Ravenscraig, Inverugie (discussed below), the possibility of a major cross-slab of ninth or tenth century date at Skellybogs does not seem at all far-fetched.

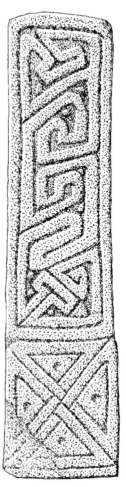

13.6 Relief-carved 'pillar', Fyvie III (Crown Copyright: RCAHMS; SC 1090346: drawing John Borland).

Further evidence of substantial relief sculpture of about this date from Buchan survives built into the wall of Fyvie parish church (fig. 13.6), beside the symbol stones mentioned above.[23] It was found in the nineteenth century by the minister of Fyvie, the Revd A.J. Milne, built into west end of the church as the lintel of a doorway. He had it removed and fixed against an exterior wall of the church at the foot of some steps, in which position it was seen by Romilly Allen (Allen and Anderson 1903, 194–6, fig. 211). Since then it has been built into the east gable wall of the church. Romilly Allen states its measurements to have been 5' by 1'4" by 11" (1.52 x 0.41 x 0.28m). He describes it as 'a pillar' of red granite 'sculptured in relief on one face' with two panels of geometric ornament. In the larger upper panel is key-pattern, identified by Romilly Allen as a 'much distorted' form of his no. 899. Below is a squarer

23 And another, from the vicinity of Rothiebrisbane, on the other side of the Ythan,

panel with a cruciform pattern identified by Allen as a triangular interlace, no. 724 with circular dots in each of four triangular loops. Our difficulty lies in knowing how much confidence to place in Romilly Allen's silence regarding the other three faces. Were they broken ? If intact, were they bare ? There is no obvious sign of fracture at either top or bottom edge, but in the stone's current position it is hard to tell.

If the stone were incomplete it might be part of a cross-shaft (unusual, though not unprecedented, north of the Mounth) or the side of a major cross-slab: the angular geometric ornament on one side of the 3m tall Maiden Stone, Drumdurno, Aberdeenshire (Allen and Anderson 1903, 190–1) provides a local parallel for the latter. If, however, as Allen seems to imply, the Fyvie stone is complete, then it can have been neither of these. Its post-medieval re-use as a lintel may point to its original function, or, if not an architectural piece, then it may be part of a composite tomb monument or piece of church fitting, but if so, its form is unparalleled (for Scottish examples of these types of sculpture see Henderson and Henderson 2004, 197–211). Whatever its original form and function the Fyvie piece is exceptional and implies that in the ninth or tenth century, there was an ecclesiastical site of some importance here.

Skellybogs/Grassiehill may seem an obscure location for a piece of major sculpture. Yet although it stood far from any church site, it appears, nonetheless, to have stood in a nodal point in the ecclesiastical landscape. In the late twelfth or early thirteenth century it acted as a boundary marker, a role it had probably served since its erection two or three centuries earlier. It apparently stood beside the road at the point where the traveller crossed into the territory of Fedderate. This land does not appear to have belonged to either the early or the Cistercian monastery, but rather to have remained in the hands of the Clann Channan mormaers of Buchan until Earl Fergus chose to dispose of it. Nonetheless it was within the parish of Deer and to encounter such a major cross at this juncture would have served as a vivid reminder that one had now entered Deer's ambit. The Skellybogs cross lends important support to the view that the twelfth century parishes embodied older territorial units, in this case going back to the tenth century, at least. A very similar example is found further south in Aberdeenshire in a reference in an early fourteenth-century charter to the march of the forest of Cordyce. The boundary is marked at one point by *crucem et magnum lapidem in via regia* 'the cross and great stone on the King's road' which stood just south of a ford called *Achynaterman* 'field of the *termonn* (boundary)', approximately 4.5km due south of Dyce parish church. The cross has not survived, though it is commemorated in the name Corsehill (RCAHMS 2007a, 147).

The subsequent breaking-up of the Skellybogs cross and its re-use in a bridge, is something seen elsewhere in the corpus of early medieval sculpture. A particularly interesting parallel is provided by the Sandyford (or 'Mountblow') cross, Dunbartonshire, which was rescued from use as a footbridge around 1757. It appears to have stood by the old Roman road where it crossed a burn which itself was an important ecclesiastical boundary, the cross's original function having been, perhaps, to announce the start of the *termonn* of Old Kilpatrick church less than 1km away (Driscoll, O'Grady and Forsyth 2004, 150–1). Of course the distance from Skellybogs/Grassiehill to Old Deer is far greater than this—approximately 7km—and the boundary is likely to have been of a different nature.

A literary reference to the erection of crosses on the boundaries of monastic lands is preserved in the early twelfth-century 'B Version' of the St Andrews foundation legend. It recounts how Hungus, king of Picts, granted a large body of land—encompassing all of Fife east of a line from Naughton to Largo—to Bishop Regulus for the building of churches and oratories. According to the legend, king and bishop first perambulated seven times the boundary of this *parochia* and then had twelve stone crosses set up along it (Taylor 2000, 116).

INSCRIBED CROSS(-SLAB) FRAGMENT, RAVENSCRAIG, INVERUGIE

Also from a boundary location, but at the opposite end of Deer's sphere of influence, comes the remarkable fragment recently discovered at Ravenscraig steading, Inverugie (NK 0985 4887). The stone was discovered by chance in 2003 when a passer-by spotted it protruding from the upper courses of a derelict drystone wall (Shepherd 2003), the retaining wall of the steading's midden. A careful search of the wall and others in the vicinity failed to uncover any further fragments.[24] It is now on display in the Arbuthnot Museum, Peterhead.

The top and bottom edges of the stone have been split, parallel and square, indicating it has been severely trimmed down to form a rectangular building-block which has subsequently broken (the right edge is very uneven). The carving is worn and there has been a generalised loss of definition consistent with the stone having stood exposed to the elements for an extended period. It was the left edge, weathered and lichen-encrusted, which was protruding from the wall at the time of discovery but it is nonetheless largely intact, as is the adjacent face. The right-hand edge and reverse have, however, been lost entirely. The current maximum dimensions of the stone are 258mm in height and 310mm across, but it appears to be only a small fragment of what was once a substantial cross-slab or cross-shaft. Its full thickness has been preserved and this is 150mm. The stone is a pink sandstone with gritty

24 Ian Shepherd, pers. com.

13.7 Inscribed cross-slab fragment, Ravenscraig (Crown Copyright: RCAHMS; SC 1094917).

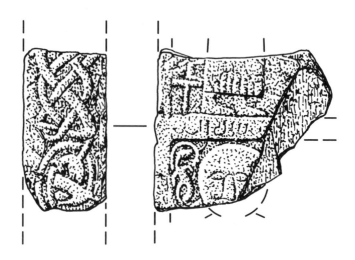

13.8 Inscribed cross-slab fragment, Ravenscraig (Crown Copyright: RCAHMS;
SC 1092050, drawing: John Borland).

inclusions, identified as Middle Old Red Sandstone containing coarse clasts and iron-staining, of a type fairly local to the area, although granite is the main rock type in the vicinity of Peterhead (Suzanne Miller, Dept. of Geology, National Museums of Scotland).

Decoration

The carving on the front face, which consists of two panels separated by a horizontal inscribed band, is executed in deep relief and organised on three planes: the background, the middle-ground—occupied by flanking motifs—and the foreground—occupied by the two main motifs and the inscribed panel. The upper panel is dominated by what could be the bottom of a cross-shaft or, alternatively, a robed figure. The lower portion of this motif is damaged. There is a sequence of parallel vertical lines which may be intended as the fringe of a garment, but could be later gouging. Borland sees two feet below the fringe, pointing to the right (fig. 13.8). The small flanking motif on the right is hard to interpret. It could be the lower part of a small cross, but appears more like a T-shaped pedestal supporting what could be a robed figure, with part of the hem of a garment and a single foot pointing towards the central figure. If part of a human figure the scene could be Longinus and Stephaton flanking the crucified Christ—a motif depicted on free-standing crosses from Abernethy[25] and Camuston, Angus (note the one-legged stance of the flanking figures on the latter)—or Christ flanked by John and Mary, as on the free-standing cross Monifieth 4 (Henderson and Henderson 2004, 145). Without further defining attributes, however, the identity of both primary and subordinate figures remains unknown (if indeed they are figures!).

The lower panel is clearer. It consists of the incomplete head of a figure, flanked to the left by a small interlaced strap animal. The head, which is aligned with the left edge of the main motif of the upper panel, is carved in high relief and has a rounded, massive quality. Its gaze is impassive and penetrating. The nose is prominent and wedge-shaped, and is flanked by half-moon eyes with defined eyebrows. At the tip of the nose the cheeks are delineated with a curve, perhaps to indicate a moustache. There are faint traces of hair, parted centrally and sweeping across to the temples. There is a glimpse of a hunched shoulder, probably indicating a heavy mantle. The figure would have extended right to the margin. The space above the figure's shoulder is occupied by an interlaced quadruped with elongated beak which faces upwards towards the figure and bites a strap, perhaps its own body, perhaps an object such as a chair back (cf. fig. 2.4) or a crozier.[26] Even although it is badly worn it is clear this creature was an accomplished composition. With its slim neck and swelling body it elegantly undulates and

25 Though there Christ's legs are bare below the knee.   26 I owe the latter suggestion to Ian Scott.

entwines to fill the irregular-shaped space. Although carved more shallowly than the head, the creature nonetheless has a rounded quality.

Even allowing for only the minimal reconstruction of width, the head is not centrally placed. If the figure is not central then it is unlikely to be Christ crucified. It is surely too massive to have been one of twelve apostles, as at Tarbat, even if arranged in two rows of six, as at Dunkeld (fig. 2.10). The lack of a cowl precludes identification as one of the three women present at the Crucifixion/Resurrection, as at Abernethy, and in any case the figure appears to be male. There are a number of parallels for paired frontal figures on crosses and cross-slabs from Angus and Perthshire. The Hendersons (2004, 143–5) have identified a composition of paired, seated, robed figures— reproduced on cross-slabs from Lethendy (fig. 2.9), Aldbar and St Vigeans 11—as Christ sitting at the right hand of God the Father (Psalm 109; Matthew 22:44). At Lethendy and St Vigeans the pair is surmounted by an angel, representing the Holy Spirit, but there is no trace of it on the Aldbar stone, so its apparent absence from the Ravenscraig stone may not be fatal to such an identification. But there are alternatives: the paired, nimbed, book-holding figures on the free-standing cross from Camuston, Angus, are Evangelists. Other paired frontal figures are Zacharias and the Angel who flank the cross on the reverse of St Vigeans 11 (noted above) and the nimbed angels on the shaft of the cross-slab from Brechin, interpreted by Henderson as saints Peter and Paul (2000, 41). Note however that the Ravenscraig figure lacks a nimbus. Peter, as patron of the medieval parish in which Ravenscraig is situtated (*Inverugie Petri*, or Peterugie), would seem particularly appropriate, but his association with Inverguie may not be as old as the Ravenscraig cross. The Deer Notes (III) record the donation of land 'for the consecration of a church to Christ and to Peter the apostle' in the year 1131/2 (see Taylor, *infra* 278). It has been suggested[27] that Deer was originally the mother-church of an area much larger than the medieval parish of Deer which included what was to become the medieval parish of Inverugie Petri (Peterugie). The Deer record may mark the origin of the separation. If so, then at the time of the erection of the Ravenscraig cross, it may have stood within the paruchia of Drostán's Deer.

Perhaps the closest visual parallel for the Ravenscraig figure comes from the free-standing cross Monifieth 4, although the figures on the lower panels there are unidentified (Henderson and Henderson 2004, 145; Allen and Anderson fig. 275, p. 265). Below a Crucifixion are a pair of frontal figures wearing ankle-length mantles and holding unidentified objects, below them is another pair with knee-length garments and drinking horns, and finally at the base David the harper. There are also similarities with the unidentified figures on the reverse of Kirriemuir 1. If not simply a space-filler, the interlaced

27 Taylor (*infra* 279), following Cowan (1961, 46).

13.9 Detail of inscription, Ravenscraig fragment.

creature at Ravenscraig may provide a clue as to the figure's identity. Its face is pointing up towards the top of the figure's head, which may be a gesture of acknowledgement. If the head had been placed centrally then this could have been Christ between the beasts but the fact that it is not leaves the interpretation of the composition open.

There are occasional examples from Ireland of crosses carved with non-Biblical scenes of more local significance, for instance what appears to be the founding of the monastery depicted on the east face of the Cross of the Scriptures, Clonmacnoise (Harbison, 1992 vol. 1, 49). Aitchison argues that what is being depicted here, and on certain other Irish high crosses, is the marking out of the *termonn* of the monastery jointly by saint and king. Furthermore he suggests that the Forteviot arch from Perthshire may depict a similar foundation scene (2006, 192–201), but no other examples have yet been identified in Scotland. If Ravenscraig is a possible case of such 'non-Universal' imagery, then the figure may be Drostán himself, perhaps accompanying Colum Cille.

The side of the slab is decorated with geometric ornament. There is no dividing border to match the one on the front, but there is a corresponding break in the design. Above is the lower portion of a simple four-strand interlace composed of a smooth rounded band. Below is the upper portion of a knot of zoomorphic interlace which is now difficult to read. The vertical margins are damaged and it is hard to say whether their knobbled appearance is the remains of a carved pattern, or simply wear.

Inscription

The inscription occupies the flat horizontal band between the upper and lower panels. The band is approximately 35 mm in height and the letters are on average about 25 mm tall. There are no ruled guidelines. Only the opening letters of the text have been preserved—a portion of unknown length having been lost at the break—and only a few of these are still legible. The first 65mm of the band has quite worn smooth, the subsequent 65–70 mm is better preserved, thereafter the carving is very worn. There are traces of at least six letters but only the middle two or three can be read with any confidence.

Little of the first letter survives but there are traces near the bottom of the band of the lower arc of a curved letter: **o, s, e** or **c** (or, less plausibly, **a, b, d**). The following letter is very faint, but may also have had a curved lower stroke. There is, however, the hint of a vertical stroke which stops just short of this curve. If not a separate letter (**i**) then it is hard to see what this character might be, unless it is two conjoined or ligatured letters. The third letter is clearer, apparently the vertical stroke of an **i** with wedge-shaped top. It does not appear to be joined to the previous letter (and is therefore not part of an **h, m** or **n**). There is the hint of a curve overhanging the bow of the next letter this could be the hook of a minuscule **s**, but this would imply a congested layout with overlapping letters.

The next two letters are the clearest of all and are not in doubt. First there is an open-bowed, upright '**d**', with a wedge-shaped ascender and a down-stroke which reaches the line. The gap between the return of the curved stroke, which terminates in a wedged serif, and the upright is almost half the width of the bow. This letter, the most complete, is 25 mm in height and 20 mm in width. It is an elegant piece of lettering and gives a clue to the original calibre of the inscription. The fifth letter is an open-bowed, half-uncial **r** with up-turned, 'fish-hook' loop. The bottom of the vertical stroke and the top of the bow have been lost but the letter is not in doubt. The sixth letter is less well preserved; there are traces of a circular stroke, **o** or **c**, perhaps, or, since it is somewhat straight-sided, **u**. There is a break in the surface immediately beyond this and any further trace of lettering is lost.

The following tentative readings may be proposed:[28]

[..][i]D*R*[o]—   or   [..][i]D*R*[u]—

The segment is too short and damaged to allow even the language it is written in to be identified. There are few comparanda in Scotland, but the preferred language for roman alphabet inscription appears to have been Latin.[29] This parallels the situation in Wales where all but one roman alphabet inscription is in Latin. The formulae which appear in post-seventh-century Welsh inscriptions are diverse but the most common opening is a personal name, of the patron or commemorand, which is perhaps what we should look for here. Other openings include *crux xpi*, *in nomine*, and the mark of the cross '+', but it is clearly none of these. In Ireland the range of formulae is more narrow, but almost exclusively in Gaelic. The most common Irish openings are *or(oit) do/ar* 'a prayer for', and *bendacht ar* 'a blessing on', neither of which would fit

28 The following conventions are observed: R legible letter, *R* damaged but legible letter, [R] damaged character, reading tentative, [.] one illegible character, [—] missing portion of

here. The most common function of inscriptions on crosses and cross-slabs in Britain and Ireland, is commemorative: they record the names of the patrons who had them erected and/or the people in whose memory they were made. Scottish examples of this type of inscription include Lethnot, Tarbat and Dupplin (Okasha 1985, Higgitt 1982, Forsyth 1995). A smaller number of texts 'label' the carving which they accompany, for instance CRUX XPI at St Donnán's, Eigg (Fisher 2001), or S MARIA M(ATE)R XRI at Brechin (Okasha 1985, 49–51; RCAHMS 2007b). The position of the Ravenscraig inscription in amongst the carved images points to the latter as the more likely. This position, on the horizontal frame of a carved panel, is seen on a number of Anglo-Saxon crosses. Examples include labels of the figures depicted— MARIA at Inglesham (Okasha 1971, 82), S(AN)C(T)A MARIA at North Elham (104), IHS XPVS Dewsbury II—and quotations from scripture relating to the scene depicted—for instance, Dewsbury III with its phrases from the Vulgate text of the miracle of the loaves and fishes (66–7).[30] Perhaps the closest parallel of all to the Ravenscraig fragment is provided by the early eighth-century Ruthwell Cross, with its series of ten roman alphabet texts arranged above and to the sides of the panels (Okasha 1971, 108–12). On this model the surviving section of text at Ravenscraig could be only part of a longer text arranged over several horizontal borders (there is no trace of, nor room for, inscribed vertical margins to the panels here). It is worth noting that on the Anglo-Saxon examples the text is always placed *above* the scene to which it refers, a precedent which makes it more likely the Ravenscraig text relates to the figure in the lower panel.

Given how little survives of the inscription it is perhaps unwise to indulge in an attempt at reconstruction, but if the first two letters are taken as *sc* then we may read [SC]IDR[O][—] which it is tempting to reconstruct as *S(an)c(t)i Dro[stan*—], either for *Sancti Drostani* (genitive), 'of Saint Drostán', or, if there were originally two figures: *Sancti Dro[stanus et Columba]* 'Saints Drostán and Colum Cille'. This would work equally for the reading [SC]IDR[U][—], for Drustan is a familiar variant of the name, which derives, in fact, from **Drustagnos* (Sims-Williams 2003, 30, 169).[31]

Although not enough of the text survives to establish its meaning, nor even its language, there is enough remaining to confirm the calligraphic quality of the lettering. It is written in a two-line (majuscule) display script which draws on book-lettering for its wedge-shaped ascenders and the sweeping curve of

unknown length.   **29** As seen at Tarbat, Brechin, Lethnot, and Dupplin. Only St Vigeans is not obviously in Latin. The fragmentary Fordoun inscription is indeterminate. **30** There is a single example of a non-descriptive text in such a position, the dedication and maker formula on the reverse of the tenth-century cross-slab from Alnmouth. The now illegible text in a similar position on the front may, however, be descriptive (Okasha 1971, 47–8).   **31** Against this interpretation is the possible vertical stroke above the curve of the second letter.

its **d** and **r**. It bears a general similarity with the lettering on the lost stone from Papa Stronsay, Orkney (Stuart 1856, pl. xlii; Okasha 1985, 56–7) and the St Vigeans 'Drosten stone' (Okasha 1985, 59–61), but the parallel is not close. The form of R at St Vigeans, with angular horizontal stroke, contrasts with the notable curve of the Ravenscraig R.

Discussion

The Ravenscraig stone is another to have endured 'multiple lives'. The midden wall at Ravenscraig steading is unlikely to have been its first modern resting place and it was probably cut down for use in some other structure in the vicinity, perhaps Ravenscraig Castle, a tower-house built in 1491, which stands 300m to the NW.[32] There is good evidence from elsewhere in Scotland, for instance Whithorn and St Andrews, that early medieval sculptured stones were being cut down for building use as early as the twelfth and thirteenth centuries when iconoclasm would not have been a motivating factor. Other losses were more ideologically driven, such as those which occurred in the 1560s and 1640s at the hands of Presbyterian Reformers (see Henderson and Henderson 2004, 215, 218–211). Indeed, seventeenth-century iconoclasm appears to have been particularly vigorous. Henderson notes that the meeting of the General Assembly of the Church of Scotland which took place in St Machar's cathedral in Aberdeen in 1640 passed an act 'anent the demolishing of idolatrous monuments' requiring all presbytries to report on their diligence in this matter. The Ruthwell Cross was one known casualty of this act and there will have been others whose demolition went unrecorded (Henderson 1972, 171). If the Ravenscraig stone bore a Crucifixion, it would have been perhaps more vulnerable to such a fate than the less blatant iconography of other sculpture. The Hendersons note that most of the extant images of the Crucifixion on early medieval Scottish sculpture have been vandalised (2004, 146).

Wherever it had been previously, we may assume that it is unlikely to have moved far from where it was first erected. The immediate area appears to have had a strategic significance over a long period and this may give a clue as to the stone's original context and function. The place where it was found is on a terrace (10m OD) overlooking the river Ugie, as it wends its way through a ravine before finally disgorging into the sea at Inverugie. There is no indication that there was ever a church or chapel in the vicinity—references to the church of Inverugie are thought to relate to Peterhead old parish church just under 4km to the south-east (see Taylor, *infra* 278)—but there have been a succession of secular power centres along this short stretch of the river. Ravenscraig lies on the south bank of the Ugie opposite Castlehill of Inverugie, site of a late twelfth-century earthwork castle (motte).

---

32 CANMORE: NK04 NE 1.

The choice of location is a natural one. The high, precipitous banks of the river at this point provide protection and make the structures all the more imposing. The coastal topography has altered somewhat due to the accumulation of sand, even since the eighteenth century, but the successive fortifications at Inverugie/Ravenscraig occupy highly defensible positions along the short stretch of higher ground between the coastal dunes and what, in pre-Improvement times, was a large expanse of moss stretching far inland towards Longside and Deer. Command of the crossing point of the Ugie here would allow north-south coastal and east-west riverine traffic to be monitored and controlled. The significance of this location is heightened yet further by the fact that the Ugie forms the boundary of the parish at this point. Beyond, on the north bank, is St Fergus (Longley), which is not only a separate parish, but was—until the boundary re-organisation of 1891—in a separate county, being a detached portion of Banffshire.[33] It appears not to have been part of the medieval earldom of Buchan. Although these administrative arrangements are documented only from the fourteenth and fifteenth centuries they are likely to perpetuate older patterns of lordship which raises the possibility that this was an important political boundary already at the time the Ravenscraig cross was erected. If Taylor is right about the mother-church status of Deer vis-à-vis the territory of the later parish of Inverugie Petri, Ravenscraig would have stood at the eastern limit of its paruchia at an important entry point. In this it can be seen as a counterpart to the *crux medici* at Skellybogs at the opposite end of Deer's territory.

Although only a small fragment of the Ravenscraig sculpture survives, it is sufficient to establish that it would have been a major monument of high quality. The fact that it bore an inscription marks it out as particularly exceptional. Only eight inscribed crosses or cross-slabs are known from eastern Scotland.[34] The massive, rounded quality of the carving and, especially, the frontal stance of the figure align Ravenscraig with later crosses and cross-slabs such as those from Dunkeld, Abernethy, St Vigeans, and Brechin for which dates in the ninth, tenth, and even eleventh century have been proposed (e.g. RCAHMS 2007b).[35] These are all major monasteries which enjoyed royal patronage—including from the dynasty of Clann Custantín

---

33 Along with its detached portion (subsequently a separate parish) Fetterangus, which was later (before 1618) absorbed into Deer parish (see Taylor, *infra* 277). **34** In addition to Ravenscraig, there is: Brechin, Lethnot, Fordoun, St Vigeans, Tarbat (Okasha 1985 and refs), Dupplin (Forsyth 1995), Crieff (Forsyth and Trench-Jellicoe 2000). Ian Scott has drawn attention to a possible inscription on the Shandwick Stone, Easter Ross (pers. com.). The horizontal frame above the spiral panel on the reverse of the cross-slab has two letters in relief—**I R**—followed by traces of incised, rune-like characters. Whether or not these are likely to be early medieval I have been unable to verify personally. **35** A connection which Marner has adduced in support of his theory of a Dunkeld origin for the Book of Deer (2002, 28). On Crinán, see Woolf 2007, 249–52.

meic Cináeda—as, we know, did Deer. According to the Chronicle of the
Kings of Alba (Hudson 1998) Brechin was founded by Cináed II (king of
Alba 971–95), the father of Mael-Coluim II (king of Alba 1005–34) patron of
Deer in II.7. The latter was father-in-law to Crinan abbot of Dunkeld.[35] The
parallels between the Ravenscraig fragment and the others mentioned may be
due to a general similarity of date rather than to specific institutional
connections, but in the twelfth century Dunkeld interest in Deer is attested by
Deer record III which refers to the giving of a pledge to the abbot of Dunkeld
in relation to the gift by the mormaer of *pett meic Gobraig for the consecration of a church dedicated to Christ and Peter. The abbot of Dunkeld
was, in some sense, the 'head' of the Columban family in Scotland, and his
involvement in this transaction presumably implies that by this date Deer was
in some way part of that family, and subject to his oversight (see Broun, this
volume). The church mentioned in text III has been identified as the old
parish church of Peterhead, and the land as Grange a short distance to the
west (Taylor, this volume). It is of particular interest, then, that a century
earlier a Clann Custantín meic Cináeda dynast had an interest of some sort in
this very piece of land. Record II.7 records the gift by Mael-Coluim mac
Cináeda of a king's *cuit* ('portion') in *pett m*a*c Gobraig. If a date as late as the
early eleventh century were accepted for the Ravenscraig fragment then one
could postulate a link with this transaction: the erection of such a fine
monument in the landscape would be a most fitting reminder of a king's
generosity. If, however, an earlier date, say ninth or early tenth is preferred—
and which the rounded form of the script would tend to support— then the
fragment attests instead to the wealth and artistic connections of Deer's more
local patrons.

The above parallels with sculpture from south of the Mounth should not
obscure links between the Ravenscraig fragment and northern monuments,
including the remarkable cross-slab from Elgin, with its Evangelist iconography,
and the Maiden Stone, exceptional in the North-East in its commitment to
frames (Henderson 1972, 173). The latter seems a particularly worthy
comparison as the Hendersons view it as an 'unambiguously clear statement
about specific rights, sealed as it were with the impress of the symbols and
validated by the authority of the Church ... The claim and its validation
would be further underwritten by the grandeur of the scale and the brilliance
of the sculpture' (Henderson and Henderson 2004, 177).

QUERNSTONE, SKILLYMARNO

Finally, though not a sculptured stone, nor indeed a monument at all, it is
worth mentioning an early medieval stone found recently on one of the land-
holdings of the *clerici* of Deer. This is a large quern-stone, found about 2004

13.10 OS 6" map, 1st Edition (1874) Aberdeenshire and Banffshire, Sheet xiii.
Detail showing possible watermill remains, South Skillymarno.

by William Fowlie, farmer of Auchrynie, while digging for a water pipe at approximately NJ 958 520. The stone is an upper quern-stone and the lack of a socket for a handle indicates that it came from a horizontal water-mill. It was found below the surface in a watery zone of dark organic material 1' deep and 8' across (0.31 x 2.44m). The OS 1st edition 6" map shows a water course in this area, which emanates from an area of boggy ground controlled by a sluice. This water-course was formerly the source of water supply for the farm (William Fowlie, pers. com.) and is shown on the map flowing down to meet the burn which ran between Skillymarno and Auchrynie and formed the boundary between Deer parish and Fetterangus.[36] The area is now open field, but the OS 1st edition shows a collection of buildings, named 'South Skillymarno', immediately to the north (fig. 13.10). These are not marked as, and were therefore not functioning as, a mill on the 1870 map, but the layout of enclosed pond, sluice, lade and other structures is suggestive of former mill-workings and worthy of archaeological investigation.

36 Although now part of Auchrynie farm (which was in Fetterangus parish), this land was formerly part of the lands of Skillymarno (Deer parish), (William Fowlie, pers. com.).

Horizontal mills, and their associated water-supply system of reservoir, dam and channels, have been described as 'among the most advanced techno-logical developments of early medieval agriculture' (O'Sullivan and Downey 2006, 36) and 'undoubtedly the most complex piece of technology which an early Irish farmer would regularly encounter' (Kelly 1997, 482). They improved the grinding of grain and allowed processing on a scale beyond that of domestic subsistence. Although horizontal water-mills are well known in the Northern Isles and in areas of the Highlands and Islands under Norse influence, they have not been the subject of much archaeological scrutiny elsewhere in Scotland.[37] References to mills in medieval Scottish charters are, however, frequent and they must have been widespread. Of course, the Deer property records themselves mention a mill (II.4) when they record the gift of *pett in mulinn* 'the holding of the mill', presumably together with the mill itself. This is a different mill to the one proposed here, perhaps, as Stuart suggested, the old mill on the South Ugie to the north of the church (1869, l) (see Taylor, this volume).

In contrast to Scotland, early medieval horizontal mills have been very well studied in Ireland, where almost a hundred are known, predominantly in parts of the south and east where 'arable farming and grain-processing were most intensive in the early medieval period' (O'Sullivan and Downey 2006, 37). About half of the known mills have been dated archaeologically and although these dated mills range widely in date, most were constructed in the period 700–1000. Indeed half the dated mills were constructed in the century 750–850. Although rare after the tenth-century there are, however, later examples from the twelfth and thirteenth centuries which are attributed to the newly-arrived Continental monastic orders (O'Sullivan and Downey 2006, 37). There is also detailed literary evidence for watermills in early medieval Ireland (Lucas 1953), including a seventh-century law tract written specifically on 'legal aspects of milling and mill-construction' (Kelly 1997, 483). It is clear that in Ireland mills were often owned collectively by several people, although high-ranking individuals might have their own mills. The largest mills were owned by professional millers (Kelly 1997, 484). Archaeological evidence shows that mills were sometimes located at monasteries, most famously at Nendrum, Co. Down, where the milling complex was tidal-powered.

On the basis of the Irish dating comparanda it seems likely that this pro-posed horizontal mill was already in existence when the lands of Skillymarno on which it stood were given to the *clerici* of Deer by Cormac son of Cennéitech (V.2) in the 1120s or 1130s, unless, that is, it was subsequently built by the Cistercians when they fell heir to the estate.[38] The quern-stone,

---

37 It has been conjectured that remains at Auchindour, Aberdeenshire may have originated as a medieval horizontal mill (Yeoman 1988).   **38** The only ecclesiastical presence in the area is 'Lady Well', a former holy well, dedicated to the Virgin Mary at NJ 9623 5233

the only surviving trace of it, is an important reminder of the agricultural underpinnings of the monastic economy and that the raison-d'être of the land grants recorded in the Book of Deer reason land was to enable the production of food.

CONCLUSIONS

With the possible exception of the cross-marked symbol stone from Deer, all of the early medieval sculptured stones from Buchan have survived into the modern period built into the fabric of a church or other secondary structure. Indeed this may be true even of the Deer stone itself, if, as suggested above, it was built into the walls of the Cistercian abbey. To reflect on the contingent, not to say accidental, nature of the recognition and recovery of these stones is sobering and should give us pause. Especially when we note that of the ten attested in Modern times, two were subsequently lost—or destroyed—as recently as the mid-ninteenth century. It is impossible to quantify the retrieval rate of early medieval sculptural fragments, and difficult even to compare rates between regions, an exercise which would need to consider numerous variables including differing local patterns of agricultural improvement, iconoclasm, antiquarian activity, and modern development. As the Hendersons note, however, 'the overall picture must be one of absolute losses, of which we will never know the content' (2004, 218). The situation is even more extreme in the case of ecclesiastical metalwork. Little of this survives from anywhere in Scotland but only a very few pieces are known in connection with the North-East. An enshrined Gospel book was held at Banchory-Ternan on Deeside until the early sixteenth-century. Believed to be Ternan's own copy of a single gospel its cover was described as ornamented with gold and silver (Simpson 1943, 86). Ternan's 'Ronnecht', a bell of early type, still hangs in the East Church at Banchory. On Donside, recent work on the small, house-shaped reliquary known as the 'Monymusk' reliquary has indicated that its association with Monymusk—identified as the monastery of Nér (Clancy, *infra* 368)—may be genuinely ancient after all (Caldwell 2001). It is from these isolated, disparate survivals that we must attempt to regain a sense of the lost material culture of the Church in the North-East.

Yet even taking into consideration regional differences in survival, there is a genuine lack of *de luxe* sculpture from Aberdeenshire as a whole. Only five symbol-inscribed cross-slabs (i.e. Romilly Allen's 'Class II') are known from Aberdeenshire—about 7% of the national total—and only two further cross-slabs without symbols (i.e. 'Class III'), an even smaller percentage of the total.

(immediately over the former parish boundary in Fetterangus). Its site was noted by the Ordnance Survey in 1870 (OS Name Book No. 68, 5) but there is no trace of it today.

This is in marked contrast to the numbers of 'Class I' symbol-stones: about a third of the national total of these come from Aberdeenshire (Henderson 1972, 171).[39] Henderson discusses various possible explanations for this contrast including the region's predominantly granite geology, which makes relief-carving a time-consuming and costly undertaking. She concludes, however, that the distinction principally arises from the sociology of patronage. Symbol stones are personal memorial stones, and their clustering on the richest agricultural land of the Don-Urie valley, and to a lesser extent the valleys of the Dee and Deveron, reflects the wealth of what Henderson has termed the 'minor secular land owner', or 'laymen of middle rank' (1972, 172). The patronage of this sort of person may also account for the roughly similar distribution of simple cross-marked stones ('Class IV') in Aberdeenshire. In contrast, cross-slabs were 'put up by or for an ecclesiastical institution' and reflect the interest of 'wealthy lay patrons' and 'great monastic house[s]' (ibid.). The comparative lack of such monuments in Aberdeenshire is probably because 'there is no evidence that Aberdeenshire was ever the centre of political power and so local ecclesiastical and secular wealth may never have been so great as in the two power centres—the Moray Firth area and Strathmore' (ibid.). It may be that it is less a question of absolute impoverishment—material or cultural—and more a case of wealth not being so concentrated in the hands of a small number of major magnates or major churches, but rather spread over a larger number of more modest local families and institutions. A key difference may be the comparative lack of *royal* activity in Aberdeenshire, although as the Deer records themselves demonstrate, Deer could count among its patrons both Clann Custantín meic Cináeda and Clann Ruaidrí kings of Alba.

Although Aberdeenshire lacks collections of sculpture to rank with Tarbat, Meigle or St Andrews, that is not to say that it is entirely devoid of sculpture of the first rank. On the contrary, the Maiden Stone, with its 'bravura displays of ornamental carving in granite' (Henderson and Henderson 2004, 177) has been described as 'a *tour de force*' able to 'take its place with some of the finest monuments to the north and south' (Henderson 1972, 173). The unexpected sophistication of the Ravenscraig fragment demonstrates that the Maiden Stone is not unique and its recent discovery puts a whole new perspective on the wealth and artistic ambitions of the church in Buchan. The other, more humble, carved stones from Buchan contribute their own, unique, information. The 'pillar' from Fyvie implies the existence of an important church. The Skellybogs and Ravenscraig fragments reflect the existence of an even grander foundation supported by wealthy patrons with access to stone-carvers of high calibre. The fact that the Ravenscraig fragment is inscribed with display

39 cf. the total absence of symbol-inscribed cross-slabs from Strathspey (Henderson 1972, 171).

lettering of high quality reflects not only local ability to produce fine calligraphy, but also a distinctive attitude to the role of the written word among patrons. The Ravenscraig inscription may be taken as an indication of the presence of a scriptorium, which brings us to the connection, if any, between this sculpture and the Book of Deer.

John Stuart was comfortable with the notion that the Book of Deer could have been produced at Deer itself (1869, xxi–xxv), but subsequent commentators have been reluctant to imagine that the Book's provenance reflects its origin. Jackson stated flatly: 'There is nothing to show where it was written, whether in Ireland or Scotland, whether at Deer itself or somewhere else within the Gaelic Christian world' (Jackson 1972, 9) and added, that, apart from the Gaelic property records, 'there is nothing at all to connect it with Deer' (1972, 7). While the latter is indeed true, it is somewhat unreasonable to expect the Book of Deer to proclaim its origins when the place of origin of most Insular gospel books is so hotly debated:[40] It is beyond dispute that the manuscript was created in a Gaelic cultural milieu (see Dumville 2007 and O'Loughlin, this volume), but in the past some scholars have been too ready to read 'Gaelic' as meaning 'Irish', with unfortunate results. Hughes entertained the possibility that the Book of Deer was written in Ireland and carried to the East at some later date, but viewed it as having 'real peculiarities in an Irish context' (1980, 36), peculiarities which encouraged her view that it was produced 'in some provincial scriptorium, quite possibly in Scotland' (37). Henderson has argued that the Book of Deer is not as 'peculiar' as Hughes supposed, yet there are concrete reasons to believe the book was not written in Ireland.

Geddes has discussed the sword depicted on fol.4v which she identifies as 'definitely not an Irish type' and therefore 'perhaps the strongest visual clue that the illuminations, although within the Irish orbit, were not made in Ireland' (1998, 548). This type of long sword is of ultimately Anglo-Saxon origin, although it was adopted by the Norse. An early tenth century example was found in 1860 at Gortons, Knockando, on Speyside. Geddes suggested that either the Deer artist saw an Anglo-Saxon manuscript, or a Viking sword (546). The appearance of this type of sword on at least two cross-slabs from eastern Scotland—on the famous battle-scene on the reverse of the Aberlemno kirkyard stone, and possibly also on the reverse of the cross-slab from Nigg (Laing 2001, 241–3)—implies that the type had been adopted by the Picts.[41] Whether it was the artist, or his model (at whatever remove), who substituted a contemporary form of a familiar object, the detail of the Deer sword points away from Ireland and towards eastern Scotland.

40 See, for instance, G. Henderson 1987, Brown 1972, I. Henderson 1982, contributions to O'Mahony 1994. 41 c.f. Henderson argues that the distinctively Anglo-Saxon *seax* depicted on the St Andrews sarcophagus may reflect an actual *de luxe* hunting knife given as a diplomatic gift to the Pictish king (Henderson 1998, 164).

Dumville (2007, 203) has drawn attention to another indication of ultimately Anglo-Saxon influence in the Book of Deer in the form of a 'highly unusual ligature' used throughout the main text of the Book which originated in southern England in the early ninth century. To those who express surprise that Anglo-Saxon influence might be felt so deep in the North-East, it may be pointed out that early forms of the name Kennethmont (*Kyllalchmond RRS* ii, 295)[42] indicate a dedication to St Alhmund, one of either of two relatively obscure Anglo-Saxon saints: Alhmund bishop of Hexham (d. 781) or Alhmund of Derby killed in 800, son of Alhred who was exiled in Pictland in 774 (Broun, n.d.).[43]

Marner and Geddes have accepted a Scottish origin for the Book of Deer and attempted to use parallels between its art and stone sculpture to localise its production. Marner adduced parallels among sculpture in Perthshire, including the Dupplin Cross and the Forteviot Arch (2002, 22–8) and on this basis argued for Dunkeld as the Book's place of origin. The methodological difficulty he faces is that there is very little sculpture of ninth and tenth century date in the North-East and so it is inevitable that any contemporary parallels will be from elsewhere. He appears not even to consider it an option that the Book came from the North-East, but then he was writing before the discovery of the Ravenscraig fragment.

Geddes attempted to use geometric motifs in the Book of Deer as clues as to its place of origin (1998, 541). She picked up on Hughes's identification (1980, 27) of the diagonal key patterns on folio 86r as a version of Romilly Allen's no. 1004, which he lists as also occurring on Monifieth 1, Dupplin, and Lindisfarne (Allen and Anderson 1903, vol.1 p. 359). To Hughes these were simply 'traditional patterns still in use in the tenth century' which 'give little help in locating the book' (1980, 27). Geddes disputes this, however, adducing two further examples of diagonal key-pattern much closer to Deer: on the panel from Fyvie (discussed above) and a cross-slab fragment found by the road across the Cairn O' Mount, and now at Marischal Museum, Aberdeen (Small 1974; CANMORE: NO67NE 15).[44] The Cairn o' Mount piece is a small part of what was once a large and sophisticated monument, carved in high relief and dating to perhaps the ninth or tenth century. The all-over key-pattern which covers its cross-shaft is badly worn and difficult to make out in places. Although diagonally set, it is not identical to the pattern in the Book of Deer (*contra* Geddes). The Fyvie key-pattern is an attempt to combine within a small space both rectangular and diagonal key-patterns in a single design. Pellets are required to fill the redundant spaces created.[45]

---

42 On Upper Donside, on the route north via Strathbogie to Moray. 43 On the enshrinement of Alhmund of Derby and its political significance, see Plunkett 1998, 222. 44 A fine image of this piece is available on-line at: http://www.abdn.ac.uk/ virtualmuseum (search by item number = ABDUA 39615). 45 As noted by John Borland: fig. 14.6.

Again, although there are general similarities with the Deer patterns, including the rectangular key-pattern on folios 4v and 5r, there is not an exact match. Note, however, that the arrangement at Fyvie consists of a tall panel of predominantly rectangular key-pattern set above a panel of simpler saltire-shaped interlace. This closely echoes the arrangement on the right-hand margin of Deer's folio 5r. Any attempt to use geometric patterns to localise Insular artworks is, as both Geddes and Hughes acknowledge, hobbled by the lack of comprehensive catalogues of such patterns in Ireland. Also, as Henderson reminds us (*infra* 61), with such designs, the creative exploration of logical permutations fosters the possibility of multi-genesis. Co-occurrence of pattern may be more indicative of date than of localisation, and much further work is required before chronological and geographical distributions can be established. It may transpire that the parallels between the Deer key patterns and those which feature on North-East sculptures, including the Maiden Stone, are indeed significant. The Fyvie comparison is perhaps the most promising, and, at the very least, shows a similar interest in cruciform frameworks.

Henderson highlights the relevance to the Book of Deer of 'the frontal-facing, often paired, ecclesiastical figures carved on cross-slabs in Angus and Perthshire' (*infra* 59). To her, however, these are indicative of date (late ninth or early tenth century) rather than localisation. Like Marner, she was writing before the discovery of the Ravenscraig fragment, which provides a much more local example of a frontal figure. It may be that the Ravenscraig fragment will prove a key to the localisation of the Book of Deer. Henderson has already drawn parallels between the art of the Book of Deer and cross-slabs from Dunkeld and Brechin. It is precisely these sculptures which, as discussed above, provide parallels for aspects of the Ravenscraig fragment. From the surviving description, the Skellybogs fragment/*crux medici*, with its depiction of a book-holding figure, provides a suitable context for the book-holding figures in the Book of Deer. The fact that the Ravenscraig fragment is inscribed strengthens the argument yet further.

The dearth of literary and archaeological evidence from the North-East—extreme even by early medieval Scottish standards—will always be a problem. Yet unexpected discoveries like Ravenscraig, and the physical evidence for manuscript production uncovered during recent excavations at Portmahomack (Tarbat) in Easter Ross (Carver 2004) confound preconceptions about remoteness or peripherality. As Henderson says (*infra* 63), Insular manuscripts 'do not readily proclaim their ... place of origin', and it is unlikely we will ever know for sure where the Book of Deer was produced. The evidence of 'the stones of Deer' certainly does not 'prove' that the Book was written at Deer but taken together they provide physical evidence of an economic, social and artistic context in which the creation of such an object was possible.

ACKNOWLEDGMENTS

I am most grateful to William Fowlie, Auchrynie, for his kind hospitality to two unexpected visitors; to Ian Shepherd, Grampian region archaeologist, for alerting me to the Ravenscraig stone and for facilitating my examination of it; to Ian Scott for discussing Ravenscraig with me and generously sharing unpublished drawings and photographs; to John Borland, RCAHMS, for discussing Ravenscraig and Fyvie with me and providing illustrations; to Mark Mitchell, Dept. of Archaeology, University of Glasgow, for allowing me to consult his unpublished MLitt project 'Old Deer (Buchan) environs desktop study'; to Simon Taylor for sharing with me his unpublished work on the place-names of Deer parish and commenting helpfully on an earlier draft of part of this paper; and to Ross Trench-Jellicoe for his most helpful and insightful comments on an earlier draft. Responsibility for errors and omissions remains fully mine. As ever, I wish to express my appreciation to Stephen Driscoll, not only for his assistance with the fieldwork but for his sustained encouragement of my attempts to view the landscape with archaeologist's eyes.

ABBREVIATIONS

A. B. Coll.	*Collections for a history of the shires of Aberdeen and Banff*, ed. J. Robertson and G. Grub (1843), 5 vols (Spalding Club 69), Edinburgh.
A. B. Ill.	*Illustrations of the topography and antiquities of the shires of Aberdeen and Banff*, ed. J. Robertson and G. Grub (1847–69), 4 vols (Spalding Club), Edinburgh.
CANMORE	RCAHMS on-line database (http://www.rcahms.gov.uk/)
DIL	*Dictionary of the Irish language (based mainly on Old and Middle Irish materials)*, compact edition, ed. E.G. Quin, Dublin (1983, repr.1990).
NGR	National Grid Reference
OS 6" 1st Edition	Ordnance Survey of Aberdeenshire and Banffshire, Six-inches to the mile, 1st edition. Southampton. Surveyed 1870, Published 1874.
OS Name Book	Original Name Books of the Ordnance Survey, Aberdeenshire, No.68.
RCAHMS	Royal Commission on the Ancient and Historical Monuments of Scotland
RMS	*Registrum Magnii Sigilli Regum Scottorum*, (ed.) J.M. Thomson et al. (1882–1914), Edinburgh
RRS ii	*Regesta Regum Scottorum* vol ii (*The acts of William I, king of Scots, 1165–1214*) ed. G.W.S. Barrow (1971), Edinburgh.

Note: references to property records in the Book of Deer follow the numbering of grants given in Text and Translation (this volume).

REFERENCES

Allen, J. Romily, and Joseph Anderson (1903), *The early Christian monuments of Scotland*, Edinburgh.
Aitchison, Nick (2006) *Forteviot: a Pictish and Scottish royal centre*, Stroud.
Anderson, Joseph (1889) 'Notices of some undescribed sculptured stones and fragments in different parts of Scotland', *Proc. Soc. Antiq. Scot.* 23 (1888–9), 344–55.
Anderson, M. O. A. (1980) *Kings and kingship in early Scotland*, Edinburgh.
Bannerman, John (1986) *The Beatons: a medical kindred in the classical Gaelic tradition*, Edinburgh.
Brook, Diane (1992) 'The early Christian church east and west of Offa's Dyke', in *The early church in Wales and the West*, ed. Nancy Edwards and Alan Lane (Oxbow monograph 16), Oxford, 77–89.
Broun, Dauvit (n.d.) 'Alba: Pictish homeland or Irish offshoot?', paper delivered to Foundation of Celtic Studies, University of Sydney, 2006.
Brown, T. J. (1972) 'Northumbria and the Book of Kells', *Anglo-Saxon England* 1, 219–46.
Caldwell, David H. (2001) 'The Monymusk Reliquary; the Breccbennach of St Columba?', *Proc. Soc. Antiq. Scot.* 131, 267–282.
Carver, Martin (2004) 'An Iona of the East: the early medieval monastery at Portmahomack, Tarbat Ness', *Medieval Archaeology* 48, 1–30.
Cessford, Craig (1996) 'The stones of *Apurfeirt* and *Ceirfuill*', *Pictish Arts Society Journal* 10, Winter 1996, 14–16.
Chalmers, Patrick (1848) *The ancient sculptured monuments of the county of Angus*, Aberdeen.
Charles-Edwards, Gifford (2004) 'A reconsideration of the origins of early Insular monumental lettering of the mixed alphabet type: the case of the 'Lapis Echodi' inscription on Iona', *Proc. Soc. Antiq. Scot.*134, 173–81.
Charles-Edwards, Thomas (1976) 'Boundaries in Irish law', in *Medieval settlement: continuity and change*, ed. P.H. Sawyer, London. 83–87.
Clarke, D.V. (2007) 'Reading the multiple lives of Pictish symbol stones', *Medieval Archaeology* 50, 19–39.
Coles, F.R. (1904) 'Report on the stone circles of the North-East of Scotland—the Buchan District—with measured plans and drawings, obtained under the Gunning Fellowship', *Proc. Soc. Antiq. Scot.* 38, 1903–4, 262.
Cruden, George (1799) 'Parish of Deer', in *The statistical account of Scotland, drawn up from the communication of the ministers of the different parishes by Sir John Sinclair* (1791–9, 21 vols), Edinburgh, vol. xvi, 469–83.
Driscoll, Stephen, Oliver O'Grady and Katherine Forsyth (2005) 'The Govan School revisited: Searching for meaning in the early medieval sculpture of Strathclyde', in *'Able minds and practised hands': Scotland's early medieval sculpture in the 21st century*, ed. Sally Foster, Society for Medieval Archaeology Monograph series, Oxford, 135–58.
Dumville, David N. (2007) 'The palaeography of "The Book of Deer": the original manuscript and the liturgical addition', in *Celtic essays 2001–2007*, vol. 1, The Centre for Celtic Studies, University of Aberdeen, 183–212.
Fisher, Ian (2001) *Early medieval sculpture in the West Highlands and Islands*, Edinburgh.
Forsyth, Katherine (1995) 'The inscriptions on the Dupplin Cross' in *From the Isles of the North: medieval art In Ireland and Britain (Proceedings of the Third International Conference on Insular Art)*, ed. Cormac Bourke, Belfast, 237–44.
—— (1997) 'Some thoughts on Pictish symbols as a formal writing system', in *The worm, the germ and the thorn: Pictish and related studies presented to Isabel Henderson*, ed. David Henry, Balgavies, 1997, 85–98. (www.eprints.gla.ac.uk/3447)

—— (2005) '*HIC MEMORIA PERPETUA*: the inscribed stones of sub-Roman southern Scotland', *'Able minds and practised hands': Scotland's early medieval sculpture in the 21st century*, ed. Sally Foster and Morag Cross, Society for Medieval Archaeology Monograph series, Oxford, 113–34.

—— and Ross Trench-Jellicoe (2000) 'The inscribed panel', in M. Hall, K. Forsyth, I.B. Henderson, I.G. Scott, R. Trench-Jellicoe, and A. Watson, 'On markings and meanings: towards a cultural biography of the Crieff Burgh Cross, Strathearn, Perthshire', *Tayside & Fife Archaeological Journal* 6 (2000), 154–88, at 166–68.

Geddes, Jane (1998) 'The art of the Book of Deer', *Proc. Soc. Antiq. Scot.* 128, 537–549.

Gibb, A. (1878) 'Some suggestions as to our mural antiquities', *Proc. Soc. Antiq. Scot.* 12, 1876–8, 196,

Gordon, C.A. (1956) 'Carved stone at Cross-stone, Ellon', *Proc. Soc. Antiq. Scot.* 89, 444.

Gustavsson, Helmer (1986) 'Runstenarnas Uppsala', in *Från Östra Aros till Uppsala*, (Uppsala stads historia VII), ed. Nanna Cnattingius & Torgny Nevéus, Uppsala.

Handley, Mark (1998) 'The early medieval inscriptions of Western Britain: function and sociology', in *The community, the family and the saint: patterns of power in early medieval Europe*, ed. J. Hill and M. Swan, Turnhout, 339–61.

Hall, Mark (2004) 'Culross Abbey parish church (Culross parish), early medieval sculpture', *Discovery and Excavation in Scotland* 5, 62.

Harbison, Peter (1992) *The high crosses of Ireland: an iconographical and photographic survey*, 3 vols, (Romisch-Germanisches Zentralmuseum Forschungsinstitut fur Vor-und-Fruhgeschichte, Monagraphien, 17), Bonn.

Henderson, George (1987) *From Durrow to Kells: the Insular gospel book, 600–900*, London.

—— and Isabel Henderson (2004) *The art of the Picts: sculpture and metalwork in early medieval Scotland*, London.

Henderson, Isabel (1972) 'The Picts of Aberdeenshire and their monuments', *Archaeological Journal* 129, 166–74.

—— (1982) 'Pictish art and the Book of Kells', in *Ireland in early medieval Europe: studies in memory of Kathleen Hughes*, ed. D. Whitelock, R. McKitterick, and D. Dumville (Cambridge 1982), 79–105.

—— (1998) 'A note on the artefacts depicted on the surviving side panel', in *The St Andrews Sarcophagus: a Pictish masterpiece and its international connections*, ed. S.M. Foster, Dublin, 156–65.

—— (2000) 'Towards defining the function of sculpture in Alba: the evidence of St Andrews, Brechin and Rosemarkie', in *Kings, clerics and chronicles in Scotland, 500–1287: studies in the early sources of Scottish history presented to M.O. Anderson on her 90th birthday*, ed. Simon Taylor, Dublin, 35–46.

Higgitt, John (1982) 'The Pictish Latin inscription at Tarbat in Ross-shire', *Proc. Soc. Antiq. Scot.* 112, 300–21

Hudson, Benjamin (1998) 'The Scottish Chronicle', *Scottish Historical Review* 77, 129–61.

Hughes, Kathleen (1980) 'The Book of Deer (Cambridge University Library MS Ii. 6. 32)', in *Celtic Britain in the early middle ages: studies in Scottish and Welsh sources by the late Kathleen Hughes* (Studies in Celtic History II), ed. D.N. Dumville, Woodbridge and Totowa, NJ, 22–37.

Jackson, Kenneth H. (1972) *The Gaelic Notes in the Book of Deer*, Cambridge.

Johansen, Birgitta (1997) *Ormalur. Aspekter av tillvaro och landskap.* (Stockholm Studies in Archaeology 14), Stockholm (with English summary).

Kelly, Fergus (1988) *A guide to early Irish law* (Early Irish Law series 3), Dublin.

—— (1997) *Early Irish farming* (Early Irish Law series 4), Dublin.

Laing, Lloyd (2001) 'The date of the Aberlemno churchyard stone', in *Pattern and purpose in Insular art: Proceedings of the Fourth International Conference on Insular Art. Cardiff ... 1998* ed. M. Redknap et al., Oxford, 241–51.

Lucas, A.T. (1953) 'The horizontal mill in Ireland', *J. Royal Society of Antiquaries of Ireland* 83, 1–36.

Macalister, R.A.S. (1945) *Corpus Inscriptionum Insularum Celticarum*, vol. 1. Dublin.

Mack, Alastair (1998) *The association of Pictish symbol stones with ecclesiastical, burial, and 'memorial' areas*, Balgavies.

McEwan, P.J.M. (1994) *Dictionary of Scottish art and architecture*, Woodbridge.

Milne, J. (1898) 'Place-names in Buchan', *Trans. Buchan Field Club* 4, (1896–8), 215.

Moore, F. (1998) 'Munster ogham stones: siting context and function', in *Early medieval Munster: archaeology, history and society*, ed. M.A. Monk and J. Sheehan, Cork, 23–32.

Morison, John (1845) 'Parish of Old Deer', *New statistical account of Scotland* vol. 12, Edinburgh, 138–65.

Nash-Williams, V.E. (1950) *The early Christian monuments of Wales*. Cardiff.

O'Brien, Elizabeth (1992) 'Pagan and Christian burial in Ireland during the first millenium AD: continuity and change', in *The early Church in Wales and the West*, ed. Nancy Edwards and Alan Lane (Oxbow monograph 16), Oxford, 130–7.

Ogston, David D. (1986) *White stone country: growing up in Buchan*, Edinburgh.

Okasha, Elisabeth (1971) *Hand-list of Anglo-Saxon non-runic inscriptions*, Cambridge.

—— (1985) 'The non-ogam inscriptions of Pictland', *Cambridge Medieval Celtic Studies* 9, 43–69.

—— and K. Forsyth (2001) *Early Christian inscriptions of Munster: a corpus of the inscribed stones*, Cork.

O'Mahony, Felicity (1994) *The Book of Kells: Proceedings of a conference at Trinity College Dublin 6–9 September 1992*, Aldershot.

Ordnance Survey of Aberdeenshire and Banffshire, Six-inches to the mile, 1st edition. Sheet XIII, Southampton. Surveyed 1870, Published 1874.

Ordnance Survey of Aberdeenshire and Banffshire, Six-inches to the mile, 1st edition. Sheet XXI, Southampton. Surveyed 1870, Published 1874.

Ó Riáin, Pádraig (1972) 'Boundary association in early Irish society', *Studia Celtica* 7, 12–29.

Original Name Books of the Ordnance Survey, Aberdeenshire, No. 68 (n.d.).

O'Sullivan, J. and Sheehan, J. (1996) *The Iveragh Peninsula: an archaeological survey of south Kerry*, Cork.

O'Sullivan, Muiris, and Liam Downey (2006) 'Watermills', *Archaeology Ireland* 20.3 (no. 77), 36–8.

Ogston, Prof (1912) 'Saint Machar's Cross', *Trans. Scot. Eccles. Soc.* 3, 3 (1911–12), 343–6.

Paterson, J. (1895) 'Fedderate and its possessors', *Trans. Buchan Field Club* 3, 24–26.

Plunkett, Stephen J. (1998) 'The Mercian perspective', in *The St Andrews Sarcophagus: a Pictish masterpiece and its international connections*, ed. S.M. Foster, Dublin, 202–226.

Pratt, John B. (1858) *Buchan*, Aberdeen.

Preston-Jones, Ann (1992) 'Decoding Cornish churchyards', in *The early church in Wales and the West*, ed. Nancy Edwards and Alan Lane (Oxbow monograph 16), Oxford, 104–24.

Ritchie, J. N. G. (1997) 'Recording Early Christian monuments in Scotland', in *The worm, the germ and the thorn: Pictish and related studies presented to Isabel Henderson*, ed. D. Henry, Balgavies, 119–28.

RCAHMS (1933) *The Royal Commission on the Ancient and Historical Monuments and Constructions of Scotland. Eleventh report with inventory of monuments and constructions in the counties of Fife, Kinross, and Clackmannan*, Edinburgh.

—— (2007a) *In the shadow of Bennachie: a field archaeology of Donside, Aberdeenshire*, Edinburgh.

—— (2007b) *Early medieval carved stones at Brechin Cathedral*, Edinburgh.

Shepherd, I.A.G. (2003) 'Ravenscraig Steading, Peterhead (Peterhead parish), carved stone', *Discovery and Excavation in Scotland* 4, 21–2.

Simpson, W.D. (1935) *The Celtic church in Scotland*, Aberdeen.

—— (1943) *The province of Mar*, Aberdeen.

—— (1952) *The abbey of Deer* (Official guidebook), Edinburgh.

Sims-Williams, Patrick (2003) *The Celtic inscriptions of Britain: phonology and chronology, c.400–1200*, Oxford.

Skene, W.F.H. (1867) *Chronicles of the Picts, chronicles of the Scots, and other early memorials of Scottish history*, Edinburgh.

Small, Alan (1974) 'Cairn o' Mount—a Pictish routeway', *The Deeside Field*, 3rd ser., 1, 8–11.

Stuart, J. (1856) *Sculptured stones of Scotland*, vol. I, Aberdeen and Edinburgh.

—— (1867) *Sculptured stones of Scotland*, vol. II, Aberdeen and Edinburgh.

—— (1869) (ed.) *The Book of Deer* (Spalding Club), Aberdeen and Edinburgh.

Swan, Leo (1983) 'Enclosed ecclesiastical sites and their relevance to settlement patterns of the first millennium AD', in *Landscape archaeology in Ireland* (Brit. Archaeol. Rep. 116), ed. T. Reeves-Smith and F. Hammond, Oxford, 269–94.

Swift, Cathy (1997) *Ogam stones and the earliest Irish Christians*, Maynooth.

Taylor, Simon (2000) 'Version B of the St Andrews foundation legend', in *Kings, clerics and chronicles in Scotland, 500–1287: studies in the early sources of Scottish history presented to M.O. Anderson on her 90th birthday*, ed. Simon Taylor, Dublin, 115–123.

—— (2005) 'The Abernethy Foundation Account & its place-names', *History Scotland* 5 no. 4 (July/August 2005), 14–16.

—— with Gilbert Márkus (forthcoming) *The place-names of Fife*, vol. 4, Stamford.

Thomas, Charles (1971) *The early Christian archaeology of North Britain*, Oxford.

Tocher, J.F. (1910) 'Medieval Buchan', in *The Book of Buchan*, ed. J.F. Tocher (Buchan Field Club), Peterhead.

Will, Robert S., Katherine Forsyth, Thomas O. Clancy and Gifford Charles-Edwards (2005) 'An eighth-century inscribed cross-slab in Dull, Perthshire', *Scottish Archaeological Journal* 25.1, 57–72.

Woolf, Alex (2007) *From Pictland to Alba 789–1070* (New Edinburgh History of Scotland 2), Edinburgh.

Yeoman, Peter (1988) 'Auchindoir doocot (Auchindoir and Kearn parish): post-medieval doocot and medieval mill', *Discovery and Excavation in Scotland 1988*, 13.

Youngs, Susan (ed.) (1989) *'The work of angels': masterpieces of Celtic metalwork, sixth–ninth centuries AD*, London.

The Cistercian abbey of Deer

RICHARD FAWCETT

THE FOUNDATION OF THE ABBEY

The abbey of Deer was founded for Cistercian monks by William Comyn, who acquired the earldom of Buchan through his second marriage to Marjory, heiress of Fergus, earl of Buchan, in about 1212.[1] At this time the foundation of a religious house was still one of the expected ways by which new land-holders established a firmer hold on their territories, proclaimed their elevated social standing, and provided themselves with a dynastic burial place within which prayers could be offered for their welfare in life and salvation after death. Buchan's own son by his first marriage, Walter, was to follow a similar course in founding a priory at Inchmahome after he had acquired the earldom of Menteith through marriage in 1233–4. The first indication we have of Buchan's plans for Deer is that in 1214 his petition to found the abbey was remitted by the order's chapter general to the Scottish abbots for the usual enquiry into the suitability of the site and the adequacy of the intended endowments.[2] The new house was formally established in 1219,[3] as a daughter of Kinloss, though, as was common at Cistercian sites, it is likely there were brethren on the site before then to prepare the first, possibly temporary, buildings for the full community.

At least some of the endowments of the new abbey appear to have been earlier the property of a group of clerici or secular priests, who were them-selves the successors of the first community of Deer, one possible location for which it has been suggested was the knoll known as Top Tillery, not far from the parish church.[4] It is even a possibility that a residue from that body of clerici was absorbed, whether willingly or not, into the newly established Cistercian community. If so, this makes the choice of Cistercians for the new community perhaps a little surprising. By the early thirteenth century the original ideals of that order to set themselves apart from the rest of mankind by occupying wilderness areas were certainly being less single-mindedly pursued but, where there was a need to absorb and convert existing commu-nities, the Augustinian canons might have been a more obvious choice. Since at least the 1140s at St Andrews the more flexible Augustinians had been seen as well suited to such work, and many of the order's houses, including

---

1 For a summary of what is known of the foundation of the abbey see Cowan and Easson 1976, 74. For an account of the life of William Comyn see Young 1997, 19–30.   2 Canivez 1933, 427.   3 British Library, Cotton MS Vespasian A VI fo. 59v.   4 Stuart 1869, x and xi.

Abernethy, Inchaffray, Inchcolm, Loch Leven, May Island, Monymusk and Restenneth, were on sites that had been home to earlier communities.[5] This adaptability was certainly a factor behind the way in which the Augustinians continued to receive new foundations throughout the thirteenth century and even into the following century. Nevertheless, despite the fact that the early thirteenth century was a period when new foundations were beginning to tail off for the Cistercians south of the Border, several new abbeys were established for the order in Scotland at this time, at Balmerino, Culross and Saddell as well as at Deer. It is also worth noting that Kinloss's only other daughter house, at Culross, which was similarly under consideration by the chapter general in 1214,[6] was itself established in a location that had associations with an important earlier religious history, in that case being linked with St Serf.[7]

THE MEDIEVAL HISTORY OF THE ABBEY

Very little is recorded of the abbey's institutional history. The first abbot,[8] Robert, who presumably came from Kinloss, returned to lead the mother house in 1220, and was succeeded by Alexander, prior of Kinloss.[9] In 1233 William Comyn, the founder, died and was buried within the abbey.[10] In the following year Abbot Walran died and was succeeded by Hugh, prior of Melrose,[11] but in 1235 the latter chose to return to Melrose because the climate of Deer did not suit his frail body, and Robert, a monk of the abbey, was elected in his place.[12] Another abbot brought up from Melrose who found that Deer did not agree with him was Adam of Smailholm, who preferred to return to Melrose in 1267 rather than to rule over what was described as the hovel of monks at Deer.[13] Of the other abbots of whom we know anything, at least two had to be removed from office. Abbot Henry, who had earlier been prior of Kinloss, was 'released' from the administration of his flock for unspecified reasons in 1262,[14] and towards the end of the abbey's life, in 1505, Bishop Elphinstone of Aberdeen had become involved in attempts to depose James Pittendreich, though he appears not to have resigned before 1510.[15]

The endowments of the abbey were evidently more or less adequate for its needs throughout the greater part of its history. A principal source of income was the annexed parishes of Deer, Foveran, Kinedward (King Edward) and Peterugie (Peterhead),[16] despite the objections of the order's founding fathers to such parochial approproations. Deer was granted to the abbey from the start, although in 1256 20 merks of its income was allocated to a prebend of

5 For summary details of these foundations see Cowan and Easson 1976. 6 Canivez 1933, 427. 7 Fawcett 2004. 8 Summary details of the careers of the abbots are given in Watt and Shead 2001, 54–8. 9 *Chronica de Mailros* (= Stevenson 1835, 137). 10 Ibid., p. 144. 11 Ibid., p. 144. 12 Ibid., p. 144. 13 Ibid., p. 198. 14 Ibid., p. 185. 15 Macfarlane 1985, 265. 16 For details of these annexations see Cowan 1967, 46, 70, 111, 164 and 215.

Aberdeen Cathedral. Foveran and King Edward seem to have been annexed only in the late thirteenth and early fourteenth centuries, while the date of Peterhead's annexation is unknown but probably late. By the eve of the Reformation, rentals drawn up in 1554 appear to show an adequately healthy financial state.[17] The accounts for the collection of Thirds of Benefices, which were called for in 1561 but are dated 1573 in the case of Deer, give a detailed break-down of income totalling about £2,300.[18] This places it in the middle rank of houses in general, and suggests that it was the fourth richest Cistercian house, though this may be misleading.

Nevertheless, the abbey appears to have passed through lean periods. The fact that the family of its founder became a particular target of Robert I's hostility cannot have been to its advantage, and it is likely to have suffered in his wasting of Buchan in 1308. But the house's fortunes were placed on a firmer footing soon afterwards when, in a charter of 1315, Robert granted the abbey recompense for war damage and confirmed its endowments.[19] Yet despite this, references to sufferings caused by warfare come again in 1371 when Pope Gregory XI confirmed the abbey's rights with regard to its annexed churches.[20]

The decline from initial fervour that affected a majority of religious houses in the later Middle Ages inevitably had its impact on Deer, though by the early sixteenth century there does seem to have been a sincere attempt to restore something approaching the original observances. Thomas Crystall, the highly distinguished abbot of Deer's mother house at Kinloss from 1504 to 1535, was assiduous in carrying out visitations,[21] though an argument between the two houses over the lands of Fechil may have left Deer disinclined to carry out their visitor's bidding.[22] Nevertheless, in 1531 the visitor general of the order issued constitutions and ordinances for the better rule of the Cistercian monasteries in Scotland, and Deer was a recipient.[23] Perversely enough, however, despite strongly expressed concerns about the laxity of religious life throughout Scotland, in 1534 or '35, James V sought relaxations for the Cistercians because of the particular circumstances that prevailed within his kingdom.[24]

In 1537, Abbot Robert Reid of Kinloss, a scholarly patron of humanist learning who did much to revive monastic life where he could, made another visitation and, despite a grant of certain relaxations,[25] gave instructions for the repair of the abbey buildings, starting with the choir of the church. In the same year, the abbot and monks made a pact that they would lead a regular and reformed life and would hold the income of the house in common after making due provision for the brethren and officers.[26] But while the spirit

17 Robertson 1862, 19–29. 18 Kirk 1995, 457–9. 19 *RRS* v, 335 (=Duncan 1988)
20 Simpson 1927, 185 21 Stuart 1872, xlvii and 39. 22 Stuart 1872, 28. 23 Robertson 1862, 5–14. 24 Cowan 1982, 37–8. 25 Robertson 1862, 14–16. 26 Robertson 1862,

might have been willing, the flesh showed some signs of continuing weakness, and in 1542 the abbot made a grant to the monks of an extra 8*d*. daily on flesh days and 3*d*. on fish days,[27] which is perhaps not suggestive of excessive austerity. Yet when considering such grants it must be accepted that the climate of monasticism was very different from what it had been in the twelfth and thirteenth centuries, and it would be wrong to judge the community by such practices in isolation. Certainly in other ways the last decades of the abbey's corporate life appear to have taken on fresh intellectual vigour. In 1537 it had been agreed that grammar lessons should be provided, for example, and a copy of Despauterius' text book was acquired in Paris.[28] It is perhaps also significant that Prior Robert Stephenson was one of the few Scots known to have had a knowledge of Greek.[29]

A further indication of corporate health is that the number of monks within the house remained fairly high, with thirteen monks signing a rental in 1554 and twelve subscribing a charter in 1556.[30] The abbey had probably benefited from the fact that it remained under the governance of monastic abbots until relatively late. The last abbot, John Innes, resigned as late as 1543, dying soon afterwards.[31] In his place Robert Keith, a brother of the Earl Marischal, was instituted as commendator.[32] There is nothing to show what impact this had on the morale and religious life of the house, though it is likely that the involvement of earlier abbots in wider affairs had always meant that the daily administration of the house devolved on the prior and senior obedientiaries, and it was only as the financial implications of this change of leadership took hold that the life of the monks was affected. Once established, the hold of the Keith family on the temporal possessions and buildings of the abbey was not to be dislodged and, after the death of Robert in 1551, the commendatorship smoothly passed to his nephew, a junior, who bore the same name.

THE ABBEY AFTER THE REFORMATION

The conventual life of the Cistercians of Deer was formally ended by the Reformation parliament of 1560, though the abbey continued to exist as a landed corporation under the commendatorship of Robert Keith. It is likely that at least some of the monks remained within their quarters at the abbey and continued to enjoy a financial allowance, assuming that Keith was more co-operative in this respect than some other commendators about whom we have information. Whatever the wishes of the leaders of the reformed church, it is also hard not to imagine that some of the monks would have still

16–18. **27** Robertson 1862, 18–19. **28** Durkan 1990, 125. **29** Dilworth 1995, 65–6.
30 Robertson 1862, 27–9 and 31–2. **31** Robertson 1862, 19; Dilworth 1986, 63.
32 Robertson 1862, 552–3.

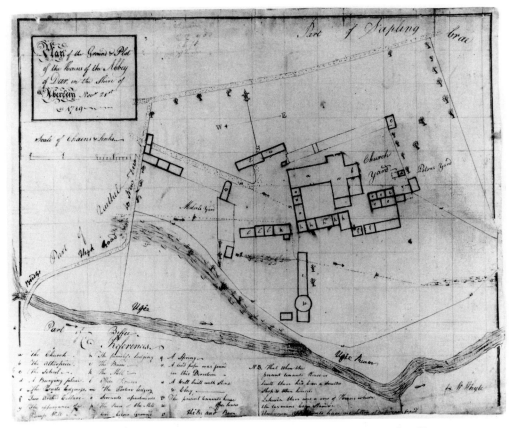

14.1 A plan of the abbey in 1789 (N.L.S. Adv. MS 30.5.22 no. 7g, reproduced by permission of the Trustees of the National Library of Scotland).

worshipped as before within the privacy of the precinct walls, though we do know that two, or perhaps even three, of the monks chose to serve in the reformed church.[33] Eventually, in 1587, probably after the community of monks had died out, the estates of the abbey were erected into temporal lordship for Robert Keith, who took the title of Lord Altrie.[34] Although Altrie married, he had no heir, and after his death in 1592 his estates and titles passed to his nephew, the fifth Earl Marischal. It is said in Patrick Gordon's *Britane's Distemper* that the earl's wife was deeply troubled by this acquisition of church property, and had a dream in which large numbers of monks were seen to be picking with their pen knives at the rock on which the family's principal castle of Dunnottar was set, a dream which was thought to foreshadow the end of the dynasty some time later.[35]

Little is recorded of the abbey buildings for many years after that, though their fate appears to have been the usual one of progressive collapse both as a

33 Dilworth 1995, 81.   34 *RMS*, v, no. 1309.   35 Dunn 1844.

result of neglect and of pillaging the building materials, as described by the author of the *New Statistical Account* in 1845.[36] But informed interest in the remains was already emerging by the later eighteenth century, and a plan sent to General Hutton in 1789 shows that the layout of the buildings was still largely comprehensible (fig.14.1);[37] it also shows that many more buildings were to be seen on the ground than is now the case. It is uncertain, however, the extent to which the names given to the buildings on the plan of 1789 related to the monastic uses or to more recent occupation. The description of a range to the north-west of the church as 'present tennants house' is clear enough, while the identification of the south conventual range as 'the family's lodging' presumably refers to the adaptation of this part of the complex as a domestic residence. But there can have been very little on the site that was still habitable by the late eighteenth century, and certainly the author of the *Statistical Account* of 1795 says the abbey was in ruin.[38] That account suggests that some investigations were taking place, since it was reported that a semi-circular Doric pillar had been found, which was presumably in fact a thirteenth-century respond. The state of ruination is confirmed by a view published in George Keith's *A General View of the Agriculture of Aberdeenshire* of 1811, which shows extensive, albeit artistically composed, ruins.[39]

By the time of Keith's view, however, the owner was beginning to take an interest in the preservation of the remains. Deer had been absorbed into the Pitfour estate, which since the early eighteenth century had been owned by a branch of the Ferguson family who enjoyed resources derived from sugar plantations in Grenada. In 1809, as an extension to the improvement of the policies of his house, James Ferguson, Member of Parliament for Aberdeenshire, enclosed the abbey within a high wall within which he set out his fruit and kitchen garden.[40] But he also took steps to preserve the abbey from further destruction. As part of this he cleared the buildings of much of the accumulated overburden, and lowered the ground within the area of the church by about three feet in order to expose its plan. It was perhaps he who rebuilt a number of doorway and window arches in the south claustral range and in the range to its south-east. In the latter, in particular, a stone with stylised foliage carving has been re-set as the keystone of a doorway.

Regrettably, his nephew and successor, Admiral George Ferguson, was less in sympathy with the medieval remains of the abbey, and in 1854 he destroyed much of what remained of the church in order to build a family mausoleum over the area of the south transept and the adjacent parts of the east conventual range (fig. 14.2). His mausoleum was designed as an austere Greek Doric temple, with its entrance front to the north. In adopting this style, Ferguson was following the lead of his predecessor, who between 1822 and

36 Morison 1845, 148–50.   37 National Library of Scotland, Adv. MS 30.5.22 7f. 38 Cruden 1795, 482–3.   39 Keith 1811, 366.   40 Smith 1875, vol. 2, p. 1062.

14.2 A view of the abbey in 1927 before the demolition of the Ferguson Mausoleum (© Crown Copyright, reproduced by permission of Historic Scotland).

14.3 Excavations within the cloister in 1927 (© Crown Copyright, reproduced by permission of Historic Scotland).

1831 had constructed a number of fine Greek revival buildings within the park at Pitfour to the designs of John Smith.[41] Smith died in 1852, but it seems at least a possibility that he had supplied the Admiral with designs for his mausoleum before his death. In building his mausoleum the admiral is also discredited with the destruction of a Pictish cross slab, which used to be set at the end of one of the ranges, but which was said to have been used in the foundations of the new building. Allen and Anderson cite this as one of the rare cases they had encountered of the deliberate destruction of a symbol stone.[42] The mausoleum itself is now gone, and the only reminder of its location is a memorial stone within the south transept to Eliza Anne Ferguson, who died on 30 August 1854, and whose death may have been the reason for the mausoleum's construction.

The Pitfour estate was broken up and the house demolished in 1926, and in the same year the remains of the abbey were acquired by the Catholic diocese of Aberdeen. With the involvement of the Ministry of Works, and with advice from Dr W. Douglas Simpson, the diocese carried out excavations on the site of the abbey church to recover the plan (fig. 14.3),[43] and also undertook works of consolidation costing about £3,000 (fig. 14.5). Subsequently, in 1933 it was agreed that the abbey should be placed in state care,[44] and further works of stabilisation were carried out. One of the first decisions that was made soon after the abbey was taken into guardianship was the demolition of the mausoleum, which was evidently in a poor structural condition. This is not a course of action that is likely to have been adopted in more recent times, though there is a certain irony in the fact that the building that had necessitated destruction of the surviving parts of the abbey church was itself in turn destroyed so as to allow the remains of the church to be seen to better advantage. The temple portico of the mausoleum did at least partly survive, however, being adapted as a propylaeum at the entrance to the precinct.[45] Continuing excavations were also carried out, and in 1939 a length of carved oak cresting was found which was presented to the National Museum of Scotland later that year (fig. 14.4).[46] Further minor excavations in the vicinity of the abbey have been undertaken on a number of occasions, most recently in 1985–6 when an area intended to be put to market garden use was investigated, and a number of potentially medieval features were located.[47]

---

41 Tait 1983, 322–331.   **42** Allen and Anderson 1903, 162.   **43** There are photographs of excavations with the date 1927 in the photograph library of Historic Scotland. **44** Correspondence on National Archives of Scotland file MW/1/524 (SC 22512/3A). **45** There are undated drawings for the re-location of the portico in the drawings collection of Historic Scotland (see fig. 16.3).   **46** National Archives of Scotland file MW/1/1044 (SC 22512/2B); Anon. 1940, 148.   **47** Stones 1986, 10.

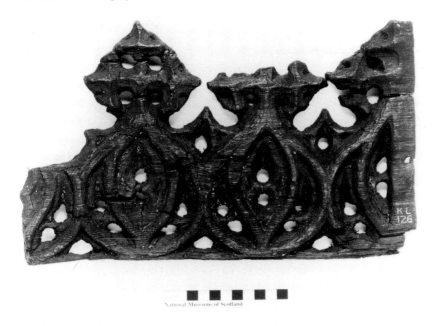

14.4 The carved oak foliate cresting found in 1939 (© Crown Copyright, reproduced by permission of Historic Scotland).

14.5 The south claustral range in the course of cutting back ivy growth in 1927 (© Crown Copyright, reproduced by permission of Historic Scotland).

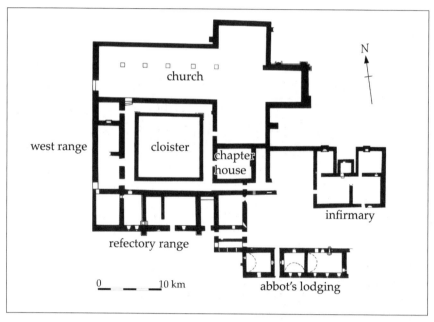

14.6 Plan of the abbey (© Crown Copyright, reproduced by permission of Historic Scotland).

THE BUILDINGS OF THE ABBEY

Except for the south conventual range and a range to its south-east, the remains of the abbey are so fragmentary that it is difficult to offer any firm statements about its architectural qualities. Beyond this, liberal measures of caution have to be applied in interpreting what remains in view of the difficulties of determining the extent of the works of consolidation and rebuilding carried out in 1809, when picturesque effect was probably cultivated more assiduously than archaeological precision. Yet further damage was caused in 1854, when parts of the masonry of the church and east range were removed in advance of building the mausoleum. Moving outside the main core of buildings, while it is not known when some of the peripheral structures that are shown on the plan of 1789 in the Hutton collection were removed, there can be little doubt that least some of those were of monastic origin. It should be noted in particular that a number of the buildings shown to the west of the church appear to have formed a courtyard in front of the abbey church. It may also be observed that Hutton's plan shows a 'porters lodging' some distance to the north-west of the church, in the position where the principal gateway to the precinct could well have been.

Nevertheless, with all these caveats, the plan of the main complex of buildings is reasonably clear, and is much as would be expected in a middle-

14.7 A view southwards across the site of the church towards the cloister (© Crown Copyright, reproduced by permission of Historic Scotland).

ranking Scottish Cistercian house (fig. 14.6). The church is on the higher ground on the north side of the main complex. It has a short aisle-less rectangular presbytery extending eastwards from a pair of transepts, each of which, on the basis of their greater width by comparison with the width of the presbytery, appears to have had an eastern two-bay chapel aisle; those chapels would have risen to a lower height than the main vessel of either the transepts or the presbytery. Nothing has survived of the arcades which presumably separated the transepts from their chapels, as are to be seen in restored state at Deer's sister house of Culross. The nave, which extended west from the transepts, would have housed the two choirs for the monks and conversi, and the rather lop-sided relationship of the nave with the transepts indicates that it had an aisle on its north side though, again, nothing of any arcade survives. There are traces of a west doorway which now appears to be asymmetrically set towards the south of the nave's central vessel, though this may be because of the way it has been consolidated. In many Cistercian houses there was a Galilee porch extending the full width of at least the central vessel but, if there was one at Deer, it has left no trace. Going beyond the basic disposition of the plan, we can see that the presbytery had buttresses slightly inset from its angles, on the evidence at the north-eastern angle; these also have the bottom chamfer of a base course and one course of ashlar facing, which continues along the north face of the presbytery. There is also ashlar facing along the footings of the south side of the nave towards the cloister, above which the wall is set back as if behind a stone bench. Elsewhere, however, much of what is seen of the church wall footings appears to be largely the result of modern rebuilding.

Amongst so much that is uncertain, it can at least be said that Deer's church plan was entirely consistent with the architectural attitudes of the Cistercians, being essentially a variant on the characteristic 'Bernardine' plan (fig. 14.7). Indeed such was the popularity of this plan type in Scotland that it was still being chosen in 1273 for the last house of the order to be founded, at Sweetheart, despite having been widely abandoned for new foundations elsewhere in Europe (fig. 14.8). The so-called Bernardine plan usually had a symmetrical pair of aisles to the nave, whereas it seems that Deer had only one; but another example of the plan with a single aisle is to be seen at Balmerino, founded not long after Deer in about 1227. There the plan is a mirror image of Deer's, with the cloister to the north of the church and the aisle on the south side of the nave. At Balmerino, where we have slightly more architectural detail surviving, the lack of correspondence of rhythm between the arcade piers and the wall shafts on the opposite side of the church strongly suggests that the aisle was a secondary addition, which was presumably intended to provide supplementary chapel space. In such cases it was easier to add a single aisle on the side away from the cloister, so that that was no encroachment on the space of the garth, and structural disturbance was minimised. There seem to have been similar considerations at a number of the churches of other orders, as at Augustinian Cambuskenneth and Tironensian Lindores.[48] At a much later date, a related consideration also applied at Cistercian Melrose, where in the late medieval rebuilding the north aisle towards the cloister retained the narrow width of the previous building, whereas the aisle on the side away from the cloister was made more spacious, and an additional row of chapels was eventually added on that side as well.[49] Assuming on this basis that the north aisle at Deer was itself a later addition, the original aisle-less plan must have been very like that at its sister house and close contemporary of Culross, the nave of which remained aisle-less throughout its history. Comparison with Culross also provides a reminder that there would have been screens at some point down the nave to separate the two choirs, and at Culross stone screens were preserved when a late medieval tower was built above them.[50]

The apparent extreme simplicity of what survives of the church at Deer probably gives a misleading impression of the qualities of the original architecture. The relationship of the buttresses to the wall, together with the

48 See plans in RCAHMS 1963, fig. 50; RCAHMS 1933, fig. 357. 49 Fawcett and Oram 2004, 93–164. 50 Fawcett 2004.

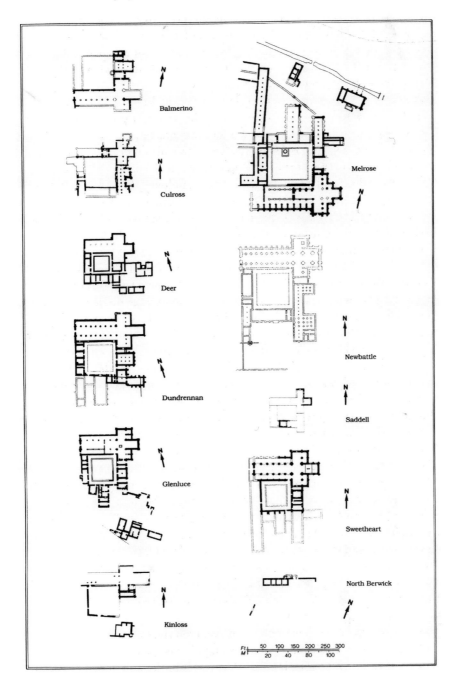

14.8 Comparative plans of the Scottish Cistercian abbeys (Martin Wilson; © Crown Copyright, reproduced by permission of Historic Scotland).

14.9 A section of small-scale decorative arcading, possibly from some liturgical fixture
(© Crown Copyright, reproduced by permission of Historic Scotland).

fragmentary base course on the south side of the presbytery, do together give
a slight hint that the architectural articulation was more sophisticated than
first appears. But the most telling clues to what we have lost are a number of
moulded stones now displayed in a modern shelter to the north-west of the
church. One of these is a finely moulded piscina basin which was evidently
damaged, and was then taken out, inverted, and re-carved on the tail of the
stone that must originally have been set into the wall, before being re-set.
Even more striking is a pair of decorative trifoliate arches with complex
filleted rolls of thirteenth-century type around their heads, which are likely to
have come from some liturgical fixture (fig. 14.9).[51] There is also a small head,
which may have been the corbel support for the hoodmould of a doorway or
window.

While it would be dangerous to draw too many conclusions from such
slight evidence, these stones do at least point to architectural detailing of
modest elegance in the first phase of building. By the later Middle Ages,
however, much of the internal impact of the building may have come from the
altarpieces, choir stalls, screens and other furnishings, many of which would
have been of richly carved and painted wood. The only hint of what we have

51 Illustrations of these are given in MacGibbon and Ross 1896, ii, 276 and 278.

lost of such furnishings is the fragment of cresting found in 1939, which was evidently designed to be slotted into the upper part of some item of framed construction intended to be seen from one side only. Likely to date from no earlier than the late fifteenth century, this shows that at least some of the furnishings in place at that time were of high quality. The tombs of the great families who had an interest in the abbey would also have been prominent, despite the earlier Cistercian discouragement of lay burials within their churches. Within the stone shelter is the head of an effigy from one such tomb, which probably dates from the thirteenth century. It has a chain mail coif and band, and there are the remains of a small kneeling angelic figure to one side of the pillow on which the head rests.

The cloister on the south side of the nave of the church is of rather small scale, but it was around this space that the three main conventual ranges were grouped. Within the cloister, running along the edges of the garth, are the footings of the inner screen walls that carried the lean-to roofs of the covered walks; these footings embody short sections of a chamfered base course towards the walks at the north-east and north-west corners. There were usually two processional doorways from the cloister into the church, aligned with the east and west walks, but only one of those doors is still identifiable at Deer, that which faces down the west walk, and there is now a reconstructed pair of steps leading up to it. The doorway may have been set within a slight salient projecting into the walk.

The main part of the east claustral range, occupying the space which extends southwards from the south transept of the church up to the inner line of the south cloister walk, is entirely taken up by the foundations of the square chapter house, the principal meeting room of the community and the second most important in the hierarchy of the abbey's buildings. Along part of its east wall are the remains of the bench which perhaps once ran around all four sides of the room. Clearly there was no provision for sacristy, library and parlour immediately adjacent to the church, as might have been expected. The chapter house seems to have projected only about as far east as the main vessel of the adjacent transept, though there is a wall to the east which appears to have enclosed a space equivalent to the depth of the chapel aisle on the east side of the transept. The function of this latter wall is uncertain, though it could represent a later lean-to building against the east side of the chapter house; the lack of bond with the south wall of the transept makes it unlikely to be an earlier east wall of a larger chapter house. South of the chapter house is a slype or passage, which extends the line of the south walk and provides access to the buildings beyond the main claustral complex, possibly by means of a covered gallery.

South of the slype, at the junction of the east and west ranges, was a room at a lower level, the main entrance to which was through a doorway with broadly chamfered jambs and sill on the east side of the range, and thus from outside the cloister. Since the Cistercians were usually quite strict in having all the main rooms required for enclosed conventual life accessible from within the cloister, the means of access could argue against this having been the day room for either the monks or the novices that was often located in this part of the range. However, a curious feature of this room is an angled window at its south-east corner, a parallel for which is to be seen in a pair of windows on each side of the calefactory (warming room) fireplace at Inchmahome.[52] One wonders if there was once also a fireplace in this position at Deer, which would mean that it may also have been the calefactory. Beyond the junction of the east and south ranges was a second passage through the east range, south of which was the substructure of the monastic latrine, which enclosed a section of the drain. Running at first floor level above the full length of this range we must assume there was the monastic dormitory, but of this nothing now survives. At the north end of the dormitory there would presumably have been a requirement for a stair directly into the church for use at the night-time services, and there would also have been the need for a stair for day-time use leading down into the cloister, but no traces are to be seen of either of these. At the southern end of the dormitory would have been the latrine.

The range on the west side of the cloister probably initially housed the conversi or lay brethren, who carried out much of the manual labour and many of the more mundane tasks of the community. But by the later Middle Ages recruitment of conversi had largely ceased, and this range was probably used for the stores of the cellarer, the obedientiary responsible for provisioning the abbey. The main body of the range was divided into three rooms, with a fourth at the junction with the south range. The northernmost chamber had a fireplace in its south wall. It is unknown if there was an upper floor on this side of the cloister.

Because of the fall of the land to the south and east, much of the south range, which faced the church across the cloister, had to be provided with a basement to bring the main rooms up to cloister level (fig. 14.10), an arrangement that also had to be adopted at Culross, where the ground slopes even more steeply. The main room in this range was always the refectory, the eating hall of the abbey, which was the third most important building in the complex after the church and chapter house. In many Cistercian houses the refectory was rebuilt at right angles to the cloister; this meant that it could be larger than the available space within the south range would allow, and it also permitted other rooms to be slotted in on each side. Amongst other Scottish Cistercian houses, this certainly happened at Melrose, Dundrennan and Glenluce, and perhaps also at Sweetheart, but it was clearly never done at Deer. The entrance to the refectory from the cloister was a

---

52 See Fawcett 1995, plan on inside back cover.

14.10 A view along the outer face of the south claustral range, compare with fig. 5
(© Crown Copyright, reproduced by permission of Historic Scotland).

doorway with chamfered jambs and sill, but with an arch that appears to be a later reconstruction; this doorway looked out along the west cloister walk.

The south range is the best preserved part of the abbey (fig. 14.11). It appears that in its final state the two storeys were separated by a timber floor rather than the stone vaulting that would be more usual within conventual buildings. This appears likely to have been the original arrangement, reflecting the relative economy with which the buildings were constructed. Nevertheless, many of the doorways and windows that are now seen in the range appear to result from post-medieval alterations, and there may have been more extensive modifications than are now evident; indeed, it seems likely that the range as a whole survived so well largely because it was later adapted for other uses. The first stages of this process of adaptation may have begun in the later Middle Ages, when we know that the monks did not always use their buildings in the ways that had been intended at an earlier period. In the strictest interpretation of the rule, for example, flesh was forbidden as an element in the monastic diet, and the Cistercians had been particularly firm in this. And yet it is clear from the charter of 1542 that there were days on which

14.11 The interior of the south claustral range (© Crown Copyright,
reproduced by permission of Historic Scotland).

flesh was eaten at Deer.[53] Since it is likely that meat eating continued to be
prohibited within the refectory, it is possible that it was consumed in other
parts of the abbey, such as the infirmary, where a more lenient diet had always
been permitted to the sick and aged brethren. We do know at a number of
English monasteries for which the documentation is more complete that a
room, sometimes referred to as the misericord, might be built close to the
infirmary to allow the monks to take meat as a normal part of their diet,[54]
while at Westminster a space known as a the *camagium* was partitioned off
within the refectory where a less strictly controlled diet was allowed.[55]

It is perhaps one sign of changed times at the end of the Middle Ages that
at the Augustinian abbey of Holyrood by 1503 the canons appear to have
given up their old refectory to the king for use as a great hall in his expanding
palace,[56] and it was unlikely they would have been able to do this if it was still
performing a necessary function in its original situation. A related situation
may be reflected in a late medieval description of the Tironensian abbey of
Arbroath, where there were apparently two refectories, one for common days
and one for feast days.[57] Since we also know from other Scottish monasteries

53 Robertson 1862, 18–19. **54** Gilyard-Beer 1958, 34. **55** Harvey 1993, 41–42.
56 Dunbar 1999, 61. **57** A description of 1517 by Sir Arthur Boece, priest of Brechin
diocese, printed in Theiner 1864, no. DCCCCXXV.

that the brethren might have come to expect to have individual dwelling houses, as was evidently the case in 1549 at Augustinian Pittenweem,[58] or to have private gardens in the case of Cistercian Melrose, Balmerino and Newbattle,[59] is it one possibility that the Deer refectory was at a late stage of its life subdivided to provide individual chambers? Perhaps a more plausible scenario, however, is that it was adapted as an element in the residence of the commendator, either before or after the Reformation, and in this connection it may be significant that Hutton's plan refers to it as 'the family's lodging'; further consideration will be given to this shortly.

Apart from the ranges immediately around the cloister, there are the remains of two buildings to their east, which provide the only surviving reminders of the many other structures that would once have served the gamut of functions that had to be housed in a self-sufficient religious community. It has to be admitted, however, that it is particularly difficult to identify the functions of such outlying buildings since, beyond the claustral nucleus, there were fewer conventions governing either where the other buildings were placed or how they were laid out. Their location and planning was therefore to a considerable extent at the discretion of the community. One of these buildings at Deer, which was of at least two storeys, is attached to the south-east angle of the latrine and extends eastwards from there. In the absence of documentation we cannot be certain of its function, but it is arguable that it was built as the residence of the abbot. In this position the letter of the monastic rule that the abbot should live in common with his monks could be observed through the fact that their sleeping quarters were inter-connected, even if only through the latrine. At Deer's mother house of Kinloss the abbot's house was evidently at the outer end of the dormitory range, because it was there that Abbot Reid greatly expanded his residence in the early sixteenth century, placing his arms above the entrance. There are also several other cases where the abbot's house appears to have been in this position, including Cluniac Crossraguel, Valliscaulian Pluscarden and Augustinian Inchcolm.

This building at Deer now consists of three originally barrel-vaulted chambers at the lower level, with a passage running through the range between the first and second chambers from the west; the vaults of the east and west chambers ran on an east-west axis, while that of the central chamber ran on a north-south axis. The lintelled-over main drain runs along the north side of the range, and the existence of a waste basin opening into this drain in the east chamber suggests that it was the kitchen; immediately above the waste basin is a water intake. The main rooms would have been at first floor level, and perhaps had a hall, chamber and oratory as their main components. There are three chutes within the wall thickness leading down from the upper storey into the drain, indicating that the upper floor was well provided with

58 Cowan 1982, 41.   59 Cowan 1982, 37.

latrines and perhaps with lavabo basins. Like the refectory range, the presumed abbot's house at Deer is relatively well preserved, though there is unfortunately less of the upper level. Also like the refectory it shows signs of later modifications. If this was indeed the abbot's house, it may be assumed that the two pre-Reformation commendators would also have occupied it. Their domestic requirements are likely to have been more extensive than those of the abbots, however, especially after the Reformation when the second of them took a wife. This could be one reason for some of the adaptations of the refectory range mentioned above since, once the abbot's house became inadequate, the adjacent refectory range would be an obvious candidate for providing supplementary accommodation.

To the north-east of the building thought to be the abbot's house are the footings of a U-shaped complex, which was connected to the south-east corner of the south transept by a wall. The main element of this is a block running from west to east that was later divided by a cross wall; north of this are two smaller rooms which, together with the main block, give the building its basic U shape, and there was a fifth smaller room in the hollow of the U. The three rooms on the north of the main block all had fireplaces. There may have been a covered gallery running from the slype in the east range towards this building, connecting with a door in its west face. The most likely function for a major group of buildings to the east of cloister is that of an infirmary, the complex that was originally intended to house the monks who could no longer withstand the full rigours of the daily round of services, and that provided a temporary lodging for those monks who were undergoing periodic blood-letting. Earlier infirmaries were most often open ward-like halls with a chapel off the east side, but in the later Middle Ages, as they acquired a wider range of functions, including the eating of flesh as suggested above, more rooms were needed. The number of rooms in this block may reflect these changes, and certainly the angle rolls of the fireplace in the north-west chamber point to a date no earlier than the fifteenth century for that part. Regrettably, with the exception of a twelfth-century infirmary partially excavated at Kelso,[60] we know very little about such buildings in Scotland, though at Glenluce Abbey there is a basically U-shaped complex of buildings to the south-east of the claustral buildings which could also have served this function.[61]

CONCLUSION

Inevitably, there has had to be much that is speculative in this brief attempt to interpret the surviving evidence for the church and monastic buildings of Deer abbey. Perhaps all that can be said with certainty is that enough remains to show

60 Tabraham 1984.   61 See Grove 1996, plan on inside back cover.

that the layout of the church and the other main buildings around the cloister conformed to what is to be expected of a Scottish Cistercian abbey founded in the earlier thirteenth century, even if parts of what we now see are the result of a number of phases of post-monastic and more modern rebuilding. There is less certainty about the outlying buildings to the east of the claustral complex, though this would probably be the case even if those buildings were more complete, and we must at least be grateful that these did survive the landscaping operations carried out by two generations of the Fergusons of Pitfour.

APPENDIX

Old Deer Parish Church

It has been generally assumed that the parish church of Old Deer was built on the site of the early monastic community. However, although this is certainly an attractive possibility, and there is a great body of evidence that sites once hallowed by worship could remain in modified use over very long periods, there is nothing in the surviving fabric of the medieval church which would either support or refute this idea. Indeed there are no identifiable features in the fabric that are likely to date from before the later Middle Ages. Nevertheless, the two-compartment plan, with its architecturally distinct chancel and nave, is perhaps unlikely to be so late; structurally undifferentiated rectangular plans were more common for parish churches by then. It is possible that this plan originated with the church that is assumed to have been granted to the newly founded abbey in 1219, part of the fruits of which were set aside for a prebend of Aberdeen Cathedral in 1256.[62] A short section of narrow chamfered base course at the north-east corner of the nave, where it meets the north wall of the chancel could perhaps be consistent with such a date.

In attempting to assess the evidence within what remains of the church, it must be borne in mind that the chancel was almost completely reconstructed in 1731, while the nave was truncated and partly rebuilt in 1789. By the time the chancel was reconstructed it had probably been out of use for worship for many years, with services being conducted in the nave. It had probably been adapted as a burial place for the heritors of the parish since not long after the Reformation, but the occasion for this latest campaign was evidently the death in 1731 of Anne Stuart, the wife of James Ferguson of Pitfour. Her imposing monument was set against the south wall, within a small walled enclosure, while Ferguson's name and the date were inscribed on a tablet on the exterior. The result was a windowless burial aisle with thinner north and east walls than the original chancel, though the original thickness is still evident in exposed

---

62 Cowan, 1967, 46.

footings. The work on the nave resulted from the construction of a large new rectangular parish church with seating for 1,200 souls in 1788–9.[63] This was largely to the west of the medieval building, but the limited area of land available appears to have necessitated the demolition of the western part of the nave, and it was reduced to an approximately square plan with a thin new west wall pierced by a central doorway. What remained was used as a burial aisle, with the principal memorial, for the Ferguson of Balmakelly family, against the south wall. Like the chancel, it is windowless, though there is evidence for three windows of various sizes on the south side, and one on the north.

The extensive rebuilding involved in those two operations left a number of architectural details still in place, but made others homeless, and one of the chief difficulties in trying to understand the church lies in deciding which are still in their intended locations and which are not. The most obviously relocated feature is a late medieval arched tomb recess towards the west end of the external face of the nave south wall, into which a number of carved stones have been set. This tomb was presumably originally within the church. A number of post-medieval memorials have been re-set in the external face of the nave north wall, while a heraldic stone has been set into the inner face of the east chancel wall. In addition to these, two medieval liturgical fixtures in the nave appear unlikely to be in their original locations. In the north wall is an arched aumbry with an encircled cross carved in the tympanum formed above a sub-arch, which appears likely to be a re-located Sacrament House. A fluted basin set within a crudely formed recess in the north jamb of the chancel arch is presumably a re-sited piscina from the chancel, or a holy water stoup from one of the entrance doorways.

But the most fascinating evidence is that associated with the chancel arch, much of which appears to relate to the rood screen and loft.[64] The chancel arch itself is a relatively small round-headed opening with chamfered arrises, and within it are slots which presumably accommodated the framing for door leaves. To its south, and best seen from within the chancel, is a blocked high level doorway, which must have given access to the rood loft; below this is a narrow mass of masonry which could have supported the stair to the doorway. Further evidence for the arrangements associated with the screen are to be seen in the south wall of the nave. A trifoliate-headed piscina presumably served one of the nave altars below the loft, while a small low-set square window that is now blocked but is externally visible would have lit this area.

Despite being so extensively modified and rebuilt, on the basis of the evidence embodied within the fabric it can be seen that enough survives at Deer to demonstrate that even a relatively small rural church might once have

63 The west gable has a tablet with the date 1789. The building history is briefly summarised in Elphinstone 1989, 15–20. 64 The evidence for this was first noted by MacGibbon and Ross, 1896, ii, 278–281.

been well equipped with liturgical fixtures and furnishings to enhance the setting of worship within it. Since they all date from the later Middle Ages, however, they cast no light on the length of time this site has been associated with worship.

REFERENCES

Allen, J. Romily, and Joseph Anderson (1903), *The early Christian monuments of Scotland*, Edinburgh.

Anon. (1940), *Proceedings of the Society of Antiquaries of Scotland* 74 (1939–40), 148.

Canivez, Joseph Marie (ed.), (1933), *Statuta Capitulorum Generalium Ordinis Cisterciensis*, vol. 1, Louvain (8 vols, 1933–41).

Stevenson, Joseph (ed.) (1835) *Chronica de Mailros* (Bannatyne Club), Edinburgh.

Cowan, Ian B. (1967) *The parishes of medieval Scotland* (Scottish Record Society 93), Edinburgh.

—— (1982) *The Scottish Reformation*, London.

—— and David E. Easson (1976), *Medieval religious houses Scotland*, London and New York (2nd ed.).

Cruden, George (1795) 'Parish of Deer', *The statistical account of Scotland*, vol. 16, John Sinclair, Edinburgh, 469–83.

Dilworth, Mark (1986) 'The commendator system in Scotland', *Innes Review* 37, 51–72 .

—— (1995) *Scottish monasteries in the late Middle Ages*, Edinburgh.

Dunbar, John G. (1999) *Scottish royal palaces*, East Linton.

Duncan, A.A.M. (ed.) (1988) *Regesta Regum Scottorum, v (Acts of Robert I)*, Edinburgh.

Dunn, John (ed.), (1844) *A short abridgement of Britane's Distemper, by Patrick Gordon of Ruthven* (Spalding Club), Aberdeen.

Durkan, John (1990) 'Education: the laying of fresh foundations', in *Humanism in Renaissance Scotland*, ed. John MacQueen, Edinburgh, 123–60.

Elphinstone, Kathleen (1989) *Deer parish church 200 years on, 1789–1989*, Peterhead.

Fawcett, Richard (1995) *Inchmahome priory* (official guidebook), (rev. ed.), Edinburgh.

—— (2004) 'Culross abbey', in *Perspectives for an architecture of solitude*, ed. Terryl N. Kinder, Turnhout, 81–99.

—— and Richard Oram (2004), *Melrose abbey*, Stroud.

Gilyard-Beer, Roy (1958) *Abbeys*, London.

Grove, Doreen (1996) *Glenluce abbey* (official guidebook), Edinburgh.

Harvey, Barbara (1993) *Living and dying in England*, Oxford.

Keith, G.S. (1811) *A general view of the agriculture of Aberdeenshire*, Aberdeen.

Kirk, James (1995) *The Books of Assumption of the Thirds of Benefices*, Oxford.

Macfarlane, Leslie, J. (1985) *William Elphinstone and the kingdom of Scotland 1431–1514*, Aberdeen.

MacGibbon, David, and Thomas Ross (1896) *The ecclesiastical architecture of Scotland*, 3 vols, Edinburgh.

Morison, John (1845) 'Parish of Old Deer', in *The new statistical account of Scotland*, vol. 12, Edinburgh and London, 138–65.

RMS *Registrum Magni Sigilli Regum Scotorum (The Register of the Great Seal of Scotland)*, ed. John Maitland Thomson et al. (1882–1914, 10 vols), Edinburgh.

Robertson, Joseph (ed.), (1862) *Illustrations of the topography and antiquities of the shires of Aberdeen and Banff*, vol. iv (3 vols numbered ii–iv, 1847–62), (Spalding Club), Aberdeen.

Royal Commission on the Ancient and Historical Monuments of Scotland (1963) *Stirlingshire: an inventory of the ancient monuments*, Edinburgh.

—— (1933) *Eleventh Report, with an inventory of monuments and constructions in the counties of Fife, Kinross and Clackmannan*, Edinburgh.

RRS, v *Regesta Regum Scottorum, v (Acts of Robert I)*, ed. A.A.M. Duncan, 1988, Edinburgh.

Simpson, W. Douglas (1927) 'The Celtic monastery and Cistercian abbey at Deer', *Transactions of the Scottish Ecclesiological Society* 8, 179–86.

Smith, Alexander (1875) *A new history of Aberdeenshire*, Aberdeen, 2 vols.

Stones, J.A. (1986) 'Abbey of Deer', *Discovery and Excavation Scotland, 1986*, 10.

Stuart, John (ed.) (1869) *The Book of Deer* (Spalding Club), Edinburgh.

—— (ed.) (1872) *Records of the monastery of Kinloss* (Society of Antiquaries of Scotland), Edinburgh.

Tabraham, C.J. (1984) 'Excavations at Kelso abbey', *Proceedings of the Society of Antiquaries of Scotland* 114, 399–401.

Tait, A.A. (1983) 'The landscape garden and neoclassicism', *Journal of Garden History* 3, 322–331.

Theiner, Augustin (ed.) (1864) *Vetera Monumenta Hibernorum et Scotorum Historiam Illustrantia*, Rome.

Watt, D.E.R. and N.F. Shead (2001) *The heads of religious houses in Scotland from twelfth to sixteenth centuries* (Scottish Record Society, new ser. 24), Edinburgh.

Young, Alan (1997), *Robert the Bruce's rivals: the Comyns, 1212–1314*, East Linton.

UNPUBLISHED SOURCES

British Library, Cotton MS Vespasian A VI fo. 59v.

National Archives of Scotland file MW/1/1044 (SC 22512/2B);

National Library of Scotland, Adv. MS 30.5.22 7f.

Deer and its abbots in the late Middle Ages

MARK DILWORTH OSB †

According to the main reference work on Scottish medieval monasticism, the history of Deer abbey is obscure until the sixteenth century, and indeed no cartulary has survived.[1] Roman records, however, provide a complete picture of ruling abbots from the early fifteenth century. Deer had been founded from Kinloss, which also lay in the North-East, and the Cistercian system of filiation gave the Kinloss abbot constitutional and disciplinary powers in such matters as visitations and abbatial elections. In the fourteenth and fifteenth centuries, however, Rome was extending its powers of provision by increasingly reserving appointments to monastic prelacies to itself. The documents reveal the erosion of the traditional Cistercian arrangements for appointing new abbots as Roman provision took over. Since an abbot was a powerful feudal lord, monastic prelacies became the target of careerist monks and of local magnates. Roman reservation and provision was a means of dealing with disputes between rival claimants but also opened a channel for candidates to pursue their ambitions, until eventually the Scottish crown and the papacy took control of monastic prelacies between them.[2]

In the following list of abbots, the documents are allowed to speak for themselves and comment will be made later. Acceptance at Rome of a resignation was usually simultaneous with provision (or mandate to provide) of the successor. Payment or promise of payment of the Roman tax for provision is not mentioned unless it adds relevant information, but confirmation from Scottish sources is added. Names are given as in the standard work on Scottish surnames[3] and comment will not normally be made on their mutilation in Roman documents. It should be noted that illegitimate birth was a bar to holding a benefice, secular or monastic, and required a dispensation from Rome. Unless this had already been obtained, an illegitimate person, like any other ineligible person, could not be elected but only postulated, and approval by higher authority was needed.

Thomas died *c*.1416

Robert Crockatt, monk of Deer, was elected by the community after Thomas's death, the election was confirmed by the father abbot (that is, the abbot of Kinloss) and he received the abbatial blessing. Robert is recorded as

---

1 Cowan and Easson 1976, 74.   2 Dilworth 1995, 12–25.   3 Black 1946.

abbot in May 1418. On 22 May 1419, after about three years of rule, Rome granted his petition to have the election proceedings ratified and himself to be provided anew. He died before 10 February 1423.[4]

Andrew de Tyrie, monk of Deer, after Crockatt's death was elected by the community *via Spiritus Sancti,* that is, by acclamation or acceptance without dissent. The election was confirmed by the father abbot and he received abbatial blessing. On 10 April 1424 Rome granted his petition to have the election proceedings ratified and himself to be provided anew despite the previous papal provision of William Bell (on 10 February 1423). Bell's provision was declared null because he did not get the apostolic letters despatched in time, Tyrie's election was also declared null, and a mandate was issued on 13 April to provide Tyrie if he was judged suitable and Deer was in fact vacant. Tyrie was provided on 24 May; he resigned as abbot to the father abbot before 25 May 1429.[5]

Arthur Callan, monk of Kinloss, born of unmarried parents, was unanimously postulated by the Deer community after Tyrie's resignation. The community petitioned Rome for his provision and on 25 May 1429 a mandate was issued to provide him if found suitable, with a dispensation for defect of birth. He is recorded in a Kinloss source as a monk of Kinloss elected abbot of Deer.[6] There was also a rival candidate, David Cran, monk of Deer, who had transferred to the Valliscaulian order on becoming prior of Pluscarden. After ruling for a year or more, he had resigned by March 1428 and in June 1430 petitioned Rome for transfer back to Deer. Three weeks later, on 4–5 July, he petitioned for technical amendments in the letters of his provision to Deer.[7] Neither his petition for this provision nor the mandate for it have survived. It should be noted that only successful petitions were recorded.

Callan in December 1432 petitioned to be provided anew to Deer, on the grounds of a possible defect in the original provision. Another rival now emerged. Andrew Symson, a Deer monk had petitioned in 1428 after Cran's resignation to be transferred to the Valliscaulian order and provided to Pluscarden, then in April 1431 had petitioned to be provided anew as he feared a possible defect in the original provision.[8] Towards the end of 1435 he attempted to displace Callan at Deer, claiming in a petition to Rome that seven years previously the latter had been provided by the father abbot despite having no dispensation for the defect of illegitimacy. Symson's petition to

4 *CSSR* I, 52–3; *A.B.Ill.,* ii, 379; Brady 1876–7, I, 172.   5 *CSSR* II, xviii, 60–1; III, 19–20; Brady 1876–7, I, 172; *CPL* VII, 346–7; VIII, 114.   6 *CSSR* III, 19–20; *CPL* VII, 114: Ferrerius *Historia*, 30. The name Callan has been chosen as it is the one in Black 1946 most similar to forms for this man found in Roman documents, one of which gave him the latin form *de Calamo.*   7 *CSSR* II, 194; III, 107–8, 116–17.   8 *CSSR* III, 268. For Symson at Pluscarden see *CSSR* II, 194, 201, 211; III, 174.

replace him was granted, as was that of a Cistercian monk of Melrose to succeed Symson at Pluscarden. A mandate was issued to the bishop of Moray and the abbot of Kinross to provide Symson if found suitable and remove Callan, who was preventing justice being done to him.[9] Symson promised to pay his tax for the provision but the mandatories must have decided against him, for Callan remained abbot until his death some time before 12 June 1439.[10]

Nicholas de Forres monk of Deer, was unanimously elected after Callan's death and had the election confirmed by ordinary authority, that is by the father abbot. Doubting if this held good, he petitioned Rome and on 12 June 1439 a mandate was issued to confirm the election proceedings if they were lawful and provide him if Deer was in fact vacant. In March 1441 Patrick Maider, Cistercian monk of Newbattle, elect and *provisus* of Deer, was at the Council of Basle, presumably seeking its confirmation of himself as abbot. Forres, however, though he delayed paying his tax, ruled until on 19 May 1457 his resignation to the Holy See, which *ipso facto* reserved subsequent provision to the pope, was accepted and he was granted a pension of one third of the Deer revenues.[11]

William Eviot, monk of Deer, born of unmarried parents, petitioned Rome for provision on Forres's resignation. He had recently transferred from the Valliscaulian order by apostolic authority. On 19 May 1457 the petition was granted and a mandate was given to provide him, with a dispensation for defect of birth. William, termed elect of Deer (which should signify that he had not been blessed as abbot), promised to pay his tax on 8 February 1458 and as abbot paid it in September.[12]

On 6 March 1458, however, Dene David Bane, abbot of Deer, was chosen in parliament to sit as a lord of session in Aberdeen and act as visitor with the remit of reforming hospitals funded by the king. He petitioned Rome claiming that Thomas Livingston, acting on authority from Cîteaux, had deposed Forres and provided him (Bane), but Eviot, even after resigning publicly, was thwarting him. Rome issued a mandate in June 1458 to summon Eviot and decide the case. Two years later an agreement had been reached: Eviot would retain the abbacy, while Bane would receive a pension for life or until his provision to a Cistercian abbey. Rome issued a mandate in August 1460 to

---

9 *CSSR* IV, no. 222; *CPL* VIII, 543–4, 568.   10 *ACSB* 19; *CPL* IX, 47. Arthur is recorded as abbot of Deer on 27 June 1439 (NAS, GD 124/1/145); this document is not the original but a copy in a later hand. Symson continued with his claims on Pluscarden (*CPL* VIII, 609; *CSSR* IV, nos. 300–1, 554).   11 *CPL* IX, 47; XI, 3222; *CSSR* V, no. 637; *ACSB*, 41–2; Burns 1962, 69. For the name Maider or Mador see Black, 1946, 574.   12 *CSSR* V, no. 637; *CPL* XI, 322; *ACSB*, 47–8; Brady 1876–7, I, 173. For the name Eviot, common at the time, see Black 1946, 248–9.

confirm the agreement if it was lawful and to make it effective.[13] William is recorded as abbot in April 1460 witnessing a charter at Deer, and also between 1463 and 1472.[14] He was abbot until his death before 16 May 1483.

James Pittendrich, monk of Deer, was provided as abbot on 16 May 1483.[15] James is recorded as abbot in 1487 and 1499–1501. Nicholas Philips(?), a Deer monk, accused him to Rome of wrongdoing and a mandate was issued in April 1505 to summon Pittendrich, remove him if the accusations were true and provide Philips in his place if considered suitable.[16] Pittendrich remained, however, and in September 1507 the king granted the lands of Over and Nether Pittendrich in Banffshire, which James had resigned, to his brother Andrew but with the abbot keeping the freehold. This was a personal and not a community transaction. His resignation was accepted by Rome on 15 April 1510. He retained half the abbatial revenues and was still alive in April 1518.[17] John Innes, monk of Deer, was nominated to Rome by King James IV on 24 December 1509 for provision when Pittendrich would resign. The provision in consistory took place on 15 April 1510. He remained abbot until 1543.[18]

These records make it possible to follow the pattern of Roman provision. No recourse from Deer to the pope in Rome or Avignon is recorded before 1419, when the abbot, elected by the community and continued in office by the father abbot according to traditional Cistercian practice, sought Roman provision, but only after three years of rule. The next three successful candidates were all elected (or postulated) in the traditional way before recourse was had to Rome. Previous monastic election was in fact acceptable to Rome, as long as it was ratified afterwards by papal provision; only in Tyrie's case was it declared null in order to allow a legal solution. A change is noticeable from 1457, but the situation at that juncture was complex, for the outgoing abbot, deposed by Cistercian authority, tendered his resignation to the holy see, which reserved to Rome the appointment of his successor. We do not know what support either candidate had from the Deer community or whether any form of abbatial election had been held. Rome appointed mandatories to judge the case. From 1483 provision was made direct and not

13 *CPL* XI, 344, 585; NAS, RH 2/6/5. fo 354; *APS* II, 47, 49. For Livingston, a Scottish Cistercian bishop, see Burns 1962, 12–13.   14 *Lords of the Isles Acts*, 105–7; NAS, GD 1/38/1; National Register of Archives (Scotland), 3094, Bundle 1/28, 67. I am indebted to the NLS Online facility, which provided these references.   15 *CPL* XIII, 826; *ACSB*, 80–1.   16 *RMS* II, no. 1698; *A.B.Ill.* II, 428–30. The accusation of 1505 is in *CPL* XVII, no. 782 and NAS, RH 2/6/3. fo. 110, where the name is transcribed as *Flaigi* and *Plirpi* respectively; the index of the *CPL* volume gives it as Philips.   17 *RMS* II, no. 3130; *James IV Letters*, no. 305; Brady 1876–7, III, 481; Public Record Office, Transcripts, 31/9/31, fo. 206; *A.B.Ill.* IV, 550.   18 *James IV Letters*, nos. 284–5, 305; Brady, 1876–7, III, 481.

through mandatories authorised to provide, and in 1509–10 the result of an agreement in 1487 between pope and king is seen, the king having the right to nominate and the pope then providing his nominee.

All the candidates, successful or otherwise, were Cistercian monks. In fact all the successful ones, apart from Callan, were monks of Deer itself, though Eviot had recently transferred from the Valliscaulian order, perhaps in order to become abbot. William Bell is fairly certainly the monk of Coupar Angus who is recorded there in 1418 and petitioned in 1425 for a dispensation from defect of birth. Both the premature provision in 1423 and the petition of 1425 describe him as a bachelor of decree.[19] In the competition for promotion, a degree and noble birth were assets, while illegitimacy, even when dispensed, was a disadvantage. Patrick Maider, after a distinguished academic career, was elected abbot of Newbattle in 1461.[20] There can be little doubt about David Bane, the formidable candidate in 1458–60: he was the Coupar Angus monk, bachelor of theology, who was abbot there 1461–80 and was made visitor of the order in Scotland.[21]

Valliscaulians were considered to be akin to Cistercians in their life and ethos, making transfer between the two orders easier. Two candidates, Cran and Symson, originally monks of Deer, had been appointed priors of Pluscarden, thus becoming Valliscaulians, then had transferred back to Deer, no doubt to be more eligible for appointment as its abbot. Being prior of Pluscarden was seemingly looked on as a rung on the ladder leading to the abbacy at Deer. One can comment that such ambition was completely alien to the Rule of St Benedict. The concern of monastic superiors to have their documents of provision completely accurate is abundantly clear, for errors gave a rival a loophole for impugning the provision and petitioning for his own. Successful candidates naturally paid their tax to the apostolic camera, though Forres delayed paying the full amount, and Symson too was apparently confident of success, for he promised to pay his tax. The abbatial vacancy of 1457 was expensive for the abbey, for in addition to Eviot's tax a pension had to be paid to the outgoing abbot and a pension and expenses to the unsuccessful candidate.

Comparison can be made between Deer and other Scottish monasteries. It is striking that all abbots up to and including Innes were monks of Deer, except of course for the Kinloss monk postulated by the Deer community. In this Deer differed from various other monasteries, where monks of other houses and even other orders secured the abbacy. In other monasteries too, it became gradually more common for a secular cleric to be provided, with the obligation of taking the habit and vows, though sometimes with a period of grace as a temporary commendator before doing so. Also, there is only one

---

19 *Coupar Angus Chrs.*, ii, 12: CSSR II, 80; Brady 1876–7, III, 481. 20 Burns, 1962, 69, CSSR V, no. 876. 21 *Coupar Angus Chrs.*, ii, 273–4; Ferrerius, *Historia*, 31.

recorded case at Deer of a claimant petitioning for the current abbot to be deposed for various kinds of wrongdoing and himself to be provided, and that was not until 1505, though it had been fairly common in the mid-fifteenth century. Unlike many other monasteries, Deer was not given any perpetual commendator, that is, a non-monk put in for life and enjoying full abbatial powers though never becoming a monk. This happened increasingly elsewhere, especially after Flodden. Similarly there is no evidence of nobles or local gentry seeking the provision of one of their own family to Deer. All this, however, was to change after 1543.

The year 1543 marked a very great change in the affairs of Deer, in that its superiors from then on were of a completely different type. For this period, too, the information is much more plentiful. In January 1543, after Innes had ruled for almost 33 years; presentation was directed under the privy seal to the pope of Robert Keith, brother of the fourth Earl Marischal, as Innes's successor when he would cease to be abbot. There was, it would seem, some confusion and ignorance of procedure for nominating to Rome. Innes's resignation was accepted by Rome on 2 May, the crown nominated Keith to Rome on the 3rd as Innes was shortly going to resign, and on the 4th crown protection was given to Innes for life.[22] On 24 June 1543 Rome provided Keith as commendator for a year and a day.[23] The crown was not satisfied and in February 1544 insisted on the commend being given in the terms of the nomination, that is, for life. Innes died at this time and Keith received the commend for life on 11 May 1544.[24] Whatever the reason, this apparently did not take effect in Scotland. In June the crown gifted the temporalities of Deer, which were in the queen's hands through Innes's death, to Keith and ordered a further letter to Rome on his behalf. He was still termed postulate (not being a Cistercian monk) of Deer in July. A year later the temporalities were gifted to a royal official until Rome should provide an abbot.[25] Then, on 9 July 1546, the bishop of Cesena made Keith's provision known. A few days later Keith promised payment of his Roman tax, in August he set about taking possession and in September the crown issued a precept for his admission to Deer.[26] It had taken three and a half years for Keith to gain full legal possession of Deer.

There are two possible, if partial explanations for the delay. Rome tended to respond less readily to the Scottish crown when the latter was in a weak position, as it certainly was in early 1543, with the queen only a few months

---

22 *RSS* III, nos. 46, 276; Cowan and Easson 1976, 74; *ERS* II, 156. For Keith's family see Paul 1904–14, VI, 43–50.   **23** National Library of Scotland [hereafter NLS], Ch 17125. This document, from the muniments of the Earls Marischal, is an instrument issued by the bishop of Cesena on 9 July 1546 making known Keith's provisions as a temporary and later a perpetual commendator. It is the source cited in Paul 1904–14, VI, 43 n. 8. My thanks are due to the Library staff for help with this diverse collection.   **24** *ERS* II, 235–6; NLS, Ch. 17124; Cowan and Easson 1976, 74.   **25** *RSS* III, nos. 830, 1290; *A.B.Ill.* II, 430–1. **26** NLS, Ch. 17125–6; Brady, 1876–7, I, 173; *RSS* III, no. 1917.

old and Arran in his first months as governor. There is also circumstantial evidence that the monks elected one of themselves as abbot, as had happened in other Scottish Cistercian monasteries. One manuscript, of uncertain value, says that Michael Pittendrich, who is recorded as a monk of Deer holding the office of warden in 1539, resigned the abbacy c.1542, and certainly on 23 March 1545 (1546 if the Scottish dating was used) the crown wrote to Rome on Pittendrich 's behalf, since the new commendator was trying to have his pension rescinded.[27] Giving a pension was the usual way of compensating an unsuccessful candidate.

Keith was said in the bull of June 1544 to be in or around his 23rd year and the crown documents in 1543 termed him Maister or Magister, denoting a graduate. This and his birth c.1522 make very possible his identification with the Robert Keith, parson of Keith (*rector de eodem*) and of the nation of Angus (north-east Scotland), who matriculated at St Andrews in 1539–40 and determined in 1540–1.[28] Nothing memorable is recorded of his fairly brief tenure of the abbacy. He attended the provincial church council of 1549 and at some point, perhaps before his promotion to Deer, he fathered an illegitimate son, the future Lord Dingwall.[29] Keith died in Paris on 25 April 1552, in the ninth year of his prelacy, and was buried in front of St Ninian's altar in the Carmelite church in Paris.[30] There is no indication of his purpose in Paris, but it is hardly likely to have been study.

Deer was experiencing what happened at other monasteries too, with a local landed or titled family tightening its grip on the abbacy. It had become increasingly common for an abbot to resign in favour of a younger kinsman (resignation *in favorem*), though sometimes retaining all authority and revenues (resignation *cum retentione*), which effectively made a kinsman heir to the abbacy. In early 1550 Keith had resigned in this way in favour of his nephew, also called Robert, son of the fourth earl.[31] No abbot or commendator of Deer, however, was ever made an important royal official, nor was Deer ever bestowed on a royal official either to give him status and income or as a reward for services rendered. No doubt Deer was spared this by being more remote from centres of government than some other abbeys.[32]

---

27 NAS, GD 86/122; *A.B.Ill.* IV, 552; II, 421; *ERS* II, 245. Some uncertainty has to remain as to the year of *ERS* II, 235–6 (see n. 21), 245, as Roman dating could perhaps have been used in correspondence with Rome. **28** *Early Recs Univ. St A.*, 142, 244; *Acta Fac. Art. Univ. S. And.*, 392. **29** *Scot. Church Stats*, 86; Paul 1904–14, III, 115–6. **30** *A.B.Ill.* IV, 19; Dempster *Historia*, no. 784; *Pap. Neg. Mary*, 415, Ep. 12. The date given in Pollen (1901) is preferred, as it comes from a letter written just a month later by Giovanni Ferrerio, the Pedmontese scholar who had taught at Kinloss. Also the date in Dempster is before Keith's ninth year as prelate began on 24 June 1551. **31** Vatican Archives, Resignationes, Series A. I am indebted for this reference to the editors of the lists of heads of monastic houses being compiled by the Conference of Scottish Medievalists. These lists will give further details on abbots of Deer from unpublished Vatican sources. **32** For the monastic background at this period in these areas mentioned, see Dilworth,

Robert Keith II was provided as perpetual commendator on 19 October 1552 at the age of fifteen.[33] He was in Paris from at least February 1554 to May 1556, as we know because during this time he signed documents there, which were then taken to Deer to be signed by the community also. Almost certainly he was pursuing studies suitable for his future role as a prelate, and the condition expressed in these documents of the grantee preserving the 'orthodox or catholic faith' would seem to indicate his personal conviction. Having returned to Scotland, he attended parliament in 1558 and was elected a lord of articles, and in August 1560 he took part in the reformation parliament.[34]

During the 1560s he played a part in public affairs, in effect as a layman, though he did so in virtue of being a spiritual lord in his capacity of commendator of Deer. In 1565 he was a privy councillor and took his father's place as a leader of an army gathered to pursue rebels.[35] He married in 1566 and in 1569–70 accepted the infant James VI, and not the exiled Catholic Queen Mary, as sole ruler of Scotland.[36] He was in effect a Protestant, though not always on good terms with the Protestant church authorities. The general assembly of 1569 refused his request to be freed from the obligation to support ministers in his lands, particularly as he had 'debursed his money to the enemies of God, to persecute his servants and banish them out of the realme'. An English report in 1570 listed him as a Protestant lord.[37] From about 1574 he attended privy council meetings fairly regularly and was clearly more acceptable to the Kirk, for in 1582–3 he was one of the 'faithfull brethren' appointed to deal strictly with persons in the north suspected of 'papistrie' and was appointed jointly by a crown commission and the general assembly as visitor of the college in Aberdeen.[38] A few years later, in 1587, Robert Keith's career as commendator ended when the monastery as a legal corporate institution came to an end, though he lived on until the mid-1590s. Information on the monastic community of Deer is not plentiful. There were 16 monks in 1539, after which their number declined slightly. In late 1557, 12 monks were resident, of whom no fewer than eight are first recorded in the 1550s, indicating that it was on the whole a young community. No later documents signed by the community as a whole have survived, though professed monks had the right, upheld by civil law after 1560, to retain their monastic quarters and so-called 'portions' or means of support. Documents

1995, 18–19, 21, 53–4. **33** Cowan and Easson 1976, 74; *A.B.Ill.* IV, 19. His career is outlined in Paul 1904–14, I, 156–9. The statement that he was 58 in 1587 (*A.B.Ill.* II, 423), cannot be correct. That would make his birth c. 1529, but he was the second legitimate son and his father was still under curators in 1530 when his marriage contract was made (Paul 1904–14, VI, 47). **34** *APS* II, 503, 525; *Diurnal Rem. Occ.* 61, 279. Detailed references for Keith and Deer in Dilworth 1997, 155–6 will not be repeated; other references are additional. [Editor: See also, Dilworth 2003]. **35** *RPC* I, 341, 379. **36** *CSP Scot.* III, 166; *RPC* I, 654. **37** *Booke Universall Kirk*, I, 153, 155; *CSP Scot.* III, 459. **38** *RPC* II, III passim; *Booke Universall Kirk*, II, 570, 624; *RSS* VIII, no 2254.

signed by the monks reveal that Deer had a prior as well as a subprior, though in many monasteries it was only a subprior who was second in command. Three monks served in the reformed Kirk as ministers, all of them in parishes not very far from Deer. One of them, Gilbert Chisholm, an older man who had been prior in the 1550s, served until 1585; the other two, first recorded in 1554, served until 1607 and 1611 respectively. In fact Deer made a greater contribution to the reformed Kirk in this regard than any other Cistercian monastery.[39] The role played by Robert Keith in this is not known.

Scottish Cistercian monasteries in the sixteenth century had a certain cohesion among themselves and the Cistercian system of filiation still operated. Kinloss, Deer's mother-house, had two reforming abbots, Thomas Crystal (1500–28) and Robert Reid (1528–53). Crystal took steps to improve monastic ceremonial—it is not clear what *ceremoniis* in Ferrerio's account refers to—at its two daughter-houses, Culross and Deer, and when a dispute arose between Kinloss and Deer over the teinds at Ellon, a church appropriated to Kinloss, the other Cistercian abbots met in Edinburgh to decide the matter. The annual general chapter at Cîteaux included Scotland in its deliberations, sometimes appointing a Scots abbot as visitor for the country and sometimes sending a visitor from France.

In the long-drawn-out visitations and negotiations in the 1530s, aimed at restoring Cistercian ideals of monastic poverty, the French abbot-visitor did not get as far north as Deer but sent comprehensive instructions for observance there. In 1537 Robert Reid, as father abbot, and Walter Malin, abbot of Glenluce and commissary of general chapter appointed to implement the visitor's instructions, visited Deer, where the abbot and community accepted their regulations. Five years later, in 1542, some modifications were made in these with the consent of Reid and Malin.[40] It seems most likely, however, that such supervision from outside became less practicable when Deer had the two non-Cistercian Keiths as superiors.

Most parish churches in Scotland were appropriated to a variety of institutions, monasteries included; the institution was technically the parson (*rector*) and received the major part of the revenues, paying a sum to a vicar to provide pastoral services. Four parishes in the North-East were appropriated to Deer abbey in this way, one of which, Deer itself, provided a yearly sum to fund a prebend in Aberdeen cathedral, though abbots of Deer did not hold this prebend themselves.[41] The two Keiths, however, did hold the prebend funded by the church of Philorth (now Fraserburgh). Robert Keith I was parson of Philorth in September 1550, Robert Keith II was provided in his place in December 1551 and was collated in June 1553. In 1570–71 the latter was in arrears with his one-third tax of Deer abbey, Philorth parsonage and

39 Dilworth, 1995, 144–5, 155–6, 163–4; *A.B.Ill.* II, 430–1. **40** Dilworth 1994.
41 Cowan 1967, 46, 215; Cowan 1995, 93, 117–8; *RSS* VII, no. 883.

the vicarages of three appropriated parishes, though Gilbert Chisholm (see above) in 1567 was receiving a stipend as a minister from two of them. Keith was still in default in 1580.[42] Then as now, professing adherence to a Church did not always induce prompt payment of one's dues.

The land holdings of Deer were large enough to form a barony, though there is no indication that it had the privileges of a regality nor of who was the lay bailie. In many other monasteries it was a local magnate who held this position for generations, sometimes with a kinsman holding the abbacy itself. As regards its revenues, Deer lay in the middle range of Scottish monasteries, with an estimated annual income of £2300 Scots, less than half that of some wealthy houses but more than twice that of some of the poorer ones.[43] Finally, one item of information highlights how little we know about Deer abbey, even in the sixteenth century. In 1524 a Dutchman from Amsterdam raised an action before the lords of council to oblige the abbot to deliver a ship and certain goods.[44] Nothing else known about Abbot John Innes throws any light on the context of this.

In 1587 Deer abbey ceased to exist in civil law. When Keith's father, the fourth earl, died in 1581, it was his grandson, Keith's nephew, who succeeded as fifth earl for Keith's elder brother had predeceased his father. A royal charter in July 1587, declaring that most of Deer's lands had been granted by the Earls Marischal and much was now held in feu by the present earl, erected the lands into the lordship of Altrie, granting the liferent to Robert Keith and possession after his death to the Earls Marischal.[45] Other titled families in Scotland were likewise the ultimate possessors of monastic property which a kinsman as commendator had feued to them, but there was perhaps no other case of the incumbent commendator being granted only the liferent. After the death of Robert Keith, Lord Altrie in the mid-1590s, Deer was completely merged into the holdings of the Earls Marischal though the monastic church remained in use as the Protestant parish kirk until the late eighteenth century.[46]

ACKNOWLEDGMENTS

The editor is most grateful to the abbot president of the English Benedictine Congregation for his consent to the posthumous publication of Dr Dilworth's paper. Also to Gilbert Márkus for his assistance in this matter and to Carol Smith for re-typing the text.

42 NLS, Ch.17129, 17132; MS 21114, nos. 51, 190, 445; *Acc. Coll. Thirds Ben.*, 221, 225.
43 Dilworth 1995, 42, 46–8; Cowan and Easson 1976, 72. For the monastic 'economy' (portions, appropriations, bailies), see Dilworth 1995, 43–4, 46–7, 78.   44 *Acts LCPA*, 207.
45 *RMS* V, no 1309. Original documents are in NLS, Ch 17167 ff (MS21114, nos 85–90); transcripts in *A.B.Ill.* II, 556–9; IV, 437–9. That the fourth earl held much former Deer property can be seen in *Books Assump. Thirds Ben.*, 457.   46 Dilworth 1995, 77–8, 84–5.

BIBLIOGRAPHY

Unpublished Sources

National Register of Archives (Scotland)
    NAS, GD 1/38/1
    NAS, 3094, Bundle 1/28, 67
    NAS, RH 2/6/3. fo. 110
    NAS, GD 86/122

Public Record Office
    PRO, Transcripts, 31/9/31, fo. 206;
Vatican Archives
    Resignationes, Series A

National Library of Scotland [NLS]
    NLS, Ch. 17124
    NLS, Ch. 17125
    NLS, Ch. 17126
    NLS, Ch. 17129
    NLS, Ch. 17132
    NLS, Ch. 17167 ff (MS 21114, nos. 51, 85–90 190, 445)

PRIMARY SOURCES

A.B.Ill. — Robertson, J. (1847–69) *Illustrations of the topography and antiquities of the shires of Aberdeen and Banff* (Spalding Club), 3 vols (numbered ii–iv), Aberdeen.

Acc. coll. Thirds Ben. — Donaldson, G. (ed.), (1949) *Accounts of the collectors of the Thirds of Benefices 1561–1572* (Scot. Hist. Soc.), Edinburgh.

ACSB — *The Apostolic Camera and Scottish benefices 1418–1488*, ed. A.I. Cameron (1934) (St Andrews University Publications, 35), Oxford.

Acta Fac. Arts. Univ. S. A. — Dunlop, A. I. (ed.), (1964) *Acta Facultatis Artium Universitatis Sanctiandree 1413–1588* (Scot. Hist. Soc., 3rd ser. vols 54–5), Edinburgh.

Acts LCPA — Hannay, R.K. (ed.), (1932) *Acts of the Lords of Council in Public Affairs 1501–1554*, Edinburgh.

APS — *The Acts of the Parliaments of Scotland*, ed. T. Thomson and C. Innes (1814–75), Edinburgh.

Booke Universall Kirk — Thomson, T. (ed.), (1839–45) *The Booke of the Universall Kirk: Acts and Proceedings of the General Assemblies of the Kirk of Scotland* (Bannatyne Club, 4 vols), Edinburgh.

Books Assump. Thirds Ben. — Kirk, J. (ed.), (1995) *The Books of Assumption of the Thirds of Benefices*, Oxford.

Coupar Angus Chrs. — Easson, D.E. (ed.), (1947) *Charters of the abbey of Coupar Angus,*

CPL — *Calendar of entries in the papal registers relating to Great Britain and Ireland: papal Letters*, ed. W.H. Bliss et al. (1893–), London.

CSP Scot. — *Calendar of the State papers relating to Scotland and Mary, Queen of Scots 1547–1603*, ed. J. Bain et al. (1898–1969), Edinburgh.

CSSR — *Calendar of Scottish supplications to Rome*, ed. E.R. Lindsay et al. (1934–97) (Scot. Hist. Soc.), Edinburgh.

Dempster *Historia* — *Thomae Dempsteri Historia Ecclesiastica Gentis Scotorum*, ed. D. Irving (Bannatyne Club, 21, 1829), Edinburgh.

Diurnal Rem. Occ.	Scott, A.G. (ed.), (1833) *A Diurnal of Remarkable Occurents* (Bannatyne Club), Edinburgh.
Early Recs Univ. St. A.	Anderson, J.M. (ed.), (1926), *Early records of the University of St Andrews* (Scot. Hist. Soc., 3rd ser. vol. 8) Edinburgh.
ERS	*Epistolae … Regum Scotorum*, ed. T. Ruddiman (1722–4), 2 vols, Edinburgh.
Ferrerius *Historia*	Wilson, W.D. (ed.), (1839), *Ferrerii Historia Abbatum de Kynlos* (Bannatyne Club, 63), Edinburgh.
James IV Letters	Hannay, R.K. and R.L. Mackie (eds) (1953) *The letters of James the Fourth 1505–1513* (Scot. Hist. Soc. 3rd ser. vol. 45), Edinburgh.
Lords of the Isles Acts	Munro, J., and R.W. (1986) *Acts of the Lords of the Isles*, ed. J. and R.W. Munro (Scot. Hist. Soc.)
Pap. Neg. Mary	Pollen, J. H. (1901) *Papal negotiations with Mary Queen of Scots*, ed. J.H. Pollen (Scot. Hist. Soc.), Edinburgh.
RMS	*Registrum Magni Sigilli Regum Scotorum*, ed. J.M. Thomson et al. (1882–1904), Edinburgh.
RPC	*The Register of the Privy Council of Scotland*, ed. J.H. Burton et al. (1877–1898), Edinburgh.
RSS	*Registrum Secreti Sigilli Regum Scotorum*, ed. M. Livingstone and others (1908–), Edinburgh.
Scot. Church Stats	Patrick, D. (ed.) (1907) *Statutes of the Scottish Church* (Scot. Hist. Soc., 54), Edinburgh.

REFERENCES

Black, G.F. (1946) *The surnames of Scotland*, New York.

Brady, W.M. (1876–7) *The episcopal succession in England, Scotland and Ireland 1400–1875*, (3 vols).

Burns, J.H. (1962) *Scottish churchmen and the Council of Basle*, Glasgow.

Cowan, I.B. and D.E. Easson (1976), *Medieval religious houses: Scotland*, London.

Cowan, I.B. (1967) *The parishes of medieval Scotland* (Scottish Record Soc. 93), Edinburgh.

—— (1995) *The medieval church in Scotland*, ed. James Kirk, Edinburgh.

Dilworth, M. (1994) 'Franco-Scottish efforts at monastic reform 1500–1560', *Rec.s Scottish Church History Soc.* 25, pt 2 (1994), 215–20.

—— (1995) *Scottish monasteries in the late Middle Ages*, Edinburgh.

—— (1997) 'Scottish Cistercian monasteries and the Reformation', *Innes Review*, 48, 144–64.

—— (2003) 'Deer abbey's contribution to the Reformed Church', *Innes Review* 54, 216–25.

Paul, J.B. (ed.) (1904–14) *The Scots peerage* (9 vols), Edinburgh.

Index

Aberdeen 142–3, 343, 349
Aberdeen Breviary 363, 375, 378
Aberdour 136–7, 252, 280, 346, 363, 382, 391, 407
Abernethy 400, 402
Abersnithock (Eglismonithoc) 369 (fig. 12.1), 370–2, 385, 412
Aboyne 373, 374, 392, 412
Abriachan 369 (fig. 12.1), 372
achad 133, 283–4, 293, 299
Achad na glerec 136–7, 289, 310–11
Achad toche temni 133, 136–7, 288, 310–11, 330
Aden 288, 294, 301
Adomnán 15, 84–5, 385, *Vita Columbae* 81, 84–87, 201, 365, 381 *Betha Adomnáin* 85
Afforsk 374, 412
Aikie Brae 276
Alcuin of York 88
Aldin alenn 140–1, 310, 329
Altrie (*Alterin*) 134, 136–9, 287 (fig. 9.2), 290–1, 289–91, 299, 301–2, 309–12, 329–31, 352–3, 355
Altrie, temporal lordship 101, 285–6, 443, 472
Ammonian sections 7–8, 11, 13
Anderson, A.O. 282, 339
annointing 72–76, 88
Aubrey, John 100, 102
Auchmachar (*Acchad madchor*) 140–1, 299, 302, 310–11, 338, 414, 287 (fig. 9.2)
Auchnavaird 302

báidid (*bádud*) 133, 332–43 *passim*
baile, bal- 284, 293
Ball domin 140–1, 292, 302, 309, 311, 338
Banchory-Ternan 372, 383, 392, 429
Banff 142–3, 343, 349
Banff, sheriffdom of 277, 425
Barrow, Geoffrey 275, 324
Bede, *mormaer* of Buchan 136–7, 286
Betha Adomnáin 85

Betha Choluim Cille 85
Bethelnie 371, 369 (fig. 12.1)
Biffie (*Bidbin*) 136–9, 253–4, 287 (fig. 9.2), 294, 298–9, 302, 309, 311, 330–1, 356
Black, Ronald xiii, 146–7, 151, 157
Book of Deer *see* Beer, Book of
Book of Deer Project xv
books, depicted on sculpture 415, 433
Borgstrøm, Carl Hj. 182–8, 214
both 362, 376 (fig. 12.2)
boundary markers 398, 405–7, 411–12, 414, 416–17
Bradshaw, Henry 3–4, 99, 103, 104–13
brithem 134, 138–9
Bróiccín 142–3, 339
Brown, Hume 321
Brown, Julian 40
Brown, Michelle 40–2
Bruide mac Bile, king of Picts 85
Bruxie, *see* Altrie
Buchan 142–3, 162;
caput of earldom 279; deanery 279; Gaelic spoken in, 343; name 229–30; parochial structure 275–80, 276 (fig. 9.1); Wasting of 441
Buile Shuibhne 84–5

Caesarius of Arles 74
Cáin Domnaig, 'the Law of Sunday' 79, 87
Cainnech son of the son of Dobarchú 138–9, 290, 292, 330–1, 337–8, 343, 345–7, 351, 355
Cairnbanno 287 (fig. 9.2), 402
Cannech 233–4
Canonum Hibernensis 86
cathair 133–4, 136–7251–2, 346, 391
Cathal son of Morgann 136–9, 289–91, 330–1, 337–8, 349–52, 355
céli Dé 81, 369, 371, 374, 391
Chisholm, Gilbert, prior of Deer 101
church organization 339–40, 342, 390–2
Cistercian order 439–41, 450–1, 453–5, 471
Clanchy, Michael 327–8

Clann Channan 140–1, 292, 337, 348, 351–2, 355, 416
Clann Chinaeda meic Ailpín 326, 356
Clann Custantín meic Cináeda 425–6, 430
Clann Morgann 140–1, 288, 291, 333, 337, 339, 348, 351–2
Clann Ruaidrí 364, 430
clerici de Der 99, 142–3, 328, 330, 345–6, 349, 356, 391, 413
Clerkhill 289–90
cloch 399, 402
Cloch in tiprat 136–7, 281–2, 286, 310–12, 329, 399–401
Cloch pette mc Garnait 136–7, 281–2, 286, 310–12, 329, 399–402, 406
coirthe 294, 309, 311, 398–9, 402
Colbain, mormaer of Buchan 140–1, 223, 332–3, 339–40, 348–9, 413
Collum 228–9
Columban paruchia 426
Comgell son of Cainnech 140–1, 292, 295, 348, 351, 398
'Common Gaelic' 181–97, 241
communion 67, 69–71, 79–80, 89
Corindu 375–7
Cormac, abbot of Turriff 142–3, 339
Cormac son of Cennédig 140–1, 299, 428
Cormac, bishop of Dunkeld 138–9, 142–3, 344, 348
cross-marked stones ('Class IV') 374, 379, 405, 412, 430
Cruden 279
Crux medici 413–6
cuit 133, 231–3, 315–17, 329–31, 349–53
cuitid 227, 231–33
Culi son of Baíthín 138–9, 290, 329, 355

dabach (davoch) 133, 138–41, 293, 297–8, 339–42, 345, 355
Dál Riadic migration paradigm 184–5
dalta 134
David I 138–9, 142–3, 275, 328, 330, 342–3, 345–6, 349, 356
davoch see *dabach*
Deer, Book of, gospel-book
  Anglo-Saxon influence 432, Apostle's Creed 53, 90, art 'imperfections' 49, 62, biblical text 3–29 *passim* 32, 62,
  binding 106, codicology 67, 135, 335, dating 67, decorated initials 8ff), 42, descriptions 104–5, digitization xv, 105, 'discovery' 104, editing 105, figure style 33, 36–7, function 32, 62, 68, geometric decoration 44, 433, intellectual context 7, 13–14, 37, 62, exemplar 13, 33, loans of 105, Marginalia 56, 134–5, 140, possible Pictish origin 53, provenance 57, 62–3, 98, 431, relation to Iona 14–15, repair 106, scribe also the artist 32, 63, carelessness of scribe 4–5, 8, 13, 62, script 67, text 'imperfections' 51, 88, 181
Deer, New, parish 275
Deer, Book of property records 118 (fig. 5.1); diplomatic edition 121–6; hands 170–1 (146–74, 177–8 *passim*); spellings, by ear 195–6, 198–201; function 196, 329, 342; orthographic 'errors' 197, 199, 200; palaeography/codicology 343–9; text and translation 136–43
Deer, Old
  church 287 (fig. 9.2), 400–1, 459–61, 472
  glebe 289–90
  kirkyard 400
  Minister's Mound 401
  parish march burn 297
  parish 275
  Top Tillery 439
Deer, place-name 136–7, 210–13, 275–6, 303, 309
Deer, Cistercian Abbey of 99
  abbots 440, 463–6
  archaeological excavations 445 (fig. 14.3), 446
  architectural fragments 444, 452 (fig. 14.9), 453
  books belonging to 99–100
  buildings 448–59 (figs. 14.5–11)
  buildings destruction 403, 444
  buildings preservations 444–5
  charters destruction of 100
  community life 441–2, 454–8, 470–1
  contents of library 99–100
  dissolution 99, 101, 442, 468

endowments 440–1, 459, 471

Ferguson mausoleum 403, 444–5 (fig. 14.2), 446, 448

foundation 414, 439

income 441, 472

later medieval charters 100

location 287 (fig. 9.2), 411

modern ownership 446

oak cresting 446, 447 (fig. 14.4), 453

plan 443 (fig. 14.1), 444, 448 (fig. 14.6), 451 (fig. 14.8)

possessions of 278, 284–6, 288, 294, 299, 402, 416

Registers 99–100, 442

repairs 441

transition from earlier foundation 285, 413, 439

Deer, pre-Cistercian foundation

cult of saints 90

foundation legend 275, 280–1, 286, 363–5, 402

geographical position of 279, 286, 400–1

nature of community 99, 391

parochia 279, 285–7 (fig. 9.2)

depictions in Book of Deer: facial hair 44; swords 44–8, 48n; possible inkwell 53; books 53, 433

Derevan 276–7

Deveron, river 280, 295

Diack, Francis 235, 238, 240, 243–4

Dickinson, W. Croft 321–2

Domnall son of Giric 136–7, 314, 330

Domnall son of Ruaidrí 136–7, 330–1, 356

Domnall son of the son of Dubaicín 138–9, 336–8, 351–2

Donchad 216–18

Donchad son of Mac-Bethad son of Ided 131, 414

Donnachac 216–18

Donnachach son of Síthech 140–1, 333, 339

Drostan 230

Dubuice, see South Ugie

Dunkeld 138–9, 142–3, 344–5, 426

Dunlichitie 373

Dyce 369 (fig. 12.1), 373–4, 379

e(p)scob 134, 228

Earl's Hill, Ellon 349

eccles (egles-) 369–70, 391

edbarta 133, 136–40, 332, 336–8, 349–50, 352–3

Ednie see *Etdanin*

Eglismonichto 370

Ellon 142–3, 221–5, 279, 339, 348–9, 405, 409–10 (fig. 13.5), 471

Elrick (*ind elerc*) 138–9, 296–298, 303, 309, 311, 356, 287 (fig. 9.2)

Etdanin 138–9, 229, 291, 309, 311, 330, 352

Éte daughter of Gille-Míchél 138–41, 278, 292

Eusebian canons 7, 13–14, 32

Eva daughter of Gartnait 140–1, 332–3, 339–40, 348, 413

Evelyn, John 101

feast 138–9

Fedderate 277, 287 (fig. 9.2), 297–8, 414, 416

fer léginn 134, 138–9, 391, 409

Fergus, earl of Buchan 298, 413, 416

Ferguson of Pitfour, Admiral George 403, 444–6

Ferguson of Pitfour, James 410, 444

Fetterangus 277, 287 (fig. 9.2), 379, 407–9 (fig. 13.4a)

Fetternear 275–6, 368–9 (fig. 12.1)

Fife 332, 348, 366, 368, 375

Fischer, Bonifatius 5–6

foithir, fetter- 278, 280, 368

Fordoun 376, 387

forinsec 340–1

Formaston 368, 369 (fig. 12.1), 371, 373–4

Foynesfield 369 (fig. 12.1), 372

Furene 298, 309, 311

Fyvie 407–9 (fig. 13.4bc), 415 (fig. 13.6), 416, 430, 432–3

Gaelic dialects 159, 162, 166, 179–264 *passim*

Gaelic linguistic features

ae for *ai* 202–5

araes 205–6

contraction of hiatus 190–1

dental fricatives 225–8

dropping of quiescent consonants and vowels 200–1

Gaelic linguistic features (*contd*)
  eclipsis 241–59
  lowering/breaking of vowels 207–10
  merger
    lenited and unlenited *l* 228–9
    palatal and non-palatal *n* and *m* 229–30
    palatal and non-palatal *rr* 231
    merger of *dh* and *gh* 231–3
    merger of final unstressed palatal *gh*
      and *ch* 233–40
  nasalisation, see eclipsis
  raising of vowels 201–5
  reduction of consonant groups 228
  reduction of long unstressed vowels
    218–25
  sandhi 240
  smoothing of vowels 213–14
  svarabhakti/epenthesis 214–18
Gaelic Notes, *see* Deer, Book of, property
  records
Gale, Thomas 99, 101, 103
Garden, Prof. James 102
Garnait 228
Gartnait son of Cainnech 138–41, 278, 292,
  343, 346–8, 351, 355
Gille-Petair son of Donnchad 142–3, 339
Giric 314
Grange 278
Grant, Alexander 325–6, 355
Grian's Well 286, *see also* St Drostán, well

horizontal water-mill 427–8
Hughes, Kathleen 4, 36–7, 41, 44–5, 53, 56,
  67

iconoclasm 424
Innes, Cosmo 318–23, 326–7
inscriptions
  ogham Afforsk 374, 412, Brodie 376,
    Formaston 368, 369 (fig. 12.1), 371,
    373–4; roman alphabet: Anglo-Saxon
    423, Brechin 423, Eigg 423, Fordoun
    376, Irish 422–3, Lethnot 414,
    Ravenscraig 421 (fig. 13.9), 422–4,
    Ruthwell 423, Welsh 422–3
Insular gospel-books in general 37
Invercruden, *see* Cruden
Inverugie Petri, *see* Peterugie

Iogenan the Pict 383, 385
Iona 14, 81, 85, 87, 363, 365–6, 386

Jackson, Kenneth
  edition 119, 131–2, 134, 145–51, 162,
    314; reviews of *Gaelic Notes in the
    Book of Deer* xiii, 146, 188–9
  views on: administrative system
    314–5, 322–7, 330–46 *passim*, 349–55
    passim; Gaelic language 167, 170–1,
    174, 179–264 *passim*; *Nér* 367;
    provenance 431; scribe's training 181
Jastrzçbski, PA. 403 (fig. 13.4), 404–5, 410
joint-grants 330–2

Keith family, Earls Marischal
  (commendators of Deer) 101, 285,
    290, 442–3, 468–9, 471–2
Kingedward 278, 286, 440–1
Kinnedar 378, 414
Kinneff 374

lann- 278, 372, 379
Latin charters 313, 327–8, 333–4, 342–3
Logie 377–8
Longley, *see* St Fergus parish
Lonmay 278
Lumphanan 372
Lurchari 140–1, 295, 310, 329

Macbain, Alexander 320–1
Mac-Bead 212, 227
Mackie, James 322
Mackinnon, James 321
Mael-Brigte son of Cathal 136–7, 291, 330
Mael-Coluim 229
Mael-Coluim son of Cinaed (king of Alba)
  132, 138–9, 297, 314, 340, 352, 355,
  364, 426
Mael-Coluim son of Cuilén 136–7, 330–1,
  338, 356, 364n
Mael-Coluim son of Mael-Brigte (king of
  Alba) 138–9, 283, 296–7, 314, 356, 364
Mael-Domnaig son of Mac-Bethad 131,
  138–9, 241–1, 414
Mael-Fhéichín 140–3, 339
Mael-snechta son of Lulach (king of
  Moray) 138–9, 283, 296, 338, 355, 414

Maitne, sons of 142–3, 339
manuscripts
  Barberini Gospels 48, 50
  Book of Cerne 32, 50
  Book of Dimma 33, 68, 71–2, 75, 77–9,
    90–5
  Book of Durrow 33, 41
  Book of Kells   33, 37, 41–2, 44–6, 52,
    55–6, 63
  Book of Mulling 42, 71–2, 75, 77–9,
    90–5
  Cadmug Gospels 33
  Cambridge-London Gospels 42
  Celtic Psalter 42
  Durham Gospels 42, 54
  Echternach Gospels 33, 36, 38 (fig. 2.3),
    41
  Garland of Howth 43 (fig. 2.5), 45
  Lindisfarne Gospels 33, 41–2, 61
  Macdurnan Gospels 41, 44, 46, 49,
    54–5, 63
  Macregol Gospels 48
  Royal Bible 50
  St Augustine's Gospels 50
  St Chad's Gospels at Lichfield 37, 39
    (fig. 2.4)
  St Gall Gospels 33, 36, 41, 44, 54
  St Petersburg Bede 42
  St Petersburg Paulinus of Nola *Carmina*
    46–7 (fig. 2.6)
  Southampton Psalter 35 (fig. 2.2), 36–7
  Stowe Missal 71–2, 75, 77–8, 91–5
  Trier Gospels 41, 55
  Turin Gospels 55
Marjorie, countess of Buchan 414, 439
Marr 229–31
Matain son of Cairell 136–7, 290, 329, 355
metalwork 429
Methlick 279
Migvie 369 (fig. 12.1), 372–4
mills 291–2, 427–8
Minister's Mound, Old Deer 401
Monastery of Tallaght 81–2, 84
Monymusk 369 (fig. 12.1), 371, 373–4, 385,
    391 reliquary 429
Moore, John, bishop of Ely 102–3
morair 322–4
Morgann son of Donnchad 142–3, 339

mormaer 133, 136–42, 220–1, 315–56
    passim, 363
Mortlach 389
Muiredach son of Morgann 136–7, 288–9,
    330, 354

Navigatio Brendani 84
Nér 367–8, 370–1, 374, 391
New Deer parish 275

O'Rahilly, T.F. 182–3, 185–8, 190, 214,
    218–19, 226, 367
Oengus son of the daughter of Lulach 314,
    342
ogham, *see* inscriptions
Old Deer, *see* Deer, Old
Old Statistical Account, Old Deer parish 410
Orti 136–7, 298, 309, 311

Penitential of Finnian 86
Peterhead, *see* Peterugie
Peterugie 278–9, 364, 391, 420, 425, 440
pett (pit-) 133, 282–3, 284
Pett in Mulenn 136–7, 291–2, 310, 311, 330,
    428
Pett m͞c Garnait 131–2, 136–7, 252, 283,
    288, 310–11, 330
Pett m͞c Gobraig/Cobraig 131–2, 136–9, 240,
    253, 278, 283, 288, 310–11, 338, 426
Pett Malduib 283, 310–11
Philorth parish 407
physicians 414
Pictish administrative/territorial terms:
    *uotir 277–8, 280, 368, *pett* 133, 282–3,
    284
Pictish symbol stones 373, 379, 404–7
Pitfour (*Pet ipúir*) 140–1, 292–3, 303–4,
    310, 311, 338, 287 (fig. 9.2), 444, 446
Pitlurg 295–6, 304
place-names, translation of 281–2
pocket gospel books 4, 62, 68, 80
poets 414
Poppleton manuscript 167, 203, 206, 220–1,
    235
property records, *see* Book of Deer,
    property records
prophetic dream 443
Prose Rule of the Céli Dé 82, 84

Quartalehouse 287 (fig. 9.2), 294–5, 304, 398
quern-stone 426–9

Ralph of Diss' genealogy of the Kings of
     Scots 203, 206–7, 216, 236
Rathen 280, 375
Ravenscraig 424–5, cross(-slab) 417–26, 418
     (figs 13.7–8)
ritual purity 81–7
ros-benact 260
Robertson, E. William 315–18, 321–7, 353
Robertson, Joseph 105
Rogers, John 275
Ros abard 138–9, 297–8, 304, 310–11
Rule of Carthage 87
Rule of Tallaght 84
rune-stones, Sweden 412

sacart 132
saints cults 366
sen 260
sí 260–3
Simpson, W.D. 365–16, 446
Skellybogs (cross) 413–6, 433
Skene, John (1543–1617) 319–23
Skene, W. F. 315, 317, 319–21, 323, 324,
     327, 350–1
Skillymarno (*Scali merlec*) 140–1, 287
     (fig.9.2), 299–300, 304, 310–11, 338,
     quernstone 426–9
South Ugie, river (*Dubuci*) 140–1, 212–13,
     290–1, 295, 305, 309, 329, 400, 424
St Andrews foundation legend 417
St Fergus parish (Longley) xiv, 278–9, 425
saints
     Adomnán 15, 84, 385, *Betha Adomnáin*
          85, *Vita Columbae* 81, 84–7, 201,
          365, 381
     Austroberta 74
     Columba 90, 136–41, 275, 363–5, 385,
          402, 421, 423, *Vita Columbae* 81,
          84–7, 201, 365, 381, *Betha Choluim
          Cille* 85
     Colum Cillr, *see* Columba
     Drostán 90, 136–41, 154, 230, 275,
          363–5, 380 (fig. 12.2), 382–5, 387,
          402, well 286, 392, 400–1, 421, 423
     Ethernan 375–7 (fig. 12.2)

     Fergus 378–81 380 (fig. 12.3), 384, 387,
          392, relics 379–80
     Finnan 369 (fig. 12.1), 370–2
     Gartnait 376 (fig. 12.2), 378
     Genovefa 73
     Gervadius (Gerardine) *see* Gartnait
     Machar 376 (fig. 12.2)
     Mael Ruba 386 (fig. 12.4), 387–9
     Marnock (Mo Ernóc) 299–300, 386
          (fig. 12.4)
     Martin of Tours 73
     Mo Luag 386 (fig. 12.4), 387–9, 392
     Moling 85
     Monegund 73–4
     Nathalan, see Nechtan
     Nechtan 367–75, 369 (fig. 12.1), 385,
          391–2
     Ninian 365–6
     Palladius 300, 387
     Patrick 84, 294
     Peter 138–41, 364, 420
     Serf 440
     Talorcan 376–7 (fig. 12.2)
     Ternan (Torannán) 383, 385, 386
          (fig. 12.4), 387, relics 429
     Uoloch (Wallach) 376–7 (fig. 12.2)
sculpture
     Aberlemno 415, 431
     Abernethy 419–20, 425
     Aldbar 53, 59, 420
     Brechin 58, 59, 415, 420, 425, 433
     Cairn o' Mount 432
     Camuston 419–20
     Cordyce (lost) 416
     Crux medici 413–6
     Deer (lost) 402–5, 410–11, 446
     Dunkeld 59, 60 (fig. 2.10), 420, 425, 433
     Dupplin Cross 432
          Elgin 57–8, 426
     Ellon 405, 409–10 (fig. 13.5), 471
     Fetterangus 407–9 (fig. 13.4a)
     Fortevoit arch 421
     Fyvie 407–9 (fig. 13.4bc), 415 (fig. 13.6),
          416, 430, 432–3
     Invergowrie 61
     Kinnord 373
     Kirriemuir 420
     Lethendy 53, 59–60 (fig.2.9), 415, 420

Lethnot 414
Maiden Stone (Drumdurno) 416, 426, 430
Monifieth 61, 419–20, 432
Mountblow (Sandyford) 417
    Nigg 58, 415, 431
    Pictish (general) 57–61, 429–30
Pictish symbol stones 373, 379, 404–7
Portmahomack (Tarbat) 59, 415, 420
Ravenscraig 417–26, 418 (figs. 13.7–8)
Ruthwell Cross 423
St Andrews 58, 61
St Vigeans No. 11 53, 415, 420, 425
Tyrie 407–9 (fig. 13.4d)
Wester denoon cross-slab 58 (fig. 2.7–8), 61
Whithorn, Peter Stone 412
see also cross-marked stones
standing stones 294, 329, 398–400
Stephenson, Robert, prior of Deer 100, 442
Stuart, John 107–9
    Book of Deer 3, 134, errors in 15–17, 19–20, 23–6, 28–9,
    Sculptured Stones of Scotland 403–4
    views on: administrative system 316, 330–1, biblical apparatus 8, interpretation of art 46, place-names 275, 292, 428, property records 328, provenance 57, 431
sword 44–8, 431

Tarves 279
Teaching of Mael Ruain 86
thanes 317–26, 354–5
Tírechán 71
toísech 134, 137–42, 213–14, 315–56 *passim*
tonsure 381
Top Tillery 439
Tractatus Hilarii in Septem Epistolas Canonicas 78
Tullich 371, 373–4, 385, 392, 405
Turgot, *Life of Margaret* 89
Turriff (*Turbrud*) 138–9, 142–3, 220, 279–80, 391, 409 sculpture 407–9 (fig. 13.4e)
Tyrie 280, sculpture 407–9 (fig. 13.4d)

Uineus, abbot of Nér 367–75, 369 (fig. 12.1), 391

Vita Columbae 81, 84–7, 201, 365

Watson, W. J. 236–7, 239, 255, 261, 277, 292–3
wells 286, 312, 377, 379, 392, 400–1, 412, 421, 423
White Cow of Crichie (standing stone) 398–9
Whithorn 412
William Comyn, earl of Buchan 99, 414, 439
wives as grantors 330–3, 347, 414